The Death and Afterlife
of the
North American Martyrs

The Death and Afterlife of the North American Martyrs

EMMA ANDERSON

HARVARD UNIVERSITY PRESS

Cambridge, Massachusetts

London, England

2013

Library of Congress Cataloging-in-Publication Data

Anderson, Emma, 1970–
The death and afterlife of the North American martyrs /
Emma Anderson.
pages   cm
Includes bibliographical references and index.
ISBN 978-0-674-05118-8 (alk. paper)
1. Jesuits—North America.   2. Jesuits—Missions.
3. Christian martyrs—North America.   I. Title.
BX3707.A53   2013
272'.909713—dc23   2013009723

To my holy trinity—Mark, Sophie, and Danny
My three wise men—Simon, Peter, and John
And in loving memory of Mimi Bonnefoi

Contents

The Death and Afterlife
of the
North American Martyrs

Prologue

THE SMALL CROWD clusters around the altar. Their many-hued faces are uniformly turned toward the skull of revered saint and martyr Jean de Brébeuf, a missionary killed in an elaborate death-by-torture ritual in March 1649. Each pilgrim patiently awaits the chance to kneel in prayer before the relic. Competition is most intense for the coveted spot at the end of the altar, where Brébeuf's skeletal face is fully visible. There, one can meet with one's own gaze the shadows of his empty eye sockets in a kind of Christian *darshan,* or exchange of auspicious glances. The lucky ones who have made it as far as the *prie-dieu* lean forward to kiss the reliquary's enclosing glass. Some longingly touch their finger-tips or rosaries to it, as if to dissolve the transparent barrier. At the back of the throng, photographers sway gently from side to side like trees in the wind, angling for a better shot. They are careful not to jostle those pilgrims who, despairing of getting any closer, kneel directly on the church floor to say their rosaries, their prayers ascending in competing accents of Mandarin and Tamil.

Outside this sacred oasis of calm, the post-mass church is a riot of noise and motion. Children, defrosting after the formality of the mass, caper in liberated glee, their birdlike shrieks punctuating the decorous mumble of adult prayer. The life-size, recumbent statues of the dead Brébeuf and his fellow martyr, Isaac Jogues, perpetually lying in state in the east and west transept, never fail to fascinate these youngest pilgrims. Some lie on the red carpet, eyes closed, arms folded across their chests, in imitation of the statues' posture, their small bodies reflected in the smudged glass separating them from the saints. As children are photographed standing by the polychrome Our Lady of All Nations statue, their innocent questions rise like querulous balloons in the church's echoing vault: "Dad, who is that man? Why is he sleeping?" Father Patrick Coldricks, a Jesuit priest originally from Goa, India, who now resides at the Midland Martyrs' Shrine,[1] is on hand to answer pilgrims' queries and direct traffic. He explains to a stocking-footed Hindu pilgrim that it is forbidden to ascend into the sanctuary, the holiest part of the church. Sensing the man's acute disappointment, Coldricks, with the air of a magician producing a rabbit from his top hat, removes a holy card depicting the martyrs from the breast pocket of his clerical suit and presents it to the pilgrim. Accepting it with a delighted smile, the man spontaneously throws his arms around the surprised Jesuit.

Veneration of the martyrs' relics is abruptly interrupted as two youths, clad in the green T-shirts of shrine staff, arrive to escort the skull on its latest adventure. Carefully, they carry the gold-and-glass reliquary from the building's shadowy interior out into the brilliant summer sunshine, where the saint's chariot awaits. It is an elaborate float honoring the Canadian martyrs, to which is coupled another, dedicated to the martyrs of Vietnam, represented by costumed pilgrims holding their relics. Small children, dressed as angels, perch on the "clouds" that decorate each. The skull having been ceremoniously installed, the two floats, pulled by the shrine's ancient green pickup, begin their slow devotional circuit of the grounds, moving with all the formality and love of a father walking his daughter down the aisle. Preceded by an altar boy bearing an elaborate processional cross, they are hemmed in on all sides by camera-clutching pilgrims singing Vietnamese hymns in honor of their martyred patrons. Parents in particular hover close, watching to ensure that their small angels do not tumble earthward. Their pilgrims' progress is watched with interest by two Ukrainian Canadian women, arrayed in brightly embroidered traditional dress. One fills a bottle with holy water from the decorative metal cistern by the gift shop, while the other languorously indulges in a cigarette, blowing the smoke like profane incense above her intricately decorated hair.

"Agnus Dei, qui tollis peccata mundi: miserere nobis . . ." The rhythm of women's singing matches their surging progress along the green and gold of the forest path. At the front of their brigade's disciplined ranks, a handmade cloth banner depicts their patron saint: Joan of Arc. Resplendent in silver armor, *la Pucelle* blazes in the sunlight only to be extinguished in the trees' heavy shade. Many pilgrims, as they walk two by two, caress their rosary beads as they march and sing. Others have holstered them on belts or backpacks so that they swing jauntily back and forth in time to the brigade's uniform marching, their pendulum motion duplicating that of the long ponytails sported by the group's youngest members. As the column moves further into the woods, the nuns leading the snaking cadre seem almost to disappear into the verdant darkness. Their long black habits make them living woodland shadows, invisible save for the impossibly white Cheshire-cat smiles of their flashing sneakers.

Suddenly, amplified shouts drown out the women's hypnotic hymn of praise. The banner of Saint René Goupil, martyred patron of the pilgrimage's adolescent male "safety officers," appears suddenly over the ridge. Clad in a Day-Glo orange vest, their newly visible leader screams the saint's name into his bullhorn in a sort of religious war cry. "Saint René Goupil," he shouts, the tendons in his young neck stretched tight, his voice near breaking. "Pray for us!" thunder his companions like a breaking wave. "Saint Isaac Jogues!" his amplified voice shouts, yet louder: "Pray for us!" scream his respondents, "That we may be made worthy of the promises of Christ!"

Starting at the larger-than-life statue of seventeenth-century Jesuit martyr Isaac Jogues, erected by the shores of Lake George, New York, this pilgrimage of nearly 200 men, women, and children will traverse seventy miles of the upstate's noisy highways and sun-dappled woodland paths. They are following, they believe, in the bloodied footprints of Jogues and fellow martyr, René Goupil. Walking hard and sleeping rough, their "Pilgrimage of Restoration" purports to retrace the very path the two saints followed after their capture in August 1642 by Mohawk warriors. Their long trek will triumphantly conclude at Our Lady of Martyrs Shrine in Auriesville: the very site on which these men are believed to have shed their life's blood for the Catholic faith.[2] Mindful of the martyrs' incomparably greater agony, pilgrims of both sexes, walking in their sex-segregated brigades, humbly offer up their own lesser sufferings, dedicating their cramps and calluses, boredom and blisters, as reparation for their own sins and for those of their families.

Many also seek to atone for what they see as the ongoing "genocide" of abortion and the crassness, vacuity, and violence of America's secular culture, dispensed through the twin sewers of the mass media and the public education system.

As Saint Joan's brigade emerges from the dark woodland path into a hummocky meadow, the confident fullness of their song breaks, snagging like knitting that has missed a stitch. Their disciplined marching likewise devolves into an every-woman-for-herself scramble over the wet, treacherous ground. The long-haired teen marching beside me stops singing altogether, clumping her rosary beads mutely together in her closed fist. When she glances shyly at me, I jump at the chance to whisper a quick question, demanding what the pilgrimage means to her. After a moment of reflection, she quietly confides: "I do it because there are still some things worth fighting and dying for. Sometimes you need to stand up and say . . ." But the girl's comments are interrupted when the nun in front of us—a Slave of the Immaculate Heart of Mary—whirls around in a blur of black to snap: "Don't you two have your rosaries with you? We are trying to pray here! Show some respect!"

Who Are the North American Martyrs?

Despite their striking contrasts, both of these pilgrimages, the celebration of Vietnamese Canadians at the Martyrs' Shrine in Midland, Ontario, and the daunting annual journey of ultraconservative American Catholics across upstate New York to Our Lady of Martyrs Shrine in Auriesville, are intended to honor the lives, deaths, and legacies of "the North American martyrs": René Goupil, Isaac Jogues, Jean de la Lande, Antoine Daniel, Jean de Brébeuf, Gabriel Lalemant, Charles Garnier, and Nöel Chabanel. This small group of Frenchmen, composed of six Jesuit priests and two *donnés* (or lay assistants sworn to support their mission), fell at the hands of competing native confederacies, Iroquois and Wendat,[3] during the 1640s, a turbulent decade scarred by epidemic warfare and social dislocation. As conflict between the Jesuits, the Wendat, and the Iroquois deepened, all three groups would draw upon their respective religious worldviews to interpret and reframe their painful sufferings and struggles.

Though all eight Europeans died violently, their collective characterization as simply "the North American martyrs" camouflages the contrasting circumstances under which each man died. Two of the eight perished during the elaborate torture rituals routinely inflicted by native combatants throughout the colonial Northeast on selected war captives. Two others fell as casualties of war in the escalating Iroquois raids on the vulnerable southerly Wendat villages in which these Jesuit missionaries were stationed. Three were held captive by the Iroquois and later executed with little ritual fanfare, while the final Jesuit was the victim of an unwitnessed robbery-murder.

Though these slain men were unofficially celebrated by their surviving Jesuit colleagues as saints and martyrs in the immediate aftermath of their deaths, their path to official recognition by the Roman Catholic Church was a long and arduous slog. It was not until 1930 that they would receive the ultimate honor the Vatican can bestow on its children: canonization.[4]

It is important to understand that there was nothing inevitable about the elevation of these eight particular individuals as martyrs. On the contrary, their isolation from the much larger pool of Christians, both French and native, who died during this bloody and unsettled period in North American history was an artificial, subjective, and inherently unfair process. Some individuals whose *causa* was enthusiastically championed in the 1650s had fallen into almost total obscurity by the nineteenth century, while others, largely overlooked or eclipsed at the time of their deaths, would receive belated appreciation hundreds of years later. Candidates who were as or more deserving of recognition as Catholic martyrs were sometimes excluded from consideration merely because their deaths occurred at politically inopportune moments for the colonial Jesuits, while others seem to have been discounted largely because of their ethnicity. For despite the fact that aboriginal[5] Christians in the 1640s died in far greater numbers than did European Catholics, falling in their scores alongside the eight men eventually canonized, no native martyrs have as yet been recognized by Rome.[6] By the 1960s and 1970s this apparent racial bias would deeply trouble both observers of and participants in the cult[7] of the North American martyrs, native and nonnative alike.[8]

This book differs in several important ways from others written about the North American martyrs. First, it begins its story at the conventional end point of the traditional hagiographic narrative. Most works on the martyrs focus on their lives as Catholic missionaries arduously seeking to convert the native peoples of North America. Their bloody deaths, in such accounts, serve merely as a convenient narrative crescendo: the triumphant, dramatic climax of their years of dedicated, courageous service.[9] This work, however, *begins* with an analysis of these figures' deaths and goes on to explore their tumultuous collective "afterlife." As I am using it, this word refers not to these figures' attainment of some otherworldly paradise but rather to their continual remembering and reinvention in the popular, protean collective imagination from their time to our own.[10]

Second, this work seeks to explore *multiple* interpretations of the martyrs' deaths and legacies, some of which fall well outside the familiar Catholic devotional perspective that has for centuries dominated the analysis of these figures. This book recounts how these eight men, the continent's first canonized saints, have been imagined and appropriated, blamed and praised, manipulated and politicized by venerators and critics alike, both within and outside the Catholic Church, over more than three and a half centuries.

In the course of fulfilling this larger objective, this book becomes, almost accidentally, the first complete *narrative* history of the martyrs' unfolding cult.[11] But the work's commitment to highlighting the views and experiences of the martyrs' detractors as well as their devotees makes its scope significantly broader, more critical, and more ambitious. For to narrate simply a "rise," "growth," "triumph," and gradual "demise" of the cult of the North American martyrs would be uncritically to adopt the very Catholic devotional perspective that has for so long obscured as much as it has revealed about the lives, deaths, and legacies of these fascinating and multifaceted figures.

Clearly, the eight individuals canonized as "the North American martyrs" would have understood their own violent deaths as martyrdoms. By the 1640s, the colonial Jesuits expected, even welcomed martyrdom, which they saw as playing a vital role in the continent's bloody baptism for Christ. In their minds, dying for God was a high-stakes ritual drama in which their final words and actions were closely watched by eyes both earthly and heavenly: their agonies witnessed by an audience visible and invisible, mortal and immortal. The Jesuits thus sought to *perform* their deaths with as much courage as they could muster: the better to edify their fellow man, to glorify God, and to merit their proffered place in heaven. These men clearly came to see their own dramatic and violent deaths as being the golden key that alone could unlock the continent's dark heart, stubbornly closed to Christ's salvific love. Their self-understanding as martyrs, moreover, was enthusiastically endorsed by generations of Catholics, who used their deaths as the fertile locus for reflection, inspiration, and imitation. But, like a window at twilight, the pane of the past can all too easily be transformed from a means of looking beyond one's own parochial perspective into a self-reflecting, self-regarding mirror. The logic of martyrdom can instill a glorious new meaning into otherwise demoralizing debacles, transforming defeat into spiritual victory and death into eternal life. Thus, in the face of threats, setbacks, ridicule, or marginalization, North American Catholics have turned to the martyrs for comfort. In their immediate aftermath, these missionaries' deaths were used to bolster the fading morale of French colonists, who were urged to reflect on the glorious otherworldly rewards God bestowed on those who held fast to his providential plan for the conversion of the New World. After their stunning defeat at the hands of English forces in 1759, the Quebecois likewise turned to the paradox of martyrdom to inspire their *survivance* or survival as a distinct linguistic and confessional minority within the larger conglomerate of "the Canadas." Martyrdom enrobed the bitter pill of defeat in a palatable patina of moral superiority that allowed the Quebecois to see themselves as, in Leonard Cohen's phrase, "beautiful losers." Nineteenth-century American Catholics, on the other hand, eager for Protestant acceptance and approbation, used the martyrs' saga to construct an attractive alternative religious myth of origins that at once challenged the dominant Protestant birth-of-the-nation narrative and satisfied Catholics' hunger for a sense of belonging in a ferociously anti-Catholic milieu. During the Cold War, the martyrs' stalwart choice to die rather than to apostatize was seen as exemplifying the horrifying contemporary dilemma confronting Christians trapped behind the Iron Curtain and by extension all those menaced by the specter of waxing Soviet power. And still today, the North American martyrs serve as powerful symbols. At Midland, they are a lodestar for newly arrived Catholic immigrants to Canada—such as the Vietnamese, Tamil, Goan, Korean, and Filipino pilgrims who seek, through their ritual involvement at the Martyrs' Shrine, proudly to celebrate their distinctive cultural and linguistic heritage whilst simultaneously symbolically "becoming Canadian" through their embrace of these "nation-saints."[12] At Auriesville, the martyrs are increasingly venerated by a Catholic minority of quite another sort: ultraconservatives. Ethnically indistinguishable from the American mainstream, these Catholics nevertheless express a powerful sense of alienation from both a lax, lukewarm church and the depraved society in which they live. They turn for comfort to contemplation and imitation of the martyrs, whose evangelical zeal and willingness to suffer death for bearing the gospel message enflames their own ardor. For centuries, then, the window-mirror dynamic has ensured that veneration of the North American martyrs has never been totally innocent of a certain degree of unconscious self-adulation.

Though understanding the martyrdom-focused mentality of these seventeenth-century Jesuits and their latter-day Catholic followers is crucially important, their perspective must be evoked with care, lest the concept of martyrdom morph from being the *subject* of the book's analysis to an unconscious *shaper of it*. Martyrdom can be a seductive, colonizing idea, a real conceptual tar baby; its simple yet powerful axioms can easily be merely assumed rather than trenchantly analyzed, even by those dedicated to interrogating the concept's underlying assumptions.[13] It must be remembered that martyrdom is always an *interpretation* of a given set of facts, rather being "a fact" in and of itself, as failure to appreciate this important distinction can lead to the misinterpretation and misrepresentation of others' viewpoints. One example will serve to illustrate this conceptual slipperiness. During one interview with Beth Lynch of Our Lady of Martyrs Shrine, I inquired about regional native perceptions of the martyrs and their sanctuary. In response, Lynch indignantly characterized a local Mohawk traditionalist[14] as a "martyrdom denier" in what seems to have been a striking adaptation of the usual phrase "Holocaust denier." She vividly recalled him as having vehemently averred, in a public forum, that seventeenth-century Mohawk warriors *had not* slain Jesuit missionaries Goupil, Jogues, and la Lande in the 1640s. But when contacted for comment the man was wryly amused by Lynch's characterization of his words. He had not denied that these three Europeans had been killed by his people, he clarified. On the contrary, he was glad that they had been. What he objected to was their persistent characterization as guiltless "martyrs." As the agents of a foreign crown, he argued, the Jesuits had been bent on the religious conversion and cultural subordination of his ancestors. Their relentless religious hectoring of his people and their repeated, uninvited appearance in Mohawk territory had been interpreted, correctly in his view, as a threat. In the end, the elder concluded, his ancestors had little choice but to defend their land, culture, and spirituality through these three preemptive slayings. In his view, these celebrated martyrdoms were in fact justifiable homicides.[15] Lynch, however, had completely misread the man's objection to their deaths being characterized with the theologically loaded term "martyrdom" as a denial that they had been killed *at all*.

Issues of nomenclature are important, as the terminology we employ helps to shape events perceived. Mothers Against Drunk Driving has waged a largely successful campaign to replace use of the word "crash" (which neither presumes nor denies the driver's responsibility) for the traditional, more absolving term "accident" (which preemptively denies the driver's guilt), demonstrating just how many assumptions can be packed into one little word. "Martyr," from the ancient Greek for "witness," packs a similar connotative punch. Just the bare, unadorned use of this word is enough to create a strong impression of the deceased's innocence, passivity, and sanctity. It is thus a loaded term that selectively highlights one of many possible interpretations of a given deadly encounter, while subtly denying other equally plausible, interpretations. As they are used in this book, however, "martyr(s)" and "martyrdom" are terms of designatory convenience rather than theological affirmation: a neutral, one-word synonym for "slain missionaries."[16]

Use of the term "martyr" also strongly implies an anti-Christian motive in a murder. Catholic definitions of martyrdom have traditionally required not only that a Christian have been executed by forces hostile to him or her; they have mandated that the slayer be motivated *in odium fidei* or "out of hatred of the [Catholic] faith." One might think that Catholic dependency on the motivations of a martyrs' antagonist might destabilize the very foundations of martyrdom itself, as it seems to give to the church's purported enemies considerable power to award or withhold its ultimate recognition of sanctity. In practice, however, Catholic willingness simply to assume or to impose rather than to truly investigate the motives of the martyrs' murderers has rendered this potentially thorny problem moot. Centuries of hagiographers have simply imputed the necessary anti-Christian animus onto the native slayers of the North American martyrs, in the process distorting or eclipsing

other motives that did not serve their rhetorical purpose, much as commentators in the aftermath of September 11 proposed essentially self-
flattering explanations for the violence, epitomized by the iconic phrase
"they hate us because of our freedom." Even as they cried out "Why?"
survivors were quick to propose comforting explanations that reaf-
firmed their own embattled worldview. In both cases, insistence on
imposing rather than discerning assailants' motives robbed interpreters
of the opportunity to understand the genuine dynamics underlying
these infamous acts of violence.[17]

The Other Side

Thus, though this book attempts to understand how Jesuit missionaries
themselves perceived their terrifying final hours, it also seeks to com-
prehend the perspectives of those on the other side of the axe, musket,
or boiling cauldron of boiling water. In traditional historiography, the
martyrs' native antagonists have generally been cast as the cruel, barbaric "Romans" to the Jesuits' courageous "ancient Christian martyrs,"
implying that the missionaries were singled out for torture because of
their Catholic faith. But seventeenth-century native peoples, Iroquois
and Wendat alike, had their own understanding of the purpose and
mores attending death by torture. They perceived these postwar rituals
as a religious sacrifice and a political reprisal in which the enemy's entire
body politic was symbolically punished in the person of the tortured.
All too aware that had the battle gone the other way, their positions
would be reversed, captor and captive met in a stylized minuet of death
in which each hewed to mutually comprehensible rules. The reluctant
respect of one's captors could be won, and the collective honor of one's
nation asserted, through a stalwart and courageous death. Captives thus
sought to endure torture unflinching, and to antagonize rather than
appease their captors. Native prescriptions for a "good death," then, had
powerful parallels with the traditional expectations for Christian martyrs, parallels that encouraged particularly perceptive Jesuit missionaries to adapt their ritual performance to the demands of the colonial
stage.

In devotional works, the slaying of these eight Catholic missionaries
is often represented as the dark assertion of a unanimous and funda-

mentally hostile native will. More careful examination reveals that these deaths were often the subject of heated controversy within native circles, and were generally the work of a minority group acting against the stated objections of the majority. For, although some wished to kill these interloping Jesuit "black-robes," others sought to ransom or even adopt them. In one instance, a Mohawk warrior himself sustained injury during his ill-fated attempt to halt Isaac Jogues's execution. Native people's disagreements regarding treatment of the Jesuits, whether they were encountered as missionaries, diplomatic envoys, unarmed noncombatants, or war captives, suggests that their traditional categories of sacrifice and adoption were pushed to their conceptual limits by the very presence of these puzzling strangers.

Over the centuries, sharp-eyed native critics, both Catholics and traditionalists, have been quick to point out the dark side of the martyrs' cult for their peoples. Although these slain missionaries have intermittently inspired a strong sense of Catholic collective identity and solidarity, it has been aboriginal peoples who have paid the price for these uplifting morale boosts. In the nineteenth and twentieth centuries, native people in both Canada and the United States were increasingly controlled and coerced by the nonnative majority. Displaced from their traditional lands and systematically restricted to reservations, their traditional ceremonies were outlawed. Native children were forced to attend educational institutions designed to effect their cultural, religious, and linguistic assimilation to the white mainstream.

In many cases, the specter of the martyrs was used to justify the need for these audacious interventions in native culture. Ritual reiteration of the gory details of the martyrs' deaths insisted, even in the face of the actual and symbolic violence being systematically perpetrated against native North America, that the "real" danger, now as then, was posed by ungrateful "savages" all too prone to lashing out against the white benefactors who sought only to "save" and "civilize" them. This troubling history has led native critics of the martyrs' cult to compare the sheer scope of the horrors endured by native peoples under centuries of colonialism with this small handful of long-ago celebrity deaths. But such protests, while they strongly contest the martyrs' claims to sanctity, themselves perpetuate the logic of martyrdom, which accords moral superiority to victimhood. Their critiques, then, do not repudiate the concept of martyrdom so much as they apply it to their own individual circumstances and the collective historical experiences of their peoples as a whole.

A Note on Style

This book seeks to evoke as well as to inform, objectives that I see as being so complementary as to be virtually two aspects of the same thing. In my view, trenchant analysis need not preclude vivid description, nor thinking eclipse sensing and feeling. Many of the events this book describes, particularly the episodes that spawned the martyrs' cult, their violent deaths, were dramatic and powerfully emotional, both as they originally occurred and as they have been renarrated and reenvisioned in the imaginations of centuries of the Catholic faithful. Indeed, the "spectacular"[18] quality of these deaths and their visceral, empathic, and corporeally charged appeal to those who have "witnessed" them through the (often distorting) media of art and literature have been major reasons why these figures have enjoyed such a prolonged and fascinating afterlife. Dryly narrating these men's deaths and the cult and the controversy they inspired in a dry and bloodless prose would, in my view, undercut rather than enhance readers' comprehension both of the instigating events themselves and the vital question of why they have mattered to so many for so long. In writing this book, then, I sought to make the past palpable: to evoke the texture of lost time and to recreate the nuance of individual perspectives. I wanted to communicate not simply how the martyrs, as spiritual and cultural symbols and realities, have been *understood* but, more broadly, how they have been *experienced*. I wished to explore the curious alchemy that occurs when people imaginatively engage with these enigmatic figures—whether in wondering reverence or frustrated protest—entangling them with their personal preoccupations, contemporary concerns, and individual identities. For this reason, I supplement analysis with narration and description of people and places, experiences and events, particularly in the opening of each chapter, inviting the reader into the time period being evoked and the perceptions and perspectives of its critical actors. It should be noted, however, that these more episodic and anecdotal passages are just as firmly grounded in the historical facts as are the more conventional, analytical sections of this book. On those rare occasions where gaps in the historical record force me to speculate, these are clearly noted.

Even as this book seeks to sketch, in broad strokes, how various linguistic, national, confessional, political, and ethnic groups have championed and critiqued, appropriated and transformed the martyrs and their legacy, it does this by relating the stories of key individuals. Rather than working in faceless and unsatisfying generalities, this book eschews the encyclopedic for the intimate. Though this work's wide temporal scope, spanning almost 400 years, has obliged me to employ both historical and ethnographic methods, each has been deployed with the identical aim: to identify the martyrs' key devotees and detractors from the seventeenth century to the present and to present their seminal contributions. The genesis, transmission, and transformations of the images and rituals, texts, and traditions that have sustained popular imaginative engagement with the North American martyrs would simply not have been possible without the seminal interventions of a handful of key individuals in each era. Although most of this book is written in the conventional third person (spliced with passages that narrate events from the assumed perspectives of different historical actors), its final chapter (like the opening sections of this prologue) adopts a vivid first-person perspective, taking the reader along as a vicarious participant-observer in three contrasting contemporary pilgrimages to the places made holy by their association with the martyrs in the United States, Canada, and France.[19] This work, then, presents both the quick and the dead, twinning lush historical portraits of the martyrs' long-dead advocates and critics with the voices of the still-living players in their ever-evolving, ever-contested cult.

1

A Spectacle for Men and Angels

STANDING BEFORE THE LEATHER DOOR FLAP of the Mohawk longhouse where he had been peremptorily summoned, the gaunt Jesuit paused, mentally forming one last prayer of thanks and of promise to his God. Despite the warning from his fellow French captive, donné Jean de la Lande, to ignore the command, Isaac Jogues was glad he had come. Much of the last four years of his life, it seemed, had been spent in preparation for the moment he suspected, and even half-hoped, had finally arrived. There had been so many false starts and so many unexplained reprieves. So many others had died instead of him. The very night of Jogues's first capture more than four years earlier, Eustache Ahatsistari, the Wendat Catholic leader of the doomed expedition to Huronia from Québec, had been selected for ritual torture, expiring after hours of grueling torment.[1] Two months later, Jogues had witnessed his companion and assistant, René Goupil, brained with an axe.[2] Bestowing a blessing on his fallen friend, he had quickly knelt, exposing his own bent head to receive a similar blow, but had been tersely bidden to rise. Evidently, it had not then been his time. God, in visions, had told him as much, himself inflicting heavy, punishing blows on his servant with his "switch or rod" before drawing Jogues close for "consolation wholly divine and entirely inexplicable."[3] His Divine Majesty had decreed that Jogues must endure this extended period of testing and trial to atone for his own sins, and those of others.

Many times Jogues had felt the wings of the angel of death gliding feather-soft against his body, only to teasingly withdraw. Many times he had commended himself to his God. In the aftermath of his initial torture, his badly damaged fingers had become so infected that they pulsed with maggots, and he staggered in a fever in which he seemed neither asleep nor awake, neither living nor dead.[4] Throughout his first, lengthy imprisonment at Ossernenon, the village of his Mohawk captors, Jogues had been haunted by the specter of starvation because "he would never eat of flesh sacrificed to the devil."[5] He had endured innumerable threats from those who found his unusual behaviour— particularly his daily withdrawal to the village periphery to pray alone, sometimes for eight or ten hours a day—deeply unsettling.[6]

Jogues's successful escape in August 1643 had been fraught with a thousand perils.[7] Protracted negotiations between the Dutch and the Mohawk left his fate in doubt making him, naked and wounded in his insecure hiding place, more vulnerable to discovery with every passing day. His lengthy ocean voyage back to France, he reflected, had merely brought him into a deeper kind of danger, that which threatens the soul rather than the body. Robbed of all his possessions by English pirates, he was helped by strangers to make his way inland to the Jesuit residence in Rennes, where he was initially taken for a pitiable beggar.[8] When his true identity was revealed, the dramatic reappearance of one long feared dead in some remote corner of New France had caused a veritable sensation. With an involuntary wince, Jogues remembered the barrage of publicity: a papal commendation,[9] an imperious summons to court, invasive curiosity about his mutilated fingers, and the embarrassment of being venerated as a living "martyr of Jesus Christ."[10] Worst of all had been the uniform incredulity and shock when he shyly expressed his dream of returning to Canada. He remembered all too well how his auditors' eyes, glowing like candles in a window, had abruptly shuttered in incomprehension and dismay. How much better to be here, in the valley of the shadow of death, than to wax fat and self-satisfied in France! Here he could be both a missionary and a diplomat, carrying a message of salvation and of peace to these benighted savages ignorant of both true civilization and of Christ's redeeming love. Surely such a glorious mission was worth his life's blood? Jogues remembered his words, uttered three weeks earlier as he left his Jesuit companions at their headquarters of Sainte-Marie among the Hurons, hundreds of miles to the northwest: *"Ibo et non redibo:* I go, but I shall not return."[11] Quietly, he repeated them to himself one last time before pulling back the longhouse's leather door flap.

Entering, Jogues sensed but did not see the sudden movement off to his side. Dimly he discerned figures moving, heard scuffling on the cabin's dirt floor, felt the whistle of a missed blow near him, heard an exclamation of surprise and anger. Abruptly, someone was slammed into the longhouse wall, and then there was silence. Now. Now, surely, it must finally be time. Jogues stood, mutely waiting, all his senses straining. He waited.

Making Meaning of Menace

In 1640s North America, the Iroquois, an alliance of five distinct aboriginal nations living south of the St. Lawrence River,[12] and the Jesuits or "Society of Jesus," the Catholic missionary order founded by St. Ignatius Loyola a century earlier,[13] both felt profoundly persecuted. Each group[14] was menaced by terrors that not only endangered their existence but also undermined their sense of collective purpose, threatening their identity and integrity as a community. While terrifyingly tangible, these threats were all the more disorienting because they also posed serious conceptual challenges. The Iroquois, lacking immunity to European diseases such as smallpox, had been decimated by waves of epidemic. Such dramatic population loss threatened social chaos and called into question the efficacy of traditional approaches to healing. But the Jesuits also faced a parallel assault on their sense of safety and success. During the 1640s, they faced both increased Iroquois incursions northward into the territories they had come to regard as their own and a growing resistance to their ideas from the very native nations they had targeted for intensive Christianization efforts. Having naively assumed that the Wendat confederacy of Georgian Bay[15] would unhesitatingly embrace their Catholic faith, the Jesuits now confronted the grim reality of sporadic violence within as well as outside their mission villages.

Faced with these challenges, the Jesuits and the Haudenosaunee[16] responded in much the same manner: by determinedly reasserting the meaningfulness of their respective traditional approaches to the great mysteries of suffering, death, and the afterlife. The Iroquois turned to soul return and sacrifice, twin concepts that had long served as the lodestars guiding their postwar ritual practices. The Jesuits, inspired both by the spectacular and grueling forms of ritualized death that they witnessed in native North America and by their profound religious desire to suffer and die for the conversion of New World souls, turned to the master motif of Christian martyrdom as a fresh source of inspiration and guidance in these troubled times. These competing conceptions of the "good death" had both striking convergences and marked contrasts. But, throughout the tumultuous 1640s, they would fit together like the cogs of a dark machine, each animating and driving on the other.

Whereas the Jesuits saw martyrdom as the fearful portal through which they must pass into a glorious and eternal afterlife, the Iroquois, Orpheus-like, sought to lure their beloved dead back to the terrestrial plane. By capturing prisoners in warfare, they symbolically stormed the afterworld to rescue their dead kin. In a time of high mortality, they reasoned, only accelerated conflict could address their serious population loss. Taking more captives would help them resuscitate the scores of souls drowned in punishing waves of epidemic, as the dead could then return to these new host bodies and resume their rudely interrupted lives as family and community members.

Engaging in a war on behalf of the dead necessarily involved the sacrifice of some young, healthy warriors. Their choice to risk their own lives so that the beloved dead could once again walk this good earth, retrieved from the shadow lands and restored to the arms of kith and kin, was seen as a laudable sign of dawning maturity in these young men. This resurrection-through-adoption thus restored not simply the dead but the Iroquois conceptual order itself, threatened by the hideous dislocations of pandemic.

Through adoption ceremonies, the Iroquois urged the deceased to resume, in the bodies of war captives, their prior identities and occupations. Adoptees were thus called by the names of the deceased and were invited to reabsorb the recounted memories, preferences, and habits of their former lives taking their place in the constellation of family relationships.[17] Leadership skills were expected in captives hosting the spirit of the charismatic departed, while those who had been marginalized figures of fun in their previous lives passed on this dubious legacy to the adoptee who had the misfortune to re-enflesh them.[18] Many prisoners rewarded their captors' incorporative efforts with lives of unimpeachable loyalty toward their new families and nation, fighting on the side of their adoptive communities against their former, biological kin.[19]

But, for the Iroquois, soul return was always coupled with sacrifice, demographic replenishment with ritual reprisal. Even as they sought, through violent confrontation, to bring back their dead, they also sought to avenge previous losses at the hands of their enemies. Because of these dual motivations, aboriginal postwar practices culminated in two asymmetrical rituals: the torturous destruction of the few and the ritual integration of the many. Immediately upon capture, all captives deemed capable of making the long trek to the victor's territory were loaded with booty. Those who could not make such an ambitious journey, such as the seriously wounded, the elderly and sick, and children in the precarious intermediate stage of their development—too heavy to be carried but too young to keep up with the group independently—were summarily executed, a fate that also threatened those who could or would not keep pace along the way. Awaiting all surviving captives at their final destination was the gauntlet, a preliminary form of torture in which captives of both genders and all ages and the entire victorious village—men, women, and children—participated. Captives were forced to run between two parallel lines of adversaries who kicked, beat, and otherwise abused them.[20] Then the ultimate fate of each individual prisoner—adoption or destruction—would be decided by the victorious community. Whereas women and children were almost automatically selected for ritual integration into the community,[21] male captives faced the additional threat of death by torture. Their very desire to augment their depleted communities through forceful adoption logically limited the number of male captives the Iroquois would have been willing to sacrifice to a symbolic few.

The victims of postwar torture in native North America were expected to greet suffering with stoicism, and even defiance: to not go gentle into that good night. Those undergoing ritual torture were expected to telegraph their courage through their endurance of pain, acceptance of their imminent death, signaled through the singing of their personal death song and participation in the mutual exchange of trash-talking insults, challenges, and threats. Victims of torture were admired for giving as good as they got in these verbal exchanges. Dying, they would threaten the inevitable revenge of their own nation for their death, predicting its ultimate victory and darkly presaging the day when the current roles would be reversed and the torturers of today would become the victims of tomorrow. How would the tormenters fare, the tormented provocatively demanded, when the shoe was on the other foot?[22]

These forbidding rites of suffering and of death were not the exclusive prerogative of the Iroquois confederacy but were practiced by the majority of aboriginal nations of colonial North America. Victors and vanquished generally colluded with one another in these rituals, together creating an exacting, stylized minuet of death in which each group affirmed the shared values of courage, stoicism, loyalty, and defiance, even as it asserted its own honor. All native nations, moreover, respected the same basic behavioral protocols for torturers and the tortured: alternating periods of intense torture with breaks for the captive to rest, eat, and receive compliments on his performance to date. Anticipating that they might face deadly torture, aboriginal adolescents prepared themselves accordingly. Indeed, many of the practices that helped young would-be warriors to gain a reputation for bravery or self-control within their own communities—clutching hot coals, enduring prolonged fasts and sexual abstention and braving "polar bear" swims in the heart-stopping cold of frozen lakes—also served as preparation for possible capture and ritual torment. Finally, all nations shared similar motivations for this ritual punishment, as all reverenced the larger connotation of sacrifice present in these complex and deadly rituals. By slaying a representative individual, his entire nation was symbolically punished. Torturers often coordinated their victims' final breaths to the rising or setting of the sun, suggesting that their lives were a sacrifice to the sun.[23] But they also kept something of their victim's spirit for themselves. In acknowledgement of an exceptionally courageous death, the exemplary qualities of the deceased were conserved in the bodies of the living through acts of postmortem cannibalism. Just as those captives chosen to live bore within their bodies the souls of the returning dead, so the courage of the ritually slain lingered within those who consumed their flesh.

For their part, faced with a situation in which danger seemed ubiquitous, the Jesuits resolved to suffer and to die so that others might spiritually live. The earliest Jesuit writings penned in New France was blithely optimistic, even Edenic, as the Jesuits confidently forecasted the easy conversion and "civilization" of native groups. Jesuit confidence in the ease of their mission reflected their pride in what they saw as the self-evident beauty and truth of their Christian message. Appreciative of native intelligence and earnest defenders of aboriginal spiritual capacity, early Jesuit missionaries to Canada predicted that, once they had gained the linguistic wherewithal to present their message elegantly and coherently, entire aboriginal nations would quickly be brought to Christ. In their initial incomprehension of native cultures, the Jesuits characterized them in terms of their supposed deficits as *ni foi, ni loi, ni roi*— "without faith, without laws, without king." All that was needed, the Jesuits blithely concluded, was the wholesale importation of the Gallic church, monarch, and legal code, which they assumed that native peoples would readily adopt as their own.

But as their engagement with native North America deepened, and the strong attachment of aboriginal people to their own spiritual and cultural traditions became more apparent, these predictions were revealed as naive illusions. As the Jesuits settled in for a long, hard campaign of Christianization, their visions of New France, and of themselves, slowly but subtly began to alter. Increasingly, Canada was presented in metaphors less redolent of Eden than of Golgotha, as "one long continuation of crosses and sufferings": its very geography and climate providing the ideal environment for penitence and self-chastisement.[24] By the 1640s, then, the writings of Jesuit missionaries cast themselves not as triumphant evangelists but as living martyrs, despised and menaced by those they came spiritually to rescue, a rhetorical change that shifted the focus from the conversion of native peoples to the suffering servanthood of the missionaries themselves.

Intimations of violence in their colonial world were, strangely, not completely unwelcome to the Jesuits. Turning to the words of early Christian writer Tertullian, who characterized the "blood of martyrs as the seed of Christians," Jesuit Paul Le Jeune saw martyrdom as the missing link in the Jesuits' heretofore disappointing campaign to convert a continent:

> We have sometimes wondered whether we could hope for the conversion of this country without the shedding of blood; the principle received, it seems, in the Church of God, that the blood of Martyrs is the seed of Christians, made me at one time conclude that this was not to be expected—yea, that it was not even to be desired; considering the glory that redounds to God from the constancy of the martyrs, with whose blood all the rest of the earth has been so lately drenched, it would be a sort of curse if this quarter of the world should not partici-

pate in the happiness of having contributed to the splendour of this glory.[25]

Jesuit blood must flow to fertilize native propensities toward Catholicism, which could flower only after their sacrificial deaths. Only by these desperate measures could this implacable northern wasteland, he intimated, be transformed into a fruitful garden of aboriginal Catholics.

Martyrdom "in the fires of the Iroquois"[26] thus became seen by the Jesuits as a way both of anchoring themselves to this forbidding country and of sacralizing its earth. Perishing in "the way of this place" would forge an adamantine link between the martyr, the spiritual beneficiaries of their deaths, and the holy place where they had laid down their lives. Many missionary personnel, both male and female, penned "vows of stability" to remain in Canada, through which they sought to align their sometimes reluctant hearts with what they felt to be an inexorable Divine Will. Using their own blood as ink, as if to make more palpable their promise, missionaries vowed: "I am as ready to give all my blood, as I have this one drop."

Despite its evident terrors, then, death by torture at native hands had certain attractions for seventeenth-century Catholic missionaries. Dramatic, even spectacular, such a death prompted the inevitable comparisons with the horrid ends met by the ancient Christian martyrs. How better for the Jesuits to convey their seriousness of purpose than by risking such a fate? Being in Canada was truly a "martyrdom of the will" that violated all natural tendencies to self-preservation.

Christian prescriptions for the behavior of a martyr overlapped substantially with native expectations for a good death. Like native torture victims, martyrs were expected voluntarily to endure or even to embrace torture and suffer with stoicism if doing so was necessary to remain constant in their faith. Singing one's self-written obituary, one's personal death song, aligned easily with Christian expectations that valiant martyrs would pray and sing even in the flames.[27] Even the traditional warnings made by native prisoners of the chastening the captors would soon receive at their natal community's vengeful hands found a parallel in martyrs' ritual pardoning of those who persecuted them.

Martyrdom also represented something of a prudent investment of suffering in the imagination of seventeenth-century Catholics. For them, hellfire was not an antiquated or obscene idea, but a terrifying reality.

Martyrdom thus represented, for some, an *attractive* gamble: a sort of Pascal's wager of pain. Hours of intense suffering on earth could well shave off eons in purgatory or an eternity in hell. While it is hard to imagine in our own epoch of spiritual grade inflation, in which the most supine and lukewarm lives are seen as meriting eternal bliss, in the seventeenth-century heaven was the automatic portion of no soul, and even great saints, such as Theresa of Avila, expected to burn, if only for a time.[28] As Catholics played a deadly serious game of snakes and ladders with their eternal fates, sliding sinuously away from the celestial rewards with their sins and mounting gradually heavenward by dint of meritorious actions (and the grace of God), martyrdom was the single longest ladder on the playing board. Dying for God was a steep and perilous stairway to heaven.

Clash of the Rituals

Both the Jesuits and the Iroquois, then, rallied during dangerous times thanks to their insistent reassertion of inherited ideas regarding suffering, death, and the afterlife. But their persistent and generally unwelcome presence in one another's lives also tested the inventive limits of martyrdom, soul return, and sacrifice as coherent concepts. Even as the social instability and chronic tension caused by the presence of the other group heightened the need for their pristine performance, their mutual ignorance of their assigned role in the alternative ritual drama forced reluctant adaptations and compromises that unnerved both communities. For these rituals of death and rebirth, despite their violent, coercive aspects, were ultimately spectacles that relied for their efficacy and impact on the scrupulous performance of normative roles by all participants, protagonists and antagonists alike. The role of the saintly martyr dying for the conversion of the "heathen" or that of the noble warrior risking his own life to resuscitate his communities' dead imposed a rigid set of expectations upon the martyr's "slayer" or the Iroquois's "adoptee." But, in their mutual ignorance of the other's worldview, each group often misunderstood their assigned role in their antagonists' ritual life, causing both consternation and forced ritual improvisation.

The experiences of Jesuit missionary Isaac Jogues clearly illustrate the mutual frustration of thwarted expectations on both sides of the Iroquois-Jesuit encounter. In all but the final of Jogues's lengthy encounters with the Mohawk, his captors denied him that which, in his own mind, would have made his suffering—and indeed his whole life—meaningful: the martyrs' palm. As perhaps the most radical advocate of the Jesuits' renewed emphasis on the spiritual power of martyrdom for the conversion of the new world, Jogues had assiduously prepared himself for death by torture at Iroquois hands. But he waited in vain for this terrifying sequence of events to unfold. Though, alongside other captives, he repeatedly endured grueling preliminary rounds of torment at each new Mohawk village they entered, leaving him with missing and disfigured digits,[29] Jogues's treatment—despite a number of frustrating near misses—failed to escalate into the glorious martyrs' death that he had long envisioned.[30]

But if the behavior of his captors thwarted Jogues's expectations that they should serve as his deliverers unto life eternal, his own conduct precluded the easy performance of either of the Mohawks' traditional postwar options of ritual adoption and deadly sacrifice. Indeed, the very quality of defiant difference that would have enabled Jogues properly to perform his role in the death-by-torture scenario doomed him to failure as a would-be adoptee, thus quashing his chances of formal reception into the Iroquois body politic. For, although sacrificial victims were encouraged to remain intractable even unto death, compliance and conformity were expected from those chosen to live. Acceptance as a new member of the community was based on behavior.[31] Adoptees were expected quietly to extinguish their own identity and to adapt quickly and uncomplainingly to life with their new adoptive families.

This Jogues either would not or could not do. Though he sought to display "Christian meekness" toward his captors, his Catholic orientation to daily life made his behavior, in Iroquois terms, simply too bizarre and threatening for him to contain the returning soul of any self-respecting Mohawk.[32] Aspects of Jogues's behavior that for him were as natural as breathing, such as his inability to bear arms, clerical celibacy, hours spent in meditative prayer, and employment of characteristically Catholic postures and gestures, made him a deeply unsettling, puzzling figure for many villagers, decisively marooning him outside the magic circle of Mohawk communion.

Jogues's inability, as a Jesuit, to bear arms either in hunting or in battle caused consternation by challenging Iroquois conceptions of appropriate gender behavior, raising doubts about his masculinity and cutting him off from valuable opportunities for male camaraderie and bonding.[33] His refusal to share food with his captors because of his oft-stated concern that its ritual consecration to the Iroquois pantheon had rendered it unfit for any child of God to consume also marked Jogues as a defiant outsider. So did his stubborn unwillingness to marry, which denied his captors one of their most effective methods of postadoption captive integration. Moreover, though many seventeenth-century native groups, including the Iroquois, practiced periodic sexual abstention, often before hunting or warfare forays, voluntary lifelong celibacy, such as that practiced by the Jesuits, was highly unusual.[34] Because the objective of temporary native celibacy was the accretion of power, the black-robe's permanent eschewal of sexual congress was, understandably, quite threatening. What kind of formidable spiritual potency was the missionary honing by indefinitely denying himself any sexual outlet?

To the priests' formidable appetite for abstention was matched his seemingly insatiable lust for privacy, which caused both curiosity and concern in this tightly knit, collectivist culture. Jogues frequently escaped to his favorite hillside haunt at Ossernenon's periphery where, even in winter, he would kneel in the snow for hours mysteriously muttering and jabbing at his face and chest in front of two pieces of crossed wood. This behavior suggested, to the missionary's many repulsed observers, frighteningly malign intentions. Was he trying to kill them with his odd gestures and whispering? Was he thwarting their hunting with his spells? Traditional Haudenosaunee religion had a deeply unflattering designation for those who skulked alone, muttering and mysterious. Jogues must be a witch.[35]

Iroquois perceptions of Jogues were also shaped by the mixed commentary of their many Wendat adoptees, who presented the Jesuits as powerful sorcerers who could both help and harm, and by the calumnies of Dutch Protestants. In the absence of any systematic Catholic evangelization before the mid-1650s, the Iroquois were forced to rely on these back channels for information about this novel religion.[36] Though the Dutch intervened on several occasions to rescue French prisoners from their captivity among the Iroquois,[37] they also endangered them, wittingly or unwittingly, by their very public contempt for Catholic ritual practices, such as the use of holy water or the sign of the cross. Though it was likely that they meant only to convey that, from a Protestant perspective, these practices were inefficacious or idolatrous, the Iroquois appear to have intimated that a clear and present danger resided in these sinister gestures. Indeed, René Goupil's 1642 death has traditionally been attributed by Catholic historians to his making the sign of the cross over the head of a child, an action that apparently met with the fear and indignation of the boy's grandfather.[38]

The material paraphernalia of Catholicism also aroused suspicion. Jogues's mass kit, which he left in Ossernenon during his summer 1646 diplomatic mission, was blamed by many Mohawk for causing devastating crop failures. It is likely that the missionary's explanation of the purpose of this ritual paraphernalia—the celebration of the Eucharist, or the ritual consumption of the transubstantiated body of the God-man—would have exacerbated rather than alleviated Iroquois fears.[39]

Distrust of Jogues, enkindled during his long captivity in 1642–1643, was reignited by the missionary's diplomatic missteps in the mid-summer and fall of 1646. Entrusted by both the Jesuits and French civil authorities to extend the olive branch of peace to the Iroquois so as to reestablish a safe east-west corridor for trade and travel, Jogues badly muffed the opportunity, awakening rather than assuaging Mohawk fears and suspicions by revealing an uncanny knowledge of local geography, which was seen by his hosts as a provocative threat.[40]

Given that they likely saw Jogues as both a threatening sorcerer and an unmanly misfit, it is not surprising that his captors vacillated in their treatment of him during each of their three successive encounters. Their chronic indecision forced the missionary himself to up the ante, nudging his captors into the role he wished them to assume in his envisioned ritual drama simply by his successive and persistent returns to their enclave.

The intensity of Jogues's longing for martyrdom can be seen in the difficulty with which he decided, after more than a year of captivity, to escape his Mohawk captors, in August 1643. His strong sense of discomfort or regret seems to have remained with Jogues throughout his time in France and even after his return in the spring of 1644 to the relative safety of first Québec, and then Wendake.[41] Only in his persistent courtship of the Iroquois during the last six months of his life did

Jogues appear to find any relief from the sense of anomie and failed purpose that seems to have haunted him from the early days of his 1643 escape.[42]

The late-afternoon sunlight of October streamed into the large long-house in two smoky shafts, making elongated, ethereal pillars from the twin ventilation holes in its ceiling to its tightly packed dirt floor. It shone around the hanging leather door flap, to which the glances of the assembly occasionally flickered, as if in expectation of an imminent arrival. The smell of supper, bubbling in copper pots over the longhouse's twin fires, mingled invitingly with the smell of the wood smoke, and the warmth inside was in pleasant contrast to the crisp tang of the autumn air outside. The dinner invitation had already been extended, and the arrival of its purported guest of honor was tensely awaited. But belying its surface normality, the atmosphere was uneasy, strained. Even after endless councils, the fate of Isaac Jogues was undecided. Unanimity, the goal of any Iroquois conclave, had proven elusive and the tension was palpable.[43] As they waited Jogues's arrival in the longhouse, sidelong, evaluative glances and whispered exchanges punctuated the unnatural silence.

In the endless counsels held over the last few days, there had been points of agreement. All the clans—Wolf, Bear, and Tortoise alike—agreed that adopting Jogues was not an option. Tolerating the priest's presence in their cabins during the long winter months was not an attractive prospect. All the villagers vividly recalled his bizarre behavior and his unpredictable shifts from meek subservience to high-handed indignation as he upbraided them for their supposed faults in the name of his unknown God. During his previous lengthy captivity, Jogues had been simply another mouth to feed—though his bizarre scrupulosity meant that he consumed little or nothing. And then, after a year, he had successfully escaped. Such a man did not seem to merit the backhanded compliment of a warrior's prolonged death by torture.

But if he did not deserve ritual sacrifice and was too stiff-necked to be integrated successfully into the community, then what was to be done with him? Some had argued for ransom, others for execution. The Mohawk majority, comprised of the Wolf and Tortoise moieties, favored the former. Opposition came from within the internally divided Bear clan. Though reluctant to reignite the controversy, a tall youth, aware that this might be his last chance to state his case before the missionary's arrival, argued one last time for ransom, his voice breaking abruptly into the hush. By bargaining for the Jesuit's life, he reasoned, the community stood to profit. But his words faced the forceful opposition of an older, powerfully built warrior. Back in the community for a third time, he argued, Jogues was not just a nuisance, he was dangerous. Did the assembly not remember the strange box he had left behind after his last visit, which, when it had been forced open, caused the latest outbreak of the disease and famine that had ravaged their people? They must not be sidetracked by greed into letting that kind of witchcraft go unpunished. No, it must be death.[44]

The sudden flood of fading sunset light into the longhouse, created by the belated arrival of the missionary pulling back the leather door curtain, caught everyone off guard. As the summoned man, advancing several steps into the longhouse, said something in his strange, birdlike language, the powerfully built warrior strode purposefully forward. Realizing his intent several seconds too late, his younger opponent hurriedly flung himself between the man and Jogues. Thrusting out his arm to knock away the descending axe, the youth was wounded and, knocked off balance, crashed into the longhouse wall. Though he staggered quickly to his feet, his hand clasped over the deep gash in his arm, it was already too late.

At last, Jogues's patience did not go unrewarded. He felt the soft feathers languorously brushing against his body, not pulling away, but lingering, drawing him into a deeper embrace. When death came, the hatchet blow to the back of his bald pate, much like that which had smitten Goupil, killed him before his body hit the ground. The older warrior had abruptly ended the prolonged debate about the missionary's fate with a great swing of his axe that neatly cleaved Jogues's naked scalp.

The Curtain Falls on the First Act

If the Jesuits had, by the 1640s, created a deeply compelling case for martyrdom as the key to unlocking New France's dark and resistant heart, then its most ardent proponent and first priestly victim was Jogues himself. Convinced that he could best contribute to the conversion of native North America through a martyr's death, Jogues had persistently battered at Iroquois doors until his desires were finally consummated. On the morrow, his young donné, Jean de la Lande, a native of Dieppe, would meet an identical fate. The black-robe's death was thus bookended by the deaths of his lay assistants, as René Goupil had been slain during Jogues's initial capture in 1642.

All three of these executions were, from the Iroquois perspective, anomalous. Failing even to approximate the ritual contours of traditional postwar practices, they were atypically quick and unceremonious. Moreover, these slayings *cannot* be characterized as an expression of the community's unified, implacable will. Rather, they were controversial actions of a Mohawk minority. Indeed, it is perhaps in their deaths that these missionaries' utter failure to communicate across the cultural chasm is most evident, a failure that is only underlined by the postmortem treatment of their remains. Seen as troublemakers whose antisocial behavior had precluded their adoption into the Iroquois body politic, the three were decapitated. As a warning to other unwelcome outsiders, their severed heads were impaled upon the palisades of Ossernenon.[45]

But, for the Jesuits, death was death. Although the trio had not undergone the full gamut of ritual death by torture, Goupil, Jogues, and la Lande had nevertheless endured dramatic, difficult ordeals ending in their execution. Jogues's compelling account of the death of Goupil and of his own thirteen-month captivity among the Iroquois in 1642–1643, published in the *Jesuit Relations,* strongly engaged the empathy of his readers with its poignant combination of present suffering and future uncertainty. His travails attracted valiant new soldiers of Christ who likewise longed to spot the snow of Canada with their blood for the greater glory of God.[46]

The fact that these three men were slain in Mohawk territory, far removed from the civic and religious capital of New France at Québec, and farther still from Wendake, the primary theater of Jesuit missionary activity, has had important implications for their veneration, both at the time of their death and in the centuries since. In the seventeenth century, the remoteness and danger of Iroquoia[47] precluded any possibility of obtaining these men's remains to preserve as holy relics. Moreover, in the centuries since their deaths the interpolation of an international border between the evolving entities of "the United States of America" and "Canada," which effectively separated their death site from those of their successors in Wendake, would come to inflect these three particular deaths with special meaning. For their rediscoverers in the nineteenth century, this trio were, by virtue of where they had died, quintessentially *American* saints.[48]

So fell the first three of eight figures who, nearly 300 years later, would collectively be canonized as North America's first Catholic saints and martyrs. But though the curtain had rung down on the first, Iroquoian, scene of a two-act drama of Jesuit death, it would soon reopen on renewed tableaux of carnage in Huronia.

Marked for Death in Wendake

Throughout the winter of 1646–1647, the fate of Isaac Jogues was unknown outside Iroquoia.[49] But when the truth finally emerged, his martyrdom was celebrated "with a Mass of Thanksgiving rather than a Requiem for the repose of his soul."[50] Jogues's death was seen as the sine qua non of a missionary's fidelity to his calling, a signal mark of God's grace and favor, and as a critical investment in the long-term religious health of the colony. Jogues's example pushed Jesuit conceptions of colonial martyrdom in a far more volunteerist direction: from mere passive resignation in the face of danger to the more ardent, active courtship of a violent demise.[51] Henceforth, Canadian Jesuits would die in self-conscious imitation not only of Jesus, but also of Jogues. The missionary's voluntary return to Canada following his desperate 1643 escape and his deliberate retracing of his own bloody footsteps back to Kanienke,[52] the land of the Iroquois, despite his apparent foreknowledge of the fate that there awaited him, made him, in Jesuit eyes, the first martyr of New France.[53]

But the battle was now on to be his successor. In private correspondence to family members in France, as well as in their published works, individual Jesuits stationed in North America vied with one another to express their passion and preparedness for martyrdom, which they often referred to as a "palm," "crown," or "garland." When reporting the violent deaths of missionaries, converts, and colonists alike, they often opined that the slain were "more to be envied than pitied," and sought to prepare their own family and friends for the likelihood that they too might not survive the coming storm.

Some Jesuits openly fretted about what their status as the quick, rather than the dead, said about their spiritual fitness. Writing to his brother Pierre in France, missionary Nöel Chabanel shared his vivid disappointment that a last-minute personnel reassignment had denied him the violent death awarded his colleague Gabriel Lalemant:

> Your Reverence has been very near to possessing a brother a Martyr; but alas! in the mind of God, to merit the honor of Martyrdom, a virtue of another stamp than mine is needed. . . . I . . . was sent upon a Mission more remote and more laborious, but not so fruitful in Palms and Crowns as that of which my cowardice has, in the sight of God, rendered me unworthy. . . . The ravages of the Iroquois throughout this country will perhaps, someday, supply what is wanting. . . . Remember me at the holy Altar as a victim doomed, it may be, to the fires of the Iroquois.[54]

Others sought to prepare themselves physically, mentally, and spiritually to grasp the palm should it be extended to them. Jean de Brébeuf, the longest serving missionary in New France and most respected veteran of Huronia, escalated, during the latter years of his life, his already daunting regime of self-punishment, which encompassed flagellation, the wearing of a hair shirt, and strict limits on food consumption and sleep. Visions of a scourged and crucified Christ enflamed Brébeuf's already fervent desire to suffer with and for his savior. But Brébeuf's actions can also be read as a deliberate program of self-hardening to ready himself for torture, a practice typical of many young Wendat and Haudenosaunee, who tested their own limits with fire and ice to prepare for battle and its tortuous aftermath.[55]

Brébeuf's behavior during the 1640s so convinced his community that he was destined for a martyr's death that, concerned that his body might be destroyed, his colleagues persuaded him to donate a vial of his blood while he yet lived, that they might revere it as a relic in such an eventuality.[56] This action signaled their receptivity to his mystical prophesies, which had become ever more urgent and gloomy as the decade progressed. In one vision, in something of a reverse Passover, Brébeuf witnessed his own cassock and those of his Jesuit colleagues being sprinkled with the blood of Christ, marking them for a holy death.[57]

Those who received Brébeuf's red rain were as envied as those whose portals were smeared with safety in the Exodus story. In martyrdom-obsessed Huronia, it was being passed over by the angel of death that was caused lamentation, not his visitation.

The Jesuits' emphasis on preparing themselves for violence in the wake of Jogues's death was all the more appropriate in that many of their number increasingly faced a double threat to their safety. To the looming threat of Iroquois invasion was coupled the prospect of peril within the very mission villages they had established throughout Wendake. Though these missions may not have been the unqualified success they had worked for and dreamed of, Jesuit success in winning a small but ardent Catholic minority had divided the tight-knit, clan-based Wendat confederacy religiously, culturally, and politically. This widening cleavage would have tragic results for this heretofore unified, prosperous, and dominant people. But the Jesuits would also reap the dire consequences of the spiritual divisions that they had deliberately introduced.

A House Divided

The Wendat people of the 1630s and 1640s shared many of the fears and preoccupations of both of their sometime antagonists, the Iroquois and the Jesuits. Like the Iroquois, their distant southern kin, the Wendat had been weakened by crucifying waves of epidemic, the result of European diseases to which they had no immunity. But, like the Jesuits, the Wendat were increasingly concerned about the Iroquois threat to their southerly flank. And yet though they alone faced the double threat of invasion *and* epidemic, the Wendat were unable to respond by unanimously turning to traditional explanatory motifs such as soul return or martyrdom. Their religious division precluded collective articulation of a satisfying explanation for their current crisis that would allow them together to chart a common way forward. Rather than going on the offensive to recoup their human losses, like the Iroquois, or hallowing their fallen as spiritual victors, like the Jesuits, the Wendat experienced, in the decade before their nation's final collapse, a bitter internal struggle. Factions within their divided communities advanced mutually incompatible explanations of their present predicament and advocated competing solutions to this daunting triple threat of disease, war, and disunity. Of this ghastly trio, it was the specter of their own division that most haunted the Wendat as they fully realized it undercut their ability to effectively confront these other challenges. And yet both the traditionalist majority and the Catholic minority persisted in attempting to persuade—or force—the other faction to adopt their own analysis of the present and prescription for the future.[58]

Oddly enough, when it came to identifying the cause of the epidemics, the Wendat were firmly united. Virtually everyone blamed the Jesuits.[59] Missionary immunity to these illnesses, their self-presentation as powerful shaman, and their characterisation of epidemic as God's punishment of Wendat obstinacy in rejecting Christianity made this universal attribution a natural assumption.[60]

This fragile unanimity soon collapsed, however, as the Wendat considered the thorny issue of how best to respond to the threat posed by the black-robes. For, surprisingly, blaming the Jesuits for outbreaks of pestilence did not automatically generate violent opposition to their presence or even the rejection of their Christian message. Drawing upon traditional beliefs that only the supernaturally powerful agent who precipitated an illness could ritually reverse it, Wendat converts turned to the Jesuits for the remediation of the very scourge they were thought to have unleashed. These new Christians interpreted baptism as a physically curative rite capable of restoring corporeal health in *this* life rather than a ceremony securing one's salvation in the next.[61]

This unique perception of the sacrament was all the more innovative given that baptism was strongly associated by both Jesuit missionaries and Wendat traditionalists with death. The Jesuit gatekeepers of this transformative Christian ritual were concerned lest baptism inadvertently be administered to those whose subsequent apostasy would profane the sacrament, threatening not simply their own salvation, but that of the celebrant who had so unwisely chosen to admit them into the Church. Thus, baptism was typically administered only on a Wendat's deathbed, with its sacred water followed in close succession by the holy oil of the viaticum. Closely associated with a Christian infant's reception into the earthly church militant in seventeenth-century France, baptism more often heralded an adult neophyte's ascendance into the heavenly church triumphant in Wendake.

Given both the prevalence of devastating epidemics and missionary fondness for end-of-life baptism, Wendat traditionalists quite rationally argued that the ceremony was a sinister piece of sorcery whose watery cross actively marked an individual for death.[62] Curative interpretations of baptism were thus the perspective of a minority, whose optimistic assessment of the sacrament as a healing balm bore within it the dark seeds of disenchantment. Should the ritual fail to fulfill its purported promise of health and happiness, enthusiastic supporters of the Jesuits could be transformed into their most adamant enemies.

Traditionalist perceptions of Jesuit malevolence were further reinforced by the dreams and visions of many in the period who claimed to have peeked behind the missionary mask of beneficence and glimpsed something altogether more disturbing. In one particularly sensational allegation, a native woman claimed during a near-death experience to have glimpsed the Christian heaven before her soul was returned to her body. She described it as a place of torture in which Christians delighted in visiting hellish torments upon the unlucky converted.[63] Jesuit insistence on God's wrathful punishment of sinners and their apparent relish in vividly describing hellfire would have made her dream convincing to Wendat auditors.

Such revelations led some Wendat to advocate the direct confrontation of these malevolent sorcerers, arguing that, despite its obvious dangers this was the only responsible long-term option. In a desperate bid to save their people from what they saw as the unwholesome, divisive influence of the Jesuits, traditionalist radicals and ex-converts launched a series of ill-fated, low-level attacks against both missionaries and converts with the aim of killing or driving out the black-robes, thus restoring their communities' former religious and political unity. In 1637, for example, traditionalists accused a number of prominent missionaries, including Jean de Brébeuf, of sorcery, a capital crime in Wendat society.[64] Though the accused nimbly thwarted death, their preservation was largely due to the strong desire of the Wendat majority to continue their political and economic alliance with the French rather than reflecting their disbelief in the credibility of the allegations.

Neophyte Christians were far more vulnerable to intimidation than were their missionary mentors. Unlike the black-robes, Catholic Wendat could not threaten trade sanctions or appeal to the backing of the colonial government. Though the slaying of leading Wendat Christians, such as the charismatic Joseph Chihoatenhwa in 1640, was often conveniently attributed by their communities to perfidious Iroquois raiders[65] (an assertion that the Jesuits, despite their suspicions, were powerless to refute[66]), it is likely that they were the secret victims of their own kith and kin, who saw their voluntary alignment with the malign sorcerers of a foreign faith as putting them beyond the pale of toleration.[67]

Traditionalists' alarms did have a basis in reality. The creation of a small but vocal Wendat Catholic minority struck deeply at the ritual ties that bound the community together. New Catholics' stubborn refusal to participate in the reciprocal practices that had long been the sinews of community cohesiveness left the circle of perfect participation, heretofore taken for granted, heartbreakingly incomplete, decisively transforming subsistence, marriage, and burial patterns.

Converts shunned "eat-all" feasts, both on the basis of both their supposed "gluttony" and their framing in traditionalist terms as an act of thanksgiving for the animal's sacrificial self-donation. They refused, even in situations of dire famine, to hunt on Sundays, and generally rejected traditionalist suitors in favor of marrying fellow Christians. Most seriously, they attempted to withhold the remains of the baptized from the communal internment with their traditionalist kin during the Feast of the Dead, an elaborate festival of disinterment, mourning, and collective reburial that was perhaps the most important single facilitator of Wendat collective identity.[68]

To these disruptions of community's ritual life they added a restless and determined evangelism. Wendat Catholics were often spirited and vocal about their new faith. Ardent and determined, they harassed family, friends, and neighbors with the evidence of their supposed sins, urging them to convert forthwith. Lest their boycotting of traditionalist ceremonies be misunderstood, they lashed out with stinging invectives against the old ways and energetically advocated the reinvention of Wendat society along Christian lines.

As the specter of a full-scale Iroquois invasion loomed, the divisions introduced by the Christian minority were no longer seen as simply annoying, high-handed, or hurtful but as deeply dangerous. By forming a countercommunity within the community, Wendat Catholics imperiled their people's political cohesion, spiritual unanimity and military strength in the teeth of this increasingly serious external threat.

By 1648, the deepening crisis led a small group of traditionalists and Wendat ex-Catholics to take decisive action. The hour was too late, they argued, for gradual consensus-building or for the endless talk of a witchcraft trial. They must strike quickly and decisively and force the Jesuits to permanently leave their homelands. For these Wendat radicals, missionary culpability in the ills endangering their society made their slaying or ejection from Wendake an imperative, even if this precipitated a shift in the Wendat's long-standing economic alliance with the French.

In a desperate, last-ditch effort to remake Wendat foreign policy through a single, fateful assassination, six traditionalist leaders in April 1648 took a solemn pledge to "kill the first Frenchman they could find alone."[69] They anticipated that this action would so appall and frighten the Jesuits that they would abandon Huronia. In their absence, it was hoped that the Wendat Catholic faction would either collapse entirely, or at least be significantly weakened. Traditionalists could then negotiate a diplomatic solution with the Iroquois and approach their Dutch allies to serve as their new source of European trade goods. Moving against the Jesuits would thus be a game changer, signaling the Wendat's final break with the French. In one fell swoop, they could thus defeat the black-robed sorcerers, court the Iroquois diplomatically, and religiously reunify their troubled confederacy.[70]

First Blood

On April 28, 1648, they struck. Their victim was twenty-two-year-old donné Jacques Douart, who was abruptly cut down in full daylight, virtually within sight of the fortified Jesuit headquarters of Sainte-Marie-among-the-Huron. But, though Douart's body was left lying as a mute threat,[71] his death did not accomplish what the radical traditionalists had hoped. Although they had been correct in thinking that the position of the isolated Huronia Jesuits was tenuous, they had themselves failed to appreciate the strong preference of the pragmatic Wendat majority for maintaining economic, if not religious, links with the French. Despite the Wendats' deep linguistic, cultural, and spiritual ties to the Iroquois, with whom they shared a common history and language, long-entrenched patterns of conflict and reprisal between the two groups proved difficult for many Wendat to surmount. Given the objections of the Wendat majority, radical traditionalists were forced to back down and offer the hated Jesuits rich compensation for the donné's death.[72]

In accepting these presents, however, the Jesuits paid their own heavy price: sweeping Douart's inconvenient death under the metaphorical rug. In any other circumstances they would likely have celebrated the young man's untimely demise as a Christian martyrdom.[73] But their own complicity in accepting compensation for his assassination rendered this possibility moot. They had, after all, accepted the thirty pieces of silver. Thus, though Douart's death occurred a full three months prior to that of the next casualty, Jesuit priest Antoine Daniel, who fell in the first battle of the long-anticipated Iroquois invasion, it would be Daniel rather than Douart who would be celebrated as the first martyr of Huronia. But if the Jesuits thought that their diplomatic smoothing over of Douart's murder would eliminate the continued threats posed by radicalized traditionalists and Wendat ex-Catholics, they would soon be proved wrong. Over the next nineteen months, these factions would play a pivotal role in three of the five remaining martyrs' deaths.

Throughout 1648, the Jesuits remained transfixed by Brébeuf's menacing vision of a huge cross in the sky, floating northward from the land of the Iroquois: a cross that was, he noted ominously, "large enough to crucify us all."[74] Given the increasing frequency of Iroquois incursions into Wendat territory, this vision seemed to be closer than ever to realization. Much as Jogues had lingered outside, gathering himself before throwing open his life's last door, the Jesuits of isolated Wendake waited, standing on the false peace that stretched out below their feet, as thin and insubstantial as the treacherous April ice on the Saint Lawrence River. Any false step on its fragile surface threatened abruptly to crack open its icy jaws, hurling the unwary into its frigid, watery gullet and death.

Even when the much-anticipated onslaught came, it was still a shock. On July 4, 1648, the Wendat village of Teanaostaye/Saint-Joseph fell abruptly to Iroquois attack. Many Wendat were dispatched in a devastatingly effective surprise ambush by Iroquois forces that had silently amassed during the night. They attacked at dawn, while some inhabitants still slept and other attended the day's first mass. As their presence was detected, chaos ensued as warriors belatedly rallied to repulse the invaders, who had already breached their palisades. Those who could fled did so, while children, the sick, and the elderly desperately tried to hide, "the cries of infants as yet unaccustomed to prudent fear betraying their hiding-places."[75]

As Saint-Joseph's pastor, Antoine Daniel's self-assigned task in the melee was the last acts of spiritual care for those he thought of as his flock, a mission that made flight as unthinkable to him as fighting alongside the Wendat warriors. As the village burned, Daniel hurriedly baptized neophytes by aspersion and conferred general absolution, rushing to complete the ritual formulae so his catechists could escape capture or death by the raiders. The priest's unexpected emergence from his log church, still arrayed in his clerical vestments, temporarily stalled the Iroquois advance, but once the shock of this unfamiliar apparition diminished, his body quivered with arrows like a latter-day Saint Sebastian, his final dispatch accomplished by a musket ball to the chest. Daniel's corpse was then immolated, like a burnt offering, in his own sanctuary, which had been set ablaze with Teanaostaye's other wooden structures. Of the eight men who would, in 1930, be canonized as the North American martyrs, Daniel was the fourth to fall and the first in Huronia.

Seventeen months later, Charles Garnier, another Jesuit missionary, would succumb in a similar early morning raid on the Huron village of Etharita. Like Daniel, Garnier was, according to Wendat witnesses, cut down in the midst of performing his priestly duties under fire. Badly wounded with a musket shot, he was still apparently able to crawl to administer the last rites to a gravely injured Wendat Catholic. He was then executed, much as Goupil, Jogues, and la Lande had been, with a single ax blow to the back of his head. Both Daniel and Garnier fell alongside scores of other men, women, and children, both Christians and traditionalists, in the midst of a violent attack on the villages in which they were stationed. They were in no way singled out for their fate. Casualties of war, they were slain in the course of battle, as Iroquois invaders fought to establish control of the targeted Wendat villages. Both died the battlefield deaths of unarmed noncombatants.

Having struck this devastating blow at Teanaostaye in July of 1648, the Iroquois would again become quiescent, contenting themselves with minor raids until their next major offensive in mid-March 1649. Over the winter, the fragile ice of peace seemed once again slowly to form. Yet just under the surface, the dark waters were always moving.

"A Cruel Death, if Ever There Was One in This World"

Bloody and naked, the two Jesuits knelt praying before the torture stakes to which, tethered, they would soon end their lives. Their knees stained the granular white-gray snow of March a dull red. Their vision obscured by the haze of blood and sweat that clouded their eyes, they reverently groped with mutilated fingers the rough wood of the stakes, kissing the New World crosses to which they would soon be fastened, anticipating that their reassuring solidness would hold up their bodies, weakened from hours of torture. They were a mass of wounds and burns, their faces masked with smears of dried black blood against which their eyes and teeth gleamed startlingly white. On the nude chest, shoulders, and back of each was a distinctive black-and-pink tattoo: a pattern of large, asymmetrical shapes equidistant from one another, the imprint of the necklace of red-hot axe-heads that had charred and seared their flesh.[76] Turning to Jean de Brébeuf, his senior colleague, the soft-spoken young Parisian Jesuit Gabriel Lalemant voiced the sentiments felt by each as they prepared themselves during this brief respite for their final ordeal: "Today we are become a spectacle for men, and for angels."[77] They were so close now to death, and so much depended on their dying well. For the glory of God, for the conversion of the "infidels" and "apostates" who tortured them, for the edification of the Wendat "flock" captured with them and for the salvation of their own souls they must be stalwart and unflinching to the end.

Though it seemed a lifetime ago, the intervening minutes stretched on the rack of suffering, it had only been five hours since their capture, with a number of Wendat survivors, in the aftermath of the desperate dawn battle for the mission village of Saint Louis, at the epicenter of Huronia. Startling abruptly into consciousness in the inky cold of the pre-dawn hours, Brébeuf's breath had made ghosts even inside the small missionaries' cabin. Was it a distant shout, the faint smell of burning, or the nudge of his guardian angel that had aroused him? He was unsure, knowing only that upon awakening he was plunged into a palpable sense of danger as shockingly tangible as if he had fallen from the safety of a boat's deck into the icy chop below. Adrenaline surging through his body, Brébeuf paused only briefly to kneel in urgent prayer, genuflecting as he rose. Darting to the door, he scanned the horizon. The faint orange glow he detected to the south was coming from the wrong direction to be the dawn and was too early. Taenhatentaron/Saint-Ignace,[78] the neighboring village, he deduced, must already be in flames, sacked by Iroquois intruders. His own settlement of Saint-Louis or the Jesuit headquarters of Sainte-Marie to its west would be the next logical targets for invasion. The ordeal that had for years twisted the threads of his religious imagination on its dark loom now seemed imminent. Could he faithfully perform the role he had so often rehearsed, deep in the inner recesses of his mind? Before charging off to prepare for the desperate hours that would follow, Brébeuf inhaled deeply, mentally bracing himself against the cross of Christ. Addressing the crucified one who had, in the past months and years, haunted his visions "bearing his Cross, or indeed, being attached to it,"[79] he prayed for strength during the coming tribulations.

Brébeuf's premonitions were soon proven correct by the arrival of Saint-Ignace's wounded escapees, and even before full dawn, the onslaught was upon them. As the palisades of Saint-Louis were being breached, Brébeuf and Lalemant performed with all the reverent dispatch they could muster the exercises of their faith, hastily baptizing catechumens and absolving neophytes, much as Antoine Daniel had done nine months before. They sought spiritually to ready the evacuees, mostly women and children, for their desperate journey in the predawn darkness over the snows to the safety of the fortified Jesuit headquarters and to assist Saint-Louis's defenders in putting on the armor of God before battle. Both priests elected to stay with the largely Christian enclave of male defenders, led by the noted warrior Estienne Annaotaha. Like Brébeuf, Annaotaha, a fervent Catholic, had received mystical presentiments of the forthcoming attack and had made a general confession of his sins only days before.[80] Realistic regarding their slim chances of successfully defending the settlement, the village's native Christian leadership and the two Jesuits resolved to die well and together. Asked Annaotaha: "could we ever abandon these two good fathers, who for us have exposed their lives? . . . Let us then die with them, and we shall go in company to Heaven."[81]

As predicted, the battle, though fiercely fought, proved short and decisive. By 9:00 that morning, the church and longhouses of Saint-Louis, like those of Taenhatentaron only hours earlier, were engulfed in flames. In the pearly overcast of the mid-March morning, grim lines of tethered prisoners struggled to keep their footing through the drifted, uneven snow as they were marched southward to the site of the Iroquois's earlier victory, their staggering progress poignantly similar to the hurried evacuation of Saint-Louis women and children hours earlier.

In the ashes of Saint-Ignace, Wendat and Jesuit captives alike endured the same treatment that had been meted out to Isaac Jogues seven years previously. Stripped naked, they were forced to run the gauntlet formed by twin lines of assembled Iroquois warriors, who punched and kicked them as they staggered, reeling from blow to blow, down the narrow way between the hostile rows. Then their fingernails were torn out. Because of their inscrutability, these sufferings were doubly excruciating. As mere preliminary torture, they were the universal fate of all prisoners and thus revealed nothing about whether an individual had been chosen for adoption into the community or designated to endure sacrificial death by torture. Like Jogues before them, the missionaries and Wendat captives were forced to wait as their ultimate destiny was weighed in the scales of the Iroquois.

In a hastily convened council amid the still-smoking buildings, the victors assembled. Their spirits were high. From their perspective, things could not have gone more smoothly. The only unsacked settlement of any strategic importance in the immediate area was Sainte-Marie, which they were confident they could take on the morrow. It was quickly agreed to bring most of the captured Wendat to their homelands for ritual adoption. Their honorable performance in the morning's fighting, even grossly outnumbered, had only heightened these captives' value in their captors' eyes, and the Iroquois were jubilant. Once remade ritually through adoption, the Wendat captives would be invaluable assets in future battles. Indeed, today's engagements had only reinforced the Iroquois's already strong confidence in the efficacy of their ancient rites of ritual inclusion and identity reassignment: for some of the most assiduous assailants of Taenhatentaron and Saint-Louis were its own prior residents. Wendat from this very area, likely friends and family of the current prisoners, they were the former catechists of Brébeuf himself.[82]

For most of the heavily guarded Wendat captives, their early morning trek from Saint-Louis to Saint-Ignace was only a foretaste of the daunting weeks-long slog that now awaited them. Though many lives had been spared by the Iroquois ruling of adoption over execution, danger still lurked. Amnesty applied only the able-bodied in the huddled cluster of guarded prisoners, their naked bodies goose-fleshed in the cutting winds. Those who were badly injured or judged unable to make the demanding journey still faced summary execution. In the days and weeks ahead, Wendat causalities would continue to mount as those prisoners unable to match the pace set by their conquerors would be quickly dispatched so as not to slow the group's progress.[83]

Enthusiastic about adopting the defeated Wendat villagers, whose cultural patterns and language so closely matched their own, the Iroquois were more equivocal regarding the captured Jesuits. The missionaries' infamous refusal to bear arms precluded their being honed from Catholic ploughshares into Iroquois swords. Their puzzling and unnatural celibacy, moreover, prevented their flesh being the instrument through which deceased Iroquois husbands could return to comfort their grieving widows. But as men highly esteemed by the French, their capture had a certain political and propagandistic value, making ransom an attractive option. An influential senior warrior among the invaders argued strongly for the two missionaries' preservation and eventual redemption, even putting up as collateral two of his own necklaces of wampum, currency that had a strongly symbolic as well as material value.[84] And so, by midmorning, the weighty matter of the captives' fate appeared to have been settled in favor of life virtually across the board, with only the most damaged destined for quick and unceremonious dispatch.

Meanwhile, ignorant that they had been earmarked for preservation, the group of mostly Catholic captives sought to rally one another's spirits in the face of possible death by torture. Echoing Annaotaha's words of Christian solidarity in life and death before the battle of Saint-Louis, Brébeuf promised the faithful heavenly glory in return for the steadfast endurance of what he clearly expected to be their last, and crowning, moments on earth:

> My children, let us lift our eyes to Heaven at the height of our afflictions; let us remember that God is the witness of our sufferings, and will soon be our exceeding great reward. Let us die in this faith; and let us hope from his goodness the fulfillment of his promises. I have more pity for you than for myself; but sustain with courage the few remaining torments.

They will end with our lives; the glory which follows them will never have an end.[85]

"Echon," the Catholic Wendat captives replied, using Brébeuf's Wendat name,[86] "our spirits will be in Heaven when our bodies shall be suffering on earth. Pray to God for us, that he may show us mercy; we will invoke him even until death."

Ironically, it would be these very public prayers and exhortations, undertaken to stoke the fires of their Christian courage in the face of a frightening fate, that would become the very factor precipitating that end. The ardor of these Catholics' spiritual preparation for their anticipated ordeal seems to have played a critical role in reversing the decision to let all the able-bodied captives of Saint-Ignace and Saint-Louis, including the two black-robes, live.

He heard the familiar voice long before he saw the missionary. It rang out, through the dense and shifting smoke of the smoldering longhouse ruins—persuading, commanding, invoking, beseeching—the same voice that had so engaged his own youthful imagination with fascinating and disturbing descriptions of hell and paradise. Echon. Though it seemed a lifetime ago, he had sat up talking with this man long into the night, their voices low and intimate in the glowing darkness fireside, heedless of those who slept in the humped forms of the longhouses under the clouded moon, their bodies slumped like children's toys abandoned in midgame. As the embers glowed, casting ruddy reflections on the copper kettle suspended over the dying fire, they spoke of the creation of the earth and the life of the world to come, the adventures of Aatahensic, the first woman on earth, and of Adam, the first man.[87]

Even then, he recalled, the man had been a better talker than a listener. Though he gave his full attention, considering, inevitably his mouth would draw itself into a tight line and his gray brows arc together in a sharp frown. His eyes, though always alert, would grow abstracted in the firelight: you could almost hear him thinking of his riposte, planning his next speech. Talking, he was another man, the spell of reflection abruptly broken by his animated gestures, which sketched images into the spark-filled air. His themes were always the same. He beat at them like a blacksmith arcing his hammer toward the anvil, the full weight of his arms and shoulders bludgeoning the red-hot metal into its assigned shape. Hell. Repentance. Baptism. Suffering. Glory.

The man recalled, with a sudden flush of shame, how he too had been gradually shaped. Like a glowing bar of metal, he too had been molded, made into the missionary's tool. Persuaded by these persistent lies, convinced of the hidden realities of which the bearded man seemed so passionately certain, he had allowed himself gradually to stop speaking, to listen. So long ago, before his new life as an Iroquois, this man's fingers had lightly traced on his forehead the cool cross of baptism.

And now, even now, Echon was still at it. Through the sullen, lingering smoke he could see Echon haranguing his slight, bearded colleague and the praying Wendat who surrounded him. Even nude, bloody, and disheveled, his voice still held the same level of authority and conveyed the same absolute certainty. As he spoke, his familiar, beautiful lies once again unfurled like bright banners above the battlefield: "God is the witness of our sufferings! Let us die in this faith!" Always the same battering themes. Why were they listening? Why had he? It was enough.

The man shouldered his way through the crowd until his gaze locked on those familiar eyes. Almost gently, he addressed his former catechist: "Echon, you say that baptism and the suffering of this life lead straight to Paradise. You will go there soon, for I am going to baptize you, and make you suffer well."[88] The man turned to the blazing fire, the symbolic center of any Wendat village, where the ubiquitous copper kettle hung on its trivet. Carefully upending its boiling water three times over the missionary's head, he intoned: "Go to heaven, you are well baptized." He ended his improvised torture ritual by reminding Brébeuf of the Jesuit's own oft-repeated claims, the words bubbling up from his long-term memory as if from a subterranean stream: "you see plainly that we treat you as a friend, since we shall be the cause of your eternal happiness, thank us, then, for these good offices we give you, for the more you suffer, the more will your God reward you."[89]

As unprecedented as they were—boiling water not being a traditional torture technique—this unnamed ex-Huron ex-Catholic's ritual actions abruptly reversed the decision to let the two missionaries live and rapidly escalated the pace and scale of their torment.[90] In an attempt to prevent Brébeuf's annoying proselytization, his torturers cut off his lips. When this proved inefficacious, his tongue was seared with hot metal objects. But his persistence in speaking, despite these serious injuries, prompted its eventual amputation, filling the missionary's mouth with blood that flowed like a warm, salty drink down his throat and dribbled down his chin, making Brébeuf's beard a bloody mat. His thighs and calves were then slashed and burned and his jaw smashed. As his strength began to wane, his scalp was pulled from his skull.

Brébeuf's behavior through these ordeals was, according to the Wendat witnesses who lived to escape and to report it, extraordinarily courageous. Even in the midst of his torture, he apparently used his voice only to pray, preach, and exhort. Otherwise, he "suffered like a rock, insensible to the fires and the flames, without uttering any cry, and keeping a profound silence, which astonished his executioners themselves: no doubt, his heart was then reposing in his God."[91] During the final moments of his life, Brébeuf's heart was pulled from his chest and distributed among those who sought to imbibe, with his flesh, something of his courage.[92]

Lalemant's fate was similar, though in addition to these shared torments, he was also burned and blinded. Physically frailer than his robust older colleague, Lalemant endured sporadic torture until the next day, giving up his ghost only at dawn on March 19, 1649, when his heart, like that of Brébeuf, was ritually ingested.[93]

The Many Meanings of March 1649

Particularly for Brébeuf, who had been in Huronia for years, as opposed to Lalemant's mere months, the events of March 16, 1649, represented a valuable and long-awaited opportunity to display religious fidelity to the twisted figure suffering on his cross. Brébeuf knew the Christian script of martyrdom by heart and was ready at a moment's notice to step onto its stage, into the drama observed "by men and by angels." In accepting the gauntlet thrown down to him from heaven by the newly martyred Jogues, Brébeuf was determined faithfully to perform his long-sought role as a martyr until his last breath. Just as Jogues effectively accelerated the process of his own martyrdom by repeatedly returning to Kanienke, Brébeuf seems to have sealed his own fate by his stubborn determination, despite numerous warnings, to preach and to pray. It was likely Brébeuf's own evangelical zeal that ultimately doomed him and Lalemant. His persistent prayer and audacious religious harassment of his captors eventually unraveled the amnesty brokered by his would-be Iroquois rescuer, whose redemptive wampum was unceremoniously returned to him in the aftermath of the missionaries' extended executions.[94]

And yet Brébeuf's conduct on that day also displayed his strong awareness of the values and practices of the aboriginal milieu in which he had lived for nearly two decades. A longtime observer of aboriginal postwar ritual, he was intimately familiar with their dynamics. Indeed, the genius of Brébeuf's behavior under torture was that it simultaneously fulfilled and transformed two very different sets of religious and cultural expectations. His courage spoke to the ancient expectations placed on Christian martyrs for fidelity under duress even as it fulfilled pan-aboriginal conventions for the postwar behavior of captives. The constant prayer his tormentors tried so hard to arrest was *his* death song. Brébeuf's hectoring evangelism served the same function as traditional "trash talk," simultaneously infuriating his captors even as the missionary's determination to persist in provocation despite their violent retribution earned their grudging respect. By meeting aboriginal expectations, Brébeuf morphed Christian martyrdom to better reflect New World realities. In so doing, he sought to inspire his Wendat flock to win these laurels for themselves while planting Tertullian's seeds in the hearts of his tormentors, seeds that might, in due course, flower into Catholic fervor.

For Iroquois traditionalists who formed the majority of the participants in the events of March 16–17, 1649, the postwar treatment of Jean de Brébeuf and Gabriel Lalemant was business as usual. Although they doubtless saw the missionaries' captivity and death as meaningful, their purported meaning would have been informed by their own traditional concepts of soul return and sacrifice, rather than the anti-Christian animus that would be misleadingly attributed to them by centuries of Catholic commentators. Though the Iroquois were by no means hermetically sealed from Christian influences, the exact congruity of the treatment accorded these two Jesuit missionaries with that endured by countless aboriginal prisoners of war demonstrates that traditional motivations and protocols were dominant in the Iroquois's perception and treatment of the pair.[95] Much like the more numerous Wendat prisoners with whom they had been captured, the two missionaries experienced firsthand the inexorable working through of the traditional stages of Iroquois postwar protocol: enduring capture, the gauntlet and preliminary torture, and then waiting as their conquerors weighed their fates of death or adoption. Their scales, however, were heavily weighted in favor of living captivity over ritual destruction, and even in the case of the black-robes the Iroquois made the near-routine determination of life. It was only belatedly that this majority ruling would be reversed by a small but significant group within their ranks. Ex-Wendat ex-Catholic adoptees would overturn their verdict as brusquely and suddenly as they upended the kettle of boiling water over the tensed and waiting shoulders of Brébeuf and Lalemant.

The "Rage of Tyrants"?

The Jesuits' conceptual model of martyrdom was based largely on the persecution of the early Christians by the Roman state. Though many rhetorical attempts would be made during the coming months, years, and centuries to force Brébeuf and Lalemant's Iroquois captors to wear the gladiatorial sandals of ancient martyrs' Roman persecutors, the two scenarios of ritual torture and death were, despite their similar elements of violence and spectacle, more different than alike.

Iroquois insistence on the absolute control of the conquerors in decisions regarding the fate of the captured posed one of the greatest adaptive challenges for the would-be martyrs of the New World. The ancient Roman context accorded the individual Christian dissident considerable agency in the circumstances of his or her death (including whether the death occurred at all). At bottom, the state's persecution of its tiny Christian minority was an attempt to reestablish the religious uniformity of the Roman Empire by enforcing observance of the cult of the emperor and the worship of the ancient pantheon of divinities.[96] Whether an individual Christian conformed to this demand through religious capitulation or death was, for the state, ultimately unimportant. This indifference as to means gave Christian dissidents a high level of agency in the torture process as, at any moment, they could arrest their torment by acquiescing to forceful demands that they apostatize.

Indeed, much of the ritual drama of early Christian martyrdom arose from audience awareness that martyrs, by refusing to abjure their faith, were effectively torturing themselves. It was their *choice* to suffer this torment: a choice endlessly repeated in the elongating seconds of escalating pain that became the basis of the martyrs' reverent celebration by their fellow Christians. They had opted for death, even the tortuous death of the arena, over religious dishonor.[97]

The logic of aboriginal postwar practices in seventeenth-century North America, however, did *not* accord torture victims this high degree of control or agency. Nor did death by torture seek to force the transformation of a prisoner's political or religious identity: that was the goal of its sister ritual, adoption. Because ritual torture sought to punish selected captives for their non-Iroquois identity, rather than to transform that identity, it is likely that even if Brébeuf or Lalemant had offered to abjure their Catholic faith in exchange for their lives, this proposal would have been seen as irrelevant or (given the Iroquois's limited direct exposure to Christianity) even incomprehensible. The missionaries' voluntary renunciation of their cherished beliefs would not in any way have addressed the Iroquois's *own* underlying religious and political motivations in torturing them, which followed a logic not predicated on or influenced by the Christian worldview. The Haudenosaunee engaged in their ancient rites of soul return and sacrifice to augment their depleted body politic and to punish their enemies for previous assaults on it. They were not acting *in odium fidei,* nor were they attempting to force the missionaries, whose arcane views were largely unfamiliar to them, to recant them.

Iroquois captors, like the Roman martyr-makers of old, could and did grant reprieves at any time during the lengthy torture ordeal: transforming suffering victims into honored kin. But this exercise of clemency was, like torture itself, designed to emphasize the absolute control of the victors over the vanquished.[98] Decisions about who would be adopted and who would be sacrificed were the jealously guarded prerogatives of the conquerors alone. Any attempt by captives to influence their fate would be regarded as an egregious breach in normative relational dynamics, as their designated role was not one of bargaining but courageous defiance in the face of imminent death. Denied the ability to control whether they lived or died, exemplary aboriginal prisoners of war thus refocused all of their energy on the *manner* of their death, the one element still within their control.[99] Scorning a clemency beyond their power to achieve, prisoners verbally and nonverbally transmitted their disdain for and defiance of their tormenters, behaviors that, ironically, often resulted in the granting of the mercy they had so definitively rejected.

Jean de Brébeuf seems to have understood this. The fact that neither he nor Gabriel Lalemant sought to negotiate with their captors, either for their own lives or for the lives of those captured with them says as much about their understanding of seventeenth-century Iroquois culture as it does about their commitment to Christianity. Rather than craving mercy, Brébeuf's speech and gestures were, like that of an aboriginal prisoner, calculatedly provocative. Much as native captives had done for centuries, the two missionaries embraced the limited agency available to them by strenuously controlling their own reactions so as to script their own demise. They modeled their comportment under torture on both aboriginal standards for captives and Christian expectations for martyrs, in the process boldly grafting a Catholic meaning onto their elaborate obedience of native norms. Granted the extended ritual ordeal that Jogues had been systemically denied, Brébeuf and Lalemant tailored Christian martyrdom to the special circumstances imposed by aboriginal postwar practices.

As they doubtless intended, the two men's exacting conformation to aboriginal ideals of captive behavior impressed their torturers. Whereas the decapitated heads of Jogues and la Lande were displayed on the palisade spikes of Ossernenon, signaling their ritual excision from the Mohawk body politic and serving as an unambiguous warning to other meddling outsiders, the hearts of both Brébeuf and Lalemant were ritually ingested, suggesting, through their reception of this ultimate postmortem complement, that they were successful in breaching the cultural divide. Though hagiographic commentators have often presented the cannibalism of these sacred hearts as the apotheosis of native barbarism, their outrage cannot hide the strong parallels with Catholic practice. Over the centuries, devout Catholics have preserved, kissed, touched, and even consumed Brébeuf's relics.[100] Like the Iroquois, they too sought to experience and to preserve his spiritual essence in their own living flesh.

For the Iroquois majority, then, Brébeuf and Lalemant were foes allied with a rival aboriginal group, who were made to pay the price for previous Haudenosaunee casualties. As Frenchmen, they represented a nation that had, virtually from their establishment of the first permanent settlement at Québec, violently engaged the Iroquois and, sometimes purposefully and sometimes inadvertently, worked counter to their interests. By focusing their missionary efforts largely in Huronia, the French Jesuits had made the fateful decision to ally themselves with the Iroquois's traditional foes, the Wendat. Having chosen to bind themselves to the Wendat politically, economically, and religiously, they had become in Iroquois eyes their proxies, subject to the same ritual rules as their allies in war and its aftermath.

Inverting Baptism

Yet for a small but significant minority of participants in their ritual slaying, the two missionaries were far more intimate enemies. In their torture of the black-robes, this small contingent of ex-Wendat ex-Catholics forged a new form of postwar torture that simultaneously reflected and rejected their Christian past: dramatizing their repudiation of Catholicism by ritually referencing the sacrament of baptism. Though they likely numbered only a few men, these former catechumens of Brébeuf were pivotal in tipping the scales of Iroquois justice to favor the missionaries' spectacular slaying over their peaceable adoption or ransom.

The powerful influence of these assimilated captives is also evident in the unusual venue where this torture took place: in the ruins of sacked Taenhatentaron, in the heart of Wendake, perilously close to the Jesuit stronghold of Sainte-Marie. Had traditional Iroquois protocol been followed, the missionaries, even if condemned to death, would have been repatriated to Iroquoia before being sacrificed. The seemingly impromptu decision by ex-Wendat ex-Catholics to torture the Jesuit duo in situ has been interpreted by some as a deliberate attempt to demoralize surviving Jesuits and their Wendat Catholic allies.[101]

Who were these young Wendat men who put their own distinctive twist on the torture of Jean de Brébeuf and Gabriel Lalemant? Not even the earliest and most detailed accounts give their names. We are told only that they had at one time embraced the Catholic faith under the tutelage of Brébeuf and been baptized at his hands. Sometime before their capture (or possible defection) to the Iroquois, they had apparently publicly renounced their newly adopted faith in favor of returning to traditionalism and had become vocal critics of the Jesuits and the Wendat Catholic faction.[102]

Ideologically, these young men were of much the same stripe as the radical traditionalists who had been involved in the slaying of Jesuit donné Jacques Douart only eleven months earlier and in the confessed robbery-murder of Jesuit missionary Nöel Chabanel by Louis Honareenhax, a self-proclaimed Wendat apostate, which would follow a scant nine months later. In fact, Honareenhax, much like Douart's killers, seems to have been part of a group that had taken a similar vow to "kill the first Frenchmen that they saw."[103] The traditionalists who had targeted Douart were still seeking, before the commencement of all-out war with the Iroquois, to find a political solution that would avert the crisis, rid Wendake of the Jesuits, and unite their polity once again under the spiritual banner of traditionalism. Given the changed military and political context, the apparent agenda of Brébeuf, Lalemant, and Chabanel's slayers was decidedly less ambitious. But if they could not hope to rid Huronia of all the Jesuits, they could still vent their profound personal disenchantment with Catholicism on its black-robed representatives through these men's individual torture and killing.

Questioned as to his motive in Nöel Chabanel's slaying, Louis Honareenhax, a baptized Catholic, apparently replied that he had "killed Father Nöel, out of hatred of the faith; for, since he and his family had embraced the faith, all kinds of misfortunes had befallen them." This confession (particularly given its strikingly convenient wording!) belatedly set Chabanel on the path to sanctity alongside his seven companions, as Honareenhax's frankly stated animus against Catholicism, its personnel, and its sacraments elevated the incident, in Jesuit eyes, from a simple robbery-homicide to an *in odium fidei* martyrdom.[104]

Unlike Louis Honareenhax, the anonymous handful of Wendat ex-Catholics who tormented the two Jesuits at Taenhatentaron/Saint-Ignace in March 1649 left no words explaining their motives. But they *did* effectively encode their complaints into their ritual actions. Though their behavior broadly conformed to traditional torture practices, the slight modifications to customary protocol made by these "apostates" gives this encounter between Brébeuf and his former catechumens the air of a secret conversation in which the common yet controversial sacrament of Catholic baptism was referenced and ritually debated in the face of a largely uncomprehending Haudenosaunee majority. The long-standing Wendat contention over the nature of Catholic baptism, long a bone of contention between Wendat traditionalists and converts, became ritually visible in the missionaries' torture at the hands of their former flock.

Buried in the ritual subtext of the torture inflicted on Brébeuf and Lalemant is a complex and multivalent association of baptism, suffering, and death. The strong association between baptism and death, as we have seen, was well established in Wendat culture. Affiliation between this sacrament and torture, however, was of more recent provenance. Though the Jesuits were eager to wipe out what they saw as the barbaric savagery of native postwar torture rituals (even as they simultaneously sought to profit from it as Christian martyrs), both they and secular colonial officials lacked the coercive power over even their native allies that would make this goal achievable. Unable to enforce a moratorium on this deeply entrenched, pan-native practice, the Jesuits contented themselves with making the baptism of consenting enemy captives a sort of ritual "prequel" to their traditional ritual destruction, which they were generally powerless to prevent. Unable to preserve captives' earthly lives, missionaries focused on the salvation of their immortal souls.[105] But, in the hands of their former catechumens, what were for the Jesuits the inherently opposed rituals of baptism and torture became fused into a seamless performance that transformed the contested Catholic sacrament into an improvised form of ritual torture.

The elements of ritual subversion in their baptism of Brébeuf and Lalemant suggest that this ex-Wendat cohort intended to telegraph their dramatic public repudiation of their former ritual incorporation into the Christian fold by presiding at a sort of "anti-baptism" or "un-baptism" affected through violent infliction rather than docile reception.[106] In mimicking the baptismal rite's threefold administration of holy water and reminding Brébeuf, their former catechist, of the necessity of the sacrament for entry into paradise, these "apostate" Wendat effectively reversed their former roles as its passive recipients by themselves appropriating the status of sacramental celebrants.

Through their actions, these men not only ritually negated their own earlier baptisms but also challenged Wendat converts' strong association of the sacrament with healing and survival. If they had accepted the sacrament because of their belief in its worldly benefits for themselves or family members, as Honareenhax appears to have done, then their actions ritually voice the disappointment of cruelly thwarted expectations, an interpretation that their use of the sacrament to inflict suffering and their sarcastic reaffirmation of the sacrament's otherworldly benefits would seem to support. In defiance of the usual script, in which a healthy Jesuit administered the sacrament to a dying Wendat, these men—defiant survivors of baptism, war, and captivity—used it to speed the end of a doomed missionary, their intimate enemy.

It is likely that these ex-Catholics were grimly aware of the horror that their status as "apostates" would have aroused in Brébeuf. Jesuit logic would have held him, as the ritual celebrant of their baptisms, partly responsible for their subsequent profanation of this sacrament by their deconversion. It is difficult to think of another means whereby these men could have more effectively tortured the missionary than by their flaunting before him, in his dying moments, their unrepentant apostasy and mockery of the sacrament's supposed objective efficacy. Such an action called the meaning of Brébeuf's whole career into question, even as it robbed him of any remaining time to ameliorate the situation.

But perhaps Brébeuf would have taken some small comfort from the fact that with their words and actions (particularly their threefold pouring of the boiling water, in the name of the Father, the Son, and the Holy Ghost), his tormentors betrayed their continuing retention of key doctrines of the very faith they had supposedly repudiated.[107] Moreover, what these men said to him was, from Brébeuf's perspective, true: in making him suffer and die they *were* speeding him heavenwards. In praying for their repentance, Brébeuf in his final moments tried to ensure that his elevation was not at the price of their eternal condemnation.

Eight men, all of them European, would eventually be selected out of what had been a decade of carnage and confusion to receive, centuries later, the ultimate recognition of the church through their beatification and canonization as martyr-saints. The eight would be composed of Isaac Jogues and the two lay assistants, René Goupil and Jean de la Lande, who had accompanied him to Kanienke and death; Antoine

Daniel and Charles Garnier, dispatched in the performance of their religious duties on the battlefield during early-morning Iroquois raids; Jean de Brébeuf and Gabriel Lalement, the only two who had grasped the sought-after, though elusive, end of death by torture; and Nöel Chabanel, who was, like the unacknowledged Douart, victim of a Wendat vow "to kill the first Frenchman we find alone." Their deaths were understood by those who participated in them, on either side of the ax or hatchet, water or musket, in starkly different, yet subtly interconnected terms. The hybrid events that they together created out of their sometimes competitive, sometimes cooperative conceptions of martyrdom and sacrifice, baptism and soul return, demonstrate both mutual incomprehension and subtle flashes of profound understanding, which marked the often deadly communication among these three groups in the 1640s.

And yet, placed against the drama of two aboriginal nations' struggle to survive as coherent societies through debilitating epidemic, war, and the social, cultural, and religious changes that accompanied European contact, this handful of celebrated deaths recede from their accustomed place of historiographic centrality to become mere vignettes within a sweeping aboriginal narrative of survival and change. Nor does the significance of the missionaries' final hours, within this wider aboriginal context, retain its conventional hagiographic characterization. Although these eight deaths, and the many hundreds of others whom their subjective selection as significant has pushed only deeper into the shadows of history, remain religiously meaningful, the underlying cultural and psychological purposes of aboriginal postwar torture and adoption ceremonies force us to acknowledge that the native concept of soul return, ritual sacrifice, and physical incorporation are as important to our understanding of their fate as is the more familiar Christian concept of martyrdom. One view, however, does not ultimately trump or negate the others. All are important. All are true.

2

The Blood of Martyrs
Is the Seed of Christians

THE NEWLY PROFESSED NUN lay prostrate on the dark church's cold stone floor. A single candle flickered in its red glass sconce, signaling the presence of the consecrated host, which, displayed in its encircling monstrance, glowed red-gold in the dim light. Arms outstretched, the new sister's body echoed the cruciform position of her bridegroom's on this, their wedding night. Above the altar, his nearly nude form hung, stretched in suffering, limbs alternately drenched and shadowed in the flickering rosy light. Though it was early May, the unforgiving granite chilled the side of her face like a winter grave. The thin veil covering her newly shaven head was a poor substitute for the warmer weight of the thick hair that, until this morning, had hung halfway down her back.[1] Though numb with cold, the young nun smiled in private triumph. Making her night vigil in the seaport city of Nantes, on the west coast of France, she was already half a country away from her home in Bayeux, Normandy. Soon she would venture yet further, boarding a vessel that would bear her across the Atlantic in fulfillment of her dramatic blood-signed vow "to live and to die in Canada, should God open the way to me."[2] Her looming departure for New France marked the culmination of the adolescent's determined four-year campaign to defy the wishes of her family by seeking to serve in a country increasingly infamous for the danger faced by its missionaries. Though the young woman's prone position ritually symbolized her perfect submission to Christ, Catherine de Saint-Augustin's indomitable will, spiritual ambition, and religious precocity were far more evident than any yielding compliance on this, her sixteenth birthday.

Even as Catherine prostrated herself before the sacrament in Nantes, across the Atlantic and hundreds of miles west of Québec's silver steeples, Jean de Brébeuf, deep in prayer, assumed a similar cruciform posture. For years the fifty-five-year-old missionary had been haunted by encounters with his suffering savior and the repeated apparitions of a threatening southern cross.[3] As Catherine prepared to depart for Canada in May 1648, the crisis in Huronia was deepening and the spiritual lives of its missionaries increasingly reflected their sometimes eager, sometimes fearful anticipation of the violence that seemed to menace them from all sides. In preparation for the imminent holocaust his visions presaged, Jean de Brébeuf silently rededicated himself with each mass he celebrated: mentally repeating the words of the solemn self-consecration he had first penned in his own blood:

> I make a vow to you never to fail, on my side, in the grace of martyr-dom, if by your infinite mercy you offer it to me some day, to me, your unworthy servant . . . my beloved Jesus, I offer to you from to-day . . . my blood, my body, and my life; so that I might die only for you.[4]

Catherine de Saint-Augustin, the teenaged Hospitalière nun, and Jean de Brébeuf, the hardened Huronia veteran, would together forge one of the most unusual and productive spiritual partnerships in the late seventeenth-century Catholic world.[5] Though Catherine arrived in New France seven months before Brébeuf's bloody death, the two would never meet in the flesh. Theirs would be a mystical union of the living and the dead, linked by the words and memories of the man who knew and loved them both: Paul Ragueneau, Brébeuf's erstwhile supe-rior and Catherine's influential confessor. It would be Ragueneau, chief architect of the early martyrs' cult in New France, who would plant the seed of his own reverence for this fallen missionary in the fertile ground of Catherine's imagination, where in due time it would flower, bearing mystical fruit.

Their intense relationship benefited all three members of this pecu-liar spiritual love triangle. As the most junior and only female member, Catherine perhaps gained the most.[6] Her powerful connection with Brébeuf, who served as her spiritual director from beyond the grave dur-ing the last six years of her life, enabled the young nun to present herself as his earthly heir and accomplice, imaginatively recasting in feminized terms the putatively masculine path of martyrdom. At Brébeuf's behest,

Catherine assumed the role of voluntary victim for Canada, secretly suffering at the hands of demons to assuage God's righteous anger at the colony's sins. Her communion with the revered martyr bought her entry into largely masculine corridors of power during her lifetime and positioned her for veneration alongside her mentor after her own death at the age of only thirty-six.[7]

But Brébeuf's memory and legacy also stood to benefit from the ritual innovations and fervent mystical imagination of this young nun. Although memorialized by many, including Ragueneau, who reverently documented the events of Brébeuf's long life and dramatic death, Catherine's appropriation of the fallen Jesuit was less historical than charismatic. She was less concerned with the details of the martyr's personal past than how he could pragmatically address the current and future concerns of the colony. Her richly detailed visions of the deceased saint, radiating light and bearing the traditional palm frond of a martyr, seemed to the spiritual leadership of New France independently to confirm their pious suspicions of Brébeuf's august heavenly status and to promise his powerful intercession on their behalf, energizing his infant cult. Catherine's pioneering use of Brébeuf's relics to heal, convert, exorcise and protect popularized his veneration in Québec by presenting him as a powerful presence capable of miraculously intervening to help ordinary *habitants*.[8]

Paul Ragueneau was the linchpin of this odd triple alliance. His emotional recollections of Brébeuf's life and violent death served as the primary spiritual glue that bound Catherine to his fallen mentor. For Ragueneau, however, the benefits of this association consisted more of psychological catharsis than spiritual upward mobility of either the pre- or postmortem variety. In his young confessee, he gained what was perhaps his most responsive audience as he attempted to articulate the meaning of the profound suffering Jesuit and Wendat alike had endured in the horror-filled years of 1648–1650. In Catherine he found a partner whose talents and strengths perfectly complemented his own and who helped him to discharge his deeply felt debt of honor to the dead by establishing their cult in the hearts and minds of French Catholics on both sides of the Atlantic. In old France, narratives of the martyrs' lives and deaths were integral to attracting new recruits for religious service in Canada, recruits who, like Catherine, sought to follow in the martyrs' bloodied footsteps. In New France, the martyrs' epic was positioned as a lodestar of meaning and even hope for colonists in a dangerously unstable environment. After Catherine's death in 1668, Ragueneau would also memorialize the young nun, writing a biography that richly documented her inner spiritual life, particularly her mystical alliance with Brébeuf.

And yet the public reception of Ragueneau's *Vie de la Mère Catherine de Saint-Augustin*, published in Paris in 1671, intimated the development of a growing threat to the nascent cult of the martyrs (and of Catherine) in the country of their birth, a threat that would only intensify over the course of the eighteenth century. Although it was perfectly in tune with the waves of spiritual ardor that had washed over France in the 1630s and 1640s, Ragueneau's recitation of Catherine's dramatic inner life would, in the later seventeenth century, encounter open incredulity as much as reverent imitation, playful mockery as well as prayerful reverence.[9] This open questioning of claims of extraordinary religious experience would only intensify in the years leading up to the French Revolution. This shift into skepticism in the Gallic motherland, coupled with the profound disruptions caused by the 1759 conquest of Québec by the English, would pose significant and unforeseen challenges to the survival of the fragile martyrs' cult that Ragueneau and Catherine had together forged. The maelstrom of war and revolution that thundered first across New France, then Old, seemed to sound the death knell of a cult whose once cohesive narrative was beginning to fray.

Catherine and the Idea of Canada

It had been a long struggle for Catherine de Saint-Augustin—born Catherine Symon de Longpré—to take her place on the stone floor of l'eglise de Notre-Dame de Toute-Joye. She had had to fight hard to win the right to celebrate her sixteenth birthday as a professed nun and to keep her solitary night vigil far from her protective Norman family, as the Canada-bound ship waited for her in the bay below, its sails tightly furled. Catherine needed to meet the legal minimum age of profession before departing for Canada, occasioning the brief sojourn in Nantes.[10] But as young as she was, Catherine had nurtured the idea of service in New France for at least four years. Admitted on the coattails of her older sister, Françoise, Catherine entered the gates of the Convent of Mercy in Bayeux at the age of only twelve.[11] The prepubescent postulant was heard pertly to remark to the novice-mistress, who had the temerity to question her vocation: "I am firmly determined in the idea that assuredly I will be a religious . . . do to me all that you will, you will not deny me the habit, and I will not leave this place except to go to Canada."[12] The de Longpré sisters' shared desire to serve in New France sparked a serious crisis within their shared family and religious community when Catherine adamantly refused to yield to either their entreaties or their tearful threats.[13]

Catherine's youthful imagination had been strongly engaged by a country that, for her, was completely literary. Her impressions of this distant, mysterious land were shaped almost entirely by narratives penned by colonial Catholic missionaries. The *Jesuit Relations*—yearly accounts that narrated the events, both spiritual and temporal, of the Canadian colony during the previous year—made particularly compelling reading.[14] Replete with dramatic accounts of conversions and miracles and descriptions of the beliefs and practices of aboriginal people, the *Relations*, darkly haloed by the omnipresent threat of violence, enjoyed a wide reading audience within and even outside pious circles in France who appreciated its glimpses into a distant, fascinating, and frightening world.

As she avidly read the *Relations*, Catherine mapped her own spiritual and personal preoccupations onto the rhetorical landscape of Canada. The country's strong association with the periphery and with the privation that schools sanctity strongly appealed to this young woman, who sought to make a dramatic statement of her desire to serve and suffer for Christ. Merely following family footsteps into the local convent was not enough for her, as this was merely a seamless, lateral movement from one de Longpré enclave to another. Catherine had been exposed from an early age to the practical realities of what would become her future vocation as an Augustinian nursing nun because her maternal grandmother, Renée Jourdan, who raised Catherine, ran her pious household as a makeshift hospital and poor relief center.[15] Ensconced in the family convent in Bayeux, Catherine enjoyed the company of her elder sister and her aunt, its founder and mother superior. After being widowed, her grandmother would also take the veil, snugly enclosing the adolescent in a religious "family" almost identical to the biological one that, with her initial vows, she had supposedly left behind in the "World." Choosing Canada may thus have been Catherine's way of expressing her willingness to sacrifice both her natal country

and her two "families" to commit herself wholly to the service of others, a gesture most other young postulants could make simply with
their preliminary vows.

But her vocation for New France also allowed Catherine freely to
indulge her already fierce religious ambition. Aware that her grandfather, Jean Jourdan de Launay, had prophesied that his youngest grand-
daughter would become "a nun, a great servant of God, one of great
courage, and a saint,"[16] Catherine may have felt that serving the inhabitants of austere and distant Canada as a missionary nurse would help
her to achieve her cherished childhood ambition and to fulfill her grandfather's words in one fell swoop.

Devotional texts, then, that described Canada as a place of temporal
danger and spiritual treasure, a new desert of penitence, and the forging
ground of the saintly, led inexorably to the crisis that would convulse
the de Longpré family in the mid-1640s. Catherine's parents were so
fiercely opposed to their youngest daughter's departure that her father,
Jacques Symon de Longpré, presented a petition to the Parliament of
Rouen to prevent it, motivating Anne of Austria, the queen regent, to
intercede on Catherine's behalf.[17] To royal interference was added saintly
involvement, that came, appropriately enough, through the same medium that had precipitated the crisis in the first place. It would be the
textual intervention of the newly martyred Isaac Jogues that would
change the family's attitude from angry bitterness to holy resignation.
Depressed about Catherine's intransigence, her father happened to leaf
through the recently published *Jesuit Relations* of 1647, which recounted
Jogues's "double" martyrdom, much of it in the deceased Jesuit's own
words.[18] Fascinated, de Longpré read of Jogues's initial capture and torture by the Iroquois, his yearlong captivity and dramatic rescue by
Dutch colonists, and his eventual escape to France.[19] Lingering over the
pages, much as his pious daughters had done before him, their father
learned that Jogues's disfigured and missing fingers had earned him the
tears of Anne of Austria—Catherine's would-be savior.[20]

This powerful textual encounter with Isaac Jogues "deeply affected"
de Longpré, filling him with shame for his angry resistance to his daughters' evident vocation for Canada. Wondering "Is it true that they suffer
so nobly for God in those countries?" he emphasized: "I wish my two
daughters to go there. I refused one, and now I give them both."[21] De
Longpré's change of heart was not entirely free from the pious fear that

to stand in his daughters' way might negatively affect his own pros-
pects for prosperity in this life and salvation in the next.[22] Even from
beyond the grave, Jogues had once again upped the ante of martyrdom.
Through his textual legacy, Jogues had forced de Longpré belatedly to
recognize the beautiful inevitability of his daughter's calling to her religious responsibilities in Canada's *via dolorosa*.

Catherine's departure on the *Cardinal* on May 27, 1648, seemed to
have settled the protracted family conflict in favor of the determined
teenager.[23] But if she had hoped that putting the Atlantic between her
and her biological and religious families would staunch the flow of
deep emotions that her departure had unleashed, she was sadly mis-
taken. Catherine's crossing merely changed the *medium* of these ongoing
tensions from face-to-face into epistolatory confrontations.[24] Though
she would spend the rest of her short life in Canada, Catherine's family
and the sisters in religion she had left behind in Normandy never
ceased to implore her to return. The young nun's strong temptation to
acquiesce was one of the most grueling and unexpected of the many
Canadian crosses she was to bear. Writing after Catherine's untimely
death, her mother superior wrote that the adolescent's choice to leave
her family, for whom she felt "an extreme gratitude and tenderness . . .
was like tearing out her own heart," as was leaving "the Community of
Nuns at Bayeux, where she was loved by everyone."[25] Catherine's powerful homesickness, initially a response to the profound culture shock
of finding herself a cloistered nun "here at the end of the world,"[26]
would find its ultimate resolution only in her mystical relationship
with Jean de Brébeuf during the final six years of her life.

In the meantime, Catherine was initiated into the very literary con-
spiracy that had so ably beguiled her. The circumstances of Catherine's
call to Canada and her August 1648 arrival at Québec, on the point of
death from a shipboard fever, were lovingly detailed in the very publication that had awakened her own ardor, the *Relations*:

> The youngest of the three Nuns called Mother Catherine de St. Augus-
> tin, was at the very gates of death,—or rather, the gates of Paradise. But
> her Spouse wished to try her still longer by sufferings, and he restored
> her health. Her vocation to this new world is rather remarkable. Her
> zeal led her to desire Crosses with affection; and her father, who feared
> the danger . . . strongly opposed her departure. . . . This poor little
> Dove was in great distress.[27]

With her overseas voyage, Catherine had moved from spectator to actor, symbolically stepping out onto the brightly lit stage of the great colonial drama she had, for years, longingly watched from the wings.

But Catherine confidently authored her own texts as well as starring in those of others. Her deceptively calm and cheerful letters home (whose tone and contents were starkly contradicted by the young nun's agonized and tearful confessions to her spiritual director that she wished for nothing more than to flee the colony) display Catherine's rapid transformation from an Old World consumer of colonial devotional literature into one of its youngest Canadian producers. Gradually the adolescent learned to spin the straw of her often difficult daily struggles into the gold of smooth and inspiring prose. Her letters never failed to articulate her love for her adoptive homeland and her mystical intimation of the spiritual destiny it provided:

> It is not that I believe that I would not be happy if I were to return to France, or that I would not be content there, or that God would not give me occasions to suffer and to become a great Saint, if I follow the graces that he would there give me, but when I reflect that He has called me to this place, I believe that he meant me to have something in particular in this country, given that he has given me here all of this satisfaction and contentment, where there is nothing else other than God. And this I can assure you . . . there is no need to search for anything other than God alone, for in Him we find everything that is most wonderful and agreeable.[28]

Though Catherine's confessions and her letters thus sharply contradicted one another, both were likely sincere. Ambivalence was inevitable as Catherine attempted to adjust to the difficult new life she had fought so hard to be able to experience. A desire to convince *herself* as well as her reader, a sense of filial duty to reassure her worried elders, and perhaps the prideful wish to justify her own dubious decision all played a role in Catherine's studied literary presentation of her unfolding life in New France.

False Calm and the Coming Cross

In view of the deteriorating political and military situation, Catherine's second thoughts about coming to Canada were certainly well justified. During her first year in New France, the colony would face its most devastating setback to date. Long-standing tensions between the Huron, the French, and the Iroquois would erupt into vicious conflict that would decimate the Wendat, sweeping them from their traditional homelands around Georgian Bay. This dramatic upsurge in armed conflict turned prosperous Jesuit missions into charred ruins and left a number of their black-robed denizens dead.

And yet, as a cloistered nun in the easterly enclave of Québec City, Catherine was almost as far removed from fresh news of Huronia as she would have been in France. Fear of Iroquois attack had almost completely cut off the travel routes that permitted communication and exchange between the colonial capital and the Jesuits who manned the westerly Wendat missions over 570 rugged miles distant, creating an ominous silence even more unsettling that actual news would have been. This eerie false calm and the pronounced sense of insecurity it fostered would have done little to reinforce Catherine's crumbling sense of religious vocation in a country whose harsh realities were proving to exceed even their most dramatic rhetorical presentation in the copies of the *Jesuit Relations* she had so eagerly thumbed through in Bayeux.[29]

Even though Catherine was now on the same side of the Atlantic as Jean de Brébeuf, the events of their daily lives thus unfolded in utter isolation from one another. Even the profound gulf of death proved easier for the two to traverse than the deafening silence created by the Iroquois blockade or the daunting obstacles of Canadian geography. March 16, 1649, then, unfolded much like any other day for Catherine de Saint-Augustin. Untroubled by intimations of doom for the man with whom her "spirit" would one day "find a unity,"[30] she awoke as usual at 4:00 a.m. so as to be ready to participate in 4:30 religious service of Prime.[31] After briefly kneeling in prayer alone in her cell, she hurriedly dressed and donned her veil. Tucking her wooden belt rosary into the crook of her arm to stop its beads from noisily clacking together, she glided swiftly past the dormitory where the invalids under her care still slept in the predawn darkness. At 6:00, in the gray gloaming of a Canadian March dawn, Catherine quietly made her first rounds, checking on each patient in the *salle des pauvres,* helping the wounded and the ill to take their breakfast, to bathe, or to move their bowels. By the time she had attended to the needs of the last patient, Brébeuf and Lalemant had already been captured and were making their final march over the frozen path from Saint-Louis to Saint-Ignace and their deaths.[32] After lunch, as the Hospitalières gathered in their private parlor to say their chaplets, their hushed, familiar words smoothly ascending to heaven, Brébeuf and Lalemant knelt to embrace their torture stakes.[33] And, as the placid early afternoon routine of the Augustinians once again unfolded its familiar rituals—the examination of conscience, public reading, and constant care of the sick—Jean de Brébeuf endured his tortuous final hours.[34] By late afternoon, when Catherine's contralto voice rose in Compline, she was serenely unaware that her hymns served as a distant and inadequate requiem for the now deceased Jesuit. At 7:00 in the evening, as the sisters knelt to pray alongside *les pauvres* and dusk gathered around the log convent, drawing an end to the short, late-winter day, Brébeuf's half-burnt body lay cold in the March snows, shrouded only by the encroaching darkness.[35]

It would not be until six months later, with the delivery of Ragueneau's *Relation* to Québec in September 1649, that its residents would learn the gruesome fates of Brébeuf and Lalemant. But, like patchy radio static, this brief blaze of news was followed by resumed silence as Québec hunkered down for another long winter's wait. Not until the next July would their vigil be broken in earnest, when Paul Ragueneau, superior of the now defunct Huron mission, led a desperate, ragged, and pitifully small band of haggard Jesuits and emaciated Wendat into the settlement. Only then could Catherine compare the horrors conjured by her imagination with the memories of the gaunt survivors evacuated from Huronia.

The Return of Ragueneau

Ragueneau had presided over an unfolding nightmare. In Canada for fourteen of his forty-two years, the unassuming priest had steadily worked his way up through the Jesuit ranks, becoming superior of the Huron mission on the eve of its greatest crisis.[36] Burdened with the responsibility for a number of crucifying decisions, he had also personally witnessed much horror. Ragueneau had watched the settlements of Wendake fall one by one to the Iroquois throughout 1648 and early 1649, culminating with the loss of both Saint-Louis and Saint-Ignace on a single day. He had seen the smoke from these burning villages rising into the sullen early morning skies on March 16, 1649, and touched, in horror and in wonderment, the mangled, heartless remains of Brébeuf, whom he had long regarded as both a personal mentor and as a living saint.[37] He had made the heartbreaking decision, in May of that year, to burn the Jesuits' laboriously built headquarters of Sainte-Marie, lest it too fall into Haudenosaunee hands, and ordered the recently interred remains of Brébeuf and Lalemant to be boiled in lye so that their holy relics could accompany the Catholic community into its ignominious exile.[38] As safe flight to Québec was deemed all but impossible, Jesuit survivors and those Wendat, mostly Catholics, who preferred to remain in their company (rather than seeking refuge with native neighbors or surrendering to the Iroquois) retreated northward to the dubious refuge of Île Saint-Joseph. Unable to harvest sufficient provisions, they there endured a winter of such extreme privation that it halved their numbers. Ragueneau was thus forced to witness the suffering and death of hundreds of men, women, and children: people whom he perceived as his personal responsibility to protect. Although he appreciated that the greatest tragedy of those years was the displacement and dispossession of the Wendat confederacy, Ragueneau wept less for their loss of autonomy and territory than he did for the destruction of his own embryonic native church.[39]

Upon their belated arrival in Québec, the traumatized survivors of this winter of horror became the Hospitalières' newest patients. Wrote Marie de Saint-Bonaventure, Catherine's mother superior, of these new arrivals:

> Each year has its own cross; and this last has the heaviest, in the ruin of the country of the Hurons by the Hiroquois, who have laid it waste by fire, massacred most of its people, and compelled the remainder to take to flight, and to disperse themselves in all directions. Almost all were Christians. These are they whom our Lord afflicts, and makes of them so many victims for Paradise. . . . Here are four hundred of these poor Christian Hurons taking refuge in Kebec, and cabined near the gate of our Hospital, to which they come every day for holy Mass. I have never before seen such poverty or such devotion.[40]

The Paul Ragueneau who returned to Québec in the summer of 1650 and almost immediately assumed responsibility for Catherine de Saint-Augustin's spiritual direction was thus a man haunted by the tragic events of his recent past and deeply committed to articulating what he believed to be this tragedy's profound religious meaning. Following his promotion to the position of superior of the entire Canadian mission in 1650, Ragueau became even more determined to rewrite the fall of Huronia as an epic of inspiring courage and—incredibly—of hope for the future. Even as he assumed a heavier administrative burden, Ragueneau poured much of his energy into writing, rhetorically reframing recent history so as to restore the morale of his deeply shaken Society. Though his reassurance was arguably necessary for the colony's political stability, extrapolating meaning from horror was also a deeply felt personal call of duty on behalf of colleagues whom Ragueneau deeply respected and mourned profoundly.[41]

Making Martyrs

The alchemical rhetoric of martyrdom, already prevalent in Jesuit writings, had found in the events of 1648–1650 its greatest explanatory challenge and, in Ragueneau, its greatest advocate. In his writings, the deaths of his fellow black-robes and the holocaust of the infant Wendat church became the sacred harbingers of an imminent flood of future conversions rooted in these seminal events, which he presented as a source of spiritual pride and strength. Speaking of the recovery of the bodies of Brébeuf and Lalemant, Ragueneau wrote:

> they found there a spectacle of horror,—the remains of cruelty itself; or rather the relics of the love of God, which alone triumphs in the death of Martyrs. I would gladly call them, if I were allowed, by that glorious name, not only because voluntarily, for the love of God and for the salvation of their neighbor, they exposed themselves to death, and to a cruel death, if ever there was one in the world,—for they could easily and without sin have put their lives in safety, if they had not be filled with love for God rather than themselves. But much rather would I thus call them, because, in addition to the charitable dispositions which they have manifested on their side, hatred for the faith and contempt for the name of God have been among the most powerful incentives which have influenced the mind of the Barbarians to practice upon them as many cruelties as ever the rage of tyrants obliged the Martyrs to endure, who, at the climax of their tortures, have triumphed over both life and death.[42]

Was not the blood of martyrs, he asked, truly the seed of Christians? Ragueneau's resounding "yes" to this question echoed his strongly affirmative answer to the most commonly and nervously whispered question of the early 1650s: whether, after the fall of Wendake, the French colonial enterprise in Canada was still viable.

Ragueneau desperately sought to shore up the fading morale of a traumatized colony by encouraging it to see the past through the lens of martyrdom. But he also wished to win for his fallen friends the formal recognition of the church as its newest saints and martyrs. His moving, influential accounts of his colleagues' pious lives and horrid demise thus attempted to demonstrate that their deaths were martyrdoms in the strict canonical sense: that is, that they had been slaughtered *in odium fidei*.[43] In his massive 1652 document, which would come to be known as *le precieux manuscrit*, Ragueneau painstakingly assembled eyewitness testimony of those who had been privileged witnesses of the martyrs' saintly lives or blessed deaths and of those who had "seen and touched"[44] their recovered bodies after their edifying ordeals. In meticulously assembling and preparing the evidence necessary for his colleagues' eventual beatification, Ragueneau's chosen role in their emergent cult was essentially historical, legalistic, and forensic. He addressed the elites of Paris and of Rome: those whom he believed had the skill and influence to shepherd his fallen friends' *causa* successfully through the Vatican's byzantine bureaucracy.

The violent incidents Ragueneau highlighted in his copious writings were carefully selected to illustrate his overarching thesis that the events of 1642–1650 displayed the workings of a mysterious but "ever-adorable" divine providence that had seen fit to winnow the Huron church and to martyr not only individual Jesuits but their larger Society, and New France as a whole.

But Ragueneau faced a number of difficult challenges in his bold attempts at textual canonization. He had to carefully mold his data to make his interpretation seem not merely logical but inevitable. Without displaying undue defensiveness, he had to explain his common categorization of "martyrdom" as a series of deaths as motley as combat casualties, summary executions, and robbery-murders: to justify his elevation of demise by deliberate ritual torture and simple exposure to the elements.[45] At the same time, Ragueneau had to subtly preclude his readers' interpretation of these incidents as cases of merely "being in the wrong place at the wrong time" by presenting them as the magnificent, intractable unfolding of God's holy will. To this end, he emphasized missionaries' mystical premonitions of and spiritual preparation for their bloody ends, stressing their voluntary acceptance of their destined deaths and their understanding of the necessity of suffering in God's providential plan to convert the New World. To this end, Ragueneau also accentuated the essentially *pastoral* nature of Jesuit motivations in choosing to remain with and spiritually serve their Wendat flocks, even in peril. Likewise, he emphasized the positive, even miraculous outcomes of their self-sacrifice on the spiritual lives of survivors. For Ragueneau's rhetoric to be persuasive, it was essential that he eclipse these men's ethnopolitical identity as Frenchmen with their *religious* identity as Jesuits. Should he fail, Ragueneau's readers might perceive these deaths as mere red threads within the larger tapestry of life in 1640s New France, which would doubtless dilute their appreciation of these deaths as essentially *spiritual* events.

In the weighty tomes he produced in the early 1650s, Ragueneau also had to justify his decision to exclude from elevation as martyrs those who had died under similar but politically inconvenient circumstances. In several cases, the Jesuits had deliberately looked the other way as members of their communities, both donnés and native Catholics, either died at the hands of anti-Jesuit agents within the community or met mysterious ends. As far back as 1640, the Jesuits had refrained from probing the suspicious death of Joseph Chihoatenhwa of the Wendat village of Ossossané. One of the first and most fervent Huron converts to Catholicism in Wendake, Chihoatenhwa was referred to by friends and foes alike simply as "the Believer" in recognition of his powerful attachment to Catholicism. Chihoatenhwa appears to have attributed his deathbed recovery from a serious illness to his baptism, a perception that motivated both his lifelong loyalty to the Catholic Church and his controversial efforts to promulgate Christianity. A lightning rod among his people, Chihoatenhwa was seen alternatively as an admirable evangelist, an ambitious social climber, and a dangerous traitor who had voluntarily aligned himself with Jesuit sorcerers. Thus many commentators have speculated that Chihoatenhwa was the likely victim of radical Wendat traditionalists within his village who opposed the spread of Christianity.[46] But the Ossossané Jesuits (including those who themselves would be elevated as martyr-saints) accepted the Wendat leaders' attribution of the murder to Iroquois raiders in order to maintain the community's fragile, uneasy peace. In choosing not to probe further the violent demise of the man who had long been the sole and passionate voice of native Catholicism in his village, the Jesuits effectively denied Chihoatenhwa the crown of martyrdom, both then and since.[47]

Ragueneau also had to handle with especial delicacy the more recent slaying of Jacques Douart, who would probably have been presented as a martyr under other circumstances. But prioritizing their own safety and the continuation of their faltering mission, the Jesuits had chosen to accept the compensation offered by his killers, which made the latter-day celebration of his martyrdom awkward. Always, then, Jesuit framing of martyrs' deaths had political considerations. Those whose deaths they could not halo with an aura of religious significance, they discreetly deemphasized, despite their marked similarities to the slayings they glorified as martyrdoms.

In his justificatory writings, Ragueneau also had to find a way to turn traditional native motivations for violent engagement, guided by concepts of soul return and sacrifice, into the *in odium fidei* he would need to make martyrs. In narrating the missionaries' deaths, Ragueneau deemphasized their captors' obvious ambivalence about the fate of their prisoners. Jogues's slaying was the initiative of an adamant minority who were actively opposed by the Mohawk majority. The deadly torture of Brébeuf and Lalemant likewise appears to have been initiated by a small group of ex-Wendat ex-Catholics, whose bold and unusual ritual actions preempted their earlier redemption. But Ragueneau's partial truths were not all deliberate. In many cases, not all of the circumstances of the missionaries' deaths had come to light when he was writing *le precieux manuscript* and other textual cornerstones of the early canonization efforts. Evidence from both witnesses to and participants in these deaths would trickle in only gradually over a period of years. Though these belated testimonials add subtlety and nuance to our understanding of these incidents, because of their late advent they were not included in the most canonical and supposedly comprehensive accounts of the deaths, which had already been written and published. Because these earliest primary texts have, in turn, served as the basis of most secondary works, these important later additions to the story were unintentionally excluded from later accounts.[48] Indications that the deaths of the martyrs were controversial: eliciting bargaining, hot debate, and even physical confrontation within native communities are often entirely absent, even in contemporary scholarly works.

These convenient elisions allowed the interpretively crisper, though less accurate, emphasis on the putatively anti-Christian motivations of the martyrs' captors to be emphasized across the board. In the hands of textual and visual redactors of the martyrdoms, native ambivalence or dissention was generally ignored in favor of an interpretation that strongly stressed *in odium fidei*. Thus, even when there were multiple contemporary explanations of native motives in a given death, anti-Christian interpretations have invariably been preferred. For example, primary documents penned in the aftermath of René Goupil's death offer competing theories regarding the motivations behind his murder. Some postulate that he was killed in retribution for Iroquois losses at the hands of the French, while others attribute the donné's death to his persistence, despite multiple warnings to desist, in making the sign of the cross over the heads of Mohawk children. In hagiographic literature the latter explanation has been the vastly preferred one, with the other hypothesis often going totally unmentioned. Similarly, despite the violent skirmish that preceded Jogues's attempted assassination, which led to the serious wounding of his would-be Mohawk defender, his execution has traditionally been painted as the unanimous will of a community whipped into a frenzy of anti-Christian hysteria by their fears of the dark magic unleashed by the missionary's mass kit, allowing the complexity of Jogues's death to be reduced to a more clear-cut case of *in odium fidei*.

One thing Ragueneau did not feel the need to justify was his near total exclusion of native Catholics from his calls for canonization. Though he reports the stalwart deaths of Wendat and Algonquin Catholics in panegyric terms, he does not consistently refer to them as martyrs for the faith. Framing only European deaths as "martyrdoms" makes a wholly unjustified distinction between the sufferings of the eight missionaries and the unrecognized agonies of the far more numerous group of native Catholic captives. It also ignores the fact that, in cases of internal persecution, native Catholics were always more vulnerable to violence than were the Jesuits. Ragueneau's blithe near-exclusion of aboriginal candidates for sainthood had a chilling effect on their recognition as martyrs down through the centuries. None of the many native Christians who suffered alongside the canonized martyrs have yet received comparable recognition from the church.[49]

Building a Mystery

As the object of Ragueneau's spiritual direction, the then eighteen-year-old Catherine de Saint-Augustin presented a microcosm of the challenges he faced in the colony at large. His direction of her thus mirrored, in important ways, his larger strategy of outreach to Québec's jumpy and disillusioned religious elite. By 1651, Catherine, like many others, was expressing serious doubts as to the colony's ability to survive the bitter blow it had been dealt with the fall of Wendake and continued dangers posed by a triumphant and uncontained southerly foe. Writing home, she observed: "we are in no hurry to finish the rest of our buildings, because of the uncertainty in which we find ourselves regarding whether or not we will long remain here."[50] To address the young nun's pessimism and strong desire to return to France, frequently expressed in her confessions, Ragueneau needed to enumerate powerful and attractive reasons for her to remain.

As he got to know Catherine, Ragueneau realized that he needed to appeal not simply to her highly developed sense of religious duty but also to her equally powerful spiritual ambition. He thus invited her to connect her own unfolding story with the sweeping narrative of sacrifice and redemption in the New World that his own writing was attempting to construct. In particular, Ragueneau encouraged Catherine to perceive her original decision to come to Canada and her ongoing (if embattled) commitment to stay as a heroic sacrifice that echoed the martyrs' own voluntary surrendering of their lives for Christ.

Ragueneau soon discovered that he had in Catherine an enthusiastic and creative ally in the formation and dissemination of the martyrs' colonial cult. Her pragmatic focus as a nursing sister working with the diseased and dislocated formed a perfect complement to Ragueneau's more scholarly role, effectively expanding the reach of the embryonic cult.[51] Ragueneau fought for the martyrs' cause on paper. But Catherine's chosen weapon was their relics, particularly those of Jean de Brébeuf.[52]

To prompt Brébeuf's miraculous intervention in the daily trials of the ill and injured under her care, Catherine manipulated the modest piece of his bone that she kept on her person at all times. This relic became as homely and familiar a part of her nursing regimen as bandages or bedpans. By prayerfully grating Brébeuf's bone, like a celestial seasoning, into the soups and beverages she served *les malades* under her care, Catherine obtained spectacular cures, conversions, and exorcisms that were then credited to the wonder-working power of the colonial saint.[53]

Perhaps her most celebrated ritual intervention involving Brébeuf's relics was Catherine's 1665 conversion and healing of a wounded French Protestant soldier, which received enthusiastic notice in both Jesuit and Hospitalière publications. The miraculous transformation of this obstreperous patient, whom Jesuit father Le Mercier characterized as "one of the most obstinate we have seen here," into a "lamb who asked to be instructed, received into his mind and heart the influences of our Faith, and made public adjuration of heresy with such a fervor that he himself was astonished" was attributed to Catherine's surreptitious garnishing of his food with Brébeuf's relic, "reduced to powder."[54]

Catherine was not the only one to use the martyrs' relics in this manner. The Jesuits also employed them to cure maladies both corporeal and spiritual, particularly in mission contexts.[55] But Catherine's daily work with those in mental and physical distress, her access to a sizable relic, and her central location in the colonial capital, which facilitated the quick dissemination of alleged miracles, made her easily the best-known colonial figure to do so.

Through her ritual use of the bones Ragueneau had personally ordered preserved, Catherine emphasized the ongoing presence and power of the fallen Jesuits and their undiminished concern for "their" colony. Ragueneau's reasoning was legalistic and historical: his case for the martyrs' heroic sanctity was made on the basis of what had already happened. Catherine's, however, was charismatic: based on what she could impose upon the saints to deliver in the here and now. Ragueneau, in his writings, rhetorically appealed to the horrifying punishments already inflicted on the martyrs' bodies, whereas Catherine demonstrated the miraculous transformations their holy remains could even now work on the bodies, minds, and souls of those still living. Catherine's ritual performances, moreover, were aimed at a popular colonial audience of Catholics and non-Catholics, French and aboriginal people, rather than Ragueneau's European clerical elite. All could judge for themselves, she implied, the veracity of the miracles worked by these holy bones using the evidence of their own senses and experiences. Together, then, through written words and ritual actions, Ragueneau and Catherine de Saint-Augustin forged a cult that would outlive them both.

"Leave the Ax Far Away"

At the same time that Ragueneau was trying to reassure a traumatized colony that it would in fact survive (and, indeed, prevail) he was simultaneously pondering the best way to defuse the ongoing threat of Iroquois aggression. Convinced that evangelical rather than military conquest was the best approach, Ragueneau reasoned that if the Jesuits could convert the hearts and minds of their sometimes enemies, they would then peacefully triumph over them. Iroquois Christianization was not simply a religious duty, he intoned, but an important aspect of the colony's self-defense.

One might expect that in their high-stakes religious courtship of the Iroquois confederacy the Jesuits would diplomatically gloss over their host's past acts of violence against their religious order. But precisely the opposite is the case. In a series of discourses penned for oral delivery, Jesuit orators directly confronted their Haudenosaunee listeners with their previous acts of aggression against their black-robed number, colloquially referred to by the Iroquois as "the Charcoal."[56] The Jesuits insisted that they did not bring up the fallen out of a misguided desire for revenge, but because they wished to share the Christian message that had motivated their ministry and to persuade the Iroquois to eschew violence:

> It was not a long time ago that your mind and our mind lived far apart. We wished, "Let the Iroquois live forever," but you wished, "Let all the Charcoal be dead." Every day we prayed for you. . . . We were taking care of you, protecting you . . . but you were continually angry at us. . . . Quit your cruelty. . . . Let it be that you stop making lakes of blood. . . . Leave the ax far away, the ax that you use to hit humans with. Let it be that you cause to be extinguished the fire you put humans in. Knock over those pots you put humans in. Love all countries where people live. Look at each other peacefully as you would live.[57]

Though seemingly paradoxical, confronting Iroquois listeners with the travails of the martyrs and the suffering they had caused other native peoples actually appealed to the strong bond of honor and mutual respect that often formed between the torturer and the tortured in Iroquois contexts. By reminding Haudenosaunee listeners that their black-robed brothers had suffered well, the Jesuits appealed to an intimate, preexisting relationship, born in blood, that had a complex ritual etiquette of its own. Stressing the martyrs' manly courage also played upon the Iroquois notion that baptism hardened resolve and constancy in the face of pain.[58] In their speeches, the Jesuits exploited their shared, painful history with the people of the longhouse to establish an intimate rapport with their listeners and to leverage it for the church militant.

Jesuit travels throughout Iroquoia during the 1650s and 1660s brought them into contact with many for whom the martyrs' deaths were not a new story, but rather a vivid memory. These encounters often yielded important new information regarding their colleagues' final hours and offered a particularly attractive opportunity for conversion. If the Jesuits could induce the martyrs' very *slayers* to receive the faith, then Tertullian's famous edict, "the blood of martyrs is the seed of Christians," would become true in a particularly gripping way. It would prove that "the blood of these apostolic men had not been shed without fruit. . . . The most precious was the conversion of those who had shed it."[59] The religious transformation of the very warriors who had wielded hatchets and musket, torch and fist against the saintly representatives of the one true faith would justify the Jesuits' turning to the alchemical logic of martyrdom to generate optimism regarding the colony's future and underline the wisdom of evangelical courtship (as opposed to military confrontation) of the Haudenosaunee. Finally, conversion of the martyrs' killers would reflect posthumous glory on those they had slain. In their delayed acceptance of the faith, these Iroquois would become like the Golgotha centurion who belatedly testified, in wonder and in fear: "Truly this man was the son of God."[60]

As Catherine's father had read in the *Relations* of 1647,[61] prior to her controversial departure for Canada, Isaac Jogues's purported killer had already become one of this illustrious circle of repentant former martyr-makers. The heavyset Bear Clan man had allegedly administered the arcing blow that had finally sent the missionary to his long-awaited heavenly reward. Captured in a skirmish with the French and their aboriginal allies in 1647, Jogues's killer was himself condemned to death by the latter. While he awaited his sentence, he was given to the French, at their request, for safekeeping and religious instruction. The burly condemned killer surprised his Gallic captors with his alacrity in embracing Catholic dogma, giving "marked evidence of his belief, and asking pardon of God for his transgressions." Duly prepared, the man "was baptized, and was made to bear the name of Father Isaac Jogues, whom, as some said, he himself had killed."[62]

The man's ritual adoption of Isaac Jogues's name interwove Iroquois notions of soul return with Catholic concepts of baptism. Captives chosen for ritual adoption into Haudenosaunee communities took on the name of the deceased community member they were tasked with revitalizing. It is likely, then, that Jogues's apparent slayer would have understood his new name as not merely *honoring* the man he had slain but actually *incarnating* Jogues's spirit in his own living flesh. For the French Catholic community, on the other hand, the man's redemption echoed the biblical transformation of Saint Paul, who, called by Christ, went from persecuting to leading the early Christian community.

The days of the new Isaac Jogues, however, remained numbered. Despite Isaac's rehabilitation as an exemplary Christian, the French were unable to persuade their allies to reverse his death sentence.[63] Much like his namesake, the second Isaac Jogues would die violently, and as a Catholic. In his last words to the French who had converted him, he apparently thanked them for being "the cause of my going to heaven."[64] Already martyred twice over, through the living death of his harsh captivity in 1642–1643 and his actual slaying in 1646, Isaac Jogues would go to the stake once more in the person of his namesake.

Jogues's killer was not the only participant in his death whom the French would encounter in the years following his 1646 slaying. They also met the young man who had attempted to save the missionary by grappling with his heavily built assailant. Impulsively thrusting out his arm in an attempt to ward off the death-blow, he had himself become wounded in the process.[65] Having traveled north to Trois Rivières, the youth regaled the French there with his story. Nicknamed *Le Berger* or "the Shepherd," the Mohawk adolescent, like his former antagonist, enjoyed a certain celebrity in colonial circles as Jogues's attempted rescuer. Many interpreted the young man's courageous wounding as having ensured his salvation: "This blow, received through charity, was perhaps the stroke of his predestination, for it may certainly be believed that this good Father obtained from our Lord, in Heaven, the salvation of this man's soul, in return for his attempt to save the Father while in the body."[66] In 1649, *Le Berger* was taken to France, the homeland of the man he had tried to save. He would die as a Catholic on Gallic soil, having asked for baptism on his deathbed as he succumbed to an unfamiliar European illness that he lacked immunity to fight off.[67]

The new wave of evangelical activity across Kanienke in the 1650s also uncovered participants in other martyrs' deaths. In August 1656, Jesuit Réne Ménard, on a mission to the Cayuga, encountered an ailing warrior whose face was marred by a massive growth. It was none other than the man who had, seven years earlier, attempted to ransom Brébeuf and Lalemant with his own wampum.[68] Like Jogues's killer and his would-be savior, this man also ardently embraced Catholicism, with his conversion being similarly interpreted as "the fruits of the charity that he formerly displayed towards Fathers Brébeuf and l'Allemant."[69] Baptized "Lazare," he became an early pillar of the Cayuga church.[70]

Bizarrely, the notion of a special relationship existing between a slayer and his victim, coupled with the prestige and rapt attention showered on those able to claim this form of peculiar, violent intimacy with the martyrs, generated at least one false claim of involvement in their deaths. Ogenheratarihiens, nicknamed by the French "Cendre-Chaude," or "Hot Cinders," was one of the most famous Iroquois advocates of Catholicism in the 1670s. He was particularly celebrated for the eloquent extemporaneous homilies, which he often delivered outside, speaking from the natural pulpit of a high tree branch.[71] Perhaps the centerpiece of Ogenhereatarihiens's rhetoric was his vivid description of his spiritual transformation from the one-time slayer of Brébeuf and Lalemant into their most ardent venerator. But some commentators have cast a jaundiced eye on Cendre-Chaude's dramatic claims. Historian Henri Béchard feels that his relative youth in the 1670s casts doubt on his claim to have taken part in the bloody events of March 1649.[72] But while Ogenheratarihiens's self-promotion as a martyr-slayer may have been false, the very fact that he would make it demonstrates the peculiar prestige to be obtained thereby and vindicates the Jesuit decision to emphasize rather than downplay their order's suffering at Iroquois hands in their Catholic courtship of the Six Nations.

Although the Jesuits did attract some influential Iroquois to Catholicism in the 1650s, their endeavors bought the colony merely a lull in conflict rather than a permanent cessation of hostilities. By the early 1660s, concern about an imminent Iroquois attack of the colonial stronghold of Québec was once again so intense as to prompt the nightly evacuation of both cloistered female orders to the less vulnerable Jesuit residence. Once again, the colony's days seemed numbered.[73] Shaken by his Society's evangelical failure in Iroquoia and concerned that colonists' fears of invasion were eroding the edifying sense of religious mission he had worked so hard to inculcate, Ragueneau now adopted a much harsher line regarding the Haudenosaunee. In 1662, he left Québec for France to argue at court that the crown must immediately invest militarily in its northerly colony's defense or risk seeing it forever ruined. Though he envisioned a speedy return to New France, once on Gallic soil Ragueneau was reassigned to a domestic position representing the interests of the Canadian mission. He would never see Catherine or Canada again.

"My Spirit Found a Unity with This Holy Man"

However, having labored to bring forth his penitent's strong devotion to his own spiritual mentor, Ragueneau could now observe with satisfaction as his influence, coupled with his absence, bore mystical fruit.[74] Physically separated from the older Jesuit who had had such a profound impact on her spiritual development,[75] Catherine would now forge a similar intimate partnership across the divide of death with Jean de Brébeuf. Much as her living confessor had done, her new "celestial spiritual director" would woo her to participate with him in an urgent shared mission.

Prior to his departure for France, Catherine had "known" Brébeuf only through Ragueneau's mediating memories and her own ritual use of the martyr's relics. But with her spiritual director's absence overseas, Catherine's diffuse sense of spiritual connection with Brébeuf began to blossom into something more intense. If these figures' triangular relationship was a colonial North American recasting of the Passion, with Brébeuf as its Christ, then Catherine's place in the drama was not that of Mary Magdalene, the spiritual intimate of its male lead, but rather of

Saint Paul, the outsider who, never having met Jesus in the flesh, became indelibly linked to him through visionary experience alone.

Catherine's first encounter with Brébeuf occurred only six weeks after Ragueneau's departure and was easily the most lavish of her visions of the deceased Jesuit:

> On the 25th of September, 1662, after communion, I thought that I saw before me Father Brébeuf, all brilliant with light, wearing a crown shining with glory, and in the place of his heart a dove as white as snow, which showed the gentleness and meekness which this servant of God has demonstrated during his life. This dove had written on each of the great feathers of his wings the seven gifts of the Holy Spirit and the eight beatitudes. In one hand he carried a palm, and in the other he pointed at the said dove. He was wearing a long alb and he had a stole of golden embroidery and gleaming white pearls, and seemed to me to be all surrounded by rays of light.[76]

Her inaugural vision confirmed Brébeuf's status as a martyr by using all the conventional symbols of Christian iconography. Catherine envisioned the deceased missionary bearing a martyr's palm frond, the traditional symbol of those who have died for the faith, and further emphasized Brébeuf's suffering with his gesture to the white dove replacing his missing heart, ingested in the aftermath of his death. His heavenly reward is visually intimated by the rays of light with which he is surrounded and the glory of his attire.

Never again would Catherine "see" Brébeuf in such magnificent or distanced terms. With time, he would become less an external presence than an intimate part of her inner life, a key player in her inner drama of stormy spiritual ambivalence, temptation, despair and ultimate triumph. As Catherine's descriptions of Brébeuf evolved to present him less as an independent force than as an aspect of her own best self—a sort of spiritual superego—he became progressively less and less visually distinct.[77] From her initial preoccupation with the visual details of the saint's attire and expression, she gradually comes to couch his presence in tactile rather than oracular metaphors. In the evocative analogy of her mother superior, Catherine comes to sense Brébeuf's presence "as a blind man, when near the fire, is sure that the fire warms him, and that he is not far from it."[78] Little by little, Brébeuf is less "seen" than "sensed":

The frontispiece from Paul Ragueneau's *La Vie de la Mère Catherine de Saint-Augustin* (1671), depicting a cross-bearing Catherine confidently interceding for sinners with the heavenly court. She is accompanied by her heavenly spiritual director, Jean de Brébeuf (the small kneeling figure in the clouds above her head).

(Houghton Library—Hyde Collection [1600–1800], Harvard University)

> In making my thanksgiving after holy communion, I sensed that Father Brébeuf was present, and wanted me to listen to something. . . . My resistance notwithstanding, my spirit found again a unity with the presence of this holy man. . . . I sensed the presence of this good Father in a manner which was very intimate, even though there was in it nothing visible or exterior.[79]

But to dismiss Brébeuf merely as an external name that Catherine affixed, through modesty or psychological dissociation, to her own best tendencies would be to miss an important, though contradictory, aspect of their relationship as the nun herself experienced and represented it. For, internalized or not, Brébeuf had lost nothing of his autonomy, authority, or spiritual potency. Catherine's relationship with the deceased Jesuit was, in fact, far from harmonious. Particularly in its early stages, it was punctuated with fierce struggles for dominance between the nun and her celestial visitor. Catherine frequently complained of Brébeuf "forcing" or "compelling" her to act contrary to her will, leading to her sharp resentment of him:

> At the time of the prayer and of the mass, Father Brébeuf made me pray to God . . . in ways which he suggested to me word for word, and did not give me the liberty to resist him or to disobey him, such that my obedience was very constrained and forced. He had me start with act of adoration, which I repeated, despite myself, several times, that God would be glorified by all of his creatures. . . . Finally, when he allowed me to complain, I said: "Monsieur! I will not say, like Job, that you torment me admirably, but I resent the heaviness of your hand, and its cruelty." . . . The same Father Brébeuf made me repeat many other acts, finally, for the conclusion, himself said to God for me those things that it wasn't possible for me myself to say, and I said that I also wanted them, and agreed with all my heart, but then, it wasn't possible for me to say a word to the contrary.[80]

Simply discerning who Catherine is referring to when she uses "I" in such passages is a difficult task. Throughout her mystical association with Brébeuf, Catherine also experienced what she described as demonic interference, if not outright possession, by forces that brought malignant physical, psychological, and spiritual effects in their wake.[81] Though Paul Ragueneau, in his 1671 biography of Catherine, defensively denied the ability of these demonic besiegers to conquer the innermost citadel of her soul, leaving his protégé with a valiant if diminished selfhood,[82] Catherine's own observations of her internal realities were far less rose-tinted.[83] In her own writings, preserved in Ragueneau's text, Catherine often used the first-person pronoun to express contradictory perspectives, even on the same event or idea, illustrating the extent to which she experienced her will and identity as fractured and effaced by the demonic presence within her. Moreover, in contrast with Ragueneau's systematic denials, Catherine grimly and frankly acknowledges that the demonic blasphemies and impurities of her hellish guests did, on occasion, align uncomfortably with her own thoughts and feelings.[84]

Some of Catherine's most gripping descriptions of her painful, forced servitude, however, allude not to her routine torture by demonic forces but rather to being obliged by Brébeuf to observe the sacraments:

> I have an extreme horror of approaching the Holy Sacrament. In truth, I would rather be in the hands of the Iroquois, and enter into their fires [i.e., be tortured], than to receive Our Lord, as the pain at that point is beyond what I can express. And this is the principle cause of my pain, to see myself obligated despite myself to suffer union which Our Lord condescends to make with me, in giving himself to me. When I am feeling a very great hatred towards [Christ], I cannot suffer this union as anything less than a type of martyrdom.[85]

Catherine's audacious inversion of treasured Catholic concepts—particularly her conflation of communion with martyrdom—illustrates how, in her writing, Satan sometimes seizes the quill.

Her internalized figure of Brébeuf, then, can be seen as the holy counterpoint of Catherine's demonic infiltration, a force capable of "counterpossessing" her and compelling her religious observance against her own compromised will. When she was not complaining of the "heaviness of his hand, and its cruelty," Catherine gratefully credited Brébeuf with keeping her on the spiritual straight-and-narrow by enabling her to perform the heavy slate of religious responsibilities expected of her despite the ferocious resistance of her obsessive demons.[86] Brébeuf's interventions thus allowed Catherine to keep her demonic infiltration a secret from her sisters-in-Christ and even from her mother superior, who learned with great surprise of Catherine's struggles only after her early death.

But Catherine also paid a heavy price for Brébeuf's intervention in the form of a prevalent sense of dissociation from her own most virtuous actions. She ultimately credited a male, invasive force for her own valiant attempts to keep up the demanding daily round of her duties, both religious and practical, which comprised her life as a colonial nursing nun while simultaneously coping with apparitions both celestial and infernal.

"Who Will Have Pity on Me?"

But even as Catherine portrayed herself as wholly enslaved to Brébeuf's powerful and often persecuting will (which she either detested or adored depending on the waxing or waning of resident evils within her) she also articulated a profoundly reciprocal sense of Brébeuf's needy dependency on her. Catherine's initial vision of the saint in glory presents him as an unambiguously imposing and magnificent figure— until he speaks. Then his wistful desperation offers a bizarre contrast with the power connoted by the symbols of his martyrdom, his rich attire, and his heavenly surroundings:

> "Who will have pity on me? Who will comfort me? . . . What great pain it gives me to see the country for which I have worked so hard, and where I have shed my blood, become a land of abomination and impiety," and he addressed himself to me in particular, saying: "Sister of Saint Augustin! Do you have any compassion for me? Would you please help me?"[87]

It is in Brébeuf's pathos that we see Catherine's unique contribution to the construction of his postmortem character. This is something completely new. As presented by Ragueneau, Brébeuf was a figure to be venerated for his power and emulated in his sanctity. Any poignancy surrounding him resulted from the venerator's knowledge of the horrifying suffering he endured in his final hours and not, as Catherine would have it, from his current saintly helplessness, peering down like a mournful bird at unfolding events in Canada from his magnificent celestial perch.[88] But Catherine was forced to stress Brébeuf's heavenly impotence and desperate desire for a partner in the reform of Canada because only these circumstances rendered her own emergent role possible. As her intimacy with Brébeuf deepened, Catherine became increasingly confident in articulating their shared goal: to protect their adopted country, through spiritual mediation and voluntary suffering, from the myriad internal and external threats that continuously menaced it.

Catherine's perception of Brébeuf as a figure of despairing magnificence requiring her active aid drew on centuries of female visionary encounters with Christ in which awe and pity commingled to pique renewed religious fervor. Her emergent vision of Brébeuf reflected the psychologically compelling contradiction of powerful powerlessness that was at the heart of Catherine's personal Christology. Her spiritual experiences allowed Catherine to craft dramatic encounters in which the roles played by her, Brébeuf, and Christ became increasingly overlapping.

Convinced by Ragueneau's theological forensics in his magisterial *precieux manuscrit,* as well as by the evidence accrued by her ritual experimentation with his relics, Catherine perceived Jean de Brébeuf as a true martyr and colonial Christ figure. Following centuries of precedent that stressed the similarity of martyrs' deaths to the slaying of the God-man they revered, she wrote: "I was moved to thank our Lord Jesus Christ for all of the graces he had given to Father Brébeuf, but most of for having made him [Brébeuf] comparable to Himself by his suffering."[89]

But it was not just in his painful death that Brébeuf resembled his heavenly master. The deceased Jesuit's palpable anxiety regarding the spiritual state of Canada, whose sinfulness rebuked his recent sanctification of its soil with his blood, echoed Christ's rebuke of sinners, whose negligence of their religious duties mocked his own salvific death. Brébeuf's reaching out to Catherine for assistance in purifying the colony markedly resembled Christ's ongoing mystical intervention into salvation history through the agency of his saints. In Catherine's religious imagination, both Christ and Brébeuf were anxious onlookers of the spiritual lives of their Canadian followers, eagerly watching to see whether their self-sacrifice would be honored and emulated or ungratefully spurned. The increasingly apocalyptic tenor of Catherine's visions in the early 1660s only heightened the similarity of these two celestial male figures, each of whom, in their anger and their sadness, both demanded and entreated New France's spiritual reformation and retribution.

The fluidity of identity that existed in Catherine's mind between Christ and Brébeuf can also be seen in her demons' analogous reaction toward the ritual objects that incarnated their spiritual presence in the material world. The unwillingness of Catherine's internal demons to tolerate the proximity of the deceased Jesuit's holy bones is comparable to their inability to share her body with the Real Presence of Christ:

> At the beginning of holy Mass, in going to take the relic of Father Brébeuf, and carry it to my mouth to kiss it, my arm wouldn't move and I couldn't make it approach my mouth no matter how hard I tried. . . . They [the demons] have a great hatred and an extraordinary rage against this holy Martyr.[90]

Catherine as Brébeuf's Heir

Catherine saw Brébeuf in Christlike terms. But she also stressed the correspondences between the martyr's story and her own.[91] Catherine clearly perceived herself and was increasingly seen by others as Brébeuf's terrestrial heir and surrogate, understanding her emergent role as a vicarious victim for Canada's sins as congruent with Brébeuf's 1649 martyrdom, despite the obvious dissimilarities between the two scenarios. Brébeuf's ordeal, of course, was graphically physical: in the final hours of his life the captured missionary had endured a variety of painful torments that left his body a shattered, charred, and heartless wreck. Analogizing his death at the hands of flesh-and-blood aboriginal antagonists to her own circumstances as a living, cloistered nun, then, required all of Catherine's rhetorical finesse.[92]

Fortunately, the transposition of male, physical torment into vicarious female agony had a venerable history within Catholicism, with perhaps the best example being the seven dolors of the Virgin, which emphasize her sharing in her son's pain by first anticipating and then witnessing his torments, an experience that has been seen by some Catholics as having its own redemptive value. Catherine's appropriation of martyrdom was also aided by her close childhood reading of the *Jesuit Relations* and her mentorship by Ragueneau, both of which encouraged her to see her daring in braving the perilous Atlantic passage to this austere "land of crosses and of penitence" as a "living martyrdom."[93]

But the identity of her antagonists also required transformation. The realities of Catherine's claustration—as well as the failure of the much-feared Iroquois invasion of Québec to materialize—necessitated that her martyr's torment take place at the hands of an insubstantial foe who could magically materialize, undeterred by the convent's strong log walls. But this difficult casting problem had already been solved by Catherine's ongoing demonic infiltration, which perfectly addressed the need for a terrifying yet invisible foe. The seamlessness of Catherine's substitution of "demons" for "Iroquois" is revealing of the already prevalent tendency to associate aboriginal peoples with the forces of darkness and disorder. The postmortem popularization of Catherine's story served only to reinforce the literal demonization of native peoples.[94]

Nailed to the Cross of Canada

During the last six years of her life, spent under Brébeuf's celestial spiritual tutelage, Catherine's Christological visions intensified: their simultaneous expression of just anger and helpless sadness mirroring the dynamics of her original encounter with Brébeuf. Catherine often saw the wounded Christ. Typically, the gash in his side was so deep that she could perceive within it his beating heart.[95] The piteous extremity of Jesus's suffering pushed to the limit Catherine's own ascetic exercises. Witnessing Christ being flagellated in a dream, Catherine then rose in a half-trace and scored her own back so severely that "I thought that I would be utterly overcome by the heaviness of the blows raining down upon me."[96]

But Catherine's was also an angry Christ. On New Year's Day of 1663, she saw Jesus as a mighty judge bearing a vial of divine wrath in his hand. As he prepared to spill it over Canada in chastisement for the colony's sins, his strong arm was held back by a phalanx of saints, Brébeuf among them. Though the enraged heavenly king was temporarily appeased, this apocalyptic vision, the first of many Catherine would experience during the last years of her short life, absolutely terrified her.[97] The apparent fulfillment of Catherine's frightening revelations by a violent earthquake that shook Québec several weeks later greatly increased the young mystic's credibility in the eyes of the select male elite in on her visionary secrets.[98]

Just as in her relationship with Brébeuf, Catherine's sense of imitative communion with Jesus was discouraged by his majestic wrath and galvanized by his physical or emotional suffering. Brébeuf had truly entered Catherine's inner, imaginative world only when she began to

empathize with his helpless sadness regarding his adopted country's religious laxness and accepted his invitation to help redeem it. Catherine's
Christological visions, similarly, crystallized her identification with a
suffering rather than punishing savior.

In communing with Brébeuf to the extent that their identities
seemed almost to merge, and in constructing her spiritual destiny as a
continuation and a fulfillment of his, Catherine was able to resolve her
own long-standing doubts about her identity and mission in Canada
and to make sense of the disturbing spiritual symptoms to which she
seemed prone. Catherine effectively rewrote the Christ story in dupli-
cate, first by relating it to a local martyr, Brébeuf, and then by usurping
it, through a series of imaginative transpositions, for herself. Casting
herself as a Christlike victim of Christ's own righteous anger against
the colony, she sought to redeem others' sins through her own sinless
suffering, defining her mission in explicitly Christological terms.[99]
Communicating her painful attachment to her adoptive country to the
religious and biological family who yet clamoured for her return home,
she wrote that:

> She was attached to the cross of Canada by three nails which she could
> not ever detach herself from. The first nail being the will of God, the
> second, the salvation of souls, and the third, her vocation in this coun-
> try, and the vow which she had made to die here. . . . She added that
> even if all of the other religious wanted to go back to France, if she was
> permitted, she would prefer to remain here alone to consume her life
> in the service of the poor savages and the sick of this country.[100]

Catherine's strenuous mystical life, coupled with her physically demanding work as a nurse, fatally compromised her always fragile
health. On April 20, 1668, she took to what was to be her deathbed,
complaining of severe chest pains.[101] Eighteen days later she was gone,
never to reach her thirty-seventh birthday. Always precocious, always
impatient, always eager, she had now gone first into glory, leaving her
older sisters, sisters of the flesh and of the vow, to mourn her premature passing.

The Death and *La Vie de la Mère*

Catherine's death occasioned an outpouring of grief and nostalgia from
her Augustinian sisters on both sides of the Atlantic.[102] Having long

vied with one another over Catherine's loyalties, Bayeux and Québec now joined in mourning her. Those who had known her as the pert Norman adolescent enthralled with the notion of Canada, and those who had labored beside her within the walls of the Hôtel-Dieu de Québec, patiently staunching the flow of blood, applying compresses, and soothing fever dreams all testified to her competent, compassionate work as a hospital nun.[103] These sterling virtues, coupled with her apparently irresistible feminine charms in both character and appearance, had won the respect and effusive affection of her sisters in religion, many of whom judged her to be a saint purely on this basis.[104] Marie de Saint Bonnaventure de Jesus, Catherine's mother superior at the time of her death, gushed:

> From the very first interview, we esteemed her a precious treasure for this house. Her outward bearing had a charm that was the most attractive and winning in the world: it was impossible to see her and not love her. Her nature was one of the most perfect that could have been desired: prudent, with simplicity; keen of perception, without curiosity; sweet and gracious, without flattery; invincible in her patience; tireless in her Charity; amiable to all, without undue attachment to any; humble, without being mean-spirited; courageous, without any haughtiness. . . . We were well aware that her bodily weaknesses were great and constant, and we saw that she bore them like a saint—always with a calm countenance, diffusing a joy full of piety in the hearts of those that saw her.[105]

But Catherine's death also wrung back the curtain on a hitherto hidden part of her life. For the first time, her astonished female colleagues learned of her desperate struggles with demons and intense postmortem partnership with Jean de Brébeuf.[106] While she lived, Catherine's visionary adventures had been kept on a need-to-know basis: effectively restricting her secret to the colony's powerful male elite. Catherine's role as Brébeuf's terrestrial mouthpiece permitted her to command bishops in his name. In March 1664 she imperiously summoned François Laval to participate in a special novena that she had planned to culminate on the fifteenth anniversary of Brébeuf's death.[107] Adored by her female peers for her humble service to the injured and ill, Catherine also enjoyed unparalleled prestige and power in the eyes of the priestly elite who were aware of her communication with the heavenly beyond and of her secret role as "a victim for Canada."

But Catherine did more than hitch her own spiritual wagon to Brébeuf's rising star. Indeed, it was she who helped *his* star to rise by transposing his cult into a whole new temporal key. In the hands of Ragueneau, its senior celebrant, the newly founded cult of the martyrs was essentially past-oriented. Motivated and informed by his own deeply personal memories of his mentor, Ragueneau sought to establish beyond the shadow of a doubt that Brébeuf's conduct, in life and in death, made him, canonically speaking, a martyr of Christ. But, having never met him in the flesh, Catherine was not preoccupied with the martyr's past. Rather, she was more interested in what wonders he could work, through her ritual intervention, both now and in the future. His miraculous transformation of illness into health and heresy into true belief demonstrated both Brébeuf's lingering attachment to New France and its people and his power to remonstrate with heaven to safeguard the physical and spiritual health of the colonial body politic.[108] Thus, though both Catherine's and Ragueneau's chosen roles in the promotion of the martyr's cult were persuasive, her preferred medium was ritual and his was textual. Only after her death did this pattern alter. After Catherine's premature passing, Paul Ragueneau sought to ensure her immortality in the only way he could. Much as he had done with his beloved martyrs, he "textualized" her, creating in his 1671 *Vie de la Mère Catherine de Saint-Augustin* an intriguing conglomerate of biographical analysis and generous chunks of her always animated letters to him: letters describing the central mystical relationship of her life—her heavenly liaison with Brébeuf. By writing the young nun's life and preserving, through her quoted letters, the fresh uniqueness of her voice, Ragueneau turned Catherine into a text. The circle was complete.

Herself seduced by reading *The Relations* into leaving France forever, Catherine now progressed from being a fish to being a hook. Her own life as a colonial religious, recounted by Ragueneau, would become new literary bait enticing others to dedicate themselves "to Canada and to God."[109]

Intimations of the Coming Storm

Even in 1671, when Ragueneau's *Vie de la Mère* first appeared in Paris, the first tiny tremors of what would become a seismic shift in traditional French attitudes to Catholicism were already making themselves felt. To be sure, some readers responded much as they would have a

generation earlier, during the peak of Gallic interest in the heroic do-
ings of Canadian missionaries. Then, Ragueneau's attribution of Catherine's painful toothache to a tiny resident devil inside the enamel, and
his admiring relation description of the 1663 earthquake as "angels
shaking the four corners of the earth," would likely have been received
with uniform awe and reverence. But Ragueneau had, perhaps, missed
his moment. Stranded in France and homesick for Canada, his home of
twenty-six years, Ragueneau was caught off guard by the ridicule with
which his earnest claims were greeted by many. Those who were not
openly incredulous, questioning the naiveté of both Ragueneau and his
deceased confessee queried the theological orthodoxy of Catherine's
mysticism.[110] The high period of French Catholic revivalism, still peaking in Canada, could no longer count on the breathless Gallic audience
it had come to expect. Canadian missionaries' sense of being locked in
a desperate, life-or-death struggle between good and evil and their longing for direct mystical contact with the divine no longer resonated with
the increasingly secular tenor of even Catholic circles within France.
The flames of Canada's ardent heart no longer kindled an answering
spark in that of its mother nation.

The incredulous reception of Ragueneau's work during the last three
decades of the seventeenth century only hinted at the scope and audacity of the coming revolution, which would forever change the relationship between the Catholic Church and the country that had traditionally claimed the honorary position of being its "eldest daughter." Across
the convulsed nation, churches would burn or, in exquisite derision, be
turned into stables, the smeared shit of donkeys profaning, unimagin-
ably, their inner sanctums. The carefully sculpted marble heads of saints
would be neatly decapitated, like an overzealously pruned rose garden.
The ancient tombs of aristocratic families, their scions interred in vaults
under the church's floors or arrayed behind decorative cast-iron fences
in the nave, would be plundered. The yellowed bones of local aristocrats
would be scattered or mixed with those of their defilers' triumphal picnic lunches among the violated remains. Their skulls would lie cheek by
jowl with empty wine bottles, their tombs flecked with crumbs.[111]

The living did not fare any better. In Brittany, an isolated priest, the
ironically named l'Abbé Pierre-Paul Guillotin, lived inside the massive
hollow of an ancient oak during the worst of the revolutionary violence, kept alive by food donations from nearby villagers. Members of

both the religious and political elite hid or fled the unpredictable mob violence and the inexorable process of formal trial and execution as the old, familiar order was turned upside down.

Like a slender candle guttering in the rising wind, the infant cult of the Jesuit martyrs in France winked out amid the militant chaos of the Revolution. Nourished in the previous decades through the still-popular *Jesuit Relations,* the memory of these colonial fallen had been popularized throughout Europe through the publication, in the original Italian, of the memoirs of Francesco-Giuseppe Bressani, a Jesuit missionary to Canada who had himself endured capture and torture by native peoples in 1644.[112] Their memory was also kept green by Bohemian Jesuit Matthias Tanner's encyclopedic Latin work describing and illustrating the gory fates endured by Jesuit missionaries worldwide. In France, the cult's flame had been fanned by the many religious among the friends and families of the martyrs, who besieged their Canadian acquaintances for illicit relics. But while Brébeuf's skull reposed safely in the Jesuit residence at Québec City, snugly preserved in its French-made silver reliquary, the femur of Gabriel Lalemant, revered on a Parisian altar, was seized by an invading mob and used triumphantly as a weapon of iconoclasm.[113] The cult of the Jesuit martyrs would not return to their Gallic birthplace in any significant way until after their canonization almost a century and half later, in 1930.[114]

The French Revolution, Martyrdom, and Art

The revolutionary ethos sweeping across Europe imperiled not simply the modest cult of these colonial martyrs, but the very concept of martyrdom itself and how it had traditionally been represented in the visual arts. The majority of artist-revolutionaries, most famously Jacques-Louis David, transcribed ancient notions of martyrdom into a new, political key, figuratively prising the halos from the heads of Catholic saints to encircle the brows of his own revolutionary heroes.

To some degree, this kind of visual borrowing of Catholic motifs was inevitable, though often ironic, as the Catholic visual paradigm had shaped even the consciousness of those who now rebelled against it. Take the enshrining of a small, spritely, smiling statue of Voltaire in what looks for all the world like an ancient saint's niche on Paris's Hotel de Ville. The application of this time-honored method of displaying religious statues on church facades to the enshrinement of the Catholic Church's archcritic was probably unreflective, rather than a serious attempt to position Voltaire as a sort of secular saint of reason. If conscious, it was likely adopted with very much the sort of twinkling humor that Voltaire's miniature self seems so mischievously to embody.

But other evidence suggests a much more deliberate borrowing. Admittedly, David often turned to the classical rather than the Catholic repertoire for inspiration. But his intimate postmortem portrait of Jean-Paul Marat, murdered by Charlotte Corday in his bath, owes much of its visual impact to its brazen appropriation of Catholic artistic convention. The position of Marat's body, gracefully inclined like a latter-day deposition from the cross, his expression, in which pain and resignation commingle, and the reverent play of gold-tinged light over his nude torso all plunder centuries of Catholic martyrdom art. In appropriating them, David also accepted an aureole of associations that implicitly cast revolutionary "martyrs" in terms similar to their Catholic cousins: as good men unjustly slain by cowardly enemies threatened by their beliefs. Like Catholic martyrdom art, the mixture of pity, awe, and outrage inspired by the idealized image of the slain was meant to forge in the viewer sympathy for their cause and a matching resolve themselves to hold to it, regardless of the personal cost. Even as the Catholic Church was being shaken to its core by the open hostility of many revolutionaries, the iconography of martyrdom continued to play a critical role in shaping how revolutionaries both perceived and publicly presented themselves. Though trenchantly questioning other Catholic conventions, many continued to turn the ancient association of suffering and sanctity to own their rhetorical advantage.

Not all artists across revolutionary Europe, however, applauded the adaptation of Catholicism's visual canon into compelling propaganda for popular political uprisings. The generator of some of the most audacious and disturbing images ever painted, Francisco José de Goya, scornfully rejected the sanctification of violence to serve either religious or political ends. In contrast with his French contemporary, Goya boldly broke the strong traditional taboos of martyrdom art, which intentionally and systematically censor the inherent violence of its subject matter in order to preserve the viewer's fragile identification with the imperiled figures it seeks to valorize. He created nightmarish canvases that graphically depict torment, systematically dehumanizing both the perpetrators and victims of torture.

Francisco Goya's undated work, *Cannibals Preparing Their Victims*, boldly eschews the entrenched conventions of martyrdom art, which typically downplay suffering and physical disfigurement in favor of saintly stoicism, choosing instead to imagine the ignominious aftermath of the missionaries' slaying.

(Musée des Beaux-Arts et d'Archeologie, Besancon, France / Giraudon / The Bridgeman Art Library)

That Goya demonized victimizers was not unusual. On the contrary, martyrdom art often highlights the perverse delight of the tormentors of Christ and his martyrs in their odious work, displaying their base cruelty or uncomprehending scorn for the condemnation of the Christian viewer. Goya's dehumanized presentation of the martyrs, however, broke with centuries of tradition, as it enshrined repulsed horror rather than reverent awe at the heart of the viewer's experience.

Two of Goya's most obscure works, *Cannibals Preparing Their Victims, or the Bodies of Brébeuf and Lallemant Being Skinned by Iroquois in 1649* and *Cannibals Contemplating Their Victims*,[115] portray the martyrdom of the two famed martyrs of Huronia. But for these descriptive titles, one would not know whom the painting depicts, so determinedly has Goya reduced his subjects from martyrs to meat.

Gone is virtually every aspect of the conventional body language of sanctity so effortlessly employed by Grégoire Huret in his iconic 1664 etching *Preciosa mors quorumdam Patrum é S. I. in nova Francia*.[116] Huret's masterwork would come to be the most popular single image of the Jesuit martyrs. His etching compresses time and space to depict in a single image ten missionary deaths that took place far apart—both in space and in time—from one another. Not only would it be reproduced countless times over the course of more than three centuries, but its figure grouping and treatment of individual missionaries would inspire endless imitation.[117] Huret depicts each man in his final moments: mutely communicating his patient acceptance of suffering and his prayerful preparation for his immanent death. Despite the fact that the work ostensibly depicts the martyrs' torture, all ten men are portrayed as dignified, physically intact, and stoically expressionless.[118]

Grégoire Huret's etching *Preciosa mors quorumdam Patrum é S. I. in nova Francia* remains easily the most widely reproduced image of the North American martyrs. Alongside the European martyrs, the artist also celebrates the courageous death of Algonquin Catholic Joseph Onaharé (the small, staked figure in the center background).

(Library and Archives Canada/C-002077)

But in Goya, gone are the kneeling figures, hands folded in prayer; gone are their submissive downcast gazes, visually telegraphing obedience even unto death; gone is the eternally descending axe, the musket balls captured forever midflight. Rather than suspending the action just before the final death blows descends, Goya presents us with the slaying's gory aftermath. But unlike David's elegiac evocation of the dead Marat, itself influenced by centuries of swooning deposed Christs and pincushioned Saint Sebastians, there is no lingering here on the mute dignity of their spent limbs. In these twin works, the martyrs are but shapeless, helpless lumps, mere meat in the process of being flayed and dismembered.

In *Cannibals Preparing Their Victims*, the viewer is confronted with a hanging body in the process of being flayed by a standing male nude. Two sitting men are bent over the other body, disemboweling it. The anonymity of the cannibals' victims is heightened by the fact that neither man's face is visible, leaving the viewer no means of determining which martyr is which. Which body is Lalemant's? Which Brébeuf's? It is impossible to say: their individuality has been stripped off by Goya in a move as neat and as brutal as their painted flaying. As the artist, Goya completes the grim striptease intimated by the Jesuit's discarded robes, strewn willy-nilly about the cave. Next comes their systematic skinning by their painted antagonists, the ostensible subject of the painting. Implicit in both is their dehumanization, the last and most cruelly ignominious transformation.

In Goya's companion piece, *Cannibals Contemplating Their Victims*, the martyrs have disintegrated still further. The same nude man who winkingly flayed one of the slain in *Cannibals Preparing Their Victims* now sits astride a large boulder, gesticulating wildly. In one hand he clutches a severed arm; in the other, he dangles a severed head by its hair.

As aptly expressed by Robert Hollier, Goya in these two works "evoke(s) the sacrilege without invoking the sacred."[119] He graphically denounces the romanticization of violence, whether suffered or inflicted, by refusing visually to link it with a larger narrative of ultimate (earthly or spiritual) triumph. Here, as in his better-known works, many of which also address themes of man's inhumanity to man, Goya expresses a bitterly pessimistic view of human nature and its propensities for selfishness, cruelty, and self-deception.[120] Intended not as an indictment of the Jesuit's historical slayers, but as a larger reflection on human propensities, Goya doubtless sought to portray the asocial cruelty that he saw as pulsing eternally just beneath the thin veneer of civilization.

But, by the same token, by portraying these twin martyrs as inanimate, spent, lifeless, by refusing to halo them with intimations of immortality, Goya serves notice that he will not allow martyrdom to perform its familiar work of reconciling sufferers with their suffering, or of encouraging violent campaigns to further their cause. His paintings are nothing less than a stark repudiation of the concept of martyrdom, root and branch. By stripping away the censorship and religious rhetoric of traditional hagiographic images, Goya confronts us anew with the depersonalization and meaninglessness of violent death. If he causes his viewer to turn away in horror, he has achieved his objective.

From the eye rolling and snickers that greeted the Paris publication of Ragueneau's paean to Catherine de Saint-Augustin, the martyrs' foremost disciple, to Goya's uncompromising deglamorization of their martyrdom, the intellectual and aesthetic soil of late seventeenth- and eighteenth-century Europe had grown inhospitable to the continued growth the cult of the colonial missionaries. But if the climate was unconducive in Europe, it was positively perilous in New France. Daily, if not hourly, in the early 1660s, Catherine de Saint-Augustin and Paul Ragueneau had awaited the end of their colonial world. More than once Catherine steeled herself, in dreams, to save the Holy Sacrament from the fire that she anticipated Iroquois invaders would set in the wooden walls of her log convent. And yet the long anticipated overrunning of Québec by the Haudensaunee never took place. The city survived, only to face, in 1759, a yet more formidable foe.

The Battle of the Plains of Abraham is almost as famous for its brevity as for its outcome. But this battle of only fifteen minutes, ending in an English victory over France, was preceded by a long period of rivalry between the two Old World titans for control of the New. Four years before the decisive conflict, the Acadians had faced mass expulsion from their homelands in eastern Canada because of the English crown's suspicions regarding their loyalty, suspicions only intensified by their fervent (if sometimes anticlerical) Catholicism. Deported en masse, many separated from their family, nearly half the shipboard

Acadians died in the squalid conditions aboard the overcrowded vessels and were buried at sea. Those who survived faced the often open hostility of their reluctant hosts, both in the American colonies and farther afield.

In Québec, the sad fate of the Acadians fueled fears of what the English might do should they successfully conquer the far more populous *habitants.* As they endured privation and periodic bombardment, awaiting help from the motherland that never materialized, some Quebecois turned to the comforts of their faith, erecting the small, glorious eglise de Notre Dame de Victoire to commemorate her heavenly protection of the city against British invaders in the late seventeenth and early eighteenth centuries.[121] But attributing their continuing safety to divine intervention was a double-edged sword, making their eventual defeat, when it came, even more difficult to accept. Amid the booming of the cannons, the terrifying sounds of splintering wood and collapsing stones echoed the inescapable questions: Why was God permitting this to happen? Where were the colony's heavenly protectors? Where was Saint Joseph, popularly credited with preventing the sacking of Sainte-Marie-among-the-Hurons in March 1649? Where was the Virgin, who had so staunchly defended her children only forty-eight years previously? Where were Brébeuf and Jogues and their companions, whose ongoing concern for the well-being of the colony in and for which they had shed their blood had led them to shower it with miracles and healings, warnings and prophesies? In numb disbelief, many shaken Quebecois must have repeated to themselves the words of Christ on the cross, fingering them like a bitter rosary: "My God, my God, why have you forsaken me?"

In the end, Quebecois fears that they would be treated like the luckless Acadians proved groundless. Their far greater numbers necessitated a different approach on the part of the new government: religious toleration rather than confessional expulsion. The new administration's need to appease the conquered Quebecois, particularly given the rumblings of revolution in the American colonies, led to the anomaly of the Catholic Church being tolerated in Québec while it was still illegal in England, a state of affairs excoriated by American revolutionary and arch-anti-Catholic Benjamin Franklin. The new colonial regime cautiously asserted itself in some religious matters, claiming the right to appoint bishops and restricting male Catholic orders from recruiting new members. By 1800, this latter policy led to a dramatic withering of the Society of Jesus. Attrition, aging, and the successive deaths of the original Jesuits finally led to the personification of the entire Canadian Society of Jesus in a single man, Jean-Joseph Casot. As he lay dying in the Augustinian's hospital, Casot was all too aware that the entire Canadian Society was expiring with him. He thus entrusted to the solicitous ministrations of these faithful daughters of Catherine de Saint-Augustin both his failing flesh and the Jesuits' chief worldly treasures: sheaves of seventeenth-century documents describing the martyrs' lives and deaths, along with what little had been salvaged of their holy bones.

Together, the conquest of Québec in 1759 and the French Revolution three decades later seemed to have spelled the ruin of the martyrs' small and fragile cult in both North America and Europe. The English victory on the morning of September 13, 1759, had struck a shattering blow to the Quebecois conception of the world and their place in it. Practical and psychological adjustments to the reality of the conquest were dwarfed by the conceptual conundrum it posed. More devastating than even the more ferocious English assault was the powerful anomie occasioned by a prevalent sense of divine desertion.

In Europe, meanwhile, intellectual, cultural, and artistic shifts had transformed popular consciousness in such a way that the mystical epic of Canadian heroism fell on newly suspicious ears. Moreover, given the ubiquity and unpredictability of violent death across a politically unstable Europe, the martyrs' horrifying ends no longer seemed particularly exceptional. While some revolutionaries adopted the traditional visual and rhetorical iconography of Christian martyrdom to laud their own heroes, more radical European voices utilized the ubiquity, severity, and senselessness of politically and religiously motivated violence to create paintings that critiqued rather than reinforced the ancient tropes of martyrdom.

Given the defiant repudiation of centuries of Catholic tradition in France and the decisive defeat of the ancien régime in Canada, the future of the martyrs' cult looked grim indeed. The Canadian Jesuits seemed to have breathed their last with Casot, leaving the Augustinians, like latter-day Catherines, to mourn their loss and venerate their relics. Yet out of this apparently complete collapse of meaning in the Old World and the New, the cult of the Jesuit martyrs would rise again in the nineteenth century: reestablishing itself not only in the francophone enclaves that had originally nourished it, but triumphantly conquering new audiences in the anglophone world.

3

Souvenirs des Jésuites

CLUTCHING HIS HAT, from which he thoughtfully shook the snow, the priest was led by Madame Légaré through the long downstairs hallway to her husband's studio. As he made small talk with the artist's wife, following her swishing skirts down the length of an echoing corridor garnished with gloomy, gilt-framed paintings, he could hear the voices of the Légarés' five children faintly floating down to him from upstairs.[1]

Twirling his hat nervously in his hands, the priest was somewhat ill at ease. The artist he was going to meet, Joseph Légaré, was a well-known supporter of the *Patriotes,* French Canadian nationalists who, five years earlier, in 1837–1838 had staged a series of abortive uprisings against the British regime. Légaré, if he recalled correctly, had even spent a brief stint in jail for subversion.[2] Though the priest had previously been assured by no less a personage than Monsignor Joseph Signay, the bishop of Québec,[3] that the smoothness and assurance of Légaré's religious works, displayed in churches throughout the city, made him the right artist for this important ecclesiastical commission, the priest was nevertheless acutely uncomfortable.

Arriving at the studio's heavy wooden door, Geneviève Légaré gave a quick knock and entered. His back turned, her husband was working by the window to take advantage of the day's soft, snow-muted light. Légaré was putting the final touches on a painted banner for the new civic organization he had recently helped found, the Société Saint-Jean-Baptiste.[4] The goal of the Society—summed up in the slogan Légaré was busily gilding: *Nos institutions, notre langue, et nos lois*—was to continue the struggle for French Canadian sovereignty. As he turned to greet his guest, Légaré, in a characteristic gesture, quickly ran his fingers through his short, prematurely white hair, making it stand on end above his thick black brows like the quills of a *porc-épic*.[5] On another man, the effect would have been droll. In Légaré's case, however, his disheveled locks stood in stark contrast to the calm, watchful wariness of his dark eyes. A self-made man who had started his artistic career varnishing carriages,[6] Légaré was a prominent voice in the civic and political life of the city and had something of a reputation for not suffering fools gladly.

Politely declining his hostess's offer of refreshment, the priest hastily explained his bishop's proposal to Légaré. The painting he was there to commission was to be a surprise gift for the Jesuits, in recognition of their Society's historic recent return to Canada, and should commemorate their heroic predecessors, Brébeuf and his brethren. Becoming more comfortable as he warmed to his theme, the priest emphasized that Légaré's piece should be at once elegiac and expectant. Even as it memorialized the courage of the Jesuits in New France's heroic past, it should anticipate the new feats soon to be undertaken by their heirs, the contemporary sons of Loyola. Légaré nodded abstractly, eyes narrowed, as the priest rambled on. He was only half listening. Having gotten a sense of what was wanted, he was already mentally translating his clerical visitor's somewhat abstract conceptions into the visual details of his planned composition.

Priests and *Patriotes* in 1840s Québec

Though likely perceived by Légaré as simply another routine consultation with a prospective client, the commissioning of what would become *Souvenirs des Jésuites de la Nouvelle-France* represented something of a watershed in the religious and political history of Québec.[7] The fact that the work was to commemorate the Lazarus-like return of the Jesuits to Canada was in itself enough to make the piece historically significant. This commissioning of a prominent and unrepentant *Patriote* by a sitting bishop of Québec City also symbolically marked the dramatic ascendency of a specifically Catholic form of French Canadian nationalism, clerico-nationalism. In the coming decades, this new ideology

Joseph Légaré's *Souvenirs des Jésuites* was commissioned to celebrate the return of the Jesuits to Québec in the 1840s. Its haunting memorial objects prophesied the romantic resurgence of interest in the martyrs' cult in French Canada and the United States during the nineteenth century.

(Musée de la civilisation, collection du Séminaire de Québec, photograph Idra Labrie Perspective, 1994.8676)

would exploit the legacy of the colonial Jesuit martyrs to craft a creative, providentialist interpretation of the ongoing and painful realities of conquest.

By 1843, when the painting was commissioned, the *Patriote*'s short-lived dream of a successful military uprising by French Canadians against their English overlords was stillborn. It had been five years since their last armed skirmish with government troops and two since the controversial Union of the Canadas, which, for the first time, made French Canadians a minority within a larger, agglomerative entity. Reasons for the failure of the abortive revolution of 1837–1838 were complex.[8] But critical factors included the rebels' lack of adequate coordination and their staunch opposition by the Roman Catholic clergy, who sternly threatened *les Patriotes* with excommunication. Their continued defiance led to the emergence of lonely tombs far from any church: the last, unshrivened refuge of Patriotes who had defied both church and state.[9]

The Catholic Church opposed armed insurrection in Lower Canada not because it was unsympathetic to the fervent nationalism of French Canadians, but because it resented the usurpation of its role as the putative leader of Quebecois society by an upstart populist movement. It was also uncomfortable with what it perceived as dangerous undercurrents of anticlericalism within Patriote ranks. To priestly ears grown accustomed to tales of Gallic outrages against the clergy, the slogans and ethos of the Patriote movement seemed disconcertingly familiar.[10]

But the church courted as well as commanded the Patriotes. Church officials coupled statesmanlike advice with religious threats; counseling that armed insurrection against the colonial government was counterproductive to the rebels' own stated goal of furthering French Canadian interests. Triumphantly pointing to its own historic coup in winning official toleration of the Catholic faith following the 1759 conquest, the church argued that it was far wiser to build cordial relations with the government, relations that would allow the successful negotiation of more equitable treatment. Though this policy of tactful diplomacy was regarded by some Patriotes as distastefully craven, by the time Légaré met the bishop's messenger, armed insurrection was indeed a thing of the past.

But French Canadian discontent was not. The founding of the still influential Société Saint-Jean-Baptiste by Légaré and his younger colleague, the self-taught historian François-Xavier Garneau, represented the Patriotes' grudging acknowledgment that political pressure might be more *utile* in their struggle than armed resistance. But it was also testimony to the smoldering anger and alienation occasioned by defeat and occupation. Many of the rank and file would have agreed with Garneau's bitter complaint: "Foreign domination is the greatest affliction a country can suffer."[11]

Thus, by the early 1840s, the church had decisively won the debate over how opposition to the government should be expressed: politically and nonviolently. What was much less clear was whether the church would win the forthcoming battle for the soul of French Canadian nationalism. As Légaré interacted with his clerical visitor, he would have been aware that his own moderate but secularly inflected nationalism was still comfortably dominant, if only because more religiously tinged visions of French Canadian nationalism—visions his own images would unwittingly help to bring into being—were in their merest infancy.[12] Even as Légaré stood pondering his new commission, his influential friend Garneau was scribbling out the first edition of his landmark multivolume *Histoire du Canada*. The *Histoire* praised the glories of the French Revolution and attributed the 1759 loss of New France exclusively to secular factors, rather than painting it as an act of God.[13]

In the decades that followed, however, such liberal, secular views would increasingly be eyed askance as French Canadian nationalism was reimagined in a bold new confessional key. The great drama of the defeat of New France and the ongoing marginalization of French Canadians would become firmly set within a Catholic interpretive framework that both affirmed its pathos and, through the inverting logic of Christian martyrdom, transformed the dross of failure into the gold of spiritual and moral victory.

This shift would be masterminded in large part by one man, Ignace Bourget, the powerfully authoritarian bishop of Montreal, who would dominate the Quebecois church for decades. As one of the opening gambits of his bishopric in the early 1840s, Bourget masterminded the triumphal return of the Jesuits by appealing directly to the Society's heroic record of suffering and service on Canadian soil. Canada, he affirmed, had never ceased to venerate the memory of the martyrs and eagerly sought the return of the spiritual "descendants of Fathers Brébeuf, Lalemant, Jogues and others who had honored our country with their suffering."[14] The return of the Jesuits, the importation of other French religious orders and skyrocketing domestic vocations would dramatically change the overall ethos of daily life in Lower Canada. Taking charge not only of the pastoral but also of the temporal needs of the Quebecois, the church would assiduously knit together an extragovernmental cradle-to-grave safety net of Catholic education, health care, and social services.[15] Clerical ascendency in Lower Canada would also lead to the challenging (and eventually the near muzzling) of the vibrant secular nationalism that Légaré and Garneau had expressed in the 1830s and 1840s.

Yet even as secular and clerico-nationalists clashed on how best to interpret their shared past, the imagery, language, and logic of martyrdom would prove broad enough to appeal to both constituencies. Indeed, throughout the nineteenth and into the twentieth century, religious and political articulations of martyrdom in Québec would be mutually reinforcing. Whether it was the *in odium fidei* slayings of Jesuit missionaries in the 1640s, the tragic overrunning by the Haudenosaunee of Adam Dollard des Ormeaux's small band of outnumbered *habitants* at the battle of Long-Sault in 1660, or the doomed attempts of *les braves* to save their colony, the rhetoric of martyrdom offered a clear distinction between the victorious evil and the saintly defeated that appealed to both of these warring factions.

Minorities and the Martyrs

In the nineteenth century, both French Canadian and, for the first time, American Catholics would utilize the dimly remembered legacy of the small group of seventeenth-century Jesuit martyrs to articulate their own sense of collective identity in their negotiations with more dominant groups within their respective societies. Both Catholic minorities perceived themselves as despised outcasts marooned within fundamentally hostile encapsulating cultures. Thus, for both Catholic enclaves in the bracing circumstances of the mid-nineteenth century, the martyrs' lives and deaths were never of merely antiquarian interest, but rather were seen as being charged with urgent contemporary relevance. Over the course of the nineteenth century, the martyrs would come to symbolize the preferred contemporary self-image of each of these national entities.

But despite common strategies for collective self-definition, there are obvious differences in the nature of the minority status of American and French Canadian Catholics and in how and why these groups appropriated the martyrs to serve as an embodiment of their collective identity. The French Canadian experience fostered both collective self-confidence and a kind of belligerent insecurity. Within their own borders, francophone Catholics formed a tight-knit, homogeneous culture. But within the larger entity created by the 1842 Union of the Canadas, they had become a linguistic and confessional minority.

Many French Canadians would doubtless have seen their plight as similar to that of Jonah and the whale. The mere fact of being swallowed by the great sea beast, they might have reasoned, did not make

Jonah a part of it, or vice versa. Like Jonah, their mission was to prevent their assimilation into the entity that had enveloped them and, if possible, to give it a bad case of indigestion while they were at it. The martyrs became a means of shoring up a defiantly different (and morally superior) collective identity that served to distinguish French Canadian Catholics not only from anglophone Protestant colonial authorities but also from other subjugated groups with whom the governing powers liked to lump them, such as native peoples. The pain-wracked figures of the martyrs became a way to assert their own deeply felt sense of distinctiveness within the wider society into which they had been so reluctantly subsumed. The martyrs' cult became something of a "keep out" sign, designed to assert, protect, and promote French Canadians' confessional, linguistic, and "ethnic" differences from the majority culture.

The situation of American Catholics was completely different. Though nineteenth-century immigration from Ireland, Italy, and Eastern Europe boosted Catholics' demographic profile in the United States (which itself fed anti-Catholic paranoia), Catholic immigrants were geographically dispersed throughout the country and confined almost exclusively to urban areas. Though small majority-Catholic enclaves did emerge, linguistic and theological divisions between competing immigrant churches (particularly the notorious rivalry between the Irish and the Germans) meant that ethnic Catholic communities inevitably existed in the plural. Powerful ideological and theological differences also existed between those who wished to maintain the linguistic and cultural distinctiveness of these Catholic enclaves and those who wanted to forge a distinctively "American" Catholic Church, transcending European ethnic for American civic identity, and the Old World for the New. These cleavages precluded American Catholics' consolidation—like their Quebecois coreligionists—into a formidable united bloc.

The tone of the martyrs' cult in the United States was also markedly different. If the unofficial slogan of the reemergent martyrs' cult in Québec was "keep out!" its mantra in the United State was "let us in!" Whereas French Canadians utilized the martyrs to symbolize their cultural distinctiveness and dignified moral superiority in defeat, American Catholics saw these figures as a golden key that could unlock minds and hearts long hostile to them. Parading before the public saintly Catholic figures whose courageous acts of Christian nation-building had graced the earliest pages of American history might serve to defuse the always bristling and sometimes shockingly violent anti-Catholicism so prevalent in nineteenth-century America. If French Canadian Catholics sought to defy the Protestant majority, then American Catholics sought to appease it.

Prophesy in Paint

Throughout the winter of 1843, Joseph Légaré labored on his clerical commission.[16] Returning to his chilly studio after hearty, fire-lit suppers *en famille,* he would work on the painting, imagining himself in the still, somewhat claustrophobic air of the well-appointed clerical study he had created as its fictitious setting. Rather than simply depicting the deaths of the martyrs, as had Huret,[17] Légaré attempted something more ambitious, creating a tableau about martyrdom and memory: a haunting still life that evoked the martyrs' paradoxical, unstable presence and absence, destabilizing present and past. Prescient regarding the important role that absence, memory, and loss would play in the nineteenth-century resurrection of the martyrs, the objects Légaré selected for this memorial work proved prophetic in presaging how the returning Jesuits would seek to commune with their fallen predecessors. Légaré's coloration of his lugubrious library is strategically dark, allowing these portals of mystical connection with the saintly dead—a book, a window into eternity, and a silver reliquary bust—to glow with a muted, unearthly light. In the left foreground, the open Charlevoix volume, its pages a blaze of white in the dim interior, lies open to the illustrated title page, inviting the viewer to read of the martyrs' famous exploits. In the background, the spines of other volumes are tantalizingly visible, and a glinting crucifix emerges only reluctantly from the shadows. Framed by rich red velvet curtains, Légaré's window onto the past reveals the eternally unfolding martyrdom of three missionaries at the hands of their native tormenters. Introducing an element of dramatic human action within a miniaturized romantic landscape, this element complicates the painting's classification as a simple *nature morte,* as does the haunting, inescapable, dead-yet-alive presence of Jean de Brébeuf. His silver *tronc-reliquaire* dominates the entire composition with its central placement and shimmering palette of soft, pewtered grays, highlighted with a few sparing silvery splashes. The bust is painted from slightly below, allowing Légaré to maximize the impact of the martyr's commanding, yet ambiguous expression.

In *Souvenirs*, Brébeuf's is a triangulated gaze. Through the window, his ever-dying eyes confront those of his viewer. The shadowed recesses of his skull's empty eye sockets, visible through the oval window of the reliquary bust, seem a subtle negation—or is it an intensification?—of his silvery stare above. Of these three elements, book, window, and bust, it is Brébeuf's triune gaze that promises the viewer spiritual communion. But the possession and veneration of his relics would be the last of these three "doors of perception" that would open to the Jesuits. Until 1925, their attempts to resurrect the cult of the martyrs and to forge a future worth of their legacy would express itself primarily through research and writing (prophesied by Légaré's invitingly open volume), and by missionary efforts among native peoples in Huronia and the opening West, symbolized by his open window onto an eternally recurring past of pain and promise.

The Pen and the Past

Légaré's painting, *Souvenirs,* was presented to newly arrived Jesuit Félix Martin in May 1843 by secular clergy eager to welcome back the black-robes.[18] In Martin, his tableau had found its ideal connoisseur. The painting's focus on the glories of the colonial Jesuits and its dreamy, faintly menacing theme of the inescapability of memory would cast its eerie spell over the French priest who, as "the foremost archivist and foremost modern historian of the Society of Jesus in Canada,"[19] would seek himself to reawaken memories of the martyred missionaries.

An 1848 daguerreotype captures Martin's unique features. He sits, protectively hunched over an open book, his large, heavily hooded eyes peering out suspiciously from under his biretta. But though the very shape of his mouth forms a shallow smile, and his first name means "happiness," this frozen Félix seems neither particularly content nor especially friendly. Posing with his truest friends—those printed on vellum and bound in leather—the priest's testy, unwelcoming expression suggests that he has been disturbed in the midst of his contemplation by an irritating visitor, like Coleridge prematurely roused from his pleasure dome by the unfortunate interruption of the "person from Porlock."[20] With its self-consciously literary props, the portrait seems to place Martin in Légaré's lugubrious library as its especial denizen or tutelary spirit.

Almost immediately upon arriving in Canada, Félix Martin commenced a laborious treasure hunt to find the widely dispersed flotsam of his shipwrecked Society. In the summer of 1844, barely a year after his arrival in Canada, he hit the biggest pay dirt of his archival career. While visiting the Hospitalière nuns of the Hôtel-Dieu de Québec, Martin

Père Félix Martin, who founded the Archives du Collège Sainte-Marie. The rediscovery, centralization, publication, and translation of seventeenth-century manuscripts recounting the gory deaths of the colonial Jesuits excited new interest in these figures in the nineteenth century, prompting renewed calls for their canonization.

(Archive of the Jesuits in Canada)

retrieved the myriad manuscripts that had been confided to their care by the dying Casot, the last Jesuit of the old order. The jewel in the crown was Ragueneau's 1653 *precieux manuscript,* in which he lovingly detailed the martyrs' virtues and their heroes' deaths.[21]

As Martin, like a clerical magpie, amassed textual treasures, he began to need a suitable nest in which to deposit them. His need was met with Bishop Bourget's urgent request that the Jesuits found an institution of higher learning in Montreal, to be called "Collège Sainte-Marie." Bourget hoped that it would be Pierre Chazelle, the restored Jesuits' urbane bilingual superior, who would found and nurture his Sainte-Marie-to-be.[22] But, uncooperatively, Chazelle had fallen wholly under the spell of the Sainte-Marie-that-was: the ruins of the Jesuits' seventeenth-century headquarters deep in Huronia, which he had visited the same summer as Martin's archival breakthrough. His visit to the Jesuit ruins nourished Chazelle's mystical conviction that he was being called to imitate his martyred predecessors in ministering to the native peoples of ancient Huronia and beyond, ultimately leading to the creation of two distinct theaters of Canadian Jesuit activity that mimicked the division of medieval monks into "active" and "contemplative" orders. Under the austere direction of Félix Martin, Lower Canada became the seat of the "contemplatives," who communed with the martyrs by painstakingly studying the sepia words they had penned, in blood and in ink. Upper Canada, under Chazelle, became the rugged enclave of the "actives," who would emulate the martyrs' missionary labors.[23]

In founding the Archives du Collège Sainte-Marie, Martin had made the hushed space of devout scholarship so convincingly realized by Légaré in paint into a living, three-dimensional reality. Here, scholars could commune with the martyrs' memory, researching dynamic new works that ventriloquized or interpreted their long-stilled voices. Established some four years before the rest of the college, the archives were the beating heart around which the rest of the institution's embryonic body would gradually coalesce.[24] The repository's emergent status as one of the preeminent caches of early North American manuscripts made it an obligatory research stop for a continental, confessionally diverse clientele: drawing anglophones as well as francophones, Americans as well as Quebecois. Indeed, the breadth and quality of Sainte-Marie's holdings forced even the incorrigible anti-Catholic Francis Parkman grudgingly to genuflect northward. It would be this diverse medley of scholars who would popularize the martyrs' story for a new generation on both sides of the international border. This not only revitalized the martyrs' cult, but greatly expanded its reach linguistically, geographically, and confessionally. A genuinely North American cult would spring from this archival seedbed as, for the first time, the martyrs' story would germinate beyond Catholic confessional boundaries to intrigue and edify Protestants.

The reestablishment of the Society of Jesus as a continental rather than a national initiative and its headquartering in New York rather than Québec from 1846 to 1879 served to broaden the archives' *Catholic* client base.[25] The "father of American Catholic history," John Gilmary Shea, would spend two years as a Jesuit novice at Collège Sainte-Marie under Martin's supervision. Though he ultimately decided not to take his vows, this experience not only enhanced his skills as an archivist and historian, but influenced his characteristic framing of Catholic history in broadly continental terms. In establishing the archives, then, Martin had not only found a suitable vault for his treasure: he had also established a historiographic armory capable of outfitting his successors with the interpretive weapons and archival training they would need to take the fight for the martyrs' cause into a twentieth century he himself would not live to greet.

The Rise of Quebecois Clerico-Nationalism

The dramatic devotional revolution led with such forthright self-assurance by Bishop Ignace Bourget in nineteenth-century Québec had both intellectual and institutional components. Intellectually, nineteenth-century clerico-nationalism belatedly offered an attractive, optimistic, and self-flattering theological response to the confusion and despair occasioned in Quebecois breasts by the 1759 conquest. This positive interpretation was in contrast both to the church's own previous analysis of the defeat and to secular interpretations that pragmatically (and thus, to Bourget, atheistically) explored military, economic, and demographic causes for English preeminence.

Initially, French Canadian Catholics' acceptance of the fundamental dogma of God's providential control of history had forced them to consider the dreadful possibility that, precisely because God had allowed it to happen, their defeat must represent his "adorable will." Taking a page out of Catherine de Saint-Augustin's hermeneutic playbook of the century before, they blamed Québec's sinful straying for this man-made disaster in much the same way as the young nun had regarded the earthquake of 1663 as a frightening divine chastisement.

But in the decades following the French Revolution, the most imaginative theological readers of political tea leaves articulated a radical new interpretation of the event: the defeat of New France was intended not as a punishment of pious French Canadians, but rather as a means of politically severing them from the godless leadership of their mother country, lest they spiritually perish alongside it. The uncomprehending agents of a divine plan, the English had been used in 1759 by an all-knowing God who prudently sought to sever the umbilical cord binding this tender New World babe to its whorish apostate of a mother. Seen from this perspective, Québec's submission under a foreign yoke was, paradoxically, a sign of God's far-seeing, providential care. Left in chaste, isolated splendor, Québec's pristine Catholicism would serve as a model of true religious fidelity in a lost and fallen world. Rather than plaintively asking why God had abandoned them, clerico-nationalists suggested, the Quebecois should "thank Providence for snatching Canada from the godless country which was tearing its altars down."[26] In the nineteenth century, clerico-nationalism's mantra that Québec had been chosen to witness to the eternal truths of Catholicism in a world run mad with apostasy and revolution would become the preferred means of distinguishing Quebecois identity from the dominant, anglophone culture that surrounded it, while simultaneously insisting on its ideological and historical separateness from France.[27] The religious patina of the theory assured an important role for the Catholic Church in French Canadian *survivance,* or the effort of *les Canadiens* to survive as a distinct linguistic, confessional, and cultural nation within the larger entity of Canada.

Clerico-nationalism thus asserted the preeminence of the Roman Catholic Church in every facet of daily life in Lower Canada, both motivating and justifying a massive institutional and personnel expansion beginning in the 1840s and reaching its zenith at the turn of the twentieth century. The newly arrived French religious orders recruited for service by Bourget, augmented by dramatically increasing domestic vocations, made male and female religious the living stones of Fortress Québec. For over a century, from the 1840s until the 1960s, the church would preside over Québec's educational system, health care, and social services, forming a virtual Catholic shadow state.[28]

Quebecois clerico-nationalism was undergirded by another, more universal Catholic movement, ultramontanism, which emphasized the ultimate and unifying power of the Holy See. The movement's emphasis on "looking towards Rome" for guidance subtly questioned the authority of its anglophone Protestant conquerors. Québec's obsequious ritual submission before Rome suggested that the Vatican was the ultimate temporal as well as spiritual authority. Ultramontanism also served ostentatiously to distance Québec from its French motherland, still suspect for its ongoing republican and anticlerical sentiments, and from Gallicanism, France's traditional form of Catholic nationalism. Bourget's lavish embrace of ultramontanism is perhaps best illustrated by his ambitious construction of a smaller-scale reproduction of St. Peter's Basilica and its audacious placement in the anglo-Protestant heart of Montreal. Bourget also instituted Roman-style clerical garb and raised a Canadian mini-army of Zouaves to defend the pope's then substantial holdings from the onslaught of godless Italian nationalists in 1868.

Clerico-nationalism's new messianic reading of Québec's history and future invited a fresh look at the martyrs. Initial interpretations of the 1759 defeat, of course, implicitly questioned the reality or value of the martyrs' supposed protection of the colony they had consecrated with their blood. For had it not fallen into the hands of the enemy? But now that the defeat of New France had been revealed to be a disguised and paradoxical victory (much like the martyrs' own), their cult regained something of its ancient luster.[29] The Rumpelstiltskin logic of martyrdom, able to spin the straw of military defeat into the gold of spiritual superiority, suggested that the colony's collective humiliation was not meaningless but transformative, and that, paradoxically, New France had been saved *through* her destruction. The slaying of the martyrs and the fall of Huronia in the 1640s thus became seen as a prophetic forewarning of the events that would follow just over a century later, much as, in Christian terms, the sacrifice of Isaac "presaged" Christ's death on the cross. The martyrs gave a much-needed specificity and pathos to an otherwise vague sense of French Canadian Catholic *messianisme,* incarnating and personifying this nebulous theohistorical theory.[30]

Clerico-Nationalist Intimidation of Intellectuals

Clerico-nationalism's rise was swift, moving from historiographic obscurity in the 1840s to a taken for granted dominance by the 1850s and 1860s. As it gained in power, it became the new historical orthodoxy to which all Québec intellectuals were expected to conform. Under Bishop Bourget, intellectual freedom that ignored its responsibility to bolster the clerico-nationalist status quo was robustly condemned as both politically subversive and religiously sinful.[31] Indeed, "liberty" itself was often condemned, during this epoch, as the false value of the enemy whose true face was not the red-tuqued, fresh-faced Marianne, but the blood-soaked *tricoteuses:* elderly French women so famously immune to human compassion that, ensconced at the foot of the guillotine, they knit their way through the ghoulish spectacle of executions, pausing only to howl for another head. Liberty, opined Bourget, inevitably brought only violence, chaos, and apostasy in its crimson wake.

Few Quebecois intellectuals would have the strength to stand against clerico-nationalists' determined and coordinated challenge to those voices who dared to write outside the halo of church approval. Joseph Légaré's longtime associate and ally, François-Xavier Garneau, would become one of their first targets. A strong French Canadian nationalist, a secularist, and a self-taught historian, Garneau was younger and more urbane than Légaré. But he was also more sensitive and far less self-assured, leaving him psychologically vulnerable to the church's thundering condemnations of his work.

Before clerico-nationalism's meteoric rise in the mid-nineteenth century, Garneau's secularly inflected historiography had been considered moderate and mainstream.[32] The young historian presented the defeat of Québec as a tragic historical accident rather than the working out of an obscure divine plan, and sought carefully to untangle the complex political, economic, and military factors for Québec's fall. For Garneau, France's fatal indifference to its northerly colonial offspring was the direct result of Québec's small size and modest economic productivity, which he blamed, in turn, on confessional restrictions on immigration to the colony. In Garneau's view, the colonial "Catholics only" policy had had ironic results. New France's obsession with religious purity had fatally limited its demographic and economic expansion, leading inexorably to its unceremonious sacking by English Protestants.[33]

As the ideological tide turned, Garneau was accused by his increasingly powerful detractors of consorting with the ideological enemy, brazenly criticizing the church, and denying the hand of God in history. His enthusiastic support for the failed Lower Canada uprisings of 1837–1838 and his sympathetic portrait of the French Revolution as a fight for greater freedom for the masses were vituperatively condemned.[34] His spirited attacks on the more authoritarian religious figures of New France, such as its iconic first bishop, François Laval, were particularly controversial. With little imagination, Garneau's coded complaints about Laval could be applied to the leonine Bishop Bourget's own clerical clampdown.[35]

Garneau was also accused of damning the martyrs, the elaborate figureheads adorning the clerico-nationalist prow, with faint praise. But his supposed sins against them were those of omission only. Though brief, Garneau's presentation of their lives and deaths in his *Histoire* was scrupulously respectful.[36] Indeed, he lauded them with many of the same superlatives as did his clerico-nationalist competitors. Yet though he celebrated the martyrs' physical courage and noble goals, Garneau confined the martyrs unambiguously and "with premeditation"[37] to the past, eschewing the historiographic fashion to present their fate as prophetically forecasting that of their people, lauding them as symbols of the physically vanquished but spiritually undefeated soul of New France.

Goaded by his sins, both real and imagined, against the new clerico-nationalist orthodoxy, Garneau's enemies unabashedly howled for his head. "He writes like a Protestant!" spat the *Journal de Québec,* enunciating the ultimate insult: one that connoted not simply the horror of apostasy but the disgusting cowardice of "ethnic" betrayal.[38] Even Garneau's supposed friends were influenced by the sharp criticism his works provoked by midcentury. Some allegedly bought and burned as many copies as they could find of the first and most incendiary edition of his *Histoire du Canada,* claiming to have done so not simply to stop the spread of Garneau's heresies but to save their friend from any further harassment and humiliation by the church.[39]

Faced with his near-unanimous condemnation and haunted by his own insecurities, Garneau eventually knuckled under. His unprecedented submission of his work to receive the imprimatur of his bishop in 1859 marked the beginning of the end.[40] Now, even if Garneau had the temerity to express unorthodox views, his clerical editors could excise them as assiduously as a picky child removing raisins from his toast. But, having been achieved, clerical oversight was now unnecessary. Reconciling himself to the changing theological currents of his time, Garneau had begun belatedly to self-censor, and himself now lit the match that would burn his earliest and best work.

The church's arrogant bullying of the soft-spoken young historian, coupled with the farce-like contours of the infamous 1869 "Joseph Guibord affair," in which Bishop Bourget retaliated against a defiant liberal by refusing him burial in consecrated soil, scandalized and radicalized as many late nineteenth-century intellectuals as they intimidated.[41] But what the church had sown in its campaign against Garneau, it would reap tenfold in the fearless figure of the blisteringly anticlerical Benjamin Sulte. If secular nationalist history had come into the nineteenth century with a lamb, it would go out with a lion.

Sulte clearly saw his paschal predecessor as something of a martyr for liberal truths, noting bitterly: "they persecuted Garneau right to his deathbed!"[42] But given the virtual certainty of his own condemnation by the church, Sulte saw little reason for diplomacy. Thus, whereas Garneau had merely consigned the martyrs politely to the past, Sulte boldly challenged every aspect of their waxing cult.[43] Though he made the necessary obeisance, stating that "the names of Brébeuf, Lalemant, Daniel are surrounded by a radiance of greatness which even time will not diminish,"[44] Sulte provocatively painted the colonial Jesuits as naive, overreaching, and selfish. In their single-minded obsession with the conversion of native North America and their foolhardy determination to risk their own lives to effect it, he argued, the Jesuits had unfairly exposed a generation of French Canadian settlers to protracted danger without their consultation or consent.[45] Innocent *habitants* who wished merely to survive and prosper in the New World had been sentenced to horrifying suffering by an absurd Jesuit policy that for too long eschewed military for evangelical conquest: "Alongside every one of the Jesuit martyrs, we can place forty Canadian martyrs—men, women, and children bludgeoned, flayed, burned, and tortured in ways just as horrible as were Fathers Brébeuf and Lalemant; but history hardly bothers with them."[46]

Not only had the *habitants* suffered the same tortures in far greater numbers than the Jesuits, Sulte argued, but their status as martyrs was actually *more* legitimate than the murky *causa* of the black-robes. For Sulte, it was a clear-cut case of martyrdom pursued is martyrdom denied. Because, in his view, the Jesuits had recklessly thrown themselves into the teeth of death, running "to martyrdom as soldiers sent as cannon fodder," they had carelessly broken the commandment that a Christian martyr must neither *seek nor evade* martyrdom.[47] By contrast, the habitants had been "led to the slaughter against their will. . . . The colony—a handful of farmers, poor and helpless—paid dearly for those [missionary] errants."[48]

Contemporary Jesuits, Sulte complained, only compounded the crimes of their predecessors by jealously guarding the title of "martyr" exclusively for their own. It was clear to Sulte that, in refusing to extend the palm to the simple laymen whose heinous deaths had been caused by their own Society's negligence, this new generation of black-robes had inherited the selfish self-regard of their colonial counterparts. Their attempt to defend a distinction without a difference, Sulte opined, made truth itself a martyr. In an era dominated by the dubious orthodoxies of clerico-nationalism, Sulte thundered, "distorted and bloated legend currently replaces history." Only those like him, ardent secular nationalists unafraid of clerical defamation, dared to challenge facile falsehoods: "We who are neither French from France, nor priest, and who do not fear ecclesiastical censure, *we* write the truth."[49]

Sulte thus passionately countered those clerico-nationalist writers who were working to effect French Canadian identification with the Jesuit martyrs. But in his equation of suffering with spiritual fidelity and moral superiority, Sulte did not so much challenge the concept of martyrdom as to argue that its benediction had graced more colonial heads than was generally acknowledged.

The defamation that Sulte had grimly predicted would not be long in coming. Like his hero, Garneau, Sulte would be inaccurately decried as a "Protestant." His outraged clerical opponents used all their influence to ban his work, blacken his name, declare him persona non grata at public events, and call for his "repentance" from his "pseudohistorical falsehoods."[50] Offered an honorary degree from the University of Toronto, Sulte proudly accepted, though his acclamation by anglophone

Protestants in Ontario served only to deepen his defamation in *la belle province*.[51]

Strange Bedfellows

Despite their adamant differences and sharp exchanges, secular and clerico-nationalists nevertheless left traces of their own thought on that of the other camp. Just as in ship-to-ship fighting the keel of one boat, scraping and shuddering against the other, forcefully tattoos its own paint onto the hull of its rival, so the two historiographic camps' favorite themes and ideas rubbed off on one another. As the century progressed, these rivals would articulate startlingly similar ideas about what constitutes a glorious death and how that death should be memorized by its grateful beneficiaries. The religious language of martyrdom would come to color political "martyrs' cults," particularly that of the doomed *braves*. These French Canadian soldiers were widely venerated for their belated 1760 victory over English forces, a victory all the more poignant for its inability to reverse the tide of history. But the process of transference would be a mutual one. The solemn, emotional pageantry that attended secular ceremonies marking the solemn internment of the long-lost bones of these political "martyrs" would find echoes in the twentieth-century "translation"—or movement through space from the custody of one group to another—of Jesuit relics.[52]

Secular and clerico-nationalist ships were also tacking in the same direction on at least one issue: their perception and presentation of native peoples. Regardless of their stripe, historians in Lower Canada were, as early as the 1840s and 1850s, articulating a far less sympathetic and nuanced portrait of native peoples than they had even a generation earlier.[53] As the century unfolded, the basically sympathetic stance of famed eighteenth-century Jesuit historian Charlevoix—whose volume had been chosen by Légaré to symbolize mystical communion with the martyrs through scholarship—would morph into the condemnatory and racist language of the American historian Francis Parkman and his Quebecois counterparts from Benjamin Sulte to Abbé Lionel Groulx.[54] Though otherwise an astute challenger of clerico-nationalist orthodoxy, Sulte's new historical drama, which effectively substituted *habitants* for the traditional Jesuit missionaries, needed aboriginal antagonists every bit as much as Jesuit historians had done.[55]

Sulte's reprinting of seventeenth-century *voyageur* songs, one of many projects he undertook to foster French Canadians' pride in their heritage, only reinforced popular stereotypes of native people as menacing and violence-prone. One of the most haunting of these repopularized ballads, *Quand un Chrétien se détermine à voyager,* listed the dangers and difficulties that beset the poor *voyageur,* counseling his religious resignation:

> When a Christian decides to travel
> He must think of the dangers that will beset him
> A thousand times Death will approach him
> A thousand times he will curse his lot during the trip. . . .
>
> Then do not swear in your wrath, rather think of Jesus
> bearing his cross. . . .
>
> When you are travelling in the great forests,
> the Indians will attack you. . . .
>
> If you wish to brave their fury, wait no longer,
> but pray to your guardian angel to protect you.[56]

Moreover, though Sulte and Groux represented, respectively, anti-clerical and clerico-nationalist extremes, each sought to defend French Canadians against what they saw as insulting suggestions of their racial, cultural, and linguistic admixture or *metissage* with native peoples. This unanimous rejection of their shared past with native peoples led, in the early twentieth century, to the changing of thousands of native names for hamlets, lakes, rivers, and mountains across Québec to saints' names,[57] and made the articulation of pro-native views in Québec increasingly rare as the century progressed.

This ideological hardening was also evident in the visual art of nineteenth-century Québec, including that of Joseph Légaré. In 1828 Légaré had burst onto Québec's artistic scene with his award-winning "historical" painting *Le Massacre des Hurons par les Iroquois.*[58] Art historian Gillian Poulter notes that this painting "may be read as . . . a condemnation of the British conquest. . . . Légaré may be understood as presenting a nationalist visual history to augment the written history of his associate, François-Xavier Garneau."[59] In this political allegory, Légaré did not hesitate to use these mighty, yet ultimately defeated "Huron" warriors as a powerful symbol of French Canadian national identity, painting them as also being noble, Catholic, and doomed. Less flattering stereotypes of the Iroquois, such as their supposedly inexorable lust for conquest, allowed them Iroquois to stand in for the victorious British, creating a disguised but, for the French Canadian viewer, unmistakeably negative statement about English collective character, the validity of their victory and, ultimately, their fitness to rule.

But Légaré's willingness to link French Canadian identity, even allegorically, with that of a native nation would not long survive the 1842 return of the Jesuits. In the flurry of Jesuit-related paintings and sketches that he generated during this period (most of which probably originated as Jesuit commissions),[60] Légaré created imagery that generally cast the relationship between aboriginal peoples and the French as one of ferocious, unjustified, and one-way violence supposedly motivated by native peoples' inherent bloodlust.[61] This darker vision is on display in both *Souvenirs* itself[62] and the larger oil *Le Martyr des Pères Brébeuf et Lallemant,* which effectively enlarged the earlier painting's small and bloody window into the past.[63] Legare's new preoccupation with depicting native-on-European violence gradually eclipsed his more nuanced, ambivalent presentations of aboriginal people, notably his haunting, *Mona Lisa*–like portrait of native woman Josephte Ourné.[64]

Gillian Poulter has compellingly argued that French Canadian artists of the mid-nineteenth century sought to counter in their own work the strong tendency of Anglo-Canadian artists to depict *habitants* and native figures in a way that visually blurred their cultural and ethnic distinctiveness.[65] In the eyes of such artists, she argues, the two groups seemed equally exotic, making both fitting fodder as "picturesque" touches in their artwork.

As its guiding principle, the picturesque employed sharp visual contrasts between supposedly "modern" and "archaic" elements or twinned untrammeled "nature" with sophisticated "culture." By visually fusing the Quebecois and First Nations through the strategic use of props common to both groups, such as sashes, pipes, and canoes, and by associating all of these ambiguous *métis* forms with the archaic and with nature, anglophone artists stressed the two groups' similarities and shared status as newly conquered peoples doomed to inhabit only the margins of the now-dominant anglophone Protestant culture. The presence of these "curious" figures in picturesque art thus supplied the same kind of de rigueur "local color" routinely lent to European works by "mysterious" gypsies or by ruins, whose romantic dilapidation gave a poignant, Ozymandian indication of their former glory.

Poulter suggests that Légaré's turn toward European-aboriginal violence as a subject matter for his own art was a calculated response to this latent political message. How better to insist on the distinction between French Canadians and native peoples than by stressing their history of conflict rather than congress?[66] Depicting the deaths of the Jesuit martyrs remained among the most visually and emotionally charged means of highlighting the two groups' separate histories and identities, however interbraided they might be. Viewer identification with the figures of Légaré's suffering missionaries was only intensified by the halo of associations that clerico-nationalists would weave between them and the martyred Quebecois body politic as a whole.

Nineteenth-century martyrdom scenes were far more racialized than their seventeenth-century predecessors. Though drawing heavily on earlier depictions, particularly Huret's iconic 1664 etching, these new, romantic adaptations of earlier imagery were as black and white in their conceptualizations as they were colorful in their palettes. To the seventeenth-century visual canon, these later artists added a heavy tincture of race, sharply contrasting the skin tones of European victims and native torturers. Huret's original etching renders all figures, French and aboriginal alike, in the same cross-hatched hue. By contrast, Joseph Légaré's 1843 oil, *Le martyre des pères Brébeuf et Lalemant,* makes his two Europeans palely blaze like twin comets in the darkness of the surrounding forest, in sharp contrast to the earthy chestnut hue of their torturers.[67] In this one visual symbol, Légaré intimated the martyrs' luminous sanctity and the wide racial and moral gulf separating them from their aboriginal tormentors.

Étienne David's 1868 lithograph, *Mort héröique de quelques pères de la Compagnie de Jésus,* which more directly pirates Huret, followed Légaré in differentiating the skin tone of the respective actors. David also used more emotionally intense facial expressions than had either earlier artist, a trend that would further intensify in twentieth-century art, in which Europeans' saintly resignation would increasingly contrast native peoples' supposed anger and ferocious joy.

David also eliminated from his copycat composition Huret's placement, in his center background, of the figure of Algonquin martyr

Though clearly based on Huret's *Preciosa mors,* Étienne David's *Mort héroïque de quelques pères de la Compagnie de Jésus* sharply distinguishes native and European actors by skin tone, emphasizes its actors' emotions, and eliminates the presence of native martyr Joseph Onaharé, who disappears in a puff of smoke.

(Library and Archives Canada/C-004462)

Joseph Onaharé, a Christian convert allegedly tortured to death in 1651 for his faith. But in the simplified, racialized art of the nineteenth century, which posited only saintly European sufferers and their ferocious native aggressors, the presence of a native martyr such as Onaharé threatened to undermine its sharp dyads.[68] With Onaharé's airbrushing, the last visual reminder of the presence and suffering of those native Christians who fell alongside European missionaries in the 1640s and 1650s disappeared from the visual canon.[69]

Replaying the Past in Huronia

If Félix Martin symbolically took up residency in Légaré's library with his founding of the Archives de la Collège Sainte-Marie, Pierre Chazelle passed through *Souvenir*'s symbolic open window into the landscape haunted by their deaths. In July 1844 he traveled by canoe from Sandwich, Ontario, northward into ancient Wendake, visiting and preaching to the native peoples of the upper Lake Huron region as he went. The climax of Chazelle's impromptu "pilgrimage" came as he knelt in prayer beside the crumbling walls of the original Sainte-Marie, thus becoming the first Jesuit to set foot there in almost 200 years.[70] With the mission complex's uneven stone foundations moldering like the jawbone of some ancient beast that had cast itself up to die on the river banks, the scene that met Chazelle's eyes resembled one of Joseph Légaré's improbably romantic landscapes come to life.[71]

Writing his superior general Jan Roothaan in Rome, Chazelle advocated the purchase and restoration of the ancient site:

> May God grant that soon the ruins of Sainte-Marie be ours and profaned no more! . . . Shall I ever be privileged to announce to Very Reverend Father General that Sainte-Marie of the Hurons exists, that I have said mass there? . . . The altar would be quickly built, and then a little sanctuary. And I still have hopes of finding St. Ignace, where Fathers de Brébeuf and Lalemant were martyred. A few acres would suffice and could easily be bought. Thus, Father, we would have in Upper Canada two pieces of property very, very dear to our hearts.[72]

Under Chazelle's leadership, and in response to the urgings of Bishop Power of Toronto, who was concerned for the spiritual care of native souls in his vast and rugged diocese, the restored Jesuits returned to "their old native missions of northern Ontario,"[73] an area that, though it did indeed include ancient Huronia, also broke new mission territory "stretching between James Bay and Manitoba."[74] Jesuit Father Jim Kelly, a contemporary Jesuit serving a largely native diocese in northern Ontario, stresses that mission work in Huronia was perhaps the *least* practical of the many options available to Jesuits eager to interact with potential native converts in 1844.[75] For their return to northern Ontario necessitated that the Jesuits divide their already thin ranks into two geographically separate units, and that those missionaries working in the west do so in English, a second language for most. As Kelly points out, the restored society did have other options. They could have played a pastoral role at Ancienne Lorette near Québec City, where Wendat survivors had settled after their long flight eastward. Spiritually nourishing the descendants of those who had suffered alongside their martyred idols would have been a natural move for

Jesuits hungry for connection with the Society's storied Canadian past. The Jesuits could also have partnered with the Oblates of Mary Immaculate, a newly arrived, energetic, and populous male religious order bent on expanding the boundaries of Catholic missionization across the prairies and into the far north. Such an adventure would perhaps have been closer in spirit to the ambition and gusto of the Jesuits' own seventeenth-century forerunners.[76] The fact that they pursued neither of these eminently logical options, opting instead to surrender to the magnet-like pull of Wendake, suggests strongly that *where* their missionary work took place was more important to the returning Jesuits than which aboriginal group they addressed.

For, although they were clustered around the Huronia of old, these new missionary outposts did not serve the same native client base as had their seventeenth-century predecessors. By the end of the seventeenth century, in the decades immediately following Wendat dispersal from their traditional homelands, the Anishnabe or Ojibwe people had gradually wrested control of these lands from their Iroquois conquerors.[77] Yet despite the Jesuits' change of aboriginal audience they nevertheless perceived these new missions as heroic resumptions of the martyrs' long-interrupted work.[78]

Returning Jesuits' tendency to frame their Society's renewed presence in Canada as a continuation of their colonial predecessors' mission led them to inflect their relationship with contemporary native peoples with heavy overtones of prospective martyrdom: casting themselves as intrepid servant-victims and their wary native hosts as essentially hostile and potentially violent. Moreover, because they longed to emulate their saintly predecessors, any possibility of danger, however faint, was welcomed with alacrity.

Following his pilgrimage to Sainte-Marie, Chazelle participated in a fraught parlay with the Anishnabe of Walpole Island, thirty miles northeast of Windsor, Ontario. Purportedly there to apologize for the zealous actions of two junior Jesuits, who had rashly cut down a sacred grove to make way for an unwanted church, Chazelle hoped to convince his offended and reluctant hosts to permit the mission's foundation. The two parties politely addressed one another in a formal exchange designed to encourage frank expression while checking strong emotions. As the senior Jesuit, Chazelle engaged both Oshawana, an elderly warrior who had fought alongside Tecumseh in 1813, and a younger chief, Petrokeshig.[79]

Oshawana opened the debate by skillfully playing upon the providentialist assumptions of his Jesuit interlocutor, which saw history as being inexorably shaped by the Divine Will. The native elder suggested that contemporary ethnic, linguistic, and religious diversity *must* reflect the wishes of the creator and should therefore be respected by his children:

> You come, my brother, thinking you will teach us Wisdom. But don't believe that savages are fools. They have the knowledge that they need. The Great Spirit has not left them in ignorance: he has given them great gifts; he has given them wisdom. . . . My brother, we are not all alike, our blood is not the same and our languages also bear no resemblance to each other. . . . Who created these differences? The Great Spirit created them from the beginning, he who does all things, according to his will. You can well see, then, that we each must have our own way of thinking of the Great Spirit and of speaking to him.[80]

Oshawana's ringing defense of religious pluralism and the right to spiritual self-determination echoed centuries of similar traditionalist arguments put to Samuel de Champlain, Gabriel Sagard, and the martyrs themselves. But Chazelle countered that Christianity was not one respectable religious option among many but the sole and unique truth that offered the only possibility of morality in this life and eternal bliss in the next. Petrokeshig, his younger interlocutor, then took the lead, contrasting the spiritual steadfastness of the Ojibwe with the foolish violence of those who had recklessly slain their own savior:

> My brother, you also received great blessings from your Ancestor; but I believe that you did not keep them faithfully, and that is undoubtedly why the Great Spirit sent his son, who came to bestow new blessings on you. However, you did not want to believe him: you hated him, you mistreated him, and you made him die. But I, a savage man, did not need his visit, because I have kept my Ancestor's blessings.[81]

As the lengthy rhetorical minuet played itself out, all three participants became frustrated, and each resorted to threats. In trying to express how deeply unwelcome the Jesuit enterprise at Walpole would be, Petrokeshig obliquely stated: "if you persist in your resolution I do not know what might happen. Sometimes a storm arrives suddenly, without a noise: it brings thunder, rain, and hail: it cannot be resisted. I hope, my brother, that nothing bad will happen." But by handing Chazelle a sort of anticipatory martyr's palm, Petrokeshig had unwittingly played into his powerful guest's hands. The fierceness of traditionalist opposition to the mission only confirmed the senior Jesuit's evaluation of its importance, even as the breath of danger introduced by his words seemed to confirm the symmetry between Chazelle's own small band of black-robes and the seventeenth-century martyrs whom they sought to emulate. Rather than discouraging the superior, the chief's warnings had—paradoxically—only sweetened the deal. The holy mission of securing Anishnabe souls must and would proceed as planned, Chazelle intoned grandly:

> I do not fear you, my brother, no, not at all. . . . When men wish to hurt me, the Great Spirit is kind to me. A Black Robe is never prouder and happier than when the enemies of Prayer persecute, mistreat, and especially, cause his death in the name of Prayer.[82]

Nor did the Jesuits need Ojibwa permission to establish their mission, Chazelle retorted, having previously received it from government officials. As the Anishnabe were not the true masters of their own domain, this parlay was a mere formal nicety with no binding force.[83]

Denied their say in a dialogue that Chazelle had contemptuously dismissed as meaningless, the Anishnabe would nevertheless get their revenge. A mysterious fire in 1849 burned the controversial mission to the ground, though the blaze caused no loss of life.[84] Even as traditionalists dramatically conveyed their continued opposition to the Jesuits' presence, they denied the missionaries what they seemed to crave most: the glory of martyrdom. But the Ojibwe could not prevent Chazelle from dying with his boots on. Barely a year after his Pyrrhic victory at Walpole Island, Chazelle succumbed to a fever, dying in an ill-fated attempt to found a mission at Sault Sainte-Marie, having impatiently waved off the concerns of those who would have nursed him further in Green Bay, Wisconsin.[85]

Les Braves et les Martyrs

Barely before Joseph Légaré's paint had dried, his prescription that the returning Jesuits should embrace the martyrs' legacy through historical study and reengagement with the native peoples of Huronia had begun to be fulfilled. His third painterly prophesy, intimated by his prominent positioning of Brébeuf's reliquary bust, decreed that the Jesuits should commune with their heroes through the reverent contemplation of their earthly remains. But the painter's final prediction would not come true for some seventy years after Legare's death, and then only partially. Jesuit veneration of their colonial predecessors' meager relics was hampered by their jealous hoarding by other religious orders, both in Québec and overseas. It was only in 1925, with the martyrs' beatification, that the Jesuits felt emboldened to demand a "brotherly sharing" of the martyrs' relics. During this process, Brébeuf's skull would be surgically bisected, with the Jesuits taking possession of the left lobe, and the right remaining with the Augustinians.[86] But Brébeuf's silver bust would forever elude the black-robes, who would possess only Legare's masterful painterly reproduction of it. To this day, the bust remains locked in the Hospitaliere's private treasury in Québec City. Alone on its small dedicated altar, the light from the opaque mullioned windows, reflected upward by the snowy altar cloth, slides and fades, slides and fades over Brébeuf's silver face with the alternation of sun and clouds, giving the impression of changing expressions on his impassive, shining countenance.[87]

Though Légaré can be faulted for this prognostic failure, his influence would decisively shape the contours of the lavish ritual procession with which the Jesuits would triumphantly celebrate their reclamation of Brébeuf's demi-skull in November 1925. The painter's own lovingly planned 1855 funeral procession for the abandoned bones of his beloved *braves* anticipated in striking detail the ceremonial "translation" of the Jesuit relics through the same Québec City streets some seventy years later.[88]

For the two years before Joseph Légaré's 1855 death at the age of sixty, he and François-Xavier Garneau would collaborate to produce an emotionally affecting public spectacle that blurred the political and religious valences of martyrdom.[89] Using image and text, respectively, artist and historian worked diligently to resurrect memories of the hard-fought but ultimately inefficacious postconquest battle fought by *les braves*: French, *Canadien*, and native soldiers whose decisive victory some seven months after the Plains of Abraham should have reversed the historic defeat of New France.[90] Though Légaré's dramatic memorial

painting of the battle[91] and Garneau's poignant descriptions of the soldiers' heroic deeds fermented public sympathy for *les braves*, it was Garneau's grisly discovery of unburied human remains in an overgrown
ravine near the battleground that fully engaged public interest.[92] Recovering and respectfully burying these abandoned remains, dis-
gracefully "exposed to the profanations of bystanders,"[93] and erecting
a fitting monument to these secular heroes became a pressing civic
priority.

Légaré personally designed each detail of the elaborate funeral procession for the recovered bones. It featured an impressive cortege of no
fewer than six black-draped horses pulling a disproportionately large,
elaborate tent carriage, complete with a massive domed cupola sheltering the sacred remains during the procession. Legare's own painting
of the battle was also prominently displayed on this *char funéraire*,
which stopped frequently to acknowledge the belated gratitude of the
public for *les braves'* tragically inefficacious sacrifice.[94] Orations for the
fallen, made before an estimated crowd of 25,000,[95] used all of the familiar tropes of martyrdom, assuring listeners that despite their defeat,
les braves were the recipients of a splendid moral victory and the gratitude of a nation.[96] Collective public veneration of these military martyrs
of 1760, like that of the Catholic martyrs of the 1640s, strengthened the
Quebecois's sense of being a distinctive and morally superior people
who had survived and triumphed over enemies both temporal and
spiritual.[97]

Légaré would not live long enough to witness the unfolding of his
lovingly planned ceremony, dying only four days before the scheduled
interment of *les braves*.[98] But his fanciful cupola would long stand guard
over his heroes' battleground burial site. Cornelius Krieghoff, his
chief painterly competitor, captured the memorable image of a man
and woman briefly pausing by the roadside, presumably in acknowledgment of the gravesite. The weathered, graying remnants of Légaré's
fanciful pagoda: his last, memorable contribution to the public life of
his city, dominates his rival's painting.[99]

Légaré loomed large over the 1925 *apothéose* of the martyrs,[100] as
this ritual "translation" of their bones strikingly mirrored the event he
had organized, but not witnessed. Having been carefully bisected by
one of the era's leading surgeons and married to a wax mold to give it
the illusion of completeness, Brébeuf's half-skull was ready for its tri-

umphal public translation ceremony. A matched team of glossy black horses, sporting black-dyed ostrich plumes on their foreheads, clip-clopped slowly along the winding cobblestone streets of Old Québec, just as they had in 1855. In the black and gold open carriage, the hard-won relics were displayed for the gathered crowds by the triumphant Jesuits. In this religious variation of Légaré's blueprint, the processional pauses were masses in which the civil and ecclesiastical elite of the city and beyond rubbed shoulders with the hoi polloi and schoolchildren, who had been given the day off in order to be able to attend the festivities. Only the emotional tenor differentiated the two. The 1925 *apothéose des martyrs* was as triumphant and celebratory as the 1855 interment had been somber and funereal.[101]

Though secular and clerico-nationalists were often avowed enemies participating in epic historiographic battles so vicious that they wrecked careers, ruined friendships, and even resulted in the unthinkable revenge of disinterment, each group sought to stress Quebecois's cultural, religious, and linguistic differences from both native peoples and the English Protestant majority in which they were now embedded. Both groups extended to their deceased heroes the most superlative and luxuriant garlands of praise possible, leading each to trespass on the rhetoric and ritual of the other, such that political and military "martyrs" *les braves* became haloed with religious associations, even as the Jesuit martyrs took on increasing political significance as the reigning symbol of Quebecois collective consciousness.[102]

American Catholics Discover the Martyrs

It is astonishing, given the complete domination of the martyrs' cult by French Canadians from its inception, that it would be *American* Catholics who would spearhead the ultimately successful campaign for their beatification and canonization. Gathering at Baltimore in 1884 for the Third Plenary Council, the American Catholic hierarchy moved that three colonial figures: Jesuit priest Isaac Jogues, donné René Goupil, and Mohawk-Algonquin Catholic Catherine Tekakwitha merited official recognition by Rome for their heroic sanctity. The Council's confident elevation of this holy trinity was part of a larger campaign by the U.S. Catholic hierarchy during this period to assert the fundamental compatibility of Catholicism and "American" values.

By the mid-nineteenth century, it had become commonplace for American Protestant historians and educators to insist upon the supposed historical and ideological link between Protestantism and American exceptionalism. This hugely influential mythic narrative of American origins linked Puritans' and Pilgrims' seventeenth-century search for religious liberty in the New World with the eventual dawning of American democracy, making Protestantism central to the evolution of American identity. Catholics, then, were unceremoniously excluded from Protestants' self-satisfied self-celebration. The onus was on them to show that they truly belonged in America: a task made more difficult by the three contradictory allegations that mainstream historians often lobbed against Catholics. Protestant historiography typically presented Catholics as ignorant "Johnny-come-latelys": foreign, undereducated undesirables unfamiliar with or actively hostile to American values. This view sneered: "you're not truly American, you just got here." But perversely, nineteenth-century historiography also cast Catholics as the colonial "bogeymen" of American history, fusing Protestant fascination with the "mysterious" and "irrational" rites of the church with their paranoia of the "predatory" military genius of Catholics' native allies (many of whom were themselves Catholic) to create the impression of a papist juggernaut bent on the extirpation of Protestant North America. This historiography countered Catholic claims to Americanness with the objection, "you're not American: you are the evil "other" that threatened the survival of our fledgling nation." Finally, Protestant propagandists presented contemporary American Catholics as the unreflecting, zombie-like victims of unscrupulous papal mind control, suggesting that Catholics were unfit psychologically for participation in the glories of American individualism, democracy, and freedom, concluding: "you cannot be American, you are the unthinking product of an absolutist, authoritarian religion."

This popular presentation of Catholics as malign outsiders who, because of their foreignness, backwardness, and unquestioning loyalty to Rome represented a threat to the American way of life, was unfortunately not simply a historiographic staple. It had virulent real-world effects.[103] During the nineteenth century, American Catholics faced the ugly, organized denunciations of the anti-Catholic American Party, popularly known as the "Know-Nothings." Nor was anti-Catholic violence unknown. In 1837 Boston, animosity against Catholics reached such a fever pitch that an angry mob, enflamed by sensationalist allegations that Roman Catholic institutions routinely held vulnerable young Protestant female converts against their will, burned an Ursuline convent to the ground.

Nineteenth-century American Catholics responded in a range of ways to these hurtful imputations of their outsiderhood. Some ethnic Catholics saw this virulent hostility as a reason to further wall themselves off linguistically and culturally, turning away from a mainstream Protestant culture that they felt would always reject them. But the dominant response of Catholic America, from the archbishoprics of Minnesota to the gritty streets of the urban Northeast, was to demonstrate, sometimes diplomatically, sometimes defiantly, that they *did* fully belong in a country that persisted in seeing them as suspect. Through spirited scholarship, spectacular public performances, the creation of new sacred spaces, and the canonization, both official and unofficial, of Catholic figures from "early America," they sought to demonstrate the compatibility of Catholicism and American identity.

During the nineteenth and early twentieth centuries, the figure of Columbus became a kind of unofficial patron saint for those Catholics who wished to show that their claims to be American were actually more ancient and illustrious that those of Protestants. Columbus, as the purported "discoverer" of America, began to be memorialized by Catholics across the country as a self-conscious rebuke to a historiography that preferred to cast the arrival of Puritans and Pilgrims as the beginning of American history. The Italian explorer's secular canonization, with the official 1937 establishment of Columbus Day as a national holiday, had Catholic crowds gleefully jamming the streets each October. As they marched with their confraternities, bearing aloft their silken banners, these Catholics were defiantly performing their American identity in a "more ancient than thou" ritual of ostentatious belonging that forced Protestants to acknowledge a patriotic debt of gratitude to one not of their faith. More than just an expression of blended or mutated "civic religion," these clamorous parades represented the noisy aspirations of Catholics to be fully accepted members of American society on the coattails of their own yet more venerable "founding father."

But as popular as Columbus was among nineteenth-century Catholics, he could not fulfill their growing, restless desire for an *official*

"American saint." Even as Bishop Ireland and others hubristically put the American church forward as a model of modern, adapted Catholicism,[104] many within the hierarchy's ranks openly envied the saint-rich ranks of the more traditional European church. "What is a nation without patrons or shrines?" sighed one.[105] What would better symbolize the "arrival" of the American Catholic Church than by having "their own" receive the Vatican's imprimatur?

American attention thus came to focus upon the fallen Jesuit missionaries who had left their mutilated remains as grisly markers claiming the soil of colonial North America for Christ. As with Columbus, by championing the *causa* of the martyrs, American Catholics could simultaneously combat the most endemic historiographic attacks against their faith, lopping off all three heads of the anti-Catholic hydra with one neat blow. The Jesuits' ancient pedigree on North American soil (like that of Columbus) spoke directly to the perception of Catholics as undesirable new immigrants. Their mission of "Christianizing and civilizing" the continent's native peoples—a still relevant goal for many Americans in the 1880s—spoke to their benign intentions and important contributions to the nation's history. The martyrs' frontiersmen-like endurance and stoicism and their choice of death above dishonor spoke eloquently to the dark imputation that Catholicism undermines individual freedom through unmanly subjugation to a central religious authority.[106]

From 1884, when the martyrs were first nominated as potential saints, until 1930, when they were canonized, their American advocates worked assiduously on their behalf in the disparate fields of historical scholarship, archeology, and Vatican diplomacy. Even as the martyrs' historical defenders told their story for the first time in English to an intrigued American audience, archeologists were laboring to discover the ancient Mohawk village of Ossernenon, where these giants of the American church had perished. Meanwhile, the official vice-postulator of the martyrs' *causa* traversed the long, lonely, and perilous path towards securing their canonization.

Historians and the American Martyrs' Cult

Two American historians, contemporaries who were born and died within months of each other, would together introduce the romantic lives and perilous deaths of the Jesuit martyrs to a broad American audience. Protestant Francis Parkman and Catholic John Gilmary Shea were both denizens of the Archives of Collège Sainte-Marie in Montreal, which had become something of a cross-border, bilingual gentlemen's club for archaeologists, historians, and antiquarians of all political stripes and confessional persuasions.

"Boston Brahmin" Francis Parkman was perhaps the best known and most respected American historian of the second half of the nineteenth century, though his reputation has more recently been clouded by the virulent racism that mars much of his writing, as well as allegations that he deliberately distorted his sources for ideological ends.[107] Born into a wealthy family of New England Protestants, Parkman, despite childhood ill health, enjoyed the natural world and projecting himself imaginatively into a romantic and colorful past. Steered by his family into the law, Parkman never practiced, though its rigors might well have suited what was by all accounts his confrontational, somewhat arrogant personality, his flair for drama, and his indubitable way with words. Rather, Parkman threw himself into his childhood dream to "write a history of the American forest and her peoples." His incredible productivity as a scholar was due in part to his inherited wealth, which enabled him to have rare manuscripts from distant archives copied or translated, and to a trio of loving women—his wife and two daughters, who aided him when "the enemy"—a lifelong nervous malady that at its worst made him unable to bear daylight[108]—laid him low. Like Milton's daughters, they laboriously copied down Parkman's whispered words in hushed and darkened rooms.

John Dawson Gilmary Shea, the other important popularizer of the martyrs' story in mid-nineteenth-century America, was born into a New York Catholic family as genteel as that of the Boston Parkmans but characterized by penury rather than privilege. Like Parkman,[109] Shea suffered from delicate health throughout his life, though in his case constitutional frailty was coupled with grinding poverty and the constant anxiety of providing for his family on an inadequate salary gleaned from writing commissions and ill-paid editorial work.[110]

Shea's celebrated career as a historian and his apparently cherished role as a husband and father were both somewhat unexpected. The man who would become recognized as "the father of American Catholic historiography" was, like Parkman, trained as a lawyer, though he spent part of his youth seeking ordination as a Jesuit priest. The death of both of his parents in quick succession in the early 1840s seems to have been a key factor propelling the young Shea to enter the Jesuit novitiate and to take the middle name "Gilmary" (meaning "servant of [the Virgin] Mary") in a public, if cryptic, affirmation of his Catholic identity.[111]

Fordham University, the site of Shea's early studies, was also chosen as the first headquarters of the new Jesuit "province of New York-the Canadas." The reconstituted Society had deliberately ignored international borders in favor of retaining the continental contours of their predecessors' presence. The novitiate's 1850 move to Montreal made Shea a protégé of none other than Félix Martin, with whom he would work closely over the next two years, and whose biography of Isaac Jogues he would later translate into English.[112] Though Shea ultimately chose to leave the Jesuits in prior to ordination, the years he had spent as a novice would decisively shape his distinctive historiography. The internationalist Jesuit bent would influence Shea's own blurring of national boundaries in his narration of North American history, leading him to present *all* of the slain seventeenth-century Jesuits as "American" heroes, not just those who fell on the soil of his native New York state. Even as a layman, Shea saw it as his God-given task to serve mother church by popularizing its heroic history in North America, highlighting Catholic contributions to the development of the continent.[113]

For decades Shea and Parkman engaged one another in print. Despite illness, poverty, and personal tragedy, each would amass a long list of influential works on America's early history, works in which the martyrs played a pivotal and highly symbolic role. Yet though they shared a fascination with these figues, and were informed by many of the same primary sources, Shea and Parkman would paint fundamentally different portraits of the American past and Catholics' role in it.

Beautiful Losers

A strong proponent of a racialist and religious Manifest Destiny, Parkman's work is suffused by his guiding assumption that the workings of Divine Providence were behind both the piteous, ongoing destruction of North America's original peoples, the "Indians," and the earlier, fated fall of absolutist, idolatrous New France. For Parkman, history was the story of a continent-wide battle between two unequal European powers, England and France, and the native inhabitants who were inherently inferior to both. Parkman saw Anglo-Saxon Protestants as the favored children of God because of their inherent ethnic superiority, greater "manliness"[114] and, most importantly, their Protestant faith. Protestantism's supposedly superior truth, rationality, and respect for the individual conscience were seen by Parkman as informing the emergent virtues of the American nation.[115] As God's elect, Protestants were destined to expand their benevolent control westward across the continent.

Parkman unapologetically doomed the continent's native people to inevitable extinction, in what his severest critic, Francis Jennings, calls a historiographic "justification for genocide."[116] He saw native people as both racially inferior and as unable conceptually to adapt to changing circumstances: "The Indian is hewn out of a rock. You can rarely change the form without destruction of the substance. . . . He will not learn the arts of civilization, and he and his forest must perish together."[117] Parkman lost few opportunities to denigrate native actors, even when he had to distort the historical record in order to do so.[118] His presentation of native character invariably stressed its supposed changeability, childishness, and propensity toward violence, a point he underlined rhetorically by fanciful animal comparisons: his "tigerish" or "wolfish" native attackers never simply walk, they "prowl"; they do not merely yell, they "howl like savage beasts."[119] But even as he overemphasized the importance of combat in native cultures, Parkman denied aboriginal warriors his recognition of their admirable prowess: painting their warfare as a thoughtless free-for-all innocent of any overarching strategy and their postwar practices as revoltingly bestial. Speaking of the Iroquois, Parkman declaimed:

> Had they joined to their ferocious courage the discipline and the military knowledge that belong to civilization, they could easily have blotted out New France from the map, and made the banks of the St. Lawrence once more a solitude; but, though the most formidable of savages, they were savages only.[120]

For Parkman, native people were, like the American landscape itself, a rugged, daunting obstacle to white progress, to be bested and surmounted.

Though Parkman also saw the French as lesser than their English conquerors, for him their inferiority was not inherent but intellectual. As Parkman saw it, the French had erred by stubbornly wedding themselves to religious and political absolutism, undermining their independence and their "manhood" by slavishly submitting themselves to both pope and king: "Populations formed in the ideas and habits of a feudal monarchy, and controlled by a hierarchy profoundly hostile to freedom of thought, would have remained a hindrance and a stumbling block in the way of that majestic experiment of which America is the field."[121] Faced with these racially and religiously inferior antagonists, Parkman suggests, the triumph of Anglo-Saxon Protestantism in North America was inevitable, assured, and, indeed, ongoing.

Parkman's strongly positive perception of the lives and deaths of seventeenth-century Jesuit missionaries to New France thus presented him with a conceptual conundrum. The martyrs displayed the very qualities of formidable courage, zeal, and "manliness" he most admired. Indeed, in Parkman's own frequent struggles with his crippling malady, he seems to have turned for inspiration to the courage of these tortured Jesuits. But how could the Catholic Church, which demanded the unmanning of all of its members through their unthinking submission to the credulous dictates of a religious oligarch, and further sapped the vitality of its elite by forcing upon them an unnatural celibacy, have produced men of this caliber? If their faith was false and idolatrous, how could it have equipped them to suffer so stoically and to die so masterfully?

Parkman never fully came to grips with this contradiction. Nor did he resolve the yet more personal paradox of being simultaneously the martyrs' fierce critic and their most ardent admirer. Sometimes he argued that the martyrs were manly *despite* their religious training, attempting to uncouple their Catholicism from their courage. Elsewhere he intimated that the martyrs' endurance of torture was facilitated by their schooling in systematically ignoring their bodily needs as celibate Catholic priests. On other occasions he seems to have accepted that their genuine religious zeal, though grounded in a false faith, did indeed motivate their courageous actions and succor them in their time of trial. Most often, perhaps frustrated by his own ambivalence, Parkman would pen passages characterized by acerbic ambiguity as he attempted to balance his lavish praise of these individual Jesuits with an equally brusque repudiation of their Catholic faith. Having described in horrifying detail the torture of Brébeuf, Parkman intoned:

> Thus died Jean de Brébeuf, the founder of the Huron mission, its truest hero, and its greatest martyr. He came of a noble race,—the same, it is said, from which sprang the English Earls of Arundel; but never had the mailed barons of his line confronted a fate so appalling, with so prodigious a constancy. . . . In him an enthusiastic devotion was grafted on an heroic nature. His bodily endowments were as remarkable as the temper of his mind. His manly proportions, his strength, and his endurance, which incessant fasts and penances could not undermine, had always won him the respect of the Indians. . . . The truth is, that, with some of these missionaries, one may throw off trash and nonsense by the cart-load, and find under it all a solid nucleus of saint and hero.[122]

At the end of his *Jesuits in North America*, Parkman used the martyrs' deaths to symbolize the demise of their fervent dream to render North America culturally French and confessionally Catholic. Asserting that that "the contest of this continent between Liberty and Absolutism was never doubtful," he mused:

> the Jesuits saw their hopes struck down; and their faith, though not shaken was sorely tried. The Providence of God seemed in their eyes dark and inexplicable; but from the standpoint of Liberty, that Providence is as clear as the sun at noon. Meanwhile let those who have prevailed yield due honour to the defeated. Their virtues shine amidst the rubbish of error, like diamonds and gold in the gravel of the torrent.[123]

Much like Leonard Cohen, who more than a century later would characterize Catherine Tekakwitha as a "beautiful loser," Parkman cast the martyrs as having failed in the audacious task they had set themselves. While it might have been a poignant and heroic failure, it was a failure nonetheless. The laurels Parkman offered the martyrs were those of consolation rather than of victory.

The very ambiguity of Parkman's views on the martyrs led to a mixed reception of his work by Catholic readers on both sides of the border. Many French Canadians were affronted by Parkman's playfully provocative swipes at the church, such as his withering criticism of the "peasant" religiosity of colonial Jesuit Pierre Joseph Marie Chaumonot. Wrote Parkman: "the grossest fungus of superstition that ever grew under the shadow of Rome was not too much for his omnivorous credulity."[124]

The Quebecois were also offended by his insulting inferences that the French, like native people, had been doomed by God himself first to defeat and then to assimilation into the rightfully dominant anglophone majority. Parkman's Manifest Destiny was a root-and-branch repudiation of Quebecois's own clerico-nationalist creed (which, of course, it closely resembled). His confident prediction of francophone assimilation was particularly unwelcome in an atmosphere that defensively promoted French Canadian *survivance,* particularly in the expanding francophone diaspora in New England.[125]

By contrast, Parkman's American Catholic readership often selectively focused on his bouquets rather than his barbs. Some saw the very fact that this important historian had deigned to research Catholic figures as indicating a slight opening in the historigraphic door, heretofore used to shut Catholics out of full participation in American public life. Among the small nucleus of scholars and priests who had begun to rally around the banner of the martyrs, there was a view that Parkman (perhaps inadvertently) gave more than he took. Indeed, for some the very reluctance of Parkman's admiration for the martyrs made his public affirmation of their virtues all the sweeter. Parkman became something of a favored example of the martyrs' ability to convince even the most hardened and incredulous soul of their sanctity. At the martyrs' long-awaited canonization in 1930, Parkman was recognized as an important latter-day witness to their heroic virtue, a characterization he would likely have testily disputed had he still been living.

Forging an American Catholic Myth of Origins

John Gilmary Shea, like Parkman, was a providentialist, seeing the events of human history as being having been divinely ordained in keeping with God's salvific plan. Like his Protestant rival, he was quick to read a sweeping religious significance into the landmark events of the American past. But Shea asserted the unimpeachably *Catholic* nature of early American history, starting with Columbus. Like a pugilist piling on the punishing blows, Shea provided example after example of the Catholic pedigree of celebrated American figures. Going further back in time and farther afield geographically than had Parkman, Shea constructed a Catholic historical trajectory explicitly to challenge the dominant Puritans-into-Americans rhetoric of his Protestant rivals:

Who discovered and colonized Greenland and had a cathedral church and convent there? . . . Leif Ericson, a Catholic, with his Catholic Norsemen, followed by Catholic bishops and priests. As to Christopher Columbus and his Catholicity there is no question. Who explored the Atlantic and Gulf Coast of the United States? Catholic Navigators: John and Sebastian Cabot; John Ponce de Leon; Pineda, first to see the Mississippi and name it the River of the Holy Ghost. . . . Who explored the Mississippi from its northern waters to the Gulf of Mexico? The Catholic Franciscan, Hennepin. . . . Who discovered and named the St. Lawrence? Cartier, a Catholic. Who made it known to the Upper Lake? Champlain, a Catholic, the first to map its course.[126]

Able to read both Spanish and French,[127] Shea rewrote American history in continental terms, redirecting his reader's attention from the fateful voyage of the *Mayflower* to that of the *Santa Maria*. He demonstrated the vital, organic connections between U.S. history, narrowly defined, and the national epics of both Canada and Mexico, claiming all as "American."

Shea's providentialism differed from that of Parkman and his own northerly coreligionists in being more purely confessional. His writing lacked the "ethnic" specificity of Parkman's Anglo-Saxon Manifest Destiny and of Quebecois clerico-nationalism. Indeed, Shea deliberately broke the strong association between French cultural identity and Catholicism by insisting on the always variegated nature of the New World church, unfailingly including Catholics of a variety of ethnic and linguistic stripes—French, Spanish, native, and English—in his massive tomes. By uncoupling the Gallic from the Catholic, Shea also avoided the historiographic dead end of 1759 for a fresher, more future-focused approach. Unlike the already determined outcome of the French-English struggle, he intimated, the real contest between Protestants and Catholics for the religious dominance of the continent was only just beginning. Shea was firmly convinced that America's future was a Catholic one. Though sidelined, defamed, and marginalized, American Catholics would, like the martyrs themselves, ultimately triumph.

Writing in his landmark 1855 work, *History of Catholic Missions among the Indian Tribes*, Shea argued that though historians were quick to grasp the heroism of the martyrs' lives and deaths, they often failed to acknowledge the still-flowering results of their efforts in native hearts and minds.[128] It was in the glowing embers of native peoples' still-ardent Catholicism, Shea suggested, that the blazing glory ignited by colonial Catholic missionaries could yet be glimpsed. Shea's inclusion of the contemporary native faithful as an integral part of his Catholic Manifest Destiny contrasted both clerico-nationalist stress on the history of Quebecois-native conflict and Parkman's contemptuous assertion of native people's inherent racial inferiority and essential irrelevance to the nation's future.

Shea was a key figure in the American rediscovery and popularization of the life and legacy of native convert Catherine "Kateri" Tekakwitha, who embraced a particularly austere, mystical form of Catholicism in the 1670s.[129] Tekakwitha's childhood was tumultuous: scarred with disease, bereavement, war, and waves of disorienting social and religious change. The child of an Algonquin adoptee and a Mohawk father, she barely survived a smallpox outbreak that struck her natal village in the early 1660s, claiming the lives of both her parents and her younger brother. Her scarred skin and weakened eyesight would stay with Tekakwitha as constant reminders of this early trauma and loss.[130] Having converted to Catholicism and fled northward to the Catholic enclave of Kahnawake, Catherine would die at the age of only twenty-four, succumbing to the scourge's lingering effects, exacerbated by her own indulgence in penitential austerity. Following her death, Kateri enjoyed a popular reputation for sanctity and wonder-working in colonial Catholic circles, veneration openly encouraged by her Jesuit mentors.

Capitalizing on the fact that this ardent young Catholic had been born in the same Mohawk village—Ossernenon—in which the Auriesville martyrs had met their deaths, Shea revived the seventeenth-century rhetorical tradition that cast the young Mohawk maiden as the martyrs' symbolic spiritual child. Though Tekakwitha was born a decade after the death of Isaac Jogues and Jean de la Lande in 1646, Shea nevertheless presented her as Tertullian's promised "Christian seed," born from the martyrs' fecund blood.[131]

Like Parkman, Shea reveled in describing aboriginal culture as dark and debauched. But whereas Parkman postulated an essential, unchangeable native barbarism, Shea traded on assumptions about native "savagery" to highlight the objective efficacy of the Catholic sacrament of baptism. Much like a peddler of laundry detergent demonstrating the efficacy of his wares on the filthiest of articles, Shea triumphantly presented the "lily of the Mohawk" in glowingly exceptional terms that stressed her near-miraculous purity and piety amid the supposed squalid debauchery of her natal culture.[132] Thus, though Shea saw "Kateri's" conversion as ultimately trumping her racial identity, his ethnocentric assumptions about the inferiority of native culture nevertheless played an essential role in creating the rhetorical contrast he so enthusiastically exploited.[133]

As the leading Catholic historian of his day, John Gilmary Shea deeply influenced the men and women, lay and religious, who formed the gelling nucleus of the American cult of the martyrs, to whom he had a deep devotional and emotional attachment.[134] His commitment to revealing for his reader the awesome panorama of a continental Catholic history, a commitment shaped by his early experiences with the border-blind Jesuits, ensured that he presented all eight of the missionaries later singled out for beatification and canonization as "American."[135] But Shea's framing of the martyrs' story in such broad and inclusive terms was in considerable tension with other Catholics' exclusive interest in the three martyrs who had "become American" by fervently preaching, praying, and dying on U.S. soil. The fact that René Goupil, Isaac Jogues, and Jean de la Lande had suffered and died within the territorial boundaries of the contemporary United States made them, in the eyes of some members of the U.S. hierarchy, especially powerful symbols of American Catholic identity.

The Search for Ossernenon

Much like Bishop Bourget, whose dream of defiantly establishing a mini–Saint Peter's in the heart of Anglo-Protestant Montreal was finally realized in 1892, American Catholics in the late nineteenth and early twentieth centuries sought to claim public space as Catholic space through ambitious building projects, such as the multi-decade construction of Bishop Ireland's impressive Cathedral of Saint Paul in 1915 and the founding of centers of Catholic higher education, such as Notre Dame in South Bend, Indiana (1842) and the ever-expanding campus of the Catholic University of America in Washington, D.C. (1887).

But a very different kind of sacred space was being sought in upstate New York in the 1880s. The quest was on for ancient Ossernenon, the seventeenth-century village that was both the "altar-stone of American martyrdom"[136] and the birthplace of a future saint. There, it was neither the proud towers of a new church nor the hard-fought establishment of an imposing Catholic institution that sacralized space, but something incomparably more powerful and primordial. Somewhere on a long-forgotten hill was the hallowed ground on which four individuals—Goupil, Jogues, la Lande, and Tekakwitha—had made their bloody exits and entrances onto this worldly stage, pawns in a divine choreography that plotted their every salvific move. There Catholic blood—martyrs' blood—cried out from the ground for memorialization, veneration, and protection.

Ossernenon's seekers sought to create in the wilds of upstate New York an "American Lourdes," where the ancient dynamics of pilgrimage would inculcate popular devotion to these four figures, helping to convince an ever-skeptical Vatican of their evident sanctity. The establishment of a cultic center on the very site of the martyrs' earthly sufferings seemed, to the martyrs' supporters, an indispensable strategic step in obtaining these figures' eventual canonization.[137] This early and intense preoccupation with sacred space distinguished the American martyrs' cult from its older French Canadian counterpart.[138]

The romantic quest for those hidden sites that the martyrs had hallowed in their living and their dying was rivaled only by historical writing in the strong appeal it exerted across confessional lines. It brought together Protestant and Catholic archeologists, linguists, topographers, and historians from both sides of the international border, who collaborated closely to locate these mute and overgrown sites. Because the identification of seventeenth-century native villages relied so heavily on literary evidence, the hunt was as much epistolary parlor game as fieldwork exercise, prompting a brisk exchange of maps and letters, manuscripts and artifacts and, always, advice and encouragement. But even with its evident collegiality, the identification of Ossernenon would prove to be a difficult, time-consuming, and contentious process, and its ultimate success, though strenuously defended for more than 120 years, is still by no means certain.

Leading the search was New York State archaeologist General John S. Clark, a military topographer tapped, following his retirement from active duty at the end of the Civil War, to help the Jesuits locate this ancient site. Tenacious and disciplined, yet opinionated and emotional, Clark's observations and opinions would be critical in siting Ossernenon and in the subsequent development of Our Lady of Martyrs Shrine.

As well as being a military man, Clark was a native (in both senses of the word) New Yorker. Of Seneca extraction,[139] he had spent virtually all of his off-duty life in the state, much of it trying to uncover the remains of his ancestors' palisaded "castles."[140] But neither Clark's Iroquois ancestry nor his fascination with exploring the archaeological remains of their villages predisposed him to anything approaching sympathy toward precontact native religion and culture, which he brusquely dismissed as "devil worship."[141] As a "devout Presbyterian,"[142] Clark's Christian sympathies lay entirely with the ill-fated Jesuits, whom he unselfconsciously idolized even across the not inconsiderable confessional barriers of his time.[143] Though clearly and proudly identifying himself as a Protestant in correspondence with Catholic collaborators, he nevertheless vowed:

> You can rest assured that anything I can do, or any information that I possess will be cheerfully given, esteeming it a great honour to contribute in even the slightest degree to the elucidation of the history of the sacrifices and sufferings of the eminent representatives of the Christian Church.[144]

As was typical of a period in which professional archeology was still in its infancy, Clark's attempts to identify ancient Ossernenon were almost completely topographic. Having narrowed down possible sites on the basis of textual and cartographic evidence and by careful triangulation from already-known village sites, Clark and his assistants would systematically search for evidence of native habitation, such as pottery shards, beads, hatchets, and pipe bowls. Final confirmation was then sought by unearthing rotten post stumps indicating the onetime presence of a wooden palisade.

Handling objects that had not been touched by human hands for more than 200 years often inspired considerable emotion in searchers. Writing to John Gilmary Shea in 1877, Clark solemnly enclosed with his letter a hatchet head he had retrieved at one of several sites he was then investigating as being Ossernenon:

> It certainly came from the ground where Jogues, la Lande and Goupil met their deaths and may be the very instrument used. I never had a relic that I prized more highly and take the greatest pleasure in presenting it to you, believing that you will appreciate its value.[145]

The passionate definitiveness with which Clark made this statement was later belied, however, by his equally strong conviction that the site at which he had retrieved the hatchet was not, in fact, Ossernenon, making it merely an interesting artifact rather than an actual relic. Much of Clark's copious correspondence during the years in which he sought the ancient site reveals a similar oscillation between joyful confidence and agonized doubt, particularly regarding the authenticity of what was quickly becoming the preferred site near Auriesville, where the number of artifacts discovered seemed suspiciously small. He was likely uncomfortably aware that, in the words of Jesuit priest and former board member "Father Richard Fisher," "there are a lot of hills and valleys in northern New York."[146]

But as the Third Plenary Council of 1884, the venue in which these saintly figures would be formally nominated loomed, Clark's statements become markedly more definitive. As the Jesuits arranged to purchase the steep hillside lot near Auriesville, the general's role shifted from one of active investigation to one of comforting reassurance. The time for expressing doubts was over. After Our Lady of Martyrs' 1885 foundation, further archaeological investigation seemed imprudent, as it might throw Clark's original identification into doubt. Thus, despite the photograph of shovel-wielding Jesuits (improbably clad in black cassocks and lacy surplices) that graced the cover of *The Pilgrim* in the summer of 1952, thorough archaeological investigation at Auriesville has been conspicuous in its absence.

In establishing a shrine where pilgrims could imaginatively commune with the martyrs on the very spot where their blood had supposedly been shed, American Catholics had done something truly unprecedented, anticipating similar Canadian developments by more than two decades. From among a continent of splendid Catholic heroes celebrated by Shea and Parkman, the Third Plenary Council selected three who had the most visceral and proven link with America in its strictest territorial sense: Jogues, Goupil, and Tekakwitha. Though born Frenchman, the two missionaries, a priest and a layman, had become honorary Americans by exsanguinating the soil of upstate New York with their life's blood. Tekakwitha's claim was more straightforward. Born in the very village where they had died, she was—like the village's purported discoverer, General Clark—a "native American" twice over. Much like Kateri, then, the American canonization campaign was born

Three cassocked and surpliced priests (left to right, Fathers Schumann, Goggins, and Devaney) turn the first sod in a short-lived 1952 excavation at Auriesville. Appearances to the contrary, archaeological work at the site has been superficial.

(Our Lady of Martyrs Shrine Archives, Auriesville)

at Auriesville. Refusing to be disheartened by the absence of the martyr-related relics, art, artifacts, and manuscripts that virtually littered Québec, Americans had gamely made the most of what they did have: sacred space.

But even as American Catholics beat their Quebecois counterparts to the punch by nominating a slate of distinctively *American* candidates for sainthood, winning the "space race" in the bargain, these impressive victories came with a then unrecognized cost. By tying the nascent American cult of the martyrs to a remote hillside in upstate New York, its advocates had unwittingly articulated its importance in merely regional terms. In the years to come, the martyrs' advocates would have to struggle mightily to transcend the very regionalism and geographical specificity in which had been so important to Auriesville's founders.

Collaboration, Conflict, and Canonization

If a shark stops swimming, then it will drown. Perpetual motion, even while asleep, is the cost of maintaining its life. Tirelessly, inexorably, and smoothly cutting through the ocean's dark depths, where day and night, sleep and waking are one, the shark never rests. Always, its silvery gills move gently in and out in a hideous mimicry of breath. Its lidless eyes point forward and its antenna-like tail, reading the currents, constantly makes small course corrections, controlling its sinuous progress through the water. The martyrs' foremost American promoter from the 1890s until his death in 1948, Jesuit Father John J. Wynne seems to have taken the peculiarities of the life aquatic as a model for his own tireless and inexorable advocacy on behalf of these colonial American saints. Relentless and meticulous, organized and disciplined, Wynne had a coolness and precision that was somewhat shark-like. Particularly in his youth, with his clean-shaven, aquiline profile, colorless eyes, rare smile, and close-cropped, white-blonde hair, he even looked a little like a shark. A multitasker who maintained the most meticulous standards for his own performance, even as he continuously acquired demanding new responsibilities, Wynne was doomed to constant disappointment by the comparable slovenliness, lack of discipline, and devotional lukewarmness that invariably surrounded him.[147]

As an advocate for the martyrs,[148] Wynne always played the long game. Where others might pause to celebrate any hard-won victory along the way, grateful for reaching even a small rocky ledge as they traversed the steep and unforgiving summit that was the canonization process, Wynne barely paused metaphorically to wipe the sweat from his brow before continuing his inexorable ascent, working day and night when necessary. Always, he planned for the next step, the next goal, calmly, smoothly, and seamlessly moving from one task to the next, endowed with a punishing work ethic that more than matched his audacious ambition on behalf of these holy figures. His personal goal was nothing less than the establishment of a truly national devotion to all eight martyrs across the length and breadth of the United States. Driven by this lofty imperative, where others saw hard-won victory, Wynne saw only new vistas of challenge.

In Rome on June 28, 1930, the very eve of the martyrs' canonization, following thirty-nine years of uninterrupted work on the martyrs'

Father John J. Wynne, who tenaciously pursued the canonization of the
North American martyrs for almost forty years.

(Our Lady of Martyrs Shrine Archives, Auriesville)

behalf, Wynne did not celebrate by taking a well-deserved glass of
wine at a candlelit table in some local *trattoria,* or spend his evening in
grateful prayer. Rather, the restless general of the American canonization campaign planned, as always, for the next step. Post-canonization,
he would redouble his efforts to expand the cult of the martyrs beyond
its traditional foothold in the American northeast and, indeed, beyond
the confessional boundaries of Catholicism itself. Wynne sought to
ignite a blaze of devotion within Protestant as well as Catholic breasts

that would thaw mutual suspicions, permitting a glorious new era of Catholic involvement at the forefront of American public life. Seeking to turn the "here today, gone tomorrow" publicity of the canonization into lasting gains for the cult, Wynne penned a carefully phrased letter to the American Catholic hierarchy even as, all around him, Vatican City bustled with last-minute preparations for the opulent ceremony on the morrow:

> Quite often it happens that when Servants of God are beatified or can-onized, there is a brief display of enthusiasm and devotion, but little or no concerted effort to make either permanent. Now that the first Sons of the Church to labor, suffer, and die for the Faith on the soil of North America have been enrolled in the Calendar of the Saints, we owe it to their memory, and to our own spiritual advantage, to cultivate a deep and abiding devotion to them . . . .they stand out . . . among the heroes of our early history and command the admiration and veneration of all alike, of whatsoever religious affiliation . . . it will gratify His Holiness to know that the newly canonized, to whom he is so earnestly devoted, are specially honored in the land consecrated by their devotion and generous blood.[149]

American Catholics' provocative initiation of beatification proceed-ings for Jogues, Goupil, and Tekakwitha in 1884 had galvanized the tardy French Canadian Catholic hierarchy into similar action two years later when, at the Seventh Council of Québec in 1886, they put forward their own slate of candidates to receive Rome's official imprimatur as saints and martyrs: Jean de Brébeuf, Gabriel Lallemant, Charles Garnier, and Antoine Daniel.[150] This countermove inaugurated a fascinating period of conflict and collaboration between Canadian and American Catholics as they together attempted to convince a sometimes skeptical or disinterested Vatican of the justice and urgency of their heroes' cause and, given the glut of Gallic names atop the official list of would-be saints, to articulate their distinctive North American identity. Together, they would argue that the martyrs were unambiguously New World rather than Old World figures who should be identified with the con-tinent of their death rather than that of their birth. Brought together both by the intimately interconnected lives and afterlives of the figures they collectively revered, as well as by the imperative of maintain-ing a united front in the grueling, protracted negotiations with Rome, relationships between Catholics across the international border were characterized by genuine mutual regard and a spirit of common purpose. And yet their civility was also sorely tested by linguistic differences, theological tensions, and nationalist jealousies. Even as Catholics on both sides of the border cooperated by emphasizing what brought them together—their shared confessional identity and the geographical and historical linkages as fellow North Americans—they also used the martyrs to demarcate a shrill and narrow nationalism: questioning, disparaging, or ridiculing the claims of the other nation to "ownership" of these saintly figures or unfavorably contrasting "their" saints with that of their rival nation. Much like siblings, the Canadian and American Catholic hierarchies were often allies. They worked together to get their way from a demanding, distant patriarch and to comfort one another in the face of his inexplicable decisions and infuriating delays. But they also competed fiercely with one another to articulate their own, often contrasting, identities and agendas, and to compete for the limited attention, affection, and approval of their shared parent.

John J. Wynne was part of the fray virtually from the beginning. Though his professional and scholarly life encompassed many unrelated responsibilities, Wynne's efforts on behalf of the martyrs over almost four decades would have constituted a demanding full-time job for a less driven individual. His labors began in 1891 when he was concurrently appointed the martyrs' official promoter and the director of the expanding shrine at Auriesville.[151] They intensified in 1923 when he became vice postulator[152] of their cause, responsible for shepherding the process through their collective 1925 beatification and 1930 canonization. During these eventful decades Wynne attempted, like a circus gymnast, to navigate diplomatically the tightrope of sometimes tense relations with both Rome and Québec while simultaneously orchestrating a relentless, media-savvy publicity campaign to cultivate devotion to the martyrs at the most popular level possible, including among Protestants.[153]

The early leaders of the American cult of the martyrs had had three simple and intimately related goals: to nominate a slate of recognizably "American" candidates for sainthood; to find Ossernenon, site of their dramatic entrances and exits into salvation history; and to establish a shrine there to honor them. But Wynne, virtually from the first moment of his involvement, was bent on transcending the very regionalism that

Our Lady of Martyrs' foundation had inadvertently helped to establish. Like Shea, Wynne was border-blind, seeing all of the candidates nominated for sainthood in the 1880s as being "American" in the broadest sense. To him, the martyrs' strong personal and historical connections with one another, their shared fate, and their operation in a common colonial world innocent of the international borders subsequently superimposed on it precluded these figures' artificial separation from one another and their appropriation along narrow, nationalist lines. In all of his published work, Wynne refers to the group of eight collectively as the "North American" martyrs, an umbrella term he coined and popularized.

This is not to say that Wynne was not an American Catholic patriot, because he was. But unlike others involved with the emergent American martyrs' cult, Wynne's nationalism did not lead him to express a preferential devotion for the saints most tangibly associated with his home state of New York: Jogues, Goupil, Tekakwitha,[154] and, somewhat later, Jean la Lande. Rather, Wynne's Catholic patriotism led him to perceive *all* of the nominees as "Americans" and to seek to make them better known across the *entire* United States. Throughout his career, Wynne would tirelessly fight narrow nationalist interpretations of the martyrs' cult which, in his mind, both artificially and dangerously detached the three Auriesville martyrs from their brothers in Christ across the border.

Wynne's deliberate and conscious continentalism was motivated by both theological and practical factors. Informed by the strongly collective ethos of the Catholic doctrine of the Communion of Saints, Wynne does not appears to have seen the process of canonization as inherently competitive, with one would-be saint's success coming at the expense of others. Rather, all of his actions and writings testify to his idealistic belief, not in a pragmatic limited good, but rather in a spiritual domino effect in which the Vatican's formal recognition of the first American saints would facilitate the ease of this process on its subsequent repetitions. Wynne's fierce loyalty to the martyrs thus did not blind him to their potential usefulness to the postmortem spiritual careers of other would-be American saints, particularly his beloved Catherine Tekakwitha. Indeed, in his canonization-eve letter to the rest of the American hierarchy, one of Wynne's chief arguments was that the warmth of American Catholics' reception of their newly minted saintly octet would, more than any other single factor, help to ensure the success of other American candidates for the ultimate honor of sainthood: "For the advancement of several causes for beatification now pending, of Mother Seton, Bishop Neumann, Bishop Laval, Father Andreis, Mother Duchesne, Venerable Mary of the Incarnation, much will depend on the devotion with which we celebrate this canonization of the martyrs."[155] Wynne idealistically believed that the canonization process, despite its flaws, was inherently cooperative, a rising tide that floats all boats, rather than competitive, favoring some over others.

And yet there were pragmatic as well as principled reasons for Wynne's determined resistance to what he perceived as the balkanization of the cult of the American martyrs. As a shrewd player of the long game, Wynne readily perceived the danger of a facile and narrow nationalism prompting American Catholics to voluntarily, even proudly, accept the short end of the stick. Wynne saw that patriotism and a misguided regionalism might lead American Catholics to establish a "rump" cult to just the three Auriesville martyrs, two of them laymen, who had left no extant relics, a situation that would be to their profound spiritual and practical disadvantage in both the short and long term.[156] Not only would such a division place the American cult at a considerable numerical disadvantage vis-à-vis the larger, five-man Canadian cult, but this distancing could also disastrously dissociate the Auriesville trio from the wonders that might yet be worked by the bones of their brothers.

Because of the violent and lonely nature of their deaths, only three of the eight North American martyrs, Brébeuf, Garnier and Lalemant, had left behind any corporeal remains to be venerated. As all three of these men had died in what later became Canada, the distribution of relics across the international border was fundamentally lopsided in a way that could not easily be corrected. Even after French Jesuits had kindly addressed Auriesville's long-standing relic deprivation, this did not alter the fact that these remains were not those of the men who had fallen in ancient Ossernenon.

As the comparatively light burden of proof required by beatification[157] was replaced by the more trenchant requirements of canonization, which demanded postmortem miracles, Wynne cannily foresaw that American Catholics, by perceiving the three Auriesville martyrs as the only "real Americans," might inadvertently prevent their heroes' indirect accreditation with any future miracles these relics wrought.[158] Only adamantine insistence on the primordial, unbreakable unity of the group of eight men, Wynne intimated, would help to avoid a situation in which relic-rich Canadian Catholics might choose not to share credit for the cures so obtained, attributing them solely to the actions of "their own" saints. Even Wynne's open, conciliatory stance, in effect, guaranteed nothing. In this matter, the Canadians were holding all the cards.[159]

Wynne's prognostications proved prescient and his cautious continentalism salutary. Just as he had foreseen, Brébeuf's bones, in the five years between the martyrs' beatification and canonization, did indeed figure prominently in two ostensibly miraculous cures. Attributed to the intervention of the North American martyrs as a group, these wonders paved the way for their collective recognition as full saints. By insisting on the power of the eight as a group, Wynne had helped to ensure that the relic-less Auriesville cult had not, through its own hubris, disconnected its wagon from the Canadian cult's relic-rich star and the possibilities of further spiritual advancement it promised. His canny continentalism had garnered for the Americans a major strategic success.

But in his cherished dream to spark a genuinely grassroots cult of the North American martyrs outside the country's northeast, Wynne was less successful. Though he himself had served as a director of Our Lady of Martyrs, Wynne remained concerned that the very specificity of "that most sacred spot" could be as used to demote the martyrs to figures of merely a regional interest, irrelevant to the spiritual lives of Catholics living further away, where they were less susceptible to the magnetic pull of the martyrs' mystical blood. His concerns seemed realistic, given that even would-be boosters of the American martyrs' cult seemed unconsciously to circumscribe its scope. For example, even as one clerical author in 1909 expressed his wish that "pilgrimages [to Auriesville] become more than merely local," his own article dictated only that "all Catholics *within reasonable distance of Albany* should desire someday to see the Shrine and visit the hill and see the rock and river and Ravine sanctified by the suffering, penance and prayer of a Jogues and Goupil."[160]

But Wynne's efforts to counteract regionalism were unexpectedly hamstrung by the Vatican itself. In his 1925 beatification decree, Pope

Pius XI readily acknowledged the martyrs' national significance in Canada by making the newly beatified octet's right to public veneration across the country automatic, despite the fact that all five deaths had occurred in a small region of western Ontario. But he chose not to do the same in the United States, expressly permitting public veneration of the newly beatified only in New York State. Should American dioceses outside New York wish to obtain this privilege, their bishops first needed to make a formal application to the Holy See to do so.[161]

One can only imagine how frustrating Pius's decision must have been for Wynne, tempering his triumph at the martyrs' beatification with a tinge of weary bitterness as he contemplated how greatly this ruling had set back his own private cause of taking the martyrs' cult nationwide. For, while the episcopal application to request public veneration of the martyrs was not a particularly onerous piece of paperwork, it did put the onus on individual bishops to take the initiative in a matter that the pope himself seemed to have indicated was of merely regional interest, putting Wynne, as their advocate, in the uncomfortable position of seeming to second-guess the pope regarding these figures' significance. Convinced that if the American hierarchy demonstrated indifference toward the martyrs it would ruin their chances of canonization, Wynne used his most adroit diplomatic skills to persuade bishops to make the application on behalf of their diocese, even offering to complete the paperwork on their behalf.

Response to Wynne's overtures was underwhelming. Although some dutifully went through the motions, others were openly indifferent or even actively hostile to his pleas. Cardinal Dennis Doherty of Philadelphia not only refused to cooperate but openly questioned the American pedigree of the martyrs, derisively dismissing them as "Canadians."[162] Archbishop Gannon of the Erie Diocese also objected and, in the years to come, would lead an (ultimately abortive) attempt to beatify a rival large group of Catholic missionaries: Jesuits, Franciscans, Sulpicians, and Dominicans who had served and died exclusively within the geographic confines of the contemporary United States. Their reactions have led Kathleen Cummings to remark that "rather than welcome the canonization of Jogues and Goupil as the *fulfillment* of the long search for their first saint, U.S. Catholics evidently interpreted it as reason to approach that quest with renewed vigor."[163]

Evidently, in the decades between the figures' initial nomination in 1884 and their triumphant canonization in 1930, the "soft northern border" assumed by continentalists Shea and Wynne had hardened for many. While the almost forty-year process from these figures' initial nomination in the 1880s to their final declaration had been relatively short by Vatican standards, it had nevertheless been long enough for other would-be saints to appear on the hagiographic horizon[164] to challenge the martyrs for preeminence in popular devotion, undercutting the cult even at the height of its success. To some, these new candidates for sainthood seemed fresher, more modern symbols through which to represent American Catholicism to itself and to the world. As more recent figures, they resonated with their lives of contemporary American Catholics in a way that the martyrs, as distant colonial figures, simply did not. The life of Elizabeth Anne Seton, for example, a late eighteenth-century American-born convert to Catholicism, seemed a powerful indication of the ultimate compatibility of the Catholic faith with American identity and values. Mother Frances Cabrini, an Italian, and Bishop John Neumann, a Bohemian, as immigrant religious who had dedicated their recently ended lives to working with the sick, the dispossessed, or the urban poor, seemed to offer an even more applicable model of contemporary, compassionate American Catholicism in action. By contrast, the martyrs seemed the relics of a long-vanished past. Though Wynne attempted to boost the cult of the martyrs by warning that the warmth of American Catholics' reception of them would help to kindle the Vatican's enthusiasm for creating more American saints, many continued to see these cults as competing, rather than cooperative, and contrasting, rather than compatible.

But even stymied by both Rome and prominent American bishops, Wynne *still* did not give up on expanding the geographic reach of the martyrs' cult to make it truly nationwide. In an "ends justifies the means" move, he duplicitously stage-managed the appearance of a thriving national cult to try to spark the appearance of the genuine article. Convinced that he must demonstrate for the Holy See American Catholics' passion for their martyrs or risk their cause stalling short of sainthood, Wynne turned to national Catholic confraternities such as the Knights of Columbus and the Catholic Daughters of America for their assistance in awakening American Catholics' ardor in their newly elevated heroes.

In the most brazen and successful of all his similar spiritual ponzee schemes, Wynne communicated with national Knights of Columbus officials to suggest that they take as the official theme of their 1926 Columbus Day celebrations the lives and deaths of the North American martyrs as part of his campaign to effect their canonization. To facilitate their efforts, he sent out what were effectively press kits with sample speeches about the beatified martyrs that, as suited this Catholic nationalist holiday, concerned the martyrs' inherent "Americanness," whose story he presents as "appealing to the American mind and heart and transcending every barrier of prejudice."[165] Wynne advised local Knights to ask prominent Protestants to serve as their keynote speaker at these purportedly homegrown events, mining the ranks of regional politicians, university professors, and members of local historical associations. According to Wynne, involving the local non-Catholic elite would subtly proselytize those selected to do the honors, underline the martyrs' historical and "civic" importance, and broaden public awareness of the martyrs outside an exclusively Catholic context. Wynne's suggestions for homey local touches that the Knights or the Daughters could implement were designed to make the events seem like genuinely local, spontaneous, and lay-run initiatives rather than what they actually were: a centralized, top-down campaign spearheaded by Wynne himself. Having provided his proxies nationwide with all that they needed to run a successful *homage* to the martyrs, Wynne then carefully harvested the fruits of his own labors, assiduously clipping out newspaper articles regarding successful events from Texas to Idaho. These he disingenuously presented to the press and the Vatican as evidence of a growing cult of the martyrs nationwide, totally omitting any mention of his own role as their puppet master.

Yet Wynne was not being completely cynical. Here, as with many of his other tactics, sincere devotion and astute politics seem to have gone hand in hand. In attempting to ferment a genuinely grassroots cult, Wynne's motto appears to have been "fake it until you make it." He seems to have acted in the hope that, by introducing Americans across the country to the story of the martyrs, encouraging them to organize impressive events in their honor, and facilitating the widest possible publicity of these events, he was merely kick-starting something that might soon take on a viable life of its own. Like a lifeguard administering CPR, Wynne was merely maintaining the nascent cult's vital signs until it could breathe for itself. Soon, he prayed, the surging vitality of genuine local devotion would obviate the need for his ongoing intervention.

Like his predecessor, John Gilmary Shea, Wynne saw the martyrs' story as an ideal way to promote Catholicism to non-Catholics, to show-case the greatness of the continent's Catholic past, and to demonstrate the fundamental compatibility of Catholic and American values. Un-like Shea, whose work sometimes betrayed his bitterness at Catholics' collective exclusion from the historiographic mainstream, or that of his Quebecois counterparts, who used the martyrs' cult to highlight their countercultural identity and values as distinct from those of the Protestant mainstream, Wynne sought to create a "big tent," cross-confessional, national cult. When writing for a broad audience, he de-liberately presented the martyrs' story in broad "civic" and "historical" terms that he felt would be especially appealing to Protestants. Wynne was unfailingly magnanimous, inclusive, even courtly toward non-Catholics, particularly socially prominent or intellectually influential Protestants, always highlighting their contributions to the cult and in-viting their renewed or deepened involvement. Like Matteo Ricci, the seventeenth-century Jesuit missionary to China, Wynne gunned for the elite, hoping to win for his spiritual heroes upscale new clients in whose reflected political glory and economic clout they could bask.

Yet even as he genuinely reached out across confessional lines, Wynne's writing subtly but profoundly manipulated the figure of "the Protestant" to serve his own rhetorical ends. Just as his popular publi-cations "translated" the devotional, Catholic cult of the martyrs into an idiom calculated favorably to impress a Protestant reading audience, Wynne also reinterpreted the behavior and perceptions of Protestant promoters of the martyrs into terms more readily appreciable by his Catholic lectors. Sometimes he would emphasize, even exaggerate the Protestant incredulity of the individual he was describing such that their appreciation of the martyrs seemed well-nigh miraculous. For example, in presenting Francis Parkman, Wynne contrasts the histori-an's well-known animosity toward the Catholic Church with his high praise for the courageous steadfastness and masculine courage of the martyrs, suggesting that the clearest possible proof of these figures' sanctity is their ability to impress this reality on those who are con-genitally the least willing to admit it.[166] But Wynne also took the opposite tack, routinely translating individual Protestants' strong interest in the martyrs into Catholic terms, almost always describing them as their "venerators" or "devotees." Even as he presented Parkman as a ravening über-Protestant, Wynne simultaneously cast him as the humble client of the martyrs, suggesting that it was only Parkman's embryonic faith in these figures that "eased his suffering and enabled him to produce his noble works in spite of ailments and even blindness."[167] It was the martyrs who had sustained the struggling Parkman throughout his recurrent bouts with his debilitating malady, Wynne surmised, so that he could serve as the fated instrument of their glorification.

From 1884, when the American Catholic hierarchy launched the opening salvo in the fight for canonization, to 1930, when the triumphal strains of the *Te Deum* in honor of the newly created saints vibrated through the crystalline Roman air, the shape, size, and personnel of the emergent cult of the North American martyrs underwent important changes, the result of the continental poker game played for decades between the Canadian and American Catholic hierarchies. The American's opening 1884 bid, which provocatively proposed only American-associated figures—Goupil, Jogues, and Tekakwitha—was raised with the Canadian's counternomination of Jean de Brébeuf, Gabriel Lalement, Charles Garnier, and Antoine Daniel two years later.

Even in these initial "hands," it is revealing who was being excluded from consideration. Figures whom both Paul Ragueneau had valorized in text, and Grégoire Huret in image, as equals of the eight men eventually canonized were permanently jettisoned. Jesuit Anne de Nöue[168] had been prominently featured in Huret's 1664 etching, which depicted him kneeling in prayer, the very position in which his frozen body had been found. Lauded by Ragueneau as a "martyr of charity," de Nöue had become disoriented on a night errand to bring the sacraments to a dying native Catholic and had subsequently frozen to death, the victim of the unforgiving harshness of the Canadian winter. His summary exclusion from the canonization sweepstakes signaled the late nineteenth-century narrowing of martyrdom to its canonical bare bones: those who fell to the deadly violence of other human beings motivated by hatred of the faith. By the same definitional token, "confessors," or those who had suffered torture but ultimately survived, such as Jesuits François-Joseph Bressani and Simon Le Moyne, were also dropped from consideration at this juncture, despite the fact that both were better-known figures than many of the more obscure martyrs.

Native martyrs were also notable in their absence from the nomination process. Although they too had been killed by non-Catholics, aboriginal Catholics do not appear to have even received serious consideration for official elevation. The sole native candidate for sainthood nominated during this decades-long process was Catherine Tekakwitha, who already stood out from the pack by virtue of her sex and the fact that she was not a martyr. Her 1884 nomination at Baltimore formally, if temporarily, linked Catherine's *causa* to her fellow "Americans" Jogues and Goupil, using the venerable rhetorical associations of Tertullian. Enthusiastically regarded by American Catholics as a powerfully "authentic" symbol of their "archaic," "indigenous" roots in the continent, Tekakwitha's nomination was more coolly received in Québec.[169] Intent upon proving their own "purity" from native influences or admixture, the French Canadian hierarchy was loath to back the candidacy of a young native woman at the possible expense of their preferred French Jesuit candidates. Caught in the crossfire of the contentious, protracted negotiations between the Quebecois and the American Catholic hierarchies, Catherine's *causa* was eventually detached from that of the martyrs, freeing her to follow her own scenic—though ultimately successful—route to sainthood.

In 1906, Canadians and Americans both "doubled-down," each seeking to enlarge their respective numbers of nominees through the proposal of one additional candidate each.[170] Deprived of Kateri, the Americans nominated Jean de la Lande, the long-ignored donné who, like René Goupil in 1642, had accompanied Isaac Jogues to Kanienke, and to death, in 1646. In response, the Canadian hierarchy saw and raised them yet another slain French Jesuit, Nöel Chabanel, rather than taking the opportunity to elevate a native Catholic. Algonquin Catholic Joseph Onaharé, whose gruesome 1651 death at the hands of his tormentors had been immortalized by Huret, would have been an obvious candidate, as would the compelling Wendat convert Joseph Chihoatenhwa, murdered under mysterious circumstances in 1640, making him perhaps the first martyr of Huronia. Chabanel's revulsion toward native people was so famously intense that only his blood-written "vow of persistence" to remain in Canada kept him from fleeing in horror back to France. Though, like Chihoatenhwa's death, Chabanel's

December 1649 murder was unwitnessed, he was nominated and eventually canonized nonetheless. The last Canadian nomination was thus a piece of cynicism unmatched since the seventeenth-century Jesuits had sacrificed donné Jacques Douart on the altar of utility.

These initial negotiations inaugurated a fascinating period of conflict and collaboration between Canadian and American Catholics. Together attempted to convince a skeptical and disinterested Vatican of the justice and urgency of their heroes' cause. Given the glut of Gallic names atop the official list of would-be saints, the martyrs' advocates stressed their distinctively *North American* identity: arguing that these Jesuit missionaries were unambiguously New World figures who should be identified with the continent of their death rather than that of their birth. Brought together both by the intimately interconnected lives and afterlives of the figures they collectively reverenced, and by the imperative of maintaining a united front in the gruelingly protracted negotiations with Rome, Canadian and American Catholics regarded one another with genuine mutual respect. Working together, they learned to stress their geographical and historical continuities as North Americans, and to emphasize their shared confessional identity as Catholics. But this spirit of common cause did not always protect their relationship from linguistic sensitivities, theological tensions, or nationalist jealousies. Both Canadians and American Catholics routinely used the martyrs not only to buttress their own, narrower sense of national identity, but also to question, disparage, or ridicule the claims of the other nation to "ownership" of these figures. Wrangling over primacy and privilege of their respective saintly patrons would lead to some of the bitterest, most unseemly infighting between Canadian and American Catholics. Ironically, these ugly, unchristian incidents became more common late in the *causa*'s progress when, assured of immanent victory, both sides moved to prematurely dismantle the cooperative partnership necessary to achieve it.

The Canadian Christ and the American Apostle

Even as the roster of would-be saints was expanding in the early twentieth century, a putative hierarchy was being established within their ranks, within the eight as a whole, and within the two geographical-historical subgroups: that of the three "Mohawk martyrs" who fell in the early to mid-1640s in upstate New York, and those of Huronia, the five who perished in western Ontario in the escalating warfare of 1648–1650. Tensions between Canadians and Americans in this period were often ignited over petty jealousies concerning the relative priority and merits of the two men who had come to be regarded as the putative leaders of the two national subcults: Isaac Jogues, the American apostle, and Jean de Brébeuf, the Canadian Christ.

Among the American subgroup of three men, Isaac Jogues's preeminence was something of a foregone conclusion due to his priestly status and dramatic, extended story, much of which was written in his own preserved hand. The story of the twice-martyred American Apostle, who endured the trauma of capture, a lengthy captivity, a skin-of-his-teeth escape, and celebration by the crowned heads of Europe before returning, like a moth to the flame, to Mohawk country and his fate lacks for nothing in its drama or the pathos of its narrative arc, particularly in contrast with the more truncated stories of his compatriots, Goupil and la Lande. More than for the details of his actual death, which, though long anticipated, was relatively quick and anticlimactic, Jogues has been venerated for his volunteerism: the fact that, though he anticipated his recapture and murder, he persisted in his plans. His was the agony of anticipation: not just once but many times over he waited for the long-delayed blow to fall.

Among the Canadian contingent, Jean de Brébeuf's easy dominance seemed equally inevitable, though, as a priest among four other priests, his preeminence was not as easily explained by the lay-clerical divide. Celebrated by Francis Parkman as "that masculine apostle of the Faith,—the Ajax of the mission,"[171] it was Brébeuf's commanding physical and psychological presence that led his to his preeminence in Canadian Jesuit circles during his lifetime and in his hagiographic afterlife. Like that of Jogues, Brébeuf's voice speaks to us vibrantly out of the wealth of his literary corpus. Simultaneously mystical and plainspoken, his is a voice that is equally at home describing lofty, prophetic visions and pragmatically addressing the small details of Canadian life, such as how best to keep sand and water out of the bottom of a canoe. His expertise in such minutiae speak to the length of his immersion in the woodlands of northeastern North America—at sixteen years, the longest New World career of any of the eight men, a fact that, along with his impressive mastery of native languages, favored his casting as the most indigenized of all of these putative "North Americans."

But above all it was the protracted, spectacular nature of his death by torture that seems to have given this Norman a peculiarly profound hold on Canadian imaginations. In contrast to all but one of the other martyrs—Gabriel Lalemant, who was captured and suffered alongside him—Brébeuf's death was prolonged rather than perfunctory. It was not his fate to be summarily dispatched by a single hatchet blow, like Jogues, la Lande, Goupil, or Chabanel, or cut down by a musket volley, like Daniel or Garnier. Rather, Brébeuf endured hours of torment before succumbing to his accumulated injuries. If Jogues's was a martyrdom of anticipation, then Brébeuf's was one of physical and spiritual endurance. The combination of the dramatic, eyewitness accounts of his death, related by escaped Wendat captives, seconded by the mute confirmation of his recovered body, has allowed Brébeuf's devotees to piece together the events of his final hours with startling clarity. The preservation of his relics, moreover, has afforded them a particularly potent and intimate form of access to their saint.

In the 1920s, as beatification seemed ever more assured, nationalist tensions regarding the relative preeminence of these two figures—Jogues, the American apostle, and Brébeuf, the Canadian Christ—became noticeably more pronounced on both sides of the border. How the group of saints should be depicted visually, and the order in which their names should be officially listed in the calendar of saints, though seemingly trivial, became hotly debated issues. The dynamics of this deepening national competition can be glimpsed in a long epistolary exchange in the 1920s between Wynne and the martyrs' preeminent iconographer, Mother Mary Margaret Nealis, a Canadian nun and creator of the Midland Shine's famous altarpiece. *The Glory* depicts the eight martyrs in the clouds, surrounded by angels, surmounting the gruesome scenes of their earthly torment below. Before serving as the altarpiece of the Midland Shrine, Nealis's *Glory* was displayed as the official portrait of the North American martyrs at their beatification in Rome in 1925.

The tone of these unofficial cross-border exchanges between Wynne and Nealis—his letters crisply typed on onion-skin paper, hers written in a flowing copper plate script on rich linen stationery embossed with

the Sacred and Immaculate Hearts—was unfailingly cordial and con-
vivial, even decorously flirtatious. And yet these informal exchanges—
generally brief, businesslike, and action-oriented on his side, longer,
more effusive, and more descriptive on hers—are valuable indicators of
emergent hot-button issues over the visual and textual priority of these
rival saints in the five-year period between their 1925 beatification and
their 1930 canonization.

Wynne initially contacted Nealis as part of his post-beatification
quest to commission an altarpiece for the Auriesville Shrine. His con-
descending, even incredulous praise of Nealis's artistic competency and
her boldness in depicting the martyrs' violent deaths illustrates the
casual, thoughtless sexism that Nealis faced as she chose to express her
spirituality as a cloistered nun through the production of publicly displayed religious art:

> I have had a chance to show [the copy of Nealis's painting] to several of
> the community and they all admire it. First they say at last we have
> something in a pious picture that is not mawkish, or sentimental. Then
> they admire every detail, above all, the spiritual expression of the
> faces. Then, they ask who did it, and when I tell them they say I am
> only fooling. "How on earth could a nun do that," they say.[172]

Nealis's response was not only good natured, it also provides considerable insight into her view of artistic production as a means not simply
of glorifying the martyrs but of identifying and empathizing with them
psychologically and spiritually. In her response, she reflected:

> In the scene below it cost me *terribly* to make those wild Indians tortur-
> ing and killing your holy brothers. Some of the nuns laughed at my first
> attempts because my Indians seemed to be apologizing to their victims
> for hurting them, or begging them to step aside so as not to get struck,
> so I *had* to make them ferocious.[173]

And yet, while Wynne was lavish in his praise for Nealis's treatment
of her subject, he ultimately rejected the notion of copying her painting
to serve as the Auriesville altarpiece because of the relative placement
of the figures of Brébeuf and Jogues. Regretfully, almost apologetically,
Wynne explains that her composition would simply be unacceptable
in the American context. As a Canadian artist, Nealis had enshrined
Brébeuf as its highest, largest, and most central figure. Despite his own
continentalist leanings, which led Wynne strongly to prefer depictions

of all eight saints together, and to be largely indifferent to their relative placement, he displays an uncomfortable awareness that other Americans would want Jogues to predominate. Wrote Wynne: "you understand, of course, why we had to have for the United States a painting that would bring out . . . Jogues and his companions." In the end, Wynne commissioned an altarpiece that, though it was obviously based on that of Nealis, made Jogues its visual centerpiece.[174] Nor were Canadians any less susceptible to this nationalistic posturing, proving particularly sensitive about, of all things, the order of the saints' listed names. Wrote one senior Canadian cleric of the Americans' temerity in placing Jogues's name before that of Brébeuf:

> This sounded to me like the rankest nationalism and it gave a very distorted impression of the martyrs. To refer to the eight as St. Isaac Jogues and companions would be like calling the Apostles Saint Jude and his companions. . . . It more or less ignores the saints martyred in this archdiocese, the ones whose lives are far more significant and whose deaths are much better attested.[175]

Sadly, as Brébeuf and Jogues came to signify the collective Catholic consciousness of "their" respective nations, the preferential elevation of one came to be seen as an unforgivable insult to the other.

By the 1930 canonization, the issue of the comparative visual prominence of the two competing saints had become so incendiary that radical measures had to be taken. As Pope Pius XI, borne on a litter, sheltered under a silken canopy, and cooled on the hot June day by acolytes bearing large ostrich feather fans, made his slow way up the central aisle of St. Peter's to perform the canonization mass, his gaze fell not on a single portrait of all eight martyrs, but rather on two dark-hued paintings on either side of the massive nave. One depicted, in somber tones, the American martyrs: Jogues, Goupil, and la Lande, the other their Canadian competitors: Brébeuf, Lalemant, Garnier, Daniel, and Chabanel. Undercurrents of competing Canadian and American nationalisms, long held in check by the necessity of unanimous action to achieve these figures' improbable elevation, had, with the success of the mission, emerged emboldened into the Roman sunlight.[176] In the decades to come, bereft of a common purpose, these nationalist divisions within the wider cult would only deepen.

With this visual division of the eight into rival national camps of three and five, and all that it symbolized, the idealistic, continentalist spirit of celebration that Wynne had been so assiduously working for was taken away from him at what should have been his moment of greatest triumph. The admonitory rather than celebratory tone of this canonization-eve letter to the American Catholic hierarchy demonstrates that Wynne himself was all too aware of this. Long an opponent of the factionalization of the martyrs' cult into competing national articulations Wynne, despite his official position as the American vice-postulator, had proven powerless to hold the octet together during their final elevation.

Wynne's "last service"[177] on behalf of his beloved martyrs was the erection of a larger-than-life statue of Isaac Jogues by the shores of Lake George, New York, in 1942. Posed as if in mid-stride, an imagined wind blowing back his cloak, the giant American Apostle clutches in his mutilated hand a cross that he holds benevolently aloft. True to form, Wynne had managed, with his usual urbane and diplomatic charm, to garner widespread support among the New York State Assembly for the project, which was enthusiastically backed by Protestants and Jews as well as Catholics. It is at the base of this statue that contemporary ultraconservative Catholic pilgrims gather to begin their seventy-mile walking Pilgrimage of Restoration along the imagined path of the captive Jogues himself. Singing and praying and bearing their banners aloft, they see the suffering they court in traversing twenty miles a day on foot as a reparation for the nation's accumulated sins. Gathered together from the four corners of the country, they wind through the hills of upper New York State southward to Auriesville. These brigades of ultraconservative Catholics who believe, in the words of one participant, that "the martyrs died for Jesus, and for America" are virtually all that remains of Wynne's once-powerful linking of the cult of the martyrs and American nationalism. Had his astonishingly hard work on behalf of the martyrs been repaid in proportion to the effort he expended their names might, even now, be on the lips of every American Catholic.

The canonization process, which demanded that the American and Quebecois hierarchies work conjointly to convince the Vatican of the justice of their cause, awoke powerful nationalistic impulses within each, creating subterranean currents of tension, competition, and conflict as well as the more visible dynamics of collaboration and mutual support. Like a rumble in the jungle between a tyrannosaurus and an albertosaurus at the end of the dinosaur era, while the conflict allowed each powerful reptile to flex their sinewy muscles at one another, victory for either could only be pyrrhic in the face of their mutual, looming extinction. Many of the fears and jealousies that each had expressed in relation to the other throughout the long fight for canonization would likewise, in the decades to come, doom both the French Canadian and the American cults of the martyrs to increasing irrelevancy.

On the American side, the early emphasis on sacred space at Auriesville, coupled with the pope's decision to limit automatic public veneration of the newly minted American saints to New York State, effectively worked against the continuing growth of the cult of the martyrs despite Wynne's hard-fought campaign to undo the damage done. Though the Auriesville Jesuits, like Wynne, remained optimistic about the cult's rosy future, completing work in 1931 on a massive circular church that one of their number had seen in a vision, in the years to come the challenge would become to fill the 10,000-seat white elephant.[178] Afire with spiritual enthusiasm in the afterglow of the 1930 canonization, the Auriesville Jesuits had massively overbuilt. When "a few gather together in my Name" in the cavernous vastness of the "Coliseum," they are typically outnumbered by empty pews that seem a rebuke, and haunted by hollow echoes that intimate their failure to fill the building, one-sixth of a mile in circumference, with devotees.[179] Since 1931, only a choice handful of special events (such as the 1952 pilgrimage-concert of the famous Von Trapp family) would fill the massive building to capacity.[180] Though conceived in a dream, the round church belied the aphorism "build it and they will come."

On the Quebecois side, the hierarchy's initial response of fearful jealousy to the Americans' 1884 initiative and their instinct to try to guard the martyrs as their exclusive property proved prescient. For the rapid anglicization of the martyrs' cult by both American and English-speaking Canadian Catholics did indeed number its days in *la belle province*. Facilitated by the translation of primary sources and the Anglophone authorship of popular secondary works, such as those of Parkman, Shea, and Wynne, the cult's increasing resonance and popularity outside Québec would make it a less viable vehicle to communicate the ethic, linguistic, and confessional distinctiveness of Quebeckers.

The 1885 foundation of the Auriesville Shrine also signaled, if only distantly, the end of Québec's dominance of the martyrs' cult. As the decades wore on, the province's lack of a similar shrine would increasingly put it at the sidelines of the martyrs' veneration, as their twin shrines at Auriesville and Midland Ontario came to be the best-known symbols and centers of their cult.

As they stood side by side at the June 1930 canonization, watching the apotheosis of figures they had together helped to define as decisively New World rather than Old World figures, French Canadian and American Catholics were perhaps at the apogee of their respective cults to the martyrs they had helped to magnify and honor. Another entity was waiting in the wings to challenge both of them for the leadership of the martyrs' cult in North America. The English Canadian cult of the martyrs, though in its infancy at the time of the canonization, was slowly but surely coming into its own. Its fervor would gradually drain away the distinctiveness of the martyrs long beloved by French Canadians, while its focus on sacred space, much like that of its American cousins, would help it to gradually eclipse French Canadian leadership of the cult in Canada. In their outreach to Protestants and their determined linking of the martyrs' cult with Canadian nationalism in the postwar period, these anglo-Canadian Catholic leaders would finally achieve, in their own nation, Wynne's long-cherished dream.

4

———————————◆———————————

For Canada and for God

I T WAS PROBABLY the single most engrossing thing ever to have happened in the sleepy town of Midland, on the shores of Ontario's scenic
Georgian Bay. In the hot, languorous summer days of July 1949, the
town was abuzz with excitement over the lavish pageant celebrating
the three hundredth anniversary of the martyrdoms of Jean de Brébeuf
and Gabriel Lalemant, set to open in just a few days.[1] The hype, even
away from its epicenter at Midland, was virtually inescapable, the spot-
light white-hot. One veteran newspaperman, half admiringly, half impatiently, called the pageant "the most publicized event in the history
of Canadian journalism."[2] Most of the town was involved with the
production, as crew, suppliers, hosts, or cast—be they "Maidens of New
France" or "Indian dancers." During the seemingly interminable dress
rehearsals, the whole town became a sort of extended "green room."
Rising young Canadian soprano Louise Roy caused a sensation when
she dropped into a local coffee shop still wearing the full makeup,
long black braids, and ostentatious feathered war bonnet that was part
of her improbable assemble as "Cornflower"—the native female lead
in the production. Featuring an orchestra, a professional corps de bal-
let, and a cast of over five hundred extras, most of them local—and
Protestant[3]—the lavish four-hour production, held in a natural outdoor
amphitheater on the grounds of Midland's Martyrs' Shrine, was the
brainchild of flamboyant American Jesuit writer, director, and fervent
anti-Communist Father Daniel Lord.[4]

Though written by an American, *Salute to Canada* was an unabashed
celebration of the hard-won sense of Canadian national identity
and patriotism that had emerged like a phoenix from the ashes of the

Father Daniel Lord (center), the author, songwriter, and director of the elaborate 1949 musical *Salute to Canada,* surrounded by his lead actors, Louise Roy, Bill Barnet, and Jack Harbour. Lord promoted the martyrs as heroic historical figures who were the shared heritage of all Canadians, regardless of their confession.

(Archives of the Midland Martyrs' Shrine)

Second World War. The production was an attempt to restate, in wide and confessionally inclusive terms, the message of the martyrs for the rising Cold War generation of Canadians. Lord's production, buoyed by rousing song and dance numbers and punctuated by endless costume changes, had in its lengthy running time two separate but linked climaxes. The first was, perhaps, to be expected: the victorious apotheosis of the martyrs. Like an old-fashioned tableau, the eight men triumphantly appeared on the highest of the three stages, replicating their poses in Mother Nealis's iconic altarpiece, *The Glory.*[5] Their reappearance, whole and living after their tasteful offstage slaying, so positioned that the floodlit silver spires of the Midland Martyrs' Shrine glinted behind them in the darkness, asserted the familiar Christian sentiment that faithful suffering merits heavenly rewards.

But lest the audience dismiss the martyrs' sacrifice as being irrelevant to its own contemporary civic and religious lives, the play's second, unexpected climax dramatically revealed the applicability of these ancient lessons to their own postwar world. Playing on the double meaning of the word "red," Lord's choreography called for the piece's übervillain, a "bloodthirsty Iroquois medicine man," to strip off his traditional garb at the height of his frenzied "war dance," revealing his true colors as a modern-day Red Army soldier. As he was joined by sinister ranks of torch-bearing, jackbooted Communists, who menacingly surrounded the audience, time was transcended, past became present, and spectators were forced to choose sides in the contemporary struggle between good and evil as Lord understood it. By theatrically threatening his audience, the Jesuit director invited them to consider whether they would have the courage, like the Canadian martyrs of long ago, to lay down their lives "for Canada and God."[6]

The Second World War's legacy of shared service and suffering encouraged postwar Canadians to think nationalistically, stressing their common civic status and duties rather than their confessional divisions. The martyrs' calculated appeal to a shared Canadian identity in the postwar era facilitated their recasting as the pioneering purveyors of civilization and of Christianity to benighted seventeenth-century natives howling in the wilderness. Such inclusive language presented the martyrs less as Catholic oddities, reeking of incense, then as the shared legacy of all (white) Canadian Christians, fostering ecumenical collaboration long before the confessional thawing conventionally attributed to Vatican II.

The specter of Communism also facilitated the cult's calculatedly broad appeal. In the 1940s and 1950s, the martyrs were recast as those who had successfully stood up to the "red menace" of their own time: the Iroquois. Canada's postwar mission of defending nation and faith from the Communist minotaur thus helped to forge a sense of their common cause both with the martyrs and with one another. But even as anti-Communism whitewashed confessional differences between Canadians, it also sparked novel new expressions of ethnic Catholic identity at the Midland shrine. The postwar era witnessed the establishment of "ethnic pilgrimages" by many European immigrant groups who came to Midland to pray for the liberation of their homelands, to indulge in the religious rituals long denied them and to foment a new understanding of the martyrs' urgent contemporary relevance as anti-Communist firebrands.

Other factors that facilitated the broadening of the martyrs' cult were largely serendipitous, such as the unexpectedly enthusiastic Protestant response to the Jesuits' archeological exploitation of the ruins of Sainte-Marie, the ancient headquarters to which they themselves had set the torch. The cult of the martyrs that took shape in the ancient heartland of Huronia was, like that of Auriesville, land-rich and relic-poor. Like their American counterparts, English Canadians were virtually forced to commune with the saints in the spaces sanctified by their historical presence, an activity that coincidentally proved congenial to Protestants, who typically regarded relic veneration with incomprehension or distaste.

Commerce and education also played important roles in contributing to the martyrs' daring confessional boundary crossings in the 1940s and 1950s. Particularly during the postwar boom, tourism in beautiful Georgian Bay was increasingly promoted by a range of business, civic, media, and transportation interests. Midland's silver-spired church and the romantic ruins of Sainte-Marie, adjacent to it, began to be promoted as a "must see" on any tourist's itinerary. Even as the martyrs' religious and political reputation was being sharpened on the whetstone of Communism, their alternative image as benign nondenominational Canadian founding fathers was being exploited commercially by media and transportation giants. In postwar Canada, the line between pilgrimage, tourism, and education was blurring, sometimes intentionally, sometimes inadvertently. Devout pilgrims, curious public school children, tourists, and summer cottagers alike flocked to the shrine and its abutting ruins, drawn by shrewd advertising campaigns and dramatic radio plays, by boat and rail "package tours," by newspaper articles and spectacular pageants, and by parochial and public school field trips. The almost evangelical copy of hard-bitten journalists, ad execs, and tourism and transportation officials, whose business trips to Midland were frequently disrupted by inconvenient religious awakenings, also helped arouse consumer desire to visit the hallowed shores of "Huronia" in an urge that had both spiritual and commercial potential.

These new postwar tourist-pilgrims were joined at the altar rail, on the dig site, and in the open-air theater by another important new "client group": children. During the postwar years, the story of the martyrs became required reading for public as well as Catholic schoolchildren, as it was now considered part of the civic *patrimonie* of all young Canadians. Protestant as well as Catholic schoolteachers would come to count on the martyrs' violent, romantic tale to stop juvenile eyes from drooping during seemingly interminable history lessons. Many also saw the martyrs as reflecting the treasured wartime virtues of self-sacrifice, discipline, and dedication. Their curricular enshrinement as important historical figures in public-school textbooks not only cemented the martyrs' broadening cult, but also ensured its intergenerational transmission.

It is tempting, given the bitter history of confessional tension in Canada, to linger on the cozy inclusiveness of the postwar martyrs' cult. It is affirming to explore the myriad ways in which the martyrs, coming to serve as an intraconfessional symbol of Canadian collective identity, opened up a much-needed dialogue between Protestants and Catholics. But the deconfessionalization of the postwar cult of the martyrs in Canada had a dark side. In large part, the common ground discovered by white Canadian Protestants and Catholics was achieved by casting native peoples as their common enemy. French Canadians in the nineteenth century had used the rhetoric and imagery of the martyrs to stress the ethnic, linguistic, and cultural differences they saw as distinguishing themselves from native peoples. Now white anglophone Canadians also used the martyrs and their legacy as means of expressing a complex mixture of emotions toward native people, constituted of curiosity, fear, animosity, attraction, and paternalistic concern. While the martyrs were presented as noble pioneers who "undertook to teach the redmen that there was something more to life than eating and sleeping and killing,"[7] native people of both the past and the present were cast as the "ignorant, squalid, and low-living"[8] recipients of white benevolence and charity. Rhetorical recourse to the martyrs, moreover, allowed white Christian Canadians to claim a sort of eternal victimhood at the hands of the "ravenous rabble"[9] even as they honed their own renewed ideological onslaught against native culture. Identifying with the martyrs' eternal suffering at the hands of bestial "savages" allowed postwar Canadians to ignore (or even to justify) their deeply damaging and unsolicited interventions into the lives of many First Nations peoples.[10]

Pageantry and Patriotism in Postwar Canada

> We've got a land to brag about,
> To sing and wave a flag about,
> A land we love as God has loved before us.
> Girls are fair here; men are square here,
> And the folks, God love 'em,
> There is none above 'em,
> You're a bright land, full-of-light land,
> You're Canada, Canada!
> Salute to you!!

So run the lyrics of the opening song from Lord's 1949 musical block-buster, *Salute to Canada*. Initially, it seems something of a puzzle that a pageant designed to celebrate something as particular as the three hundredth anniversary of the deaths of four Roman Catholic martyrs would be couched in such broad, nationalist terms as to merit the title *Salute to Canada*. But the show's hearty, cringe-inducing patriotism must not discourage analysis of the play's sophisticated structure and urgent message. The show's insistently patriotic themes, however deliciously cheesy, are central to Lord's trenchant agenda. He manipulates his audience's sense of collective identity and its relationship to time and space to create a new, broader constituency for the martyrs' cult in Canada: mimicking in microcosm important developments that were inexorably resculpting its dynamics. Lord's play urged both audience and cast to look past the divisions of confessional difference to the shared allegiances made possible by Canadian patriotism. For all of its artless sexism ("men are square here!") and naive nationalism, there was something quite subtle about the underlying structure of Lord's extravaganza, which played with the dualities of historical and devotional time, manipulated the twin imperatives of venerating and imitating the martyrs, and brought together the commercial and the eternal, the sacred and the profane.[11]

Like an old-fashioned passion play or the earlier, less elaborate outdoor pageants that had been enacted at Midland during the previous decade,[12] Lord's production affirms that salvation history had, in the story of the martyrs, unfolded in historical time on Canadian soil. The death of the martyrs, the destruction of Sainte-Marie, and the fall of Huronia, though tragic events, were ultimately a meaningful and triumphant part of God's plan. If the Jesuit mission to the "Huron" was a failure, this was the failure of the cross, where apparent death and humiliation mask a deeper reality.[13] So far, so conventional. But then Lord starts to play with time, allegiance, and collective identity, structuring his pageant as an extended dialogue between two pairs of children: a Wendat boy and girl who, having been killed in the 1649–1650 fall of Huronia, know nothing of what has happened since their deaths, and a contemporary Canadian boy–girl pair who, though aware of the current state of Canada, are lamentably ignorant of its earlier history. The play is thus conceived as a process of mutual illumination, whereby contemporary white Canadians and the native peoples of a bygone era work together to understand the complex links between past and present.[14]

Using this narrative device, Lord loops the past around to meet the present, making a palpable, electric connection between his audience members in 1949 and the martyrs who had walked the same soil three hundred years earlier. Lord suggests that the martyrs' sacrifice was absolutely necessary for the present-day reality of Canada to exist as a moral entity, recasting Tertullian's epigraph in an unexpectedly nationalistic direction:

> These Canadian Martyrs and Pioneers, who died for Christianity and to bring civilization to the savages, are pioneers in the realest sense, whose death is the fertilizing influence out of which emerges a great nation. Hence we do not tell their historic story as much as we present their influence upon us who are the inheritors of their heroism.[15]

For Lord, this point about the ongoing, contemporary effect of the martyrs was so critical that he not only repeated it in numerous press conferences, but had these sentiments prominently printed in the play's program. Making the martyrs the symbolic founding fathers of contemporary Canada gave them a greater hold on the loyalty of Lord's cast and his audience by presenting their respectful recognition as a *civic* duty incumbent on Protestants as well as Catholics.[16] All Canadians are bound to the martyrs by the same obligatory debt of gratitude, Lord intoned. By presenting the martyrs as patriotic, rather than purely religious figures, Lord was at once acknowledging and encouraging their political and Protestant appropriation.

Lord's time-defying trick of turning the "red menace" from a quasi-ethnic to a political designation, and from something safely rooted in the past to a real and present concern, raised the question of how one is to approach the saints. Lord's play balances veneration with imitation: coupling admiration of the martyrs' inimitable act of country-founding heroism with a clarion call to contemporary Canadians to imitate their courage in the face of a new threat to God and country. Lord posited that the eternal struggle between good and evil, civilization and barbarism, bravely fought by the martyrs in the 1640s, continued in the contemporary struggle between the Western forces of freedom, democracy, and Christianity and the Soviet juggernaut of repression, autocracy, and atheism. In insisting that his audience not only acknowledge and respect the martyrs' sacrifice but themselves confront a similar threat, Lord emphasized a long-standing theme in Catholic piety—the imitation of Christ and the saints—tacitly admitting that perhaps imitation of martyrs came more naturally to Protestants than their veneration.[17] Presenting the martyrs not simply as historical figures deserving of reverence but as relevant models for contemporary Canadians' political and religious behavior, Lord rejected the limiting term "pageant" for his production. Confronted with the word, Lord would strongly demur, clarifying that the play was

> not strictly a pageant. . . . A pageant usually presents accurate history. . . . This type of production presents the spirit of a place, a movement, a group of men . . . the meaning as we would understand it today. . . . At the end, the hope is that the audience will realize: That apparent tragedy can be the beginning of real greatness . . . That the willingness to die—to lay down one's life for one's friend and the cause in which one believes—is as important today as it was three hundred years ago . . . That Red Perils change their shape but continue to strike at God, Christianity, and democracy . . . That what the Martyrs did was to the lasting glory of Canada . . . and what modern men and women do means the future progress of Canada.[18]

Canadian Protestants and the Martyrs

The war and postwar years witnessed a crescendo of Protestant creative interest in the martyrs. Extras, dancers, and scrim painters participated enthusiastically in Lord's extravaganza. Celebrated Methodist poet E. J. Pratt penned his magisterial epic poem *Brébeuf and His Brethren*.[19] Protestant publicist F. E. D. "Davey" McDowell bestowed on the martyrs a more dubious immorality in his raunchy but wildly popular novel

The Champlain Road. "Crusty Baptist" Wilfred Jury led the archaeological excavation of Sainte-Marie-among-the-Huron, the ruined Jesuit headquarters, and would design the historical reconstruction that would rise on its ruins in the 1960s.[20]

Jury's exploration of this seventeenth-century site, however, was possible only because of the sacrifices made by earlier generations of martyr-boosting Protestants. When the Society of Jesus, in the persons of Félix Martin and Jean-Pierre Chazelle, returned to Huronia, local Protestants proved eager to welcome and to aid them. Midland's Anglican minister and amateur historian, Reverend George Hallen, guided Martin to the overgrown, romantic ruins of Saint-Marie, his family's preferred picnicking spot.[21] Local Protestant farmers William Playfair and William Shepherd obligingly sold the Jesuits parcels of lands containing the ruins of Sainte-Marie and the hill that rose above them, the future site of the Midland Martyrs' Shrine. They personally financed and prayerfully dedicated a memorial to identify and commemorate the martyrs on the site where they had lived and worked. Had non-Catholics opposed Jesuit acquisition of this property or blocked the building of the successive shrines that rose in 1907 and 1926,[22] then the Jesuits' extravagant dreams would have been stillborn. But government official Charles McCrae, in his address at the 1926 ceremony dedicating the Midland Martyrs' Shrine, spoke for many of his fellow Canadian Protestants when he cast Jean de Brébeuf and Gabriel Lalemant as "heroes of Church and State." Intoned McCrae: "appreciation of the work they did and the great sacrifice they made is not confined to members of any one Church. People outside the Catholic Church are every bit as proud of those two pioneer noblemen as those in it."[23] His reframing of the martyrs as "pioneers" who brought European "civilization" and Christian beliefs to a bloody, barbaric "frontier" prophesied the accelerated deconfessionalization and nationalization of the martyrs' cult in the postwar period."[24]

Ethnic Pilgrimage and Anti-Communism at Midland

Nationalism was the new key in which the martyrs' anthem would be sung in the postwar period. Protestantization was the outcome of attempts—from both sides of the confessional aisle—to recast a Catholic cult in broader, more patriotic terms. But if nationalization was the sought-after outcome, and Protestantization was simultaneously a product of and a means to achieving it, then fear of Communism was a critical, yet largely unacknowledged catalyst of both. Some contemporary Jesuits have been tempted to write off the anticommunism of the martyrs' postwar cult—so memorably enacted in Lord's 1949 extravaganza—as a "flash in the pan" or "an American import."[25] This is perhaps understandable given that the abuses of the McCarthy era remain so unattractive, and that the postwar period's characteristically apocalyptic brand of Marian anti-Communism seems now both dated and paranoid. Yet even a cursory examination of the *Martyrs' Shrine Message,* the devotional magazine of the Midland shrine, from the immediate postwar years to the 1970s, reveals that anti-Communist interpretation of the martyrs was a preferred rhetorical means of making them relevant to the uncertainty and fear of "the atomic age." While Canadian Catholics, like their American counterparts, appropriated Our Lady of Fatima's apparent prophesy of her forthcoming conversion of Russia to articulate a typically Marian anti-Communism,[26] both national groups also utilized the martyrs as a familiar lens through which to view contemporary threats. Canadian Catholics prayed to "our glorious Martyr Patrons of Canada" for many things. But a favorite entreaty of the era was "to beg them to ward off from our shores the persecutions which the Church is undergoing in Europe."[27] Homilies on this theme were common on both sides of the border, and articles were often shared and reprinted in the respective shrine publications, demonstrating a preoccupation that transcended borders.[28]

The perceived threat of Communism, then, served as a persuasive argument for the necessity of national unity at the same time that it gave the martyrs a welcome new relevance. Communism was the contemporary cloud against which the martyrs' vaulted courage and defiance blazed out all the brighter.[29] Appropriated as models of how best to respond to this new threat to Canadian Christianity and democracy, the martyrs were seen in broadly Christian terms as a potent symbol of those "dragging out a miserable existence behind the 'Iron Curtain'"[30] and in Catholic terms as active intercessors on their behalf.

Fear of the hammer and sickle in the late 1940s and early 1950s, then, helped to foment the new, nationalistic image of the Canadian martyrs as firebrands of anti-Communism. But the same force also created a devotional renaissance among Eastern European immigrants and refugees that would decisively shape the shrine's material culture, self-image, and sense of mission. Midland's geographical proximity to the holy sites where Brébeuf and Lalemant, Chabanel, Daniel, and Garnier had laid down their lives made pilgrimage there "natural" for "Polish, Slovak, Slovene, Czech, even Chinese pilgrims who know what persecution is . . . came to pray . . . for relatives and friends in danger." The advent of so-called ethnic pilgrimages in the postwar period would broaden the shrine's reach from its traditional Irish Catholic majority–French Catholic minority base[31] to make the shrine the buzzing Catholic polyglot it has remained ever since. As well as preserving archetypically European Catholic rituals and material culture at the Midland shrine, these pilgrimages would emerge as one of its most characteristic, distinctive, and profitable postwar features.

During and after the war years, Canada absorbed a flood of Eastern European immigrants, many of them Catholic. Some had been displaced

A Polish pilgrimage at Our Lady of Martyrs Shrine in Auriesville in August 1965. Such events were very popular at both the Midland and Auriesville shrines in the years after World War II, as Eastern European pilgrims gathered to pray for relatives caught behind the Iron Curtain.

(Our Lady of Martyrs Shrine Archives, Auriesville)

by the war. Some sought greater economic opportunity. Others were fleeing active persecution for religious or political activism.[32] Clustering in ethnic ghettos in Canada's larger cities, refugees of the Soviet bloc saw the Canadian Catholic church as their natural ally and advocate. They took advantage of its spiritual consolations and practical assistance in the forms of financial relief and language lessons. Fusing an urgent political activism with traditional Catholic devotionalism, many immigrant Catholics from Poland, Hungary, Czechoslovakia, and other Eastern European nations sought to perform on Canadian soil the same devotional patterns that had been forced underground in their "red-ruled homelands."[33]

The religious energies of many immigrant communities in Toronto quickly came to focus on the nearby Midland Martyrs' Shrine, located ninety-eight miles due north of the metropolis. There, by reestablishing the familiar European rhythms of penitential and petitionary pilgrimage, they could direct the attention of both God and man to the plight of family members still overseas. Moreover, by synchronizing their pilgrimage with protests organized by resistance movements overseas, such events could make a political as well as a religious statement.

The Midland Martyrs' Shrine was more than amenable to the urgency of new immigrant spirituality. Indeed, the two forces—the shrine and the immigrants—would prove to be for each other both wax and seal. Immigrant spirituality would, over the years, indelibly mark the physical space of Midland. In the postwar period, its verdant grounds would ring with foreign languages, unfamiliar hymns, and novel rituals as new Canadian Catholics "performed their ethnicity."[34] As the tides of pilgrimage receded, the devotional jetsam of its passage would remain, marooning at the shrine both costly gifts and humble: from an ornate silver "Slovak" cross or a costly reproduction of the Polish Black Madonna to the rosaries, photographs, flowers, and notes wedged in the crevices of its outdoor statues by ordinary pilgrims. Whether big or small, these tokens were more than simply expected gifts of guests to a host; they were defiant statements of belonging and ownership, which gradually transformed the shrine's look and feel into a cosmopolitan polyglot.

In response to the immigrants' self-understanding as persecuted Christians in forced exile, the martyrs were presented as emblems of unfailing faith under religious persecution and as sympathetic intercessors for the plights of those faced with atheism's reckless hate. The presence of exotic "ethnic" pilgrims at the shrine offered Catholic Canadians a sense of being united with them against a real and present danger to their own beliefs and way of life, a danger that dragged in its train the possibility of contemporary martyrdom. As the Canadian Catholic majority intimated that they, like these recent immigrants, might soon be "called upon to suffer persecution, to be a martyr in some way or other, like Christ, like the Canadian Martyrs, like the Christians who languish behind the 'Iron Curtain,'" they became a natural, sympathetic audience in these touching spectacles of solidarity.[35] To pilgrims' publicly expressed concerns regarding the safety of their overseas family members was added newspapers' shameless fear-mongering that the Midland pilgrimages attracted the ireful attention of Communist spies. In 1956, the *Telegraph*'s headlines blared: "Red Agents Watch Poles at Midland!" alleging that the 10,000-strong Polish religious gathering had been infiltrated by "Communist intelligence agents" who sought to observe and photograph them, with threatening intent.[36]

Even as the shrine was permanently marked with the exotic presence of "ethnic" pilgrimages, so these pilgrims were also impressed with the image of the martyrs, their new and powerful Canadian intercessors. Themselves tempered in the fires of persecution, it was argued, the Canadian martyrs understood the lives of Christians "behind the Iron Curtain." Urging newly arrived Eastern Europeans to pray for the liberation of their homelands and the defeat of Communism through the intercession of these Canadian martyrs became an important aspect of their "Canadianization."

From Martyrs' Hill to Midland

Much the same constellation of circumstances that had prompted the "spatialization" of the American cult were also operative in English Canada. Given that northwestern Ontario was as distant as Auriesville from the rich mother lode of martyr-related artifacts conserved at Québec, Ontarians, like their American counterparts, were forced to "make do" with sacred space. In the decades to come, however, their ability to claim that the sainted martyrs had lived and died in this area would prove itself a powerful plus: facilitating the Midland shrine's Protestantization and its mutually profitable relationship with the world of commerce and of education.[37]

Canadian devotees of the martyrs began their search for sacred space with a considerable advantage in that they knew the location of Sainte-Marie, the Jesuit headquarters that had served as the onetime home of all eight men. It was simply unmistakable. Despite persistent legends that pillagers of Sainte-Marie's ruins would be haunted by the martyrs' vengeful ghosts, settlers seeking an easy source of predressed stone had nevertheless ravaged them. Despite this, even in 1855 the ancient foundations, still standing "two to four feet above ground,"[38] were easily discernible. Yet, though martyr aficionados readily acknowledged the critical importance of Sainte-Marie, some still yearned to discover those yet more sacred spots where each martyr had individually laid down his life. Decades before the silver steeples of the Midland shrine rose on the crest of the hill overlooking Sainte-Marie, Canadians would establish a humbler chapel, Martyrs' Hill, founded on the putative death site of the double martyrdom of Jean de Brébeuf and Gabriel Lalemant: Taenhatentaron/Saint-Ignace.

Father Arthur E. Jones, the identifier of the site, was General John Clark's Canadian counterpart. Much as Clark had done in his long quest for Ossernenon, Jones faced the daunting task of discerning from scant evidence the long-vanished location of the seventeenth-century native villages in which the martyrs had perished. Like his American colleague, he attempted to match the missionaries' terse, fragmentary descriptions of village locations with clues in the contemporary landscape.

But despite their common challenge, the two men cut vastly different figures. Even in his sixties, as Clark scoured the rolling hills of northern New York State, he remained every inch the soldier: slim, disciplined, and upright. Jones, conversely, was a morbidly obese Jesuit scholar who was far more at home at his desk, twiddling compasses and calculating distances, than in the field, observing the lay of the land. Indeed, his massive bulk meant that "he was unable to do much climbing or digging himself." Having hired a horse and buggy to convey him as close as possible to these remote sites, Jones would regale his driver with historical and archaeological anecdotes while taking a few anticipatory glances into his bulging picnic basket.[39]

But by 1903, Jones's armchair calculations nevertheless appeared to have borne fruit. He identified a site in a farmer's field near the present-day community of Waubaushene, Ontario, as having once been Taenhatentaron/Saint-Ignace, the Wendat village where both Brébeuf and Lalemant had been put to death. Four years later, the Jesuits established a "rough wooden chapel, spacious but not artistic" on the site.[40] Because of its slight elevation, the little church would come to known as "Martyrs' Hill."[41]

Despite its relative isolation, the little chapel soon established a growing reputation for extraordinary cures.[42] Sundays at the hill attracted as many as a thousand miracle-seeking pilgrims. Locals ventured to the site on foot or by horse and buggy. The rich came by private auto, braving the pitted, narrow farm roads. But finally, to accommodate the demand, the Canadian National Railway (CNR) added a "Miracle Stop," close to Martyrs' Hill, to its itinerary.[43]

A homely, anonymous "Shrine Diary," kept during the summer of 1911, provides an intimate insider's look at the rhythms of life at Canada's first shrine established in honor of the martyrs.[44] To read its fluid, anonymous copperplate is to experience whiplash, even within the confines of one small, lined page, between the sublime and the mundane. On one side of the note paper, the anonymous diarist records her witnessing of the miraculous cure of one Père Poussin:

> I will not attempt to describe the miracle, as I presume the Reverend Father himself will forward a written statement to those most interested in the cause of the Canadian martyrs, suffice it for me to say that we who have talked to the Rev. Father were much edified by his description of the miracle God had worked in him. . . . It was a spiritual inspiration and we feel that the Canadian martyrs will be greatly glorified by the miracle.[45]

On the facing page of this paean of praise to the martyrs is scrawled an impromptu shopping list: "stove black, lard, coffee" in the same hand.

And yet the ritual life of the Martyrs' Hill Shrine, which seemed, after fourteen years, to be so well established, was quickly drawing to a close. Curiously, the sanctuary's demise was at the instigation of the same man responsible for its original establishment. On his deathbed in January of 1918, Father Jones confided to his confessor that he entertained doubts regarding the authenticity of the Martyrs' Hill site.[46] Unsure whether he had erred in his identification, he could not bear to depart this world without unburdening himself.[47]

Pilgrims at "Martyrs' Hill," the first Canadian shrine established in honor of the martyrs in 1907. The site became so closely associated with miracles during its eighteen years of existence that rail giant Canadian National established a "Miracle Stop" on its route to serve pilgrims.

(Archives of the Midland Martyrs' Shrine)

Jones's about-face regarding the authenticity of Martyrs' Hill must have raised a number of puzzling questions in the minds of its longtime local clients, particularly regarding the miracles that had, for some twenty years, flourished there. In popular consciousness, this unassuming space had proven itself to be holy ground in the most impressive way possible. Though pilgrims would doubtless have acknowledged that it was God alone who was responsible for producing the blessedly unnatural events that had unfolded on the hill, they would also have argued that *where* God chose to answer pilgrims' prayers was significant. The fact that he chose to respond to the martyrs' collective interventions on behalf of their clients at the purported death site of two of their company was doubtless seen as a strong validation of both the (as yet uncanonized) martyrs' sanctity and the site's authenticity.

In Catholic contexts, miracles always prompt a kind of holy forensics, a reading of the tea leaves to determine who, what, or "where" was responsible. Unlike Protestants' belated return to a belief in the miraculous, based on their new appropriation of the biblical Jesus's wonderworking powers, Catholic miracle narratives have always em-

Père Jacques Dugas (right), a devotee of the martyrs, applies the martyrs' relics to Gerald Henry (center), Midland, 1926.

(Archives of the Midland Martyrs' Shrine)

phasized not simply their ultimate source but the blessed channels through which divine grace chooses to flow. The people, places, and things that act as conduits for this continual outflowing of divine love from the godhead to afflicted persons are themselves seen as holy and worthy of veneration.

Saints are attractive to the Catholic laity for many reasons, including their personal narratives and their extraordinary virtues. But one of their most attractive characteristics is their effectiveness in serving as mediators between the divine and the profane worlds, and their effortless permeation of the membrane separating the living and the dead. It is on this basis that many Catholics choose the agents through whom they will direct their prayers. An elderly Frenchwoman, the aptly named Mimi Bonnefoi, taught me this. Many a day during the three months I lived across the road from her blue-shuttered house in Josselin, Brittany, I would be recruited to serve as Mimi's "troisième jambe"—her third leg—gently supporting her arm as she made her accustomed trek through the village to the doctor's office, where she stayed for a brisk fifteen minutes, and the Basilique, where she lingered three times longer, first in front of the fulsomely dressed statue of Notre

Dame de Roncier, where she would invariably light a blue candle, and then before the mass-produced plaster statue of Sainte-Thérèse de Lisieux, where she would light a white one. I would sit and watch Mimi's unvarying routine: witnessing her lips moving in inaudible prayer, her head dipping and bobbing in silent, decisive punctuation, her well-worn beads slipping though her tremulous fingers. I would watch the colors from the stained-glass windows wink like bright jewels off her spectacles and slide their liquid glow lovingly over her slight frame. One day, as we hobbled home, I asked why she invariably isolated these two saints from the pantheon of holy figures honored at the church to receive her unchanging prayers for healing. Without waiting for her answer, I excitedly bombarded her with subquestions: "Was it because both these figures were women?" "Was it because they were local figures?" Mimi stopped her faltering progress over the cobblestones to look at me, and her warm brown eyes crinkled into a smile that encompassed both my eagerness and my stupidity. "Non," she said, "c'est parce qu'elles sont vraiment plus efficace"—"No, it's because they work much better."

This rough-and-ready calculation of the sanctity of persons or places from their effectiveness at channeling divine intervention is not simply a lay phenomenon. The religious use similar logic. In 1917, just a year before Jones's agonizing deathbed doubts, an English priest acquired an anonymous relic he believed to be that of Brébeuf. He wrote to Mère Beaupré of Québec, the longtime custodian of Brébeuf's other relics, anxious to establish its provenience and ownership. In her response, Beaupré did not bore the priest with dry abstractions regarding the bones' minutely recorded chain of custody. Nor did she mummify him in ecclesiastical red tape. Her response reflected the same spiritual pragmatism of Mimi or of Martyrs' Hill. She simply challenged her British interrogator to prayerfully invoke Brébeuf's intercession while applying the relic to the Catholic invalids of his parish. If the unproven bone shard worked miracles, she explained, it was assuredly Brébeuf's relic.

For the faithful of Martyrs' Hill, to worry overmuch about the trifling details of seventeenth-century topography in the face of God's indubitable blessings, showered so copiously on them there, seemed perverse, if not sacrilegious: like looking a spiritual gift horse in the mouth. But for the dying Jones, any doubt regarding his identification of the site was intolerable. How could he die in peace, knowing that he might inadvertently have established the martyrs' cult on quicksand? Better to refound the shrine adjacent to a location whose archaeological pedigree was immaculate and unquestionable: Sainte-Marie.[48]

His confessor agreed. It would be the very priest who had administered Jones his last rites, Father J. M. Filion, who would virtually single-handedly spearhead the shrine's relocation to Midland: serving as the new shrine's chief fundraiser, architect, foreman, and first director. The child of an Irish mother and a French-Canadian father, Filion had grown up a fervent devotee of the martyrs. As a boy, he had venerated them through play, casting his friends as the "Indians" to his "missionary."[49] Ambitious and bilingual, Filion was a rising star among the Canadian Jesuits, having been tapped to serve as the youngest provincial in their history. Tall and quiet, with a gentle, refined face, Filion often carried a breviary to conceal the loss of two fingers on his right hand.[50] Though his disfigurement evoked that of Isaac Jogues, his spiritual hero, Filion's injury was the result of a more prosaic accident in high school shop class.[51]

In 1918, when Filion first become provincial, the Canadian Jesuits under his leadership were increasingly restive, divided by the growing nationalism within Quebecois Jesuit hearts and beset by linguistic tensions.[52] As his last action as the leader of the entire Canadian Society in 1924, Filion supervised his society's careful dismemberment. In a move eerily reminiscent of the craniotomy that would be performed on Brébeuf's skull a year later, Filion divided the Society linguistically into two separate and unequal subgroups, assuming leadership of the smaller new English-speaking division, the "Vice-Province of Upper Canada."

Thus, though Filion's decision to move the martyrs' shrine was prompted by Jones's stricken deathbed confession, this strategic relocation also reflected his wider linguistic and professional priorities. By relocating Martyrs' Hill from the francophone enclave of Waubachene to English-speaking, largely Protestant Midland, Filion was ambitiously attempting to broaden the cult outside its traditional cultural and linguistic base and to wrest for himself the mantle of its leadership, long the prerogative of local *franco-Ontarien* clergy.[53] Filion had great things planned for his martyrs and was determined to obtain what *he* saw as the strongest possible theological, spatial, linguistic, and logistical undergirding for their cult. Founding a new shrine adjacent to ancient Sainte-Marie, he felt, would emphasize the Jesuits' storied past, permitting the new sanctuary to bask in its reflected glory as the most ancient European ruin in Ontario. Greater proximity would also allow him subtly to ratchet up the pressure to acquire and excavate the Sainte-Marie site.[54] By boldly claiming this prominent Midland hillside as unambiguously Catholic sacred space, Filion was serving notice that the martyrs (much like himself) would no longer be confined by linguistic, confessional, or cultural barriers.

But even as Father Filion gamely mustered the materials, money, and manpower to make his ambitious new shrine a reality, the search was on for the *real* Saint-Ignace. If Martyrs' Hill had not marked "that most sacred spot" where Brébeuf and Lalemant had died, then the genuine site was still somewhere out in the wilderness awaiting discovery. Taking up the challenge of finding this lost "altar of Canadian martyrdom"[55] was Alphonse Arpin, a Waubachene woodsman. Though unable to read or write, Arpin had the enviably intimate knowledge of the local topography that Father Jones had lacked. Arpin's illiteracy, moreover, proved more easily surmounted than Jones's debilitating girth. Arpin had family members read him those sections of the *Jesuit Relations* that described the comparative locations of seventeenth-century Wendat villages until he knew the information by heart. Having identified potential settlement sites on the basis of topographical indexes, he then verified his choices by measuring, in French "leagues," the distances between them, navigating deer paths pushing a bicycle wheel he had ingeniously equipped with a cyclometer. In this way, Arpin systematically narrowed down which of the ancient villages could be the elusive Saint-Ignace.[56]

Having arrived in this way at a single, preferred site, Arpin sought final proof: turning not to archaeological confirmation, but divine intervention. Earnestly imploring the martyrs for the miracles and wonders they had poured down on Waubachene, he prayed for a sign in the midst of the meadow he believed to be Saint-Ignace. Immediately, related Arpin, blazing fireballs erupted out of the ground. Astonished, the woodsman contacted Filion, who decided that the two should conduct another devotional experiment at the site. Consigning two unmarked holy cards to plain white envelopes, the pair sealed and buried them, one near where the fireballs had emerged from the earth, the other at a competing village site. When they returned a week later to disinter the cards, the one buried at Arpin's Saint-Ignace was mysteriously impregnated with reddish blotches, though its envelope remained unblemished. For Alphonse Arpin, this Houdini-like apparition of "blood" was yet another miracle, proving that he had indeed corrected Jones's earlier error and found the holy ground on which the martyrs had perished.

Arpin's efforts opened the door for Wilfred Jury's exhaustive excavation in 1952, which unearthed the archaeological remains of more than twenty longhouses. Obviously, there had been a Wendat village on the site. But was it the long-sought-after Saint-Ignace? Then, as now, the question evokes controversy. Once bitten, the Jesuits are, understandably, twice shy and chary of making a definitive determination. In private documents, if not public statements, caution abounds, with "Saint-Ignace II's" authenticity being periodically questioned in internal reports.

Nevertheless, hoping for the best, the Society acquired the tree-ringed meadow as a pilgrimage site. Weekly outdoor masses are said during the summer months and a few modest memorials have been erected, including a plaque honoring Arpin's efforts in identifying the site and rustic wood crosses at the supposed sites of Brébeuf and Lalemant's torture stakes.

But even as he witnessed, alongside Arpin, events he interpreted as miraculous, Filion's priority remained the establishment of the new Midland Shrine. Concerned lest devotion flag without a clear cultic center, he wanted to move quickly. The new director's vision for his twin-spired sanctuary owed much to his French Canadian heritage, as its stone facing and silver spires are highly reminiscent of a Quebecois parish church. Filion was also adamant that its wood-clad vaulted ceiling be made so as to resemble an overturned canoe. But otherwise, he could not be too picky regarding the thrown-together shoestring shrine. Though the final result was impressive, the church was fabricated on a dime, using donated materials, other institutions' postrenovation leftovers, and whatever relics could be salvaged of Martyrs' Hill. Because of their secondhand provenance, most of the donated windows and decorations had nothing whatsoever to do with the martyrs.[57] Indeed, at the shrine's 1926 dedication, only a few statues and Mother Nealis's iconic portrait identified the site as one honoring the newly

Pilgrims make the stations of the cross following the opening of the still-incomplete Midland Martyrs' Shrine Church in 1926. Situated on a hill, the new shrine overlooked the ruins of Sainte-Marie, the Jesuits' seventeenth-century headquarters.

(Archives of the Midland Martyrs' Shrine)

beatified martyrs. Over the years, as funds permitted, the shrine would commission new works to illustrate the martyrs' lives and deaths and convey more emphatically their institution's unique identity and purpose.

But even as Filion stood surveying the double-time construction frenetically under way on the lip of the hill, his gaze kept drifting to the still-neglected ruins of Sainte-Marie. In an attempt to "turn Catholic minds from the Waubaushene Shrine to the Old Fort," Filion held what he termed a "monster pilgrimage"[58] to Sainte-Marie the year before his sentinel church's eyes would open: holding an outdoor mass for thousands to celebrate the martyrs' triumphal beatification.

Under Filion, the Canadian cult of the martyrs had been taken in a decisive new direction. His bold relocation from Martyrs' Hill to Midland and his success in finally acquiring the Sainte-Marie site were important preliminary steps in expanding the cult's postwar appeal to anglophone, Protestant majority culture. The excavation of Sainte-Marie (and the historical recreation that would later come to tower over its reclaimed ruins) fired the imagination of Canadian Protestants. Many felt more at home there than they did in the ornate, incense-laden precincts of the shrine, amid side altars boasting bejeweled reliquaries and walls poignantly festooned with layers of abandoned crutches.[59] The ruins of Sainte-Marie, because of their strong historical interest, evocative incompleteness, and one-step remove from the "Catholic space" of the shrine, came to be a fertile site of Protestant encounter—whether historical, patriotic, or devotional—with "their" martyrs. The skeletal remains of the buildings where the martyrs had once lived were, for many Protestants, more evocative relics of their still-tangible presence.

Yet the Protestant-friendly atmosphere of Saint-Marie was a product not just of what it lacked, but also of what it had. For many years, Wilfred Jury, the site's chief archaeologist, was a daily fixture.. His bracing combination of deadpan humor, no-nonsense work ethic, and understated Protestantism permeated the open-air site like a teabag infusing a cup of hot water. His presence and authority served as a comforting signal to other Protestants of the seemliness of their developing interest in the martyrs as both historical figures and as models of a distinctively Canadian Christianity. Despite his Jesuit overlords and papal commendations,[60] Jury's oft-stated mission in excavating Sainte-Marie was a conspicuously secular one: to uncover new information about early Canada. Jury's deliberate and determined positioning of his contributions as scholarly and civic suggested that the historical importance of these seventeenth-century Jesuits as Canadian "pioneers" effectively trumped their specifically *Catholic* identity. Jury's lighthearted relationship with the Jesuits, on conspicuous public display through continuous banter, provided an attractive blueprint for interconfessional relations in the postwar period. Jury teasingly accused his Jesuit assistant of "deliberately prolonging . . . devotions to dodge the heavy work of digging," to which the priest retorted that he was attempting to intercede for Jury's Protestant soul, already flirting with eternal damnation.[61] This low-key stand-up routine demonstrated for confessionally mixed audiences that religious differences need not impede personal friendships and that even cherished beliefs and practices could easily withstand gentle teasing by those that do not share them.

God and Mammon

Mammon also contributed to the martyrs' confessional boundary cross-ing in the 1940s and 1950s. Particularly during the postwar boom, tourism to beautiful, historic Georgian Bay, with its Martyrs' Shrine and romantic ruins, was increasingly promoted by a range of business, civic, media, and transportation interests. In 1949, Father Lally, the shrine's then director, crowed that it had received the "unsolicited privilege" of being designated one of the top five tourist attractions in Ontario—alongside traditional favorites such as Niagara Falls and the Parliament Buildings in Ottawa—giving it pride of place in a fifteen-minute government-sponsored tourism short.[62] The martyrs' growing cross-confessional appeal as national "founding father" figures was increasingly exploited by Canadian communication and transportation monopolies such as the Canadian Broadcasting Corporation and the CNR.

The war years and postwar period were the heyday of the martyrs' evocation through the commercial radio drama. A bizarre conglomera-tion of education, entertainment, and advertisement, cemented together with a chummy, folksy gaiety that seems, in our own more ironic age, so forced as to be unintentionally comic, radio dramas were cheerfully didactic, informing Canadian listeners how they should regard Hu-ronia's historic sites. Like astute telemarketers, their writers anticipated listeners' possible objections to visiting Sainte-Marie and the Martyrs' Shrine, addressing them directly in their scripts. A 1939 radio play al-lows the auditor to eavesdrop on a conversation taking place in the car of "the Gordons," who "full of vim and health"[63] are discussing the itinerary of their Huronia vacation as they zoom along:

> *Ken:* Are we really going swimming in Georgian Bay this weekend, Dad?
> *Dad:* We are, my lad . . . then we'll . . . drop down into the lovely little town of Midland. From there we'll drive out about three miles to a place that I don't think you'll ever forget, the world-famous Martyrs' Shrine.
> *Mom:* You know, Dad, I've always wanted to see that.
> *Ken:* So have I, Mom. You know the story of the Jesuits' work among the Hurons has always had a great thrill for me! It's odd, but although all that happened 300 years ago, Dad, it seems ever so much more real and thrilling and closer than all the political stuff in Canadian history from 1840 on.

Dad: It's a tremendous story, that amazing account of the Jesuits' work in Huronia from 1615 to 1650. No matter what a person's religion is, he can't help feeling the thrill in what the faith and courage of the Jesuits accomplished among the Hurons. We'll try and visit a lot of the very places where the Canadian Martyrs lived and did their heroic work.[64]

The program's message to its listener is clear: by spending quality time together in this natural Arcadia, overflowing with opportunities for cultural and personal enrichment, the Gordons will strengthen their family bonds. Visiting the Martyrs' Shrine and Sainte-Marie will reinforce their identity as proud Canadians as they learn more about their nation's heroic history. As tourists, the Gordons are performing their patriotic duty by stimulating Canada's economy. Swell!

As this breezy radio drama demonstrates, the martyrs' cult profited not only from a bridging of confessional boundaries but from the virtual erasure of the always blurry line between pilgrimage and tourism. In emphasizing the historical, archaeological, and entertainment value of Sainte-Marie and the Martyrs' Shrine (and discreetly assuaging Protestant fears that they could somehow "catch" Catholicism there), the religious nature of the sites was often seriously underplayed. Even the *Martyrs' Shrine Message,* the shrine's own newsletter, often presented these sites as appropriate destinations as much for the curious novelty seeker or "the cottager seeking to fill in a rainy Saturday" as for the respectful patriot, hopeful invalid, or genuflecting devotee. The cult's simultaneous confessional broadening and political appropriation aided immeasurably in this blurring of sacred and profane.

This commercialization of the martyrs' cult was not generally seen by Jesuit leaders as a threat to its fundamental integrity. No Jesus-in-the-Temple histrionics took place against these contemporary "money changers." On the contrary, Canadian Jesuits generally interpreted the glare of media, government, and commercial interest in the martyrs as positive, if not providential: triumphantly recounting the latest public relations coups to one another in internal correspondence.[65] Father Thomas Lally, shrine director in the critical years 1928–1953, embodied this pro-publicity attitude when he apparently greeted a startled newspaper reporter with the ingenuous words: "I knew you would come. . . . I have been praying for the help you offer me."[66]

From the Jesuit perspective, the synergetic blending of tourism and pilgrimage could work in both directions. If pilgrimage could "descend" into "mere" tourism, then, by the same logic, a tourist's curiosity, properly nourished, might well flower into devout veneration. Popular culture, though often fatuous or puerile, may well disseminate the martyrs' message to the hearts of the otherwise unreachable. Shrine officials, in agreeing to host tourists hot off their Great Lakes cruise boat or the CNR's scenic whistle-stop tour, sought to subject these happy holidaymakers to an evangelical alchemy: turning the dross of their idle, snapshotting curiosity into the gold of true reverence.

The Midland Jesuits soon proved themselves masters of public relations, manifesting the same combination of ostentatious showmanship and pragmatism more often associated with the business world. Jesuit showmanship was most obvious in their high-profile slate of tercentenary events in 1949, notably Lord's ambitious pageant, and in their skillful manipulation of the media to promote these events. Indeed, the project's Jesuit publicists succeeded in creating such buzz around the production that the hype itself became the subject of media attention. Writing in the *Georgian Tourist*, Frederick Helson states:

> Newspaper men agree that never, certainly not in the last 20 years, have the "drums been beaten" as they were for the shrine pageant. Advance stories started nearly a year before the event. Feature story piled on picture spread as the event neared—and radio and magazines picked up the refrain. Not even the Canadian National Exhibition has been plugged as was this shrine pageant at Midland.[67]

Agents of the mass media, tourism, and transportation industries were thus seen by the Jesuits as potential allies rather than the corruptors of their own purely spiritual message. Although aware of commercialism's demeaning dangers, then, the Midland Jesuits preferred to think of it as affording them new, exciting avenues for widespread, popular, and bracingly modern evangelization.

Solomon and Sheba

The Jesuits' confidence in their ability to effect this subtle alchemy on their visitors was only reinforced by the site's often remarkable impact on even the most hard-bitten. Journalists, ad execs, tourist agents, and transportation officials exposed to Sainte-Marie or the Martyrs' Shrine sometimes became "true believers" in the martyrs, creating synergetic products that had both commercial and religious dimensions.

F. E. D. "Davey" McDowell is perhaps the best example of this phenomenon. A Protestant and resident of the Georgian Bay area, McDowell served as a senior executive in the CNR's regional public relations office for virtually his entire adult life. Inspired by the tumultuous religious history of the area in which he lived and worked, McDowell wrote a truly awful "historical romance," *The Champlain Road,* which unaccountably won the nation's top literary prize, the Governor General's award, in 1939, vaulting him to nationwide fame. McDowell's pulp fiction went through several printings and was eventually adapted into a successful Canadian Broadcasting Corporation radio play of the same name. It aired in 1949, during the tercentennial celebrations of the martyrdoms of Brébeuf, Lalemant, and Chabanel and the fiery destruction of Sainte-Marie.

The Champlain Road faithfully narrated the familiar, even stale tale: detailing once again the tragic collapse of the Jesuit missions and the demise of the "Huron" nation itself in the holocaust of fire and death that was 1649–1650. A *danse macabre* of bloodless caricatures, *Road* almost mechanically manipulates the faded devotional stereotypes of the mystical missionary, the manly donné, the pitiable "Huron" Christian, and the maniacal, bloodthirsty Iroquois. But McDowell's uninspired work did have one feature that set his retelling apart from any other, before or since: his willingness to pair his all-male cast of historical actors with an entirely fictional female character: the lissome and imperious Arakoua, a traditionalist Wendat "warrior-princess." Much like Gina Lollobrigida, the curvaceous 1950s pinup who played a Queen of Sheba bent solely on Solomon's seduction in the Yul Brynner film *Solomon and Sheba,* Arakoua springs full blown from the masculine id like a kind of obscene Athena. Arakoua's unrepentant "paganism" and her aristocratic status as a "Huron princess" give her—much like Lollobrigida in *Sheba*—glorious license to endlessly issue curt sexual demands to the slavering men surrounding her and to ask (presumably rhetorical) questions about her own desirability while parading about in little or nothing. In the radio play, mere seconds after having been saved from captivity among the Iroquois by the manly donné "Godfrey," she coos: "it is indeed Arakoua that you have saved. Look at me. Am I not wholly desirable in your eyes? Am I not beautiful?"[68] In creating Arakoua, McDowell had found a way to bring together two sets of stereotypes into an unwholesome embrace: the cinematic bombshell of the sexually insatiable, "untamed pagan" queen[69] and the tired types of hagiographic literature. McDowell's novel, then, is a kind of literary *poutine* in which the dry, stale fries of his turgid devotional prose are smothered in a rich, forgiving gravy of sex.[70]

McDowell's raunchy retelling of the martyrs' story, its luridness redeemed in the eyes of many by the prestigious honor it had received was, perhaps unsurprisingly, a resounding commercial success. As both a novel and radio drama, *Road* was often credited with arousing its readers' and listeners' desire to visit the hallowed shores of "Huronia," an urge that had both spiritual and commercial potentialities, as McDowell was doubtless aware. For the rest of his long career with the CNR, McDowell would expertly leverage the considerable power of the rail giant to serve the shrine and Sainte-Marie by providing the infrastructure, publicity, and prestige they needed to develop and thrive.

But this "cross-promotion" also worked in the other direction. Writing in his company rag, the *Canadian National Magazine*, McDowell used Sainte-Marie to reflect glory on the CNR:

> Three centuries of history converge at Fort Ste. Marie, and the age that knew the bark canoes of early French flotillas is taking form beside that symbol of modern transportation, the railway track and bridge. The Canadian National System has the distinction of being the only railway on the continent which runs over the outer defences of what was once a large pioneer fortress of the French regime.

Contrary to the biblical injunction, McDowell did serve two masters, God and Mammon, and consistently used each to benefit the other.

The increasingly cozy relationship the shrine was constructing with the forces of the world did prompt uneasiness in some Jesuit hearts and minds. Even as Father Daniel Lord or shrine ally "Davey" McDowell were forging a place for the martyrs within popular culture, drawing liberally on its stock themes, motifs, and characters (from communist übervillains to pagan femme fatales), other Jesuits worriedly portrayed contemporary movies, novels, and advertisements as siren-like temptations treacherously drawing unwary Catholics to wreck themselves on the rocky shoals of immorality. Jesuit John McHugh, writing in 1947, expressed his doleful opinion that the "appalling tragedy of social immorality is a disaster" that posed more deadly risks than even Communist Russia.[71] The *Martyrs' Shrine Message*, often complicit in the era's relaxation of the pilgrimage–tourism divide, also periodically roused itself to warn its Catholic readership of the need to guard their purity from the filth of a popular culture that "reeks of disrespect of the human body"[72] and encourages the "paganism of pleasure-seeking."[73] For the writers of these articles, the radio, movies, and advertising were not amoral forces to be harnessed and used for the shrine's advantage but powerful beacons of immorality to be resisted through abstention, prayer, and reparation. Indeed, some Catholic writers went so far as to compare the church's unequal struggle against the Goliath of popular sleaze as a contemporary form of martyrdom: "Our persecution may take on one of many forms. It may be an objectionable movie, a suggestive picture, soft music, a bad companion . . . or any of the other hundred human weakness."[74] Some Canadian Catholics thus felt continuously confronted by an unscrupulous, seductive, and "venomous"[75] media—a sexy, tempting, and voracious figure much like McDowell's Anakoua—even as Catholic senator Joe McCarthy terrorized both Fifth Avenue and Hollywood with his thundering oratory, sweeping condemnations, and anti-Communist blacklist.

Other critics quietly decried the rather worldly definitions of "success" and "failure" that were becoming normative in shrine circles during the postwar years. Some rebuked shrine officials for their shameless tendency to crow about the prestige of the dignitaries they had hosted, the masses of spectator congregants they had drawn, the number of glowing newspaper articles they had generated, and the amount of revenue they had taken in as proof positive that their campaign to put the martyrs at the forefront of Canadian consciousness was a roaring success. Obliquely warning the Jesuit leadership of Midland to assume a more becoming modesty, they asked, "What does it profit a man to gain the whole world if he loses his soul?"[76]

The Jesuits' harshest critic of their accommodation with "the World" would be one of their own. The passionate outbursts of Father Denis Hegarty, a blustery, black-haired Irish Jesuit who arrived at the shrine in 1949 would barely be kept in check by his vows of obedience to his religious superiors. An ardent opponent of postwar trends toward the commercialization and Protestantization of the martyrs' cult, Hegarty would be something of a crown of thorns for six successive shrine administrations uniformly determined to continue their cozy relations with the media and their ecumenical accommodation of other Christian confessions.

Repeatedly injured during his World War II service as a Catholic chaplain to the Canadian armed forces, Hegarty was assigned to the Martyrs' Shrine following his demobilization and prolonged convalescence.[77] On the advice of his doctors, he was ordered to assist Wilfred Jury in the excavation of Sainte-Marie, as it was hoped that the fresh air and exercise would aid in his rehabilitation and mitigate his ongoing tendency toward depression. Though initially ignorant of the martyrs, Hegarty quickly fell under their spell, becoming an ardent devotee and a champion of their celebration in unequivocally *Catholic* terms.

Both Hegarty's profound sense of identification with the martyrs and his desire to protect them from Protestantization likely stemmed from his scarring childhood experiences of interconfessional conflict in Ireland. Remembering the frightening and violent Protestant attacks endured by his Irish Catholic family prompted Hegarty to remark, "When one has to be ready to die for his faith, it becomes a very real thing, not just a catechism lesson."[78]

Hegarty's profound distrust of Protestants and his determination to defend what was for him the martyrs' inescapably *Catholic* identity virtually guaranteed that he would clash with Jury, Sainte-Marie's irascible Protestant excavator-in-chief. From the beginning of their relationship, the pair's repeated disagreements on seemingly trivial technical matters intimated the more profound and ongoing ideological battle between these two strong personalities. Because for Hegarty, the uncovering of these holy ruins could be nothing other than the most sacred of duties, Jury's tendency to articulate the dig's mission in educational, historical, or patriotic terms, however well meant, was not only misleading but impious.[79]

Perhaps to compensate for what he saw as the gradual and dangerous leaching of Catholic content from Sainte-Marie's self-presentation, Hegarty took it upon himself to give homilies to visitors, becoming infamous in Canadian Catholic circles for his powerful rhetorical evocation of the martyrs' torture and death. "Black Denis" Hegarty's presentation never varied, whether he was delivering it to his Jesuit superiors or to a group of impressionable elementary school students.[80] Standing beside a rough cross erected at Saint-Ignace II, on the site where his nemesis, Wilfred Jury, had uncovered a burnt wooden pole, an artifact that Hegarty interpreted as being Brébeuf's torture stake, the black-haired, black-browed, black-gowned priest would so graphically evoke the horrors the missionaries suffered that on more than one occasion children in his audience fainted or become physically ill.[81] The climax of Hegarty's homilies was always the same and, despite its repetition, it was always dramatic. Reaching into his cassock pocket, while thundering that martyrs' blood had sacralized this very spot,[82] Hegarty would hurl holy medals depicting the martyrs onto the soil at the base of Brébeuf's cross, transforming them into secondary relics.[83] Caught up in the drama Hegarty had created, his auditors would scramble for these treasures with all the alacrity of children harvesting the bounty of a burst piñata. Even Pedro Arrupe, the Jesuit's superior general or "Black Pope," was reduced by Hegarty's theatrics to combing through the muddy grass on his hands and knees to claim his own holy token.[84]

Hegarty's intense devotional performances at both excavation sites underlined his message of Catholic exclusivism. The priest's rhetorical reveling in the martyrs' torments and his transubstantiation of medals into relics were deliberately unaccommodating of non-Catholic sensibilities: indeed, they seemed designed as much to shock Protestants as to awe Catholics. Hegarty's unvarying determination to preach the same message regardless of the age, confession, or rank of his auditors is reminiscent of the outrage of eighteenth-century Franciscan missionaries to China who, offended by the suave accommodation of their Jesuit counterparts to the local culture, expressed their displeasure by bawling "Christ and him crucified!" Hegarty's vivid and disturbing homilies were his own cry of protest against what he perceived as the shrine's slouching toward adulteration and misguided accommodation.

Hegarty's most cherished dream was to find the graves of Brébeuf and Lalemant, which the *Jesuit Relations* claimed were somewhere on the site of Sainte-Marie. This would, essentially, be the search for an empty tomb because the two saints' charred and broken bodies had rested in this grave for for barely a month before being disinterred and boiled in lye so that their bones might accompany the Christian community in their desperate flight to Île-Saint-Joseph. But for Hegarty, the fact that the missionaries' flesh had apparently been reinterred in the original gravesite was more than enough to make it holy ground.[85] On August 16, 1954, after five years of searching and praying, his prayers

Jesuit Father General Pedro Arrupe kneels in prayer at the foot of the rough cross purportedly marking the site of Jean de Brébeuf's 1649 martyrdom, 1977. Looking on from behind the cross (wearing a hat and glasses) is Jesuit Father Denis Hegarty.

(Archives of the Midland Martyrs' Shrine)

joined with those of a cadre of Catholic children selected specifically for the purpose, Hegarty's dream was finally realized.[86] Overcome with emotion, Hegarty held the small lead plaque that would confirm his find. Originally affixed to Brébeuf's casket, it read, in old French "P. Jean de Brébeuf, brûsle par les Iroquois le 17 de mars l'an 1649."[87] Discovering Brébeuf's resting place was undoubtedly the highlight of

Hegarty's entire life, which had encompassed more than its fair share of religious strife, war, depression, injury, and illness.[88]

It was a success made all the sweeter by Jury's departure. Left alone to stride over his sacred sites unchallenged, Hegarty's discovery of Brébeuf's grave must have seemed nothing less than the divine vindication of his uncompromising, ultra-Catholic approach to interpreting the site. But despite the priest's lifelong savoring of this moment, any impression of victory over his longtime nemesis was illusory. Jury's departure was due less to Hegarty's triumph than the end of his contract.[89] In the years that followed, it would be Jury's interpretation of the contested archaeological site, rather than Hegarty's, that would rise again in wood and stone, immortalizing the Protestant archaeologist and linking his name forever with Sainte-Marie as "the house that Jury built."[90] By contrast, Hegarty's brief moment in the sun as the discoverer of Brébeuf's grave proved fleeting as both his beloved Society and his own body conspired to silence him. His health, never robust, was further compromised as he developed throat cancer and gradually became unable to speak, thus denying him what was perhaps his principal pleasure: the performance of his graphic homilies before crowds of onlookers at Sainte-Marie and Saint-Ignace II.[91]

Undeterred, Hegarty started to write, committing to paper his own archaeological interpretation of the ruins of Sainte-Marie, which contrasted Jury's in many respects. But, weary of Hegarty's tenacious questioning of Jury's authority and his findings, the shrine administration quashed publication of his work of twenty years, preventing the publication of *Band of Brothers*. During the final twenty-nine years of his life, "Black Denis"[92] was a resident of the Jesuit Province Infirmary, his achievements forgotten and perspectives dismissed by all but a few.

But Hegarty left one lasting legacy at the site, a victory for his contention that Sainte-Marie should always be primarily a pilgrimage site. In 1964, the Jesuits realized that recourse to the deep pockets of the provincial government was the only way to resurrect Sainte-Marie from her ashes. But they demanded, as a condition in what amounted to a transfer of power, that pilgrims wishing to pray at Brébeuf's grave be exempted from entrance fees to the historical recreation, and that pilgrims be able to access this site separately, via a specially constructed bridge. Though silenced by throat cancer, Hegarty had made his point loud and clear.

The Martyrs in the Classroom

If you ask any Canadian over the age of forty "Who is Jean de Brébeuf?" chances are that they will be able to tell you, particularly if they paid attention in school. Until relatively recently, even the largely Protestant students in Canada's public schools were taught about the martyrs as part of their baseline education in Canadian history. Beginning in the postwar period, the martyrs' story was seen as an indispensable part of a child's education, not simply because of the alleged importance of this episode in Canadian colonial history, but also because it arguably formed an invaluable addition to a child's patriotic consciousness, and aided in their moral development.

Education, even more than commercialization, was a key way in which the martyrs' cult was nationalized and "Protestantized" in postwar Canada. Though the mass media arguably reached more people (and certainly a broader cross-section demographically), it could not guarantee their undivided attention or unquestioning acceptance in the same way that classroom teaching did. Learning about the gruesome details of the martyrs' torture and death at aboriginal hands, moreover, had even more of an emotional impact at a young age, as children lacked the ability critically to evaluate the story and its sources or to consider the reasons why it was being recounted. To judge from the fact that the experience is often vividly remembered even decades later, encountering the martyrs in the Canadian classroom was often a fascinating, if disturbing, experience.

Institutionalizing the martyrs in the classroom normalized them by making them a familiar part of students' everyday experiences. The martyrs were present through the lurid etchings of their death agonies, portrayed in students' dog-eared textbooks. In Catholic schools, their portraits hung on the classroom walls in glory or in agony, or both. The martyrs bequeathed their individual names to schools. The silver letters that proudly spelled them out would be lost in the clouds of chalk dust rising like incense as the oversized erasers were pounded clean against the school's outer walls. The martyrs' story became indelibly associated with other school memories and sensations: the industrious, hopeful smell of freshly sharpened pencils; the agony of fingers pinched in a lift-top desk; the comforting, squashy familiarity of a homemade peanut-butter-and-jelly sandwich liberated from the depths of its warm brown-paper bag; the itch of a demure, pleated wool skirt and knee socks. Enshrined in the curriculum, which bequeathed on them a sort of indefinable, taken-for-granted-ness much like the "because it just is, that's why" of times tables, the martyrs were rediscovered afresh each year by a new cadre of students. Teachers and students, then, were pivotal in accelerating the confessional broadening of the martyrs' cult in the postwar years and ensuring its intergenerational transmission. The martyrs' inclusion under the aegis not only of parochial but of public school education signaled that they had truly emerged as nationalized figures beyond the chrysalis of Catholicism.

Although all students met the martyrs in the familiar spaces of their classrooms, some Ontario students "went to" the martyrs as well. Students of the greater Toronto area often visited Sainte-Marie on school field trips, both when it was an active archaeological dig, and later, when the site had been fully reconstructed. From their inception, interestingly, these field trips were more common in public than Catholic schools,[93] confirming the impression that Sainte-Marie was a venue uniquely suited to Protestant preferences. Voicing a mixture of satisfaction and concern, Jesuit Father Frederick Lynch wrote, in 1949:

> One is impressed with the eagerness with which non-Catholic students and their professors are coming in increased numbers each year, to Old Fort Ste. Marie, from all over Ontario. The Department of Education has even sent certain collegiate groups, calling it "An Experiment with Visual Canadian History." It would seem regrettable then if Jesuit pupils should leave our schools with less knowledge of this phase of our history than have the Protestant pupils.[94]

Popular fascination with the unfolding archaeological puzzle presented by Sainte-Marie drew children and their educators to the site, as did Wilfred Jury's measured public pronouncements regarding the site's educational and historical value for all Canadians. Educational trends that stressed the importance of experiential, authentic learning also facilitated this surge of interest.

Initially, however, Sainte-Marie's pedagogical programs were very uneven. By random chance, visiting school groups could either be exposed to Jury's understated civic-mindedness or to Hegarty's darkly baroque devotionalism. Some students were encouraged to handle flint arrowheads, tour test trenches, and ask questions about archaeology, while others would be left trembling, shocked and awed, in the wake of Hegarty's rhetorical juggernaut.

Following Sainte-Marie's reconstruction in 1968, the public school–Catholic school gap in visitation numbers widened even further. This may have reflected the fact that Sainte-Marie-among-the-Huron was now a purportedly secular, government-run institution, with the umbilical cord that had long attached it to its mother institution, the Martyrs' Shrine, having been cut. Nourished for decades by the Jesuits' blood, sweat, and tears, Sainte-Marie was able to be born only with the midwifery of deep-pocketed external agencies.

In the decades that followed, the shrine's daughter site would become more and more independent. Though initially strongly resembling its sole parent in its overall ethos, with the passing decades Sainte-Marie would increasingly come to challenge the shrine's traditional presentation of the deadly encounter between European Jesuits and native peoples in the mid-seventeenth century by striving to present a more balanced picture of the effects of contact on both groups. In Sainte-Marie's ethos, as well as its physical layout, then, Jury had the last word over Hegarty.

The Martyrs and Masculinity

Whether in the classroom or on site, the educational incarnation of the martyrs' cult was at once universal and pointedly masculine. Although all postwar schoolchildren were taught about these figures, their stories were often presented as being especially attractive to or relevant for boys and young men. "Because boys are won over by daring, charmed by manliness, our presentation of the lives of the Canadian Martyrs to them cannot fail to produce a good effect in their lives, and give more glory to God," reasoned Jesuit educator Father John O'Neill.[95] The textbooks, devotional works, newspaper articles, and homilies of this period agreed, taking it for granted that the stories of the martyrs' "thrilling heroism" and their desperate struggles against the elements and "hostile natives" would (or should) be of especial interest to boys and men. The martyrs, then, came to be presented as icons of masculinity at the same time that they became representatives of Canadian nationalism and as spiritual bulwarks against Communism. Though their virtues of courage and zealous faith remained the duty of *all*

Catholics, in practice these qualities were rendered in the shorthand of "manliness."

Representing the martyrs as icons of a hearty Canadian masculinity ("men are square here!"), devotional articles in the 1940s and 1950s increasingly focused on their physicality. While descriptions or depictions of martyrs are by their very nature somatic, as a key part of their story revolves around their endurance of suffering and death, this era witnessed a particularly intense preoccupation with the martyrs' corporeality. Descriptions of the eight missionaries focused less on their personal or spiritual qualities than on their masculine bodies: their "ropy muscles," "Herculean strength," "giant frame,"[96] or "upright stance."

Jean de Brébeuf was singled out for particularly intense somatization.[97] In the postwar literature describing him, from E. J. Pratt's epic poem *Brébeuf and His Brethren* to penny devotional pamphlets, Brébeuf is never simply a man: he is inevitably "a giant veteran and leader,"[98] "rock-like" and "massive." Radio plays in which he is featured invariably call for a "deep recitative."[99] Less physically imposing missionaries, such as Antoine Daniel or Gabriel Lalemant, who fit less obviously into this masculine mold, were made exemplars of the mental toughness and determination which "every boy," regardless of his phenotype, can cultivate. "Even in the weakness of Daniel, a boy recognizes that pluck which would be an asset to any football team," opined the *Martyrs' Shrine Message*.[100] Much was made of the martyrs' ability to bear heavy loads on portage, to thrive on little or no food or sleep, to endure the "rude shelter" of native peoples, to withstand the constant irritants of smoke and insects, to walk long miles in captivity, and, of course, to bear torture stoically. Such faithful fortitude had always been lauded as part of the rhetoric of martyrdom, but its purpose in the postwar period broadened. As well as exhibiting the martyrs' Christlike suffering, it highlighted their masculine comfort in the rugged outdoors. As Canadians strived to articulate their collective identity as a nation, many focused on the role of the country's physical terrain in shaping the distinctive character of its inhabitants. Forbidding, beautiful, treacherous, and—above all—northerly, Canada was a land that demanded much from those who would live there, schooling them in endurance, fortitude, and stoicism. The martyrs, as archetypal "Canadians" and as model men, were crowned in this era with stinging haloes of blackflies and given the calloused hands of *voyageurs*.

This pronounced postwar emphasis on the martyrs' physicality didn't mean that their psychological, spiritual, or emotional qualities went unrecognized or uncelebrated, but rather that these abstract qualities were themselves enrobed in fleshliness. The ardent faith of a Charles Garnier is made tangible in his "glowing eyes," "gentle smile," or "priestly gestures," as facial and physical attributes, stance, and gestures were made to serve as the sort of visible or outer casings or symbols for inner contents in a kind of somatic shorthand. Intangible qualities like honesty, openness, and fearlessness were embodied in Brébeuf's imagined "straightforward gaze." Like John Wayne, the martyrs' physical comportment, demeanor, and gestures were made to communicate their ethos, character, and strict morality, rather than their words. Ironically, given that historians value the martyrs and their Jesuit companions for their very "verbosity"—the sheer volume of the writing they left behind—postwar popular culture rendered the martyrs as laconic and physical as the heroes of "Westerns." In playing—like Father Filion—their own game of "martyrs and Indians" in the 1940s and 1950s, then, Canadians were taking their cues from wider popular culture.

The political situation also affected the masculinisation of the martyrs, and the calculated pitching of their cult so as to appeal to Canadian schoolboys. The martyrs' purported virtues of strength, endurance, determination, and mental toughness were the very qualities that educators sought to inculcate into the rising generation of anti-communist cold warriors. While female embodiment of these sterling values was never discounted, it was tacitly assumed that, in the face of the Communist threat, it would be men—strong, faithful, and courageous men, like the martyrs—who would be needed to oppose it. As articulated within and outside classroom walls in the 1940s and 1950s, then, the image and legacy of the martyrs sharpened and sensitized participants' perception of gender in much the same way that it both heightened their patriotism and dampened their confessional identification. The martyrs' cult became a venue for performing masculinity as well as telegraphing patriotism and uncompromising anti-communism.

The Dark Side of Ecumenicalism

Strange things were happening in the Martyrs' Shrine parking lot. Under a surly sky and bruised clouds, which intermittently emitted a chilling, needle-like rain, a bizarre and motley group had assembled, its numbers seemingly doubled by the reflections in the puddles dotting the black asphalt. Biretta-sporting, cassocked Jesuits; Mohawks in buckskin vests and full Plains-style warbonnets; camera-draped reporters in their drab suits and fedoras mingled, sharing small talk, of which there was always enough to go around; and umbrellas and cigarettes, which were always in short supply. Because of the inclement weather, the ritual script that had dictated the interaction of the three groups had been scrapped, and a mild, "hurry-up-and-wait" confusion reigned while a new agenda was hastily contrived.[101] Finally, the various teams were given their marching orders. The newspaper reporters were dispatched, in a cloud of tobacco and winking flashbulbs, to wait in a phalanx at the top of the steep stairs leading to the church's open double doors, where they joined Brébeuf and Lalemant, who also watched this "memorial reenactment" of their own final hours from their saints' niches high on the church's facade. It was hoped that the reporters' virtual bird's-eye view would ensure dramatic photos of the scene unfolding below, where, in a kind of religious square dance, each cassocked Jesuit was being sandwiched between two native "captors," who were instructed to seize him by the arms. The resulting three-man-wide processional snake of Jesuit "martyrs" flanked by Iroquois "warriors" was meant symbolically to reenact the capture and torture of Brébeuf and Lalemant some 300 years earlier.[102]

The original, more ambitious plan had been for these "captives" to be manhandled by the Iroquois along a three-mile woodland path, the very trail believed to have been traversed by the two missionaries from their capture at the Wendat village of Saint-Louis to Taenhatentaron/Saint-Ignace II, the site of their deaths. This "token bondage,"[103] as it was described in one contemporary newspaper account, was thus itself a mere token of the event as originally conceived. Gamely continuing the expurgated ritual, each "captive" priest, led by the example of Jesuit provincial John Swain, brought his hands together in the ancient attitude of prayer while simultaneously lowering his head, signifying his salutary resignation to God's will in the face of the symbolic violence of his "captors'" clutches. Lit up by the popping of press photographers' flashbulbs, the first threesome—the tall, slight, and pale Swain, flanked by two shorter, fantastically arrayed Mohawk chiefs—solemnly initiated the "curious procession's"[104] slow movement forward, the downcast heads of the Jesuits forcing their escorts to conduct them safely over the wet tarmac and up the steep steps into the waiting mouth of the church.

The tercentenary events held at Midland during the summer of 1949, which both commemorated and "replayed" the deaths of Brébeuf, Lalemant, Garnier, and Chabanel, display the range of ways in which native people in postwar Canada were excluded, manipulated, scripted, and ventriloquized by the martyrs' cult. Native participation in these memorial events could have provided an opportunity, through dialogue, for a deeper exploration of what had transpired in 1649. But the presence of aboriginal people was stage-managed in such a way as to affirm rather than challenge the new ecumenical orthodoxy, which presented saintly white "civilizers" senselessly killed by marauding and irrational "Indians."

In these commemorative events, the suitability of native responses was never left to their own initiative. Instead, aboriginal leaders were invited to perform roles that had been scripted (or, given their invariably nonverbal nature, "blocked") for them by a white religious elite that sought to exploit their visual presence, gestures, and song rather than to solicit their perspectives or interpretive input in any substantive or meaningful way.[105] There quite literally to be "seen and not heard," the roles assigned aboriginal peoples in these ritual dramas either sentenced them to replay "their ancestors'" bloody and shameful deeds, cast them as latter-day penitents for these horrid events, or both.

In their silencing of native participants during these commemorative events, the Jesuits found a powerful ally in the postwar press. Even after the chummy mixing that had preceded the ceremony, the ideal milieu for facilitating the rapport, newspaper reporters generally failed to interview (or, in many cases, even to identify) aboriginal participants in their articles on the event. Despite their prominent—nay, essential—role in the ritual, it does not appear to have crossed the collective mind of the assembled media to solicit native perceptions of the event. Moreover, in the dramatic photographs that accompany the often sensationalistic coverage (the *Ensign* newspaper headline shouted: "Iroquois Invade Midland!"[106]), Jesuit "captives" are invariably identified by name, and often title, whereas the native "captors" with whom they are shown interacting remain nameless.[107]

In a "symbolic reenactment" from 1949 of the captivity and martyrdom of Brébeuf, Lalemant, and Garnier, two Mohawk chiefs from Caughnawaga, identified as "Chief Flying Feather" and "Chief Bright Moon," manhandle Jesuit provincial John Swain up the steep steps to the church at Midland's Martyrs' Shrine.

(Archives of the Midland Martyrs' Shrine)

Rather, postwar reporters lazily slotted native peoples into premade rhetorical categories, preparing articles that were the journalistic equivalent of the new fad for easy at-home dining, TV dinners. Served with an appealing side dish of imagery, journalists' intellectually lazy coverage freeze-framed First Nations in the past. Two particularly popular interpretive flavors for representing native involvement in the tercentenary year of 1949 were the "descendants of their slayers" motif and the "triumph of Christianity" trope.

In the first, contemporary native people were rhetorically associated with the infamous deeds of their supposedly murderous ancestors. This is only to be expected, given that commemorative ceremonies often called on them to "reprise" their people's putative role as the martyrs' captors and killers. Journalist Mary Nowak's summary of native participation is typical: "In full regalia of feathers and buckskins, a group of Iroquois worshipped at the Midland Martyrs' Shrine, praising God whose missionary servants their ancestors had massacred in Huronia country 300 years ago."[108] This rhetoric manages to connote a sort of inherited biological taint, much like the mark of Cain, which brands the inherently violent Iroquois as eternal rebels against God's grace.

Journalists routinely added to this impression by profoundly distorting the Mohawks' centuries-long relationship with Christianity. Some audaciously presented their participation in the 1949 ceremony as a belated, albeit dramatic embrace of Christ and as erstwhile "proof" of the ultimate productivity of the martyrs' pious self-sacrifice on behalf of native peoples. But presenting the Iroquois as the recently redeemed enemies of God, won over through these cathartic commemorative rituals to the side of the light disingenuously ignored the historical depth of their engagement with the faith, including their successful eighteenth-century petition of the Vatican for a dispensation allowing the performance of mass in their own language. Nevertheless, postwar media coverage of the Iroquois's presence at tercentennial events insisted on celebrating their peaceful cooperation in the event as a critical "Christian Victory":[109] a final "triumph of the faith" the martyrs had sought to establish in old Huronia.

Although profoundly uninterested in native participants' words, which threatened to reveal individual, considered perceptions of contemporary events, reporters were enchanted by their image, particularly in supposedly "traditional" garb.[110] Indeed, reporters' reluctance to interview native people seems to have been in inverse proportion to their enthusiasm for photographing them. The silent presence of aboriginal peoples—in person and on film—facilitated the projection of the media's own fantasies upon them, trapping them in a romantic, precontact past. Images of aboriginal peoples were unapologetically used by both the media and devotional writers as "a vivid touch of colour"[111] in a striking throwback to the nineteenth century's "picturesque" aesthetic.

"Davey" McDowell's 1949 puff piece on Sainte-Marie for *Canadian National Magazine* is a classic example of what we might term "picturesque revival." Its cover photograph features contemporary native people in supposedly traditional dress posing alongside a CNR train halted on its trestle, which then cut over the ruins of Sainte-Marie's outer bulwarks. Much like a mid-nineteenth-century painting, the photo seeks to create a jarring juxtaposition by its purported contrast of "the past" and "the primitive" with CNR's gleaming state-of-the-art technology. Lest readers miss the point of the image, McDowell's article is quick to spell it out for them, casting these native peoples as living ghosts: "Their ceremonial dress gave a vivid touch of color to the past that was a part of Forte Sainte Marie, but there were memories not unmixed with a touch of tragedy. . . . In such a way did sunlight and shadow play upon Fort Ste. Marie over the void of three centuries." Imagery of native peoples in the 1940s (though now photographic rather than painterly) was, in true "picturesque" fashion, used to consign aboriginal peoples to a vanished past.

But in the summer's most hotly anticipated commemorative dramas, native people did not need to be so tightly controlled. For that matter, they need not even participate, having been replaced by whites. In *Salute to Canada*, the stock devotional roles of the murderous Iroquois traditionalists and the weak but devout "Huron" Christians were largely outsourced to white actors.

Sadly, this total replacement of natives by whites wasn't even that much of a leap. The Midland Jesuits had so tightly controlled aboriginal participation in its other commemorative rituals during the summer that Lord's jump to a formal theatrical script was simply the next logical step. Moreover, media coverage of these events had so strongly equated "nativeness" with costume—namely, the inauthentic and sometimes outlandish Plains gear unwittingly sported by many Iroquois participants—that the old aphorism of the "clothes making the man" seemed, in this era, particularly apt.[112] United in their desire to avoid genuinely engaging contemporary aboriginal perspectives, opinions, and ideas in any meaningful way, the postwar Jesuits and an unimaginative and complicit media reduced native identity to a prescriptive performance complete with a mandatory script and costume. These two signifiers made it easy for virtually anyone to "play Indian."[113]

In Lord's 1949 spectacular, virtually none of the native roles, even those of the many extras, seem to have been played by native people.[114] The absence of aboriginal participants on set gave Lord even more leeway to play out common fantasies of native people as sexy, vanished, and violent. Lord made "Cornflower," his native lead, a sensuous

"Indian princess" in a more decorous echo of McDowell's lascivious Arakoua. More profoundly, the entire structural conceit of his drama presupposes that the Wendat are a wholly vanished people. With the Huron having tragically fallen alongside Brébeuf, it is up to the contemporary Canadian schoolchildren to explain to the long-dead "Huron girl and boy" what has happened in the centuries since their deaths. The notion of the Wendat as a romantically doomed people wholly swept away in the torrent of 1649–1650 had its roots in devotional tropes of their national downfall as an amplified echo of the Jesuit martyrdoms. But the myth of total Wendat extinction also served as a convenient excuse not to consult the living community in matters vitally affecting them.

But it was in the figure of the Iroquois medicine man that Lord succeeded most effectively in uniting pop culture and devotional stereotypes of native peoples. Casting him as the adamantine foe of the martyrs reinforced popular perceptions of the contemporary Mohawk people as the renegade enemies of Christ, a reading that took on political force when this character was recast in contemporary terms as a "Red" agent within Canadian gates. Lord's time-traveling transformation was doubtless meant in strictly metaphorical terms, as he sought to exploit the multiple contemporary resonances of the word "red." As a dramatist and a priest, Lord sought to challenge the complacency of his audience by daring them to imagine themselves in a position where the same constancy and courage displayed by the martyrs would also be required of them. Lord was likely unaware that his rhetorical wordplay might impugn the recent wartime service of First Nations. Aboriginal Canadians had fought and died in World War II in record numbers, serving a nation that would deny them the right to vote until 1968, using the logic that treaty "privileges" were incompatible with democratic prerogatives. But by using the Iroquois as symbolic shorthand for the antidemocratic, anti-Christian forces that were popularly perceived to be menacing postwar Canada, Lord drew a magic circle delineating "us" so as to exclude native people from its charmed interior.

Although the postwar "Protestantization" of the martyrs' cult shows it at its most attractively dynamic and open, the inability of its leadership to engage in any meaningful way with native peoples clearly demonstrates the limits of this inclusivity. Aided and abetted by a media that lazily shoehorned native people into preconfigured rhetorical tropes, the Jesuits preferred simply to capitalize on the photogenic presence and gestural eloquence of native people than to solicit their perceptions of the events being commemorated in any meaningful way. Together, they created roles for native people that were so hollow that the substitution of native participants by white actors in Lord's scripted tercentennial drama seemed merely the next logical step.

Wendat Desecration

In 1947 and 1948, as the uncovering of Sainte-Marie's ancient ruins received national media coverage, another archaeological site was being excavated only a few miles away, near Perkinsfield, Ontario. Kenneth Kidd of the Royal Ontario Museum was in the process of systematically disinterring the remains of more than 680 seventeenth-century Wendat men, women, and children from the "ossuary" or mass grave in which they had been laid in 1636.

In his 1953 article describing his excavation at Ossossané,[115] Kidd bemoaned the increasing rarity of native ossuaries, noting, seemingly without irony, that "few had escaped detection and pillaging."[116] He stressed the scientific and historical value of the site, noting that Jean de Brébeuf himself had witnessed the original internment of these remains in 1636 , an event that had motivated the missionary to pen what remains today the most exhaustive description of the "Huron Feast of the Dead." In making this point, it is likely that Kidd sought to benefit from the intense public interest aroused by the contemporaneous archaeological exploration of early Jesuit sites, using it to justify his wholesale violation of a site sacred to the Wendat people without their consultation or their consent.[117] In defiance of Wendat custom, these ancient bones would be kept aboveground for scientific study until 1999.

The excavations at Sainte-Marie and Ossossané thus occurred in parallel and would have seemed similar to any contemporary observer, given their neat grids, painstaking test trenches, and carefully sifted dirt. And yet both the sites themselves and the remains uncovered at each were perceived and treated in remarkably different ways by their excavators.

Both sites had been places of protracted encounter between European Jesuits and the Wendat. Ossossané, one of the most important "Huron" settlements of the early seventeenth century, had been the home of Joseph Chihoatenhwa, a Wendat convert to Catholicism whose murder—likely the work of his own people—had been conveniently laid at the door of the Iroquois. Following Chihoatenhwa's martyr-like death, however, Catholicism flowered at what became known as "the Christian village."[118] Ossossané's unusually powerful Christian minority was infamous for disregarding their people's traditional emphasis on collective decision making in favor of strident insistence on mandatory conformation to Christian norms within its precincts.[119]

But despite Catholic ascendency, traditional burial patterns still held sway in the Ossossané of 1636. Prior to their reinterment, the bodies of all those who had died during the previous decade were disinterred, stripped of putrefying flesh, washed, feasted, mourned, and ceremonially reclothed. Although Brébeuf argued vociferously that baptized Catholics should be interred separately from their traditionalist kin, he was overruled and forced to witness the burial of some "fifteen or twenty" Wendat converts in the common mass grave.[120] Present not simply as an observer, then, but as a religious cocelebrant, Brébeuf chanted his own *De profundis* over the bodies of these Wendat Catholics. Ossossané, then, was a place of testy and often traumatic religious contact. It could best be described as a majority-traditionalist, minority-Christian Wendat community that accommodated a handful of Jesuit missionaries.

Sainte-Marie, by contrast, was founded in 1639 less as place of religious contact than as a place of respite, where weary priests, exhausted from their labors in far-flung missions, could rest and spiritually refresh themselves. And yet, though it was originally envisioned as a European enclave, Sainte-Marie attracted a sizable native contingent virtually from its inception. Though the native presence there waxed and waned, native numbers consistently dwarfed those of the French. At its apogee, French inhabitants numbered only sixty-eight men, including priests, donnés, soldiers, and laborers.

Wendat converts who breathed their last at Sainte-Marie were buried European style in individual graves and in a recumbent posture rather than the traditional Wendat fetal position, with its intimation of rebirth. Clutching rosaries in their skeletal hands, the dead awaited eternity alongside Jacques Douart, the young donné killed in 1648 during a flashpoint in the growing tension between traditionalist radicals and the Jesuits.[121]

Both Ossossané and Sainte-Marie, then, were places of religious commingling and conflict in which Europeans and Wendat, traditionalists and Catholics, together coexisted and clashed. But the complexity of each site's history was not reflected in archeologists' treatment of skeletal remains at each site. Though arguably of as much "scientific" interest as the Ossossané remains, Sainte-Marie's dead were studied in situ during the site's excavation, rather than being disinterred. Though separated by centuries of turbulent history and the unbridgeable reality of death, excavators at Sainte-Marie seem to have felt honor-bound to respect their Christian burial.[122] Gazing into the vacant eye sockets of these Catholic dead, excavators may have felt something akin to Jean de Brébeuf's own sense, in 1636, of memento mori: "Having opened the graves, they display before you all these Corpses, on the spot, and they leave them thus exposed long enough for the spectators to learn at their leisure, and once for all, what they will be some day."[123] But the presence of the same number of Christian remains at Ossossané did not prevent the site's professional pillaging. There, the powerful bonds of shared religious affiliation were abruptly snapped. The unfamiliar interment rituals of Wendat traditionalism and the "utter disorder and confusion in which the bones were found"[124] seems to have aided Ossossané's excavators in maintaining a wary emotional distance. Indeed, there is an almost comical refusal in Kidd's writing to acknowledge the true nature of what he is excavating, as can be seen by his preference for the oblique term "osteological material" to characterize the human remains that he was daily disentangling.

Plans for each site also differed considerably. Sainte-Marie's excavation was undertaken largely to provide the necessary information for the site's eventual restoration. Though there were nationalistic, educational, and commercial motivations involved, at base the Jesuit quest to resurrect their order's ancient headquarters was a religious one: the redemption of a holy site tragically sacrificed in the desperate circumstances of 1649. Ossossané, by contrast, was perceived merely as a scientific gold mine lacking any of the reverence normally accorded a cemetery or burial site. Though the excavation was justified partially by what it would reveal about the diet, lifestyle, and health of the "ancient Huron," it does not seem to have occurred to the Royal Ontario Museum that archaeologists should have consulted contemporary Wendat regarding this decision to so roughly wake their sleeping ancestors.

Moreover, no plans were ever made to reinter the bones following the conclusion of their study.

Comparing the concurrent excavations of Sainte-Marie and Ossossané reveals a now familiar story regarding the limits of imaginative identification in postwar Canada. In these years, Canadian Catholics and Protestants tentatively took the first steps into a brave new world of interconfessional consultation and cooperation with one another in shared educational, commercial, and archaeological ventures, which had as their primary goal to honor the martyrs, increasingly interpreted as being the common heritage of all Canadians. The broadening and "Protestantizing" of the martyrs' cult in the postwar period expanded Catholics' and Protestants' understanding and experience in a way that defied traditionally strict confessional lines for a nationalistically in-flected sense of shared Christian identity. The cult's broadening of the martyrs' appeal in ways that both deliberately and inadvertently ap-pealed to Protestants led to their rearticulation as nationalistic "heroes of Church and State" in English Canada from the 1940s through the 1960s, in both high culture and the unabashedly populist radio dramas as characteristic of the period as ladies' "motoring scarves." But this euphoric sense of a shared identity was by no means universal, as it was based not on the bedrock of common humanity but on the far more limited basis of a common religious orientation. This was a decidedly *Christian* ecumenicalism. Archaeologists' unwillingness to extend to non-Christians the same attitude of respect and imaginative sympathy highlights the strongly Christian assumptions that underlay their de-termination of whose space is sacred and whose remains inviolate.

The cult of the martyrs in postwar Canada became progressively more Anglicized and Protestantized, and Midland gradually gained more and more widespread acknowledgment as the Canadian cult's epicen-ter. For the first time, English-speaking Catholics, in a manner mirror-ing Father Filion's wresting of the local cult from francophone Catholic Waubachene to anglophone Protestant Midland, would challenge the French Canadian hierarchy for leadership of the martyrs' cult. In a sense, the Anglophone cult won the war without firing a shot. It had administered the coup de grâce to its French Canadian counterpart simply by coming into being. The martyrs had long been seen by the Quebecois as a particularly apt symbol of their own national fortunes: their provocative combination of apparent defeat transformed by faith into spiritual victory a fitting symbol of the defiance-even-in-defeat that was at the heart of Québec's distinctive brand of religio-political *messianisme* and its ultramontane self-presentation to its apostate French motherland, its suspicious English overlords, and its Vatican protectors. But the enthusiastic adoption of *"les martyrs de la Nouvelle France par les maudit anglais"*—not to mention the anglophones' puzzling courtship of *"les Protestants, calice tabarnacle"*[125]—immediately made the martyrs a less fitting symbol to express Québec's linguistic, confessional, and historical distinctiveness. Anglophone Canadians' wholehearted postwar embrace of the martyrs, then, virtually ensured the cult's long decay and eventual abandonment in Québec, even by many Jesuits there.

The unimaginative high-handedness with which native roles in the cult had been dictated—or in some cases preempted—by white actors would also, in time, find a response. Native people would not remain quiescent in the face of a cult that had so systematically excluded them, misrepresented their history and, through the mandatory assimilative onslaught of residential schools, forced its sometimes pernicious assumptions on their children. In the decades to come, Catholic and traditionalist native peoples in both Canada and the United States, particularly members of the nations historically connected to the martyrs, would begin systematically to challenge the traditional interpretations and imagery of the martyrs' cult and the wider assumptions on which it was based, to protest its often insensitive and inaccurate scripts for their participation in it, and to challenge its presentation of their literal and figurative ancestors. The anglophone "spatialization" of this cult in the late nineteenth and early twentieth centuries in both the United States and Canada would ensure that much of this often difficult process of confrontation and dialogue would take place at the Martyrs' Shrine in Midland and its American twin in Auriesville, New York, rather than in Québec.

5

Bones of Contention

THE DRIVING RAIN beat down on the heads of the thousands assembled by the outdoor altar.[1] Gusts of wind sent autumn leaves scurrying along the ground, slapped soaked tendrils of hair against drenched faces, and suddenly turned umbrellas inside out, exposing their fragile, radiating metal spines, like the delicate skeletons of sea urchins. Though it was only late September, it was cold. Noses were raw and reddened. Some eyes streamed as rain and wind-induced tears comingled. Even as they shivered, many pilgrims worried that the inclement weather would delay the historic ritual they had gathered at the Midland Martyrs' Shrine to witness. Billed as Brébeuf's long-anticipated "return home" ("a little the worse for wear,"[2] as one newspaper reporter waggishly remarked), the outdoor mass would transfer the left lobe of Jean de Brébeuf's skull[3] from the custody of the French Canadian Jesuits of Québec City into the keeping of their English Canadian counterparts at Midland.

Pilgrims' fears of cancellation proved baseless. As if on cue, the wind abated, the rain ceased, and the ceremony started on schedule and in full sun. Brébeuf's skull, in its gold-and-glass reliquary, was carried in procession on a crimson cushion borne by four Knights of Columbus in full regalia.[4] The elaborate gestures of donation and equally munificent words of grateful reception were performed as planned.

Père René Latourelle, an elderly Jesuit theologian and the author of a volume on Brébeuf,[5] represented the French Canadian donors of the demi-skull. His remarks reflected on the joy of what he called Brébeuf's "homecoming":

Here, in this region, Brébeuf arrived in 1626, becoming the first Catholic saint to set foot in Ontario. . . . *Here,* he preached the Gospel to the Hurons and the Neutral Nation. . . . *Here,* he pronounced his vow to accept martyrdom if God granted him that gift. . . . *Here* he suffered martyrdom with his companion, Gabriel Lalemant. *Here* he *was,* and *still is* fully at home.[6]

In their turn, the Midland Jesuits praised the generosity of their francophone counterparts and, in the one subtle dig of the event, thanked them for finally bringing to an end the shrine's long quest for a major relic of "the Father of the Faith in Ontario."[7] Provincial Eric Mclean expressed the hopes of many present in saying that this symbolic sharing of the bones of the man who for so long had meant so much to both linguistic communities would bind French and English more closely.

As the final notes of the last hymn faded into the September sunlight, there was a perilous wave of movement as hundreds of pilgrims spontaneously rushed forward toward the exposed reliquary. Even after order had been restored and more decorous queues established, some still-sodden pilgrims waited more than an hour to fix their gaze on the sightless eye sockets of Jean de Brébeuf.[8]

Human remains are the ultimate liminal objects, acting as a gateway between this life and the next, simultaneously affirming and denying the reality of death. Bones are often seen as the fulcrum of an individual's identity, affording those that view or handle them a sort of intimate communion with the deceased. Père André Metz expresses just this sense of embodied connection as, reverently caressing a portion of Brébeuf's hip bone, the major relic of his religious community, the Rouen Jesuits, he imagines the saint striding over a Canadian countryside he himself has never seen.[9] Full of a kind of spiritual magnetism, bones are the material medium through which the deceased may manifest their still considerable power. But bones can also be a terrifying symbol of absence and loss. Seeming to deny transcendence, they are a snuffed candle, a silenced voice. Simultaneously helpless and formidable, dead and alive, bones can kindle the spiritual presence of the deceased or remain perversely anonymous and disquietingly mute. In their naked vulnerability, they often generate powerful impulses to protect them from abuse, from despoliation.

Dry bones—of revered saints, of one's ancestors, of important historical figures—can, Ezekiel-like, inspire the formation and transformation of spiritual or social bodies politic. Although ostentatious reverence for human remains is most evident within Catholicism, with its ancient cult of saints' relics, attachment to the bones of one's ancestors or cultural heroes is common across religious and cultural traditions, and is particularly intense in native spiritualities. Collective action on behalf of bones can thus bring communities together to venerate and protect the beloved deceased. But it can also rip them apart. Precisely because of the powerful, disquieting emotions they unleash, human remains can easily become dangerous "bones of contention." Fostering disputes regarding custody, treatment, or "meaning," remains can thus fracture as well as unite the groups that seek to control them. Because bones' living advocates often view the deceased's identity as in some way continuous with their own, different ideological or spiritual commitments within the group can lead to jarringly discordant ideas about who the dead really were and to equally sharp disagreements about what they want from the living. Imaginatively enfleshed with the interpretations and identities of those who handle, kiss, view, or protect them, bones provide a concrete, emotional symbol that serves as the locus of collective identity.

Two translations that took place in the 1990s, the 1992 transfer of Brébeuf's severed skull from Québec City to Midland just described and the reverent reburial of 681 Wendat skeletons by their descendants in 1999, signaled important power shifts that profoundly affected the martyrs' cult. Exploring the fate of these various bones of contention and establishing why they were shuttled through space, passing from the possession of one group to another, will illuminate a number of critical cultural and religious sifts in late twentieth-century North American society.

Generally, translation denotes a shift in two groups' relative power, with the remains' receivers being in the ascendancy. Wendat success, by the end of the millennium, in shifting contemporary attitudes about the morality of scientific institutions continuing to cling to the ancient remains of native peoples over the protests of their descendants is an excellent example both of aboriginal people's growing political power and of the theory that the reception of relics indicates a waxing influence. But in other cases, translation can represent renunciation. The passion evoked by bones can wane as they cease to be a focal point for group identity. Even hard-won, formerly cherished relics can lose their status as other objects or ideas become more important signifiers of collective identity. In this case, relics are discarded and donated like so much outgrown clothing.

Is this what happened with the 1992 transfer of Brébeuf's skull by the Quebecois Jesuits? Was their donation of the left portion of Brébeuf's cranium really a magnanimous act of spiritual generosity? Or was it a covert renunciation: their last "onstage" gesture in a cult that they no longer saw as relevant to their collective identity, either as Jesuits or as Quebecois?

An Outgrown Cult

In search of answers, I visited the skull's Jesuit donors at their headquarters on the cobblestoned Rue Dauphine in Old Québec. Maison Dauphine is an imposing mid-nineteenth-century gray stone building, attached to a smaller church located just inside the ancient city walls.[10] Outside the complex that serves both as the Jesuits' residence and their outreach center for homeless and addicted youth, the clip-clop of horses' hooves and the cheerful jingling of their harnesses echo down the narrow street. Horse and carriage rides, a favorite activity of tourists visiting the historic old city, depart from the Porte Saint-Jean just a few feet away. The jauntiness of the bright ribbons and artificial flowers braided into the horses' manes and the tourists' childlike excitement stands in sharp contrast with the overcast day, gray stone, and bleak expressions of a small group of Goth teens who cluster, smoking, around Maison Dauphine's entranceway.

Nodding them a greeting, I enter and am immediately received by my host, Père Gilles Morisette, a tall, white-bearded Jesuit priest. Barely has he shaken my hand and dispensed the expected pleasantries before he launches into an account in rapid-fire French of the 1992 skull donation. I follow him, listening intently, as we navigate this Jesuit rabbit warren. The narrow darkness of the hallway is intermittently relieved by bright art-rehab paintings on its walls. Gesturing as he walks, Morisette describes the skull's renunciation as coinciding with a wholesale reorientation of his religious community in the early 1990s:

> As [our] community diminished, the provincial head of the Jesuits
> asked Michel Boisvert . . . a young Jesuit, to oversee a new orientation
> for Maison Dauphine. The old community certainly had not greatly
> promoted the devotion to the holy martyrs, even though they had half
> of Brébeuf's skull. When Boisvert started, the house became a place for
> street youth. I have the impression that Michel Boisvert called [the Je-
> suits at Midland] and offered the skull because it wasn't really doing
> anything here. . . . He must have thought to himself that it would be
> more useful in Midland. . . . They have a *real* sanctuary in Midland.[11]

Though Brébeuf's skull was the most significant and coveted of the
religious items translated during the community's reinvention of themselves, he went on, it was far from the only martyr-related item to be
jettisoned during this period. Virtually everything moveable, including
even Joseph Légaré's long-treasured *Souvenirs,* were also unceremoniously ditched, resulting in the apparent erasure of the martyrs' cult at
Rue Dauphine.[12]

This thorough house cleaning, however, left one huge exception.
Removing a large bundle of ancient, oversized, St. Peter–style keys
from a hook on the wall, Père Morisette unlocks the door separating
the Jesuit complex from its exquisite adjoining church. Moving through
the white-painted sacristy out into the sanctuary is like going back in
time. Because, as Père Morisette notes, "the chapel remained as is even
though the house was re-oriented," the building preserves, as if in
amber, the overheated emotional tenor of the martyrs' cult in Québec
in the period just after their 1930 canonization. The chapel features "les
Martyrs Canadiens" so extensively that the entire building is like a
massive walk-in reliquary. Around the railing of the choir loft runs the
golden legend, surrounded by blue fleur-de-lis: "O Saints Martyrs Canadiens, Priez pour Nous."[13] Lozenges of brightly colored light fall on
the dramatic, recumbent statues of Brébeuf and Jogues, which lie under each of the side altars,[14] eyes closed, hands clutching triumphal
martyrs' palms. Behind Brébeuf are the words of his own blood-scribbled
promise: "I make my vow never to turn from the grace of martyrdom if
it be offered me" appears in gold. On the ceiling, a fresco depicting a
cross exuding eight drops of blood, one for each martyr, is surrounded
by rampant red maple leaves and golden fleur-de-lis.[15]

It was to this historic church that Brébeuf's newly acquired half-
skull was ceremonially borne in 1925, in its open carriage, to the cheers

of assembled holiday throngs. Acknowledged in the pages of the *Martyrs' Shrine Messenger,* the *Pilgrim,* and other devotional publications as the third major site in North America dedicated to the martyrs, it was often cast, in vaguely St. Petersburg–like terms, as their "Winter Shrine,"[16] where devotees could visit the martyrs (in person, as it were) should the urge inconveniently overwhelm them during the long seasonal closure of Midland and Auriesville. But, Père Morisette hastily assures me, this era is long over, if, he provocatively suggests, it ever really began. Though the church attracts a modest number of visitors annually—generally tourists interested in religious art or seeking a quiet place to sit and rest their weary legs—Morisette is adamant their interest in the martyrs is tepid at best: "Long has the devotion been small. I have never come here to the church to answer any questions about the martyrs."

The apparent disinterest of casual visitors in the martyrs so ostentatiously honored in this jewel-like church is matched by the indifference of their hosts. For the contemporary Jesuits who live just feet from them, the church's antiquarian treasures, drenched in the pathos and piety of another era, have clearly lost their power to inspire. Though he politely points out items that may be of interest to me, his guest, Père Morisette is clearly bored by the statuettes and reliquaries he so dutifully shows me. As he guides me back through the sacristy door, he ruefully admits that, in all the years he has lived at Rue Dauphine, he has visited the church on only a handful of occasions. Yet though this "tourist site,"[17] as he disparagingly refers to it, remains the public face of Maison Dauphine, it is definitely not the beating heart of the contemporary Jesuit mission. That honor belongs to a small, interior "domestic chapel," the private worship space of the Jesuits and their adolescent clients. Windowless, simple, and dimly lit even in the day, it represents the complex's true inner sanctum. Dominated by a large, gaudy statue of Saint Jude, the patron saint of lost causes, the floor of the homely chapel is littered with cots and sleeping bags that accommodate, around the clock, the homeless teens who are the Jesuits' main pastoral focus. The fact that young drop-ins seeking safety and sleep are enshrined, quite literally, in the Jesuits' private sanctuary powerfully demonstrates the shift in emphasis from veneration of the ancient "nation-saints" of the 1920s and 1930s to frontline social service work, a shift marked, perhaps significantly, by the exodus of Brébeuf's bones. The translation of the saint's skull arguably freed these Quebecois Jesuits from the claustrophobic weight of their past, allowing them to embrace unencumbered a future-focused social agenda.

After showing me the church, Père Morisette led me through a series of Escher-like staircases to a dusty private parlor on the top floor of the Jesuits' residence. In this aerie we were joined by his young colleague, Père Roch Lapalme. In the formal interview that followed, both Jesuits, despite their generation or more between them, were equally adamant that Brébeuf and his brethren were in no way relevant to their contemporary identity or mission as Quebecois Jesuits. On the contrary, their evaluation of the martyrs' lives and deaths, though always polite, was trenchantly critical. Though Lapalme and Morisette acknowledged that the martyrs have loomed large in the Canadian history of their order, they presented these missionaries as the being the *antithesis* of their own beliefs and commitments as Jesuits in the twenty-first century. Though the martyrs' legacy continues to shape their collective identity, it is thus an identity forged in opposition.

Initially, both Jesuits blamed their shared estrangement from *les saints martyrs canadiens* on the temporal and theological chasm separating seventeenth- and twenty-first-century Québec. Given the ever-changing ethos of sanctity, Morisette suggests, the martyrs could not help but become irrelevant:

> What we call holiness—it is very circumstantial. It belongs to a certain era, to specific years. After that, it becomes almost irrelevant. Think of any saint . . . 50 or 100 years later, they're no longer relevant. . . . Once you leave that time frame, their lives no longer make sense. They don't witness to anything anymore.

Mainstream contemporary Catholicism, Lapalme opined, has largely repudiated its former emphasis on self-purification through suffering.

But as our conversation unfolded, it became increasingly clear that it was not simply the deep historical divide that made the martyrs problematic figures for these Quebecois Jesuits. Had that been the case, Morisette would have been unable to nominate the martyrs' virtual contemporaries as his personal heroes:

> I found it very interesting to read about the discovery of a new world, the intercultural relations. That is more admirable than being killed.

That spoke to me. We had admirable Jesuits. Such as Marquette. . . .
They lived in much the same way as those early martyrs but [their pur-
pose] was to open a new territory. There is something monumental
about them. Their human experience is very beautiful—to go to the
Amerindians and adapt to the culture. That is the missionary style that
makes sense to me. . . . They were adventurers rather than martyrs.
They are admirable, in my opinion, as long as they are alive. For me the
martyrdom is an excess, there was really no need.

Morisette's startling comments implicitly connect a missionary's purported stance toward other religions and his fate in a shared, dynamic
intercultural world. Both priests castigated the martyrs for failing to
share in their own values of religious openness and toleration, implying that the martyrs were bumblers whose insensitive missionization
techniques led to an entirely predictable retribution. Morisette is attracted by Marquette because in him he sees a reflection of his *own*
values of openness and survival, adaptation and spiritual growth.
Conversely, for him the martyrs symbolize religious intolerance and
cultural confrontation, values justly repudiated by their "excessive"
and "unnecessary" deaths. For Lapalme, too, these martyrdoms are not
a heroic spiritual apotheosis but a tragic and preventable "misunderstanding": the direct result of their failure to engage in the genuine religious dialogue long demanded by their native hosts. For both priests,
the violent deaths are an indictment less of the martyrs' native slayers
than of the martyrs' unwillingness to truly engage with the native societies that hosted them.

The two Jesuits' obvious allergy to religious imposition in the
seventeenth-century contact arena reflects the overall orientation of
contemporary Quebecois Jesuits, though this is an ironic reflection.
Even as the duo expressed admiration of Marquette's intercultural
openness, they themselves avoid evangelization of First Nations as a
matter of policy. Said Morisette:

When I first came to the Jesuits in 1962 or 1963, there were two young
Jesuits—and each went to reserves. Another Jesuit said that he would
like to go work in those communities. But when he talked to the provincial, he said no. It was a ministry that was absolutely not valorized.

Though there were practical reasons for this policy, including the language barrier between the francophone Society and the English-
speaking Mohawks of Kahnawake, for example,[18] its principle cause is

strong Jesuit concerns that continued attempts by the Catholic Church to shape native religious life are fundamentally paternalistic and lack respect for aboriginal people's religious sovereignty. Eschewing spiritual engagement with native populations seems to be the contemporary equivalent, for Lapalme and Morisette, of the religious give-and-take they so admire in actors like Marquette.

Despite their lack of connection with contemporary native groups, the Jesuit duo's critiques of the martyrs' cult echo those of many native Catholics. For example, both decry the apparent racism of Rome's saint selection process. Père Morisette suggested that the Vatican's failure to recognize that both French and aboriginal Catholics paid the ultimate price for their faith during the turbulent 1640s was a dreadful mistake that has understandably restricted the cult's appeal:

> There were many Christian Amerindians [who also died]. We should have done a massive canonization. Name one [Amerindian martyr], there were lots! There is absolutely no reason [that they shouldn't have been canonized]! They were Christians. They were in the same situations. It is clear that this is a great weakness of those events, not to signal this. In the church, it was always the Fathers and Sisters [that are canonized]. But it is never that simple in reality. . . . This [omission] has made the movement of the French Canadian martyrs very weak. It would be greatly different if it were a broader movement.[19]

By ignoring those native Christians who fell alongside the martyrs, Morisette argued, Rome had not only turned its back on these Catholic heroes but had reproduced the offensive stereotype of "good Frenchmen being killed by wicked savages" that he remembered as a staple of his elementary-school education in the 1950s.

Morisette and Lapalme agreed that Quebecois Jesuits' aversion to missionary work with aboriginal peoples has, over the past fifty years, been a critical difference in orientation between themselves and their anglophone Jesuit counterparts: "It was not in the spirit of [Quebecois] Jesuits to continue to invest in those areas. As you say, in English Canada, they've continued. The next generation [there] worked very hard. That was not the case here. . . . Missionization is no longer our principle purpose." Quebecois Jesuits' wholesale rejection of missionary work questions the very impulse toward converting native peoples, which was the martyrs' very raison d'être. For Morisette and Lapalme, the continuing missionization of First Nations by their anglophone colleagues is a distasteful exercise in religious paternalism that is grounded in old-fashioned colonial attitudes that stem from their continuing veneration of the martyrs. Quebecois Jesuits have themselves eschewed the evangelical for the pastoral. Their ministry for street youth allows them to serve those who seek *them* out, rather than attempting to impose their faith on an entire target demographic.

Père Lapalme, echoing the nineteenth-century arguments of Benjamin Sulte, suggested that the martyrs actively and selfishly sought violent death. He singled out Isaac Jogues for particular criticism, suggesting that his open-eyed decision to return repeatedly to the scene of his own earlier imprisonment and torture betrays an unseemly thirst for martyrdom:

> Jogues wanted it. . . . He was chasing after death. In the beginning of the Church, there was a current like that, [but] the Church said that this was not what was needed. When we are martyrs, it is not because we search for martyrdom. It is because we witness, we are witnesses till the end. It is not because I want to die. But, in the case of Jogues, it is a bit ambiguous. You know, he returns to France but it is like he wants to come back. His ideal was to die.

Lapalme's position reaffirms the orthodox "middle way" of martyrdom. Like the jettisoned policy of the American military on homosexuality, "don't ask, don't tell," this position mandates that Christians neither cravenly shirk from suffering nor selfishly place themselves in harm's way, deliberately seeking martyrdom. Lapalme thus openly questions whether Jogues, a canonized saint and revered member of his own religious order, can really be considered a genuine martyr.

Paul Ragueneau, writing in the seventeenth century, stressed the strong pastoral motivations of the missionaries' decision to remain as spiritual shepherds to their endangered flocks. But to this Lapalme and Morisette add their own stipulation: that this standing in solidarity must be accepted, if not initiated, by the community the missionary seeks to serve. To provide genuine spiritual solace during the group's time of trial, they argue, a missionary must be truly accepted by his community. When it is clear that this is the case, the duo's attitude becomes noticeably more sympathetic, even reverent. Lapalme affirmed that priests who remain in conflict-wracked areas should be admired for their commendable sense of religious duty rather than characterized as having a morbid death wish: "It continues to be a reality that

Jesuits are stationed in war zones. They could leave but they don't, and it is not because they want to die." Lapalme and Morisette's comments thus couple a stringent defense of their Society's voluntary spiritual service in dangerous circumstances to *willing* recipients of their ministrations with a forceful condemnation of the pursuit of martyrdom for its own selfish sake.

These two priests' perspectives have dramatic implications for the cult of the North American martyrs in its traditional Québec heartland. They unsentimentally unravel the traditional death-into-glory alchemy of martyrdom by insisting that the fate of some martyrs represents not a heavenly blessing but an all-too-human failure for which the martyrs themselves should be held largely responsible. Though the two do not go so far as to assert that the missionaries' slayers "did the right thing"—a position argued by some contemporary aboriginal traditionalists—it is clear that they place the primary blame for those deaths on the martyrs' cultural tone deafness, religious intransigence, or simple unwillingness to save themselves, thus avoiding the wholesale blaming of contemporary native people for a handful of ancient homicides that has long been one of the less attractive features of the martyrs' cult.

But as interesting as they are, these are the views of only two men. How representative are they of the perspectives of other Quebecois Jesuits and of the views of Catholics more generally across *la belle province?* Both Père Morisette and Père Lapalme presented their perspectives on the martyrs as the norm for their Jesuit peer group. But they also insisted that their attitudes reflected those of the broader Quebecois community, reflecting the unique cultural and religious shifts the province has undergone since the 1960s—shifts that have led Quebeckers to regard the martyrs, their former icons, with a far more jaundiced and critical eye than that of their anglophone Canadian counterparts. As a lifelong Catholic and a Jesuit since the early 1960s, Morisette in particular claimed a privileged vantage point on the fate of the martyrs' cult in Québec: "Well now, I am 70, and I have never known real devotion to the holy martyrs. . . . I have not [personally] known any Jesuit to proselytize on the martyrs." Pressed, he admitted to only one exception: Pere René Latourelle, the elderly Jesuit priest who played such a pivotal role in Brébeuf's 1992 translation. Both Lapalme and Morisette also stressed that the martyrs played no significant role in their religious formation as Jesuits, a statement that is all the more striking given that they went through the system decades apart.

The pair were also at pains to point out that their community's redirection of the waning energy and resources of a dying martyrs' cult into more socially oriented channels was not unique to Maison Dauphine. Similar incidents, they alleged, have taken place all over Québec in the last fifty years. Morisette recounted the stillbirth of a proposed shrine in honor of *les martyrs de la Nouvelle France* planned since the 1930s for Montreal.[20] Although ample funds existed to build the proposed church, he noted, construction did not proceed because "by the 1970s, no one was interested." The money was diverted to fund an elder-care facility named for martyr Jean de la Lande instead.

The Jesuits' failure to build the long-envisioned Montreal martyrs' sanctuary supports Père Morisette's contention that, among his fellow Quebecois Jesuits, their cult has long been on life support and that the 1992 translation of Jean de Brébeuf's skull to Midland was thus like an organ donation from an already dead patient. While the gift of the half-skull was politely couched in the language of fraternal surrender and accepted in that spirit by its recipients, there is every indication that this event represented, for the francophone Jesuits, the symbolic sloughing off of an increasingly ill-fitting skin. Their donation was a public repudiation of both the turgid triumphalism of clerico-nationalism and the cloying paternalism of "Indian missions."

As his final word on the subject of Quebecois Jesuits and the cult of the martyrs, Père Morisette recounted to me the death in the early 1960s of an elderly Jesuit priest, a lifelong devotee of the martyrs. While the priest was on his deathbed, a skeptical young Jesuit (in a striking echo of the words of Christ's tormenters to him on the cross) mockingly advised the dying man to pray to his beloved martyrs for recourse. But when he painfully gathered his breath to respond to his tormentor, the priest did not defend the martyrs' honor. Nor did he castigate his younger colleague for his lack of faith. Poignantly, he simply requested to be left alone to die in peace. Was this refusal to engage with his tormentor a tacit confession of the dying priest's own doubts in the martyrs' intervention? A bitter acknowledgment of his own inability to convince his peer of their spiritual power? It is unclear. But perhaps, with this unnamed priest, died the last believer that a vibrant Quebecois cult of the martyrs could survive the upheavals of Vatican II and *la révolution tranquille:* the rapid secularization of the province of Québec in the 1960s and 1970s.

The Martyrs and the Quiet Revolution

In the 1960s the apparatus of Bishop Bourget's Catholic shadow state, which had provided essential social services such as health care and education since the mid-nineteenth century, was systematically dismantled and its responsibilities taken over by Québec's provincial government.[21] But as profound as they were, these changes were dwarfed by the massive ideological shift underway. The Quiet Revolution was more than simply a structural reassignment of roles between the traditional power brokers of church and state. It also inaugurated a 180-degree shift in how ordinary Quebecois interpreted the church's role in their lives. Like medieval paintings of the Virgin Mary that picture her protectively sheltering miniature sinners under her long blue cloak, the Roman Catholic Church had long been affectionately regarded in Québec as the benevolent and powerful guardian of their collective identity, language, and culture. *La révolution tranquille,* however, recast the church's historical prominence along far more sinister lines: as the long reign of an insular, authoritarian patriarchy. Bitterly branding its Catholic past "le grand noirceur," or the "great darkness," this new interpretation painted saw the church as ultimately responsible for Québec's intellectual impoverishment and economic self-sabotage. Church policies previously accepted as necessary for the *survivance* of French Canadians' distinctive New World identity, such as the parochial orientation of Catholic education or the clergy's attempts to encourage large families were now seen as having delayed the advent of modernity, repressed women, and sandbagged Québec's economic development.

This new perspective led to a sometimes bitter, sometimes darkly playful attitude toward the church and its sacred objects on the part of ordinary Quebecois. For Père Morisette, the new security precautions introduced in churches during this era are particularly revealing of the new attitudes of his fellow Quebeckers. Referring to the serial thefts in the 1960s and 1970s of the heart of the recently canonized Montreal saint Brother André,[22] Morisette noted that Brébeuf's skull had to be

secured with a chain [so] no one could leave with it. There had to be
those precautions because there had been problems in Montreal with
students and Brother André. . . . It became a student challenge to steal
the heart of Brother André. . . . [One time] it took about a year before
[the heart] was returned. Well, you can see the mentality in Québec!

That students would be so bold as to repeatedly steal a relic from Montreal's famous Oratoire Saint-Joseph, apparently as a high-spirited lark,
epitomizes for Morisette the monumental shift in Québec's religious,
political, and cultural mentality during the Quiet Revolution. The act's
cheeky irreverence demonstrates how virtually overnight the church
went from being the respected and undisputed leader of most aspects of
community life to being vulnerable to subversive symbolic abuse.[23]

Morisette reminded me that these epochal shifts in Quebecois Catholics' relationship with the church took place largely in the absence of
its hierarchy. Its bishops were in Rome, fiddling with the theoretical
details of how the church should adapt to modernity, while Québec
figuratively burned. The mass grassroots movement thus preceded (and
in many ways superseded) the official, top-down reforms of Vatican II
in the province, which were too little, too late to have their intended
revitalizing effects. According to Morisette, this bloodless coup presented the returning leadership with a shocking fait accompli, forcing
them to adapt to a wholly altered religious landscape: "When they
came back, they could not recognize their surroundings. For example,
Cardinal Leger said that he did not recognize himself and could no longer be archbishop of Montréal—'I quit.' It was like that everywhere.
The bishops were traumatized."

Quebeckers' new, darker interpretation of their shared Catholic past
formulated during the Quiet Revolution led to plummeting levels of
participation in most ritual aspects of the faith, particularly mass atten-
dance. It also had huge implications for the cult of *les saints martyrs canadiens,* affecting both its popularity and its perceived relevance.[24] Viewed
from the perspective and with the priorities of *la Révolution,* the cult
seemed saturated with the blood and guilt of an earlier era, its preoccupations and ethos a kind of miniaturized *grand noirceur.*

The sidelining of devotion to the martyrs can also be seen as collateral damage in the Revolution's realignment of Quebecois collective
identity along linguistic rather than confessional lines. In rejecting the
church's traditional role as the guardian of their distinctive identity,

Quebeckers were not turning away from nationalism so much as re-
defining it in ways inhospitable to the continued vibrancy of the martyrs' cult. *La révolution tranquille* effectively replaced the messianic
clerico-nationalism of the nineteenth and early twentieth century with
a new, linguistically based nationalism.[25] No longer would Québec's
distinctiveness be perceived primarily as a matter of confessional difference. The French language, long pushed into a secondary, supportive
role in identity maintenance, would become the dominant indicator of
Québec's essential difference from the rest of Canada so quickly that,
for younger Canadians, it is difficult to imagine how it ever could have
been otherwise.

As linguistic identity gained the ascendency in Québec, the martyrs
effectively became victims of their own wild success outside the province. As early as the mid-nineteenth century the martyrs' cult, formerly
the exclusive prerogative of French Catholics, was adopted by anglophones. In postwar Canada, interest in the martyrs as the heroic forbearers of "Christianity and civilization" had allowed them to jump
confessional as well as linguistic lines, leading to the Protestantization
of this erstwhile Catholic cult. But even as these developments introduced the martyrs to new audiences, they simultaneously took a fatal
toll on the special sense of favored uniqueness the martyrs had long
given their original venerators, French Canadians. Religious figures
now favored by anglophones seemed inappropriate standard bearers
for the sense of predominantly linguistic distinctiveness that Quebeckers now wanted to express. Moreover, the martyrs' tired association
with the old clerico-nationalist notion of spiritual victory in apparent
defeat was increasingly out of step with Quebeckers' new and self-
conscious embrace of modernity, competition, and entrepreneurship.
However glazed with self-justification, the old themes of defeat and
demoralization were incompatible with Québec's new slogan: *Maitres
Chez Nous!* With this dramatic shift in sensibilities, René Lévesque replaced René Goupil in popular consciousness, and the martyrs were
pink-slipped.[26]

Thus, even if the cult of the martyrs in Québec had somehow miraculously escaped the tidal wave of secularism unleashed by *la révolution tranquille,* it would still have been at a considerable disadvantage in
competing with now entrenched anglophone articulations of the same
cult at Midland and Auriesville. Though anglophones' strong emphasis

on sacred space at Midland was simply the result of these relic-poor communities making the most of what they had, it now represented a considerable competitive advantage. By trumpeting "Saints lived here!" or inviting cross-bearing visitors to ascend the graphically named "Hill of Torture," these anglophone shrines encouraged encounter with the martyrs where they had lived and died, inviting venerators to approach their sacred geography through the age-old rubric of pilgrimage. Despite its longtime status as the leader of the martyrs' cult and the province's status as a sort of giant reliquary of martyrs' bones and historical "remains," Québec's inability to establish a vibrant central shrine in their honor has made devotion to and critique of the martyrs in this Canadian province much more nebulous and diffuse. Without a central site at which to perform either veneration or protest, the martyrs simply slipped from the everyday consciousness of many Quebeckers.

Je Me Souviens

But devotion to the martyrs does linger among the fading and the rising generations of Québec. There is the faith and fidelity of an elderly contingent of Hospitalière nuns, the spiritual descendants of Catherine de Saint-Augustin. At the Hôtel-Dieu in Québec City they continue zealously to guard against all comers the remaining right lobe of Brébeuf's skull. The sisters' jealous commitment to the ongoing custody of these remains and their oft-voiced fears that the Jesuits might return for the second half as well is in sharp contrast with the indifference of Pères Lapalme and Morisette.[27] These nuns, who measure their own custody of this relic in centuries, rather than decades, were clearly miffed that their order's 1925 donation had been so lightly discarded after a mere sixty years, eying askance the decision to pass on their *cadeau précieux* to "those Canadians" at Midland. Some sisters expressed apparently genuine confusion as to why the anglophone Jesuits would even want the relic, betraying the degree to which they see Jean de Brébeuf as meaningful primarily within a *Quebecois* frame of reference, despite the fact that for the last eighty years he has been a saint of the universal Catholic Church. Uncloistered since Vatican II, these Hospitalières sometimes jauntily combine their traditional veneration of *les martyrs* with sly, pop-culture references to the linguistic nationalism of post–*révolution tranquille* Québec. Soeur Claire Gagnon, asked why the martyrs were still so popular among her order, winkingly appropriated the slogan of Pepsi's famous 1970s Québec campaign, exclaiming, "Ici, chez nous, c'est Brébeuf!"[28]

These unabashedly populist "chez nous" sentiments resonate strongly in some perhaps unexpected quarters. Soeur Gagnon's repackaging of her enduring reverence for Brébeuf in phrases deliberately culled from the calculated commercialism of Pepsi intimates something of the new "hipness" that these early figures of Québec history have in the eyes of some young sovereigntists. At several generational removes from the raw emotion and knee-jerk anti-Catholicism of the Quiet Revolution, nationalist Quebecois youth are finding in the rubble of their discarded past some serviceable heroes and heroines of the once and future New France.

Along with these bright spots of undiminished fervor and renewed interest, there remains the not inconsequential material legacy of the martyrs' cult in Québec. More than in any other part of North America, the province of Québec boasts numerous churches, schools, and streets named for the martyrs and a wealth of statues, buildings, and institutions constructed in their honor. Even on the facade of l'Assemblée Nationale, the provincial parliament, Brébeuf's likeness is enthroned, like those of other Quebecois heroes, in his own niche. Sculpted with his arm arduously holding aloft a large cross, the expression of the biretta-sporting Brébeuf is alert, purposeful, and energetic, his lips slightly parted, as if praying aloud.

Yet Père Morisette explicitly discouraged me from reading too much into these still imposing external surfaces. He himself interprets them as simply the residue of one more era in the multilayered historical geography of Québec, like flotsam left behind by some long-receded tide of the sea of faith. Like more recently christened streets named for separatist heroes, such remnants are, in his view, simply invocations of the past rather than living monuments to some still vital ideal: "There is a parish dedicated to the holy martyrs here in Québec, but they never do anything for the martyrs. . . . There are street names in Québec that carry the names of the holy martyrs, [but] they are no better than the Boulevard Hammel or Bourassa."[29]

Francophone actors have always played a guiding role in the articulation and development of this New World cult. From the time of Brébeuf, when the urgent, passionate language of martyrdom betokened the Jesuits' attempts to understand their own inability successfully to plant the Gospel message in New World soil, to the cult's framing by Ragueneau and Catherine de Saint-Augustin, to the romantic rediscovery of the Jesuits' story in the nineteenth century and its reinterpretation in historiography and art, to their passionate participation in the epic drive for canonization, francophone figures have led the way. But at the dawn of the twenty-first century, the once buzzing cult of *les martyrs de la Nouvelle France* in Québec became something of a hollow shell. Like an abandoned wasps' nest, the impression of size and vitality one gleans from its impressive exterior is quickly belied by the emptiness and silence within. Brébeuf's 1992 "homecoming" to Midland thus represented a watershed event in the history of the martyrs' cult in North America because it arguably formalized the voluntary ritual abdication of the Quebecois Jesuits from the leadership of the cult they had long dominated.

Feast of the Dead

The long, hot wait for the delayed arrival of the Royal Ontario Museum truck had ratcheted up the native assembly's sense of anticipation to an almost unbearable degree. At the site of ancient Ossossané,[30] beside the yawning, sandy pit, the flags of each of the four assembled Wendat nations, from Kansas, Oklahoma, Michigan, and Québec, hung limply on their poles. As the long minutes ticked interminably by and the direction and depth of the pines' soft shadows gradually lengthened with the shifting sun, longing, tension, and suspense all mounted as the emotional atmosphere came to mirror the sweltering breathlessness of the August afternoon. The patience demanded of them, however, only sharpened some participants' sense of communion with their long disinterred ancestors, whom many perceived as being equally eager to consummate their long-delayed reunion with their living kin.

The truck's tardy arrival prompted, first tentatively, then insistently, the chanting of a hypnotic Wendat *Requiem*. Francis Gros-Louis of Virginia described how he felt as his anticipation finally gave way to the powerful, paradoxical emotions of reunion:

My eyes blurred from the salty tears running slowly down my cheeks. My hands trembled in anticipation of what I was about to do and my heart pounded as the realization of what I was about to participate in overwhelmed me. As the eerie funeral chant of the Huron people, "hi, hi, hi, hi, hi, hi, hi, hi, hi," rippled softly through the roadside stand of stately pines I recall a mixed emotion of great sadness and yet extreme happiness as I bent to pick up one of the 300 cardboard file boxes containing the human remains of over 550 of my Huron Indian ancestors and carried them to what hopefully will be their final resting place.[31]

Each box was individually carried under a human welcoming arch formed of elders holding aloft eagle feathers. Then it was "smudged" or purified with the smoke of the four sacred herbs—cedar, tobacco, sage, and sweetgrass—before being presented to the oldest participant present, ninety-year-old Madeleine Gros-Louis of Québec. Resplendent in a 200-year-old embroidered moose-hide collar, the nonagenarian symbol of Wendat matriarchy, protected by a canopy to shield her from the sun's fierce rays, ceremonially touched each cardboard container before the remains were amassed at the lip of the pit for the final leg of their long journey home.[32]

The gathered Wendat were aided in their sacred task by delegations of other First Nations: Cree and Anishinabe, the contemporary residents of Huronia, and Métis, including several direct descendants of Louis Riel, the famous Canadian freedom fighter. Most significant, in the eyes of many, was an Iroquois delegation.[33] The tenderness and care with which a young Mohawk father and his five-year-old son carried the bones of their people's onetime enemies seemed to many particularly touching and meaningful. Georges Sioui, a Wendat scholar and poet from Wendake, Québec,[34] remembers: "everyone transported the boxes of bones together. I remember there was a sentiment of unity. . . . Those who were enemies before the ceremony, well, that disappeared that day."[35]

While the containers of remains were being carefully unloaded and ritually welcomed, those at the bottom of the deep, blue-shadowed pit were preparing the grave fittingly to receive the bones that many present called their "grandfathers"[36] or "brothers and sisters."[37] Elders lined the pit floor and walls with cedar boughs and beaver skins and prepared food and gifts to feed and greet the returning souls. Janith English, chief of the Kansas Wyandot and a retired psychiatric nurse, remembers that these intimate moments of preparation felt timeless, suspended. The breathless, haunting quality of the hot, late August afternoon led many to feel that they were being observed by and enfolded into the wordless presence of these ancient ones. The "mind-altering meditation of our singing,"[38] English recalls, resulted in a "mental, spiritual and emotional state somewhere between this life and the next,"[39] a state in which the barriers between participants, living and dead, simply fell away.

The pit prepared, the assembly then joined in ferrying box after box from the pit's high lip deep into its sandy mouth, carefully depositing on the carpet of fur and boughs the time-darkened skulls, long tibia, and eggshell crania of children. As the afternoon passed, the pile of amassed remains came to stand over six feet high.[40] Many participants expressed their fervent hope that their ancient kin, back in the sandy soil from which they had been taken more than fifty years previously, could "finally rest. After so many years, their souls will be at peace."[41]

Occurring seven years after the translation of Brébeuf's skull from Québec City to Midland in 1992, the Ossossané repatriation dwarfed, in both its size and its significance, the earlier event. Held exactly 350 years after their final defeat by the Iroquois confederacy had exiled Wendat survivors from their traditional homelands around Georgian Bay, this 1999 event brought together their widely dispersed descendants, reuniting them on their ancestral lands for the first time in hundreds of years.[42] Huron-Wendat and Wyandott, Anderdon and Wyandot, all came together to formally resuscitate the ancient Wendat confederacy and to bury the remains of their ancestors, unearthed from Ossossané's sandy soil by Kenneth Kidd in the late 1940s. The event, even as it marked the anniversary of the Wendat's social fragmentation, defeat, and dispersal in 1649, systematically reversed them through ritual. In their return to Wendake, the refounding of their ancient confederacy, and their successful reclaiming and reburial of their ancestors' remains, the Wendat quietly affirmed their continuing existence as a people and their determination to resist any further victimization.

All present at Ossossané saw the unearthing of their ancestors' bones and the long aboveground sojourn they had had to endure as a great wrong that had been perpetrated against their people, living and dead. Even in the euphoric aftermath of the repatriation, Francis Gros-Louis freely confessed that, despite the Wendat homecoming being "the highlight of my life," he was still angry, both with those who had disinterred these particular bones and with *all* those who continue to defend scientific institutions' right to retain aboriginal skeletal remains: "No person could ever have my one in a life time experience without feeling some level of resentment towards those who see no harm in the continuing practice of keeping the human remains of Indian people in body bags or file boxes in the name of research."[43] Gros-Louis bitterly blames Kidd's decision to disinter on a still-powerful archaeological double standard that only selectively respects the sanctity of human burial, emptying the tombs of some groups even as it leaves others inviolate:

> There is absolutely no justification for treating the human remains, burial offerings, and property of our Indian people any differently than those of any other society in the 1990s. What a wonderful way it would be to enter the new millennium, the year 2000, free from the blatant injustice to a proud people whose ancestors have been too long considered anything less than equal members of the human race.[44]

Much the same sense of galvanizing indignation had prompted Francis's distant relation, Michel Gros-Louis, to initiate his formal repatriation request to the Royal Ontario Museum in 1997. In 1974, as a young man, Gros-Louis had visited the Ossossané site with his father. Reading the historical marker that marked the site, the pair were shocked to learn that all of the human remains formerly sheltered in the pit had been unearthed and were still being studied at the Royal Ontario Museum.[45] Impulsively, Gros-Louis promised his father that he would reclaim and rebury the remains of his people in the very ground from which they had been rudely ripped. Mindful of his childhood vow, he opened negotiations with the Royal Ontario Museum that eventually resulted in the 681 skeletons' repatriation and reburial. Looking back over the long process, Michel Gros-Louis reflected:

> It has been my sacred duty. I believe my ancestors have asked me to give them rest, to give them peace. It is important to return our people to their rightful resting place. According to our customs, the most horrible crime is to open a grave. We won't have any future if we don't respect our past.[46]

Themselves like the dry bones of Ezekiel's vision, the different parts of this reconstituted Wendat body politic came from across North America, each independent nation bearing its own distinctive history of repeated displacement and survival. The "Wyandotte," "Anderdons," "Wyandot," and "Huron-Wendat" who gathered near Midland were a variegated group socially, culturally, linguistically and spiritually, though they were united in feeling "compelled to attend" despite the long distances and financial sacrifices this entailed for many. The voices that warmly greeted one another in Wendat, French, and English were accented with strong Quebecois, Midwestern, and Southern inflections. Despite Oklahoma participant Jim Bland's drawled regret, "Ah wish Ah could speak Frah-nch,"[47] the bilingualism of many present ensured that communication was generally possible at this international family reunion.

Like its seventeenth-century counterpart, this contemporary Wendat Feast of the Dead combined social, spiritual, cultural, and political activities spanning several days, from preparatory, purifying sweat lodges to barbeques, activities that allowed the members of this long-estranged native family to get to know one another and to communicate something of their long and largely separate histories to an intrigued and sympathetic public and media. The Feast began with the ceremonial reentry of the renewed Wendat confederacy into its ancient homeland. A large flotilla of canoes made their way up the Wye River to land at Sainte-Marie, in the shadow of the Martyrs' Shrine, although the unfamiliarity of some with the preferred transportation of their ancestors meant that not all participants arrived dry.[48]

But the reinterment ceremony was indubitably the ritual heart of the gathering. On the eve of the third millennium, shadowed by the shattering events commemorated in that 350th anniversary year, its participants ceremonially constructed a bridge through time that brought together past and future, dispersal and reunion, living and the dead. As the Wendat descendants, bone by bone, returned the remains of their common ancestors to the Ossossané ossuary, they ritually undid Kidd's 1948 sacrilege, repeating the same time-hallowed ceremony that had witnessed here in 1636 by Jean de Brébeuf. This latter-day Feast was, in the words of many who attended it, a deeply cathartic experience, one that bound them together with the living members of other distant Wendat nations and fulfilled a debt of honor to the dead. But there was a shadow side to the unfolding of this profound ritual that went unmentioned in press coverage and scholarly studies alike, which presented the events of August 1999 as simply a feel-good story of aboriginal unity and hard-won triumph over the vicissitudes of their tragic seventeenth-century dispersal and the more recent theft of their ancestors' bones.[49]

When, in such accounts, the Ossossané skeletons are acknowledged as "bones of contention," the tug-of-war over them is misleadingly presented as having taken place between the Wendat and the Royal Ontario Museum, with the institution's relinquishment of the remains painted as portending a hopeful new era of respect for native rights.

Although this popular reading is undoubtedly satisfying, it is far from being the whole story. Like the photo negative of a much-loved family snapshot, which transforms the familiar, carefree, smiling faces into black-eyed, black-toothed strangers, recognizing the deep divisions that plagued the Ossossané repatriation of 1999 renders the event eerily unrecognizable. The Feast joyously affirmed Wendat survival and solidarity, it is true. But it also laid bare painful fault lines in the newly formed confederacy's collective identity. Like a subterranean river, these undercurrents of tension occasionally streamed to the surface, emerging abruptly into jarring conflicts that, to the distressed participants, seemed to come out of nowhere.

All present at the Ossossané pit participated in the same Feast, which by tacit agreement was modeled as closely as was practically possible on the ancient Wendat Feast of the Dead. And yet it would be equally true to say that there were as many ceremonies experienced that day as there were participants, and not simply because of the vagaries of individual perception. Small but important variations in the collective ritual were actually encouraged by its improvised, free-form, "organic"[50] nature. The Wendats' traditional eschewal of hierarchy and their high degree of respect for individual autonomy precluded the creation of a central, controlling authority to oversee and direct all ritual actions. In its absence, individual participants spontaneously made their own decisions about how best to proceed or hastily conferred with those around them. Thus, ceremonies within ceremonies began to emerge, as Christian prayers, gestures, and vocabulary unobtrusively flowered in the negative space of traditional ritual, unknown to many participants and against the explicit wishes of a few.

The Lord and the Rings

The Jesuit had arrived at Ossossané late. The Royal Ontario Museum truck had long since parked and begun to disgorge its precious cargo.

Wiping the sheen of sweat from his brow, the priest unobtrusively approached a group of Wendat women arranging boxes at the lip of the pit and asked whether he could help carry over some of those still remaining in the cargo hold. One woman replied that, although they had enough manpower for that task, he was more than welcome to bless each box as it arrived. Though the Jesuit had offered himself as simply another set of willing and anonymous hands, the elder, like a fairy godmother waving her wand, transformed him back into a priest. His ritual gestures would thus act as a Catholic counterpoint to the ceremonial greeting of the bones simultaneously being carried out by Madeleine Gros-Louis. As he sketched with fluid, linear movements of his hands the sign of the cross over each container, the Jesuit became something of a latter-day Brébeuf, who had intoned his own *De Profundis* by this very grave 363 years earlier. And yet, because of the bones' naked anonymity, *this* priest's mandate was far more comprehensive. Unable to distinguish Catholic from traditionalist femurs or to discern the beliefs that had once animated the empty skulls ranged in the boxes before him, the priest simply blessed *all* the remains in a move that some Wendat would see as lovingly inclusive and others would condemn as an unwelcome intrusion.

Meanwhile, in the dreamlike atmosphere at the bottom of the ossuary, Janith English, Eléonore Sioui, and another Wendat woman made their own preparations to receive the souls whose presence they felt gathering like storm clouds all around them. As she carefully laid out corn, berries, and handmade grave goods, English vividly recalls how her sense of time began to unwind and her personal identity seemed simultaneously to dissolve and expand:

> It could have been a thousand years in the past, or a thousand years in the present. There was a complete connection with the land, with the people, a oneness with the spirits of the past. . . . I could feel their presence. I was an onlooker, but I had the sense of thousands of other onlookers looking on too.[51]

United in their communion with the dead, the trio of female elders pledged their sisterly love for one another. From all corners of the new Wendat confederacy, they wanted their solemn promise of future friendship between their nations to be witnessed by the gathered ancestors:

> We made a solemn vow to be true sisters and to give our lives in service
> to our people. . . . Many prayers were said. . . . [We] shared the pipe and
> arranged the ashes to seal the prayers. Almost in unison, one woman
> observed: "there are so many souls here." The eldest said, "there are
> thousands of angels here.[52]

As the climax of their private ritual, English entrusted to her new sisters ancient grave goods from the 1636 interment to be included with their own gifts on the pit's decorated floor. These articles had been returned, along with the bones, by the lead negotiator for the Royal Ontario Museum, Mima Kapches. The most compelling of these artifacts were rings. These were Christian wedding rings that had originally belonged to seventeenth-century Wendat women who had been interred in the original ossuary of 1636.[53] Seeming to promise an intimate personal connection with their Wendat foremothers through the simple act of wearing what they had once worn, these ancient wedding rings were invested with an almost Tolkien-like power.

As each woman simultaneously slipped on one of the repatriated rings, dully glinting in the pit's blue shadows, English felt a powerful sense of communion with her Wendat Catholic ancestors. Herself a Wyandot traditionalist "who has also chosen Christianity," English shares the faith of her Lakota husband, who is a Methodist minister. Janith English had experienced this intense sense of connection to her Catholic roots before when donning the heavy silver crucifix she wears as part of her "traditional regalia" as a Wyandot chief, or when reading spidery manuscript accounts of her kin's long annual canoe pilgrimage to Detroit to fulfill their "Easter obligations."

But this intuited connection, experienced periodically in the past, seemed even more palpable and intense in the actual presence of these Ossossané Catholics. English felt powerfully affirmed in her own religious choices by what she perceived as their similar decision hundreds of years earlier. Like her, she explained, these men and women had perceived the fundamental compatibility of old and new religious ways and had done their best to honor both. Moved, English felt inspired to use what she termed "convert rings" as a central metaphor in her prayer, asking "that the faith that was evident in the acceptance of these rings might be accepted in thanks for the healing of the Wendat people."

English's evocation of the rings in her plea for the healing, unity, and spiritual renewal of the newly formed Wendat confederacy would prove deeply ironic, as the presence of these ancient artifacts had precisely the opposite effect. It was controversy over these rings that enabled the specter of spiritual division that had so haunted their Ossossané ancestors to return as an unwelcome guest at this new Feast. Because their ancestors' anonymous bones mutely refused to disclose their religious inclinations, the presence of what most agreed were unambiguously *Catholic* grave goods[54] took on a heightened and divisive significance. The rings, by making the invisible spiritual divisions that permeated the new Wendat confederacy tangible, thus threatened to drag their hard-won sense of unity and common purpose into undertows of confrontation and anger. Bitter controversy over these artifacts' meaning, wearing, and repatriation made heated debate over the Wendat's contemporary collective religious identity virtually unavoidable. This dispiriting debate only highlighted the different Wendat factions' ultimately irreconcilable evaluations of Christianity and its legacy.

The same rings that for English represented a comforting ratification of her own religious path were perceived by others present as the sinister talismans of a fundamentally malign faith that had brought only shattering change and suffering in its wake. Pleading with Quebecois elder Eléonore Sioui to remove the ring, a traditionalist Ojibwe elder argued:

> This [ring] was never meant to bring good luck to our people. . . . It isn't something you want to be wearing, it was brought into our culture to change us. . . . It was foreign, with the potential of harming our people. . . . It could change who we are without our consent. . . . There is a bad omen, bad luck coming from the ring.[55]

Indeed, the rings so enflamed emotions that, on two separate occasions, the female elders wearing them were allegedly accosted in an attempt to wrest them from their fingers "by force."[56] Having won the assembly's universal admiration for his important role in the ceremony, their assailant was just as globally condemned for what was perceived as a double transgression of the Wendat code of respect for elders and reverence for women. Their shared disapproval of this man's actions proved to be a rare, fleeting moment of unanimity between traditionalists and Christians.

Wendat Bones of Contention

In their clashes with each other, both Christians and traditionalists appealed to their own perceptions of the Wendat that were to inspire their competing visions of who Wendat people are now and who they should strive to become in the future.

For those at Ossossané who sought to forge an exclusively traditionalist model for contemporary and future Wendat collective identity (and native identity more broadly), the rings presented an unforeseen and deeply unwelcome complication. Some traditionalists, like the Ojibwe elder who had urged Eléonore Sioui to remove the ring, clearly accepted the Christian nature of these artifacts, though they characterized them as concretizing centuries of religious colonialism, thus casting a baleful spell over the entire gathering. But others, such as Michel Gros-Louis, questioned the Catholic provenance of the rings and boldly denied that any baptized Catholics had ever been interred at Ossossané. Such a claim, though of dubious validity, given historical evidence to the contrary, would bolster his argument that the 1999 repatriation should be exclusively traditionalist in its spiritual orientation.

Much like their seventeenth-century forbearers, some contemporary Wendat traditionalists see the advent of Roman Catholicism in Wendake as having been largely responsible for fostering the internal religious and political divisions that had led to their people's defeat and dispersal in 1649–1650. Perceiving Catholicism as a false consciousness that had led to the loss of their nationhood and ancestral lands, traditionalists thus discouraged the emergence of Catholic ritual elements at this contemporary Feast of the Dead and condemned those that did appear.

For English and other Christian participants in the Feast, however, the rings were definitive proof that Wendat Catholics were interred with their traditionalist kin in the original Ossossané pit. The presence of these native Catholic dead justified the "double blessing" of the remains by Madeleine Gros-Louis and the Jesuit priest. Though the Jesuit's involvement was an improvised, last-minute addition to the ritual, to English his presence perfectly reflected the religiously variegated nature of the original interment ceremony of 1636. Though it had followed traditionalist protocol, this ritual had also had Catholic embellishments, supplied by Jean de Brébeuf. Indeed, this Wynadot chief is quick to embrace the martyrs' mission and motivations for being among her peoples, which she sees as being rooted in their genuine love of their fellow human beings: "I do have a devotion to the martyrs. A great deal. I feel that their hearts were in the right place. Everyone says it was political, but there's more. I truly believe these were young men who had the right attitude: they wanted to spread a message of love."[57]

But English is profoundly conscious that her own positive evaluation and experience of the faith (and its ultimate compatibility with traditionalism) was far from universal at Ossossané. Many of her fellow participants at the Feast, she acknowledges, still bear as yet unhealed wounds from contact with Christian institutions, particularly its schools, wounds that have understandably made them deeply distrustful of the church and bitterly dismissive of its claims to moral authority or spiritual truth. For this reason, she discloses, some participants were upset that some of the Feast's preliminary activities were held on the grounds of the Martyrs' Shrine: "There were some who said to me: 'I will not go to the Martyrs' Shrine. I don't know how you can even go up that hill. I went to residential school.' For them it was still just too recent, too close."

But English clearly expects her own empathy to be returned. Questioned by some traditionalists for her decision to recite the Lord's Prayer in Wendat over the amassed bones in a preliminary ceremony at the Royal Ontario Museum, English unapologetically defends what she sees as her fundamental religious freedom to honor her ancestors in the manner she sees fit: "I would consider it a personal attack to the freedom of religion of the Wyandot Nation of Kansas . . . if there remained any question regarding the appropriateness of travelling thousands of miles after three and one half centuries to pray among our ancestors."[58]

The August 1999 Feast of the Dead was thus a bittersweet collective rite of passage that marked both a significant anniversary and a contemporary turning point in Wendat history. Brought together to reconstitute themselves as a living political and cultural body, the reanimated Wendat confederacy was united in its advocacy for its all-too-vulnerable ancestors. Together, they carefully reinterred the fragile remains with all the tenderness of a solicitous parent putting a sleeping child to bed. Many participants emerged from the burial pit empowered with a new confidence and determination. Some vowed to continue the work to reclaim other ancestral remains, still marooned in labs,

museums, and storage facilities across North America, while others
sought zealously to prevent the archeological unearthing of still-intact
ossuaries or to advance Wendat interests on a number of other fronts.
The sympathetic nature of mainstream media coverage of the event,
which generally coupled strong interest in the reburial ceremony with
condemnations of the 1947–1948 excavations, illustrates the wholesale
shift in the perception of native traditional culture and religion by nonnative Canadians between the 1940s and the 1990s.

But if the reburial had shown the Wendat the not inconsiderable
scope of their political power, increasing their confidence in their ability to effect meaningful change, it had also revealed disquieting disunity within Wendat ranks. Brought together by their desire to rescue
and to honor the dead, their time together had also forced them to acknowledge their deep religious divisions, which had led inexorably to
conflict over how the dead should be honored. As they once again left
Wendake, participants carried with them a sobering awareness that
these stark differences in their perspectives and identities, rooted in an
irreconcilable evaluation of the nature and ongoing effects of the native
people's pivotal encounter with Christianity, could not easily be resolved. But, though a painful one, this too was the legacy of their Ossossané ancestors.

History Lessons

The divisions so nakedly revealed in the controversy over Christian
artifacts, rituals, and institutions at the 1999 Feast are also readily
discernible in Wendat perspectives on the cult of the North American
martyrs. With many of the repatriation's events held in the shadow of
the Martyrs' Shrine spires, the Wendats' collective return to their ancient homelands also prompted the reengagement by many with what
had been a persistent and troubling theme in the Catholic educations of
their childhoods.

Georges Sioui vividly recalls his "first lesson in Canadian history,"
which he received as a six-year-old in the parochial elementary school
run by the Sisters of Perpetual Help on the Wendat reservation of Ancien Lorette, in Québec.[59] A prominent participant, along with his
mother Eléonore, in the Wendat repatriation, Sioui is a tall man with
a spare, lean frame. Gentle in his demeanor, Sioui is so soft-spoken as to

be at times barely audible, making it easy to imagine him as the shy schoolboy whose experiences he narrates.

Sioui clearly remembers the crisp fall day in 1954 when his teacher, a black-garbed mother superior, first introduced him to *les saints martyrs Canadiens*. Speaking with "a sincerity that sometimes had her close to tears,"[60] the nun succinctly presented the encounter between the doomed missionaries and the Wendat as the bequeathal of salvation and civilization on barbarians who had responded only with shocking ingratitude and bestial violence:

> Your ancestors . . . were savages with no knowledge of God. They were ignorant and cared nothing about their salvation. The king of France took pity on them and sent missionaries who tried to convert them, but your ancestors, the savages, killed those missionaries, who became the blessed Canadian martyrs. Now, thanks to God and His Church, you are civilized people. You must ask God's pardon every day for the sins of your ancestors, and thank Him for introducing you to the Catholic faith, for snatching you from the hands of the Devil who kept your ancestors in a life of idolatry, theft, lying, and cannibalism.[61]

The wimpled sister gestured with her pointer to an image of the martyrs in torment, hanging in its accustomed place of honor on the schoolroom's wall, below the blue and white fleur-de-lis of the Québec flag. Pausing, she allowed her students to observe their martyrs' tormented bodies before thundering: "Now get down on your knees, we're going to pray to the blessed Canadian martyrs!"[62]

Soundlessly, the native children aligned themselves, heads bowed, hands together, in neat rows beside their polished wooden desks. The two girls behind him, Sioui remembers, struggled to stifle their sobs. Yet, though he silently genuflected along with his classmates, Sioui's own boyish consciousness brimmed not with repentance or shame but with rebellion. Even as a six-year-old, he resented the nun's attempts to impose her own parochial interpretation of history on him and his Wendat classmates and was indignant at her distorted, disdainful portrait of their ancestors. Raised by traditionalist parents,[63] Sioui had long been exposed to a contrasting perspective on history, which kept him from obediently swallowing the bitter pill of self-hatred the nun had prescribed for him. And yet, when he told his parents about the upsetting lesson, they were philosophical. Georges must succeed in school, his father argued, so that one day he could use the tools afforded him by his Catholic education to "write some other history books": books that would contest this pernicious portrait of his ancestors.[64] And the memory of this hated history lesson *did* propel Sioui successfully through his completion of a doctorate in history at the prestigious Université Laval in Québec City. In fulfillment of his father's prophesy, he *has* written a number of works that sharply critique dominant historical interpretations of native–European encounters in colonial North America.

In 1989, Sioui took part in an Iroquois-Wendat delegation or "what we called an anti-pilgrimage" to the Midland Martyrs' Shrine and Sainte-Marie-among-the-Huron. There they sought a dialogue with the Jesuits regarding instances of historical distortions, or what Iroquois delegate Louis Hall bitterly described as "twistory,"[65] at these sites.

As a traditionalist Wendat, Sioui had considerable strategic value to the Iroquois delegation he had been invited to join. For the Midland Jesuits, Wendat Catholicity, typically conceived of as universal, enthusiastic, and uncritical, had long been the moat around their conceptual castle into which they sought to divert the rising tide of Iroquois criticism. According to Sioui, "every time [the Iroquois] tried to approach Sainte-Marie, they were told that, this is a *Huron* issue, we have never had a word of reproach from the Hurons, they are up here all the time on pilgrimage."[66] Sioui thus served as something of a human siege hammer against the intellectual defenses of Fortress Midland. His very presence met this tired Jesuit argument on its own dubious merits: demonstrating that not all Wendat *were* Catholics, nor were all Wendat satisfied with how these institutions had chosen to depict *both* native nations and their complex and bloody relationship.

Confronted by Sioui's self-presentation as a Wendat traditionalist, his Jesuit host immediately tried to strong-arm Sioui into once again embracing what the priest saw as his *true* religious heritage. Citing the Wendat's centuries-long association with the Catholic Church, his clerical interlocutor paradoxically cast Sioui's *traditionalism* as a rejection of his people's history and values: "Mr. Sioui, you are a Huron, and you are baptized . . . so you are Catholic. . . . Why haven't you taught the Christian religion to your child?" Although, unlike Sioui's black-gowned elementary school nemesis, the Jesuit was powerless to force the adult Sioui to his knees, the priest nevertheless did his best to shame the unrepentant Wendat intellectual into spiritual compliance.

Sioui quietly and politely restated his identity, defended his right to free religious choice, and powerfully affirmed his strong sense of solidarity with the Iroquois members of the joint delegation:

> I said sir, my Father (I always spoke like that to a priest because that is how I was taught), I teach my son the spirituality of my Wendat-Huron ancestors. That is his religion. It is our right to do this. . . . We are not in agreement with the way you have pulled us apart from our Iroquois kin. We have *all* suffered from being made into the "good Indians" and the "bad Indians." We [the Wendat] are tired of being seen as the good sheep who let themselves be shorn. . . . The Iroquois find it very lamentable and damaging to their reputation and their integrity as a people to continue to be described as an inadequate and irrational people.

For Sioui, the cult of the martyrs has not only negatively impacted the self-perception of countless native children by presenting them with a false and distorted view of their precontact spirituality and culture, it has also created a false and pernicious contrast between the Wendat and Iroquois confederacies. By characterizing the Wendat as the paschal Catholic victims of unscrupulous Iroquois predation, generations of nonnative historians and artists have been content to craft a simplistic, patronizing vision of the Wendat as passive, compliant, "good," and doomed. Since Paul Ragueneau, Sioui argues, Jesuit historiography has cast the Wendat, "seed-bed of the native Church," into something of an aboriginal "Greek chorus" to the central tragedy of the martyrs themselves, seeing in the fall of Huronia only a magnified reflection of the Jesuits' own suffering and sacrifice.

Moreover, Sioui argues, Jesuit attempts theologically to rationalize what he refers to as "the Wendat genocide" have gone largely unchallenged. Even secular historians have uncritically echoed Jesuit providentialism in suggesting that the Wendats' forced dispersal ultimately resulted in the wider promulgation of the Christian gospel, which they carried with them as they were thrown into the hurricane of change. For Sioui, such attempts to justify or to redeem his people's suffering for Christian ends are both grotesque and myopic.

Sioui's scholarship also boldly reassesses Iroquois motivations for engaging in escalated warfare during the 1640s, suggesting that they acted out of a sincere desire to save other native nations from the depredations of European imperialism. By forcibly incorporating fragmented and struggling peoples into their own body politic, Sioui reasons, the Iroquois were seeking to create a unified, pan-national force capable of contesting European dominance in northeastern North America. Rather than being vilified for their militancy, Sioui argues, the Iroquois of the mid-seventeenth century should be seen as the precursors of other pan-aboriginal movements, such as that of Pontiac, Tecumseh, and Handsome Lake, who also presciently anticipated the wide-scale loss of aboriginal land, power, and sovereignty and sought to check European aspirations with organized, multinational militant resistance.[67]

Sioui sees the cult of the martyrs, with its myopic focus on the fate of eight men, even as the existence of aboriginal nations hung in the balance, as being grossly disproportionate and self-serving. When his Jesuit interlocutor sought to confront him, like his history teacher of old, with the saintly sacrifice of the Canadian martyrs, Sioui countered: "There are five Canadian martyrs, right? Well, for each one of those five martyrs there is an entire nation of our Wendat confederacy that just disappeared. So why does nobody speak of them?"[68]

Who Killed Whom?

Sioui's claim that the magnetism of the martyrs' cult has distorted history and negatively influenced perceptions of native peoples (including their own self-perception) finds wide affirmation outside as well as within Wendat circles and among both traditionalists and native Catholics. His arguments resonate with particular force at Akwesasne–St. Regis, the Mohawk reservation that brings together a slice of southeastern Ontario, a sliver of southwestern Québec, and a chunk of northern New York State. The site of Iroquois settlement since at least the 1750s, the reserve has long been linked to the martyrs' cult through its tradition of pilgrimage to the Our Lady of Martyrs Shrine in Auriesville, New York, some 200 miles due south.

As suggested by its hyphenated name, Akwesasne–St. Regis is a divided community, literally and figuratively. The reservation straddles the Canada-U.S. border in recognition of the Mohawk people's prior claims to the land, which long predate the existence of either of these modern nation-states. Bisected by the international border, signs of division are everywhere on the reserve: in its two post offices, the Canadian only a scant mile from the American; in the speed limits, differently demarcated in kilometers and miles; in the street signs, which feature the Mohawk language on the Canadian side of the border and English on the American; and, of course, in the multiple flags flown. Alongside the Canadian maple leaf and the ubiquitous Stars and Stripes flies the defiant pennant of the Mohawk Warriors: a red and yellow sunburst featuring the profile of a warrior's head, complete with traditional spiked hairstyle and feathers.

Signs of ideological discord are less obvious but still discernible as flashy professional advertisements for the reserve's casino compete for the driver's attention with homelier signage that sternly reminds its reader that "gambling is not our traditional way." Invisible to all but those who live here are the less tangible barriers and boundaries caused by the reservation's contentious religious diversity, which often pit the reserve's historic, silver-steepled Catholic churches against its newer, more traditionally oriented community centers and the longhouse. Over the course of the last fifty years, Akwesasne–St. Regis has gradually evolved from a near homogeneous Catholic stronghold into a venue in which traditionalists and Catholics are, according to the estimates of both groups, roughly equal.[69] Despite this, both religious factions tend to perceive the other as dominant, hostile, and in the ascendancy.

Retired high-steel construction worker "Owen Reid,"[70] a lifelong resident of Akwesasne–St. Regis who speaks Mohawk as his first language, heartily seconds Sioui's sentiments that attention to the martyrs has eclipsed, if not denied, the reality of native people's suffering under centuries of colonialization. Though he is Mohawk and illiterate whereas Sioui is Wendat and possesses a doctoral degree, the two men's acerbic criticisms of the martyrs' cult still substantially overlap. Both contrast the mere handful of Jesuit martyrs with the staggering death toll endured by their own peoples since first contact with Europeans, though Reid references more recent incidents whereas Sioui bases his arguments on his professional historian's knowledge of the colonial period. Asked point-blank in Mohawk whether he considers the eight Jesuits to be "real martyrs," Reid, a baptized Catholic, leans forward in his chair, swallows, wrinkles his brow, and rhythmically taps his ever-present walking stick on the floor. Suddenly, he bursts out in a hoarse, rasping whisper: "Not in my eyes, no. In my mind, I don't believe in none of it. . . . Hey, who killed who, here? What's going on in this picture? Back then and still today they [the Catholic Church] like to point the finger."[71] It is perverse for the Catholic Church to continue to cast native people as the aggressors in its ongoing promotion of the martyrs' cult, Reid indignantly suggests to his Mohawk interviewer, given that it has utterly failed to take responsibility for its own exponentially more destructive, concerted, and long-standing assault on the minds and bodies of native children in its residential schools. Citing the high death tolls in these institutions, where children fell victim to malnutrition, tuberculosis, abuse, and neglect, Reid unhesitatingly casts such systemic treatment as premeditated murder, stating:

> Look how many kids they were killing just a couple hundred miles from here . . . and now [the Canadian government] paid off the native people just to say I'm sorry. . . . I can't believe some of the things that have happened. . . . I mean, I said, when I first heard it, I thought they were talking about the 1800s. It was like a slap in the face when I found out it was in 1955, 56. Our neighbours in Canada, they were still killing native people. They still had these schools that they put the kids in and were abusing them and killing them. . . . These kids that were being abused, how much hurt they were in, they watched a lot of their own brothers and sisters being murdered, being abused, being sexually abused . . . and they had to watch.

Set across the broad sweep of the centuries, Reid argues, it would thus be more accurate to characterize the Catholic Church, rather than his own Mohawk people, as the inhumane aggressor.

In making such arguments, both Reid and Sioui find affirmation from a perhaps unexpected quarter: "Sister Ursula Little." A nun and prominent member of the Kateri League, a native Catholic organization dedicated to promoting the inclusive accommodation of aboriginal peoples and their spiritual traditions within the church, Sister Ursula, like Reid, is originally from Akwesasne. Sister Kateri is a nationally sought-after facilitator of retreats and workshops and an opinionated and charismatic leader in native Catholic circles. Asked about her impressions of the contemporary cult of the North American martyrs, she flatly and unapologetically states that, as a Mohawk woman, she finds it "problematic": "I *don't* have a devotion to the martyrs. . . . There are feast days in the Church which we observe but I personally have a hard time with it. I am Mohawk, these are my people . . . so I don't identify with the martyrs."[72]

Little's personal disavowal of the martyrs, however, does not lead her, either openly or obliquely, to question the validity of their canonical status. Nor does she go as far as some Iroquois traditionalists, who argue that their people's right to religious and territorial self-defense justified their deadly aggression against the missionaries. Sister Ursula reluctantly accepts the church's sometimes heavy-handed imputation of Mohawk guilt in the martyrs' slaying. But this admission is tinged with weary impatience, like a child lying on the playground cement and saying "uncle": "We know what happened. We know what our people did. We feel bad about it. . . . But it is reality. It happened, as Mohawk people we're not proud of it. But it is over."

Though she shoulders the burden of ancestral guilt so indignantly shrugged off by Sioui and Reid, Sister Ursula does join them in suggesting that the reality of aboriginal suffering under colonialism needs to be better acknowledged in how the martyrs' story is told. The Auriesville shrine, she states, despite its siting "on Mohawk land," totally ignores the traumas her people endured there. The deadly smallpox epidemics that wracked the Mohawk body politic in the seventeenth and eighteenth centuries forced her people repeatedly to abandon their villages, even Ossernenon, in a fruitless attempt to outrun the malady.[73] Noting the strong emphasis that the shrine has traditionally placed on the holiness of its sacred soil, consecrated by the martyrs' blood, Sister Ursula argues:

> You need both sides . . . the two sides, not just the martyrs'. [The shrine] has to reflect more of the context, more about our people. This is Mohawk country, Kateri [Tekakwitha] country. It is also holy ground because our people died there, of smallpox, and some of our people were martyred too, but you don't hear about it. . . . The real miracle was that Kateri even survived. We know of lots that didn't. . . . We know that it is holy ground for both groups. But *our* people lived here.[74]

Much like traditionalists Reid and Sioui, then, Sister Ursula, a Catholic nun, overtly challenges the total preoccupation of the martyrs' cult with the demise of a handful of European missionaries at the expense of acknowledging, even tangentially, some of the deadly effects of contact on native peoples.

Marginalization and Martyrdom

For Owen Reid, leaving Catholicism seemed the best option. For much of his childhood and youth, Mohawk traditionalism was still very much

a marginal, underground movement, while Catholicism was so ubiquitous as to be well-nigh mandatory at Akwesasne–St. Regis. Reid suggests that lacking the freedom to choose his own beliefs bred within
him a false consciousness that gradually alienated him from his true
self and numbed his ability to experience authentic emotion:

> As a child, I had no choice, but inside I wasn't happy. But when I went
> back to my own culture it changed my life, my heart was happy. I
> didn't know how to be happy before that. I never had a heart. I was
> negative. When you are negative you don't have a heart.[75]

Having left the church only in his late adulthood, Reid is an admitted
neophyte in the spiritual ways of his ancestors. Despite his sense of fulfillment at having become a traditionalist, he says, he finds it hard to
fully escape the aegis of Catholicism. Ruefully, Reid admits that he is
still very vulnerable to the same sorts of shaming techniques used
against Sioui, which question the spiritual and moral validity of his
newly chosen religious path or cast him as a traitor to his people for
having forsaken the church. Reid confides: "I am just learning my culture, because I wasn't brought up with that . . . and sometimes, I am
ashamed who I am." What makes this experience all the worse, he
adds, is that his pangs of guilt and anxiety are not triggered just by memories of his Catholic past, or confrontations with overbearing clergy, but
result from his everyday treatment by fellow Mohawk, his Catholic
neighbors. Turning to his interviewer, he abruptly intones: "It is *our
own people* who are teaching me how to be ashamed of me."

But when one turns to Catholic residents of Akwesasne–St. Regis,
one finds much the same painful sense of hurt rejection. Catholics on
the reserve allege just as forcefully that it is *they* who are the primary
victims of their community's entrenched, often bitter religious divisions. Some feel that they are vulnerable to the ridicule and shunning
of traditionalists because of their stubborn commitment to a church
that is now increasingly marginal in the community life of the reservation it long dominated. As congregations' ranks on the reserve are now
constituted largely by the elderly, younger believers become particularly conspicuous targets for alleged ostracism and teasing. "Cecilia Pafford," a Mohawk Catholic in her early forties who has long been involved with the church's music program, talks about her experiences,
her usually ebullient face shadowed: "there's hatred against the Church.

We [Catholics] get picked on all the time. Longhouse people make fun of us."[76] Her eyes glazing, she says haltingly: "They shun me. They call me 'Saint Cecilia.'" Her mother, "Agnes," slips her hand into her daughter's, affirming: "It's true. She just doesn't belong."[77]

Her feelings of rejection and mockery at the hands of the traditionalists in her community have led Pafford strongly to identify with the North American martyrs, whose ancient suffering she sees herself and the whole contemporary church as symbolically sharing. Unlike Sister Ursula, whose Mohawk identity seems to preclude her identification with these European martyrs, Pafford sees them less in ethnic than in confessional terms as "Catholics killed by non-Catholics," a scenario that she sees as being equally or even more applicable today."[78] Speculating that the endemic religious tensions at Akwesasne will soon ripen into open violence, Cecilia darkly prophesies a "new age of martyrdom" just over the horizon. For her, the martyrs serve as important role models for the part she is convinced that she will be called on to play in the future:

> The Catholic Church is the foundation of this reservation. But with the whole Indian movement and rejection of Catholicism, they are trying to get rid of it. And Mohawk Catholics, they can't explain [their attachment to Catholicism] but they won't give it up. So we're going to end up with new martyrs. . . . The traditionalist rebellion is strong again. . . . They want to knock the church down, they're already starting. . . . They think that they can just criticize the priest, give him a hard time. . . . It's going to get violent . . . war is coming.

Although for many the events of the turbulent 1640s are so distant as to be almost unimaginable, Pafford sees the dynamics of religious division and mutual demonization as having cycled around remorselessly to recur again in the here and now. Her determination to hold to her faith in the face of openly expressed ridicule in the present and the violence she so clearly expects in the future have directly shaped how she understands and appropriates the lives and legacy of the North American martyrs.

The concept of martyrdom enshrines the idea that suffering or persecution confers upon an individual or a group a certain moral gravitas. It implies that victims are always morally superior to their persecutors. Though of course the targets of violence are not always moral exemplars (think of mass murderers executed by the state) nor are the perpetrators of violence always ethically repugnant (think of a rapist physically assaulted by his victim in a courtroom),[79] the logic of martyrdom nevertheless establishes a powerful equation between victimhood and moral superiority. In the popular imagination (if not the black and white of canon law), it has been the gory details of the martyrs' suffering that have been the key to their elevation, the solemn guarantor of their integrity, and the hallmark of their quiet defiance.[80] It has been this linking of injury with innocence and righteousness with woundedness that has arguably given the figure of the martyr its strange charisma and strong hold on public imagination and sympathy.[81]

At contemporary Akwesasne–St. Regis, as at the 1999 Wendat repatriation, religious divisions within native communities have shaped alternative, competing collective religious identities, which, despite their sharp differences, are often characterized by a similar sense of being misunderstood, rejected, or persecuted by "the other." Mohawk traditionalists and Mohawk Catholics alike present themselves as spiritual underdogs who are oppressed, shamed, or threatened by a religious rival who is always seen as superior in power and remorselessness.

Moreover, contemporary aboriginal critics, both Catholic and traditionalist, have quite appropriately advocated for a better historical contextualization of the martyrs' story, such that the sufferings of their own native nations—from disease, displacement, warfare, and forced Christianization—are prioritized over the scattered deaths of a handful of white missionaries. While their enumeration of various ways in which their peoples have suffered is certainly accurate, the question of "who killed who" is ultimately an attempt to fight fire with fire in a showdown of suffering that does not substantially shift the dialogue out of what are clearly Christian categories and assumptions.

That Cecilia Pafford, Janith English, or Sister Ursula Little would rhetorically don martyrs' robes is eminently logical, as martyrdom forms an important part of their conceptual "tool kit" as Christians. But what is both fascinating and poignant is that native traditionalists' self-presentation seems equally influenced by martyrdom's characteristic association of victimization with moral superiority. Even as native traditionalists kick against the pricks, defiantly contesting the deeply entrenched assumptions fostered by the martyrs' cult, their own self-presentation as the morally superior victims of white colonialism only reinforces the scaffolding of the martyrdom complex they themselves are seeking to rip down.[82] The apparently unconscious use of martyrdom tropes by those who have only with great difficulty distanced themselves from Christianity demonstrates that the concept of martyrdom continues to colonize even those who have repudiated its religious foundations. Martyrdom, then, is a sort of conceptual revenant surviving the death of Christianity in the lives of many native traditionalists.

The 1990s witnessed a number of pivotal moments in the martyrs' cult: moments marked by the movement of long-contested bones through space. Taken from the custody of one group into the safekeeping of another, these translations were just one manifestation of wider shifts in the relative power of the bones' donors and receptors. Though it was presented publicly as a munificent donation, a long-delayed response to the urgent request of their anglophone brothers, the Quebecois Jesuits' return "home-ward" of Brébeuf's half-skull was the logical ritual outcome of a series of watershed events that had occurred in Québec over the previous decades. *La révolution tranquille* had fundamentally transformed the ethos of Québec, particularly popular perceptions of the Catholic Church's long-dominant role in the province. Nor were its religious immune from these waves of galvanizing change. Between the 1960s and the 1990s, the Quebecois Jesuits would fundamentally reinvent themselves, rejecting the outmoded clerico-nationalism of the martyrs' cult for a Vatican II–inspired agenda of direct engagement with society's most vulnerable. In the process, they jettisoned once-treasured reminders of the cult they had long led.

At Ossossané, the triumphant repatriation of hundreds of Wendat skeletons that had long languished above ground marked an even more fundamental power shift. In the Kidd era, it did not even occurred to archeologists to consult with the living descendants of those whose tombs they planned to plunder. However, in their negotiations with the Royal Ontario Museum, despite the frustrating legal and procedural delays this often entailed, the Wendat were, in a sense, pushing against an open door. A wholly new sense of respectful sympathy for native autonomy and cultural sovereignty had taken hold in this and other institutions, making them only too willing to comply with repatriation requests.[83] The same mainstream Canadian press that, in the Cold War period, had been content to render native peoples "seen and not heard" now clamored to hear the stories of the long-estranged, long-dispersed Wendat nations who came back to Wendake to bury their ancient dead. Increasingly confident in their dealings with faceless, largely nonaboriginal institutions such as museums, courts, and the media, the 1999 repatriation also forced the newborn Wendat confederacy to reckon with their own all-too-evident Achilles' heel: powerful, pervasive religious divisions. As native groups sought to confront a cult that many see as having powerfully damaged their image and interests, their confidence and ambition would constantly be checked by the infuriating reality of their own internal spiritual dissension. This plurality of perspectives would be just as evident as native traditionalists and Catholics together confronted the material culture and imagery of the martyrs' twin shrines on both sides of the international border.

6

The Naked and the Dead

THE SMALL GROUP of Mohawk women hesitated on the threshold of Our Lady of Martyrs Shrine Museum in Auriesville, New York. Temporarily blinded, they waited for their eyes to adjust from the brilliant sunlight outside to the greenish, aquarium-like darkness of the building's interior. All around them they could hear the low, soothing murmur of voices as pilgrims and tourists alike scrutinized items in the glass cases or squinted at wall displays.

As her vision began to clear, one of the women, veteran elementary schoolteacher "Sarah Oldfield,"[1] found her attention drawn to a dramatic plaster diorama displayed in the center of the room, which depicted Isaac Jogues being tortured. His bearded face distorted in pain, the saint stood as if transfixed. Around him, half-naked Mohawk children were depicted in the process of worrying off his fingernails with their teeth. Horrified, the group of women stood and stared, themselves almost as still as the statues that had claimed their shocked attention. As the temporary spell began to break, Oldfield and her companions searched for an explanatory plaque that might help them better to understand the graphic display or a museum guide who could discuss it with them, but to no avail. Other visitors, some covertly, some with open curiosity, glanced at the violent diorama, then at the group of Mohawk women, and then quickly away.

Memories began to bubble to the surface of Oldfield's consciousness, and her stomach began to churn. She remembered the naked fear sometimes displayed by nonnative children when they met her at the powwows held nearby at Kahatsiohareke, the Mohawk linguistic and cultural center where she often volunteered.[2] She recalled their parents' embarrassed incomprehension of their children's evident unease: "I just don't understand why she is acting like this!" "I don't know where he is getting this from." She recollected the comment a Mohawk elder had made years earlier: "that Auriesville shrine, that's a shrine to hate." As her nausea and dizziness intensified, Oldfield ran through the museum doors back out into the summer sunlight.

The theology of martyrdom is incarnated, sometimes graphically, in the material culture of the martyrs' shrines on both sides of the border. At Auriesville and at Midland, the message of suffering and sanctity has been pressed home visually since the each of the twin sanctuaries were founded. Sparkling in stained glass, etched in marble, or formed from aging, crumbling plaster, the imagined bodies of the martyrs are memorialized: their flesh twisted in pain or wreathed with flames, eyes ecstatically upturned, hatchets or boiling water poised eternally above their waiting heads, frozen forever mid-descent. Like funhouse mirrors, the shrines multiply images of the martyrs' torment exponentially. Their torture is refracted endlessly in the shrines' churches, chapels, and oratories. It echoes throughout their lush, statue-filled grounds, through their museums, cafeterias, and gift shops.

These depictions of death are composed so as to turn the viewer's eye toward the centrally positioned martyrs as they stand, tethered to torture poles, or kneel, awaiting the coup de grâce. Often, the martyrs' heavenly reward is indicated by the comforting presence of palm-bearing angels or, more subtly, through the golden shafts of light that play approvingly over their tortured bodies.

And yet the martyrs are not alone in these pictures. On the contrary, the physicality of their native tormenters is often far more forcefully realized than the martyrs' typically ethereal presence. As they have been imagined by artists, the slayers' bodies brim with an active and vicious life. Invariably near naked, their lithe, muscular forms are inevitably of a dark or reddish hue. Caught mid-yell, mid-gesture, their faces clouded with anger, these native men's pulsating, arrested energy presents the greatest possible contrast to the martyrs' static attitudes of poised prayer and air of supernatural calm.[3] The dramatic contrasts between paleness and darkness, motionlessness and movement, re-

signed suffering and pitiless rage have only sharpened over the centuries, peaking in the very art executed to decorate their sanctuaries,
founded in the late nineteenth and early twentieth centuries.

Because these images incarnate the central message of the martyrs'
cult in such a powerful and provocative way, martyrdom art has long
been the fuse igniting impassioned native engagement with the martyrs' cult at each of these two venues. Imagery is thus central to any
discussion of how these two institutions have responded to aboriginal
critiques since the 1970s, both because the visual messages displayed
by the shrine have provoked more intense native reaction than any
other single element and because the response of each shrine to native
complaints have been in such stark contrast.

Over the last forty years, the Martyrs' Shrine in Midland, Ontario,
has gone to great lengths to transform those aspects of its martyrdom
art deemed insensitive or problematic by native peoples, even when
this has meant the jettisoning or ingenious disguise of previously iconic
pieces. At Our Lady of Martyrs Shrine in Auriesville, in contrast, the
issue of how the martyrs' suffering and deaths should be depicted continues to be intensely controversial, even as the sanctuary desperately
struggles to survive in the face of harsh economic realities and serious
administrative infighting.[4] For many who work and worship at Auriesville, martyrdom art is irreplaceable in its formidable ability vividly to
convey—at a psychological, spiritual, and somatic level—the lived immediacy of the martyrs' experience. Its proponents argue that it is only
by imaginatively placing oneself in the martyrs' place, a process facilitated through art, that the sheer audacity of their faith and courage
becomes apparent. To censor or downplay the violence of the martyrs'
fate in the name of political correctness, they argue, not only cravenly
robs these heroes of their hard-earned glory but also steals from the
viewer the invaluable moments of spiritual enlightenment that can
be achieved only through corporeal empathy and emotional catharsis.

"A Shrine to Hate"

Sarah Oldfield's flight from imagery that she felt presented her people
as being inherently and senselessly violent is far from a unique experience at the Auriesville shrine. Nor are such extreme reactions the
exclusive prerogative of traditionalist visitors. On the contrary, Mohawk

Catholic pilgrims report similar encounters, in which their previously buoyant sense of belonging at the shrine was punctured and deflated on the sharp edges of Auriesville's imagery. To the shock that characterized Oldfield's experience is thus added an intensely personal feeling of betrayal, as faithful Catholics, by their own church.

Much like Oldfield, Mohawk Catholic "Agnes Pafford" vividly recalls how the emotional tenor of her pilgrimage to Auriesville in the 1970s abruptly changed when she stumbled across a sculpted bas-relief that depicted a Mohawk man in the process of consuming a human arm. The sight dumbfounded her. If shrine officials were content to perceive and to present "us Mohawk as cannibals,"[5] then why had they invited her choir to come all the way from the Akwesasne–St. Regis reserve to sing there, she wondered. How could they remain unaware of how their gratuitous display of this artifact (itself wholly unrelated to the martyrs' story), would affect native visitors?

Responses to Auriesville's graphic imagery, whether positive or negative, seem to be amplified when they are encountered in the places that are purportedly sanctified by holy bloodshed. "Alice Duchene,"[6] a Mohawk language teacher and former nun, ruefully confesses that her own physical and emotional responses to "The Ravine" are so powerful that, despite several attempts, she has not yet been able to complete this short devotional walking circuit. "Sister Ursula Little" seconds Duchene's profound sense of alienation and horror at this site: "the Ravine *is* gruesome, it gives you the chills. . . . We all know what happened there, but do you have to dwell on that?"[7]

"The Ravine" has long been one of Auriesville's premiere attractions. Its evocative power, however, does not derive from its physical geography, which—though lovely—is unremarkable, consisting of a heavily treed gorge and sunken meadow, through which flows a small, twisting brook.[8] Rather, the site's emotional wallop stems from its spatial claims and the way in which its graphic signage and statuary have been artfully arranged so as to facilitate pilgrims' imaginative internalization of the story of René Goupil, the first of the Auriesville martyrs, at this, the purported site of his death and botched burial. Promoted by the shrine as a "vast reliquary"[9] containing Goupil's lost, holy bones, the entire site is presented as being mysteriously irradiated by the saint's hidden, holy presence.[10]

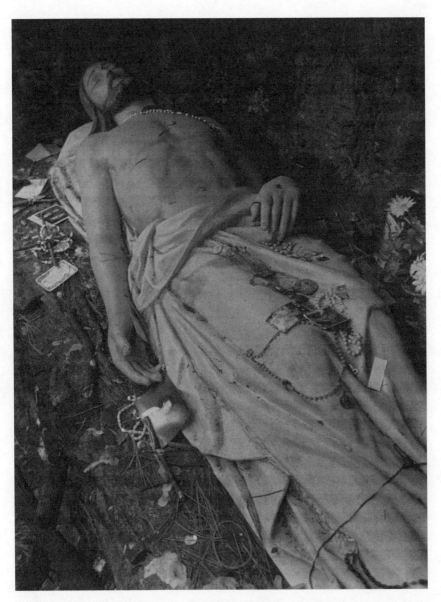

A statue of the dead Christ festooned with pilgrims' mementos lies in Auriesville's "Ravine." This woodland valley, purportedly the final resting place of the lost bones of the three "American martyrs," René Goupil, Isaac Jogues, and Jean de la Lande, often evokes strong emotions in visitors.

(Our Lady of Martyrs Shrine Archives, Auriesville, Brad Reynolds, photographer)

Treading the Ravine's sylvan path, one gradually descends into this valley of the shadow of death. Visitors read each of its scroll-shaped signs, which use Isaac Jogues's words to narrate the story of Goupil's martyrdom and its aftermath.[11] With each passing panel, the missionary's sense of danger and despair becomes more and more palpable. Each agonized litany conveys a sense of barely controlled hysteria, which the setting makes unsettlingly fresh and vivid. The signs recount the sudden, deadly attack on Goupil by "Indians with some evil design" and chronicle Jogues's fear of meeting the same fate. They candidly present Jogues's confessed inability to protect his friend or even to properly bury his body. Jogues's narration culminates in the valley's sunken dell, where the final scroll discloses his horrifying discovery of Goupil's gnawed remains, mutely rebuking Jogues from their resting place on the forest floor. There the voice abruptly ends. Coming to one's senses in the present-day clearing, one is surrounded by gloomy statues that memorialize Christ's death and entombment and forever freeze René Goupil defiantly making the sign of the cross above a kneeling native child: the very act hagiographers claim motivated his murder. Haunted by the words of the last sign, "the memory of these martyrs surrounds us everywhere: their holiness in the air, their voices murmuring in these trees and brooks, their blood upon the ground, their bones beneath the flowers,"[12] one's gaze searches almost involuntarily among the mossy tree roots and leaf-littered grass, irrationally expecting to meet a moldering skull's answering gaze.

Many who have visited the Ravine testify to its powerful ability to evoke emotional and physiological responses ranging from admiration to anger, from nausea to tears. For some, like the elderly male pilgrim who walked this North American Stations of the Cross just ahead of me, it was evidently a deeply affecting spiritual experience. As he carefully read each sign, the man was unable to check the empathic tears that ran openly down his face. For him, as for Molly Milot, an earnest, pale young Catholic from Oklahoma, the Ravine had evidently made the martyrs' passion "real" in a new and visceral way. Reflects Milot:

> It was a very special place down there. That really made it, for me. I definitely liked the Ravine the best. René Goupil was martyred in that place, and his body was buried somewhere in there, the signs talked about it. I had read about the martyrs in my history book, but when

Pilgrims solemnly regard a statue of René Goupil blessing a native child in the Ravine at Auriesville in the 1950s.

(Our Lady of Martyrs Shrine Archives, Auriesville)

you come over here and you see the Ravine, you say, wow, all of this . . . it is *really* real.[13]

But, confronted by each sign's repetitive recitation of native mendacity, Alice Duchene quickly became overwhelmed by anger and alienation:

When I walked down there I only went half way and had to turn back. I didn't like the way they highlighted the martyrs, with no consideration for the native people. . . . I turned away, but then I thought, "Why didn't they put our native people up? They were martyrs, they were murdered too. Why was it just these seven men?"[14]

Much like Sister Ursula Little, Duchene, a devout Roman Catholic, was offended that even on this, the Mohawks' ancestral land, her people were presented only as a terrifying, omnipresent threat to Christian safety. The fate of native martyrs, she noted, went wholly unmentioned: "I felt that it was a putdown. . . . There were native people that lived in that area that were killed, but that was never mentioned. There were lots of plaques, but after I read the first one I felt insulted, put down. Disconnected."

Sister Ursula Little strongly agrees that Auriesville's current visual message, at the Ravine and elsewhere, deliberately overlooks centuries of Mohawk fidelity to the Catholic Church in its ongoing choice to present her people as mere martyr slayers:[15]

They show that the martyrdoms were due to the Mohawk people at that time, but the way in which it is presented presently is very offensive. It is difficult to walk through and see how it is portrayed. More sensitivity is needed. . . . They are emphasizing the martyrdoms in the wrong way. . . . People need to know the rest of the story, otherwise we will always be "those bad Indians who slaughtered the missionaries."[16]

The shrine's lingering over the Good Friday of the martyrs' deaths, the nun argues, has distracted them from focusing on the joyous Easter Sunday that followed. The bitter divisiveness of its "us and them" narrative should be dropped in favor of a more positive message focusing on the spiritual revolution that the martyrs engendered in Mohawk hearts and minds. Asking "But all that [violence] is over. And what came of it?" Sister Ursula triumphantly answers her own rhetorical question:

What came of it? This young woman, Kateri. . . . Because of Kateri we have a Catholic faith. . . . She's a model for us, an ancestor, an elder. . . . She brought about healing. . . . You might as well say that as a result [of the martyrdoms] she became Christian. Where there's blood, from that new life comes.

For Sister Ursula, as for many other native Catholics, Catherine "Kateri" Tekakwitha personifies her people's history and identity. To her, the young saint[17] is not simply a distant historical figure who practiced a daunting regime of austerity and penitence but a living spiritual figure who provides a powerful, inspiring model for her own unfolding religious journey. As Sister Ursula sees her, Kateri was a young woman who was able to retain her identity, language, and culture while simultaneously grasping the salvific truth of Catholicism and living its ideals to a heroic degree. Sister Ursula's mission is thus to encourage the Catholic hierarchy to make a similar gesture of unity and trust by recognizing native spiritual wisdom and incorporating it into its own liturgy:

> We, as Mohawk people, have tried to be true to the Church, and live out our Christian values, our native values, which I see as compatible. . . . Some of our ways are still being characterized as witchcraft . . . but these are God's gifts to our people. . . . Our ways need to be affirmed, rather than shut down. We can't leave behind our ways, rituals, symbols . . . [they are] so meaningful, it just brings people alive and touches their spirit. When we can we must use our ritual and symbols in the liturgy. . . . We aren't watering down Catholicism, we are trying to bring in our past.[18]

The veneration of Kateri, then, has often served as a vehicle for native peoples' self-affirmation.[19] Many see in her canonization the triumphant fulfillment of their own untiring efforts. Says "Natalie Lamoureux," a Catholic laywoman and Mohawk elder: "I am sixty-seven years old, and I have been promoting Kateri for as long as I can remember. I have devoted my whole Christian life to her canonization."[20] Others, such as Sister Ursula, hope that Kateri's apotheosis will somehow end the ostracism and racism that have overshadowed too many native lives, heal their religiously fractured communities, and enkindle in native Catholic hearts a more profound sense of belonging in their church.

Sister Ursula's collaborator in confronting Auriesville's imagery is "Father Richard Fisher," a Jesuit anthropologist and former member of the shrine's Board of Directors. An affable, self-deprecating academic in fragile health, Fisher was appointed in 2006 to evaluate Auriesville's imagery after decades of complaints from native visitors. For Fisher, the issues raised by Auriesville's art touch both on the nature of truth and on the moral imperatives of the Christian message.

Concerned since his student days about the tenor of Catholic visual representations of native people, as a seminarian Fisher fought to have

stained-glass windows depicting the Jesuit martyrs being gorily assaulted by Iroquois removed from his institution's chapel. Fisher argues
that such art cannot be considered an accurate representation of the
complex historical events it purports to represent. It is too simple,
he suggests, too convenient in its predisposing its viewer to interpret
the Jesuits sympathetically as the saintly victims of an "essentially violent"[21] people senselessly bent on their destruction. Presenting a single
interpretation of these deaths and their significance does not exhaust
their meaning, he intimates, nor does it account for the fact that interpretation is ultimately a subjective judgment: "It is a martyrdom
from a Catholic perspective because [the Jesuit missionaries] chose to
be there. But is it murder? Warfare? Ultimately, it becomes a value
judgment."

Fisher feels that Auriesville's exclusive focus on a handful of European deaths unfairly presents them as "epitomizing events" that somehow crystallize or essentialize the long and often tragic relationship
between natives and nonnatives on North American soil. The very
conceptual category of martyrdom itself deemphasizes the historical
context in which these deaths occurred, the better to stress their similarity to that of Christ, a decontextualization that, for Fisher, obscures
rather than illuminates their multiple meanings.

Fisher is particularly critical of Auriesville's exhibition of violent
imagery in venues where they could be encountered by children. Much
like Oldfield, whose encounter with the Jogues diorama raised painful
memories of the fear her presence inspired in some nonnative young-
sters, Fisher argues that children are less able than adults to contextualize or critically to question what they are seeing:

> For children in particular, violence is just not appropriate. The Chil-
> dren's Museum at Auriesville used to have a picture of a Huron woman
> burning. "Can we not do this?" I said. My goal is to take out the things
> that are offensive, stereotypical, or infantilizing. "What is their con-
> nection to the story we are trying to tell here?" should be the question
> we are always asking ourselves.

But at the heart of Fisher's critique of Auriesville's imagery is his
strong concern that it blackens the reputation of a people who have already endured a long history of marginalization. Why does the shrine
insist on casting as eternal "bad guys" a visible minority struggling

with the painful legacy of colonialism and ongoing discrimination, he asks. How can this be consistent with Christ's commandments? And how can Our Lady of Martyrs Shrine be content to offend the people on whose land it rests? Taking the biblical maxim "by their fruits ye shall know them"[22] as his watchword, Fisher contends that the revelation of Christian truths cannot, by definition, result in oppression and violation. Honoring the memory of the church's saints must never trump the highest Christian calling, which is to love one another and to champion the downtrodden. For Fisher, there is no denying the damage that Auriesville has inflicted on native peoples by its stubborn clinging to bloody martyrdom art. But, like a self-inflicted wound, he argues, this decision has also hurt the shrine by negatively affecting its reputation and ultimately, perhaps, even imperiling its chances of survival. By steadfastly refusing to fully accommodate the expressed concerns of aboriginal neighbors, it has alienated important potential allies.

The extreme characterization of Auriesville as "a shrine to hate," then, is born from a powerful sense, held by both native and nonnative critics, that the imagery disseminated there discernibly affects both the perception and treatment of contemporary native people by the majority nonnative culture. Like a respirator, the art continuously breathes new life into racist stereotypes of aboriginal peoples as inherently barbaric and pitiless, wordlessly shaping the unconscious attitudes of those that behold it. Auriesville's power to wound can be experienced directly and immediately, prompting reactions of anger, horror, and nausea. But it can also occur vicariously. Oldfield's shocked tears prompted an empathic, protective response as ripples of outrage on her behalf spread throughout the Mohawk community. Thus had the shrine's imagery affected even those who did not themselves behold it.

The Hidden Imagery of Midland

There is an underside to every institution, no matter how glamorous: a secret, prosaic life of dripping faucets, threadbare carpets, and mildewed, understairs cupboards. This private world is usually known only to its true intimates: those who enter through "employees-only" doors or loading docks; those who use the steep, utilitarian fire stairs rather than swanning down the showy marble ones; those whose domain is the janitorial closet rather than the corner office.

Shrines are no different. They too have their nonpublic areas: their closed-off rooms and jammed storage closets, their boxes filled with the unwanted and the unloved, their mess. But in shrines, the squalor hidden away from prying eyes can tell an important hidden story. For these forlorn spaces contain not simply broken coat racks, stored Christmas decorations, and hideous pink armchairs, but repudiated theologies, ambivalent artifacts, and the jetsam of previous institutional incarnations. In an abandoned cafeteria kitchen at the Auriesville shrine, there are boxes bulging with copperplate correspondence dating to the 1880s. Envelopes containing telegrams from President Herbert Hoover and Pope Pius XI sit, dusty and disregarded, in the long-dry commercial sink.

And, in the basement of the priests' residence at the Midland shrine, one descends creaky wooden stairs into the greenish gloom. The small casement windows, painted on the inside with a thin layer of dust, are strangled on the outside by ivy, the brightness of the sun-shot leaves making a vivid, if monochrome stained glass. Here, in a forlorn alcove, surrounded by the overflow of miraculous crutches and canes from the church, and serenaded only by the vacant clinking of coat hangers, which our passing has disturbed into phantom movement, sits a large, vividly painted plaster bas-relief depicting the torture of Jean de Brébeuf and Gabriel Lalemant.[23]

For over fifty years, this piece enjoyed a prominent place in the shrine's church underneath the twelfth station of the cross, inviting comparison between Christ's suffering and that of his martyrs. The relief is deeply carved, so that the figures nearly emerge from their plaster backdrop. Even dulled by a thick layer of dust, the image is startling in its emotional immediacy. Though obviously modeled on Grégoire Huret's iconic etching, the two missionaries' faces are not masks of saintly resignation; they are twisted in pain, their mouths open and muscles taut. Their executioners' expressions, conversely, connote a toxic mixture of anger and twisted pleasure. One man languorously strips off the flesh of Brébeuf's calf with his knife. Once this image was wreathed in incense, rather than covered with dust. But now it sits like a dethroned king in ignominious exile.

At Midland, rejected images are not simply deposed, they are also disguised. Ingeniously adapted, they hide in the open. What the institution's current director, Father Bernard Carroll, calls "the identifying mark of this shrine,"[24] the much-reproduced Mother Nealis painting of the eight martyrs in glory, executed in the 1920s, still hangs in its accustomed place of prominence. But, like Solomon's baby, the work has been cleverly visually amputated so as to simultaneously preserve its considerable historic value while responding to escalating native complaints about its violent imagery.

In the early 1980s, in a belated response to the Second Vatican Council, the shrine church's altar was brought forward and its sanctuary redecorated in a style one employee slyly dubbed—because of its white stucco and plush red carpet—"early Italian restaurant." Displayed on the new false wall placed close to the congregation, the top two-thirds of Mother Nealis's masterwork, depicting the eight martyrs communing with sweet-faced angels in heavenly splendor, still visually dominates the sanctuary. But the painting's lower third, showing each missionary's gruesome death, is now totally hidden beneath the stucco

This bas-relief depicting the torture of Brébeuf and Lalemant, formerly proudly displayed in the church of the Midland Martyrs' Shrine, was abruptly exiled during the early 1980s to the basement of the priests' residence, as the institution began to reevaluate its imagery.

(Photo by author)

Jesuit Martyrs of Canada, Saints John, Isaac and Companions.

Mother Nealis's *The Glory,* which was ingeniously edited during the 1980s in response to complaints regarding its violent, stereotypical images of native peoples.

(Archives of the Midland Martyrs' Shrine)

that enfolds its hidden bottom like a spiky diaper. With the gilded frame reattached to the edited painting, those unaware of its original dimensions would never suspect there was anything missing. Although Father John Wynne had gallantly assured Mother Nealis in a 1925 letter, "your sermon in line and color will have its effect as long as, and wherever [the martyrs] will be honoured,"[25] her visual homily was in fact truncated a scant six decades after he had licked the envelope.

From *The Glory* to *A Sharing*

The changes to Midland's imagery in the 1980s, however, included additions as well as deletions. Having stripped away layers of antiquated agony like so much faded wallpaper, the shrine began visually to emphasize *native* giants of the Catholic faith. Under Father James Farrell, who directed the shrine from 1981 to 1996, the visual culture of Midland would become much more native-centric. Farrell's vision for Midland may have been shaped by his decades working in predominantly aboriginal communities in northern Ontario, where he maintained a wide rolodex of contacts. Known as a plainspoken homilist and a born administrator, Farrell tried to make the shrine more reflective of the *native* portion of the ongoing native-Jesuit dialogue.

Following her 1980 beatification by Pope John Paul II, Kateri Tekakwitha would become far more visually prominent at Midland. She had long been present, in miniature as it were, in the books and holy cards sold in the shrine's gift shop. But under Farrell, Kateri would, like Alice in Wonderland, be magnified exponentially, from her fairylike dimension in the modest holy cards to larger than life in the new statue he commissioned for the shrine's grounds.[26] Farrell also transformed the north transept of the shrine church into a minichapel in Kateri's honor, forming a sort of "shrine within a shrine." He also more fully integrated Kateri into Midland's ritual life, particularly its "novenas," special nine-day cycles of prayer undertaken by Catholics for special intentions. Like a convenient bridge partner, adding Kateri to the roster of the eight canonized martyrs made up the perfect number of holy figures whose intercession could successively be implored during the intense cycle of prayer and supplication.

Farrell also prominently featured the long-ignored Wendat Catholic Joseph Chihoatenhwa in his shrine redecoration, making the seventeenth-century convert central in two of his most important artistic commissions. At the same time, the Midland Jesuits sought belatedly to secure formal recognition of Chihoatenhwa's heroic sanctity by attempting to introduce his cause for beatification. To this end, they amassed primary documents, courted Vatican officials, and encouraged pilgrims to pray through Chihoatenhwa's intercession in the hopes that the long-deceased Wendat might prove his own sanctity by working a verifiable miracle.[27] Though Farrell did not directly address Chihoatenhwa's controversial death, the statue in the new Native Prayer Gardens suggestively depicts the Catholic Wendat man with his head thrown back and his arms extended in cruciform position.

Chihoatenhwa also featured prominently in a new stained-glass window commissioned for the shrine church. Portrayed deep in conversation with Jean de Brébeuf, Chihoatenhwa is captured midspeech, gesturing toward a Brébeuf who listens, deep in thought. Since its unveiling, *The Sharing* has become something of a popular new "identifying mark"[28] for Midland, rivaling if not replacing Nealis's *The Glory*, whose theological conclusions it implicitly rebukes. Reproduced at many times its original size, it now dominates downtown Midland in the form of a colorful mural decorating the grain elevators on its lakeside shipping docks.[29]

These dramatic changes to Midland's imagery resulted from a number of factors. Its transformation reflected changing theological currents and the desire of some Jesuits to "re-Canadianize" a shrine they felt had become, in the postwar years, overly eclectic. Also critical were escalating complaints from native and nonnative visitors regarding violent imagery and the influential example set in this regard by Sainte-Marie-among-the-Huron, a historical park now run almost entirely by the provincial government.

Father Bernard Carroll, the Midland shrine's current director, sees theological changes in twentieth-century Catholicism as having informed its decisive move away from the traditional visual stress on native culpability in the deaths of the martyrs. Midland's shift, he argues, mirrored the Second Vatican Council's own belated recognition that the church's casting of the Jews as "Christ killers" had provided both the historical precedent and theological justification that had paved the way for the Holocaust. A new sense of nuance, it was argued, was needed in interpreting ancient and violent events, so that an entire people

would no longer be unjustly blamed for them: "The Jews were condemned as being the killers of Christ. There were tons of historical and
social factors that contributed to that decision, as well as fear, but don't
condemn a whole people, the factors of the time played a huge role." In
the 1980s, Carroll suggests, the Jesuits at Midland made a similar realization that they too had engaged in a problematic "blame game" that
revictimized an already vulnerable sector of Canadian society:

> And it is the same thing with the martyrs, there were a number of rea-
> sons. You can't just show a tomahawk over someone's head, there were
> lots of circumstances that led to their death. The main thing is that they
> died lovingly caring for their people, and even for their enemies. The
> means of their torture is really not important.[30]

Vatican II also reshaped Catholic understandings of religious change
at both the individual and collective levels, the process conventionally
known as "conversion." Before the 1960s, the religious transformation
that had raggedly and divisively taken hold in seventeenth-century native communities was celebrated at Midland as the miraculous kindling
of light in the long-reigning darkness of ignorance and fear.

But in the Vatican II era, the language of religious transformation
itself became transformed. The Midland Jesuits began to speak of the
martyrs as having "perceived the dynamic activity of the risen Lord Jesus among these Indians, anterior to the coming of any missionary, in
their culture, their customs, and their primitive yet genuine virtues."[31]
This new notion that native peoples who had not yet heard the Gospel
were nevertheless imbued with the spirit of Christ changed the traditional picture completely. No longer were missionaries seen as bequeath-
ing to native peoples new and saving truths but rather as recognizing
those that native culture had independently evolved and from which
the missionaries themselves could learn. This new theology was perhaps most memorably captured in Pope John Paul II's much quoted but
little understood catchphrase uttered during his 1984 visit to the Midland shrine: "Christ, in the members of his Body, is himself Indian."[32]

The striking visual changes at Midland also reflected the concern of
some Jesuits that by reaching out to ethnic Catholics in the postwar
years, the shrine had inadvertently endangered its own distinctively
Canadian identity. Father Jim Kelly, a Jesuit currently working as a
parish priest in a largely Ojibwe diocese, remembers worrying that the

artifacts so generously donated by generations of pilgrims would gradually "overwhelm the shrine" to such an extent that the institution would come to be "associated with the Slovak Cross, and not the martyrs."[33] Farrell agreed. His decision visually to stress the contributions of colonial native Catholics was part of his intentional, self-conscious program of "Canadianization," which deliberately countered multicultural influences many felt had gone too far.[34]

But perhaps the most critical factor in the shrine's comprehensive visual reinvention in the 1980s was native criticism.[35] John Robinson, a tall, quiet Anishnabe Catholic active in the church's outreach ministries to native peoples in Toronto, is convinced that martyrdom art has long had a pernicious effect on the perception of native peoples. Throwing his long, gray-streaked black braid over his shoulder and leaning forward to emphasize his point, Robinson enumerates the malign messages he feels such art perpetrates:

> Those pictures always portrayed native people as being very savage. People look at that and say, the Jesuits were killed by savage people, savage native people that didn't know right from wrong: they didn't know about Jesus or God. But native people always knew about the Creator who created everything. Meanwhile they try to make it look like [the martyrs] are angels in heaven. They put the martyrs up in the clouds and the native people down at the bottom of the picture. I think that a lot of people, even today, they don't want to make native people saints because of this imagery.[36]

Deluged during his tenure by similar arguments, Father Farrell made the pivotal decision in the early 1980s to jettison "good-guy, bad-guy" imagery featuring "angelic Frenchmen and demonic Iroquois."[37]

Sainte-Marie-among-the-Huron encountered similar complaints during this era and formulated what would be a far-reaching and influential response. As a government-run institution, the historical park was seen by critics as being more amenable to the input of tax-paying Ontarians than the privately owned shrine. Critics were also quick to pounce on Sainte-Marie's stated commitment to presenting both native and European perspectives upon encounter in order to highlight instances where the institution failed to live up to its own espoused ideals.[38] Predictably, the park's artwork, which in many cases simply duplicated that on display at the shrine, received heavy criticism. But it was Sainte-Marie's dated orientation film that drew the most withering commentary.

Commissioned by the Jesuits in the late 1960s, when Sainte-Marie and the shrine were still hand in glove, the amateur black-and-white film was narrated in a ludicrous French accent that combined the worst of Inspector Clouseau and Pepé Le Pew. It presented the events of the 1640s entirely from the perspective of the Jesuits, focusing largely on the martyrdoms and the fall of Huronia, and painted the Iroquois in unapologetically menacing hues. The film's most dramatic moment was its ending, which featured an image of the burning Sainte-Marie wreathed in flame. But then, as if by magic, the historical disaster was undone—redeemed, mended. In just seconds, the screen smoothly ascended, even as the large garage door behind it trundled open to reveal the restored Jesuit complex, resurrected like a phoenix from its seventeenth-century ashes. Seamlessly bridging past and present, the film's conclusion subtly colored visitors' subsequent experiences of the site that had been so dramatically revealed to them.

Critics of the film, however, scorned these theatrics. Indignant letters condemned the film for "teaching fear and hatred of a racial group, the Iroquois, and contempt and horror toward traditional Native religion."[39] Having watched the film with a group of young Mohawks, Catherine Verrall of the Canadian Alliance in Solidarity with the Native Peoples wrote: "Iroquois young people have suffered immeasurably from the negative connotations, taught in our schools over the last century, about 'demons who killed and tortured.' . . . They have learned to feel ashamed, or under attack."[40]

Sainte-Marie's administration responded with a smooth new color slide show that adopted an omnipotent style of narration and explored Jesuit, Wendat, and Iroquois perspectives on contact, religion, and war in an evenhanded manner, eschewing hagiography for relativism in its presentation of the three groups' fateful collision in the 1640s. Rather than ending with the elaborate showmanship of its predecessor, it concluded with a somber invitation for visitors to judge for themselves whether the Jesuit advent had been for good or for ill.

Sainte-Marie's new orientation film caused some consternation at the Midland Martyrs' Shrine. One disgruntled lay Catholic compared what she considered the film's pushy "politically correct" message to that of the evil computer HAL 9000 in *2001: A Space Odyssey*. Some Jesuits were also offended by new film's failure even to mention the martyrs and stung by its stubborn agnosticism regarding the outcome of the Huronia experiment. In a statement reminiscent of Daniel Lord, whose *Salute to Canada* pageant had imagined the contemporary Canadian nation as being born from the martyrs' blood, Father Alex Kirsten, former director of the shrine, passionately asserted: "even though [the martyrs] died, it was a success. Even though the mission was destroyed, it was a success . . . and the success is: well, what is Canada today? It is a place where Christianity, Catholicism still exists, still flourishes, still grows."[41]

Yet though Sainte-Marie's commitment to presenting both native and Jesuit perspectives on contact did occasionally generate tension between the two institutions, it is undeniable that having an independent, government-funded public institution across the highway has, overall, been a huge net benefit for the Midland Martyrs' Shrine. In practical terms, it has been a tremendous boost to pilgrimage numbers, as tourist-pilgrims often visit both cross-promoted sites. More important, Sainte-Marie's self-definition as a center for native history and culture has continually challenged the Midland shrine to be tolerant and open to other perspectives, checking its devolution into either quaint irrelevance or unintended insensitivity.[42] The historical park's comparatively nuanced attention to the complex dynamics of intercultural contact has provided a balance to the shrine's more hagiographic history and near exclusive focus on the martyrs. Because of Sainte-Marie, it is simply not an option for the Midland Jesuits to feign ignorance or to deny the existence of multiple perspectives in and about the past. Midland's current director, Father Bernard Carroll, sees Sainte-Marie as having reached a laudable new level of maturity, which has beneficially affected his own institution:

> It is respectful of native peoples, showing that some disliked what the Jesuits were doing, and some liked it. It shows that Jesuits came with fire in their bellies, wanting to change native societies, but they ended up being changed. The Jesuits called [native peoples] "savages," "pagans," but also came to respect their community structures, their spirituality. They grew in respect. Both sides are presented.[43]

Between them, these four factors—theological shifts, a desire to "re-Canadianize" the shrine, native complaints, and the trail-blazing example set by Sainte-Marie—were powerful enough to dislodge the boulder-like bas-relief of the tortured martyrs from its prominent place in the shrine church and to maroon it, like a glacial erratic, in the basement of the priests' residence. Together, these elements were powerful enough visually to sever Mother Nealis's formerly iconic creation with all the elegant casualness of an experienced magician detaching his beautiful assistant's torso from her legs. Combining their clout, these factors together generated unprecedented new imagery at Midland that, for the first time, depicted native people as something other than mere bloodied cogs in the machine of martyrdom.

Brébeuf's Dream

But Father James Farrell wanted to do more than simply celebrate, through newly commissioned artwork, the spiritual heroism of the native Catholic saints of the Canadian past. He wanted nothing less than to mold new ones for the future. Re-envisioning the Midland Martyrs' Shrine less as a place of multicultural or "ethnic" pilgrimage than as the crucible for a powerful new native spiritual revival, Farrell dreamed of making the idealized Chihoatenhwa-Brébeuf dialogue of his stained glass *A Sharing* into a dynamic reality between contemporary Jesuits and native peoples.[44] Farrell thus developed two ambitious new native-focused initiatives: the Anishnabe Spiritual Centre, devoted to the forging of a native Catholic clergy; and "Indian Prayer Days," a pilgrimage for native laypeople.

Under Farrell, when Midland Jesuits spoke of "Brébeuf's dream,"[45] they were referring not to the missionary's famous 1640 vision of a menacing cross "large enough to crucify us all" but to the saint's supposed recognition of the need for a fully realized "native church," in which aboriginal Catholics would fully assume the spiritual leadership of their own communities through ordained ministry. This interpretation of Brébeuf's legacy shifts the focus from the martyr and his gory death back onto the native nations he is seen as having sought to serve and strengthen.

The Anishnabe Spiritual Centre or *Wassen-dimi-Kaning* was established near Anderson Lake in northern Ontario to train native men to become the spiritual leaders of their parishes. Their integration of native cultural, linguistic, and spiritual elements into Catholic worship was explicitly encouraged.[46] Traditional practices such as "smudging," a ceremony in which smoke from the four sacred herbs of tobacco, sage, sweetgrass, and cedar is used spiritually to purify participants, became a staple of the Anderson Lake Mass. Though seminarians were encouraged to train for the Catholic priesthood, the Jesuits, seeing clerical celibacy as fundamentally foreign to native sensibilities,[47] also sought to forge a strong male diaconate and accepted married men into training for this role. Their initiative received international exposure in 1984 when several newly minted Ojibwe deacons coserved mass with Pope John Paul II during his visit to Midland. The ritual gestures of these aboriginal men, perfectly synchronized with those of the Holy Father, implied a papal ratification of this bold new interpretation of "Brébeuf's dream."

Farrell's other new initiative, Indian Prayer Days, combined the classic spiritual aspirations of Catholic religious retreat with renewed outreach to the native Catholic community, particularly the Ojibwe enclaves that encircled Midland. But while the director used his web of contacts throughout native northern Ontario to publicize the new pilgrimage and took care of banalities such as financial support and bus chartering, he pointedly left the spiritual side of the event entirely in native hands.[48] Farrell wanted to sponsor an event that would be run by and for native Catholics. He did not want native peoples' role in their own event to be dictated to them by nonnative authorities, nor did he wish native people to "perform" for nonnative onlookers. Farrell's relinquishment of administrative and ritual responsibility to native organizers was a revolutionary departure from previous patterns of native involvement at the shrine, which were typically heavily controlled, largely symbolic, and often calculated to edify the nonnative audience rather than native participants themselves. Previous aboriginal participation at Midland was often comprised of acting out "bit parts" in someone else's spectacle: often silent, walk-on roles in traditional costume. Farrell's new approach, which coupled the privacy needed for unself-conscious worship with low-key administrative backup, would prove popular with native Catholic leaders.[49]

Speaking in a basement chapel at the Midland Martyrs' Shrine in June 2011, Ojibwe lay Catholic Jean McGregor-Andrews kicked off the annual "Native Prayer Days" with a moving, powerful relation of her recent dream involving her deceased grandson. A small woman with short, gray-flecked hair and an air of empathic warmth, McGregor-Andrews welcomed the predominantly Anishnabe gathering. The goal of this year's retreat, she stated, was to encourage each adult partici-pant to take a personal, practical, and spiritual interest in the lives the young people of their communities through prayer, counseling, and simply "being there" for them. For McGregor-Andrews, standing beside a rough, chainsaw-hewn statue of Joseph Chihoatenhwa, the drug abuse, low self-esteem, and high suicide rates plaguing native youth are merely symptoms of a wider spiritual malaise. It is religious rootlessness or "floating" that is the ultimate cause of the ills plaguing "Indian coun-try," she argues:

> This weekend is for our young people. We have to open up their spiri-tual side, whether it is the traditional way or Catholicism. How they develop their spirituality is up to them, they don't have to be Catholic, but they have to be able to relate to their Creator. If they don't have that, than there is nothing there holding them up.[50]

Though she is open to the remediation of this dangerous rootlessness through many means, Jean's preferred method is prayer through the powerful intercession of the Jesuit martyrs. Central to the event since its inception under Farrell, the martyrs are seen by many participants in Native Prayer Days as eager to confer great temporal and spiritual boons on native people, with whom they are indissolubly linked both historically and spiritually.

Many Anishnabe participants were eager to share stories of family members healed through the intercession of the martyrs. Some stories demonstrated an involvement with the shrine that has spanned gener-ations. "Olivia Desjardins," a seventy-three-year-old Ojibwe Catholic from Toronto, relates that her grandmother was healed from debilitat-ing seizures not long after the shrine's 1926 opening. Her grandmoth-er's discarded crutches, she notes with pride, were among the many that, for decades, draped the church's walls like an ugly wooden lace.[51]

For participants in Native Prayer Days, the martyr-native relation-ship cannot be neatly encapsulated in the victim-slayer dyad so familiar from martyrdom art. Rather, it finds expression in that most intimate of Catholic relationships, that between patron saint and petitioning client.

In her homilies, punctuating the weekend retreat, Jean constantly stressed that the martyrs were uniquely available to native peoples, for whom they had given their lives:

> Anyone can pray to the martyrs. . . . I pray to them every day. . . . They gave up their lives for us. . . . When you bring something here, leave it here with the martyrs and God. Alcoholism, family problems, diabetes: leave them here. Leave them here for the care of the martyrs and saints. Leave pain, sorrow, illness, hopelessness, all those inclined to commit suicide, and just leave them here.[52]

The martyrs' intercessory power, for many native participants, is only enhanced when they are approached on the "holy ground" where they lived and died. Accordingly, as part of their weekend program, the group of approximately forty-five mostly Ojibwe Catholics visited Saint-Ignace II, the grassy, tree-ringed meadow identified by Alphonse Arpin that is the alleged site where Jean de Brébeuf and Gabriel Lalemant were killed. There, in an open-walled rain structure, the pilgrims gathered to say the sorrowful mysteries of the rosary. Their prayers, recited in both Ojibwe and English, were like a sort of verbal crocheting, as the whispered rush of the syllables hooked and twisted smoothly one into the other, their monotone repetition smoothing and soothing down the initial rush of emotion at the drama and color of their words, which flashed and winked through the softer verbiage like needles: "womb," "sinner," "souls," "death," "hell," "mercy." Having said their beads, the pilgrims attentively listened to a brief lecture on the site delivered by the shrine's archivist, Steve Catlin.

After greeting them in Ojibwe, Catlin began by explaining the origin of the two prominent crosses on the east side of the field. Along with the shelter in which they stood, these were the only manmade artifacts in the large, grassy clearing. Father Denis Hegarty, during the course of archaeological work, had found the remains of four charred, deeply buried post holes that he interpreted as having been the actual torture stakes to which Brébeuf, Lalemant, and two unnamed Christian Wendat chiefs had been tied and tortured. Briefly evoked by Catlin's discourse, these native martyrs were, at least momentarily, present amid the Ojibwe assembly. Unmemorialized by any permanent monument, their nameless, faceless memory was ephemeral, ethereal, passing over the assembled company like a waft of wood smoke. The native martyrs of colonial North America have long been characterized by this elusive, evocative facelessness and namelessness, which has affected their cult at both the institutional and the imaginative level. Though some, it is true, have a comparatively full biography, more typical is their near total erasure as individuals. Some might argue that the very vagueness of these largely forgotten figures presents a powerful rhetorical advantage in connoting their larger meaning. The poignant, well-known figure of the Unknown Soldier is an abstraction that serves as the symbol of soldiers so badly butchered by war that their remains could neither be identified nor repatriated. Theoretically, the "Unknown Native Martyr" could keep a similar vigil for the memory of those whose stories are too deeply buried in the past to be retrieved.

But deeper reflection reveals that these two figures are more different than similar. The Unknown Soldier is a regretful figure of last resort, whose monument marks the final resting place of only the truly unidentifiable fragments of lost humanity. Even in the chaos of war, extraordinary efforts are often made to repatriate bodies for burial or at least systematically to retrieve, identify, and inter them closer to the fields on which they fell. Part of the Unknown Soldier's uncanny power, then, lies in his ability wordlessly to evoke the sadness of those wartime families who lost even the meager consolation of being able to bury their loved one's remains.

In contrast, our lack of knowledge regarding the names and actions of those aboriginal Christians who died in far greater numbers than the canonized martyrs and under harrowingly similar circumstances has been almost entirely due to the *lack* of care taken in recording their identities and experiences. The sense of diligent yet doomed effort that gives the Unknown Soldier his special poignancy is wholly missing here. The Unknown Native Martyr is a bloodless abstraction whose existence bespeaks indifference rather than regret.

John Robinson, who attended the June 2011 visit to Saint-Ignace, perceives the neglect of native martyrs as the by-product of a mentality that dismisses native-on-native violence in the colonial period as "business as usual"—so ubiquitous as to be wholly unexceptional: "When they looked at native peoples, they were killed by their own people, so they left them out of it. . . . They didn't even care if it was a different native nation, they figured if they were native they were native."[53]

Tribal distinctions and the nuances of traditional animosities were ignored in favor of lumping together protagonist and antagonist under
the larger label of "native," Robinson argues. Catholic authorities, he
suggests, made a deliberate decision to overlook native martyrs because
their existence threatened to complicate the native slayer–white victim
dynamic of popular martyrdom art and rhetoric. In this simplifying
shorthand, Robinson alleges, seventeenth-century native Catholics were
robbed even of their religious identity: "they recognized [the canonized
martyrs] because they were priests, they were sent to teach the native
people. But the native people were left out of it because they were considered as savages, not Christians."[54]

The End of the Dream?

Today, both native-centric programs initiated in the early 1980s by Father Farrell attract a significantly different demographic than when
they were originally established. In Farrell's time, the Anishnabe Spiritual Centre's heavy enrollment seemed to promise a real renaissance in
native Catholic leadership. Early classes, particularly those for the diaconate, were filled to capacity with native male candidates. But this
early tsunami of interest was apparently a rogue wave. Now, laments
Father Jim Kelly, graduates of Wassen-dimi-Kaning are graying, and
few new deacons have been ordained to replace them.[55] In Kelly's eyes,
Farrell's vision of a native-run church has failed:

> That dream has not come to fruition. The hope was that native people
> would claim, mark, and lead their own churches. It was part of a wider
> societal trend at the time that involved claiming their own spirituality
> and their own church. Now there is a great level of native participation
> in the church, but not a distinctively native church.

His gloomy analysis, however, pointedly ignores the program's continuing popularity among native women. Anderson Lake now prepares
mostly female candidates for the administrative, pastoral, and sacramental duties once performed exclusively by male deacons. Denied this
title because of the church's prohibition of female ordination, these
graduates are referred to as "DOS" (or "Diocesan Order of Service") and
are "mandated" to their parishes rather than ordained. Native women's

strong desire to serve despite this overt discrimination suggests that Brébeuf's dream has not so much failed as it has, once again, morphed.

"Native Prayer Days," Farrell's premiere event for native Catholic lay-people has also witnessed critical demographic shifts since its heyday in the 1980s. Though Jean McGregor-Andrews is quick to note that the event's size does not correlate with the degree of its spiritual power,[56] other Ojibwe faithful wistfully recall when the event filled the large shrine parking lot with packed buses, not a mere handful of private ve-hicles.[57] The event itself has shrunken temporally from a three-day, two-night commitment to a mere day and a half.[58]

But it is the lack of young participants is the most telling. As the middle-aged and elderly pilgrims gathered in June 2011 to pray for their communities' young people, the objects of their prayers were no-table in their absence. When McGregor-Andrews optimistically opined that the youthful targets of their ardent prayer "might one day be here at Midland praying for *their* young people,"[59] the congregation, though suitably moved, seemed ultimately unconvinced. The notion that a phalanx of young native Catholics would spring forth from Midland's holy soil like warriors from dragon's teeth, replacing their elders as they fade, wither, and finally fall seemed, even in this place of miracles, to be almost beyond belief.

Though Father Farrell's native-centric programs were, in the con-text of what had preceded them, bold and ambitious, they were also quite limited in scope. Farrell chose to engage exclusively with *Catholic* native peoples, particularly those who sought spiritual empowerment through greater implication within their church. He did not in any sub-stantial way address those who had returned to the spiritual ways of their ancestors. Farrell's preferential engagement with native Catholics would bear bitter fruit in the frigid and hectoring reception that would be accorded Wendat traditionalist Georges Sioui during his 1989 visit to Midland, a full eight years after Farrell had taken the helm.

Over the last thirty years, traditional spirituality has continued to draw native Catholics away from the faith. The ongoing refusal of the Catholic Church to apologize formally for its long involvement with na-tive residential schools, coupled with shocking revelations of the full horrors of the spiritual, physical, and sexual abuse experienced at these institutions, has increased native reluctance to participate in Catholic programming at the shrine, even when it is native-run and native-led.[60] Native suspicion and sadness has led to the development of a painful chasm between the church and native peoples, claims Father Alex Kirsten, a former shrine director. As the two regard one another across this divide, neither group is sure how to bridge it or even whether they want to. Kirsten observed: "Our relationship with the native community is at best a delicate one. . . . They don't know how to deal with it 100%, and we're not exactly sure how to deal with it 100%."[61]

Despite this serious estrangement, Farrell's optimistic vision of a shrine intimately engaged with native peoples seems poised for a comeback. Vividly reminded of their collective past in 2011 as they celebrated the Society's four hundredth anniversary in North America, the Midland Jesuits are once again claiming service of native communities as their special prerogative. Current director Father Carroll, though as painfully conscious of the rift with native peoples as his predecessor, argues that the church's past sins make its outreach to native communities a moral imperative:

> There is definitely a suspicion of the church. When I hear about this, it makes me want to reach out, to make every effort to make [native people] feel at home here. I want to know what is going on in their lives. We may have to go to them, not have them come to us. I want to try to foster reconciliation with native peoples, as they are in great pain now, with the residential schools. From the comments I hear in the community, I am not sure that they feel that they have first rights to this place [the shrine], that this is their home.[62]

Carroll is explicit that building relationships with First Nations will be both the defining feature of his tenure as shrine director and a strong priority in the future mission of the institution he leads.

In the aftermath of Kateri Tekakwitha's triumphal canonization in October 2012, the great hunger in some native Catholic hearts to see the sanctity of their spiritual ancestors officially acknowledged has not gone unnoticed at Midland. Native protests of a racial double standard in the official recognition of martyrs have also been heeded. Reflects Father Carroll:

> I wish that the native martyrs had been named . . . but we pray through *all* of the martyrs' intercession [native and nonnative]. That needs to be more emphasized and more stressed [in outreach to native peoples]

that it wasn't just the Jesuits, it was *your own ancestors* that gave their lives as well.

Under Carroll, as under Farrell thirty years ago, the Midland Jesuits are fighting to have their shrine's visual icon, Joseph Chihoatenhwa, elevated alongside his sister-in-Christ Kateri through his recognition as a "venerable servant of God" by the church. Though support for his candidacy extends all the way up the Jesuit hierarchy,[63] Carroll is keen to expand support at the grassroots level: "We want to push, and to emphasize [Chihoatenhwa's] legacy, and we want native peoples to be involved with this too. Many have a deep devotion to Kateri Tekakwitha, but don't know Joseph Chihoatenhwa. . . . We are inviting all to pray for a miracle through his intercession."[64]

But some at the shrine argue that the longed-for miracle happened well over a decade ago. Archivist Steve Catlin suggests that it was only through Chihoatenhwa's intervention that the remains of fellow Ossossané villagers were finally returned to the safekeeping of their Wendat descendants in August 1999. In Catlin's imaginative reading of these events, the devout Wendat Catholic becomes the unlikely patron saint of the largely traditionalist cultural and spiritual renaissance rekindled at his onetime home.[65] Catlin dreams of working with the Wendat to organize pilgrimages from Midland to Ossossané, which he sees as holy ground not simply for native traditionalists but all Catholics and indeed all Canadians, regardless of their religious background.

In seeking a closer working relationship with native traditionalists, Catlin is pushing Midland's model of native engagement far beyond the Catholic-only perimeters established by Father Farrell. Long a proponent of joint spiritual initiatives, Catlin was pivotal in persuading the shrine's administration to permit Iroquois and Wendat traditionalists to hold a "false-face" ceremony on the site some see as Canada's holiest ground: Saint-Ignace II. In this private ritual, descendants of those who fought on both sides came together on this former battle site to seek reconciliation and healing and to cleanse themselves and the land of its difficult past. This ceremony was unique among the hundreds held at the site in that its primary ritual focus was not on the attack's most celebrated victims, Brébeuf and Lalemant, but on the many nameless native peoples, on both sides of the conflict, who had fallen alongside them.

It remains to be seen how aboriginal people—traditionalists, Catholics, and those who feel themselves cut off from any spiritual roots, Jean McGregor-Andrew's much-prayed-for "floaters"—will respond to recently renewed attempts at conversation by the Midland Jesuits. But Carroll's advent has definitively settled at least one burning question. The incoming director firmly shuts the door on his predecessor's talk of restoring Nealis's painting to its former dubious glory:

> That would make me uncomfortable. I don't see the need for it. There was a very conscious decision that was made to hide the bottom of the painting. We were aware that it could be used prejudicially against people, and that was not what we wanted. To me, the bottom part of the painting was never important. Our focus is on the brotherhood and sisterhood of all peoples.[66]

For now, at least, Farrell's bold visual innovations at Midland will stand uncontested and unaltered.

The Impasse over Imagery at Auriesville

While the issue of violent imagery has been largely resolved at Midland, how the martyrs are presented visually remains intensely controversial at its sister shrine in Auriesville, where the patchy, inconsistent nature of the sanctuary's visual editing presents a striking study in incoherence and ambivalence. Some of the most graphic images, such as the Jogues diorama that confronted Sarah Oldfield in 1999, are no longer on public display, and the steep slope greeting arriving pilgrims is no longer referred to as "the Hill of Torture." Small signs that previously indicated with pretended precision where the martyrs' severed heads were impaled on the village palisades have likewise been retracted.

But while much is taken, much abides. Three large log crosses, emblazoned with the red legends "Jogues," "Goupil," and "la Lande," welcome the pilgrim. Amid the flickering candles of a wayside chapel, Isaac Jogues stands serenely, his mangled hands folded in prayer, his inclined head revealing the scarlet, killing gash on the top of his skull. On the exterior of the shrine's gift shop, large hand-painted tiles propose an improvised "coat of arms" for each martyr, juxtaposing peaceful Christian symbols—a Host, a chalice, a palm—with an unvarying "Mohawk" counterpoint: upraised tomahawks. Inside, Francis Talbot's

Saint among the Savages remains, in something of a devotional time-warp, the best seller it became after its initial publication in 1935. And "the Ravine," with its unnerving ability to engender both spiritual euphoria and nauseated horror remains as it has for decades, proving the maxim that "the body that is nowhere is everywhere."

The very selectivity of Auriesville's visual self-censorship is eloquent testimony to the mixed emotions it arouses at the institution's highest levels. The shrine administration finds itself caught between a Scylla and Charybdis: those who argue that the institution's art smacks of an unsavory, un-Christian racism and those who view any further "watering down" of the shrine's iconography as an unconscionable betrayal of the martyrs. Apprehensive shrine officials have thus conscientiously sought middle ground:

> In the overall picture they are probably right in asking us to, for example, update some of our exhibits, or be a bit more revisionist, or take a wider view of the history, but I do think on the other hand this is a Shrine, and it is dedicated mostly to the martyrs and what they suffered and what martyrdom means, so we have to remember that aspect and not go too far in the other direction. It is a balancing act, a tight-rope act.[67]

The administration's caution, of course, leaves both sides of the ideological divide all the more exasperated. Those who were expressly invited to serve as consultants regarding the shrine's ongoing image woes are left to conclude that their suggestions, having been solicited, are now being ignored. Meanwhile, shrine employees who advocate the spiritual benefits of "witnessing" the martyrs' agony through art complain of a repressive political correctness that hints that more exacting reforms are imminent.

In order to understand how Our Lady of Martyrs became so theologically fractured, and why imagery became her crown of thorns, we need to return to the shrine of the late 1960s. Turning back time reveals that post–Vatican II Midland was not alone in producing a leader determined to confront negative stereotypes of native people and to engage them anew in a spirit of friendship and openness.[68] Father James Farrell's Auriesville counterpart was Father Thomas Egan. Born in nearby Amsterdam, New York, Egan had been involved with Our Lady of Martyrs virtually "from boyhood."[69] His appointment as director in 1968 was thus something of a homecoming, taking him from a military chaplaincy in the rice paddies of Vietnam back to his childhood haunts.

A tall, deep-voiced man with a distinguished mane of neatly brilliantined black hair and a ready grin, Egan is described by all who knew him as charming, outgoing, and "friendly with all sides, both longhouse and Christian."[70] Noted for his ability "to traverse different worlds,"[71] Egan's appointment as St. Regis's parish priest immediately following his tenure as shrine director allowed him to pursue for a further fourteen years his pet project: facilitating Mohawk pilgrimage from Akwesasne to Auriesville.[72]

Though, like Farrell, Egan felt driven to change how native people were perceived and presented at the shrine, he addressed the issue primarily through the written word rather than, like his Canadian counterpart, mounting a concerted campaign to change his institution's imagery. In Auriesville's newsletter, *The Pilgrim*,[73] Egan challenged every aspect of how the martyrs' story was traditionally told. Generally, this publication had used native culture as merely the dark, barbaric backdrop against which the martyrs' jewel-like sanctity blazed out all the brighter. It was unusual, in its pages, for the Mohawk to be presented as anything other than the martyrs' vilified killers.[74] Outside of this familiar role, they were, to the publication's predominantly white readership, shadowy, mysterious figures, if not extinct than certainly unknown as a contemporary people with their own perspective and history.[75]

But Egan's articles changed all this. Even as the new director continued to churn out the expected homey news and brief, breezy discussions of Catholic issues, Egan wrote searching articles tracing Mohawk experiences from the time of the martyrs to the present. His pieces detailed their successive divisions and dispersions and presented their political and military vicissitudes over the centuries. Egan frankly acknowledged traditionalist and Protestant as well as Catholic allegiances and identities among the contemporary Iroquois.[76] His broad focus clearly implied that the wider context of Iroquois history should interest his readership.

Even in articles that spoke formulaically of the "heroic, self-sacrificing" martyrs or described Catherine Tekakwitha as the "lily of the Mohawk, fairest flower of their nation," Egan's new twist was evident. He directly addressed the "red-pride" arguments of native traditionalists, which portrayed native loyalty to the Catholic Church as an Uncle Tom–like internalization of colonialism. On the contrary, Egan argued, aboriginal acceptance of Christianity was entirely consonant with the maintenance of their cultural identity:

> The French Jesuits who worked in the tradition of Jogues and Brébeuf insisted time and time again that the native people of North America did not have to give up being Indian in order to be Christian. . . . Kateri Tekakwitha was an Indian through and through to the day she died. . . . Kateri therefore has a message for the peoples of our times. . . . Don't try to be someone God didn't want you to be.[77]

God, Egan stated forcefully, wants native people to be spiritually whole and culturally unbroken.

Egan also did not flinch from dictating to his white readership how they should regard contemporary aboriginal peoples, particularly the shrine's Mohawk neighbors. He sternly exhorted them to look beyond the stereotype of native people as the martyrs' barbaric dispatchers, even pointing out that the slayings of Jogues, Goupil, and la Lande were the actions of a minority within a single Mohawk moiety and should not be used to libel their descendants. In piece after piece, he pounded home his message that his white readership must acknowledge native people as their fellow human beings, respect them as American compatriots, and warmly embrace them as members of the body of Christ:

> Having known the Mohawks these many years I would find it difficult to think of them in any other way than as brothers and sisters in the Lord, precious in his sight for their many talents, accomplishments, and loyalty to the Faith, a people who contributed mightily to the development of both Canada and the United States. I pray that many of our pilgrims who come here to honour the martyrs and Kateri may also enjoy the privilege of knowing the Mohawks as personal friends.[78]

Egan cast native fidelity to the Catholic Church as a model *all* pilgrims would do well to follow, urging them to "draw inspiration from the loyalty of the Catholic Mohawks, Hurons, and Algonquins who 300 years ago were living the faith most heroically in this area."[79]

Egan's voice reverberates out of the past full of passion, urgency, and sincerity. It seems odd that a man so obviously dedicated to rehabilitating the image of aboriginal peoples at his institution could have been so blind to the often gratuitously violent imagery of native people that

Father Thomas Egan, director of Our Lady of Martyrs Shrine from 1968 to 1981, pictured with Esther Phillips and her son Angus. Egan was a voice of reform at Our Lady of Martyrs Shrine. But his failure to adequately consult native groups and his blind spot regarding his institutions' controversial images undercut his efforts.

(Our Lady of Martyrs Shrine Archives, Auriesville, Ray Hoy, photographer) surrounded him every day. Egan must have walked past the Jogues torture diorama that so horrified Oldfield. He doubtless glanced at the cannibalistic frieze that upset Agnes Pafford dozens, if not hundreds of times. Yet, curiously, Egan seems to have been oblivious to these visual echoes of the textual antinative stereotypes he ferreted out with such alacrity in the pages of *The Pilgrim*.

Because of Egan's blind spot, the material culture of Our Lady of Martyrs thirty years after the conclusion of his reforming tenure has lost none of its ability to shock, offend, and alienate. Moreover, in contrast with Father Farrell's campaign, which permanently changed the visual landscape at Midland, Egan's textual legacy was easily effaced. For all their freshness and urgent idealism, his ardent essays appealing for a new kind of relationship with native North America were easily consigned to the scrap heap of history. Enduring the insult of sitting in dusty boxes in the disused industrial kitchen of the defunct shrine cafeteria, they only narrowly escaped the injury of being thrown out altogether.

Mohawk Pilgrimage

There was only one major exception to Egan's persistent privileging of text over image: his insistent inclusion in *The Pilgrim* of photos of native visitors, captured mid-whirl in dance or open-mouthed in song or prayer.[80] Not content to limit his campaign for native–white rapprochement to the printed word, Egan—much like Farrell—sought to encourage a renaissance of aboriginal involvement at Our Lady of Martyrs.

Labor Day weekend, the closest secular holiday to the feast day of the North American martyrs, thus became an important seasonal event for many on the St. Regis reservation. Recalls Sister Ursula: "We always went to the celebrations that day. With the display of dancing, it was a time you were affirmed and felt proud. It was good. We had mass and our Choir singing."[81] In her memory, those long-ago, late-summer days at Auriesville are something of a lost Eden. The nun fondly remembers Egan as affirming that native Catholics should remain grounded in all aspects of their natal culture, including traditional spirituality. In both his incorporation of Iroquois symbolism and ceremony into the mass and his warm welcoming of Mohawk traditionalists, Egan seemed to the young Sister Ursula to embody the Catholic Church's postconsular attitude of empathy and inclusion. She remembers nostalgically that the annual pilgrimage engendered within her a powerful sense of fulfillment, peace, and promise, sentiments that nourished her dawning religious vocation.

But other Mohawk Catholics responded very differently to the priest's exuberant experiments with white–native and traditionalist–Catholic rapprochement at Auriesville and Akwesasne. "Cecilia Pafford," who sang at Our Lady of Martyrs as a child and adolescent throughout the 1980s, vividly recounts the intense frustration she felt worshipping there. For her, the inordinate attention given to trivialities such as native participants' dress signaled a disquieting obsession with surface appearances at the expense of profound truths:

> It just didn't feel like a mass to us. No one introduced themselves to us. They never talked with us, or told us why they were doing these things. I was never told what was going on, or why. They wanted a show! They said, "This is what the people want to see, this is what Father wants. . . . We're going to take you there, wear ribbons, wear feathers, we'll take your picture." I didn't know why I was there.[82]

White organizers were more interested imposing *their own* vision of native identity upon Mohawk Catholic participants than in trying to understand how the participants *themselves* experienced their identity, Pafford alleges. Had they asked, she would have told them that reverent participation in the Mohawk mass is at the center of what it means to be a both a Catholic and a Mohawk. Pafford credits the Catholic Church with preserving the language of her people with its 1710 papal dispensation, which permitted worship in the native vernacular more than 250 years before Vatican II.[83] More than culture or even religion, she argues, it is language that is most integral to individual and collective identity: "Language gives you your worldview, your whole way of thinking. Who you are is determined by your language."[84] Confronted by Mohawk traditionalist claims that their ways are more integral to Iroquois identity than is Catholicism, Pafford is quick to counter that: "Iroquois traditionalists can't speak the language. They have the feathers, the leather, but they need Catholics to teach them their own language."[85] Because Mohawk collective identity is essentially and inescapably linguistic for Pafford, the Mohawk can only be strengthened as a people when they ritually reconstruct the same choral cathedral—the Mohawk mass—first erected by their forbearers in the eighteenth century.[86] It is in this way that they can connect with their fundamental identity as a people.

But alterations to the Mohawk mass were commonplace at Our Lady of Martyrs Shrine. Egan's determination to open Auriesville's doors to Mohawk traditionalists as well as Catholics and to break down barriers of mutual suspicion between white and native pilgrims resulted in something of a motley crew participating in these events. The ancient ritual's traditional rhythms were thus frequently punctuated by discordant elements, from the recitation of the Lord's Prayer in sign language to the performance of traditional Mohawk social (as opposed to ceremonial) dances. To Pafford, these unwelcome interruptions represented a blasphemous interference with something primordial and sacred: "now the whole purpose is totally defeated. . . . You just killed the solemnity."[87]

Along with other native Catholics, Pafford found herself questioning the leadership—and even the piety—of those who would countenance such radical changes to her beloved liturgy. Though Egan doubtless intended these services as a valuable opportunity for aboriginal–white congress, his lack of consultation with native Catholics regarding liturgical deletions and additions left Pafford feeling more like an unpaid participant in a religious variety show than the cocelebrant of a mass. Indeed, the Catholicism Father Egan was inviting ambivalent Akwesasne–St. Regis traditionalists to rejoin was one that was increasingly unrecognizable to Pafford.

Adding to Cecilia's strong sense of "being in Hollywood" was the "plastic-y and fake" sanctuary of Auriesville's unusual round church, the Coliseum, where her choir stood during masses. Meant to evoke the ancient Mohawk village of Ossernenon, the two-tiered log structure, in the center of the round church, represented its architect's fervid imagination of what a seventeenth-century palisaded "Mohawk castle" should look like. Facing radiating ranks of wooden pews ambitiously designed to seat a congregation of some 10,000 souls, the dramatically lit sanctuary was bedecked with solemn statues of the martyrs and topped by the emaciated figure of Christ on the cross. The

The interior of the Coliseum, Auriesville's massive round church. Completed in 1931, the Coliseum is one-sixth of a mile wide and has a capacity of over 10,000.

(Our Lady of Martyrs Shrine Archives, Auriesville)

structure enclosed the sacristy,[88] the hub of much clerical fidgeting with candles and censers, as priests popped in and out of its multiple doors like rabbits entering and leaving a warren. It is little wonder that Pafford remembers this improbable log assembly as being "more like a stage than an altar." Gazing out from her station high in the "castle" into the ranks of a largely white congregation, Pafford had the unsettling sense of being on display for the curious. She often fantasized, as an adolescent, of shouting: "Hey! We're all supposed to be praying, so why are you staring?"[89]

As Pafford gradually began to realize she had been brought to Auriesville less for her own religious edification than that of white visitors, she came to see the pilgrimage less as a spiritual quest than as a commercial opportunity. Denied the chance to express her spirituality

A Mohawk choir sings in the "Mohawk Castle" sanctuary of Our Lady of
Martyrs' Coliseum. Some native participants in masses at Our Lady of
Martyrs during the Egan era objected to frequent alterations to the traditional
Mohawk mass, the strong emphasis on wearing supposedly "traditional"
costume, and the curious gaze of nonnative pilgrims.

(Our Lady of Martyrs Shrine Archives, Auriesville)

authentically, Cecilia and her teenage friends began to hawk Mohawk
handicrafts at the shrine, reasoning, "at least we have a place to sell the
baskets again. . . . We can make some money on this. . . . The bus is
paid for, so let's do this little trip."[90] The Mohawk adolescents also got a
modicum of amusement from pulling the wool over the eyes of "the
tourists." Straight-facedly, they wove outrageous tall tales about life at
Akwesasne–St. Regis for their white auditors. Secure in the knowledge
that their rapt audience could not discern the difference, they made up
nonsense words to traditional Mohawk songs.

   In attempting to involve the Akwesasne Mohawk more intimately
in the life of the Auriesville shrine and simultaneously to confront white
pilgrims' vision of them as mere martyr slayers, Father Egan was evidently well meaning. But he seems seriously to have underestimated
the complexity of what he was taking on. The Mohawk of St. Regis,
both Catholic and longhouse, understand the relationship between the
church and native traditionalism in a variety of complex ways. Attitudes

run the gamut from Sister Ursula Little's understanding of two spiritual paths as entirely compatible to the strict exclusiveness of Cecilia Pafford and her mother, Agnes, who feel that combining distinct religions denies *both* traditions the understanding and respect they deserve.

By making dialogue with the growing traditionalist movement his highest pastoral priority, Father Tom Egan became a hero for Sister Ursula, both then and now. In facilitating events at which she felt both her budding Catholic vocation and the fullness of her Mohawk identity were warmly acknowledged, Egan bequeathed to the young nun her life's mission—to facilitate greater Catholic acceptance of native spirituality under the aegis of Kateri Tekakwitha:

> Our rituals don't have to be used just in the longhouse, it can be used in the church also. . . . [When we do this] we aren't watering down Catholicism, we are trying to bring in our past. In earlier years we were doing this, but now the picture has changed. . . . What we were doing, it has all been undone.[91]

In Sister Ursula's analysis, it was his successors' abrupt retreat from Egan's inclusionary outreach that has "divided the faith community" on her home reservation, significantly deepening the stark rift between Catholics and traditionalists. Even if the church were to once again embrace Egan's inclusive stance, she laments, "so many have already been hurt . . . it would be hard to bring back people who have been pushed away."

From the Paffords' perspective, precisely the opposite is true. Though mother and daughter both recognize that Egan's outreach to traditionalists was intended to adjudicate growing religious tensions in the community, they are equally adamant that his naive strategy did more harm than good:

> The traditional movement was there during his time. [Egan] was trying to keep people Catholic. He kept them temporarily, but they were already going. He made the Catholic and longhouse division more apparent. He illuminated it. . . . He was counting heads and not looking at the heart at all. He was trying to make us one, but instead it emphasized the divisions. He said: "we have to build bridges," and we said "no, the native way is to shake hands and part ways." You can't put it together. To cram it together is more disrespectful than to let it fall apart.

Egan's wrongheaded attempt to accommodate traditionalists, claim the Paffords, not only threatened the cohesion of the Mohawk mass and the religious integrity of the Catholic faith, it also eroded the dignity of traditionalists, by effectively trying to make them into something they were not. Despite Egan's published admonition, "Don't try to be someone God doesn't want you to be," they argue that the well-meaning priest ultimately failed either to recognize or to respect important baseline distinctions between these two spiritual traditions and their proponents.

On the surface, Egan's attempts to invigorate Mohawk pilgrimage to Auriesville seem similar to the "Indian Prayer Days" that Farrell established at Midland. But the scope, purpose, and management style of the two events were very different. Farrell's decision to restrict his new programs exclusively to native Catholics may have seemed a limiting, even parochial demarcation at the time. But this allowed Farrell neatly to avoid navigating the bitter theological divides inside native communities, divides that are all too apparent when we compare the views of Sister Ursula and Cecilia Pafford. In making native traditionalists the major focus of his pastoral attentions, Egan failed to score any lasting gains among them, even as he simultaneously alienated native Catholics, his "base." Conservative Catholics like the Paffords quickly became resentful of the priest's wooing of traditionalists, feeling that their own spiritual needs should be higher on his list of pastoral priorities. Admits Agnes, "we were getting offended and angry. 'What about us?' we thought. The lost sheep were refusing to come back."

In trying to design events that were as much about ameliorating white racism as about fostering native participation, Egan also failed to respect aboriginal participants' need for autonomy and privacy, needs that Farrell had anticipated and tried to honor at Midland. In the end, by trying to make his events all things to all people, Catholic and traditionalist, native and white, Egan managed to alienate everyone except those Catholic inclusivists, like Sister Ursula, who were already theologically aligned with him. Finally, Egan's baffling failure, during his thirteen-year tenure, to address Auriesville's violent imagery ensured that the issue would linger like an unexploded land mine, causing continued controversy, dissension, and distrust at the shrine he had once led.

During his decades of service, Egan served as something of a living bridge between Akwesasne and Auriesville, a connection abruptly severed with his death in 1994. "Except for him," notes Father Richard Fisher, "there was no connection. . . . The St. Regis pilgrimage broke down. . . . Egan had a lot of social ties, and that connection is important. . . . No one else had the same connections."[92] Levels of native participation at Our Lady of Martyrs dropped precipitously and have never since equaled the heights under his direction, as Egan's successors allowed his flawed but exuberant experimentation with native engagement to wither on the vine.

In Egan's absence, old patterns of thinking and writing about native people were quick to reassert themselves. Mere months after taking over, his successor, Father Boyle, wrote a Christmas pastoral that resuscitated all of the crude native stereotypes lulled into somnolence under Egan. Seeking to arouse the reader's sympathy with Jogues's miserable martyr's Christmas in 1642, he wrote:

> A captive for almost five months, living among people who ignored or distrusted Jesus and His Name . . . his Christmas joy could only spring from faith. . . . Jogues' exile and isolation gave him a special way of following Our Lord in poverty, in loneliness. . . . On Christmas Day his Bethlehem was a rude Indian shelter filled with smoke and vermin, as his Calvary would be a hill in the Mohawk Valley.[93]

Scoring Ossernenon's trees with the mark of the cross, Boyle wrote, Jogues symbolically exorcized the land, willing Christ's "enemies, the pagans . . . the demons . . . that rule far and wide" to "flee before it."[94]

The directors who succeeded Boyle were even more overt in their contempt for native sensibilities and in their refusal to give quarter to aboriginal critiques of their institution, however politely expressed. Father John Marzolf became infamous among the shrine's staff for his outspoken, Marie Antoinette-esque dismissals of native perspectives. "If they don't like the Shrine, then let them go join the Kateri League instead," he apparently retorted, referring to the native Catholic organization dedicated to the Catholic enculturation of native traditional spirituality.[95] When angered, the turbulent priest was not above recommending native departure for yet warmer climes. Longtime shrine employee Dorothy Domkowski remembers Marzolf as "pretty much telling the Indians they weren't invited to the Shrine anymore."[96]

"Yes," affirms her colleague Beth Lynch, "he basically said, 'They can go to Hell.'"[97]

Fonda, Auriesville's Sainte-Marie

Systematically stonewalled by Auriesville's increasingly defiant "take it or leave it" approach, native groups seem to have long since given up attempting to communicate their concerns to its administration. After Egan, his shrine gradually let slip the precious connections he had established with aboriginal communities, and a widespread sense of alienation, if not outright animosity, came to characterize relations between the shrine and its native neighbors, both traditionalist and Catholic. Native disenchantment with Our Lady of Martyrs was facilitated by the nearby presence of another prominent Catholic institution: one that honors a native saint and is only too happy to engage with contemporary native peoples.

The National Shrine of Saint Kateri Tekakwitha is located only four miles west of Auriesville, across the Mohawk River. Founded in 1938 by the Order of Friars Minor, it marks the purported spot of Kateri's 1676 baptism, just as Auriesville claims the honor of being her 1656 birthplace.[98] Like Sainte-Marie-among-the-Huron in Ontario, Kateri's shrine in Fonda, New York, was once an active archaeological site. Its first director, Father Thomas Grassman, was a professional archaeologist who led an ambitious dig from 1950 to 1957 that unearthed the remains of a seventeenth-century Iroquois village, composed of several longhouses encompassed by a surrounding palisade.[99] Because their ancient outlines remain clearly staked today, contemporary visitors can "enter" the longhouses' imaginary walls and wonder at these ancient structures' prodigious footprints.

Just as Saint-Marie serves as Midland's local competition and sometime ally, so Fonda is Auriesville's regional rival. But whereas the moderating influence of Sainte-Marie steered Midland into its current stance of sensitivity to native concerns, Fonda's vibrant nearby presence seems only to have hardened attitudes at Auriesville. For Kateri's shrine exemplifies an alternative approach to working with and for aboriginal peoples, which has proven to be more successful than anything Auriesville has been able to muster, even under Egan. Both native and non-native respondents are unanimous in their perception that, of the two sites, Fonda is by far the preferred venue for native visitors. Even Sister Ursula, who so nostalgically remembers her youthful experiences at Our Lady of Martyrs, nevertheless states unequivocally: "More of our people go to Fonda than Auriesville."[100] Cecilia Pafford and Natalie Lamoureux also readily acknowledge their true preferences: "Father Egan organized pilgrimages to Auriesville, but I always wanted to be at Fonda."[101]

Lamoureux is a member of the Kateri League and sits on the Board of Directors at Fonda. But this ardent Mohawk Catholic is also an enthusiastic, informed participant in traditionalist longhouse ceremonies at Akwesasne. Drawing on her decades of experience at both venues, she contrasts the guardedness at Our Lady of Martyrs with the warmer responsiveness of "our" shrine:

> We [Mohawks] don't deal with Auriesville, just with Fonda. We wanted to make sure our Shrine [that is, Fonda] had the right history, the right images. It seems like [at Auriesville] all kinds of people are there. There isn't much for native peoples. They don't sing in our language. Fonda is more homier, it is better for our people.[102]

Lamoureux can cite many instances in which her concerns not only received a hearing but were immediately addressed by Fonda's Franciscan administration. Confronted by a long-standing display of Iroquois "false-face" masks, the Mohawk elder quietly approached then director Father Kevin Kenney. She explained: "I don't think that this should be on display, because it is still going on. It's not a part of history, it still exists." Kenney not only acquiesced to her request that the display be removed, he also voluntarily repatriated the religious artifacts, returning them to the Akwesasne–St. Regis Mohawk.[103] The Franciscans proved just as amenable to native direction in ritual matters. Natalie gently reprimanded another priest for his well-meaning attempt to incorporate native traditions into the mass by burning sweetgrass in place of incense: "Please don't do this until you know how *we* do it! We should be doing it ourselves."[104]

Receptivity to native engagement at Saint Kateri's shrine has led to a cordial working relationship with local First Nations and to a far higher level of native participation there than at Auriesville. At Fonda, aboriginal peoples participate in events that they have helped to organize and shape. This spirit of open dialogue and working together is missing at Our Lady of Martyrs and was even under Egan. Cecilia Pafford's anxiety that something precious was being lost with the adulteration of the Mohawk mass and her anger at serving as a living prop in white fantasies of "Indian-ness" may well have sparked important changes had she communicated them frankly to event organizers. But the attitude of successive Auriesville administrations has clearly dampened native willingness to express dissatisfaction. Even Lamoureux, who communicates so clearly and confidently with the Franciscans at Fonda, is unwilling to voice even minor concerns to Jesuit officials at Auriesville, a fact that speaks volumes about the different "rules of engagement" at the two sites.[105]

Asked point-blank why Fonda enjoys greater success in attracting native participation, Auriesville official Beth Lynch is quick to suggest that it is merely the identity of the saints venerated at the respective shrines that makes the critical difference. A quick-witted former journalist, Lynch suggests that it is "only natural" that Mohawk Catholics be involved in celebrating "one of their own." As a recently canonized figure, Kateri is still basking in the afterglow of her ecclesiastical honeymoon. Her venerators can still link their decades of devotion to her cause with her triumphant vindication in October 2012. By contrast, Lynch glumly admits, Auriesville can boast only a phalanx of deceased white missionaries, violently killed at the hands of native peoples, no less. As these figures received the terminal degree of their own sainthood over eighty years ago, she implies, it is unfair to expect the same level of animation from their advocates. Although Lynch's line of argument clearly has a defensive function, there is a grain of truth in this rueful characterization. Like a bud, the still emergent Kateri cult promises a yet fuller flowering, whereas that of the martyrs seems withered and past its prime.

There is a palpable ambivalence in the way Lynch and others at Auriesville speak about Kateri and her shrine and in how they frame the likelihood that the cult of this newly canonized "Mohawk Saint" will come to eclipse that of the martyrs locally, nationally, and internationally. On the one hand, Our Lady of Martyrs officials individually express apparently sincere devotion toward Catherine Tekakwitha. Collectively, too, Auriesville embraces Kateri and profits thereby. Chastely clasping her ubiquitous lily, the native convert has been a prominent part of Auriesville's iconography virtually since its founding. Tekakwitha has long had her own dedicated museum on-site at Our Lady of Martyrs, and its large gift shop boasts far more Kateri-related religious paraphernalia than it does martyr-related items. So striking is this imbalance in devotion detritus, in fact, that the uninitiated might easily be convinced that they had somehow made a wrong turn on the highway.

Auriesville advocates for Tekakwitha consistently seek to channel her growing popularity in a way that will benefit their own saints, hitching the martyrs' tired wagon to her rising star. Seizing on Tertullian's familiar dictum linking exsanguination to conversion, they rhetorically link the popular native figure to the three "Auriesville martyrs." Of course, Kateri never met Jogues, Goupil, and de la Lande, as all three men were slain a full decade before her birth. But Auriesville advocates make much of the fact that she was allegedly born on the very ground fecundated by their martyrs' blood. Casting Kateri as the martyrs' spiritual child or "Christian seed," they adeptly claim the remarkable spirituality of this young woman as one more laurel for their own saints' brows.

The theological interpretation of Kateri advanced by many at Auriesville is in sharp contrast with that expressed by many of her native devotees. Mohawk Catholics like Natalie Lamoureux and Sister Ursula Little see in Tekakwitha the inspiration for their own contemporary agenda, which stresses the ultimate compatibility of native traditional spirituality with an ardent, undiluted Catholicism. They glimpse in Kateri something of the elusive wholeness and peace they seek in their own fractured spiritual and social lives. For walking the middle way between traditions can be a dispiritingly lonely experience. Though Lamoureux's presence in the longhouse is accepted despite her known Catholic commitments, she is the only remaining member of her large extended family to retain a connection to the church: "all of the members of my family have gone over to the longhouse way."[106]

But Auriesville interpretations of Tekakwitha seize on the very elements of her story downplayed in native retellings of her story: disjuncture and discord. Her blue eyes flashing as she gestures, Lynch argues that those who present Kateri as maintaining her Mohawk cultural identity after her conversion dilute and denigrate the most miraculous aspect of her story: the completeness of her religious transformation. In Lynch's reading, the young Mohawk-Algonquin convert not only chose

Christianity over traditionalism but had to struggle mightily against her own kith and kin to do so, eventually choosing the bitter path of exile. If conversion is, as some native Catholics claim, the peaceful interweaving of formerly disparate traditions, she asks, then were such extreme measures necessary?[107]

Beth Lynch's reading of Kateri's legacy transposes it into much the same spiritual key as the anthem Lynch sings to her own spiritual heroes. Though not a martyr, she argues, the young convert nonetheless suffered humiliation and forced relocation because of her religious commitments. It was Kateri's determination to follow Jesus whatever the consequences, Lynch suggests, that is the special mark of her often misunderstood religious genius. Reinterpreted in this light, Kateri becomes highly relevant to contemporary conservative Catholics, who see themselves as targeted for similar persecution and mockery in a fallen and cynical world: "Kateri was living in a pagan world, just like us. She is our model."[108] Both contemporary native Catholics and Catholic conservatives, then, tend to read their own identity and characteristic preoccupations into this figure from their shared past.

Lynch's strong disagreement with what she sees as native Catholics' counterfactual presentation of Kateri's life and legacy profoundly affects her analysis of the Fonda shrine. Those who seek to make Kateri an icon of syncretism, she feels, have unwittingly opened up her cult to a host of unwholesome and un-Catholic influences. In Lynch's reading, Fonda's stress on Kateri's retention of her native culture becomes the adder's kiss of a resurgent "paganism" on the chaste breast of Catholicism. Appreciation of Kateri's femininity, Lynch feels, can encourage an unholy "feminism," even as emulation of her "native communion with nature" ushers in "pantheism." In this subtle way, then, Lynch is able to use Fonda's very popularity against it by implicitly questioning its propriety and orthodoxy. Auriesville's unwillingness to paint itself in the fashionable, sexy hues demanded by "the World," Lynch seems to suggest, makes it the dowdier but more righteous of the two sister shrines. Like the wise virgin, waiting with her heart and lantern alight, she will be ready to greet the returning bridegroom. Her sibling's flame, by contrast, left unguarded, will flicker and die.

But such a critique can cut both ways. For her part, Natalie Lamoureux perceives seventeenth-century Jesuit missionaries as religious bigots incapable of understanding, let alone appreciating, the religious riches they encountered in native North America:

> The martyrs, their perception was inaccurate. They couldn't understand that it was possible to blend Catholicism and traditionalism. . . . My perception was that the Black Robes didn't understand our ceremonies. To us it was a sacred thing, but they thought it was war dances. . . . I have no problems blending the two. My mother is a clan mother, my two brothers are faith keepers . . . and I do both. I attend the naming ceremonies, and the winter ceremony, and the false face ceremonies, and no one there gives me a hard time. . . . I always take my eagle feather and pray with it.[109]

Lamoureux suggests that both the martyrs and the shrine later established to honor them are fundamentally hostile to her native culture and averse to contemporary, progressive trends toward ecumenicalism and interreligious dialogue.

Both the Midland and Auriesville shrines, then, have a local competitor and ally that has decisively influenced their institution's self-perception and self-presentation. Sainte-Marie, the "daughter" of the Midland shrine, has since its institutional maturation in the 1980s exerted, with its own focus on native and Jesuit experiences of religious contact, something of a moderating influence on its mother. But Fonda has been unable to do the same for Auriesville. Perhaps it is the shrines' shared status as such that leads those at Our Lady of Martyrs to perceive the Saint Kateri shrine as an upstart rival, a popular younger sister, rather than a potential ally for joint initiatives. Perhaps the institutions' mutual alienation is due to the narcissism of small differences between the Jesuits and the Franciscans. Perhaps it is because of simple, petty rivalry between the religious figures each strives to honor. But one thing is certain: though Fonda presents a compelling alternative model of how a Catholic shrine can solicit and utilize input from native people both within and outside the church, its lessons have been pointedly ignored at Auriesville.

Sarah Oldfield, we recall, had fled from the Auriesville shrine in tears after encountering a statue of Isaac Jogues being tortured by Mohawk children. She returned several months later, determined to express her concerns about the display directly to the shrine's administration. She wanted to tell them that the diorama falsely essentialized centuries of white–native encounter by casting native people as eternal and irrational antagonists. She wanted to argue that such provocatively violent imagery reduced the complexity of traditional Mohawk culture to one aspect of its postwar practices. She wanted to convey that the Our Lady of Martyrs imagery had continuing, real-world effects on her people, predisposing nonnatives to regard contemporary Iroquois people with fear, animosity, or contempt.

Oldfield expected that these arguments would be readily comprehensible to the shrine's administration, even if they disagreed with her. But, in meeting with shrine director Father John Paret, she encountered a communicative disconnect that was as disturbing, in its own way, as the instigating incident had been. Though polite, even courtly, Paret clearly did not understand her arguments or even concede her right to voice them. As she struggled to convey to the uncomprehending Jesuit how she felt *his* imagery was hurting *her* people, Oldfield had the unnerving sense that her words were bouncing impotently off an invisible force field surrounding the shrine director. Unable to penetrate Paret's bubble with her critical shafts, she eventually left, discouraged. Throwing her purse over her shoulder as she bent her head under the light drizzle, Oldfield wearily wondered why she had even bothered returning to Auriesville.[110]

In the person of John Paret, Oldfield had been confronted with an understanding of time and truth deeply incompatible with her own, stranding their tentative, wary dialogue on the shoals of mutual incomprehension. Unlike critics of Auriesville's violent imagery, who are guided by a conventional, historical sense of time and who seek to understand a given event by assiduously tracing both antecedents and aftermath, Paret lives in "devotional time." Immersed in this theological view of history, Father Richard Fisher argues, Paret and other Auriesville officials do not share the view that martyrdom art is

> cruel and stereotyped. . . . They just don't think about the implications. . . . It is not that they're insensitive, it's just that they

don't get it. They are not trying to perpetuate negative stereotypes of native people . . . but they are the inheritors of the 1950s, 1960s stress on martyrdom. . . . They just don't see what the images are doing.[111]

In contrast with historical consciousness, devotional time elevates certain encounters or events on the basis of their apparent conformity with atemporal or eternal ideals. The guiding question is not "how representative is this incident of centuries of encounter between native people and Europeans?" but rather "does this violent death conform to the example set by Christ and his martyrs?" Martyrdoms, from this perspective, are not so much "historical events" as they are eternal verities existing "above" or "outside" banal reality, verities that pierce periodically into profane time like the hierophantic elevation of the Host during mass.

Because they are essentially unrooted in the history that hosts them, these events can easily be transplanted to flower anew in alien eras. Indeed, the continued vitality of the cult of the North American martyrs owes much to this temporal creativity, which has allowed these deaths to speak anew to the changing theological, cultural, and political circumstances of each successive generation of devotees. Imaginative transplantation has allowed the martyrs to preside over the clerico-nationalist conquest of Québec, to battle the "red menace" of Communism, and, contemporaneously, to embody both the imperative of intercultural dialogue and the defiant defense of eternal Catholic verities in the face of an increasingly secular and pluralistic North American culture. Without devotional time, the martyrs, marooned in their own era, would quickly have receded from collective Catholic consciousness, becoming increasingly tiny figures in the rearview mirror of history.

For Father Paret and others at Auriesville, the art that memorializes these moments of sacred suffering shares in the original event's time-transcending qualities. The "eternal now" presented in martyrdom art—the suspended, frozen moment between the beginning of a violent gesture and its inevitable end—can serve as a temporal envelope into which devotees can slip themselves in order to witness and even vicariously experience the martyrs' suffering. In such moments of contemplation, viewers, through imaginative empathy, merge their own flesh with the suffering body of the saint, the searing universality of pain serving as the electric medium of this communion. In the intensity of this martyr-focused experience, other figures in the image simply drop away. The very elements of the Jogues diorama that had commanded Oldfield's shocked attention, the crouched figures of the seminude Mohawk children clustered around the saint, gnawing on his fingers, had become almost invisible to John Paret. Long accustomed to casting native peoples simply as torture delivery mechanisms, as impersonal providers of the requisite suffering needed to manufacture a martyr, it was inconceivable to Paret that these painted figures could also persecute the contemporary Mohawk community. As they together gazed at the diorama that was the focus of their dissension, Paret and Oldfield were, in a very real sense, not seeing the same object.

Just as their understandings of time diverged, so too did their comprehension of truth. For Oldfield, truth is inescapably multiple. Her experience as the member of a minority group whose perspectives on history have often been ignored or unacknowledged has essentially forced her to appreciate that there is always more than one side to any story. By contrast, Paret's understanding of truth is absolute. Just as he perceives the martyrdoms as reflections of eternity rather than as accidents of history, so truth, for him, is singular and unchanging. From Paret's perspective, what is most needed at Auriesville is not the accommodation of alternate perspectives but the bringing of the recalcitrant to see the light and be transformed thereby.

Martyrdom art is a powerful tool in this evangelical battle, because it shows what the followers of the truth have been prepared to endure rather than betray it. For Paret and his contemporary Auriesville acolyte Beth Lynch, these sublime "snapshots" of the martyrs' agony, "taken" in the moments just before the martyrs' deaths, memorialize what they most cherish about these figures: capturing the martyrs' move from mortality into transcendence, highlighting their quietly defiant courage, and celebrating their ultimate spiritual victory. Lynch is adamant that even in the name of cultivating better relations with native peoples, the martyrs' suffering cannot be downplayed or denied:

> What is important to me as a Catholic is that people have to understand the suffering in order to understand what martyrdom is. We can't just say that they died, or they were killed, or they were hit in the head. We

don't know what suffering is, here in our cushy, spoiled lives here in
America . . . so there has to be some indication of what they went
through, without making it bloody and gory. It is not like any of us are
strangers to brutality. . . . You know, Joan of Arc was killed in the same
town where Isaac Jogues went to seminary, killed by her own people.
So as I tell the story I am not slamming the Native Americans.[112]

The notion that the shrine should further dial down its violent martyrdom art, for Lynch, represents the ever-present temptation toward
theological adulteration, a temptation the martyrs also faced but stoically resisted. For Lynch, the martyrs' outstanding characteristic was
their refusal to compromise their beliefs and practices, even when immersed in a "pagan" culture:

Even with their conversion of the natives, [the martyrs] didn't compromise anything, they weren't saying, OK, you can keep doing this
and this. No. You can't. You have to take only one wife, you have to
stop the cannibalism. . . . They didn't compromise. . . . From what I
can tell in all that I have read, [the martyrs] didn't ever compromise
anything.[113]

Their choice, as she sees it, of death over religious dishonor speaks
volumes to contemporary Catholics struggling to hold to eternal truths
in a world full of doubt, cynicism, and change. Like the martyrs,
Catholics must be prepared to endure the uncomprehending scorn of
the fallen and the lost as they champion unpopular verities. Ultimately, one does not show respect for or love of the other by affirming
their false views in the name of political correctness, Lynch argues.
One demonstrates it by bringing them into a fuller appreciation of the
one singular truth, which shines out from the martyrdom art derided
by critics. Hiding what the martyrs suffered would deny pilgrims of
all ethnicities, including native people, the experience to vicariously
witness and be transformed by the martyrs' pain and ultimate
exultation.

The ongoing debate over martyrdom imagery at Auriesville, then, is
not a quibbling one. Father Fisher's terse characterization of the debate
as unfolding between "those who want to contextualize [the martyr-
doms], and those who want to cast moral culpability on a whole group
of people" frames the issue as a struggle between "good" contextualizers
and "bad" blamers. What is at stake is whether the shrine will continue,

through the display of historically skewed and overtly racist imagery, to contribute to the further victimization of an already vulnerable segment of the American population, an agenda that is obviously far from Christlike. But Lynch's equally heartfelt comments about "self-loathing"[114] Catholics who have turned their back on the church's true teachings implies that those seeking to modify the shrine's material culture are all too willing to sell out Catholic truth to the facile demands of political correctness. For her, the issue is whether Auriesville will continue in its sacred mission of allowing visitors vicariously to witness their uncompromising perseverance in the faith, even in the face of death itself.

While the Auriesville administration presents itself as taking a mediating position between zealots on either side of the issue, proponents of martyrdom art are clearly in the ascendency. Officials' comments invariably stress the dangers of "going too revisionist" rather than highlighting the perils of historical distortion or racist stereotyping. Pro-art employees at the shrine enjoy the implicit backing of ultraconservative Catholic groups such as the Pius X Society and the National Coalition for Clergy and Laity, organizers of thriving pilgrimages to Auriesville. Like Beth Lynch, these groups venerate the martyrs for what they see as their willingness to die rather than give up their cherished theological principals. Despite their sometimes fraught relationship with the shrine's administration, ultraconservative pilgrims, given their numbers and their passion, are ideally positioned to influence the imagery debate at Auriesville in the future.

Both Midland and Auriesville have their cobwebbed cupboards that contain, alongside yellowing pamphlets and mildewing lost-and-found articles, gory and incongruous caches of rejected artwork and signage, like the detritus of some improbable shipwreck, washed in on the ebb and flow of public outrage. "HILL OF TORTURE" blares one uprooted sign, the dirt still clinging to its stake. Scores of paintings are there, too, taken down and turned to the wall like naughty pupils in a strict schoolmarm's classroom. In these forsaken spaces, only the silent dust or the spinning spider witnesses the martyrs' frozen last moments of prayer and of agony. There are no more empathic shivers of rapture or of revulsion. And yet, despite their consignment to a similar ignominious limbo, the status of these jettisoned items seems, at each shrine, to be subtly different. At Midland, their dust is a shroud, their basement a crypt. At Auriesville, however, their displacement may well be temporary. The growing influence of ultraconservatives might yet effect a triumphal restoration of these rejected images. Their current sleep is perhaps that of the chrysalis rather than the tomb.

7

Pilgrims' Progress

THE SOUND OF LATIN PLAINSONG, high and thin, permeates the gray, early morning chill and is answered by the sweet, intermittent soprano of birdsong. Pine needles bite deeply into my knees as I kneel with some 200 pilgrims, many of them children and young people, on the damp grass. Together we gaze expectantly uphill at the make-shift altar installed under an imposing figure—a giant statue of Isaac Jogues.[1] Caught midstride, the Jesuit saint's frozen gaze greets the dawn horizon. One of his mutilated hands clutches a cross, while the amputated digits of the other are upheld in a protective gesture of benediction high over the outdoor congregation. The freshening wind tosses the autumn leaves and toys with the banners of the assembled "brigades," their bright illustrations honoring, among others, Joan of Arc, the child seers of Fatima, the Immaculate Heart of Mary, and Isaac Jogues himself. The banners are held by two rows of adolescents separated by gender and standing, like bridesmaids and ushers, on either side of the outdoor altar. The breeze gently lifts the edges of the lace mantillas worn on the bowed heads of many female pilgrims and flaps the white tent protectively erected over the golden reliquaries and candelabra on the outdoor altar, flickering the candles' flames. The rich odor of incense wafts from censers swung by altar boys, mingling with the tang of the dried pine needles lying in tawny profusion on the grass. To the rear right of the congregation, a tall adolescent makes his confession. Even kneeling, he dwarfs the seated priest carefully listening to his whispered words. Young pilgrims—the very youngest resting in their parents' arms—silently and stoically watch the unfolding mass, listening as the quiet Latin alternates between the deeper tones of the

four priests, arrayed in embroidered purple, and the higher counterpoint of several black-clad nuns—Slaves of Mary Immaculate—who
lead the congregational responses.

Abruptly, the gentle drone of Latin is replaced by harsh, amplified
English as the mass's chief celebrant, Canon Andreas Hellman, speaking through a bullhorn, begins his vernacular homily.[2] The assembled
pilgrims, he states, are on the brink of commencing a most sacred task.
Following this early morning outdoor mass they will begin their
seventy-mile trek "in the very footsteps of the martyrs," following the
purported path taken by René Goupil and Isaac Jogues, who were
marched back to the Iroquois homeland in the Mohawk Valley after
their capture on the banks of the St. Lawrence River during the summer
of 1642. A "Pilgrimage of Reparation" for individual, societal, and institutional sins and a symbolic spiritual "reconquest of America" for Christ,
their arduous journey will meander along sylvan paths, dusty back roads,
and beside seedy strip malls until the pilgrims reach the holy ground
sanctified by the blood of the man depicted in such a heroic manner.

Like the martyrs themselves, Hellman intones, the assembly are
"soldiers of Christ" who stalwartly endure the incomprehension of a
world that does not share their faith. Their fervent commitment to the
magisterium and the ancient Latin rites of the church has often earned
them the scorn of their family and neighbors,[3] even fellow Catholics:
"so many of our friends and our relations . . . have shown surprise, resistance, contempt when we have shown who we are as Christians. . . .
They thought that we were of their generation, they thought we were
also children of this world, children of Satan." The gathering's collective persecution, he acknowledges, has already brought them close to
Christ, but this connection will only deepen upon their arrival at
Auriesville:

> We have at this point already the bloody standard of the cross not only
> planted in our midst, but in our hearts. If that is not the case, this will
> happen by the end of this pilgrimage, once we set foot on the holy
> ground, on the grounds that were hallowed by the shedding of the blood
> of St. Isaac Jogues and his companion, St. René Goupil.

Gesturing to the oversized statue behind him, Canon Hellman encourages his flock's collective veneration of "this giant . . . a hero, a
conqueror, a master of the spiritual life . . . His great apostle to North

America." He reminds the assembly of the ultimate source of the martyr's strength—Christ—and admonishes them to aspire to a similar emulation of their savior's life and death, during both this arduous three-day-long journey and their longer, lifelong pilgrimage in a world that ultimately is "not their home." Urging them to keep to "the straight and narrow way which is so well marked by the blood of our Lord and of his martyrs," he orders them, as they march, to "carry your weapons: your crucifix in your right hand and the rosary in your left, the name of Jesus in your heart and the name of Mary on your lips. So be it."

Following the solemn Latin rite, a hasty al fresco breakfast of instant oatmeal and hot chocolate is served, made with boiling water ladled out by female volunteers. Though simple, the hot meal is welcome, not least because the Styrofoam cup warms my chilled hands better than does the weak, early-morning sun. I try to break the ice with the women in my assigned brigade as we sit together on the grass during the few precious minutes allotted for breakfast by asking them why they wear the mantilla during mass. A pilgrim in her early twenties replies, with a toss of her long, whip-straight ponytail, that covering her head is simply a biblically mandated gesture of respect to God. Another agrees, adding that the transition to Latin demarcates the mass as a sacred time of communion with the divine, rather than one's peers:

> During the Latin Mass the priest is facing the altar, facing God, it is being directed to him. The new mass, well, it really communicates among the people, instead of toward God, it's not surprising what has grown from it, the lack of reverence. To me the Latin mass is a far superior way of giving glory to God, instead of to people.[4]

My rapport with the group quickly wanes, however, when I compare the pilgrims' mantillas to Muslim women's *hijabs* or headscarves. "They may look similar," Margaret Middleton, a middle-aged pilgrim from the Midwest told me, "but that's about it."[5] Warming to her theme, she predicts that the coming apocalyptic war between Christianity and Islam will soon force ordinary Catholics, much like the martyrs themselves, to choose between apostasy and death. She affirms that pilgrims

> need to be ready to do our part, to be ready to suffer and die. According to [Muslims] we are all infidels, so, if they became a dominant part of the society, like they are in Europe . . . well, their next step is to eliminate people who aren't Muslim and who don't want to convert.

But because Middleton had previously confided to me her belief that "we need the restoration of a Catholic America, we really need a Catholic culture," I suggest that perhaps Christianity and Islam are more similar than different, as both seek converts and desire positively to influence society. Regarding me with undisguised astonishment, Middleton almost drops her rosary. Recovering, she swiftly sketches a stark dichotomy between the two religions:

> But Catholicism is the one true faith, it is what Christ commanded. . . . The difference is he didn't say to kill anyone, he said convert with love. . . . [Muslims] take their belief system not from Jesus though, it's from Mohammad. . . . He had visions or locutions . . . which, when you look at them, were demonic, anything is demonic that is going to tell you to kill others who don't want to convert.

Our intense discussion is interrupted by deafening feedback from a bullhorn. Our attempts to continue it sotto voce meet with the disapproving stares of other pilgrims, under which Middleton quickly quails into silence. Sporting a Smokey-the-bear style ranger hat, Mike Mc-Donald, the National Coalition of Clergy and Laity's "brigadier-general," reminds the gathering that they must at all times follow the directives of their individual brigadier and the ubiquitous Safety Patrol. As pilgrimage is a collective activity, he sternly intones, individuals must resist the temptation to perform additional penitence, such as fasting, which could impede their brigade's collective progress.

After prolonged prayer, the spirited yelling of each brigade's especial chant, and the solemn aspersion of the brigade banners with holy water, the pilgrims proudly form up and march off. Children of both genders walk together, under the auspices of the Fatima seers, but adults are segregated into sex-specific brigades. As the women walking in honor of the Immaculate Heart of Mary head out, bottles of bright yellow Gatorade swing cheerfully from the nuns' belts, incongruous alongside their black-beaded rosaries and glinting holy medals. Backpacks protrude like hunchbacks from underneath their traditional wimples, and sneakers flash a startling white beneath their floor-length black habits. Behind them, the sisters' student charges, teenage girls modestly arrayed in ankle-length skirts, decorously process two by two like the animals venturing into Noah's Ark. Rallying behind a homemade banner of a grim-faced Isaac Jogues, the men of his namesake brigade perilously

National Coalition of Clergy and Laity pilgrims, bearing their banners, typically walk into the sunlight. Pilgrims walk in tightly organized, sex-segregated brigades and pray and sing virtually continually during the three-day-long annual event, which takes them seventy miles, by foot, from the massive statue of Isaac Jogues in Lake George, New York, to Our Lady of Martyrs Shrine in Auriesville.

(National Coalition of Clergy and Laity)

counterpoise quavering tenor with authoritative bass in a complex
Latin hymn, using the rhythm to set the pace for their march. Inter-
spersed among the disciplined battalions, like the rarer glint of a silver
rosary medallion amid more pedestrian beads, are priests still arrayed
in their liturgical garb of vivid purple topped with surplices of snowy
white lace. Some, like Canon Hellman, have jauntily accessorized this
ecclesiastical formal wear with wide-brimmed tilley hats and whittled
walking sticks.

Thus do the disciplined bands of nearly two hundred ultraconservative Catholics—virtually all of them white—depart on their seventy-
mile-long walk: women and men, religious and lay, children and youth,
each brigade separately intoning their respective prayers and songs, each
imploring the attentions of Christ and his martyrs, of various saints,
angels, and of the Virgin Mother of God. The solemnity of their continual choral devotions is occasionally interrupted by the terse, bullhorned directives of the Safety Patrol, a group of gangly adolescent boys
wearing Day-Glo orange vests and armed with walkie-talkies. Breaking into the rising, reedy notes of a "Salve Regina" or a "Miserere Mei,"
their giant, disembodied voices issue terse commands: "Keep to the
left of the yellow line!" "Stay right up against the fence!" The mood of
prayerful penitence is also intermittently undercut by the appearance
of the coalition's rented flatbed truck containing four Porta-Potties,
which slosh by on their shameful errand of mercy.

Sometimes, weary drivers stumble across the Our Lady of Martyrs
Shrine while looking for a tranquil picnicking area along the seemingly
interminable interstate, which winds through the scenic hills of upstate
New York between Albany and Syracuse. Exiting air-conditioned vehi-
cles into the summer sunshine, they stretch their car-cramped limbs
before exploring the Ravine or shrine museums or commandeering a
picnic table placed invitingly in the shade, near the visitor parking lot.
Similarly, casual, curious vacationers in Georgian Bay's alluring cot-
tage country emerge through the black metal gates of the Midland
Martyrs' Shrine into its statue-filled grounds seeking much the same
kind of diversion as at any other of the local tourist destinations. Smell-
ing of sunscreen and shaking off sand from the lake's beaches, they

snap photos, ask questions of the shrine's green-clad personnel, or grab a cup of coffee from the shrine's cafeteria. But although both venues thus host a number of "walk-in" tourist-pilgrims, the vast majority of visitors arrive with organized Catholic pilgrimages. The experiences of most of those who set foot on the grounds of each shrine, then, are profoundly shaped by the devotional framework imposed by pilgrimage, with its carefully orchestrated sequence of events and its inculcation of a strong collective identity and esprit. Recognizing the centrality of pilgrimage at Midland and at Auriesville but also the increasing divergence in how and by whom it is performed at each venue, I decided to participate in pilgrimages to each site to get an intimate glimpse of the dynamics of contemporary veneration of the North American martyrs on both sides of the border.

My selection of which pilgrimages to attend was based on careful analysis of which ones seem to be in the ascendancy at each site. For although both shrines share a striking similar history of postwar "ethnic" pilgrimage, dominated by Eastern Europeans, the demographics of devotion at these sites have diverged sharply in more recent decades. Though both shrines still host graying, dwindling contingents of Poles, Czechs, Hungarians, and Italians each summer, as they have for the past seventy years, the demographic vanguard at both sites has long since passed to other groups.

At Midland, the continuing vibrancy of "ethnic pilgrimage" is almost entirely due to the emergence over the last two decades of new participants. Demographic dominance has gradually shifted from early stalwarts—Irish and Italians, Poles and Portuguese—to a new Asian clientele. Filipino, Vietnamese, Cambodian, Tamil, Japanese, and, most recently, Goan Catholics from that small western Indian province all come, each on their assigned days, in motor coaches from the nearby metropolis of Toronto. They come for a day out of the city, a day in which outdoor worship on the shrine's carefully manicured grounds is supplemented by the enjoyment of traditional music, language, food, dancing, and elaborate rituals, many involving costumes, floats, and devotional processions. Unlike the graying European events, these pilgrimages are very much family affairs. Children dressed as angels or outfitted in traditional costume dart among the gloomy statuary, as bright as the flower beds they play among. English is virtually unheard as pilgrims converse and worship in the Asian languages of their homelands. Much like a traditional Italian *festa,* these events contrive to combine serious religious devotion with feasting and festivity, affirming the group's traditional cultural, linguistic, and spiritual roots even as they celebrate their survival as proudly distinct entities within Canada. These Catholic minorities are enthusiastically welcomed by the Midland Jesuits, who value the opportunity both unobtrusively to inculcate devotion to the martyrs among these new clients and to showcase how neatly their theologically liberal values of ecumenical openness align with the multicultural lodestar of Canadian politics. At Midland, the martyrs function as symbols of intercultural dialogue. To this end, it is their lives of "outreach" and "accommodation" to the unfamiliar "other" that are stressed over their grisly deaths.

At Auriesville, conversely, the torch of pilgrimage has been passed not to new ethnic or linguistic minorities but to a new breed of pilgrims: ultraconservative Catholics.[6] Groups such as the National Coalition of Clergy and Laity (NCCL) and the Society of St. Pius X make their arrival at Our Lady of Martyrs the culmination of an arduous trek, modeled on the martyrs' own difficult journey and explicitly couched in penitential and reparative terms.[7] If joyous feasting predominates at Midland, austerity rules at Auriesville. Though these ultraconservative pilgrims, like their Asian counterparts north of the border, seek to affirm through pilgrimage their minority status, it is their theo-ideological stance rather than ethnic or linguistic identity that sets them apart from the mainstream. While the Midland shrine celebrates different cultural articulations of Catholicism, it simultaneously affirms the ultimate unity of both the Catholic Church and the Canadian state. Ultraconservatives, however, use their long walk shrine-ward to shame the majority culture into reflection, repentance, and redemption (even when the majority culture is largely unaware of it). Taking as a model the uncompromising and unpopular evangelism of the martyrs themselves, which culminated in their violent deaths for the faith, these pilgrims see their self-sacrificing slog as a powerful witness of faith in a death-hardened, sin-steeped society.

To these two North American pilgrimages I also sought to add a triangulating venue that might force some of the broader (but paradoxically less apparent) similarities between them into the light. I found it by exploring the contemporary martyrs' cult in France, journeying to a small, homemade chapel privately erected to Jean de Brébeuf by an elderly circle of his French venerators. Built in the saint's hometown of Condé-sur-Vire, Normandy, the modest structure is formed from the stones of his ruined ancestral home, La Boisée. French dynamics of the martyrs cult are very different from those in North America. As distinctive as the Goan event and NCCL pilgrimage may at first appear, their family resemblances quickly became apparent when compared with the foreign complexion of the martyrs' cult in their Gallic homeland.

Children's Crusade

Those who took part in the 2010 Pilgrimage of Restoration are so theologically conservative that for some of them, the stereotypically self-evident query "Is the pope Catholic?" remains an open question. Many pilgrims feel that the "lukewarmness" and "adulteration" that they see as having crept into the Catholic Church since the Second Vatican Council have incrementally seduced even its highest leadership away from the traditional teachings they themselves revere.[8] As they walk in what they believe to be the actual footsteps of their fallen, martyred heroes, these pilgrims seek to emulate them spiritually as well, by embracing theology and ethics they see as being forged in the martyrs' image. Celebrating the Latin mass—the same mass the martyrs would have said, they tell me—they practice a Catholicism that, in its absolutism and rejection of many aspects of modernity, conforms more to the spirit of the first rather than the second Vatican Council. Stalwart practitioners of the Latin mass, they defend traditional Catholic theology, undiluted by the hand-wringing apologies and ecumenical sensitivities of the last forty years. Decrying the erosive effects of feminism on American society, they reassert, in their own lives, the validity of traditional, patriarchal patterns of authority in both the family and the church.

Although the Catholic Church as an institution has a staunchly anti-abortion stance, the NCCL addresses itself to less definitive issues involving human biology. When asked to clarify the collective ills for which they seek to atone, many pilgrims named "sins" related to sexuality and fertility: homosexuality, "immodesty," abortion, divorce, birth control, and the teaching of "sex ed" in American public schools, a practice that the group condemns as "objectively gravely evil. It is a perverse method of instruction which makes public and open those things which by nature are private, intimate or shameful. *Classroom sex-ed leads children to sin.*"[9] Ultraconservatives condemn mainstream Catholics for having abandoned their own touchstone belief that human beings must cede to God all aspects of their earthly lives, including control of their own reproductive capacities. According to the NCCL, married couples should receive cheerfully as many children as God sees fit to send and not tinker with the timing or number of their pregnancies.[10] Some extend their personal beliefs about the immorality of contraception to their working lives, seeing this as a form of witnessing to a sinful world. One longtime pilgrim employed as a nurse steadfastly refuses to gown up and assist in sterilization operations at her hospital, on the grounds that so doing would abet the patient in his or her evasion of God's gift of children. Seeking to countermand the "moral decay" they see as prevalent in American culture, the NCCL mandates a group norm that enshrines the "natural" begetting and spiritual nourishment of children at its very heart: rewarding large families with approval, praise, and support.[11]

On the eve of the pilgrimage, NCCL members gather at Cramer's Point Motel near Lake George, relishing the opportunity to indulge in the last hot shower they will enjoy for several days. In the designated "women's dorm," the exchange of news about the advanced pregnancies or recent deliveries of absent pilgrims was one of the few secular topics of conversation. The group's strict ban on birth control introduced to these informal exchanges between devout women a strong element of contingency and uncertainty. One pilgrim in her early twenties, who was to be married in a few months, was unable to answer with any certainty her friends' urgent query: "are you coming next year?" Having anticipatorily surrendered her marital fertility to God, she was unable to make firm plans, aware that this time next year she may well be expecting her first child.

Though both male and female NCCL pilgrims are dedicated to respecting God's sovereignty over their reproductive lives, their common commitment to bearing and raising large families affects them in profoundly different ways, as specific sacrifices are expected of each. Many ultraconservative Catholic women eschew careers for lives of selfless service to their husbands and children in the home. Pilgrim Mike Emig described his stay-at-home wife's average day: "my wife is a mother and a homemaker, and she spends every day making meals, cleaning clothes, teaching children. She does the same thing day in and day out."[12] But, he added, her selfless endurance of monotonous housework and consistent privileging of others' needs above her own is laudably Christian:

> In itself this is a meaningless job, but when you offer that job to God as the job he has given you to do, it becomes meaningful. Not just being a mother, but every job has unpleasant things. But when we offer all the little sufferings to God that dignifies any kind of work, all the jobs we do throughout the day.

Because of their suspicion that all but the most conservative Catholic institutions are "too liberal and watered down," many ultraconservative Catholic mothers spend their days caring not only for infants and preschoolers (as do many of their mainstream peers) but also school-age children and adolescents. The large number of children they bear and the high degree of responsibility they take for their religious, educational, and social formation makes their roles as mothers almost all encompassing.[13] At the cookout after the first long day of marching, as pilgrims busied themselves with erecting tents, tending to blisters, and feasting on the chili smoldering in large, blackened tureens, one mother sat at a picnic table with her oldest daughter, a girl in her late teens. As the two of them paged meditatively through college brochures, the woman simultaneously nursed her youngest child, a six-month-old. Around her, children between these extremes of infancy and adulthood played, screamed, and jostled for her attention. The use of birth control to restrict family size is so prevalent that most North American women, including mainstream Catholics, cannot easily fathom the challenges of this woman's experience of virtually multigenerational mothering.

Men, on the other hand, are expected to be the heads of their households, taking as their model the "kingship" of Christ. Their role is to guide and protect their families, making the final decisions on behalf of all its members and embracing as necessary mortifications the hard work, frugality, stress, and personal sacrifices that financially supporting a large number of dependents inevitably entails. Without another adult wage earner in the family, they often bear the financial burden alone. As we walked together, bringing up the limping rear of the NCCL's disciplined brigade formations, the NCCL's cofounder, Mike Meier, confided to me:

We have a nice house, but I have a pickup truck with 300,000 miles on it, and I have a fifteen-year-old car that I drive on a daily basis. We don't take the kids to Disney every year, we don't go skiing in Colorado, we have lift tickets at the local ski place, which is pretty nice. . . . You figure, hey, we're married, and marriage is for family, and so you center your life around that.[14]

Children are thus the touchstone of traditionalist Catholic life and a living barometer of how completely a married couple has surrendered itself and its future to God. The NCCL's many child pilgrims embody its collective values. Their fresh faces mutely transmit the message that God's true followers must respect his gift of life. Though several adolescents proudly sported T-shirts decrying abortion, these were, in a sense, superfluous. The very presence of so many kids, children whom the NCCL claims mainstream society would never have permitted to be born, forcefully communicates the group's commitment to allowing God to reign supreme over its member's reproductive lives.

If women are expected to be their family's primary caregivers and educators and men serve as its protectors and providers, then children are schooled to respect their parents' authority and to behave with modesty, patience, respect, and stoicism. Even the very young were expected to endure the long marches, variable weather, and interminable Latin masses of the three-day pilgrimage with uncomplaining equanimity. The Pilgrimage of Restoration offers graduated options for participation so that the experience can, in a sense, grow with the children. Often, the youngest pilgrims cut their teeth by joining in only on the pilgrimage's last, most exciting leg, the short victory lap between the shrine of Kateri Tekakwitha in Fonda and that of the martyrs in Auriesville. Having mastered this shorter sojourn, which one adolescent disparagingly referred to as the "wimpy pilgrimage," children then can graduate to walking the entire route at around seven or eight years of age. Some veterans, in their late teens, go on to become "captains" of individual brigades.

The behavior and appearance of child pilgrims reflects the highly conventional gender roles dictated by their elders. Girls dress uniformly in ankle-length skirts, eschewing makeup and wearing their hair in long, pre-Raphaelite locks. Boys are groomed for leadership roles through the Safety Patrol, which affords them the not inconsiderable pleasure of herding and yelling bullhorned directives at compliant adults. Some boys were quick to pick up on this Ozzie-and-Harriet environment of masculine entitlement. In one overheard exchange, one youth asked another, "I wonder whether those women have our dinner ready yet." His friend, playfully shaking his fists, replied, "Well, they better, or else!"[15]

Given the NCCL's strong emphasis on male leadership within the Catholic family, its director, Gregory Lloyd, makes the case that the North American martyrs speak most urgently to other men. Contemporary American popular culture, he argues, belittles and discounts fathers, consistently portraying them as unnecessary, incompetent, unintelligent, or immoral. As a result of these demeaning stereotypes, he contends: "men are becoming weenies down here [in America]. There has been a diminishment of fortitude, a focus on pleasure-seeking instead of doing what is right. Men have become couch potatoes."[16] By turning their backs on the sacred duty to protect, serve, and support their wives and children, men have abdicated the necessary, natural position of authority in the American family. Though the martyrs were celibate priests rather than married laymen, they present, for Lloyd, a much-needed corrective model. Their tenacity, courage, and seriousness of purpose should be emulated by all males, he argues, whether Catholic or not: "Brébeuf was this giant. They are literally cutting out his heart and he is yelling out encouragement to his comrades, the Christian Indians. Everyone is just astounded by his courage."[17]

But Lloyd's masculine appropriation of the martyrs was sharply questioned by other ultraconservative pilgrims.[18] In between bites of chili at the central bivouac tent, I asked Sarah Clarke whether the martyrs have a special resonance for American men. Thoughtfully fingering the massive wooden crucifix around her neck, she unhesitatingly responded:

> No. I don't think that God is sexist. I think that he requires all of us, whatever we are, to be willing to sacrifice our lives. . . . There's no difference to God. We have different roles, of course, but we are all expected to have the same burning desire in order to attain God. He doesn't let women off easy because they are weaker, or expect more from men, because they are stronger, because there are strong women, and there are weak men. . . . It has nothing to do with the nature of our particular person. . . . God created us to know, love and serve him, with no excuses.[19]

Though she had been introduced to me by Father Hellman as a "truly good woman," Clarke made it clear that, despite her own lauded conformity to the gendered expectations of ultraconservative Catholicism, she had no intention of being stranded outside the golden circle of martyrdom because of her sex. Being prepared to die for the faith is, for her, a universal requirement incumbent on all true Catholics, regardless of gender or age. Indeed, she cast the seventy-mile walk as a "school of martyrdom" that she wants each of her children to attend. Clarke prepares them spiritually for the pilgrimage on the long drive east from Michigan by playing a CD recounting the lives of the martyrs, particularly Isaac Jogues, to whom she has an especial devotion. She takes particular care to draw her children's attention to this saint's longing to convert others and his willingness to die doing so:

> St. Isaac's desire for the salvation of souls, that's exactly the kind of desire we want to instill in our children. If they have to go to the point of blood, then, well, thanks be to God. They have to be willing [to give their lives], to love God that much, because that's what he did for us.

Once a year, for a few precious days, these ultraconservative Catholic families together make a mobile, temporary community in which their values and way of life predominate. While each family is often considered a little unusual at home, in coming together they take comfort from the fact that, across the country, there are others who choose to believe and to live as they do. Mike Meier half-jokingly referred to the yearly trek as a "support group" for ultraconservatives:

> I think that the goals of most of those that are here with families is to give your children the best exposure that you can to the fact that, #1, you are not alone, #2, there are deep truths that people from Wisconsin, New York, Pennsylvania, Indiana, Oklahoma, Texas, Illinois, and Minnesota—there are people all around the country who share similar beliefs and who are sympathetic, who understand you.[20]

The pilgrimage has a strong "family reunion" feel. Most of the participants know one another, and many share friendships spanning many years. In the rare and precious intervals in which pilgrims can relax, ceasing to march, pray, sing, and eat in unison, the sacred and the social come together. At the campsites, the kids, energetic despite their long day, roam in packs, stirring up clouds of dust from the dirt roads with their running heels. Adolescents, coyly grouped in same-sex clumps on picnic benches or the grass, chat, laugh, and, from a decorous distance, flirt. Although the pilgrimage is first and foremost a religious exercise, it is also a valued opportunity for teenagers to see their friends in an environment that lacks the moral dangers that their ultraconservative parents typically associate with mainstream American society.

Though the majority of participants in this pilgrimage are laypeople, the event also attracts two groups of religious, the Slaves of the Immaculate Heart of Mary and the Canons of Christ the King. The canons, as Hellman pointedly explains, are the product of an institute established for "the orthodox, those of us who believe *everything* that the church teaches." Its graduates, having been trained exclusively in the Latin rites, are unable to conduct a vernacular mass even if asked to.[21] The Slaves were established in 1949 by the controversial American Jesuit Leonard Feeney, who was excommunicated four years later. Male and female members of this double-order wear black, floor-length robes featuring an embroidered circle of gray chains on their chests, which encircle the Virgin's Immaculate Heart, stabbed with knives and enclosed with pink roses. Nuns add to this ensemble a traditional long, peaked black veil.

Slaves' taste in liturgy and theology is as preconsular as their dress. Like the NCCL, they contend that the contemporary church has been seduced into all manner of unholy compromises with modernity, which has caused it to turn its collective back on the magisterium, the distinctively Catholic theological compass that has for centuries guided the church's God-given mission in the world. Worshipping exclusively through the Latin rites, they stress the unfashionable doctrine of *extra ecclesiam nulla salus*—that salvation is unattainable outside the Catholic Church. This formerly mainline belief was scrapped only at the Second Vatican Council. The Slaves' unapologetic consignment of all non-Catholics to hellfire defies ecumenical currents within Christianity since the 1960s and the humanistic valuing of cultural and religious "diversity" in secular society. The Slaves' determined public affirmation of this doctrine has thus led to allegations that they are inherently intolerant.[22]

Angels and Demons

As intimated by Canon Hellman's dawn homily, the religious universe of these Catholic ultraconservatives, both lay and religious, is starkly

Manichean: positing an unending war between "our divine General and King, Jesus Christ,"[23] and his archnemesis, Satan. Nor is the aptly named Hellman's reference to the Prince of Darkness a mere rhetorical flourish. The richly imagined inner worlds of these Pilgrims of Restoration resound with the creaking, leathery wing beats of demons as often as they witness the feathery resplendence of angels. For them, Satan, his legions, and the fiery reality of hell are inescapable, omnipresent realities.[24] Pilgrims' strong sense of being participants in an epic, eternal battle between supernatural entities for the soul of the world amplifies the seemingly ordinary events and emotions of daily life. Just before the 2010 pilgrimage, I emailed the NCCL's director with a few last-minute logistical inquiries. In his lightning-quick reply, Greg Lloyd informed me that I was in grave spiritual peril. These trivial details, he suggested, were a distraction sent by the Prince of Lies in an effort to sap my will to walk in the martyrs' bloody footsteps:

> All those worrisome details don't mean a hill of beans except (we have found from patient observation) to the Evil One. He uses them, coward that he is, to hide behind, to peek out from behind at every aspiring but timid pilgrim like a cruel prankster uses the cover of dark and mirrors or cheap props to frighten children at a circus. You just get yourself to Cramer Point Motel. We'll get you where you need to go from there.[25]

Even our most private moments, thoughts, and inclinations are, for these pilgrims, "public." Heavenly and infernal eyes are constantly trained on our every action. Not just in the extreme circumstances of martyrdom or of pilgrimage do we become "a spectacle for men and for angels":[26] in the mundane events of our daily lives, too, we are part of this larger supernatural struggle, an eternal war manifesting itself even in the internal theater of our own thoughts and feelings.

Pilgrims are not content to be mere passive spectators of this supernatural drama. Rather, they seek to become, through their devotional and penitential actions, an active part of the Catholic economy of salvation. They attempt to settle the wages of sin, both personal and societal, by a kind of Catholic accounting: making reparation to Christ for their own failings and those of others through prayer, penance, and pilgrimage. In the minds of NCCL pilgrims, the wellspring of merit generated through self-sacrificing suffering is like a fountain that flows into different catchment basins. Once one has properly atoned for one's faults, any excess merit will overflow and begin to fill those below, atoning for the sins of others: one's family, community, nation, and eventually the world. Though one might never know the identity of those benefiting from one's spiritual largesse, one can draw comfort from the notion that one's "sacrifice of praise and thanksgiving" is benefiting other souls, living or dead.[27]

The religious logic of reparation is intimately akin to that of martyrdom, which likewise posits that the sacrifices made by the saintly few spiritually benefit the uncomprehending many. Although Canon Hellman's early-morning homily expressed a profound sense of spiritual modesty, as he noted that Jogues's larger-than-life presence spiritually as well as physically dwarfed the pilgrims kneeling at his feet, the NCCL's self-assigned role as the generator and donor of spiritual merit undeniably has a martyr-like dimension.

Mike Emig, a layman and longtime member of the NCCL, eloquently explained to me his understanding of the importance of reparation. He and his ten-year-old-son, Joseph, kindly offered to give me a lift after a hip injury rendered me unable to walk. A quiet, serious-minded man, Emig kept his dark eyes on the road, the rosary hung over his rearview mirror oscillating gently with his route's dips and turns. His son, huddled in the back seat amid neat piles of luggage and tents, listened quietly as his father spoke:

> We can make reparation for other people's sins, as well as our own. So, we offer all the sacrifices that we make, and we put them in the hands of Our Lady. We give her a list of intentions of our own, but if someone else needs them more than what we put forward as intentions she might use our sacrifices to bring someone else back to the church. . . . She will not abuse anything that we offer to her. . . . We forget the enormity of sin, how horrible even one venial sin is . . . and, you know, we go on merrily living our lives in sin, without regards to God's rights. . . . We can never make enough reparations, and God is the only one who knows what he will accept as full reparation, and if we do too much, he will take it and apply it somewhere else. We can never do too much.[28]

Joseph shyly echoed his father's words, volunteering that his own special intention in making the seventy-mile pilgrimage was the reconversion of older siblings who have fallen away from the faith. In the minds of pilgrims, with each mile that their banners advance, each Hail Mary that is chanted, and each twinge of pain prayerfully accepted, spiritual merit is being accrued and its invisible benefits redistributed to "others" both intimate and impersonal, from lapsed family members to the whole of mainstream American society, fallen and lost on the darkening plain.

Imitating the Martyrs

Ultraconservative Catholics see the North American martyrs both as models for their individual spiritual lives and as guiding stars for the future direction of the church. Their theology and collective identity enshrines martyrdom at its very heart: in the martyrs' refusal of theological compromise,[29] ardent evangelism of native peoples, and willingness to die for their beliefs, ultraconservative Catholics see the inspiration of their own ethos and credo. Passionate evangelists committed even to the death "to carry the torch of faith and divine love," the Jesuit martyrs represent—like Jesus—an intriguing double model of fiery zeal and passive patience under persecution. Both elements of the martyrs' collective personality are relevant to how ultraconservatives perceive their relations with American secular society and the larger church.

On the one hand, ultraconservative Catholics cast the martyrs as being, like themselves, zealous, defiant, and uncompromising—even confrontational—in their intolerance of incorrect beliefs or sinfulness. Longing for a new age of righteous indignation, in the mold of Jesus casting the money changers out of the temple, Mike Meier wistfully contrasts the contemporary church's "wishy-washiness," which he attributes to "a desire to please too many at the expense of the Truth,"[30] with the "very strong, clear, manlier" language of the martyrs who, he explains, "didn't mince words!" Much like Beth Lynch at the Auriesville shrine, Meier and other pilgrims interpret the missionaries' violent deaths as the result of their refusal to adulterate their Catholic faith, even in the face of death itself. Walking the pilgrimage trail still clad in his heavy mass vestments, Canon Andreas Hellman's forehead liberally beads with sweat. Following a snaking line of singing pilgrims on a hummocky walking path that winds through field and forest, Hellman expresses his longing to bring Christ back to a society that he sees as having systematically excised his presence and influence:

It is called the Pilgrimage of Restoration . . . the restoration of the social kingdom of our lord Jesus Christ. This pilgrimage is the denial of the heresy of the separation between the state and the church. We're not Muslim so we don't want a mingling of religion and politics, but we do want the two to positively influence one another. . . . What we want is to give society back to Christ, to give Christ back to society. . . . He is not an alien, he's not an infectious disease, and our faith is not, but it is what formed a civilization. We want to restore a Christian civilization, and we understand that you can't give what you don't have. . . . If you live it, you can spread it from there. . . . We are trying to live what Christendom used to be.[31]

Even ultraconservatives' relationship with their host institution, Our Lady of Martyrs Shrine in Auriesville, is not totally devoid of confrontation and religious one-upmanship. Female pilgrims participating in the Society of St. Pius X event are infamous for their relentless attacks on their fellow Catholic women at Our Lady of Martyrs. A teenaged employee of the Shrine Museum indignantly recalls being raked over the coals for her "immodest" clothing. "Jeez!" she says, shrugging, "I was only wearing capris!" Her accusers, she remembers, were forced by their own strict dress code to wear the pilgrimage's commemorative T-shirts over heavy, knitted turtlenecks that completely covered their arms and necks. To this they added flowing, ankle-length skirts. When the young woman offered to entertain the children with a rosary game she had designed, more attacks followed. How could she even think of degrading Our Lady's sacred talisman in this disgusting manner, one demanded. Since Jesus did not play foolish games, our children do not either, another remonstrated. Relations between ultraconservatives and Auriesville were even worse before Rome brought these aficionados of the Latin mass back into full communion. Prior to that, the bishop's explicit orders kept ultraconservatives from celebrating mass in the huge, circular church on site, restricting them to an outdoor pavilion. Enraged by this exclusion, ultraconservative pilgrims would often retaliate by leaving mounds of their garbage strewn around the site as a sign of their displeasure, according to shrine officials.

But it is not all Jesus in the temple. Ultraconservatives also identify strongly with the martyrs' stoic acceptance of the horrific torments inflicted on them. Some relate to the martyrs' endurance of unjust persecution for their beliefs "at the hands of those that hate them" because they feel similarly targeted by a range of putative "attackers." Pilgrims complain that mainstream American society mocks their strong faith, pillories their countercultural lifestyle, and dismisses out of hand their sincere, heartfelt criticisms of its materialistic, cynical, and shallow ethos. Hellman draws sweeping parallels between the plight of the martyrs in seventeenth-century Iroquoia and that of ultraconservative Catholics in contemporary "pagan" America, punctuating his comments with emphatic gestures of his walking stick:

> Iroquois society was a society of death, like ours. About utility. Like Darwinism, where the strongest survive, where there is no room for love. Whoever is strongest dominates the others and whatever is judged useless is eliminated. That's how they killed Saint René Goupil, out of superstition. He made the sign of the cross over a little child and they killed him. . . . [Goupil] teaches us a great example of how to deal with this culture of death. . . . If need be, we will give our lives, we will hold our position, we will not desert. And we will sacrifice it all for the people that put us to death, either physically or spiritually, by persecuting us, by ridiculing us by putting down all priests altogether because some of us have been Judases. . . . We suffer that, we offer it up. We are inspired. We know that no matter what sacrifices we can make, it is nothing compared to what these men, the missionaries, have done.

Hellman conflates early modern native culture with contemporary American society in a parallel not intended to be flattering to either party. Both are "societies of death," he argues, pointing to their predilection for the heartless culling of the unwanted through, respectively, the torture and slaying of war captives and "murder of the unborn."[32]

The drama of pilgrimage ups the ante of the NCCL's determined confrontation of mainstream American society by giving its members a vast stage—the roads and byways of upstate New York—on which to publicly enact their faith, with all the attendant risks of mockery and denunciation that this poses. Confrontation with unsympathetic hecklers is eagerly anticipated by some NCCL members as a particularly visceral way of tasting what the martyrs underwent. At Cramer's Point Motel on the eve of the pilgrimage, one young woman sweetly warned me to be prepared for motorists to yell obscenities or throw trash at us from their moving cars. This, she smiled, must be welcomed as an opportunity to endure the very humiliation experienced by Jogues and Goupil when they walked this route in 1642.

While many NCCL pilgrims thus cast mainstream American society as their chief antagonist, others proactively present the mainline Catholic Church as marginalizing, misunderstanding, even martyring them, its most faithful children. Portraying themselves as victims of the church casts the institution as not merely negligent in the performance of its own religious duties but as actively hostile to the righteous remnant that is attempting to fulfill them. Pilgrims' dissatisfaction with the contemporary church is expressed obliquely, generally by contrasting the imagined church of the medieval past with what they see as the emasculated, adulterated institution of the present day. Sarah Clarke sighs over her chili as, in a wave of nostalgia for an era she never knew, she casts the medieval church as a commanding beacon piercing the darkness of ignorance and confusion:

> If the church were pure, she would be like a beacon of light calling all to her. But there's so much confusion these days. Since the Protestant Reformation, there's so many churches, not to mention, of course, all the other religions, like the Buddhists. So—how are we to know [what is true]? But at her height, when Christ was king, when Christendom was civilization, [the church] was the beacon in the night that everyone knew, hey, this is the truth.[33]

In Clarke's framing, religious diversity is cast as the distinctive and puzzling burden of modernity.

The perception of ultraconservative Catholics that they are, like the martyrs, part of a noble but misunderstood minority doomed to experience only moral victory is all the more striking given that in many ways they form part of a vocal faction in American political life and a not-inconsiderable force in the life of the Catholic Church. Although the NCCL's taste in liturgy is admittedly marginal, the group's theo-ideological stances on gender roles, contraception and abortion, homosexuality, home schooling, and sex education, and its disgusted condemnation of the lasciviousness and lawlessness of contemporary American culture are seconded by many Protestant evangelicals. Moreover, the notion that these ultraconservative Catholics are an embattled minority fighting against the rampant liberalism of the mainstream church completely contradicts the markedly conservative turn of the last five papacies. As much as the NCCL and its affiliates might wish to cast themselves as misunderstood prophets wandering in the wilderness, many of their views are perhaps more popular than they like to acknowledge.

The Reconquest of America

Standing in the rain in front of the surrealistically large round church, you can hear them before you see them. Distant, disembodied voices seem to come from the low clouds, their singing a complex tangle of competing Latin entreaties. Then banners crest the top of the steep hill and the first weary pilgrims come into sight. The Slaves have donned transparent, hooded rain capes so that their defiant religious fashion statement, the long black habit and veil common before the grievous misstep of Vatican II, is still visible. They look like burnt muffins encased in protective Saran Wrap. Other pilgrims sport a variety of rain gear, and adolescents, as is their wont even in ultraconservative circles, are defiantly damp and underclad, their long hair swinging like wet rope. As the Children of Fatima round out the Glorious Mysteries, rain drips from the rosaries clutched in their chilled, wind-reddened hands. Gradually, all the blistered brigades trickle in, wincing, to pool before the church's open doors. But having arrived at their much-anticipated destination, the death site of three American saints, little quarter is given for euphoria or self-celebration. Rather, organizers launch into a protracted list of rules pilgrims must observe during the two-hour Latin mass of thanksgiving to follow. Banners bowing through the open double doors, the pilgrims progress inside, brigade by brigade, and are instantly swallowed up in the maw of the enormous church. Whereas on the rainy roadsides, marching incongruously alongside cut-rate stereo marts and down-at-heel auto-body shops, their numbers seemed defiantly impressive, inside the Coliseum, designed to seat 10,000, their modest 200 souls fill only a dieter's wedge of the structure's circular pie. Taking up their stations at the ends of the long wooden pews, the adolescent banner bearers, though footsore, will stand throughout the long mass, spelling one another as they take turns to hold high Christ's royal banners in his house.

In a telephone interview some months before the September 2010 pilgrimage, NCCL director Gregory Lloyd assured me that, rather than demonizing native people as mere martyr slayers, Pilgrims for Restoration strongly identify with them:

> We have such love for the Indians, whether they convert or not. . . . We have been very inviting to the native Indian peoples, Christian or not. We don't want them to see this pilgrimage as a European thing. We try not to focus on the savagery of the deaths. We see this as the will of God. God accomplished his will through their evil decisions. We don't hold anyone accountable. We feel empathy with Indians. . . . We don't like prejudices because we have been the object of prejudices ourselves.[34]

Predicting that I would experience, during the Pilgrimage of Restoration, an outpouring of popular devotion to native converts Kateri Tekakwitha and Joseph Chihoatenhwa, Lloyd provocatively characterized the uncanonized Wendat Catholic as the "the greatest saint of the New World." For Lloyd, Chihoatenhwa's profound embrace of Christianity in the teeth of his people's disapproval makes him an even more important role model for contemporary Catholics than the North American martyrs:

> We see in him a tremendous example, especially to males in particular, not because he was tough guy, not because he was *a* brave, but because he was *brave*. He did what was right even when he was going to get hurt. Civilization can't be born without this kind of virtue.

But in stark contradiction of their director's confident expectations, the rank and file I interviewed, rather than venerating native converts, stressed native propensity to remain mired in sin long after the glory of Catholic truth had been made manifest to them. Having rhetorically tied Iroquois torture and slaying of their war victims with American culture's perverse contemporary worshipping of promiscuity and violence, Canon Hellman presented the negative perception of native culture as a necessary first step in historiographic sophistication, stating: "I am assuming that you are beyond the myth of the holy savage. . . . You have read too much about them. It is not politically correct to say it, but it is a fact."[35] Hellman's dark assumptions regarding native culture were vigorously seconded by NCCL laypeople. "The savages sometimes were sometimes rather savage, you know!" remarked Molly Milot, contrasting their barbarism with the practical and spiritual blessings imparted them by the benevolent black-robes:

> When you think what the Catholic missionaries did for the Indians, they really did help them. . . . The Jesuits, especially, came in as

ambassadors. They taught them in a more humane way than Protestants. They even taught them the basis of farming and civilization. I don't think that hurt [native peoples]. . . . I think that [Catholic missionaries] did a really good job.[36]

Pilgrims who expressed concerns about a racist double standard in the church's elevation of its martyrs were less concerned that native people had been unfairly excluded from official honors than they were worried that aboriginal candidates might receive a free pass in a sort of spiritual affirmative action. Commented pilgrim "Peter Miller," on Chihoatenhwa's *causa:* "you don't want their causes to proceed on a political basis. . . . [Vatican officials] should obviously apply the same criteria to them [as to nonnative candidates]."[37] Similarly, Sarah Clarke, though she garlanded Kateri Tekakwitha with all her traditional titles and recognized the native saint as "our shining example, the little flower of America, the lily of the Mohawk: she's our example of persevering in the faith despite the odds,"[38] nevertheless attributed her canonization to the church's caving in to the pressure of identity politics rather than to the "little flower's" inherent virtues.

Vigorously affirmed in conversations along the scenic byways of upstate New York, the negative perceptions of native traditional culture and the presentation of conversion as a desperate struggle to escape dens of debauchery and death are also officially proclaimed from the altars of Auriesville. In Canon Dolan's climactic homily, which crowned the long Latin mass, "little Sunshine" Kateri Tekakwitha is presented as heroically unique in turning to the gentle truths of Christianity rather than joining her community in their bloody worship of "War Gods":

> Little Sunshine desired to love the True God, not the Gods her people were worshipping, the War Gods. When things went badly for her people, for example, when there was famine, or disease, or war, what would they do? They would capture other Native Americans and torture them, make them scream, and their War Gods would be appeased by the screams of their victims as they murdered them. All the other people would go and watch the torturing and bloodletting, but little Tekakwitha would run away. She had a horror of this torture, this cruelty. She ran away to the woods, to the Great Spirit.[39]

Preternaturally chaste, "obedient," "pious," and "submissive," even in the face of the warrior culture that surrounded her, Kateri's religious biography is used as a means to pound home, one final time, the contrast between falsity and truth, darkness and light, which is at the heart of ultraconservative theology.

"A Real Party"

The hot late August sun beams down, its fierce glare making the silver crosses atop the spires of the Martyrs' Shrine church in Midland shine so brightly that they are hard to even look at. Persisting in doing so makes fiery purple afterimages rage on the inside of one's closed eyelids. In the deep shade of the mature trees around the outdoor "Polish altar," hundreds of pilgrims sit on picnic blankets or camp chairs, speaking animatedly in Konkani. They mill about expectantly, reading the inscriptions on the statues that mark the extremities of this outdoor "nave." There is much readjusting of saris and fanning of sweating faces with commemorative programs. Some run after toddlers to ensure that they do not pick all the flowers in the outdoor beds. Others retrace their steps to the serried rows of idling motor coaches, which linger indolently in the shrine parking lot, to retrieve cameras, handbags, or cigarettes. Though most present reside in the Toronto area, virtually all have family roots in Goa, a province in western India colonized in the sixteenth century by the Portuguese. Portuguese influence still marks Goa's indigenized Catholicism, inflects its music, and flavors its cuisine. Some pilgrims, self-importantly twaddling Blackberries, are second-generation Canadians who have maximized the opportunities afforded them by their parents and grandparents to earn advanced degrees and achieve professional success. Others are new arrivals still adapting to life in a new land, particularly its unfamiliar cold, a specter mercifully absent on this humid summer morning, so hot as to be positively Goan.[40]

The milling pilgrims await the delayed commencement of the day's devotional activities: *ladineh*, a musical rosary that will honor Our Lady of Fatima; and an outdoor mass in Konkani. Some, like my host, Father Patrick Coldricks, his appetite aroused by the teasing smell of smoldering charcoal, openly fantasize about the elaborate Goan feast, which, along with traditional dancing, will round out the day's agenda: "There are so many different kinds of sausages you will not believe it," he smiles. But when I ask the Goan Jesuit when the ladineh will start, he shrugs and offers me a sheepish grin rather than a straight answer. To the rueful laughter of Goan eavesdroppers, he loudly quips that the event is running on "IST—Indian Stretchable Time."

After much officious testing of the sound equipment, a small choir formally arrayed in black and white finally begins to sing in praise of the Virgin, and the assembly enthusiastically joins in. The rosary's ornate Portuguese-style guitar accompaniment sounds, to the uninitiated ear, much like the cheerful strains of a Mexican mariachi band. The energetic joy of the music presents the strongest possible contrast with the frozen agony of the martyrs' statues that encircle the outdoor altar.

The singing heightens the crowd's expectations. Pilgrims crane their necks to see where she is. Belatedly, Our Lady of Fatima appears, jostling along in the bed of the green Martyrs' Shrine pickup. Her hands folded in prayer and her eyes downcast, the Portuguese Virgin is gold-crowned and white-robed, her pale ivory skin a striking contrast with the darker faces of her Goan supplicants. She is extricated and, with some difficulty, hoisted aloft to receive the musical tribute of her people on a heavy, elaborately carved wooden litter. Though it is designed to be carried by four strong bearers, everyone, including Coldricks, wants to join in. Soon Our Lady is being slowly borne along by a moving mountain of men, women, and children. Because of the crush, some can place only a token finger on her litter. Though the singing is much louder now, in the presence of the Virgin, pilgrims still talk uninhibitedly among themselves. Some shout contradictory instructions as to where the procession should head, while others warn of low-hanging branches that threaten to snag the statue's fragile crown. Many, hastily removing sunglasses and mugging for the camera, demand that family members snap their picture as they help carry the Virgin Mother along.

As the ladineh winds down, preparations for the outdoor Konkani mass unhurriedly unfold. The outdoor altar is decorated with cut flowers, the golden goblets unpacked, the microphones moved. Circling the crowd, Father Coldricks commandeers six children to assist as altar servers. Though the English-language mass inside the large shrine church is just reaching its Eucharistic climax, the priest nevertheless shepherds his charges into its sacristy to be outfitted with robes and surplices. Hilarity ensues as, like Goldilocks, the children find that robes are much too big or much too small. One boy's flat refusal to sport a lavender surplice provokes giggles from his comrades. The noise generated by these wardrobe negotiations results in a long-faced priest pointedly swishing shut the heavy velvet curtains that separate the sacristy from the church's sanctuary. But his implicit rebuke of the children's high spirits is ignored as Father Coldricks and his band, now neatly outfitted, scramble out of the shadowy enclave back into the sunlight.

The event's relaxed, open atmosphere, its palpable pride in Goa's religious culture, and its strong emphasis on the importance of cultural exchange and religious tolerance reflect the personal qualities and values of its instigator, Father Coldricks, who credits his very presence in Canada to the miraculous intercession of "the Canadian martyrs." Speaking with me on the eve of the pilgrimage he will attend as both Goan guest and Jesuit host, Coldricks was by turns playful and profound during the lengthy interview and its many interruptions.[41] Because we talked during the priest's on-duty hours at Midland's central Shrine Office, his reflections were repeatedly disrupted by pilgrims who besieged him with donations and shy requests to be blessed with the martyrs' relics.

Coldricks's discussion of his intercontinental life over the past several years is suffused both with yearning and wry amusement at the perversity of his own yearning. While in India, he ruefully recalls, he longed for Canada. Now, in Canada, he harbors affectionate nostalgia for India—its sounds, colors, textures, language, and food. The priest's decision to initiate the first-ever Goan pilgrimage to Midland was thus prompted by both personal and pastoral factors. Very much aware of the long tradition of ethnic pilgrimages at Midland, he longed to showcase the cultural and spiritual richness of a Goan festival for his Canadian Jesuit colleagues, even as he sought to forge stronger ties with the Goan expat community in nearby Toronto. The priest's memories of Christmas in Goa clearly shape his expectations for the morrow:

> The mass will be in their own language, Konkani, it will be our language, our culture. I will train the director here to speak a few words of Konkani. We have a lot of Portuguese culture in our blood. . . . They will have the procession of our Lady of Fatima around the place. . . . We have a special sung rosary, ladineh, it is very beautiful. The Goans are a musical lot. Our festival season is so beautiful you cannot believe it. At Christmas the whole place is lit up with so many lights that you cannot imagine. There are stars and decorations all over the place. There is midnight mass and people having beers at the outdoor bars. It is a real party!

At this juncture, the Shrine Office's glass door swings open and a young, dark-haired pilgrim hesitantly approaches Coldricks's wooden desk in the corner of the room. She is clutching a donation envelope, which she shyly offers the priest. "Oh thank you, God bless you," he beams, "now I can go to a fancy restaurant." Nonplussed by Coldricks's ebullient joking, the pilgrim smiles cautiously. "Have a wonderful time—enjoy yourself!" he admonishes her as she turns to leave.

Even as Coldricks jokes that the young pilgrim's beauty has caused him to lose his train of thought, he strikes a more serious note. The Midland Martyrs' Shrine is at a unique juncture in its history, he asserts. It is attracting not only an increasingly diverse cross-section of Catholic pilgrims but growing numbers of non-Christian clients, particularly Hindus, who, according to Coldricks, are drawn by the site's "aura of holiness": "They have that deep reverence of devotion. They might walk up to the altar on their knees. They leave their footwear outside. They want to touch the feet of God. They can almost put us [Catholics] to shame with the way they handle the aura of holiness that the shrine offers."[42] Coldricks confides that it is difficult for him to turn them away from the Eucharist, as church policy obliges him to do:

> There are sometimes conflicts because they are not supposed to receive Holy Communion. It is a little bit unpleasant for them to understand. So now we have developed something to smooth that out. We tell them, please come forward for a blessing with your arms on your chest. Many of them have come. When I bless them I say thank you so much for coming, and they are so happy, they give you such a big hug that it is rather embarrassing, it almost brings you to tears to see this.

The priest's greatest fear is that their ritual exclusion will lead these Hindus to conclude, with Gandhi, "I would be Christian were it not for the behavior of the Christians." Coldricks quietly affirms: "What we have here at the shrine is a universal call to people of *all* diverse religions." Midland, in its treatment of these Hindu pilgrims, has the opportunity to display the open-hearted acceptance and love that are the truest reflection of both Hinduism and of Christianity.

Once again, Coldricks's reflections are cut short by visitors entering the Shrine Office. "Come in, come in, do not hesitate, this is your place!" he encourages them. The group's putative leader stutters nervously that they are Catholic pilgrims seeking a blessing. "But even if you were not

Catholics you are still most welcome!" the priest insists, rummaging through the jumbled desk drawers and drawing out a reliquary that resembles a large, concave magnifying glass. He solemnly extends it for the pilgrims to reverence and, making the sign of the cross, intones: "So with the intercession of the Canadian Martyrs, may God bless you with holiness, happiness and peace of mind in the name of the Father, Son, and Holy Spirit." As the departing pilgrims shut the door behind them, Coldricks observes wryly: "The concept of spirituality has yet to sink into us. You know, to understand that primarily we are a human being, with God's spirit in us. The rest is all politics. So why make a big hype about who is a Catholic and who is not a Catholic?"

As he crams the relics back into the messy desk drawer, I ask the priest whether he shares the pilgrims' evident belief in the martyrs' powerful intercession. Coldricks lights up, enthusing: "The thing is, my existence here in Canada is entirely due to the Canadian martyrs." His

Father Patrick Coldricks blesses Father K. T. Philip, a pilgrim to the Midland Martyrs' Shrine, with the relics of the North American martyrs.

(Photo by author)

story starts with a family tragedy: the recent death of his "Aunt Dragon," the loving but bad-tempered relative who raised him after his parents perished in an auto accident. Though he suffered her loss as an adult, her loss awoke the memory of his earlier bereavement. Sorrow rendered Coldricks virtually unable to function. As his depression deepened, a concerned cousin in Canada sent him money to come and visit. Coldrick's tough-minded superior Jesuit reluctantly accorded permission for him to accept a temporary posting to the Midland shrine:

> The Provincial from here asked me, "Would you like to work in the Canadian Martyrs' Shrine?" and I said, "There is no question. We heard all about these martyrs when we were novices with the Canadian Jesuits in Darjeeling Province. I would love to!" So I came here. I felt something totally different, the aura of the company of the Canadian martyrs. So I told my old man that I wanted to stay and he had such a fit. He wrote me a very strong letter and told me to get back there [to India]. Everyone was upset because I was going, but I said, "Alex [Father Alex Kirsten, the then shrine director], I will be back, but I have to get permission first."

Faced with his "old man's" adamant opposition to his permanent departure from India, Coldricks besieged the martyrs with his prayers, remonstrating that he sought only to serve them in the country of their death. Every morning and every night for two years, he reverently held their worn holy card, repeating its "miracle prayer" before he finally received permission to return to the Ontario shrine.

Coldricks's organization of the first Goan pilgrimage to the Midland Martyrs' Shrine could thus be cast as a personal act of thanksgiving for this long-sought answer to prayer. But despite his personal dedication to the martyrs, Coldricks does not see promotion of their cult as being the pilgrimage's primary goal. Particularly in its inaugural year, it is the celebration of Goan Catholicism, music, language, and culture that must take center stage, he stresses. Any inculcation of devotion to the Canadian martyrs should therefore be handled obliquely and subtly. He reveals that, in his own remarks on the morrow, he will highlight the compelling parallels between the martyrs and beloved Goan saint Frances Xavier, referred to simply as *goanchi saiba* or "the saint of our land":

> When people hear about the Canadian martyrs they think that they have nothing to do with Saint Francis Xavier. But they were in the same society, the Society of Jesus. They were united by the bond of Je-

sus Christ. So you can have Saint Francis Xavier and the Canadian martyrs, too. In the end, they are all the same thing.

Introduced into Goan immigrant culture through the Midland pilgrimage, the Canadian martyrs will eventually function as new *goanchi saiba*, Coldricks postulates, protecting and interceding for the community in their new home. These new saints will in no way replace the old. Rather, these heavenly companions will work together, as all are ultimately "the same thing." By stressing the similarity between new Canadian saints and the reassuringly familiar devotional figures of the Goan homeland, Coldricks subtly affirms the compatibility of being fully Canadian and fully Goan, a view that neatly aligns both with Midland's liberal theological ethos and with Canadian federal policy.

Festival versus Flagellation

Both the NCCL's journey to Auriesville and the Goan pilgrimage to Midland are events held by Catholic minority groups that feature well-attended outdoor masses conducted in a language other than English. Held at a venue honoring the North American martyrs on or near the sites where these figures lived and died, each event continually references the hallowed figures' lives and legacies, both visually and verbally. Yet these general descriptions belie sharp contrasts. The two groups are minorities in a different sense, and each defines pilgrimage in its own distinctive way. Each pilgrimage has its own atmosphere, proposes contrasting codes of conduct for its pilgrims, and models radically different rules of engagement with the shrine they visit and with society as a whole.

The Goans are a visible minority within the wider Canadian society, though theologically and liturgically they are very much within the Catholic mainstream. Only the minutest details of their personal appearance, such as both sexes' modest clothing and religious jewelry, and female pilgrims' uniformly long hair, avoidance of makeup, and wearing of the mantilla during mass, visually indicate their ultraconservative religious beliefs. Moreover, though NCCL members' belief in the superiority of the Latin mass makes them as a small minority within Catholicism, their stances on human sexuality and reproduction are shared across confessional lines with other ultraconservative Christians.

The two groups' working definitions of pilgrimage also sharply diverge. For the Goans, as for most other ethnic pilgrims,[43] the relatively short journey between Toronto and Midland on a plush, chartered bus is not considered to be an important part of the event but merely its practical precursor.[44] Typically, the motor coach, with its reclining seats and smoked glass windows, does not serve as a venue for collective devotional exercises.[45] Rather, the pilgrimage is popularly understood to start only once the buses rumble through the shrine's black gates. For NCCL pilgrims, by contrast, it is the strenuous journey that commands the lion's share of their spiritual and physical energies during the grueling three-day event. For much of their pilgrimage, it is the idea of Auriesville that inspires them, rather than the actuality. The vision of the heavenly Jerusalem, together with the example of the suffering martyrs, motivates them to crest steep hills, sleep rough, and rise early; to ignore rain in their face and in their shoes; and to endure with equanimity a pilgrim's inevitable cramps and blisters. Though many present arrival at the shrine as the emotional climax of their experience, most NCCL pilgrims do not spend a fraction of the time at Auriesville that the Goans spend at Midland.

The two events also differ markedly in tone, atmosphere, and purpose. Although the demeanor of pilgrims at both events was reverent, the Goan event was far more relaxed. Goan organizers tolerated much more noise from participants, and participants put up with a great deal more chaos from their putative organizers. Even in the midst of the ladineh, pilgrims yelled contradictory directions to the singing mountain of people bearing Our Lady of Fatima. Kids' behavior was freewheeling: as many shrieked as were silent, cried as were content. During the long outdoor mass, some children gravely stood, knelt, and sat alongside their parents, but others capered unchecked under the trees. The constant delays gave the Goan pilgrimage a loose, unstructured atmosphere. Gaps in the schedule, many of them unplanned, left ample time for pilgrims to experience the shrine for themselves, passing the time as their fancy dictated. Some chose to light petitionary candles, while others simply smoked. Some wandered the grounds, casually snapping pictures as others reverently performed the Stations of the Cross. Some shopped, snacked, and socialized, picnicking on the manicured grass, while their friends and relatives reverenced the martyrs' relics or were blessed by the on-duty priest. Others took advantage of the day's limping progress to leave the grounds entirely, traversing the special pilgrim's path to visit Brébeuf's grave at Saint-Marie, while others queued to fill plastic containers with the shrine's holy water.

The laissez-faire environment of the Goan pilgrimage, its blue halo of fragrant smoke intimating the feast to come, stands in sharp contrast to the austerity, rigor, and mandated conformity of the NCCL event. On the march, pilgrims of restoration moved as a disciplined corporate body through space. Walking, praying, singing, and even eating in unison, they demonstrated the harmonious order and laudatory self-control of ultraconservative Catholicism for a witnessing world. At dawn on the first day, the assembly was exhorted to obedience and explicitly discouraged from individual initiatives that might undermine the group's uniform devotional performance or erode the brigades' cohesion. Stopping outside of designated rest times, falling out of step with one's walking partner, or indulging in private conversation or snacks on the march were discouraged, as these self-indulgent activities could jam the pistons of ceaseless prayer, arresting the continuous minting of spiritual revenue.

Even the very youngest were expected to comply with the demanding expectations. Arriving at Auriesville wet and weary from the day's long march, children were expected to sit, silent, damp, and unfed, through a two-hour Latin mass in the cavernous Coliseum. Noncompliance with group norms provoked meaningful glares and whispered remonstrances from other pilgrims, rebukes that quickly restored the sinner's shamed compliance, even when—as was often the case—their error was completely inadvertent. Ironically, it was often pilgrims' very scrupulosity, as they nervously consulted one another to ensure that they were complying with expectations, that attracted others' condemnation.

The different emotional tenor of the two events—levity and solemnity, joy and penitence—underscore profound differences in how the groups envision the meaning and purpose of their respective pilgrimages. The Pilgrimage of Restoration is a countercultural event designed to confront mainstream society with its sloth and cynicism, sinfulness and immodesty. The event's careful sex segregation, disciplined marching, strong youth participation, and fervent affirmation of Catholic truths creates another America, projecting the world as the NCCL feels it could and should be. Their pain, they assert, is our gain; their voluntary acceptance of the walk's rigors redeems even as it rebukes the wider society's sins.

The Goan event, by contrast, is festive rather than ascetic, celebrating the world largely as it is, rather than imagining how it might be. Whereas ultraconservatives enact, in their mobile, temporary community an alternative vision both of the Catholic Church and the American dream, the values championed by Midland's ethnic pilgrimages are solidly—even stodgily—mainstream. Ethnic pilgrims and their Jesuit hosts both enthusiastically endorse the contemporary values espoused by the Roman Catholic Church and the Canadian state. Determinedly displaying the cultural, religious, and linguistic survival of their diasporic minority community, Goans affirm their culture's dynamism and portability by temporarily recreating their homeland, in miniature, at Midland. The medium of pilgrimage permits Goan immigrants to negotiate a normative collective identity even as they proudly showcase their religious, cultural, and culinary heritage for outsiders and onlookers.[46] The event's festive elements—its music, dancing, and lavish food—are thus not ancillary or incidental but as critical to their affirmation of cultural endurance as their vernacular worship. In coming to Midland, the Goans triumphantly celebrate—even worship—their ability to survive and thrive in their adopted Canadian home.

Their Jesuit hosts collude in ethnic Catholics' self-celebration. Midland's theologically liberal ethos combines the ecumenicalism of mainstream post-Vatican II theology with a self-conscious echo of Canadian federal policy. Since the 1960s, the Canadian government has increasingly stressed multiculturalism, which calls for the preservation of cultural, linguistic, ethnic, and religious diversity in Canada. Midland's hosting of ethnic Catholic pilgrimages also acknowledges the myriad ways in which Catholicism has manifested itself globally and celebrates how these international expressions of Catholic truth are increasingly manifested in a multicultural Canada.[47] States Father Alex Kirsten:

> Today's church in Canada is an ethnic church. The Martyrs' Shrine is a home for a variety of ethnic communities and a site of pilgrimage for a variety of ethnic pilgrimages: twenty-six ethnic groups come. The shrine has become symbolic of what the church in Canada is today, a multiethnic, a multicultural expression of the faith.[48]

As "a national Canadian institution," he states, it is "only natural" that the shrine reflect the federal government's expectations that new Canadians will retain the language and traditions of their homelands:

> Canada is not a melting pot. The United States is a melting pot. They acknowledge it in their own documentation. Everyone comes in and blends together and what comes out is American. Whereas Canada has always been described as a mosaic. . . . In a mosaic the pieces remain distinct . . . and that means our ethnic bits and our cultural bits have an intrinsic value. Canada values them and they are part of that Canadian image, the Canadian vision. So, in a sense, the shrine has taken that on itself. I don't know if Americans see this, but that's why we're so different.

Immigrants not only enhance the state's multicultural mosaic, Kirsten notes, they also sustain and revitalize the Canadian Catholic Church.

But despite Canada's strong rhetorical commitment to multiculturalism, racism remains a real problem in Canadian society. Father Coldricks, as a new immigrant to Canada, pointedly comments: "You may think that Canada is a perfect paradise and all, but [racism] is here too. It is a human element that we have to try to rise above."[49] Though publicly affirmed as the lodestar of Canadian federal policy, the state's much-vaulted tolerance and diversity are not always evident in everyday encounters, even at Midland. Some elderly white pilgrims, participants in the original, European "ethnic pilgrimages," often evince sincere bafflement as to why so many nonwhite pilgrims are present at the shrine. Such comments demonstrate that nonwhite pilgrims are still seen by some as "other" despite their common confessional identity as Catholics, an attitude that belies the shrine's strong emphasis on the supposed spiritual unity and brotherly love that shared Catholic identity is supposed to bring to pilgrims' encounters with one another.

Midland's townspeople are even blunter in their disparagement of ethnic Catholics' presence. Ignoring the considerable economic benefits brought by thousands of pilgrims annually, municipal officials routinely complain to shrine administrators: "*your people* have been messing up the beach again."[50] Thus, although the ethnic pilgrimages staged at Midland do not present a radically countercultural critique of society, like that of the Pilgrimage of Restoration, they do challenge Canadians to practice what they all too glibly preach.

Multicultural Martyrs

The Midland Jesuits' idealistic emphasis on multiculturalism and diversity is grounded in a particular reenvisioning of the martyrs' legacy, one that presents the strongest possible contrast with how these figures are appropriated by American ultraconservatives. While NCCL pilgrims seek to emulate the martyrs' suffering by retracing their bloodied steps to the holy site of their deaths, it is the martyrs' lives of dedicated service to the "other" that is highlighted at Midland. Whereas ultraconservatives admire the martyrs' theological inflexibility and willingness to face death before dishonor, the Midland Jesuits praise their supposed willingness to engage with and learn from native peoples.

The Midland Jesuits enshrine the martyrs as exemplars of the very intercultural and interreligious dialogue they wish to encourage on site. Icons of encounter rather than of intransigence, they are presented as purveyors of enculturation rather than as agents of "spiritual conquest." The martyrs are honored for their supposed ability sensitively to negotiate the cultural and religious differences between themselves and their native hosts. Says Kirsten:

> Our shrine's multicultural expression of the faith takes its roots right back to the martyrs. They discovered that they weren't bringing the be-all-and-end-all of knowledge to "barbarians": there was much to learn here as well. So if their attitude was that "we are bringing the best of Europe," then luckily they were open to discovering that there was a lot here that was also the best.[51]

The contrast with ultraconservatives could not be starker. The NCCL's embrace of the doctrine of *extra ecclesiam nulla salus*—no salvation but through the Catholic Church—effectively precludes their acknowledgment of the truth, legitimacy, or beauty of any other religious tradition. "Pilgrims of Restoration" often have highly negative views of other religions. Indeed, their understanding of traditional native spirituality and their understanding of Islam seem curiously similar. Both are cast as "cultures of death": as hate-filled, inherently violent traditions bent on the persecution of Christianity. For pilgrim Margaret Middleton, the rising Muslim tide that she prophesies will confront her and other "future martyrs" with the stark decision to "convert or die" is the contemporary counterpart of the Iroquois juggernaut faced by seventeenth-century Jesuit missionaries. One's clear duty as a Catholic, now as then, is to "conquer for Christ" by defiantly proclaiming the truth, even in the face of imminent, violent death. This, they affirm, is how one emulates Christ and his martyrs. Like them, one can fully live out one's faith only when one is prepared to die for it.

But at Midland, visitors are subtly encouraged to emulate Christ and the martyrs in quite a different way: by loving and serving their neighbors, Christian and non-Christian alike. Much as the martyrs putatively discerned the presence of Christ within traditional native culture, contemporary pilgrims are urged to see Jesus's face in the face of the stranger. Religious truth, assert contemporary Midland Jesuits, cannot be seen as singular or proprietary, nor can it be claimed as the exclusive prerogative of any one group. Vast, mysterious, and ineffable, truth may be glimpsed and expressed in many different idioms, including those of other religious traditions. Father Coldricks's warm embrace of Hindu pilgrims at the shrine's altar rail welcomes them not as potential converts to a singular, Catholic truth but as fellow worshippers of a shared religious reality that ultimately transcends traditions. Once one has grasped that "primarily we are a human being, with God's spirit in us," Coldricks asserts, then "all else is politics."

Native traditional religion is also seen by contemporary Midland Jesuits less as a threat to Catholic cohesion on reserves than as an alternative means of reaching toward shared divine realities. Discussing the traditionalist renaissance in native communities over the last thirty years, Father Kirsten explains: "What has happened to a lot of the younger [native] people has been a resurgence, a rediscovery of the native religions. For a lot of them that has become a focus for their search for the divine, their seeking God, or whatever." Rather than viewing non-Christians as rivals or threats, the Midland Jesuits urge visitors to build bridges of human empathy with the practitioners of other faiths, in stark contrast with ultraconservatives' advocacy of the religious "conquest" of those outside the Catholic pale and their naked nostalgia for the church's supposed medieval hegemony. The martyrs' message at Midland thus brings together postconciliar emphasis on outreach to religious "others" with secular Canadian values advocating multiculturalism and diversity. Just as NCCL pilgrims, by walking in the martyrs' putative steps, cast themselves as their contemporary heirs, so the Midland Jesuits, by presenting the martyrs as intercultural mediators, sanctify their own role in continuously encountering those different from themselves. The ethnic, cultural, and religious "otherness" of contemporary shrine pilgrims affords Midland officials the opportunity publicly to perform their espoused values of tolerant inclusiveness.

The Midland Jesuits' liberal interpretation of the martyrs' legacy thus focuses far more attention on these figures' lives than on their deaths, making events there less thanatological than pilgrimages culminating at Auriesville. The culling of the site's most violent imagery during the 1980s, coupled with the fact that the Midland shrine is not, like that of Auriesville, located on the site of the martyrs' deaths, has facilitated the turn to their saintly lives of service rather than their bloody martyrs' deaths. This deemphasis of death is arguably necessary for the liberal reinterpretation of their legacy to have any coherence. Otherwise, their murders would mutely and starkly rebuke Coldricks's optimistic notion that the spirit of brotherly love that animates all religions must invariably bring people together in a spirit of peace.

The values of tolerance, diversity, and dialogue shape not only the manner in which Midland officials present the martyrs to pilgrims but also *how* they impart information about these saints to their multicultural clientele. NCCL pilgrims see their event as a stark confrontation of the dominant society, in which its guiding values are systematically repudiated by the countervalues of the pilgrimage, with chastity replacing promiscuity, devotion displacing cynicism, and asceticism rebuking materialism. Their encounters with the shrine that hosts them can be tense, even confrontational.[52] The relationship between the pilgrimage and the wider society and church it exists to chastise, like that between a bow and an arrow, must always exist in a certain tension. For the pilgrimage to function as a countercultural event, the pilgrims must continuously highlight the divergence between their credo and that of the wider world surrounding them. At Midland, however, Jesuit hosts and ethnic guests are not pitted against one another but rather enter into a delicate negotiation involving give and take on both sides.[53] Says Kirsten: "people come with their own set of expectations, and when they are here we have a set of expectations. The task of the administration is to bring those expectations into closest possible approximation." Both groups must compromise in order to achieve a working equilibrium between beloved ethnic devotions and the veneration of the martyrs.

Surrounded by her family, pilgrim Tharini Tharmalingam weeps as she receives a blessing from Midland's shrine director, Father Bernard Carroll. In the background, Brébeuf's skull, in its jeweled reliquary, is clearly visible on the side altar.

(Photo by author)

Jesuit attempts to inculcate ethnic pilgrims' devotion to the North
American martyrs are thus handled obliquely and with considerable
caution, in the spirit of nuanced, intercultural engagement. There is no
one-size-fits-all evangelical approach. Rather, the Jesuits minutely tai-
lor each appeal to the specificities of the group, intimate knowledge of
the group's devotional emphases, and prior observation of their pilgrimages. Father Kristen confides that

> some links are easier to make than others. When the Vietnamese come,
> for example, they have a long procession that takes place on the ground.
> They have their own martyrs, the martyrs of Vietnam. So there are two
> floats. There is one for the reliquaries of the Vietnamese martyrs. And
> there is one for the reliquaries of the martyrs of Martyrs' Shrine, the
> Martyrs of Huronia. They are all in procession, and [the Vietnamese Ca-
> nadian pilgrims] make the connection that "these martyrs are just like
> our martyrs at home." That's the connection for them. The saints who
> intercede for us at home know the saints who intercede for us here.[54]

Just as the North American martyrs function in Goan circles as new
goanchi saiba or "saints of our land," so Vietnamese Canadians' perception of a heavenly friendship existing between the martyrs of their old
and new homelands is the key to facilitating their devotion to Brébeuf
and his brethren. Through such subtle courtship, Midland Jesuits gradually broaden the base of the martyrs' cult among ethnic communities.
At Auriesville, on the other hand, is it the NCCL's determined intransigence and confrontation even of its host shrine that has moved that
institution rightward.

Jean, *Vous Êtes Notre*

The winding roads of Normandy brought us through lush farm country
and alongside craggy limestone cliffs. Everywhere was the briny kiss of
the ocean, glazing the car's windshield with salt. The ribboning route
revealed, concealed, and revealed again the architectural marvel of
Mont-Saint-Michel, closer and more magnificent with every jagged
crook of the road. Marooned in the wide tidal estuary it has guarded
for more than twelve centuries, the fortified town, topped with its
monastery church, impaled the looming clouds with its proudly jutting
spire. A tiny spark of gold, glinting in the sun like the flame-tipped arrow that pierced Saint Theresa of Avila's swooning heart, was all we

could discern of the gilded warrior angel poised at the apex of its bell tower, his uplifted sword eternally poised to strike at the enemy. As we neared our destination, my husband, Mark, pulled over our rented Renault into the Saint-Lô tourism office, and we went inside to ask for directions to the small local chapel dedicated to Jean de Brébeuf. But even here, on the site's very doorstep, we were met with blank, uncomprehending stares. No one, it seemed, knew what we were talking about. Renegotiating the town's narrow, cobblestone streets, we re-emerged into farmers' fields and, after a few false starts, stumbled, almost accidentally, on the site. The late afternoon sun spread a mellow golden light over the small chapel, landscaped gardens, and ruined walls of the complex's original house and outbuildings.[55] Three poles flew the banners of Normandy, Québec, and Canada. Beside them stood an empty stone plinth, seeming expectantly to await a statue of the local saint. Waiting for us was Gilbert Gauroy, the stooped, elderly founder of a small group of lay Catholics who style themselves Les Amis de (the Friends of) Jean de Brébeuf. A reserved, formal man, Gauroy had graciously agreed to show us around the chapel his group had built at the site of the martyr's birth from stones pulled from the ruins of his ancestral home, La Boissée. Awkwardly juggling two silver-handled canes and the keys, Gauroy unlocked the door and ushered us inside.

Spotless, homemade, and appealing, the diminutive chapel is a sort of religious version of the Seven Dwarfs' cabin. Its whitewashed interior is barely large enough to house two anemic pews, a small altar displaying an elaborate golden reliquary, and a couple of amateurish paintings of Brébeuf done by our host. The chapel's humbleness speaks of determined faith, necessary frugality, and a certain flair for improvisation. One roofless section of the site's evocative ruins—stabilized rather than fully restored—has been ingeniously transformed, with the planting of flowers and strategic placement of benches, into a small, walled "prayer garden." Everything on-site, Gauroy told me proudly, has been salvaged from the discards of other churches, made by *les Amis*, or bought at local flea markets.[56] The chapel's chief treasure, a lavishly framed vial of earth from Saint-Ignace, the site of Brébeuf's martyrdom, is prominently displayed on its eastern wall. A souvenir of the Friends' pilgrimage to Canada, the earth brings the saint's story full circle by memorializing his death at this, the very spot of his birth.

Following our tour, Gauroy guided us to the home of the group's president, carpenter Pierre Bunel, where *les Amis* had assembled to meet us. The richer gold of early evening sunlight poured into his spotless kitchen through the open wooden shutters. Chickens pecked and squawked contentedly in the yard outside. Though there are a few small religious mementos on the walls, Bunel's decor is dominated by framed sepia photos of Condé-sur-Vire before the Second World War. A tall, gregarious bachelor clad in rough canvas overalls, Bunel is an affable and generous host, although initially his thick Norman accent renders him almost incomprehensible. Our Canadian French also poses difficulties for him. But generous servings of Calvados, the potent local apple brandy, help to smooth away any awkwardness and soon the conversation flows freely. With much joking and many asides, *les Amis* answer my questions about how they came to establish the tiny chapel, now a pilgrimage site for North American devotees of the martyrs.

The Friends explain that although they had long dreamt of forming an association to promote the interests of their local saint, it was a visit from a group of would-be pilgrims in 1991 that brought things to a head. The disappointed Canadian visitors publicly lambasted the small community for its failure to preserve the site of Brébeuf's ancestral home or to construct a suitable venue for prayer to their martyred native son in the village of his birth. Almost twenty year later, the memory of the dressing-down was still fresh. The allegation of impiety and neglect shamed them doubly, as devotees of Brébeuf and as Normans who treasure good hospitality as a core value. Chagrined, the newly formed *Amis* decided to force the Catholic Church finally to fulfill its promise, broken over sixty years earlier, to build a memorial chapel at La Boisée. Hooking his silver-handled walking canes over the back of his kitchen chair, Gauroy leaned forward to tell the story. In 1930, he earnestly relates, Cardinal Roullau of Québec, en route to the canonization ceremonies in Rome, led a pilgrimage to Condé-sur-Vire and presented the local curé with 30,000 francs for the construction of a modest chapel. But the Canadian contingent had barely left town before the bishop swooped in and summarily reallocated the windfall to construct a movie theater.

Though the church did reluctantly relinquish the absconded funds, the confrontation engendered a lasting animosity between *les Amis* and the parish powers-that-be. This bad blood convinced the small group that if they wanted the chapel ready in time for the celebration of Brébeuf's four hundredth birthday in 1993, they themselves must build it. Though the Friends were not young even back in 1993, together they mortared the stone, stabilized the remaining ruins, and landscaped the grounds, their exertions fueled by a never-ending stream of coffee and cigarettes. The group also sought to rally their idyllic rural community to the project behind the twin banners of Catholic devotion and pride in their local *patrimonie* but with little real success. Pierre related— more with dry humor than with any real bitterness—that the group was considered *fou* (crazy), both for their interest in the obscure saint and for taking on such an ambitious construction project.[57] Suzanne Guenon, Pierre Bunel's sister, caustically noted that although many resisted involvement in the project, they now had the temerity to criticize *les Amis* for the modest scope of the very construction they had refused to fund or support. "Where are the toilets?" they asked. "Why isn't it bigger?"[58]

In speaking to the gathered Friends, it quickly became apparent that Gallic devotion toward the martyrs diverges dramatically from North American patterns. Careful consideration of the perspectives of *les Amis* promises to make the important but often invisible similarities between the jarringly different experiences of ethnic pilgrims to Midland and ultraconservatives to Auriesville much more compellingly apparent. Despite pronounced differences in how these groups envision the contemporary legacy of the martyrs and articulate their own collective identity as their venerators, the yet more fundamental differences of the Gallic cult help to highlight their many shared assumptions.

Coming from Canada, where Jean de Brébeuf's name is a household word, my husband and I were initially taken aback by the fact that the French-born saint is virtually unknown in the country of his birth. Even those who lived and worked only a stone's throw from his little chapel seemed entirely unaware of its existence. The gloomy forecast of one Norman devotee, who dolefully presaged that "if you go to Coutances, only ten kilometers away, no one—not even the priests—will know Brébeuf's name" proved correct. By contrast, in Midland, the Martyrs' Shrine is grudgingly recognized as an important pillar of the local economy. Its iconic stained-glass window, *A Sharing*, is reproduced at thirty times its original size on the town's giant grain elevators down by the docks, and any resident can direct you to its jutting silver spires or outline for you the bare bones of the saints' story. Similarly, driving through the Mohawk Valley of upstate New York, toll takers on Interstate 90 can easily orient you to the winding regional road that has been, for the past 127 years, the home of the Our Lady of Martyrs Shrine.

Several factors explain France's apparent indifference toward her saintly native sons. First, in appealing for the veneration of French Catholics, Brébeuf and his brethren must compete in a crowded religious marketplace, which already has entrenched and venerable favorites. In contrast with saint-starved North America, France is chockablock with martyrs and homegrown religious heroes. Every ancient country church seems to boast its own cherished local saint or miracle-working relics.

Second, the much greater profundity of French historical consciousness makes these seventeenth-century figures, seen as "ancient history" in North America, into Johnny-come-latelies in the land of their birth. In North America, the coming of Europeans to the continent is often cast as the "beginning" of its religious history, a perspective that blithely ignores centuries of indigenous spirituality. In Canada and the United States, Brébeuf and his brethren have long been perceived as the venerable founders of French Catholicism and as early pioneers of European civilization in the New World. But in France, popular historical consciousness has much longer roots. Once, while waiting for hours to see the ecstatic thirty-second blur of motion that is the Tour de France, I started to talk with French spectators. Having observed several incidents of their local animosity to the British, both tourists and those who have taken up permanent residency in this idyllic corner of northwestern France, I asked them: "Pourquoi vous n'aimez pas les anglais?" ("Why don't you like the English?"). Some candidly mentioned that they resented the steep rise in local housing prices caused by rich British retirees buying local properties. Others added that these immigrants rarely make an effort to learn French or to integrate into the community, preferring to keep to themselves. At this point an elderly woman, who had been listening to the exchange while quietly knitting in her camp chair, broke into the conversation, spitting: "Ils ont brulé Jean d'Arc" (They [the English] burned Joan of Arc). The fact that the murder of this quintessentially French saint over five centuries ago was mentioned as a cause of local friction in the same breath as escalating housing prices speaks to the passion and depth of Gallic engagement with their past. In France, saints, like a good Bordeaux, seem only to improve with age. Bretons have been venerating the time-darkened, gold-haloed skull of Saint-Yves, patron saint of lawyers, virtually since his demise in 1303. The venerability of such cults gives them an incumbent's advantage over "newcomers" like the North American martyrs.[59]

The martyrs' Gallic veneration is also handicapped by the amount of time they spent away from their French homeland. Though arguably deeper than that of many North Americans,[60] French collective consciousness is also much more regional. French historians are often deeply fascinated by their own local history, while remaining stubbornly unmoved by events and figures even a little outside it. Thus, though all eight of the "North American" martyrs were born, educated, and reached maturity in France, their protracted colonial hiatus and the fact that their martyrdoms occurred overseas puts them—for some—outside the magic circle of local interest.

French hyperregionalism also explains why the martyrs' homeland cannot claim a "cult of the North American martyrs" per se. Here, Gallic dynamics of local pride and identity work against collectivization. In North America, the martyrs are venerated together, as a group. Though there has long been a pronounced tension between those who encourage devotion to all eight figures together, under their most inclusive title, and Canadian and American nationalists who especially venerate those who fell within their own country's national boundaries, even this dismemberment retains the collective nature of the cult. In France, by contrast, where the martyrs have been able to grab any kind of tenuous foothold in collective consciousness, it has been as individuals, purely at the local level. Gallic veneration of the martyrs expresses itself as a constellation of tiny, localized microcults dedicated to each individual saint in the hamlet of his birth.[61]

Judging from the collective account of *les Amis* of the founding of their tiny chapel, the French veneration of the martyrs lacks the strong supernaturalism of its North American articulation. In sharp contrast with Father Coldricks's moving assertion that the "Canadian martyrs" intervened spiritually to bring him to back to the Midland shrine, the Friends made no dramatic claims of answered prayers or saintly miracles. On the contrary, they highlighted their own efforts in the saint's service against a variety of odds. In a sense, *les Amis* reversed the traditional patron–client relationship by presenting themselves as intervening with earthly authorities on Brébeuf's behalf, rather than beseeching his heavenly intervention for their intentions.

The devotion of *les Amis* to Brébeuf also wholly lacks the strongly ideological component, whether liberal or conservative, that characterizes North American devotion to the martyrs. It is all too easy to contrast the different political orientations of pilgrimages in honor of the martyrs while overlooking their shared politicization as a basic, underlying similarity. Thus, the trenchant theological and political conservatism of NCCL pilgrims seems to present a near-total contrast with the liberal ecumenicalism and multiculturalism championed by Goan Jesuit Father Coldricks. And yet, when the ethos of each is compared with that of *les Amis,* it is the *shared* politicization of these pilgrimages that seem more notable than their respective places on the liberal–conservative divide. Midland's casting of the martyrs as relevant models for contemporary intercultural encounter are meaningless to *les Amis.* They see La Boisée not as a site of intercultural or interreligious dialogue but rather as a spiritual resting place for weary overseas travelers hungry for communion with their shared hero at his birthplace. Providing this sanctuary for fellow devotees to Brébeuf, particularly their "little cousins"—the Quebecois—is the Friends' low-key, personal way of showing hospitality and displaying their own devotion to this shared saint.[62] Moreover, unlike American ultraconservatives, *les Amis* do not perceive or present themselves as latter-day champions of the true faith against a prevaricating church and a godless, secular culture. This is all the more striking given that they have had to fight both church and state tooth and nail to found and promote their modest chapel. Nor, despite the open mockery they receive from other community members, do *les Amis* cast themselves as contemporary martyrs suffering the cruel incomprehension of the irreligious. Rather, these stories of "persecution" are related in a dry, self-deprecating manner, with an eye to their evident humor and irony.

But this is not to say that these French devotees, like their Canadian and American counterparts, do not see some reflection of themselves in Brébeuf. In their case, however, this strong sense of identification is at least as much historical and geographical as it is devotional. Though their interest in Brébeuf is articulated through religious idioms, such as the building of a chapel, the local saint serves as a kind of embodiment of their *patrimonie*. Promoting and defending him is an attractive way to express their intensely local sense of rootedness in one place and their passionate interest in how that place has evolved over time. *Les Amis* perceive Brébeuf as kin or neighbor, as someone with shared roots in the Norman soil, as a figure shaped by the local geography and culture, lending a rough intimacy to how they discuss this local boy made good. The very name of their group—the *Friends* of Jean de Brébeuf (rather than, for example, the "slaves" or "oblates" of Mary Immaculate)— captures this sense of familiar egalitarianism. A local *cantique* written to honor Brébeuf's 1930 canonization makes much of his regional identity, rather than celebrating him as a new saint of the universal church:

A Condé-sur-Vire	At Conde-sur-Vire
Naquit autrefois	was born long ago
Le Saint qu'on admire	The saint we admire
Et prie à la fois	took the Faith
Un petit village	In a little village
Nommé "la Boissais"	named "La Boissais"
Un vieil ermitage,	in an old hermitage
Des aïeux parfaits. . . .	to honorable forebearers. . . .
Jean, vous êtes notre	Jean, you are ours
Par tous vos aïeux,	By virtue of your ancestry
Soyez notre Apôtre	Be our Apostle,
Montrez-nous les Cieux!	Conduct us to Heaven![63]

Though the Friends are happy that their chapel has helped to forge transatlantic ties with his other venerators, their own devotion toward Brébeuf is predicated on the fact that, as a native son of Condé-sur-Vire, he is truly "ours."[64]

In keeping with their strong focus on *patrimonie, les Amis* often couple the story of Brébeuf with more recent and tragic events in their local history, particularly the near-total destruction that accompanied the Allied assaults of 1945. The Friends' experiences as young people during the traumatic final years of the Second World War, when Normandy became a fierce battleground between Nazi and Allied forces, have deeply colored their understanding of what it is to be Norman, linking it indelibly to suffering and destruction. Even fifty-five years later, the pain of these events is still very fresh in the minds of these elderly Friends. Like a somber presence in the room, these memories are palpable even amid the humor and camaraderie of their generous Norman hospitality.

As I talked with *les Amis* across the spotless oilcloth of Pierre Bunel's kitchen table, I was initially impatient with these more recent tales of epic destruction, viewing them as unwelcome "interruptions" or "digressions" in the discussion of Brébeuf. I grew weary of Pierre removing from the walls for our inspection his many sepia-toned photos of Condé-sur-Vire's prewar bridges, churches, and homes and of the group's seemingly inexhaustible interest in comparing these original structures with their replacements or reconstructions. Some of their recounted stories, it is true, did coherently connect Brébeuf to the battles of Normandy. René Guenon remembered how as a ten-year-old he had taken refuge with his family in "la Boissée"—then still standing—during the protracted assault on Condé-sur-Vire and how all had prayed to its former saintly occupant to preserve them from harm. But for the most part, these stories seemed bafflingly unrelated evasions of my questions. It was only with their sheer repetitiveness that the striking similarities between these tales of martyrdom and of total war started to click into place: revealing an added dimension to the Friends' strong identification—as local historians, as Catholics, and as Normans—with the martyred Brébeuf. Both sets of stories, I started to see, recount suffering, endurance, and a mitigated, tortured sort of triumph. Like Brébeuf, Normandy was assaulted, if not martyred. Her towns were destroyed and her architectural treasures decimated. The lives of many Normans were lost, casualties of the determined counterassault of besieged Nazi forces and, perhaps even more painfully, victims of the salvation-through-destruction wrought by the Allies attempting to liberate northwestern France from its long Nazi occupation. Like Brébeuf, Normandy endured systemic destruction. Its suffering was necessary for good ultimately to triumph in what has generally been cast, both then and now, as a protracted battle between the forces of darkness and light.

Like Brébeuf, Normandy has been "resurrected," though her battle scars are still plainly visible and are much mourned. Gilbert Gauroy, our elderly guide, lives literally in the shadow of the region's reconstructed cathedral in St. Lo, a town some five kilometers north of Condé-sur-Vire. He insisted that we visit it together, ostensibly to show us its stained-glass window of Brébeuf. Much like the variegated stories of *les Amis*, the structure is a strange conglomeration of mismatched elements, bringing together the recent and the venerable. The postwar design preserves what remains of the twelfth-century edifice, filling in the many gaps left by extensive bombing with stark, unadorned black schist. Deeply pockmarked with bullet holes, the church is as much a grim acknowledgment of its own irreparability as it is a triumphant assertion of survival. The church, though still standing, mourns what has been lost, even as it urges visitors to grieve not, rather find strength in what remains behind.

Nostalgia. Pathos. These two words characterize the Friends' collective recounting of the adventurous but doomed career of their local son in 1640s Canada and of the tragic destruction of their region in the all-out battle for continental domination three hundred years later. These poignant emotions—strangely at odds with the humor of our halting, Calvados-fueled exchanges—also came to the fore when this elderly group contemplated the bleak future of devotion to Jean de Brébeuf in his birthplace. These elderly Friends enjoy few of the advantages taken for granted by the martyrs' other devotees. Unlike the ultraconservatives, who are increasingly at the forefront of the American cult, or the many ethnic pilgrimages to Midland, which feature the high-spirited participation of many children and youth, the Friends do not enjoy the enthusiastic and committed participation of the younger generation. They loyally serve their local saint as individuals, rather than as representatives of their extended families. Virtually devoid of grassroots support, they are—as they themselves ruefully confess—regarded as colorful local "cranks" by the rest of their community.

Nor, like the Midland Jesuits, have *les Amis* managed to enlist the support of the government in preserving what is arguably an important historic site. Indeed, their relationship with their municipality is almost as fractious as their association with the local church. Forced to choose between the devil and the deep blue sea, *les Amis* have decided to will their diminutive chapel to *la Mairie*—the local government— instead of to the church that so reluctantly underwrote its construction. Although justifiably proud of what they, as a small but dedicated group have managed to accomplish on Brébeuf's behalf, *les Amis* are also painfully aware that local veneration of "their" saint will weaken substantially with each of their individual deaths and will itself likely expire with the demise of the last Friend. The expectant stone plinth waiting outside their modest chapel for a donated statue will likely remain forever empty.

Epilogue

THE WIND SWEPT the tiny, crystalline flakes along the ground. Smoke, ash, and snow together performed a languorous dance, veiling and revealing the indistinct forms on the ground. Here, all was white, or gray, or black: no living colors enlivened the monochrome landscape. Even the dead grass that poked above the snow was sere and brittle. The night's heavy snowfall had obscured all traces of the recent battle for Taenhatentaron/Saint-Ignace: erasing all footprints, extinguishing all flames, and softening the outline of what had once been walls. Snow lay thick on the broken, off-kilter lie of a fallen roof, on a half-burnt palisade.

The dead lay anonymous. They could have been hummocks, mere natural features of the landscape, save for the details that the scouring wind chanced to reveal. Like a mother smoothing out white bedclothes over a sleeping child, its ministering hands revealed the curve of a naked neck or the slender arch of a foot. It gently liberated strands of long, black hair from its crust of layering white to whirl and dance like something alive. High above, ravens rode the thermals like black kites cut from their strings, their harsh song distant yet distinct, its guttural tones a promise or a warning. Below, others had already begun to feast. They clustered over the snowy mounds like living shrouds, like black robes. Flapping their glossy feathers, they poked at the frozen forms with their sharp beaks, black eyes glinting. Some tugged, obscenely, at human intestines. Bending back their dark heads, they pulled the red ribbons taut, as if doing up a bloody bodice.

Death had made no distinction among those who fell during the sacking of Taenhatentaron. Nor did the snow that covered them during the tiptoeing night. First melting as it fell on their still-warm flesh, it gradually collected on their open, sightless eyes and motionless chests, veiling their wounds and erasing the pools of blackening blood beneath their bodies in its absolving whiteness. The ravens did not distinguish between saint and sinner, murdered or martyred, as they feasted indiscriminately, glad for a meal in the cruel scarcity of a Canadian March, whose bleakness always belies spring's coming.

No, it is only people who have made distinctions among these fallen. If deemed worthy of any remark by the hagiographers and historians who over the centuries have recounted these incidents, the deaths of the native many have generally been tagged as "tragic" and promptly forgotten. The more generous have included the fall of the Wendat confederacy as a sort of ratifying echo, a brutal backdrop for the martyrs' spotlit sufferings. But they, too, strategically consigned their suffering to the periphery, lest they upstage their own chosen leads in this New World drama. Historians have generally colluded with Jesuit survivors who, in the battle's aftermath constructed a "sanctity gap" to separate their slain brethren from the "hapless" or "doomed" Wendat, the subjects of their selfless pastoral attention.

This process of winnowing "the martyred" from the merely "slain" was a physical as well as a conceptual process. When possible, the Jesuits literally separated these holiest dead from the rest of the fallen for awestruck contemplation, sacred forensics, and lavish ritual interment. On March 18, 1649, for example, two days after the fall of Saint-Ignace and Saint-Louis, the Jesuits of Sainte-Marie cautiously emerged from their palisaded stronghold. Wary of Iroquois attack, they hesitantly approached the settlement's frozen ashes with the goal of identifying and recovering the bodies of Jean de Brébeuf and Gabriel Lalemant. Catholic Wendat who had witnessed the missionaries' torture and subsequently escaped their captors' clutches to flee westward to the Jesuit headquarters had recounted to the horrified Jesuits how the two had died. Their halting words, likely delivered in a state of shock, pain, and exhaustion, would become the first draft of these new martyrs' dawning legend. Thus warned of what they would find, the black-robes crouched over each body, searching among the many rendered eyeless and heartless by the marauding crows for the corpses of two Europeans, whose organs had been ritually ripped from their bodies by human antagonists. With these violent actions, they fervently believed, the duo's native slayers had unwittingly crowned the pair with martyrs' laurels and ushered them through heaven's gates.[1]

If New France's forbidding landscape, littered with the fallen, was a northerly recasting of Ezekiel's vision, then it was certainly a selective one. From among the bodies of the myriad slain during this dark decade, only eight were selected to rise again in the popular imagination and enjoy an afterlife as eventful, dramatic, and suspenseful as their much shorter lives had been. It would be the wounds of *these* particular men— Europeans rather than natives, missionaries rather than converts—that would be wondered over and touched with reverent awe. It would be *their* final moments that would be reimagined in paintings and poetry, *their* bones venerated as priceless relics. Invoked over the centuries as saints, heroes, pioneers, and, above all, as martyrs, their likeness would be installed over altars and schoolroom chalkboards alike. Looming larger than life, their solemn statues, cast in attitudes of severe benediction, would grace the lonely shores of places they had walked while alive. Shrines would rise in their memory on the western and southern extremes of the lands that, by their lives, labors, and bloody deaths, they had audaciously sought to claim for Christ, their actions as bold a witness as the crosses they habitually slashed in the living flesh of New France's trees.

A Distinction without a Difference?

The Jesuits who jealously claimed the burnt husks of their friends' bodies, then, clearly saw their deaths as qualitatively different from those of the Wendat who had perished all around them. Though many of the native slain were devout Catholics, intimately known to the Jesuits, who assiduously recorded the details of their lives, conversions, and growth in the faith, in death the Wendat were mourned merely as collective sheep to the missionaries' individual shepherds and memorialized as exemplary converts *to* the faith rather than as martyrs *for* it. But were the Jesuits justified in their myopic preoccupation with their own dead? Was it legitimate for these black-robes to lift up their own (both literally and figuratively) from the native fallen who lay, broken, all around them? Or should they have taken their cue from the snow, which gently blanketed all with the same anonymous shroud, or even from the ravens, who preyed on all of the bodies, oblivious to their race or religion?

The answer to these questions depends, at least in part, on whether the deaths of these eight missionaries can fairly be characterized as exceptional: either in terms of *how* they were killed, or *why* they were killed, or both. Looking at first at how they died, it must be asked: were these eight murders true aberrations whose unique and holy dynamics challenged standard native diplomatic, war, and postwar patterns and practices, as the Jesuits and their historiographic champions over the centuries have maintained? Or were they remarkable more for their conformity with rather than confrontation of long-established native norms?

The case for strong continuities between the deaths of the eight canonized and those native people who either fell alongside them or suffered identical fates under similar circumstances is a powerful one. Though the eight Europeans met their deaths by myriad means, convincing corollaries with numerous native victims can be made in every case. René Goupil, Isaac Jogues, and Jean de la Lande were captives of the Iroquois whose lives were unceremoniously taken when the diplomatic and military tides turned against them. French diplomatic envoys (like the ambassadors of native polities) were seen as personifying the nation they represented. They were thus vulnerable to retributory violence if the French committed any act perceived by their hosts as threatening or violent, even if it was committed in self-defense. For example, according to a contemporaneous account, Goupil may have been cut down to retaliate for Mohawk losses during their ill-fated Iroquois attack on the French settlement of Richelieu. Jogues and la Lande became vulnerable due to many diplomatic missteps, and were eventually dispatched when their efforts to effect a lasting peace between the French and the Iroquois confederacy resoundingly failed.

Two more of the eight were casualties of war. Charles Garnier and Antoine Daniel died in early-morning Iroquois raids on vulnerable Wendat settlements in which they were stationed as missionaries. As unarmed noncombatants, precluded by their religious vows from bearing arms, their battlefield deaths were thus indistinguishable from the scores of Wendat women, children, and elders who also fell, though they did not fight.

Two other black-robes also perished in the ashes of a sacked Wendat village. Jean de Brébeuf and Gabriel Lalemant, however, did not die in battle but were chosen for the grueling, honorable death generally reserved for esteemed warriors. The escalating torture they endured, from their initial "running of the gauntlet" to the ritual ingestion of their hearts, conformed impeccably—with a single, startling, and important exception: their boiling-water "baptism"—to the traditional protocols that had long prevailed in intranative encounters. In fact, these deaths can be seen as an ironic measure of Jesuit success in fully penetrating Wendat society: both because they were apparently selected to die as "honorary Wendat" and because they seem consciously to have conformed their own performances to aboriginal notions of honorable death.[2]

The last of the eight canonized, Nöel Chabanel, was the lone victim of a robbery-murder whose only living witness was his confessed killer. Though his death differed substantially from those of his seven martyred companions, his slaying has obvious parallels with other violent incidents involving both native and French victims during the same period.

On the face of it, then, the myriad ways in which these eight men were put to death bear remarkable similarities to the fates routinely meted out to native peoples—including Catholics—in far greater numbers, thus raising the thorny question of why only these eight Europeans have been honored as martyrs. But perhaps if the physical *means* by which they died did not make them special, then the *motivation* for their slayings can provide the necessary justification.

With the passage of the centuries, devotional literature and art has come to place increased emphasis on native peoples' supposed hatred of and anger toward these eight missionaries, in an effort to illustrate convincingly the *in odium fidei* traditionally needed to produce bona fide Catholic martyrs. The depicted facial expressions of the martyrs' native slayers gradually morphed from the calm inscrutability of seventeenth-century depictions to untrammeled and maniacal rage in the twentieth. In the vivid historical prose of Francis Parkman and Abbé Groulx, the martyrs' undifferentiated native assailants fairly pulse with a demented "tigerish" menace. But to judge on the basis of their recorded actions, native attitudes toward these eight missionaries encompassed a range of other emotions, including curiosity, indifference, respect, puzzlement, and sympathy.

Indeed, excluding the deaths of Garnier and Daniel, which took place in the chaotic heat of battle, making extended consultation regarding their fates virtually impossible, the question of what to do with captured Jesuit missionaries proved hotly controversial in native circles. The various fates of the eight Europeans were in no way inevitable or predetermined. Nor was violence the reflexive, unanimous action of singular, muscular native will, as martyrdom art would have us believe. On the contrary, in five of the six remaining cases,[3] the missionaries were slain by a *minority* faction within a given native body politic.

Jogues and la Lande were executed by a Bear Clan faction against the express wishes of the Mohawk majority. Indeed, Jogues's condemnation was controversial even *among* the people of the Bear. Jogues's death sentence was appealed both in words and in the desperate actions of the tall youth who was himself injured in a failed attempt to divert the deadly blow.

A small group of ex-Wendat ex-Catholics in the ranks of the invading Iroquois force who toppled Saint Louis and Saint Ignace in March 1649 took the lead in the ritual execution of Brébeuf and Lalemant. Though the Iroquois majority seemed to have decided to keep the duo alive, with a Cayuga man giving his own wampum as collateral for their lives, this Wendat faction proved to exercise an influence well out of proportion to their diminutive demographic size. Their persistent hectoring and innovative torment escalated the momentum and severity of the missionaries' torture, ultimately resulting in their deaths.

Nöel Chabanel's murder was the fruit of Louis Honareenhax's defiant vow to kill the first Frenchman they could find, a similar promise to that which had been made and fulfilled with the similar but unsanctified slaying of Jacques Douart. Honareenhax was part of a violent Wendat minority faction that opposed the majority's wish to retain ties with the French and attempted, through a small-scale and ultimately abortive campaign of terror, to force the Jesuits from Wendake and to wreak revenge on them for the insalubrious changes they had brought in their black wake.

Five of the eight missionary deaths, then, were accomplished by small minorities within larger native enclaves. Over the centuries, the perceptions and sentiments of this minority of native actors in these famous incidents have been either deliberately or sloppily overgeneralized to characterize the perspective of whole native nations. But despite this convenient or actively cynical exaggeration of these minority perspectives, they are still critically important. Not only do they exhibit strong indications of *in odium fidei,* the heart's blood of any argument for martyrdom, but they also demonstrate that, even as the escalating frictions caused by colonialism encouraged the Jesuits, the Iroquois, and the Wendat alike to turn for solace to their traditional understandings of "the good death"—whether this was martyrdom, retaliation, or sacrifice—the strains of this encounter simultaneously forced these concepts and their attendant rituals to morph, both ideologically and practically.

In some deaths, such as those of Brébeuf and Lalemant, the multiple meanings piled one on top of the other: sometimes competing, sometimes colluding. The exhibition of courage and defiance under torture translated particularly well across the cultural and linguistic divide, though this behavior could connote faithfulness to Christ, stalwartness as a representative of one's natal nation, or both. But in other cases, frustration was palpable on both sides of the encounter as each group struggled to situate the other in traditional categories into which they did not perfectly fit. Iroquois puzzlement as to how to handle Goupil, Jogues, and la Lande is so evident as to be almost palpable. The treatment of Jogues and Goupil during their 1642 captivity was far harsher than was typical for adoptees. And yet adoption's ritual flip side, death by torture, did not emerge as an alternative. Eventually, they all met compromise deaths at the hands of a dissident minority: quick executions devoid of ceremony or the backhanded compliment of prolonged torment.

As native sacrifice and Catholic martyrdom met and morphed, rituals within rituals developed. The deadly baptism that Brébeuf and Lalemant suffered at the hands of their furious ex-catechumens had a range of subtle meanings evident only to those who had undergone this ritual initiation into a Christian world of meaning. Observed by a curious Iroquois majority, who likely saw the boiling-water ordeal as an improvised variation on traditional torture (which indeed it was), these ex-Wendat ex-Catholics ritually undid their own baptisms. Themselves becoming priests, they administered a sacrament they likely perceived as having promised so much more than it was able to deliver. Like Louis Honareenhax, they probably sought to punish these black-robes for the deadly divisions the Jesuits had planted within Wendake: rendering it vulnerable to the very invasions in which they themselves had taken part, as assailants rather than defenders of their homelands. In bitterly repeating back to the Jesuits their own words, assuring them that this torturous sacrament would send them to the heaven they so longed for, the men displayed considerable knowledge of the religious tradition they so evidently were rejecting. Is it ironic or merely fitting that the three clearest cases of *in odium fidei,* exhibited in the slayings of Jean de Brébeuf, Gabriel Lalemant, and Nöel Chabanel, all took place at the hands of ex-Catholics? Was the martyrs' truest legacy that they had taught enough of their faith to enable these men to make them martyrs?

"Choice" has also proven itself the infinitely flexible friend of the martyrs' advocates, providing them with another justification for the selection of European over native candidates as martyrs. Volition is integral to martyrdom. To be a martyr, an individual must consciously and courageously accept danger and, ultimately, death.[4] To die with the necessary determined faith, martyrs must first conquer their own will to live *at any cost* as, without the Gethsemane of acceptance, there can be no Calvary of martyrdom.[5] Their hagiographers thus praise Garnier and Daniel for *choosing* to remain in their vulnerable posts despite the deepening Iroquois threat. Along with Brébeuf and Lalemant, they are credited with electing, in the face of imminent invasion, to stay with their village's native defenders to provide them with religious consolation rather than fleeing with other noncombatants. Yet should the argument be made that Wendat warriors—many of them Catholic—made essentially the same choice, to risk their lives in a doomed effort to hold their ground in the face of a larger invading force, hagiographers simply move the martyrs' choice unassailably and inimitably into their Gallic past, into which their native competitors for the martyrs' palm cannot hope to follow. In choosing to brave the dangers of a new world, hagiographers have long argued, these Europeans had already indicated their willingness to grasp the palm should it be extended to them. In creating this distinction, moreover, they imply that the native slain had merely succumbed to the savage violence endemic to their benighted, Christ-less culture, thus neatly absolving the Jesuits from either the factionalizing of Wendat society or the destabilization of intranative power relations.

But in making volition central, the martyrs' advocates walk a knife's edge. Their strong focus on individual choice only highlights those aspects of these colonial confrontations that distinguished them most sharply both from the persecution of the primitive church by Rome and the Christian-on-Christian violence endemic to post-Reformation Europe. In these classic martyrdom scenarios, torture and the threat of death are the twin handmaidens of religious coercion. Should individuals undergoing torture choose to recant their offending religious (or confessional) identity, their torment would cease. But because the motivations for aboriginal postwar torture were grounded in a fundamentally foreign religious worldview, these Christian rules were not only inapplicable, but wholly nonsensical. Even in those cases where a minority of the martyrs' killers seem to have had the requisite hatred of Christianity to make them martyr-makers, it seems unlikely that they would have ceased to torment the missionaries had they apostatized under duress. After all, the goal of aboriginal death by torture (unlike that of ritual adoption, the far more common fate) was not to *transform* the captive's identity, but to punish him for his existing identity: his belonging to a nation or an alliance of nations held responsible for causalities the victors had endured in the recent past. In native contexts, captives had no choice regarding the degree of torture they would suffer, or whether they would live or die. This was not for them to decide, remaining always the prerogative of their captor. A prisoner's restricted volition could express itself only in rigorously sculpting his or her reactions to the torturer's initiatives, a fact that Jean de Brébeuf seems to have appreciated. Given the very limited agency afforded the prisoner in native postwar rituals, it is perhaps prudent that hagiographers have generally preferred to place the martyrs' anticipatory self-offering earlier in their religious careers.

But as well as confronting the problem of too little volition, the martyrs' defenders have also had to contend with the problem of "too much." Isaac Jogues's reckless disregard for his own personal safety, demonstrated in his repeated spearheading of peace delegations into the very territory where he had suffered prolonged, near-fatal captivity, was evidence to his Jesuit peers of the ardent fullness of his desire for martyrdom. Yet to his critics at the time and in the centuries since,

Jogues's volunteerism went well beyond the mere acceptance of his fate into the active courtship of it, putting his death beyond the pale of orthodox martyrdom into its radical fringes.

Defenders of the canonized martyrs have also sought to protect them from competition from strong native candidates by emphasizing their inimitable role as Catholic priests. In the seventeenth century, the strong association of priesthood with martyrdom initially supported the doomed *causa* of a now virtually unknown Jesuit, Anne de Nöue, even as it undercut the otherwise powerful case of donnés René Goupil and Jean de la Lande. The punctiliousness of the six canonized priests in performing their pastoral duties to the bitter end has been used as a bulwark to guard defensively their proprietary claim to a special sanctity. Antoine Daniel's appearance at the door of his church in the unfamiliar glory of his priestly vestments is credited with temporarily checking the Iroquois advance, allowing some Wendat noncombatants the opportunity to flee. The wounded Garnier is likewise celebrated for his last earthly act: crawling toward a mortally wounded Wendat Catholic to administer him the last rites. Brébeuf and Lalemant are honored as much for their desperate prebattle baptism by aspersion as Saint-Louis readied itself for the dawn onslaught as for their dramatic, defiant witnessing for the faith during their extended torture. And Noel Chabanel, the so-called forgotten martyr, is remembered precisely for his mastering of his deep-seated repugnance of all aspects of life in North America, particularly native culture, in order to convert and serve native Catholics.

The emphasis on sacerdotal status softened enough by the late nineteenth century to permit the canonization of two European laymen alongside the six priests. But evidently, this opening was not large enough to permit the entry of *native* Catholic laymen.

Hagiographers' failure, over the centuries, to *seriously* consider aboriginal candidates as Catholic martyrs is particularly ironic given their own complete (and completely unacknowledged) dependency on the "Christian savages, worth of belief"[6] who were the *only* surviving eyewitnesses to the martyrs' individual deaths. Their testimony regarding these missionaries' final acts and last words is thus the rock upon which the entire martyrs' cult has been built. Without these escapees' relations of these men's "spectacle for men and for angels" their suffering, though edifying celestial eyes, would be unknown to history. But unfortunately for these seventeenth-century native Catholics, witness-ing something spiritually crucial, even world changing, is no guarantor of equitable treatment by the church. Just ask Mary Magdalene. Her urgent relation to the disciples of her unique encounter with the risen Christ, though it is the very marrow, the very fundament of the Chris-tian faith, has nevertheless not been enough to admit her to Jesus's in-ner circle in the eyes of the church. A sainted sinner she remains, not a disciple. Much the same can be said of seventeenth-century native peoples, whom hagiographers have used to testify on behalf of the mar-tyrs, but have not regarded as actually being martyrs. Thus, while their testimony is conveniently considered sound enough to found a cult on, the cult remains a cult that hallows exclusively European, rather than native, figures. But if the martyrs are lionized for their creation of a spiritual link between themselves and native Christians in life, then why should they be separated from them conceptually in death, di-vided by martyrdom accorded and martyrdom denied? Why should the recipients of these rites be any less recognized than those who admin-istered them? Consistency and logic would seem to demand that either all those Catholics who fell together during the dark decade of the 1640s are martyrs, or none are.

But this modest argument, which merely seeks fairness in how in-dividual cases of Catholic martyrdom are judged, exists alongside a far more sweeping, ambitious, and radical native critique of the martyrs' cult: one that threatens to swamp its fragile craft with the dark tides of native suffering. Reframing martyrdom as a collective, rather than an individual, experience, some contemporary native critics—both Catho-lics and traditionalists—have appropriated the language and logic of martyrdom to describe the travails of both their individual native na-tions and of indigenous peoples more generally. Pointedly asking "who killed whom?" they replace the molehill of the martyrs' isolated, indi-vidual, and long-ago deaths with the mountain of native agony: com-mon, collective, and continuing. The seventeenth-century crown of thorns worn by native North America—epidemic, internal divisions, and escalated warfare—gave way to new agonies in subsequent centu-ries, in the form of territorial displacement, forced assimilation, and always the painful struggle to retain their cultural, spiritual, and lin-guistic identity: native people's contemporary Golgotha. However, by unconsciously expressing the depths of their people's suffering through the Christian concept of martyrdom, native traditionalists who often seek only to escape from the Catholic categories of their childhoods inadvertently testify to their ongoing conceptual and emotional power.

Together, seventeenth-century historical actors on either side of musket and hatchet crafted, through their performance of violence and suffering, hybrid events. These bloody incidents displayed all participants' instinctive recourse to their respective traditional interpretations of meaningful pain, even as these other actors' irritating recalcitrance in playing their assigned roles in these composite ritual dramas forced both the rites and the concepts that underlay them to morph. The fact that these eight deaths (and many others left in the historiographic shadows by the martyrs' luminous glory) were seen from a range of perspectives as they were unfolding *must* be pivotal to any responsible interpretation of them. For the chief problem with the dominant interpretation of these men's deaths as Christian martyrdoms is not that it is *wrong* but that it is only *partial*.

Partiality is not problematic when it is frankly acknowledged as such. However, for over three and a half centuries, the martyrs' viewpoint has been presented as not simply *a* perspective on their deaths but as *the* perspective. Rather than becoming itself the *subject* of study, missionaries' understanding of the meaning of their suffering has been the normative angle from which their deaths have been interpreted. Including the putative perspectives of seventeenth-century Iroquois and Wendat participants is thus a profoundly needed corrective to the historical narrative, as their experiences of these complex events are just as critical to our analysis of them as are those of the martyrs. But in providing a competing perspective on these familiar, iconic events, I am not seeking to replace the traditional thesis with a new antithesis or to overwrite Jesuit experiences with those of native people. To do so would be to make the same mistake all over again, by presenting a partial perspective, however compelling or fascinating, as the entire truth. Truth's very power and purity lie in its modest acknowledgment of its own partiality and in its reluctance to claim a false and hectoring universality. One participant's perspective on an event cannot vitiate or eclipse that of another. Even or perhaps especially in their particularity, their variations, and even their contradictions, each retains its own unassailable validity.

Will the Martyrs' Long Afterlife Continue?

> Full fathom five thy father lies;
> Of his bones are coral made;
> Those are pearls that were his eyes;
> Nothing of him that doth fade,
> But doth suffer a sea change
> Into something rich and strange.[7]

Over the centuries, the martyrs too have had their sea changes. The generative currents of adulation and of criticism, the tides of theological fashion and political ideology, and the encrustations of collective identity have continuously transformed and transfigured the memory of these missionaries. During their long collective afterlife, which has to date endured more than six times longer than the terrestrial existence of the eight's oldest member, the martyrs have taken on ever richer and stranger manifestations. But can this protean transformation be endlessly sustained? Will the martyrs' long procrustean afterlife continue?

The answer to this question is, to some extent, dependent on the geographic venue. Barring some totally unforeseeable change, it seems safe to say that in France the afterlife of the martyrs will finally wink out with the death of the last member of their small coterie of elderly local devotees. Many factors set themselves against the flowering of the martyrs' cult in their Gallic homeland, from the very richness of French religious history and its surfeit of saints to French regionalism's dissolution into individual regional microcults. The success of the martyrs' North American advocates, during the canonization process, in "branding" them as New World figures has given them a foreign taint that has also worked against already fragile claims on regional loyalties. Moreover, the French Revolution, which in Québec would become the key to a new, messianic interpretation of the colony's devastating 1759 defeat by English forces, would in France serve merely to sweep these figures from their broken altars. It would only be after their 1930 canonization that the martyrs would again receive grudging recognition in the land of their birth. Finally, the martyrs' Gallic afterlife is impeded by the fact that in France these figures do not attract the same level of critical attention as they do in Canada and the United States. Without the probing questions and challenges of native Catholics and tradition-alists to energize debate about these figures, they quickly stagnate.

In Québec is it hard to be quite so definitive about the future of the martyrs' afterlife. For some, like the Jesuits of Québec City, the death knell of the martyrs' cult has long since rung. The advent of both Vatican II and *la révolution tranquille* has transformed their practice of Catholicism into decisively pragmatic, social, left-leaning terms. God is to be glorified and Christ emulated, not by the forcing of an aggressive Gospel message against those who have rejected it, but by the service of the needy, the rejected, the misunderstood, the unloved. Perceived as part of the detritus of a discredited past—a "great darkness"—the martyrs' cult is, for these liberal priests, long over.

In Québec, the martyrs' cult has always been deeply tied to politics. In fact, here in its birthplace, it might not be going too far to claim that their cult was essentially inspired and sustained throughout its history by the need to comfort a panicking populace, to convince them of the glory (and heavenly rewards) that came from remaining in "this few acres of snow" rather than fleeing back to France in the face of the Iroquois threat. Having kept them on the continent, the cult of the martyrs was used, in the nineteenth century, to rally a people demoralized by military defeat and uncertain about their future in the larger, agglomerative entity of the Canadas and as part of the armory of the ascendant clerico-nationalist faction, which from midcentury sought deeply to imprint Roman Catholicism in every aspect of society, where necessary squashing dissent with an iron fist. With *la révolution tranquille*, all that had been revered became discounted and discarded as the Quebecois, embarrassed regarding their past susceptibility to clerical control, have angrily rejected all that they had once venerated. But, while much of the vitriol of *la révolution tranquille* remains, there is now a new generation for whom the heroes and heroines of New France's distant past are a fresh discovery. Unbesmirched in their young minds with the stain of the "grand noirceur," there is always the possibility that the martyrs will rise again as nationalist Quebecois symbols. Indeed, with the election in 2012 of the separatist Parti Quebecois, a new tide of Québec nationalism may be swelling. Even in some of its first legislative actions, we can see that its official, French-style policy of secularization, which forbids the public display of religious symbols (an action that targets mostly the wearing of the hijab by provincial governmental employees), the load-bearing walls of cultural Catholicism were quickly made exempt from these edicts, ensuring that the massive crucifix present in the Assemblée Nationale (and Brébeuf, whose statue, among others, decorates the buildings' elaborate external façade) will remain. If young Quebecois nationalists see in Brébeuf and his brethren symbols of the distinctive cultural and linguistic heritage they seek proudly to protect, the martyrs may yet come to the consciousness of a new generation. Whether they inspire admiration or condemnation is, for the purposes of their afterlife, immaterial. The only thing it cannot sustain is indifference.

In anglophone North America, the continuing afterlife of the martyrs seems more definitively assured, though the manner in which the significance of these figures is articulated in Canada and the United States seems to be developing along strikingly divergent lines. In English Canada, the cult of the martyrs, centered at Midland, has since the postwar period mirrored both the discernible ecumenical thawing between Canada's traditional "two solitudes" (French Catholic Canada and English Protestant Canada) as well as the country's gradual opening to the nonwhite, non-Christian world, evident in its wholesale shifts in immigration policy since the 1960s and in its adoption of multiculturalism as official policy. Here, the cult of the martyrs faithfully transcribes into a distinctively Catholic key the national hymn celebrating ethnic and cultural diversity. Midland has become something of a dialogical space in which the retention of the much-vaulted cultural distinctiveness of immigrant groups can be harmonized with a homogenizing Canadianness through the acceptance of the "Canadian martyrs," who are interpreted as symbols of these themes of intercultural and interreligious communication. Although the shrine's strong emphasis on ethnic pilgrimage has been critiqued as a convenient means by which the Jesuits have attempted to elude their troubled relationship with native peoples (by diluting native people into simply one more "ethnic pilgrimage"), the shrine's echoing of widely accepted cultural and political values would seem to ensure its continued survival as an institution. The inclusion of a growing Asian Canadian diaspora since the 1990s and the youth of many of these new participants seem to indicate that the martyrs' legacy will continue, in the future, to be transmitted to an increasingly diverse Canadian Catholic recipient base. Currently, at the shrine, the still largely white Jesuit administration

sees itself as facilitating new pilgrimages, new venerators of the figures
their institution celebrates. They are themselves the contemporary
martyrs, seeking to establish bridges of understanding with culturally
and ethnically diverse groups. But it will be interesting to see what, if
anything, changes when, given the increasing dearth of Canadian-
born priests, Midland becomes an *entirely* multicultural affair, with a
staff of exclusively foreign-born Jesuits greeting an increasingly diverse
international clientele. Soon the cult of the martyrs, labeled by some
critics as the fruit of an essentially racist canonization process that systematically excluded native candidates, may be the exclusive prerogative of nonwhite Jesuit hosts and a nonwhite pilgrimage base. Ringing
out in Korean, Konkani, and Mandarin will be praise for figures who
themselves spoke only French, Latin, and Wendat. Indeed, this seems
all the more likely, given that the martyrs are no longer as prominently
featured in public school classrooms as they once were. In the heyday
of the martyrs' postwar Protestantization, their story was part of an
incipient Canadian civic religion. Knowledge of the martyrs' tale was
considered a part of any historically aware Canadian's basic education.
But in the twenty-first century, this is no longer the case. Belated sensitivity to the often deeply biased way the martyrs' story has been told
has led to it being neglected rather than rehabilitated in the Canadian
public school curriculum.

In the United States, by contrast, where the martyrs' cult never
went national or succeeded in jumping confessional borders in quite
the spectacular way it did in Canada, the cult of the martyrs has become a countercultural movement, rather than a Catholic cheerleader
for state policies. The martyrs have become, in the United States, symbols of Catholic doctrinal purity and intransigence and examples of the
way Catholicism should be lived—passionately and purely, as unapologetic and uncompromising evangelists in life and as unwavering martyrs in death. In the hands of their ultraconservative venerators, the
martyrs are held up to show how the mighty have fallen. They present
an unforgiving mirror to the unholy compromises effected as the
church colludes in its own "adulteration" as promulgated at the Second
Vatican Council. Catholic ultraconservatives are no easier on the current social, cultural, and spiritual tenor of American society, dismissing
it as heartless, shallow, crass, and virtually incapable of reverence for
the holy, the pure, and the decent, be these its long-ago sacrificed sons,

the martyrs, or those denigrated and mocked "true" Catholics who today carry their torch.

Some native people on both sides of the Canada-U.S. border still proudly hoist the banner of the martyrs. For the predominantly Ojibwe participants in Native Prayer Days at Midland, the martyrs are thaumaturgical figures who wish nothing more than to rain down blessings on "those for whom they died." For others, the martyrs are a powerful symbol of their own increasing marginality as Catholics within communities increasingly contested as the domain of traditional native spirituality. But native enthusiasm for participating in the cult of the martyrs has been dampened by many factors. Many are turned off by the alienating manner in which native people, particularly contemporary Wendat and Iroquois groups, have overtly been blamed for their martyrs' deaths. There has been the articulation, particularly since the 1970s, of public critiques of the martyrs' cult by both traditionalists and Catholics, such that participation in it could be read as a rejection of one's own people or as siding against them. There has been the martyrs' evocation in projects that have wreaked havoc in native communities, such as assimilative education, particularly residential schools.

Finally, for many native Catholics, there is also the factor of saintly competition from more appealing or attractive figures. For many native Catholics, it is not the martyrs but saintly aboriginal figures who are the preferred recipients of their devotional attentions, such as newly canonized native superstar Catherine "Kateri" Tekakwitha. The energy, dynamism, and drive many showed in the buildup to their preferred saint's 2012 canonization provide intriguing insights into what the 1920s must have been like for the martyrs' own boosters. Having secured the canonization of Kateri, native Catholics across the continent will likely mobilize in order to begin their next Sisyphean rolling of a new candidate up the steep hill of Vatican recognition. Although the attention of nonnative Catholics is still largely focused on colonial-era aboriginal candidates, such as the long-suffering Joseph Chihoatenhwa, whose candidacy for sainthood is the common cause of American ultraconservatives and the Midland shrine administration, many native Catholics are more interested in a more modern candidate for sainthood: Rose Prince. Prince, a twentieth-century Carrier woman from the interior of British Columbia, was allegedly found to be wholly incorrupt when her body was disinterred two years after her 1948

death. Incorruption has typically been interpreted by Catholics as a
sign of the deceased's great sanctity, based on a literal reading of Acts
13:35: "Thou shalt not suffer thy holy one to see corruption." Moreover,
Prince's quiet, unassuming faith, childhood disfigurement, and maternal bereavement have startling parallels with the religious biography of
Kateri Tekakwitha. Though some native people have raised concerns
about the political ramifications of venerating a young woman who
was so strongly associated with the residential school system, popular
native interpretation of Rose's role has been as someone who truly and
nobly lived the Christian message by making the experience of involuntary incarceration easier on other native children. Long eclipsed in
native hearts by Kateri Tekakwitha, the advent of Rose Prince would
seem to dim the martyrs' luster yet further.

The earth's steady, primordial heartbeat reverberated, each stroke so
primal, so shattering that it seemed that the darkened world must end.
Echoed by the distant growl of thunder, the drum's hypnotic beat was
not just heard but felt, vibrating upward from dancing feet through
swirling torso to eyes tightly closed within painted masks. The drum
forced the dancers' hearts into its own magisterial measure, commanding their very blood to course in synchronicity with its own chthonic
rhythms. At one with one another and the giant heart that moved
them all, the dancers became the living drum, the moving earth, and
the living blood that once had flowed out, long ago, upon it. In the humid darkness, the fire of the Wendat glowed like a single eye. In the
flickering orange firelight, the masked dancers' sweating bodies flowed
around it like living tears, their chanting voices undulating through
the sultry summer night. In 2007, 358 years after the battle that had
destroyed the native village that once stood here, the Wendat gathered
at Saint-Ignace to mourn the losses sustained there. Those present
grieved for all who had fallen that day: for the Iroquois, driven to attempt an audacious strategy of survival through conquest, and for their
own people, who, destabilized by division, had proven unable to resist
the advances. In the dispassion of daylight, ritual words of condolence,
the legacy of the Iroquois peacemaker, Deganawida, had been ceremoniously spoken. Now, in the darkness and through the dancing, the

gathering sought to make them real. After three and a half centuries held like a breath, they sought catharsis. As if in sympathy, the summer night itself thickened with tension as they danced. The rising, unexpressed emotion was suffocating, the humid air seeming too thick to breathe. Finally, as the dancers whirled below, the night above exploded into dangerous grief. Bolts of sizzling white lightning split the fattened air. The sky's crying jag was torrential, immediately soaking everything it touched. Streaming down the dancers' bodies, it reduced their roaring fires to vast puddles of scorched mud. Above Saint-Ignace, the very elements raged and wept, along with the gathering, for losses both ancient and recent.

Notes

Abbreviations

Archives

AMMS Archives of the Midland Martyrs' Shrine, Midland, Ontario, Canada
JAC Jesuit Archives of Canada, Montreal, Québec, Canada
OLMSA Our Lady of Martyrs Shrine Archives, Auriesville, New York, United States of America

Frequently Cited Reference Works and Periodicals

DCB *Dictionary of Canadian Biography*
DJB *Dictionary of Jesuit Biography*
MSM *Martyrs' Shrine Message*
PG *The Pilgrim*

Prologue

1. The Martyrs' Shrine in Midland, Ontario, was established in 1926 adjacent to the ruins of the seventeenth-century Jesuit headquarters of Sainte-Marie-among-the-Huron. It is located on the shores of Georgian Bay, approximately ninety-eight miles due north of Toronto.
2. Our Lady of Martyrs Shrine is located adjacent to Fultonville, New York, approximately forty miles northwest of Albany. Its somewhat elliptical name, which honors the Virgin Mary as the Queen of the martyrs, is due to the fact that this sanctuary was founded in 1885, forty-five years before the canonization of the North American martyrs. Catholic canon law forbids the public veneration of individuals prior to their official recognition as saints by the church (see Kenneth Woodward, *Making Saints: How the Catholic Church Determines Who Becomes a Saint, Who Doesn't, and Why* [New

York: Simon and Schuster, 1990], and Michael Higgins, *Stalking the Holy: The Pursuit of Saint-Making* [Toronto: House of Anansi Press, 2006]).

3. The Wendat (with variant spellings "Wyandot" or "Wyandotte") was and is the name used by this native confederacy to refer to themselves. However, they are still known to some as the "Huron," the nickname given them by seventeenth-century French colonists (see Georges Sioui, *Huron-Wendat: The Heritage of the Circle* [Vancouver: University of British Columbia Press, 1999]).

4. Recognition by the church involves climbing a daunting ladder of the canonization process, from its lowest rung (being recognized as "venerable" or a "servant of God") through beatification, when one becomes "blessed," through canonization (through which one becomes a full saint (see also Woodward, *Making Saints*). Though it is frowned upon, the *public* veneration of those as-yet-unrecognized by the church as saints is fairly common: for instance, Ronald Rudin, *Founding Fathers: The Celebration of Champlain and Laval in the Streets of Quebec, 1878–1908* (Toronto: University of Toronto Press, 2003, 11–51) explores what amounted to public veneration of Bishop François de Laval prior to his beatification. Paradoxically, even as canon law forbids veneration of renegade popular saints, canonization itself requires evidence of a strong tradition of adulation for the would-be saint.

5. Please note that the adjective "aboriginal" (common parlance in Canada) will be used throughout this work as a synonym for "native," which is perhaps more familiar to American readers.

6. Catherine "Kateri" Tekakwitha, a seventeenth-century Mohawk-Algonquin Catholic canonized in October 2012, is not a martyr as conventionally defined, as she ultimately died of natural causes rather than being killed. Though she remains a figure of controversy in some Iroquois circles (see Allan Greer, *Mohawk Saint: Catherine Tekakwitha and the Jesuits* [New York: Oxford University Press, 2005, 193–205]) she is nevertheless an important, beloved figure in the spiritual lives of many contemporary native Catholics (see Paula Elizabeth Holmes, "We Are Native Catholics: Inculturation and the Tekakwitha Conference," *Studies in Religion/Sciences Religieuses* 28, no. 2 [1999]: 153–174).

7. As used within Catholicism, "cult" simply refers to a tradition of venerating (or of spiritually honoring, as opposed to worshipping, which is reserved exclusively for God) a deceased individual with a reputation for "heroic sanctity."

8. Although colonial women—*habitants*, native Christians, and Catholic religious alike—died in circumstances comparable to that of the Jesuit martyrs, the cadre of canonized martyrs would remain as resolutely male as it is absolutely white.

9. See, for example, T. J. Campbell, *Pioneer Priests of North America, 1642–1710* (New York: The America Press, 1911); E. J. Devine, *John de Brébeuf: Apostle of the Hurons, 1593–1649* (Montreal: The Canadian Messenger, 1915); E. J.

Devine, *The Canadian Martyrs* (Montreal: The Canadian Messenger, 1923); Joseph Donnelly, *Jean de Brébeuf 1593–1649* (Chicago: Loyola University Press, 1975); Alphonse Fortin, *Les Saints Martyrs Canadiens* (Rimouski, PQ: Les Editions du Centre St Germain, 1943); Henri Fouqueray, *Martyrs du Canada*, deuxième édition (Paris: Pierre Tequi, 1930); René Latourelle, *Jean de Brébeuf* (Montreal: Éditions Bellarmin, 1993); Angus Macdougall, *Martyrs of New France* (Midland, ON: Martyr's Shrine Publications, 1972); Joseph MacFarlane, *The Mohawk Martyrs: America's First Saints* (New York: Jesuit Mission Press, 1946); Felix Martin, *The Life of Father Isaac Jogues, Missionary Priest of the Society of Jesus*, trans. John Gilmary Shea (New York: Benziger Brothers, 1885); Leon Pouliot, *Les Saints Martyrs Canadiens* (Montreal: Éditions Bellarmin, 1949); Joseph Robinne, *L'Apôtre au Cœur Mange: Une époque, un homme, une mission* (Paris: Editions Saint-Paul, 1949); Frédéric Rouvier, SJ, *Les Bienheureux Martyrs de la Compagnie de Jésus au Canada* (Montréal: Le Messager Canadien, 1925); Francis-Xavier Talbot, *Saint among the Hurons: The Life of Jean de Brébeuf* (Garden City, NY: Image Books, 1956); Francis-Xavier Talbot, *Saint among the Savages: The Life of Isaac Jogues* (New York: Harper, 1935); Gerald Treacy, *Stories of Red Skin and Black Robe* (New York: Paulist Press, 1945); John J. Wynne, *The Jesuit Martyrs of North America* (New York: Universal Knowledge Foundation, 1925).

10. Though this book is unique in exploring the evolution of perceptions of the North America martyrs as religious, historical, cultural, and artistic icons, other works have pursued a similar strategy of addressing shifting perceptions of important North American historical or religious figures. For example, see Jennifer Reid, *Louis Riel and the Creation of Modern Canada: Mythic Discourse and the Postcolonial State* (Albuquerque: University of New Mexico Press, 2008); Guy St-Denis, *Tecumseh's Bones* (Montreal: McGill–Queen's University Press, 2005); Rudin, *Founding Fathers;* Patrice Groulx, *Pièges de la Memoire: Dollard des Ormeaux, les amérindiens et nous* (Gatineau, QC: Vents d'Ouest, 1998); Norman Knowles, *Inventing the Loyalists: The Ontario Loyalist Tradition and the Creation of Usable Pasts* (Toronto: University of Toronto Press, 1997); and Sergio Luzzatto, *Padre Pio: Miracles and Politics in a Secular Age* (New York: Picador, 2011).

11. The only previous attempt to present a full history of the cult of the North American martyrs is the ambitious multivolume work of Quebecois historian Guy Laflèche, *Les Saints Martyrs Canadiens*, 5 vols. (Montréal: Singulier, 1988–1995). However, Laflèche chose not to write a narrative account of the cult's development. Rather, his volumes are a heterogeneous collection of primary sources, lists of publications related to the North American martyrs, and essays on various aspects of their cult.

12. This delightfully apt phrase is Kathleen Cummings's. Kathleen Sprows Cummings, "The Rise of the Nation Saint," chap. 2 of *Citizen Saints: Catholics and Canonization in American Culture* (in progress). Copy obtained courtesy of the author.

13. For a discussion of the difficulties in defining martyrdom, see Paul Middleton, *Martyrdom: A Guide for the Perplexed* (London: T & T Clark, 2011), 5–7; Paul Middleton, *Radical Martyrdom and Cosmic Conflict in Early Christianity* (London: T & T Clark, 2006), 1–38; Lacey Baldwin Smith, *Fools, Martyrs, Traitors: The Story of Martyrdom in the Western World* (New York: Alfred A. Knopf, 1997), 3–20.

14. As I will be using it throughout the book, the term "traditionalist" refers to native people who follow what they conceive to be the precontact spirituality of their ancestors.

15. For a similar published argument, see Richard Lundstrom, "A Hard Look at American Catholic Folklore: Mohawks, Martyrs, and Myths," *National Catholic Reporter* (May 1973).

16. The same applies for the use of the word "saint." Please note that, as well as being used as neutral synonyms for "slain missionaries," the terms "saints" and "martyrs" will also be used anticipatorily: that is, I will refer to the figures as such in the centuries before their canonization. This avoids repeated usage of verbal behemoths such as "eventually-to-be-canonized saint" or "soon-to-be-recognized martyr."

17. For an interesting reflection on martyrdom post-9/11, see Middleton, *Martyrdom*, 1–18.

18. Scholars working on martyrdom in a range of eras have noted the important role played by spectacle and its witnessing, whether immediately or "secondarily," through the intense art and texts that describe these deaths. See Elizabeth Castelli, *Martyrdom and Meaning: Early Christian Culture Making* (New York: Columbia University Press, 2004), particularly 104–133. Lucy Grig, *Making Martyrs in Late Antiquity* (London: Duckworth, 2004, 60–61), also argues for the inherent "theatricality" of martyrdom.

19. Pilgrimage organizers were contacted in advance to obtain their permission for me to attend and observe their events. I made no secret of my "outsider" status when interacting with organizers or with pilgrims, identifying myself as an academic and clearly explaining my project to interested pilgrims. All individuals whose comments were used in this book read and signed an informed consent form in which they not only gave their permission for this, but indicated whether comments should be attributed to them by name or to a pseudonym. Out of respect, I always sought to be as unobtrusive as possible during religious services and other devotional exercises and to refrain from interviewing pilgrims while they were worshipping. Formal interviews were supplemented with more intimate conversations in which I felt freer to challenge, push, and otherwise engage with my respondents.

1. A Spectacle for Men and Angels

1. Rueben Gold Thwaites, ed., *The Jesuit Relations and Allied Documents*, 73 vols. (Cleveland: Burrows, 1896–1901), 26:187; see also 31:21–23, 34–37. As noted by Allan Greer in his essay "Conversion and Identity: Iroquois Christianity in Seventeenth-Century New France" (in *Conversion: Old Worlds and New*, ed. Kenneth Mills and Anthony Grafton [Rochester, NY: University of Rochester Press, 2003], 184), though the names of native Christians such as Eustache Ahatsistari have "the appearance of a European-style pairing of a personal name and a family name . . . they were something quite different, a badge of layered identity" that paired the individual's preexisting name (in this case, Ahatsistari) with his or her new baptismal name. For more on the life of Ahatsistari, see John Steckley, *Untold Tales: Three Seventeenth-century Huron* (Ajax, ON: R. Kerton, 1981), 19–26.

2. Thwaites, *Jesuit Relations*, 31:53–57.

3. Ibid., 31:67–69.

4. Ibid., 31:29–31.

5. Ibid., 31:71.

6. Ibid., 31:73.

7. For Jogues's own narration of his escape and time in France, see ibid., 31:93–109.

8. Ibid., 31:101–105.

9. Ibid., 31:105–107. The queen had alerted Dutch colonial officials to Jogues's plight and instructed them to put him on a boat for France. See Félix Martin, SJ, *The Life of Father Isaac Jogues, Missionary Priest of the Society of Jesus*, trans. John G. Shea (New York: Benziger Brothers, 1885); Rev. T. J. Campbell, *Pioneer Priests of North America, 1642–1710*, vol. 1 (New York: The America Press, 1911), 30–31.

10. Thwaites, *Jesuit Relations*, 31:99. On Jogues's apparent dislike of his new-found fame, see Campbell, *Pioneer Priests*, 1:30–31.

11. Ibid., 31:111. Jogues had also apparently anticipated his initial capture in 1642: see ibid., 31:17–19.

12. These independent nations were linked not only politically, but also by language, history, and ideology. Fanned out across a vast territory in what is now New York and Pennsylvania, the five partner nations were (from the easternmost to the westernmost groups) the Mohawk, Oneida, Onondaga, Cayuga, and Seneca. In 1722 a sixth member, the Tuscarora, was added. Just as the Iroquois confederacy was composed of constituent nations, each nation was composed of constituent clans, which were themselves made up of "several extended families, related through the maternal line" (Alan Taylor, *The Divided Ground: Indians, Settlers, and the Northern Borderland of the American Revolution* (New York: Alfred A. Knopf, 2006), 19. See also see Tom Porter, *Clanology: The Clan System of the Iroquois*

(Hogansburg, NY: Native North American Traveling College, 1993). For further information on the culture of the seventeenth-century Iroquois confederacy, see Roger Carpenter, *The Renewed, The Destroyed, and the Remade: The Three Thought Worlds of the Iroquois and the Huron, 1609–1650* (East Lansing: Michigan State University Press, 2004); Daniel Richter, *The Ordeal of the Longhouse: The Peoples of the Iroquois League in the Era of European colonization* (Chapel Hill: University of North Carolina Press, 1992).

13. For more on the Jesuits' founding, educational and missionary emphasis, and characteristic spirituality, see John O'Malley, *The First Jesuits* (Cambridge, MA: Harvard University Press, 1993). The capitalized term "Society," as in "Society of Jesus," will be used throughout the work as a synonym for the Jesuits.

14. This two-way comparison between the Iroquois confederacy and the Jesuits does not imply parity between them. The Jesuits in colonial North America numbered only a handful of men, whereas the Iroquois were a powerful and, despite the epidemics they had repeatedly endured, a still-populous people. By comparing the two, I am simply making the point that both groups responded identically to serious threats: by making recourse to traditional religious ideas.

15. Though both the Iroquois and the Wendat are referred to as "confederacies," they are confederacies of a different type. The Iroquois was an alliance of different native nations, whereas the Wendat "confederacy" was a nation made up of independent clan-based tribes comprised of the Attignawantan, or people of the bear, the most westerly group; the Arendarhonon, or people of the rock, in the east; and the Attigneenongnahac and Tahontaenrat peoples (Bruce Trigger, *Children of Aataentsic: A History of the Huron People to 1660* [Montreal: McGill–Queen's University Press, 1976], 30). By contrast, the contemporary Wendat confederacy, formally reestablished on August 27, 1999, is more like the Iroquois model, as it reunited into one people the Huron-Wendat of Wendake, Québec, the Wyandott of Oklahoma, the Wynandot of Kansas, and the Wyandot-Anderdon of Michigan.

16. Meaning "people of the longhouse," Haudenosaunee is a synonym for Iroquois and will be used as such throughout this book. Though not yet in widespread usage outside Iroquois circles, it is the term preferred by many Haudenosaunee themselves.

17. See Daniel Richter, "War and Culture: the Iroquois Experience," *William and Mary Quarterly* 40 (1983): 528–559; Jon Parmenter, *The Edge of the Woods: Iroquoia, 1534–1701* (East Lansing: Michigan State University Press, 2010), 45–75; and Carpenter, *Renewed*.

18. The contemporary Dene Tha people of northern Alberta still see infants as embodying the returning souls of dead ancestors. See Jean-Guy Goulet, *Ways of Knowing: Experience, Knowledge and Power among the Dene Tha* (Vancouver: University of British Columbia Press, 1998).

19. The integrative power of these rituals, though impressive (see Parmenter, *Edge of the Woods*, 57), should not be overstated. See Richter, *Ordeal of the Longhouse*, 71–72, for a discussion of captive resistance.

20. Captives were required to run a gauntlet at every village visited by the returning war party as they were taken deeper into the victor's territory. For Jogues's experience of repeated gauntlet-running, see Thwaites, *Jesuit Relations*, 31:17–51. Generally, the ultimate decision of death or adoption would be taken, and the ritual enacted deep in the victor's home territory.

21. The high value of women in Iroquoian societies and Wendat societies would have made their dispatch rare. See Thwaites, *Jesuit Relations*, 33:243–245; Richter, *Ordeal of the Longhouse*, 35.

22. Richter, *Ordeal of the Longhouse;* Karl Schlesier, "Epidemics and Indian Middlemen: Rethinking the Wars of the Iroquois, 1609–1653," *Ethnohistory* 23, no. 2 (1976): 129–145; Carpenter, *Renewed*.

23. Isaac Jogues specifically mentions that Iroquois warriors thanked the sun for allowing his capture (Thwaites, *Jesuit Relations*, 31:31), and that scaffold torture generally commenced at sunup (ibid., 31:45). Martyr Gabriel Lalemant's execution, moreover, seems to have been deliberately timed so he would expire shortly after the sun's rising on March 17, 1649 (ibid., 34:147). See also Cornelius Jaenen, *Friend and Foe: Aspects of French-Amerindian Cultural Contact in the Sixteenth and Seventeenth Centuries* (Toronto: McClelland and Stewart, 1976), 123, 14. On ritual cannibalism, see Georges Sioui, *Huron-Wendat: The Heritage of the Circle,* trans. Jane Brierley (Vancouver: University of British Columbia Press, 1999), 171–174; and Georges Sioui, *For an Amerindian Autohistory: An Essay on the Foundations of a Social Ethic* (Montreal: McGill–Queen's University Press, 1992), 54–56.

24. Paul Ragueneau, quoted in Francis X. Talbot, *Saint among the Hurons: The Life of Jean de Brebeuf* (Garden City, NY: Image Books, 1956), 290. The Jesuits' preoccupation with martyrdom was widely shared by other Catholics. See Dominique Deslandres, *Croire et faire croire: Les missions françaises au XVII siècle* (Paris: Librarie Arthème Fayard, 2003), 294.

25. Thwaites, *Jesuit Relations,* 17:13. Le Jeune's conclusions were seconded in 1646 by Jérôme Lalemant: "It is credible . . . that the plans we have against Satan's empire for the salvation of these people will only bear fruit if they are soaked with the blood of some other martyrs." For martyrdom themes in Jesuit writing, see Paul Perron, "Isaac Jogues: From Martyrdom to Sainthood," in *Colonial Saints: Discovering the Holy in the Americas,* ed. Allan Greer and Jodi Bilinkoff (New York: Routledge, 2003), 153–168, 340–342; Timothy Pearson, "Becoming Holy in Early Canada: Performance and the Making of Holy Persons in Society and Culture" (doctoral dissertation, Department of History, McGill University, 2008), 64–65, 68.

26. Thwaites, *Jesuit Relations,* 35:161.

27. Brad Gregory, *Salvation at Stake: Christian Martyrdom in Early Modern Europe* (Cambridge, MA: Harvard University Press, 1999).

28. *The Collected Works of St. Teresa of Avila* (Washington, DC: Institute of Carmelite Studies, 1980), 86.

29. For Jogues's own account of his 1642 captivity and escape, see Thwaites, *Jesuit Relations*, 31:17–101.

30. Parmenter has a particularly interesting take on Jogues's captivity, particularly his repeated brushes with death and equally repeated reprieves. He sees Jogues's first captivity as a muffed ransom attempt, noting that a cryptic "note" (which used drawings rather than words to signal the number of captives taken and their future fate) was found at the scene of his capture, a note similar to those that accompanied other ransom demands (see Parmenter, *Edge of the Woods*, 56–70).

31. In the colonial northeast, ethnicity was thus not considered a barrier to full membership in a native nation. On the contrary, European captives from both New France and New England were routinely integrated into victorious native polities through adoption (see Richter, "War and Culture"; John Putnam Demos, *The Unredeemed Captive: A Family Story from Early America* (New York: Vintage, 1995), and James Axtell, "The White Indians of Colonial America," *William and Mary Quarterly* 32 (1975). Indeed, some Europeans, like Guillaume Couture, who was captured alongside Goupil and Jogues in August 1642 (Thwaites, *Jesuit Relations*, 31:25–27), went on to be elevated to positions of great esteem within their adoptive communities. Couture, for example, served briefly as a chief before returning to French colonial society as part of a captive exchange in 1645 (see Trigger, *Children of Aataentsic*, 647–648, 668. Couture's successful, if ultimately temporary, adoption demonstrates that there was nothing inevitable about the other European's rejection and summary execution. The contemporary emphasis on blood in determining eligibility for official membership in a First Nation is thus a striking deviation from seventeenth-century native norms in determining belonging, which were exclusively behavioral. See Pamela Palmater, *Beyond Blood: Rethinking Indigenous Identity* (Saskatoon, SK: Purich Publishing, 2011), and Paul Chartrand, ed., *Who Are Canada's Aboriginal Peoples? Recognition, Definition, and Jurisdiction* (Saskatoon, SK: Purich, 2003).

32. Some have seen the fact that Jogues was entrusted to the care of an older Mohawk woman, whom he referred to as his "aunt," as evidence that he was adopted by the Mohawk. This argument appears further strengthened by the fact that she intervened to save Jogues's life on several occasions (see Thwaites, *Jesuit Relations*, 34:83–85; Parmenter, *Edge of the Woods*, 57–58; Martin, *Life of Father Isaac Jogues*, 141–142). But to me it seems more accurate to view Jogues as a "public prisoner" whose unpredictable and harsh treatment sharply contrasted the more consistent care of true adoptees (Thwaites, *Jesuit Relations*, 34:53). In my judgment, the continued

strong collective suspicion of Jogues and the many times he was menaced with death prove that the missionary he was never fully accepted as part of the community.

33. The flouting of aboriginal gender norms by either native peoples or Europeans could lead to serious social ostracism. See Emma Anderson, *The Betrayal of Faith: The Tragic Journey of a Colonial Native Convert* (Cambridge, MA: Harvard University Press, 2007).

34. It was for this reason that the behavior of Catherine "Kateri" Tekakwitha, a convert to Catholicism who took a vow of virginity, was also viewed as being so unusual by the Mohawk.

35. Thwaites, *Jesuit Relations*, 31:73–75.

36. Missionary initiatives among the Iroquois had been retarded by the early missteps by the colonial French, beginning with Samuel de Champlain's fateful and deadly volley against Mohawk warriors in 1609 at Ticonderoga. See Gerald R. Alfred, *Heeding the Voices of Our Ancestors: Kahnawake Mohawk Politics and the Rise of Native Nationalism* (Toronto: Oxford University Press, 1995), 29–30; David Hackett Fisher, *Champlain's Dream* (New York: Alfred A. Knopf Canada, 2008), 256–271; Parmenter, *Edge of the Woods*, 20–21).

37. The Dutch had attempted earlier in Jogues's captivity to ransom him (see Parmenter, *Edge of the Woods*, 58–59).

38. Thwaites, *Jesuit Relations*, 31:53–59. But other contemporary observers interpreted Goupil's death as being in revenge for Mohawk casualties slain during their attack on the colonial settlement of Richelieu (see Parmenter, *Edge of the Woods*, 58).

39. Martin, *Life of Father Isaac Jogues*, 196–197. The Wendat, certainly, had been uneasy about transubstantiation, regarding the French has having brought over a rotting body that they used to make people sick (See Thwaites, *Jesuit Relations*, 12:237–239, 15:33).

40. Parmenter, *Edge of the Woods*, 67–68).

41. Throughout the book I will use "Wendake" (as does Trigger, *Children of Aataentsic*) as well as, simply for variety, the colonial term "Huronia" to refer to the Wendat homeland in the 1640s. As with my employment of "Iroquoia," the idea is to reinforce in the reader's mind the fact that these areas were, in the mid-seventeenth century, the sovereign and largely uncontested territories of these native nations. For a description of the geography of ancient Wendake, accompanied by a map, see Trigger, *Children of Aataentsic*, 27–31.

42. While Jogues was still in Montreal after his long Atlantic voyage back from France, he wrote, in response to the proposal that he should return to Iroquoia, "Yes, my father, I desire all that our Lord desires, at the peril of a thousand lives. Oh, what sorrow I should have, to fail at so excellent an opportunity! Could I endure that it should depend on me that some soul were not saved?" (Thwaites, *Jesuit Relations*, 31:107).

43. On the Iroquois's strong desire for unanimity, see Taylor, *Divided Ground*, 19–20. The fate of Jogues and la Lande had been discussed in numerous clan and intraclan conclaves without being resolved to everyone's satisfaction. The Bear clan's deadly dinner invitation to Jogues was timed to coincide with yet another intraclan meeting, presenting the rest of the Mohawk polity with a fait accompli. But, as the events recounted show, even the Bears, the moiety most adamant in arguing for Jogues's death, were divided on this issue.

44. Neither of these men's names have been preserved by history. The tall youth who attempted to intercede for Jogues, first by his words and subsequently by his actions, was nicknamed *Le Berger* (or "the Shepherd") by the French in their subsequent dealings with him. For more on his later life, see Chapter 2 of this work (and Martin, *Life of Father Isaac Jogues,* 201). His physical description comes from the impressions of French nuns who encountered him in Europe (Thwaites, *Jesuit Relations,* 36:37). The name of the missionary's slayer is also unknown. However, he took as his own the name "Isaac Jogues" in his subsequent Catholic baptism. For more on this man, see Chapter 2 of this work and Thwaites, *Jesuit Relations,* 32:23.

45. See Martin, *Life of Father Isaac Jogues,* 201; Parmenter, *Edge of the Woods,* 69–70. Parmenter interprets the execution of Jogues, la Lande, and an unnamed Wendat man as an unmistakable diplomatic signal that "war had resumed" (70). Carole Blackburn (*Harvest of Souls: The Jesuit Missions and Colonialism in North America, 1632–1650* [Montreal: McGill–Queen's University Press, 2000], 65) concurs, characterizing Jogues's as "a political killing."

46. The life of one such religious inspired by the lives and writings of Jogues, Catherine de Saint-Augustin, will be explored in depth in Chapter 2.

47. "Iroquoia" or Kanienke was, in the mid-seventeenth century, a vast territory encompassing "the area bounded by the St. Lawrence River to the north from present-day Trois Rivières to the Oswegatchie river near Prescott, Ontario; to the east, by the Adirondacks west of the Hudson River–Lake Champlain–Lake George waterway all the way from present day Albany, N.Y. to Sorel on the south shore of the St. Lawrence; and above the Mohawk River from the Hudson River to Oneida lake in Central New York" (Alfred, *Heeding the Voices,* 26). For a map of seventeenth-century Iroquoia, see ibid., 27, 34. For their territorial holdings in the eighteenth century see Taylor, *Divided Ground*, frontpiece and 5. Throughout this work, I will use "Iroquoia" (like Taylor) and "Kanienke" (like Alfred) alternately, as synonyms.

48. Of course, the legitimacy of the Canada-U.S. border has long been contested by the Iroquois, whose traditional ancestral lands straddled it, making them, in Taylor's words, "gatekeepers of a border land" (Taylor, *Divided Ground,* 8–10, 407–408). Taylor attributes white authorities' concern with

establishing and protecting this international border as being largely responsible for their accelerating attempts to control and confine native people in both Canada and the United States in the late eighteenth and early nineteenth century (ibid., 8–9).

49. Thwaites, *Jesuit Relations,* 36:23.

50. Leon Pouliot, "North American Martyrs," in *The New Catholic Encyclopedia,* vol. 10 (New York: McGraw-Hill, 1967), 506.

51. Whether Jogues's quite aggressive courtship of death fits within conventional definitions of martyrdom is debatable. Paul Middleton's work *Radical Martyrdom and Cosmic Conflict in Early Christianity* (London: T & T Clark, 2006) explores similar instances of what he calls "radical martyrdom" (in which Christians actively sought confrontation) in the earliest centuries of Christianity and finds them to be surprisingly common. Jogues's behavior seems closer to radical martyrdom than the orthodox position that, as a Christian, one must neither seek nor avoid persecution and death. For further consideration of definitional quandaries surrounding martyrdom, see Lacey Baldwin Smith, *Fools, Martyrs, Traitors; The Story of Martyrdom in the Western World* (New York: Alfred A. Knopf, 1997), 3–20), and Michael Gaddis, *There Is No Crime for Those Who Have Christ: Religious Violence in the Christian Roman Empire* (Berkeley: University of California Press, 2005), 14–23.

52. The Iroquois term for their traditional homelands, Kanienke, will be used throughout this work as a synonym for "Iroquoia."

53. For more on the perception of Jogues as a martyr, see Deslandres, *Croire et faire croire,* 291–294.

54. Thwaites, *Jesuit Relations,* 35:161. In this passage, the Iroquois are here simply the deus ex machina of martyrdom. Chabanel would get his devout wish, being slain in December 1649.

55. Ibid., 34:183. Native peoples, both traditionalists and Catholics, utilized these self-hardening techniques. In the Christian context, they took on an additional meaning: that of penitence for sin. See Allan Greer, *Mohawk Saint: Catherine Tekakwitha and the Jesuits* (New York: Oxford University Press, 2005), 119–124, and Greer, "Conversion and Identity," 175–192.

56. Guy-Marie Oury, ed., *Marie de l'Incarnation: Correspondance* (72 Sablé-sur-Sarthe: Abbaye Saint-Pierre de Solesmes, 1971), 379–380; Joseph Donnelly, *Jean de Brébeuf 1593–1649* (Chicago: Loyola University Press, 1975), 271; Deslandres, *Croire et faire croire,* 293.

57. Donnelly, *Jean de Brébeuf,* 228; Talbot, *Saint among the Hurons,* 290.

58. There seems to have been only one village where Catholics actually became the majority: Ossossané. The village in which Joseph Chihoatenhwa had been a marginal, rejected figure for his Christianity had, by 1648, become a majority Catholic enclave in which Catholics attempted to impose their beliefs and practices on traditionalists (see Thwaites, *Jesuit Relations,* 34:107, 217; for analysis see Trigger, *Children of Aataentsic,* 760–762). While

Chihoatenhwa's name has been spelled in many different ways, I have
used John Steckley's spelling.

59. Schlesier, "Epidemics and Indian Middlemen," 139.
60. Bruce Trigger, *Natives and Newcomers: Canada's Heroic Age Reconsidered*
    (Kingston: McGill–Queen's University Press, 1985), 246–247. The Jesuits'
    self-characterization as shaman was sometimes deliberate and sometimes
    inadvertent. See Anderson, *Betrayal of Faith*, especially 165–206.
61. The Jesuits' missionary predecessors in Canada, the Recollet, also re-
    ported a native tendency to interpret baptism as a curative rite. See Ga-
    briel Sagard, *Histoire du Canada* (Paris: Edwin Tross, 1866), 395.
62. Trigger, *Natives and Newcomers*, 249–250.
63. Thwaites, *Jesuit Relations*, 30:29–31.
64. While all of the Jesuits were suspected of witchcraft, Jean de Brébeuf was
    seen as being particularly dangerous (see Thwaites, *Jesuit Relations*, 19:195,
    34:185–187).
65. Ibid., 20:79.
66. Ibid., 20:95, 21:161–164, 211. The theory that Chihoatenhwa was killed
    by his own people is strengthened by the fact that he had previously
    received numerous death threats (ibid., 19:247–249; see also Trigger
    (*Children of Aataentsic*, 598–601) and Talbot (*Saint among the Hurons*, 221–
    222). Steckley (*Untold Tales*, 3–15) notes that Chihoatenhwa was re-
    ported to have sensed a threat immediately before his slaying, which led
    him to abruptly order his young nieces to run home. Had he feared an
    Iroquois ambush, Steckley argues, it is much more likely that Chi-
    hoatenhwa would have accompanied them to safety and warned the
    village of immanent attack. He suggests that Chihoatenhwa was at-
    tempting to avoid the girls being "killed as witnesses" (ibid., 13) by his
    Wendat killers.
67. However, despite the demonstrably greater vulnerability of native Chris-
    tian converts to retaliatory acts of violence by their own people, to date
    all of North American martyrs canonized have been European rather
    than aboriginal.
68. Thwaites, *Jesuit Relations*, 23:31.
69. Ibid., 33:231.
70. For an excellent analysis of radical traditionalists' motives, movement,
    and eventual defeat, see Trigger, *Children of Aataentsic*, 746–750.
71. Thwaites, *Jesuit Relations*, 33:229–249. Of the then five nations of the Iro-
    quois confederacy, the Mohawk and the Seneca played a disproportion-
    ately large role in the attacks on Wendake from July 1648 to December
    1649 (see Parmenter, *Edge of the Woods*, 72).
72. Ibid., 33:233–249. The practice of forcing the perpetrators of crimes to
    richly compensate their victim's family and survivors or "cover the grave"
    was practiced widely among First Nations, including the Iroquois (see
    Taylor, *Divided Ground*, 30–34).

73. I am not arguing here that Douart was a martyr but that he likely would have been seen as one by the Jesuits, had their political situation been less precarious.

74. Thwaites, *Jesuit Relations,* 34:163–165.

75. For an account of the battle and Daniel's death, see ibid., 33:259–269.

76. Blackburn (*Harvest of Souls,* 67) suggests that this ax handle necklace was meant to connote the rosary, but the fact that this seems to have been a fairly common practice in traditionalist-on-traditionalist torture (see Thwaites, *Jesuit Relations,* 34:39) suggests otherwise.

77. For Jogues's "spectacle" quote see François du Creux. *The History of Canada or New France,* vol. 2, trans. and intro. Percy J. Robinson (Toronto: The Champlain Society, 1952), 520; see also Joseph Robinne. *L'Apôtre au Coeur mange: Une époque, un homme, une mission* (Paris: Éditions Saint-Paul, 1949), 280. Jogues, of course, had repeated these same words to himself during his first and longest captivity among the Mohawk (Thwaites, *Jesuit Relations,* 31:43). For a general discussion of the inherently spectacular nature of martyrdom, see Paul Middleton, *Martyrdom: A Guide for the Perplexed* (London: T & T Clark, 2011), 57–65; Elizabeth Castelli, *Martyrdom and Meaning: Early Christian Culture Making* (New York: Columbia University Press, 2004), 104–133; Lucy Grig, *Making Martyrs in Late Antiquity* (London: Duckworth, 2004), 60–61).

78. I use both names because the Wendat village of Taenhatentaron was in existence prior to the establishment of the mission of Saint-Louis. I will use these terms alternatively to designate this Wendat settlement, the first to fall on March 16, 1649.

79. Thwaites, *Jesuit Relations,* 34:161.

80. Ibid., 34:129. Annaotaha survived the battle and (perhaps because of his prowess as a warrior) was initially tapped for adoption into the ranks of the victorious Iroquois. Eventually he was released in the hopes that he would persuade more Wendat to join the Iroquois confederacy voluntarily. But Annaotaha did precisely the contrary, fighting to the end of his life against Iroquois expansionism. He died alongside the much-mythologized Adam Dollard des Ormeaux at the battle of Long Sault. As John Steckley notes, Annaotaha's fascinating life has been eclipsed by the more famous European figures—Brébeuf and des Ormeaux—with whom he shared the historical stage. See Steckley, *Untold Tales,* 27–41.

81. Ibid.

82. Ibid., 34:25–33, 141–143.

83. Ibid., 34:137.

84. Ibid., 43:311–313. See also P. Henri Fourqueray, *Martyrs du Canada* (deuxième édition) (Paris: Pierre Téqui, Libraire-Éditeur, 1930, 256), who gives the man's name (perhaps mistakenly) as "Oioguen." Upon his Catholic baptism, Brébeuf and Lalemant's would-be rescuer took the name "Lazare."

85. Ibid., 34:141.

86. Brébeuf's Wendat name, "Echon," is currently held by Dr. John Steckley, the noted authority on the Wendat language.

87. Aatahansic was the primordial first woman in Wendat and Iroquois mythology. Haven fallen from a cloud toward the watery world, she was rescued by aquatic animals, who then dived down to retrieve mud from the ocean floor to make land for her to live on. Aatahensic's descendants, a pair of twin boys, would shape the surface of this new earth into its current shape.

88. Thwaites, *Jesuit Relations,* 34:28–29, my modernization.

89. Ibid., 34:145, my modernization.

90. The use of boiling water in postwar ritual torture was unheard of. Christophe Regnault, a donné and veteran of the Wendake mission, stated: "I have seen the same treatment given to Iroquois prisoners whom the Huron savages had taken in war, with the exception of the boiling water, which I have not seen poured on anyone." (ibid., 34:33). Gabriel Lalement's lengthy torture took place after that of Brébeuf.

91. Ibid., 34:143 (see also ibid., 34:191). This quotation reflects the belief of some Christians that a martyrs' seeming supernatural insensibility to pain is made possible by his or her foretaste of the "beautific vision" of God, generally experienced only in heaven itself. For an interesting analysis of how these beliefs translated into the stoic figures of martyrdom art, see Gregory, *Salvation at Stake,* 40–41.

92. Lalement's heart was removed and eaten in the same manner. Ibid., 34:147.

93. The stop-and-start nature of Lalemant's torture, which alternated torment with pauses for rest, food, and even sleep, was more typical of intranative patterns of ritual torture than was Brébeuf's more accelerated death.

94. Paul Prud'homme, in *Nos Martyrs: Jean de Brébeuf, Isaac Jogues et lears companions* (Montreal: Messager, 1929), a short publication he wrote as a guide to accompany an elaborate series of glass slides intended to present the martyrs' story to the public (a copy has been preserved at AMMS), was one of only very few Jesuit writers to mention this incident, with Henri Fouqueray (*Martyrs du Canada,* deuxième édition (Paris: Pierre Tequi, 1930, 256) being the other. Because the would-be ransoming of Brébeuf by Lazare became well known only after the most influential accounts of Brébeuf's death had already been written, and because this story was not properly indexed in Thwaites's *Jesuit Relations,* it has been largely overlooked.

95. Alfred presents Mohawk animosity toward the French in the mid-seventeenth century as stemming largely from previous evidence of French aggressiveness toward them and the fact that they had chosen to ally themselves with the Iroquois's traditional foes (Alfred, *Heeding the*

Voices, 30). Jogues himself notes the political nature of the poor treatment meted out to himself and other French captives in 1642 with his words: "they were thus enraged against the French because the latter had not been willing to accept the peace, the preceding year, on the conditions which they wished to give them" (Thwaites, *Jesuit Relations*, 31:27–29).

96. For a sensitive evocation of Roman authorities' motivations in confronting the ancient Christians, see Gaddis, *There Is No Crime*, 14–23.

97. Brad Gregory passionately attacks contemporary historians' tendency to lazily dismiss martyrs' religious passion and determination to hold firm to their faith as a form of mental illness, arguing that they must rather strive to understand the martyrs' worldview (Gregory, *Salvation at Stake*, 6–15).

98. *All* of the victors appear to have had a say in captives' fate. As is evident from the deaths of Brébeuf and Lalemant, a small subgroup within the victorious Iroquois body politic could and did exercise an influence out of proportion to their actual numbers.

99. Sioui, *Huron-Wendat*, 173–174.

100. Jaenen, in *Friend and Foe*, 143–145, notes that Jesuits often underplayed the Real Presence in the Eucharist due to fears that native people might see this as similar to postwar ritual cannibalism. Trigger, in *Children of Aataentsic*, 389–390, 537, makes a similar point. Catherine de Saint-Augustin, a key early promoter of Brébeuf's cult, used pulverized relics to cure the sick. See Chapter 2 of the current work and Dom. Albert Jamet, *Les Annales de l'Hôtel-Dieu de Québec, 1636–1716* (Québec: l'Hôtel Dieu de Québec, 1939), 148.

101. Steve Caitlin, the archivist at the Midland Martyrs' Shrine, makes this argument (recorded interview with the author, June 15, 2009). According to Caitlin, so did the late Jesuit father Denis Hegarty in his unpublished work *Band of Brothers*. Other analysts, such as René Latourelle, see the decision to torture the Jesuits in situ as being simply to fill in the time as the massed forces of Iroquois and their assimilated Wendat captives waited to assault their ultimate target: Sainte-Marie (see René Latourelle, *Jean de Brébeuf* (Québec: Bellarmin, 1993, 212).

102. Given the nature of their political beliefs, they could also have voluntarily joined the Iroquois. Trigger notes that it is unknown how much contact there was between traditionalist radicals and the Iroquois prior to the 1649–1650 Iroquois onslaught (Trigger, *Children of Aataentsic*, 722–724, 744–750).

103. Trigger, *Natives and Newcomers*, 265. The similarities between Douart's and Chabanel's killings point out the intensely political process through which possible "martyrdoms" are identified and promoted. Jesuit acceptance of compensation in this slaying precluded them from promoting Douart's murder as martyrdom. See Chapter 2.

104. See E. J. Devine, *The Canadian Martyrs* (Montreal: The Canadian Messenger, 1923), 103.
105. On the Jesuits' inability to stop ritual torture, even among Wendat Catholics, and on their baptism of captives, see Jaenen, *Friend and Foe*, 139–141, and Trigger, *Children of Aataentsic*, 713–714.
106. Thwaites, *Jesuit Relations*, 34:33.
107. Ibid., 34:29, 35.

2. The Blood of Martyrs Is the Seed of Christians

1. For a rich study of Hospitalière devotionalism, particularly its strong focus on the crucified Christ, see Marie-Claude Dinet-Lecompte, *Les soeurs hospitalières en France aux XVII et XVIII siècles: La charité en action* (Paris: Honoré Champion Éditeur, 2005), 359–381.
2. Paul Ragueneau, *La Vie de la Mère Catherine de Saint-Augustin: Religieuse Hospitalière de la Miséricorde de Québec en la Nouvelle France* (Paris: Florentin Lambert, 1671), 115, my translation. See also Jodi Bilinkoff, *Related Lives: Confessors and Their Female Penitents, 1450–1750* (Ithaca, NY: Cornell University Press, 2005), 71.
3. Francis Parkman, *The Jesuits in North America in the Seventeenth Century* (Boston: Little, Brown, & Co., 1876), 109.
4. Rueben Gold Thwaites, ed., *The Jesuit Relations and Allied Documents*, 73 vols. (Cleveland: Burrows, 1896–1901), 34:165, 167–169, 183. According to Marie de l'Incarnation, his contemporary, Brébeuf was told in a vision of his martyrdom three days prior to its occurrence (see Guy-Marie Oury, ed., *Marie de l'Incarnation: Correspondance* [Solesmes, 1971], 379–380).
5. The Augustinian Hospitalière nuns were and are a female Catholic order dedicated to care of the ill and injured (see Dinet-Lecompte, *Les soeurs hospitalières*). They will be referred to in this work as both the Hospitalières and the Augustinians.
6. Catherine de Saint-Augustin is not as well known outside *la francophonie* as her older Ursuline contemporary, Marie de l'Incarnation, because Ragueneau's 1671 *La Vie de la Mère* has not yet been translated into English.
7. Catherine de Saint-Augustin was pronounced venerable in 1894 and beatified in 1989. She has not yet been canonized.
8. Like "Canadiens," *habitants* is a term for French Canadian settlers (hence "Habs" as the popular nickname for the Montreal Canadiens hockey team).
9. See Éric Thierry, "Catherine de Saint-Augustin: Remembered from Quebec to Normandy," in the *Encyclopedia of French Cultural Heritage in North America*. The article is also available in French. http://www.amerique francaise.org/en/article-346/Catherine_de_Saint_Augustin,_Remem bered_from_Quebec_to_Normandy_.html.

10. Thwaites, *Jesuit Relations*, 52:63–65; Denise Pepin, *Chroniques pour une meilleure connaissance de Catherine de Saint Augustin* (Caen: Éditions Don Bosco, 1990), 42. Their ship would depart from La Rochelle on May 27, 1648.

11. Pepin, *Chroniques*, 41.

12. Ragueneau, *La Vie*, 31.

13. Thwaites, *Jesuit Relations*, 52:57–65.

14. Catherine would also have read the correspondence of the Québec Hospitalière nuns. See Pepin, *Chroniques*, 41; Dom Guy-Marie Oury, *The Spiritual Journey of Catherine de Saint-Augustin* (Québec: Les Augustines de la Miséricorde de Jésus, 1995), 91.

15. Ragueneau, *La Vie*, 24.

16. Ibid., 22, 44; Thwaites, *Jesuit Relations*, 42:59; Oury, *Spiritual Journey*, 34–35.

17. Thwaites, *Jesuit Relations*, 32:135. For her father's opposition and lawsuit, see Ragueneau, *La Vie*, 36; Oury, *Spiritual Journey*, 89–95. For the involvement of the queen regent in the case, see Oury, *Spiritual Journey*, 94.

18. "Double" in the sense that Jogues escaped Mohawk captivity in 1643, only to voluntarily return to Iroquoia, and his incomplete martyrdom, in 1646. "Double martyrdom" is a devotional common trope in writings on Jogues's life and death.

19. What de Longpré would have read as one long document was split into several volumes in the Thwaites edition of the *Jesuit Relations*. See Thwaites, *Jesuit Relations*, 30:205–297, 31:16–137.

20. Ibid., 31:105–107, 125.

21. Ibid., 32:135.

22. Ragueneau, *La Vie*, 36. Her mother was similarly won over. However, despite the de Longpré's new amenability, the Augustinians ultimately decided to release only one of their daughters: Catherine.

23. Pepin, *Chroniques*, 42.

24. The situation was further complicated by the fact that, though her religious community had reluctantly agreed to relinquish her, Catherine was still technically under obedience to their hierarchy, rather than that of Québec.

25. Thwaites, *Jesuit Relations*, 52:61.

26. Ragueneau, *La Vie*, 44.

27. Thwaites, *Jesuit Relations*, 32:133–135.

28. Ragueneau, *La Vie*, 44, 59–63. For Catherine's desire to return to France, see Oury, *Spiritual Journey*, 123–127.

29. Catherine's depression after coming to Canada was a common reaction. Marie de l'Incarnation had a similar response, as did Nöel Chabanel. One of the nuns at the Hotel Dieu did indeed leave for France shortly after Catherine arrived. See Oury, *Spiritual Journey*, 117.

30. Ragueneau, *La Vie*, 118.

31. The seventeenth-century Augustinians alternated their nursing duties with their observance of the traditional canonical "hours," seven daily periods of collective prayer: Matins, Tierce, Sexte, None, Vespers, Compline, Matins, and Laudes. For their assistance in determining the Hospitalière's daily schedule in the 1640s, I am indebted to Sister Marie de l'Enfant Jesus and Sister Marie-Colette of Pont d'Eglise, France.

32. Thwaites, *Jesuit Relations,* 34:127–129.

33. Ibid., 34:145–147.

34. Ibid., 34:139–147.

35. Thwaites, *Jesuit Relations,* 34:25–37, 123–157.

36. Léon Pouliot, "Ragueneau, Paul," in DCB, vol. 1.

37. Thwaites, *Jesuit Relations,* 34:127.

38. Ibid., 34:35.

39. Ibid., 34:199–201.

40. Ibid., 36:59.

41. The regard was mutual. Brébeuf also effusively praised Ragueneau. See ibid., 32:10, 61–63.

42. Ibid., 34:139–141.

43. Ragueneau was instructed to create these documents by the bishop of Rouen, who erroneously believed he had religious jurisdiction over canonizations in New France. See Ibid., 38:189. See also Julia Boss, "Writing a Relic: The Uses of Hagiography in New France," in *Colonial Saints: Discovering the Holy in the Americas, 1500–1800,* ed. Allan Greer and Jodi Bilinkoff (New York: Routledge, 2003), 211–233.

44. Christophe Regnault, Sainte-Marie's resident shoemaker, repeatedly used this phrase in his sworn testimony regarding his observation of the bodies of Lalemant and Brébeuf. See Thwaites, *Jesuit Relations,* 34:33–35.

45. Ragueneau's slate of candidates for collective canonization in the early 1650s varied in significant ways from the eight men who were eventually elevated. For more, see Chapter 3 of this volume.

46. On Chihoatenhwa's conversion, see Thwaites, *Jesuit Relations,* 15:77–99, 155, and John Steckley, *Untold Tales: Three Seventeenth-Century Huron* (Ajax, ON: R. Kerton, 1981), 5–6. On Chihoatenhwa's evangelization efforts, see Thwaites, *Jesuit Relations,* 15:101–109, 123–127, 19:133–165. On his death, see ibid, 20:79, 95, 21:161–164, 211. Bruce Trigger (*Children of Aataentsic: A History of the Huron People to 1660* [Montreal: McGill–Queen's University Press, 1976], 598–601) sees Chihoatenhwa as the victim of his own Wendat people, as does Francis X. Talbot (*Saint among the Hurons: The Life of Jean de Brebeuf* [Garden City, NY: Image Books, 1956], 290) and Steckley (*Untold Tales,* 11–14). Jon Parmenter (*The Edge of the Woods: Iroquoia, 1534–1701* [East Lansing: Michigan State University Press, 2010], 51), however, takes the attribution of his slaying to the Iroquois at face value, seeing their apparent attack on Chihoatenhwa as

a way of demonstrating to the Wendat the inability of the black-robes to protect them.

47. Those currently seeking to forward Chihoatenhwa's *causa* as a saint generally present him as a saint rather than a martyr. See Chapter 6 of this volume.

48. The attempted redemption of Brébeuf and Lalemant by Lazare, though attested to in the *Jesuit Relations* (Thwaites, 43:311–313), appears in only a few secondary accounts of their martyrdoms, such as Henri Fouqueray's *Martyrs du Canada*, deuxième édition (Paris: Pierre Tequi, 1930), 256, and Paul Prud'homme's *Nos Martyrs: Jean de Brébeuf, Isaac Jogues et leurs compagnons.* (Montreal: Messager, 1929).

49. For more on Onaharé, see Thwaites, *Jesuit Relations*, 35:222–233; Francois Du Creux, *The History of Canada or New France* (Toronto: Champlain Society, 1951), 571–574; Allan Greer, "Colonial Saints: Gender, Race and Hagiography in New France," *William and Mary Quarterly* 57, no. 2 (April 2000): 335–336, 343. On Chihoatenhwa, see Thwaites, *Jesuit Relations*, 19:151–153, 20:79–85; Steckley, *Untold Tales*, 1–17; Trigger, *Natives and Newcomers: Canada's Heroic Age Reconsidered* (Kingston: McGill–Queen's University Press, 1985), 249; and Trigger, *Children of Aataentsic*, 717. European laymen also fared poorly in Ragueneau's writing. They would become more popular candidates for formal recognition as martyrs only in the nineteenth century, with two of the eight eventually canonized, René Goupil and Jean de la Lande, being laymen.

50. Ragueneau, *La Vie*, 44.

51. Catherine also revered martyr Isaac Jogues, as he had "opened her way" to Canada, and swore a solemn oath to remain on the anniversary of his death. But Ragueneau's urging notwithstanding, she did not identify with the martyred Nöel Chabanel, despite their similar temptations to return to France. Oury (*Spiritual Journey*, 130–134) notes that Ragueneau utilized the text of Chabanel's vow of persistence as the basis of a spiritual exercise he assigned Catherine in 1654. But her temptations would abate only after she was taken under Brébeuf's celestial wing.

52. Only the relics of Brébeuf, Lalemant, and Garnier are extant. Despite a 1938 prediction by famed German stigmatic Teresa Neumann that the remains of Jogues, Goupil, and la Lande would eventually be found somewhere on the Auriesville site, this prophesy has not yet come to pass (see "Teresa Neumann Prophesies Martyrs' Relics Will Be Found," *The Catholic Reporter*, August 23, 1934, 109).

53. Thwaites, *Jesuit Relations*, 50:87–89, 123, 56:103–105; Dom. Albert Jamet, *Les Annales de l'Hôtel-Dieu de Québec, 1636–1716* (Québec: l'Hôtel Dieu de Québec, 1939), 148, 239.

54. Thwaites, *Jesuit Relations*, 50:87–89.

55. The Jesuits, however, did not use Catherine's preferred method of grating his bones into food, but either touched the relics to the afflicted area

(Thwaites, *Jesuit Relations,* 50:123) or, having "dipped" or "steeped" the relics in water, then gave the water to the invalid to either drink or apply it to their wounds (ibid., 56:103–105).

56. John Steckley, *De Religione: Telling the Seventeenth-Century Jesuit Story in Huron to the Iroquois* (Norman: University of Oklahoma Press, 2004), 129–131. Steckley has here collected and translated speeches originally written for oral delivery to an Iroquois audience.

57. Ibid. The odd cadence here is the result both of the text's many translations (from French to Wendat to English) and from the difficulty of explaining Christian concepts in the Wendat language.

58. Thwaites, *Jesuit Relations,* 31:123.

59. Félix Martin, *Catherine Tegakouitha: Iroquois Maiden,* trans. William Lonc, JAC, 2006, 53.

60. Mark 15:39.

61. Thwaites, *Jesuit Relations,* 32:21–27.

62. Ibid.; see also Félix Martin, SJ, *The Life of Father Isaac Jogues, Missionary Priest of the Society of Jesus,* trans. John G. Shea (New York: Benziger Brothers, 1885), 207. The man never directly confessed to killing Jogues. Rather, when questioned about the matter, he "hung his head, without saying aught" (Thwaites, *Jesuit Relations,* 32:25). However, this same individual was also accused by an escaped Wendat present at Jogues's slaying of having struck the deadly blow.

63. This demonstrates the fact that French colonial officials had no coercive power over aboriginal allies in such matters.

64. Thwaites, *Jesuit Relations,* 32:25. His last words thus echo the taunts of Brébeuf and Lalemant's ex-Wendat ex-Catholic tormentors, who demanded the missionaries' thanks for being the cause of their immortal joy.

65. Ibid., 36:23.

66. Ibid., 36:23, 25–27.

67. Ibid., 23–45; Parkman, *Jesuits in North America,* 305.

68. Thwaites, *Jesuit Relations,* 43:311–313.

69. Ibid.

70. Ibid., 43:139, 33–35. For every cooperatively contrite convert, however, there was an unapologetic apostate, such as Louis Honareenhax, the slayer of Nöel Chabanel.

71. Martin, *Catherine Tegakouitha,* 2006.

72. Henri Bechard, "Ogenheratarihiens," in DCB.

73. The fact that these colonial religious were prepared to take this radical step can be better appreciated when we remember that, in 1633, the Jesuits refused other female visitors, native women seeking shelter from immanent Iroquois attack, on the grounds that the presence of women represented too great of a sexual temptation. See Thwaites, *Jesuit Relations,* 5:107 and Emma Anderson, *The Betrayal of Faith: The Tragic Journey of a*

Colonial Native Convert (Cambridge, MA: Harvard University Press, 2007), 140.

74. Oury (*Spiritual Journey*, 197) and Bilinkoff (*Related Lives*, 74) both explicitly present these visions as a substitution for Ragueneau's presence.

75. Ragueneau remained in close epistolatory contact with Catherine during the six years between his 1662 departure and her 1668 death. Many of these letters are extensively quoted in his *Vie*.

76. Ragueneau, *La Vie*, 115.

77. This shift away from the visual is all the more striking given "the visual precision of Catherine's mystical graces" (Oury, *Spiritual Journey*, 178).

78. Thwaites, *Jesuit Relations*, 52:69. These words were penned after Catherine's death. Allegedly, no one in her Augustinian convent, including her superior, was aware of her the young nun's supernatural visitations, both celestial and demonic, during her lifetime.

79. Ragueneau, *La Vie*, 118–119.

80. Ibid., 123, 125–126.

81. Ragueneau avoids using "possession" to describe Catherine's spiritual symptoms, preferring "obsession." Because Catherine was not deranged, he argues, she could not have been completely possessed. Marie de l'Incarnation, another contemporary who also knew Catherine quite well, was of essentially the same opinion (see Oury, *Marie de l'Incarnation*, 746; Oury, *Spiritual Journey*, 200–201). Catherine's own words, however, connote a far graver situation.

82. Catherine also experienced demonic manifestations. Just before she saw Brébeuf, Catherine condemned one of her recent apparitions as a "false vision" inspired by Satan, explaining her initial suspicion of Brébeuf's sudden appearance.

83. Ragueneau's editing of Catherine's writing in his *Vie* appears to have been quite minimal. See Bilinkoff, *Related Lives*, 70–75.

84. Brébeuf was eventually able to convince Catherine (as Ragueneau could not) that her demonic obsession did not render her less acceptable to God; on the contrary, he was pleased by her ability to bear this burden. See Ragueneau, *La Vie*, 124.

85. Ibid., 125.

86. Psychologists, of course, would reverse the causality of Catherine's seventeenth-century mystical reasoning in this case, positing that it was Catherine's own ambivalence that led to her perception of herself as being at the mercy of two competing external forces.

87. Ragueneau, *La Vie*, 115.

88. Interestingly, Catherine also presents Saint Joseph in similarly piteous terms. Ibid., 151–152.

89. Ibid., 121.

90. Ibid., 117. Catherine associated Brébeuf strongly with the Eucharist, as she received the sacrament from his invisible hands. Brébeuf used the

presence of the Host to intimidate her demonic tormentors: "As [Brébeuf] spoke, I sensed the approach of many demons, but I saw that the Father inclined his head a little toward the Holy Sacrament, and at that moment they fled." Ibid., 115.

91. In *La Vie*, Ragueneau presents Catherine's presence in the colony as symbolically sharing the same danger being endured by Jesuits in Wendake, painting her as protomartyr for her courageous decision to come to Canada, particularly at such a young age. Ibid., 44.

92. However, many of Catherine's mystical experiences did involve considerable physical pain. Ibid., 123.

93. The rhetorical shift in Jesuit writings from living martyrdom to a more literal expectation of violent death was discussed in Chapter 1.

94. See Peter Goddard, "The Devil in New France: Jesuit Demonology 1611–1650," *Canadian Historical Review* 78, no. 1 (1997): 40–62. The association of native violence with Satan's hordes also occurred in New England and New Spain. See Jill Lepore, *The Name of War: King Philip's War and the Origins of American Identity* (New York: Vintage, 1999; Jorge Cañizares-Esguerra, *Puritan Conquistadors: Iberianizing the Atlantic, 1550–1700* (Stanford: Stanford University Press, 2006).

95. Catherine's visions bore marked similarities with those of Mary Margaret Alacoque, who saw the Sacred Heart of Jesus, profoundly impacting Catholic iconography.

96. Ragueneau, *La Vie*, 121. The odd passivity of this phrasing is due to Catherine's perception that four strong arms appeared to help her to scourge herself, leaving her back "wet with blood."

97. Ibid., 153–155. Catherine continued to experience apocalyptic visions throughout 1663 and 1664 (ibid., 152–154).

98. Other colonial religious, such as Marie de l'Incarnation, also perceived the earthquake as a divine chastisement (Oury, *Spiritual Journey*, 204–215; Oury, *Marie de l'Incarnation*, 688–689).

99. Ragueneau, *La Vie*, 154.

100. Ibid., 48. It was Ragueneau who transposed the passage into the third person.

101. Thwaites, *Jesuit Relations*, 52:75.

102. Thwaites reproduces a letter written by Marie de Saint-Bonaventure de Jesus for circulation in all the Augustinian Hospitalière communities on both sides of the Atlantic. See Thwaites, *Jesuit Relations*, 52:57–81.

103. Ibid.

104. Jamet, *Les Annales*, 155–158, 236, 238; Oury, *Marie de l'Incarnation*, 815.

105. Thwaites, *Jesuit Relations*, 52:65–67.

106. Ibid.

107. Ragueneau, *La Vie*, 120. Making these novenas around the anniversary of Brébeuf's death appears to have been something of a tradition with Catherine in the later years of her life. See Oury, *Spiritual Journey*, 218.

108. Catherine's choice to use Brébeuf's bones (even though the relics of two other martyrs, Charles Garnier and Gabriel Lalemant, were also available) likewise set a powerful precedent. Following the martyrs' collective beatification in 1925, the Jesuits would once again make preferential recourse to Brébeuf's relics in a successful attempt to obtain the two miracles necessary for their canonization. Of the many wonders his miracle-working bones allegedly performed, two healings were selected to serve as proof of his powerful saintly intercession, those of Acadian nuns Soeur Marie Georgina Robichaud and Soeur Alexandrine Ruel in 1927, both of whom had suffered from tubercular peritonitis. "Credit" for these supernatural manifestations was given to the martyrs as a group, permitting the octet's canonization in 1930. See Adrien Pouliot, SJ, *1930–1980: Il y a cinquante ans les Martyrs Canadiens étaient canonisés* (Québec: Les Pères Jésuites, 1980). This work was subsequently translated into English by George Topp, appearing as *The Holy Martyrs of Canada: Beatified in 1925, Canonized in 1930* (the publication information is the same). See also AMMS Cures dossier, E601.
109. Jamet, *Les Annales*, 237–238. See also Thwaites, *Jesuit Relations*, 52:103–109; Thierry, "Catherine de Saint-Augustin." The Hospitalières claimed that a young Parisian Jesuit had been inspired by Catherine's exploits to come to Canada, thus completing the cycle of textual inspiration and imitation begun with her own prepubescent discovery of the *Relations*.
110. Specifically, Catherine was painted as a "Quietist": that is, as one whose supernatural preoccupations had eclipsed her ritual connections with the church and broken her bonds of charity with others.
111. Both of these generalizations are based on local stories in Josselin, Brittany, where the tomb of the local aristocracy was plundered in the very manner described. The ravages of the Revolution in this small Breton town are still very visible. My thanks to Mimi Bonnefoi for these stories.
112. Bressani, like Jogues, was liberated by the Dutch, escaped to France, and once again returned to New France. He would survive the perilous 1640s and die at home in Italy in 1672.
113. I am indebted to Jacques Monet, SJ, for this anecdote. Joseph Donnelly (*Jean de Brébeuf 1593–1649* [Chicago: Loyola University Press, 1975], 293) notes that Lalemant's skull suffered a similar fate. Sent to his sisters in France, it was preserved at Sens until it, too, was destroyed during the Revolution.
114. The postcanonization cult of Jean de Brébeuf in France will be treated in Chapter 7 of the current work.
115. Robert Hollier, "Goya inspire par l'histoire du Canada," *Vie des Arts*, no. 41 (1966): 42–43.
116. This etching was first commissioned as an illustration for Jesuit historian François du Creux's syncretic work, published the same year. François-Marc Gagnon is the authority on the genesis, diffusion, and "fragmentation" of

Huret and other seventeenth-century images of the Jesuit martyrs. See François-Marc Gagnon, "L'iconographie classique des saints martyrs canadiens," in Guy Laflèche, *Les Saints Martyrs Canadiens,* vol. 1 (Montréal: Singulier, 1988).

117. Huret's work inspired a number of nineteenth-century oils and lithographs that essentially pirated his image. See Chapters 3 and 5 of the present work.

118. Mathias Tanner's illustrations in his work *Societas Jesu ad sanguinis et vitae profusionem militans* (Pragae: Typis Universitatis, 1675), like Goya's paintings, break many of the implicit taboos of martyrdom art by showing Gabriel Lalemant with coals in his empty eye sockets. Tanner's image did not have the protean afterlife of Huret's image, suggesting that he had inadvertently broken the empathic bond between viewer and subject that is at the heart of martyrdom art.

119. Hollier, "Goya inspire par l'histoire du Canada," 42–43.

120. Suzanne Singleterry. "Dystopia: Goya's Cannibals," *Aurora: The Journal of the History of Art,* January 1, 2004.

121. The Virgin Mary was credited with defeating two attempted British invasions in 1690 and 1711.

3. *Souvenirs des Jésuites*

1. John Porter, *The Works of Joseph Légaré, 1795–1855* (Ottawa: National Gallery of Canada, 1978), 10. Joseph and Genèvieve Légaré married in 1818 and had twelve children, only five of whom lived.

2. Ibid., 12–13; Mario Berland, *La Peinture au Québec, 1820–1850: Nouveaux regards, nouvelles perspectives* (Québec: Musée du Québec, 1991), 348; Jean Trudel, "Joseph Légaré et la Bataille de Sainte-Foy," *Journal of Canadian Art History* 8, no. 2 (1985): 141–142.

3. Porter, *Works,* 71.

4. Ibid., 148–150. Légaré was described in a contemporary newspaper as "one of the most enthusiastic founders of the [Québec City] Society" (ibid., 150).

5. A porcupine. Légaré's hair is disheveled in all of his daguerreotypes (see Porter, *Works,* 14, 15) and in his 1837 portrait by fellow Québec artist Jean-Joseph Girouard (ibid., 13).

6. Ibid., 10.

7. See John Porter, "Légaré, Joseph," in DCB. In his thirty-five-year career Légaré would produce more than 250 works, almost half of them for the church.

8. See Allan Greer, *The Patriots and the People: The Rebellion of 1837 in Rural Lower Canada* (Toronto: University of Toronto Press, 1993) and Jacques Monet, *The Last Cannon Shot: A Study of French Canadian Nationalism, 1837–1850* (Toronto: University of Toronto Press, 1969).

9. Serge Gagnon, *Quebec and Its Historians, 1840 to 1920* (Montreal: Harvest House, 1982), 44–45.

10. Ibid., 40.

11. Garneau, private correspondence, quoted in ibid., 33.

12. Ibid., 9–12.

13. François-Xavier Garneau, *Histoire du Canada depuis sa découverte jusqu'à nos jours*, 5 vols. (Paris: Alcan, 1913–1920).

14. Ignace Bourget's famous "Appel aux Jesuites," excerpted in Gilles Chaussé, *Les Jésuites et la Canada Français, 1842–1992* [Montréal: La Compagnie de Jésus, Province du Canada Français, 1992), 11–12, my translation. Chaussé refers to this Appel as "La Magna Charta de la nouvelle Compagnie de Jésus au Canada."

15. The classic work on the explosion of female vocations in nineteenth-century Québec is Marta Danylewycz, *Taking the Veil: An Alternative to Marriage, Motherhood, and Spinsterhood in Québec, 1840–1920* (Toronto: McClelland and Stewart, 1987).

16. For analysis of this work, see Porter, *Works*, 71–74, and Guy Laflèche, *Les Saints Martyrs Canadiens*, 5 vols. (Montréal: Singulier, 1988–1995), 1:267–268.

17. He does take this more traditional approach in other paintings of the same era, notably *Le martyre des pères Brébeuf et Lalemant* (on display at the National Gallery of Canada in Ottawa). This may also have been a Jesuit commission. For an image of the work, see Porter, *Works*, 72–73.

18. "Secular clergy" refers to those priests who are not—like the Jesuits, the Dominicans, or the Franciscans, for example—the members of a religious order.

19. Laflèche, *Les Saints Martyrs Canadiens*, 1:267–268, my translation. T. J. Campbell, in his *Pioneer Priests of North America, 1642–1710*, vol. 1 (New York: The America Press, 1911), 1, concurs with Lafleche's assessment of Martin's centrality to the reestablishment of the martyrs' cult, stating that Martin "has done more than anyone else to revive the memory of those old heroes of the seventeenth century," noting in particular Martin's important influence on the American historian John Gilmary Shea. Martin's archival, archeological, and historical endeavors twice received the support of the Canadian government. See also Peter Guilday, *John Gilmary Shea: Father of American Catholic History, 1824–1892* (New York: United States Catholic Historical Society, 1926), 20.

20. Coleridge always insisted that his completion of the poem was stymied by an unwelcome visitor, though he might just have had writer's block.

21. Horatio Phelan, "Early Huronia Shrines," in MSM, date unclear, 9. Had Martin paid better attention to the visual evidence contained in Légaré's *Souvenirs* and inquired as to which religious community had custody of the reliquary bust, he probably would have found this Augustinian treasure cache even sooner for, as noted by Julia Boss, textual and actual

relics are often preserved together. Julia Boss, "Writing a Relic: The Uses of Hagiography in New France," in *Colonial Saints: Discovering the Holy in the Americas*, ed. Allan Greer and Jodi Bilinkoff (New York: Routledge, 2003), 211–212; Laflèche, *Les Saints Martyrs Canadiens*, 1:267–269.

22. Bourget had encountered Chazelle on several occasions in both North America and Rome and had effectively headhunted him to lead the reconstituted Jesuits in the newly established Jesuit province of Québec–New York. Chazelle would have been the logical choice to establish Collège Sainte-Marie because of his previous experience in university administration in Kentucky. However, he subsequently came to greatly value Martin as well. Impressed by Martin's scholarship and unimpeachable political orthodoxy, Bourget abruptly withdrew his patronage from Quebecois historian Abbé Jacques Paquin—already a thousand pages into a proposed three-volume history of Canada—and appointed Martin to write it, justifying his change of heart on the basis of Paquin's supposed softness on *les Patriotes* during their abortive revolution (Chaussé, *Les Jésuites*, 45–46). As a Frenchman only newly arrived in North America, Martin was free from this baggage, and his experiences of persecution in Napoleonic France perfectly resonated with Bourget's adamant antirevolutionary stance (Georges-Émile Giguère, "Martin, Félix," in DCB).

23. Georges-Émile Giguère, "Chazelle, Jean-Pierre," in DCB; Laflèche, *Les Saints Martyrs Canadiens*, 1:267.

24. According to Georges-Émile Giguère ("Martin, Félix"), the archives were established in 1844, with the college itself only being formed four years later.

25. Chaussé, *Les Jésuites*, 21. For his analysis of the politics of this situation, which he felt placed French Canadian Jesuits at a marked disadvantage, see 21–23.

26. Gagnon, *Quebec and Its Historians*, 15; see also Yvan Lamonde, *Histoire Sociale des Idées au Québec, 1760–1896*, vol. 1 (Québec: Fides, 2000), 287–295, 317–321.

27. See Gabriel Dussault, "Dimensions messianiques du catholicisme québécois au dix-neuvième siècle," in William Westfall, ed., *Religion/Culture: Comparative Canadian Studies/Etudes canadiennes comparées* (Ottawa: L'Association des études canadiennes, 1985), 64–71.

28. For an excellent short exposition of the clericalization of nineteenth-century Québec, see Gagnon, *Quebec and Its Historians*, 2–5, 49–50. For an exceptional record of the visual culture of this period in Québec, see Claude Gravel, *La Vie dans les Communautés Religieuses: L'Age de la ferveur, 1840–1960* (Montréal: Les Editions Libre Expression, 2010).

29. The Jesuit martyrs were not the only figures whose luster was restored in the age of clerico-nationalism. Dollard des Ormeaux also emerged

(though somewhat later than the Jesuit martyrs and *les braves*) as a symbol of heroic self-sacrifice on behalf of Québec. But the very politicization of Dollard's legacy makes discerning fact from pious legend regarding his death in the 1660 battle of Long-Sault difficult. For more on Québec's increasingly popular "guardian angel," see Ronald Rudin, *Founding Fathers: The Celebration of Champlain and Laval in the Streets of Quebec, 1878–1908* (Toronto: University of Toronto Press, 2003), 228, 229–230; see also Patrice Groulx, *Pièges de la Memoire: Dollard des Ormeaux, les amérindiens et nous* (Gatineau, QC: Vents d'Ouest, 1998), and Guy Laflèche, *Le martyr de la Nation huronne et sa défaite avec Dollard des Ormeaux* (Laval, QC: Éditions du Singulier, 1995).

30. See, for example, Ferland, in Gagnon, *Quebec and Its Historians,* 53–54.
31. See Lamonde, *Histoire Sociale des Idées,* 336–344. Also, for an excellent study of Quebecois laywomen's internalized guilt in the clerico-nationalist era, see Christine Hudon, "Des dames chrétiennes: La spiritualité des catholiques québécoises au XIXe siècle," *Revue d'Histoire de l'Amérique Française,* 49, no 2 (1995).
32. Gagnon, *Quebec and Its Historians,* 11.
33. Garneau, *Histoire du Canada,* 157. Garneau even went so far as to suggest that if only one Christian confession was allowed to emigrate to Canada, it should have been Protestants, who were more willing and more adaptable. See also Gagnon, *Quebec and Its Historians,* 23–24.
34. Garneau, *Histoire du Canada,* 4:240–284; see also Gagnon, *Quebec and Its Historians,* 36, and Lamonde, *Histoire Sociale des Idées,* 180–181.
35. Gagnon, *Quebec and Its Historians,* 18. Like the martyrs, Laval was a figure particularly beloved of clerico-nationalists, perhaps because of his authoritarian reputation. Also like the martyrs, Laval was seen by many as an excellent prospective saint. The 1877 rediscovery of his long-lost bones by construction workers renovating the Québec City Basilica and these remains' ostentatious "translation" through the streets of Québec was so spectacular that organizers feared that they may have inadvertently crossed the line by actually venerating Laval as a saint before Rome had had the opportunity to weigh in (something that would be very much against their own ultramontaine instincts). See Rudin, *Founding Fathers,* 11–51.
36. Gagnon, *Quebec and Its Historians,* 20.
37. Ibid., 41.
38. *Journal de Québec,* March 12, 1846, quoted in Gagnon, *Quebec and Its Historians,* 140.
39. Gagnon, *Quebec and Its Historians,* 39.
40. Ibid., 42.
41. See Lamonde, *Histoire Sociale des Idées,* 363–367. Bourget denied Guibord a Catholic burial on the grounds that he had continued to belong to a

banned literary institute after it had been condemned by the church. His widow took the matter to court and won. Bourget, however, in a fit of pique, both deconsecrated Guibord's grave site and gave parish employees the day off so they could pelt the man's coffin with rocks during his reburial.

42. Ibid., 105.

43. His arguments anticipated, by a century, similar points made by Québec Jesuits today; see Chapter 5 of the present work.

44. Benjamin Sulte, *L'histoire des canadiens français*, 4th ed., 4 vols. (Montréal: Beauchemin and Valois, 1883).

45. Gagnon, *Quebec and Its Historians*, 77–78.

46. The other villain, for Sulte, was France itself, whom he blamed for abandoning and "victimizing" Québec (Sulte, *L'histoire des canadiens français*, 4:31).

47. Ibid., 3:143.

48. Gagnon, *Quebec and Its Historians*, 79.

49. Sulte, *L'histoire des canadiens français*, 3:138; Gagnon, *Quebec and Its Historians*, 80.

50. Ibid., 105.

51. Gagnon, *Quebec and Its Historians*, 107.

52. *Apothéose des Bienheureux Martyrs Canadiens de la Compagnie de Jésus: Translation des Reliques et Triduum* (Québec City: L'Action Sociale, 1926).

53. However, as historian Don Smith notes, there were exceptions. Napoleon Legendre published an article in 1884 in which he tried to imagine the history of New France from a native perspective, critiquing early French kidnapping of native peoples, their exploitation in the fur trade, and the invasion of their lands. Native violence, he stated, was often justifiable self-defense. Donald B. Smith, *Le Sauvage: The Native People in Quebec Historical Writing on the Heroic Period (1534–1663)* (Ottawa: National Museums of Canada, 1974), 45–47.

54. Despite their intellectual similarities, Sulte did not like Parkman, seeing his historiography as slighting and mocking French Canadians. Said Sulte: "the compliments he gives us are dipped in bitter ink." Gagnon, *Quebec and Its Historians*, 99, 68. The advent of theories of scientific racism made the otherwise puzzling unanimity of secular and clerico-nationalists more comprehensible.

55. Smith, *Le Sauvage*, 101.

56. For the original French text of the poem, see Grace Lee Nute, *The Voyageur* (St. Paul: Minnesota Historical Society, 1955). It is ironic, given Sulte's thesis that the Jesuits imposed their own martyrdom complex on *les Canadiens*, that this popular voyageur song has much the same dynamic. See Gagnon, *Quebec and Its Historians*, 79.

57. Smith, *Le Sauvage*, 51–58; Gagnon, *Quebec and Its Historians*, 90.

58. For the image, see Porter, *Works,* 34; and Berland, *La Peinture,* 354. For its analysis, see Porter, *Works,* 33–34; Berland, *La Peinture,* 355–358.

59. Gillian Poulter, "Representation as Colonial Rhetoric: The Image of 'the Native' and 'the Habitant' in the Formation of Colonial Identities in Early Nineteenth-Century Lower Canada," *Journal of Canadian Art History* 16, no. 1 (1994): 21–22.

60. Berland, *La Peinture,* 369–370.

61. I say generally because, in an undated painting described as "one of the oldest female nudes in Canadian painting" (Porter, *Works,* 144), Légaré celebrated the heroism of a native female martyr being killed for her faith, though commentators differ in their interpretation of the figure's identity. See Berland, *La Peinture,* 355, 357; Porter, *Works,* 144. The painting is reproduced in Porter, *Works,* 143. Obviously, this image represents a massive jump forward from Huret's tiny, ambivalent handling of Joseph Onaharé.

62. Légaré also did several other portraits of the Jesuit martyrs. See Porter, *Works,* 73, 76.

63. For the painting, see Porter, *Works,* 75, and Berland, *La Peinture,* 369. For analysis, see Porter, *Works,* 72–73, and Berland, *La Peinture,* 369–372. Berland (*La Peinture,* 369) notes that *Le Martyre* is essentially the same image miniaturized in the window of *Souvenirs.*

64. It is unclear whether Ourné was Wendat or Abnaki (Porter, *Works,* 74–75, 78). The original painting hangs in the National Gallery of Canada in Ottawa, Ontario. For a color image, see Berland, *La Peinture,* 92. For analysis, see Berland, *La Peinture,* 372).

65. Poulter, "Representation as Colonial Rhetoric," 14, 19.

66. Ibid., 22.

67. Porter, *Works,* 72–73, 75.

68. See Allan Greer, "Colonial Saints: Gender, Race and Hagiography in New France," *William and Mary Quarterly* 57, no. 2 (April 2000): 335–336, and Gagnon, in Laflèche, *Les Saints Martyrs Canadiens,* 1:79.

69. Onaharé is today almost unknown. Only rarely is his martyrdom, just two years after that of Brébeuf, celebrated in Catholic devotional literature. For analysis of Onaharé's failure to receive official recognition as a martyr, see Greer, "Colonial Saints," 323–348. For the most complete analysis to date of Onaharé's life and death, see Timothy Pearson, *Becoming Holy in Early Canada* (Montreal: McGill–Queen's University Press, forthcoming 2014), chapter 3. See also his doctoral dissertation, "Becoming Holy in Early Canada: Performance and the Making of Holy Persons in Society and Culture" (Department of History, McGill University, 2008), 134, 142–147, 157, 284.

70. Sandwich, Ontario (near present-day Windsor) would become the headquarters of Jesuits assigned to the missions of northwestern Ontario. See

Paul Delaney and Andrew Nicholls, *After the Fire: Sainte-Marie among the Hurons since 1649* (Meaford, ON: East Georgian Bay Historical foundation, 1989), 6–7. See also Chaussé, *Les Jésuites,* 13–14, and Giguère, "Chazelle, Jean-Pierre."

71. The site's romantic resonances were only sharpened by the local legend that those who had impiously dared to raid Sainte-Marie's stones were justly haunted for their sacrilege (see Delaney and Nicholls, *After the Fire,* 7).

72. Chazelle's letter is reprinted in Delaney and Nicholls, *After the Fire,* 7. See also Phelan, "Early Huronia Shrines," 8. However, despite the passion of Chazelle and other early Jesuit visitors to the site (such as Felix Martin and Joseph Hannipaux), it would be almost a century before Sainte-Marie was once again in Jesuit hands. Moreover, Jesuit merging of pilgrimage and missionization meant that "walking where the saints had walked" became defined as an almost exclusively *Jesuit* privilege, a tendency that arguably retarded the spatial development of the Canadian martyrs' cult.

73. Chaussé, *Les Jésuites,* 29, my translation; see also 13. For more on Bishop Power's role, see Frances J. Nelligan, "Modern Indian Missions," MSM (December 1955): 117–119.

74. D. Hannan, "The Modern Blackrobes," MSM 9, no. 2 (June 1945): 14.

75. Father Jim Kelly, telephone interview with the author, June 24, 2011.

76. See Robert Choquette, *The Oblate Assault on Canada's Northwest* (Ottawa, ON: University of Ottawa Press, 1995).

77. The Anishnabe are also known as the Ojibwe. Joining native groups indigenous to the area, such as the Algonquins and Cree, the Ojibwe held the area against intermittent Iroquois challenges throughout the eighteenth century (see Delaney and Nicholls, *After the Fire,* 4). Much like the Iroquois, who were also split between the United States and Canada, Ojibwe who remained in the United States faced Protestant missionization, whereas those that emigrated to Canada often became the targets of Catholic evangelical efforts. For a fascinating study of Ojibwe-Protestant hymnody, see Michael McNally, *Ojibwe Singers: Hymns, Grief, and an Native Culture in Motion* (Oxford: Oxford Unviversity Press, 2000).

78. The Jesuit notion that they were continuing the work of their celebrated predecessors was particularly strong in postwar Canada. See, for example, Nelligan, "Modern Indian Missions," 117–119; Peter J. Brown, "Manitoulin," MSM 12, no. 1 (March 1946): 7–19; Victor Traynor, "Old Huronia and the Hurons of Today," MSM 17, no. 2 (June 1953): 36–37, 60; Neil McKenty, "Aibisiwinge the Consoler," MSM 14, no. 4 (December 1950): 100–101, 116–117; Vincent MacKenzie, "The Jesuit Missions of Ontario Past and Present," MSM, 5, no. 2 (June 1941): 18, 30; D. Hannin, "the Modern Blackrobes," MSM 9, no. 2 (June 1945): 18–19; Alfred Sinnott,

"Jean-Edouard Darveau 1816–1844 First Martyr Priest among the Missionaries to the Indians in Western Canada," *The Canadian Catholic Historical Association Report*, (1950): 13–20; Cadieux, "Fondateurs du diocese du Sault Sainte-Marie," in *La Société Canadienne d'histoire de l'eglise catholique, Rapport 1942–1943*, 77–96. In his article "The Modern Apostle of Manitoulin Island: Reverend Father Eugene Papineau, S.J., 1876–1931," (MSM 15, no. 3 [October 1951]: 84), Victor Traynor stresses Papineau's desire to "emulate St. John de Brébeuf and bring these Indians to Christ."

79. Denys Dêlage and Helen Hornbeck Tanner, "The Ojibwa-Jesuit Debate at Walpole Island, 1844," *Ethnohistory* 42, no. 2 (Spring 1994): 295–321.

80. Ibid., 303–304.

81. Ibid., 312.

82. Ibid., 317. A later Jesuit commentator, Lorenzo Cadieux, would indignantly characterize the attitude of the Walpole Island Anishnabe as one of "hostilité diabolique" (see his "Fondateurs du diocese du Sault Sainte-Marie").

83. Ibid., 320.

84. Ibid.

85. Giguère, "Chazelle, Jean-Pierre."

86. A wax lobe was created for each half of the severed skull to give it the illusion of completeness.

87. Mariette Paquin, who volunteers at the Augustinian compound, testifies to the Brébeuf bust's ever-changing expression: "I find that we see his determination, his softness, and we see his joy as well. It really depends on how you look at it" (Paquin, in-person, recorded interview with the author, August 7, 2009).

88. Both of these solemn public celebrations bore marked resemblances to other "sumptuous and highly orchestrated" public rituals, such as the traditional *Fête-Dieu* or Corpus Christi processions and other ostentatious translation ceremonies, such as those of the relics of Québec's first bishop, Francois Laval, in 1877. For a fascinating study of Laval's translation, see Rudin, *Founding Fathers*, 3–51.

89. Trudel, "Joseph Légaré," 157.

90. Ibid., 145.

91. Trudel analyzes the many liberties Légaré takes with history in his painting (ibid., 168).

92. Ibid., 154, 147–149.

93. Ibid., 149, my translation.

94. Though Légaré's sketches for the funeral cortege have not survived, a Paris newspaper published an engraving of the scene. It is reproduced in Porter, *Works*, 148, and Trudel, "Joseph Légaré," 140. For analysis, see Porter, *Works*, 150; Trudel, "Joseph Légaré," 151–153; and Rudin, *Founding Fathers*, 18.

95. Trudel, "Joseph Légaré," 157. Others have substantially lower estimates of the turnout, with Rudin placing the number of spectators at 10,000 (Rudin, *Founding Fathers*, 18), a still impressive turnout.

96. Trudel, "Joseph Légaré, 153.

97. The Catholic Church's stance on *les braves* was ambiguous. Objecting that the Catholic identity of the fallen French could not be determined from their bleached bones, authorities declined requests for their internment in a Catholic cemetery, unintentionally leading to their battle-site internment site becoming secular holy ground. See Rudin, *Founding Fathers*, 19–20.

98. Trudel, "Joseph Légaré, 156. The ceremony was originally scheduled to take place on June 25, 1855, four days after Légaré's death, but was postponed until July 18 of the same year.

99. For the image, see Trudel, "Joseph Légaré," 161 (for analysis, see 160–161).

100. *Apothéose des Bienheureux Martyrs.*

101. For more on the choreography and ritual of these translation and internment events, see Rudin, *Founding Fathers*, especially 28–51.

102. This can be seen by their frequent rhetorical coupling with more "secular" figures, such as Jacques Cartier, in the Cartier-Brébeuf monument of 1889. See Rudin, *Founding Fathers*, 6.

103. See Jay Dolan, *In Search of American Catholicism: A History of Religion and Culture in Tension* (Oxford: Oxford University Press, 2002), 54–59, 92–96, 134–136, on American nativism and anti-Catholicism.

104. The initiative within the American Catholic church was later condemned as dangerous and arrogant by Rome. For an excellent account of this controversy, see Charles R. Morris, *American Catholic: The Saints and Sinners Who Built America's Most Powerful Church* (New York: Random House, 1997), 84–86, 90–93. For a fascinating reflection on American Catholics' struggle to articulate their identity, see Robert Orsi, "U.S. Catholics between Memory and Modernity: How Catholics Are American," in *Catholics in the American Century: Recasting Narratives of U.S. History,* ed. R. Scott Appleby and Kathleen Sprows Cummings (Ithaca, NY: Cornell University Press, 2012), 11–42.

105. R. H. Clarke, "Isaac Jogues," *Catholic World* (1872), quoted in Kathleen Sprow Cummings, "The Rise of the Nation-Saint," chapter 2 of *Citizen Saints: Catholics and Canonization* (in progress), copy obtained courtesy of the author.

106. Kathleen Cummings suggests that Jogues's and Goupil's apparent deaths as martyrs were also attractive because martyrs, unlike saints, did not need to work certified miracles to receive beatification, see Cummings, "Rise of the Nation-Saint."

107. Francis Jennings is one of Parkman's most stringent critics in this regard, stating baldly that "his biases are poison." Jennings, "Francis Parkman: A

Brahmin among Untouchables," *William and Mary Quarterly* 42 (1985): 306.

108. It is unclear whether Parkman's condition was neurological or neurotic. See W. J. Eccles, "Parkman, Francis," in DCB.

109. The two historians were born and died within mere months of one another. Shea's dates are 1824–1892; Parkman's, 1823–1893.

110. Guilday, *John Gilmary Shea,* 58, 28, 153. Though a highly respected historian, Shea was able to attract substantial financial remuneration only in the last years of his life.

111. Ibid., 18–19.

112. Ibid., 19–20. Despite his own poverty, Shea donated the proceeds of this translation to the Our Lady of Martyrs Shrine in Auriesville. Ibid., 129. For more on the organization of the reconstituted Jesuits, see Chaussé, *Les Jésuites,* 21–24.

113. Ibid., 28–29. Though Shea was never ordained, he retained a fondness and loyalty for the Jesuits throughout his life. On his death, one Jesuit stated: "he was one of us." Ibid., 149.

114. Though Parkman was thus a trenchant judge of the masculine hardiness of other men, he himself was often prostrate and bed-bound. For an analysis of Parkman's obsession with masculinity and race, see Jennings, "Francis Parkman," 320–321.

115. For a sketch of how Protestant historiography shaped the academic study of religion, see Michael P. Carroll, *American Catholics in the Protestant Imagination: Rethinking the Academic Study of Religion* (Baltimore: Johns Hopkins University Press, 2007), 149–157.

116. Jennings, "Francis Parkman," 316.

117. Ibid., 317. See also Smith, *Le Sauvage,* 34.

118. Jennings, "Francis Parkman," 306, 308–311.

119. See Francis Parkman, *The Jesuits in North America in the Seventeenth Century* (Boston: Cosimo, 1876), 382. Jennings ("Francis Parkman," 312, 318–319) also remarks on Parkman's animal metaphors.

120. Parkman, *Jesuits in North America,* 213.

121. Ibid., 448.

122. Ibid., 389–392.

123. Ibid., 448–449. Elsewhere he says: "if [the Jesuits] were destined to disappointment, it was the result of external causes, against which no power of theirs could have insured them" (ibid., 371). It was perhaps Parkman's sense that the Jesuits had failed that made it safe for him to eulogize them so effusively.

124. Ibid., 370. T. J. Campbell characterized this quote as being "like a shot from an ambush" (*Pioneer Priests,* 1:11).

125. Indeed, so disliked was Francis Parkman in Québec's ultramontane circles that his 1878 invitation to receive an honorary doctorate at Laval

University in Québec City had to be apologetically rescinded by his would-be hosts in the face of Catholic outrage. See Eccles, "Parkman, Francis." Much the same hostility is evident as late as the 1930s. While grudgingly aknowledging that "his *The Jesuits in North America* [has] done more to translate the story of Catholic missionary beginnings in North America into an idiom comprehensible to the vast English-speaking world than any other work[,] . . . Parkman . . . failed generally to appreciate in anything like adequate measure the true spirit motivating the lives and labours of these pioneer missionaries" (Thomas O'Connor, "Some Non-Catholic Contributions to the Study of the Canadian and American Missions," in *The Canadian Catholic Historical Association Report 1937–1938*, 13). O'Connor thus preferred to stress the contributions of Reuban Gold Thwaites, editor of the *Jesuit Relations*.

126. Shea, quoted in Guilday, *John Gilmary Shea*, 33.

127. J. L. Morrison, "Shea, John Dawson Gilmary," in *The New Catholic Encyclopedia*, vol. 13 (New York: McGraw-Hill, 1967), 167.

128. John Gilmary Shea, *History of the Catholic Missions among the Indian Tribes* (New York: E. Dunigan, 1855), 15.

129. Tekakwitha was this young woman's Mohawk name. In 1676 she was baptized "Catherine" after Catherine of Sienna. The name "Kateri" was a fairly late addition to her cult. This moniker was created for her by American writer Ellen Hardin Walworth, who in writing *The Life and Times of Kateri Tekakwitha, Lily of the Mohawks, 1656–1680* (Buffalo, NY: P. Paul, 1891, 1) used "Kateri" as what she called "the Iroquois form of the Christian name Katherine." In this work Catherine "Kateri" Tekakwitha will be referred to by all three names. For more information on the evolution of her name, see Allan Greer, "Natives and Nationalism: The Americanization of Kateri Tekakwitha." *The Catholic Historical Review* 90, no. 2 (2004): 260–272, particularly 271, and Allan Greer, *Mohawk Saint: Catherine Tekakwitha and the Jesuits* (Oxford: Oxford University Press, 2005), xi, 195–199. In 1851, as he was trying to decide whether to be ordained, John Gilmary Shea visited Tekakwitha's tomb in Caughnawaga. Guilday, *John Gilmary Shea*, 29.

130. The best biography of Tekakwitha is Greer's *Mohawk Saint*. For information on her biography and early cult, see Nancy Shoemaker, "Kateri Tekakwitha's Tortuous Path to Sainthood," in *Negotiators of Change: Historical Perspectives on Native American Women*, ed. Nancy Shoemaker (New York: Routledge, 1995), 49–67, and Kay Koppedrayer, "The Making of the First Iroquois Virgin: Early Jesuit Biographies of the Blessed Kateri Tekakwitha," *Ethnohistory* 40, no. 2 (Spring 1993): 277–306. "Tekakwitha" translates from the Mohawk as meaning "she who creeps along," a name that references her debilitating handicap (see Greer, *Mohawk Saint*, 14).

131. Her birth occurred fourteen years after the death of Réne Goupil, the first Ossernenon martyr.

132. Shea, *History of the Catholic Missions,* 273. Contemporary native peoples, Catholic, traditionalist, and those who walk both paths, often object to Tekakwitha's presentation in such exceptionalist terms. See Chapters 5 and 6 of the present volume.

133. Shea's appreciation for Tekakwitha finds no correlate in Parkman, who had no patience for female religious, even those of European extraction, and who was excoriating in his evaluation of the foremothers of New France (see Parkman, *Jesuits in North America,* 170–177). As a Catholic, a native person, and a woman, Catherine Tekakwitha would likely have met with Parkman's triple derision.

134. Indeed, Campbell (in *Pioneer Priests,* 1:1), claims that Shea "stained his life of Jogues with his own tears." Shea was a key player in the forming of the American Catholic Historical Society. Guilday, *John Gilmary Shea,* 90–95.

135. Kathleen Cummings sees American intellectuals as conceptualizing a "soft northern border" in the mid- to late nineteenth century. See Cummings, "Rise of the Nation-Saint"; Cummings, *New Women of the Old Faith: Gender and American Catholicism in the Progressive Era* (Chapel Hill: University of North Carolina Press, 2009), 32.

136. These words are taken from a monument at Auriesville.

137. The current Martyrs' Shrine at Midland was established after their beatification in 1926, though its predecessor at Waubachene was founded in 1907, as discussed further in Chapter 4.

138. Sacred space would remain peripheral in the Quebecois martyrs' cult because the sites where the martyrs had lived and died were outside of their immediate geographical purview, being located in Upper rather than Lower Canada. Only one Canadian Shrine, the ill-fated Martyrs' Hill, was founded before the martyrs' beatification, with the more celebrated, current Midland Martyrs' Shrine established only in 1926, after their beatification.

139. See PG 72, no. 4 (1961). Wynne also identifies Clark as Seneca in both his published works (see Father John J. Wynne, SJ, *Our North American Martyrs* [pamphlet, 1931], OLMSA, 20) and private correspondence (see his letter to Bishop Dunn, April 24, 1925, OLMSA).

140. This peculiar nomenclature, originally used by the colonial Dutch (see Parmenter, *The Edge of the Woods: Iroquoia, 1534–1701* [East Lansing: Michigan State University Press, 2010], 43), persists on today's signs on the New York Turnpike.

141. Clark to Campbell, undated, Clark Papers, OLMSA.

142. Robert Gaudet, SJ, "Shrine of Our Lady of the Martyrs," PG 57, no. 1 (March 1957): 18. The *New York Freeman's Journal,* in an article entitled "New York's Historic Shrine: A Visit to the Shrine of Our Lady of Martyrs at Auriesville" (anonymous, September 18, 1909), identifies Clark as the "State cartographer."

143. These barriers were visible even in how Clark refers to Catholics as "your people" in his correspondence with Catholics.

144. Clark to R. Dewey, January 15, 1884, Clark Papers, OLMSA. Clark's contributions to the advancement of the martyrs' American cult make this nineteenth-century Protestant general something of an archaeological Parkman. But Clark's recognition of the martyrs' sanctity was far less grudging than that of his fellow Protestant and his efforts on their behalf were far more deliberate than Parkman's almost inadvertent boosterism.

145. Clark to Shea, September 25, 1877, Clark Papers, OLMSA. The passionate definitiveness with which Clark made this emotional statement was later belied by his equally strong conviction that the site at which he had retrieved it was not, in fact, Ossernenon, making the hatchet head merely an interesting artifact rather than an actual relic.

146. "Father Richard Fisher, SJ" (pseudonym), telephone interview with the author, June 2010.

147. In his private correspondence, some of which is preserved at the OLMSA, Wynne confesses his bafflement as to why the Auriesville Shrine directors have never kept proper records regarding the miraculous cures that have occurred there, for example (Wynne to his father provincial, Lawrence Kelly, in 1927).

148. Wynne was also an advocate for Kateri Tekakwitha, serving as her vice-postulator. He also spearheaded the creation of the *Catholic Encyclopedia* and founded the still extant Catholic journal *America.*

149. J. J. Wynne, typewritten draft, Archives of the Our Lady of Martyrs Shrine, Fonda, NY.

150. See Horartio Phelan, "Early Huronia Shrines," in MSM, date unclear, 9.

151. The martyrs' official Promoters were Jesuit fathers J. Devine and Jean-Baptiste Nolin, both of whom played a very active role in the establishment of the martyrs' cult and in the creation of the first Canadian shrine to the martyrs at Martyrs' Hill, near Waubaushene, Ontario. The deeply devout Nolin would die in 1914 in a failed attempt to save the Holy Sacrament from the burning church.

152. E. G. Ryan, "Wynne, John Joseph," in *The New Catholic Encyclopedia,* 2nd ed. (Detroit: Thomson-Gale, 2003), 868. See also Father Francis Curran et al., *1885–1985: The National Shrine of the North American Martyrs* (Auriesville, NY, 1985), 36.

153. Wynne's writing lacks the tinge of bitterness sometimes evident in Shea, who sometimes expresses a sense of exasperation with the historical distortions and anti-Catholicism of his day, writing: "If Catholics try to bring forward some real true history they are denounced. Evidently some people love ignorance better than knowledge. . . . In the books used in the Protestant Public Schools, the Catholic element is studiously

ignored or maliciously misrepresented" (Guilday, *John Gilmary Shea,* 113).

154. Tekakwitha's *causa,* despite his efforts, languished at the expense of that of the martyrs, allowing her to take only the first step onto the three-tiered podium of sanctity during Wynne's lifetime. She became venerable in 1943, was beatified in 1980, and was canonized in 2012.

155. Wynne, public letter, OLMSA. This section was added between the canonization-eve draft and the eventual publication.

156. One contemporary volunteer at Auriesville, Lilly Fiorenza, sees the shrine's current difficulties as the direct result on the administration's decision to, in her words, "emphasize only the three at the expense of the eight." In-person interview with the author, June 2011.

157. Beatification of a martyr needs no confirming miracles, requiring merely that the martyrs' advocates demonstrate that these missionaries had died *in odium fidei.*

158. Of course, in Catholic belief, miraculous cures need not occur solely through the application of relics: they can occur through prayer alone or through other means of grace, such as pilgrimage. Late nineteenth- and early twentieth-century editions of *The Pilgrim* make it clear that clients of the martyrs and of Kateri *did* experience amelioration of their health and other problems through pilgrimage to the Auriesville site even before the martyrs' relics were available there. And yet Wynne's judgement that the American cult should not facilitate its own distancing from potentially wonder-working relics was still astute.

159. Wynne's letter to a French Jesuit, Andre Guittet (OLMSA), shows that, even after the canonization, he never stopped trying to find relics, writing in 1933 to chase down a rumor that Isaac Jogues had affected a cure through a preserved piece of his garment.

160. "New York's Historic Shrine," *New York Freeman's Journal,* September 18, 1909; emphasis added.

161. See the papal beatification decree of Pius XI, OLMSA, and John J. Wynne, "Martyrs of North America," *The Catholic Mind* 28, no. 18 (September 1930): 365–376. In this article, Wynne recalls that, during the canonization mass, the two groups of martyrs were named, respectively, "Canadenses (Canadians)" and "Neo Eboracenses (New Yorkers)" (366). By contrast, see John McCaffrey's article "The Jesuit Martyrs—Patrons of ALL Canada," MSM 15, no. 4 (1951): 110–111, 127–129.

162. Cummings, "Rise of the Nation-Saint," 16. This caustic characterization demonstrates the belated success of the Quebecois hierarchy in muscling in after 1886 to defend what they would have seen as their own prior claim to the martyrs' cult.

163. Ibid., 17. See also James Powers, ed., *Documents Pertaining to the Cause of the Martyrs of the United States* (Easton, PA: Commission for the Cause of

Canonization of the Martyrs of the United States, 1957). Wynne participated as a member of this commission, a generous act given that its organizers were so openly hostile to the cult of his own martyrs.

164. Cummings, "Rise of the Nation-Saint."

165. Wynne to Mr. Harrison, April 24, 1925, Wynne correspondence,
OLMSA.

166. Other Catholic writers such as Alan Polmaise, in his "Parkman and the
Martyrs" (*Commonweal* 12, no. 22 [October 1, 1930]: 546—548), followed
the same tactic. Polmaise states of Parkman: "No man was individually a
more potent advocate and factor in arriving at the actual canonization of
these saints than the great American and distinguished historian" (ibid.,
548).

167. Wynne, *Our North American Martyrs*, 18.

168. De Nöue was likely named to honor Saint Anne, the mother or the Virgin
Mary. French custom permitted males to take the names of female saints
(for a time, Marie was a popular choice as a second name for male as well
as female infants in France and Québec). For a short devotional sketch of
de Nöue's life and death, see "The Man Who Lost His Way," MSM (June
1946): 53, 73.

169. Greer, "Natives and Nationalism."

170. Curran et al., *1885–1985*, 39.

171. Parkman, *Jesuits in North America*, 99.

172. Wynne to Nealis, April 26, 1925, Wynne Papers, OLMSA.

173. Nealis to Wynne, May 2, 1925, Wynne Papers, OLMSA.

174. Wynne to Nealis, January 6, 1926, Wynne Papers, OLMSA. The same
expectation of primacy also motivated vocal American demands that
Jogues's name (rather than Brébeuf's) should lead the list of eight saints.
To see a photograph of this Auriesville altarpiece, see PG 55, no. 4 (Winter 1943): cover.

175. Father McCaffrey to Bishop Carter, August 9, 1969, and Father McCaffrey
to Philip Pocock, May 27, 1969, AMMS.

176. JAC, E601, envelope 3, unnamed document, discusses the commissioning
of "two new, huge paintings" for the canonization, one of the "Canadian"
and the other of the "American" martyrs, as does an anonymous article,
Item E601, envelope 3, JAC.

177. Ryan, "Wynne, John Joseph," 868. For an account of the statue's erection, see *America* 55, no. 291 (July 4, 1936).

178. For a description of the church and its symbolism, see Louis Devaney, "The
Coliseum at Auriesville: Temple of the 72 Doors," PG 80, no. 1 (1959): 1–3.
Commentators varied in their estimates of the building's capacity. Devaney claimed the Coliseum could hold 6,500 seated people, or 15,000
standing. Statistics on the church are taken from Gaudet, "Shrine of Our
Lady," 18. Curran claims seating for only 6,500 and standing room for a
further 3,500 (Curran et al., *1885–1985*, 42).

179. Gaudet, "Shrine of Our Lady," 18.
180. Curran et al., *1885–1985,* 44–45.

4. For Canada and for God

1. For studies of the role of massive pageants in shaping popular perceptions of history and religious and civic identity in Canada, see Ronald Rudin, *Founding Fathers: The Celebration of Champlain and Laval in the Streets of Quebec, 1878–1908* (Toronto: University of Toronto Press, 2003), especially chapter 4, and H. V. Nelles, *The Art of Nation-building: Pageanty and Spectacle at Quebec's Tercentenary* (Toronto: University of Toronto Press, 1999), particularly 3–17, 143–146, and 153–197. Both works explore the elaborate celebrations of 1908.
2. Frederick Helson, " 'Salute to Canada' Pageant Magnificent and Beautiful, Triumph of Canadian Talent," *The Georgian Tourist,* First Week of August, 1949.
3. Derm Dunwoody, "Midland Hillside Magic Setting for Story," *Telegram,* July 27, 1949.
4. For a brief sketch of Lord's life and accomplishments, see "Father Daniel A. Lord, S.J.," MSM 14, no. 4 (1950): 39–43.
5. Postcard of the *Salute to Canada* pageant entitled "Triumph of the Martyrs," preserved at JAC, pageant fonds.
6. *Salute to Canada* Program, July 1949, 2, preserved at JAC, E603 #3, 39.
7. Margaret Lawrence, "Ports of Call: The Shrine of the Martyrs on Georgian Bay," *Saturday Night,* July 15, 1939.
8. Frederick Griffin, "Saints in Ontario," *The Toronto Star Weekly,* July 18, 1931.
9. Francis X. Talbot, *Saint among the Huron: The Life of Jean de Brebeuf* (Garden City, NY: Image Books, 1956), 297.
10. The concept of martyrdom has always been elastic enough to encompass contradiction, even the contradiction of using holy victimhood to victimize others. For a fascinating study of the elasticity of tropes of martyrdom and their use to justify actual offensive violence against other groups in the ancient world, see Michael Gaddis, *There Is No Crime for Those Who Have Christ: Religious Violence in the Christian Roman Empire* (Berkeley: University of California Press, 2005).
11. The pageant's program coupled biographies of the martyrs with breezily secular ads for "double-fresh" Player's cigarettes, GE fridges, and priests' "summer weight" clerical suits. *Salute to Canada,* Official Program, July 1949, 2, preserved at JAC, E603 #3, 39.
12. Before Lord's 1949 blowout, the largest pageant held at Midland was the more traditional "Pageant of the Jesuit Martyr Saints" in 1937.
13. The similarity of this narrative to the clerico-nationalist epic is so obvious as to need no further comment.

14. *Salute to Canada* Program, 2.
15. Ibid.
16. Lord did not leave Protestant participation to chance. In March 1649 he visited Protestant enclaves the Kiwanis Club, the YMCA, and the Phalanx Club to drum up support. Private correspondence, Father Lally to Father McCaffrey, March 7, 1949, JAC, E603, #3.
17. For a history of Protestant attitudes to both martyrdom and to Protestant martyrs, see Brad Gregory, *Salvation at Stake: Christian Martyrdom in Early Modern Europe* (Cambridge, MA: Harvard University Press, 1999).
18. *Salute to Canada* Program, 41–42.
19. The martyrs were frequently celebrated in verse by many less-famous Protestant poets, including the Anglican minister of Midland, Rev. Warren (AMMS, letter file, 1929).
20. The phrase is attributed to Dr. R. N. Sherville in 1968 in Paul J. Delaney and Andrew D. Nicholls, *After the Fire: Sainte-Marie among the Hurons since 1649* (Meadord, ON: East Georgian Bay Historical Foundation, 1989), 57.
21. Ibid.
22. However, subterfuge was used in the acquisition of the original Martyrs' Shrine near Waubachene, Ontario. Jesuit Arthur E. Jones used a local family as the putative buyers because he anticipated local Protestant opposition (Jones correspondence, JAC).
23. Quoted in Mary James, "Stately Ceremonies Mark Dedication of New Shrine," *The Catholic Register*, July 1, 1926.
24. Griffin, "Saints in Ontario." The combination of the political and the religious at the event was also underscored by the fact that the statues of Lalemant and Brébeuf were, before their ceremonial unveiling, concealed with the Union Jack (then the Canadian flag) and the Vatican flag, respectively.
25. Jesuit Father Jacques Monet, interview with the author, March 15, 2009. The extremity of American anti-Catholicism is crystalized in Archbishop Fulton J. Sheen's characterization of the Soviet Union as "the mystical body of Satan" (quoted in James T. Fisher, *Communion of Immigrants: A History of Catholics in America* [Oxford: Oxford University Press, 2002], 121).
26. Canadian Catholics, like their American counterparts, participated in "Rosary Rallies" and listened to the "Family Rosary Crusade" and the "Rosary for Peace" programs on the radio. See Horatio Phelan, "Early Huronia Shrines," MSM, date unclear, 13.
27. MSM 13, no. 1 (March 1949): 3.
28. The Jesuit martyrs were made (secondary) patrons of Canada in 1940 (St. Joseph was Canada's first patron saint). See G. K. Mcinerney, "These Patrons: What Did They Do for Our Country," MSM 5, no. 3 (October 1941): 5–6. For examples of anti-Communist homilies, see Joseph Fallon, SJ, "The Martyrs—A Challenge," MSM 19, no, 3 (October 1955); G. Garand, SJ, "Martyrdom and Everyday Life," MSM 22, no. 1 (March 1958).

29. For an excellent general discussion of Catholic anti-Communism in North America, see Charles R. Morris, *American Catholic: The Saints and Sinners Who Built America's Most Powerful Church* (New York: Random House, 1997), 221–254; and Fisher, *Communion of Immigrants*, 123–124.

30. Garand, "Martyrdom and Everyday Life," 8.

31. Father Jim Kelly, telephone interview with the author, June 24, 2011. See also Harold Bedford, "The Ukrainian Rite: First Ukrainian Pilgrimage to Martyrs' Shrine," MSM 10, no. 3 (October 1946); A. Benelis, "The Lithuanian Cross at Martyrs' Shrine," MSM 24, no. 2 (1960): 22. Ethnic pilgrims have been credited with the survival of the Midland Martyrs' Shrine over the decades (see Michael Swan, "Ethnic Pilgrims Keep Shrine Going," *Catholic Register*, May 10, 1999.

32. For the dialogue between postwar immigrants to Canada and their host or "gatekeeper" culture, see Franca Iacovetta, *Gatekeepers: Reshaping Immigrant Lives in Cold War Canada* (Toronto: Between the Lines, 2006), 50–73, 290–294.

33. David Proulx, "Spy as 10,000 Pray: Red Agents Watch Poles at Midland," *The Telegram*, August 27, 1956.

34. Iacovetta, *Gatekeepers*, 95. Iacovetta notes that, much as at Midland, secular venues such as the Toronto Institute tended to focus on the most "quaint," "lavish," and "fascinating" (i.e., nonthreatening) aspects of their homelands' culture, such as dress, food, and dance, even as newcomers often sought to encode political commentary in these elements (ibid., 96–101).

35. Ibid., 96–101, 124–132.

36. Ibid.

37. Ibid., 57–59.

38. Delaney and Nicholls, *After the Fire*, 8–13.

39. Ibid., 20.

40. Herbert Cranston, "A Dreamer Who Made His Dream Came True: An Interview with Rev. J. M. Filion, S.J.," MSM (December 1946): 118.

41. Delaney and Nicholls, *After the Fire*, 20.

42. Ibid.

43. This suggests that officials may have exaggerated Martyrs' Hill's isolation to justify the shrine's 1925 relocation to Midland. Delaney and Nicholls, *After the Fire*, 20; see also Phelan, "Early Huronia Shrines," 11.

44. The diary was likely penned by a seasonal worker, likely a woman, in charge of tending to the temporal needs of its overnight pilgrims, *Shrine Diary*, JAC, fonds E601, #1.

45. Ibid.

46. Only three years earlier, Jones had penned a *Restatement of Proofs*, in which he defended his identification of Martyrs' Hill as Saint-Ignace.

47. Phelan, "Early Huronia Shrines," 11. Jones's was not the only such false alarm. In 1946, Jury thought that he had discovered the death site of

martyr Antoine Daniel. When this was disproven, the Jesuits sold the land and destroyed the commemorative cairn they had erected. Ibid., 6.

48. Phelan, "Early Huronia Shrines," 12.

49. Ibid.; see also Cranston, "A Dreamer Who Made," 110, 118–119.

50. "Filion, James," in DJB, 114.

51. Ibid.

52. Ibid., 112.

53. Key French Canadian leaders were the Jesuit Père Jean-Baptiste Nolin and the secular priest Père Theophilus Laboureau. The latter had overseen, a generation earlier, a grueling two-decade effort to build and dedicate St. Anne's, a Penetanguishene church dedicated to memorializing the then un-beatified martyrs. See Delaney and Nicholls, *After the Fire,* 17; David Dupuis, *St. Anne's of Penetanguishene: Huronia's First Mission* (Penetanguishene, ON: St. Anne's Building Committee, 2001), 33–39, 67–68.

54. The Jesuits did not gain total ownership of the Sainte-Marie site until 1939. See "Filion, James," 112. For a triumphal first-hand account of its purchase, see Father T. J. Lally, S.J., "Fort Ste. Marie Now Owned by Martyrs' Shrine," MSM 4, no. 2 (May 1940): 14, and Father T. J. Lally, S.J., "The Excavations of Old Fort St. Marie," *The Canadian Catholic Historical Assocation Report 1941–1942*, 15–22.

55. William Sherwood Fox, *Saint Ignace: Canadian Altar of Martyrdom* (Toronto: McClelland & Stewart, 1949).

56. Ibid. See also Fox's article by the same name in the *Canadian Historical Review* 28 (1942–1943): 43–56.

57. Ibid., 13–14.

58. Cranston, "A Dreamer Who Made," 119.

59. For a 1931 description of the shrine's interior and exterior, see Griffin, "Saints in Ontario."

60. Harvey Hickey, SJ, "Archeologist and Priest Dig to Uncover Proof Where Hurons Died," MSM 11, no. 3 (October 1947): 63.

61. Ibid. McGivern and Jury worked together on an ultimately abortive attempt to locate the place where martyr Antoine Daniel died.

62. Private correspondence between Lally and McCaffrey, March 7, 1649, JAC, E603, #3.

63. Nathaniel Benson, "History Rides the King's Highway," broadcast on CBC radio, August 9, 1939, 1. Script preserved at JAC.

64. Ibid., 1–2.

65. In private correspondence, Lally gleefully recounted the interest of the media, church officials, and school groups in tercentenary events. Lally to McCaffrey, JAC, E603, #3.

66. "Lally, James," in DJB, 179.

67. Helson, " 'Salute to Canada.' "

68. Franklin Davey McDowell, *The Champlain Road* (Toronto: Macmillan, 1939).

69. The trope of the lissome pagan queen was very common, with perhaps the most famous example being Elizabeth Taylor's Cleopatra in the 1963 film of the same name.

70. Poutine is a high-cholesterol staple of Canadian roadside snack stands, particularly in Québec and Ontario. It is made by smothering French fries in beef gravy and cheese curds.

71. John McHugh, SJ, "Brébeuf's Standard for His Hurons," MSM 11, no. 3 (October 1947): 64.

72. John O'Neill, SJ, "The Martyrs and Youth," MSM 19, no. 1 (March 1953): 16–17, 28–30.

73. Fallon, "The Martyrs—A Challenge."

74. Garand, "Martyrdom and Everyday Life," 8–9. These sentiments are echoed by contemporary Catholic conservatives.

75. O'Neill, "The Martyrs and Youth," 28.

76. Mark 8:36.

77. "Hegarty, Denis," in DJB, 130.

78. Ibid.

79. Ibid., 131.

80. Steve Catlin, recorded interview with the author, June 15, 2009; see also "Hegarty, Denis," 131.

81. Catlin interview.

82. J. G. Shaw also dramatically exploited sacred space in his booklet *Saints Lived Here: The Story of the Martyrs' Shrine* (Midland, ON: Martyrs' Shrine, 1970). Much the same dynamic is evident at the Auriesville Shrine's Ravine.

83. "Hegarty, Denis," 131.

84. Arrupe visited Saint-Ignace in 1967. Ibid.

85. The Archives of the Midland Martyrs' Shrine retains some of the graves' soil in a large pickle jar. Archivist Steve Catlin prayerfully prepares tertiary relics by burying holy medals in this soil, an activity that would have met with Hegarty's approval.

86. Denis Hegarty, SJ, "At the Grave of Brébeuf," MSM 19, no. 4 (December 1955); see also Denis Hegarty, "The Excavation of the Indian Church at Ste. Marie," *The Canadian Catholic Historical Association Report 1955*, 59–73; Denis Hegarty, "A Saint's Grave," MSM 19, no. 2 (1955), 37–38; "La sepulture de saint Jean de Brébeuf," *Relations* 14 (October 1954): 166.

87. "Hegarty, Denis," 128. Scientific analysis of this soil indicates that it has an unusually high organic content.

88. Ibid., 127–132.

89. Hegarty caustically noted that "when [Jury] declared the work completed the graves had not yet been found." Hegarty, "At the Grave of Brébeuf."

90. "Hegarty, Denis," 131.

91. Ibid., 131–132.

92. "Black Denis" was Hegarty's nickname, bestowed on him because of his thick mane of black hair. "Hegarty, Denis," 128.

93. For example, "fifty two school groups, twenty four from Catholic schools and twenty eight from Public Schools, visited the Shrine during the last two weeks of May and the month of June." Memo, "Organized Group Pilgrimages, 1955," JAC. Some groups even stayed overnight. See Kathy Fretwell, "Live-in at Sainte-Marie Realistic Return to the 1640s," *Toronto Star*, November 7, 1987, H17.

94. Lynch correspondence, February 22, 1949, JAC, E603, #3.

95. O'Neill, "The Martyrs and Youth," 30.

96. Benson, "History Rides the King's Highway," 8.

97. Among ultraconservative Catholics, where gender roles continue to be a critical way of defining identity, performing selfhood, and apportioning labor within the family unit, this lingering devotional—almost sensual— gaze on Brébeuf's imposing physique is still quite evident.

98. Benson, "History Rides the King's Highway," 15.

99. Ibid., 8.

100. O'Neill, "The Martyrs and Youth," 17.

101. According to the *Globe and Mail*, some passed the time singing in the Shrine's Inn, where a priest "beat a cheerful, lively boogey from the piano." Lex Schrag, "Celebrations at Shrine Mark Christian Victory," *Globe and Mail*, July 11, 1949.

102. Douglas Blanchard, "Indians Attend Mass, Honor Jesuit Martyrs," *Toronto Daily Star*, July 11, 1949; Mary Nowak, "Iroquois Invade Midland," *The Ensign*, June 23, 1949.

103. Nowak, "Iroquois Invade Midland."

104. Schrag, "Celebrations at Shrine."

105. Only Father Michael Jacobs, a Catholic priest of Mohawk extraction, was exempted from this silencing, presumably because his priestly vocation made him a shining example of the same, belated "Christian victory."

106. Nowak, "Iroquois Invade Midland."

107. See, for example, the photos and captions in Blanchard's 1949 article ("Indians Attend Mass").

108. Nowak, "Iroquois Invade Midland"; Blanchard, "Indians Attend Mass."

109. Schrag, "Celebrations at Shrine."

110. In many cases, this garb was anything but traditional, being instead a pastiche of Plains culture stereotypes. Some contemporary traditionalists see their people's ignorance of their own nation's distinctive clothing and other traditions as a mark of how much assimilative education and immersion in mainstream culture alienated their people from their roots.

111. McDowell, *The Champlain Road* (Toronto: Macmillan Co. of Canada, 1939), 8, 9.

112. This changing of the native dress code to better identify them as "native" in the eyes of spectators was nothing new in Canadian historical pag-

eants. Rudin notes that "so that they might seem truly exotic and play their role in the script as threats to French-Canadian settlement," the paid native participants in the massive 1908 tercentenary celebration of Champlain's founding of Québec "would be dressed as Plains Indians, brandishing tomahawks and shouting war whoops" (Rudin, *Founding Fathers*, 211). For an account of Mohawk attempts to discern their own ancestral dress, see Douglas M. George-Kanentiio, *Iroquois on Fire: A Voice from the Mohawk Nation* (Westport, CT: Praeger, 2006), 47.

113. For a thought-provoking exploration of the implications of white people "playing Indian," see Phillip Deloria's fascinating book of the same name (New Haven, CT: Yale University Press, 1998).

114. For leads that required operatic training, this was perhaps understandable.

115. Despite the similarity of their names, Ossossané and Ossernenon should not be confused. Ossossané was/is in ancient Wendake/contemporary western Ontario and was notable for being the site of the first European-style church in Ontario, and the home of Joseph Chihoatenhwa, the Wendat protomartyr. Ossernenon was the Mohawk village in ancient Iroquoia/contemporary upstate New York in which Jogues, Goupil, and la Lande were killed and Catherine Tekakwitha was born.

116. Kenneth Kidd, "The Excavation and Historical Identification of a Huron Ossuary," *American Antiquity* 18, no. 4 (April 1953): 359–379. In an address to the Huronia Historic Sites Association (published in MSM 5, no. 3 (1941): 10), Kidd enthused about the "tourist value" of the region's archeological riches while warning his audience that "we must take precautions . . . that our archaeological treasures are not plundered by mere souvenir hunters." Kidd's concerns were likely motivated by reported incidents of Wendat skulls, plundered from their ancient ossuaries, casually being displayed as curios or even callously used as flowerpots by the contemporary inhabitants of "Huronia" (see Michelle A. Hamilton, *Collections and Objections: Aboriginal Material Culture in Southern Ontario* [Montreal: McGill–Queen's University Press, 2010], 6, 20). For further information on the discovery of the Ossossané ossuary, see Frank Ridley, "A Search for Ossossané and Its Environs," *Ontario History* 39 (1947): 7–14.

117. Hamilton, in *Collections and Objections*, notes that European archeologists often justified their lack of consultation of native people with the motif of the "vanished Indian" (5–6), even as native groups frequently expressed vehement objections to grave despoliation (87–97).

118. Ibid., 105. Ossossane did become a majority Christian community during the winter of 1648, twelve years after the 1636 Feast of the Dead.

119. Ibid., 105–111.

120. But Brébeuf did win a partial victory. The remains of two Europeans, including the body of slain coureur de bois Étienne Brulé, were interred in Catholic holy ground.

121. See Patrick Kerans, "Murder and Atonement in Huronia," MSM 17, no. 2 (June 1953): 46–47, 52.

122. Ibid., 53.

123. Rueben Gold Thwaites, ed., *The Jesuit Relations and Allied Documents*, 73 vols. (Cleveland: Burrows, 1896–1901), 10:279–305.

124. Kidd, "Excavation and Historical Identification," 360.

125. "Les maudits anglais," or "the God-damned English," has been a traditional invective used by francophone Quebecois. "Tabarnacle" along with "calice" are traditional French Canadian swear words, referring to the tabernacle, the ceremonial container of a consecrated host, and the chalice, the ritual vessel in which the transubstantiated wine is served. That these words are commonly used as "swear words" says as much about the permeation of Catholicism into Quebecois culture as it does about its ambiguous place there. Usage of these traditional Quebecois epithets in the popular television show *Mad Men* will hopefully make them better known outside Québec.

5. Bones of Contention

1. Tonia Desiato, "Thousands Thank God for the Faith," *Catholic Register*, October 10, 1992.

2. Mark Bourrie, "Brébeuf Returns to Midland," *The Free Press*, September 30, 1992.

3. Only the left half of the skull was in fact returned, with the right being retained by the Augustinian Hospitalière nuns of Québec City.

4. Desiato, "Thousands Thank God for the Faith."

5. René Latourelle, *Jean de Brébeuf* (Montreal: Éditions Bellarmin, 1993).

6. René Latourelle, "Speech for Brebeuf's Homecoming," AMMS; emphasis in original.

7. Father Maclean's homily, AMMS, Fonds "Relics F2B."

8. Bourrie, "Brébeuf Returns." 1992.

9. Devotion to Brébeuf in France will be explored in Chapter 7. Brébeuf taught at the Jesuit College in Rouen for several years before he left for Canada, and the Jesuit residence there is named for him. Père André Metz, interview with the author, July 26, 2008.

10. The church was built in 1820 and the residence in 1856, according to Adrien Pouliot, "La chapelle des Jésuites" (unpublished paper, May 1983).

11. Père Gilles Morisette, recorded interview with the author, August 6, 2009.

12. Père Roch Lapalme, recorded interview with the author, August 6, 2009.

13. The translation is "Oh holy Canadian martyrs, pray for us."

14. Midland's shrine church also has recumbent statues of the saints under its side altars.

15. According to Adrien Pouliot, "La chapelle des Jésuites," these decorations were added gradually. The recumbent statues of Brébeuf and Jogues were the gift of the city and the province of Québec. The drops of blood surmounted by maple leaves and fleur-de-lis were added in 1949 in recognition of the three hundredth anniversary of Brébeuf's, Lalemant's, and Garnier's deaths. The late date of these additions seems somewhat to contradict Morisette's vehement assertions that the cult was virtually dead in the province by this period.

16. The MSM of August 1949 invited readers to "Visit Three Shrines of the Jesuit Martyr-Saints: Auriesville, Midland, and this Jesuit Chapel in Québec City."

17. The small church currently receives an estimated 3,000 visitors a year.

18. On the widespread Quebecois perceptions of Mohawks as "anglos," see Gerald R. Alfred, *Heeding the Voices of Our Ancestors: Kahnawake Mohawk Politics and the Rise of Native Nationalism* (Toronto: Oxford University Press, 1995), 17–18.

19. "Amerindian" in the preferred Quebecois term for native peoples, like the English Canadian "First Nations."

20. The planned Montreal sanctuary is also mentioned in "La Sepulture de saint Jean de Brébeuf," *Relations* 14 (October 1954): 166.

21. Although the rest of Canada also experienced secularization during this period, greater religious diversity outside Québec made the process less stark and dramatic.

22. Canonized in 2010, Brother André was a Montreal lay brother known for his simplicity, humility, devotion to Saint Joseph, and miraculous healing powers.

23. For an interesting fictional treatment of the theft of Brother André's heart, see Michel Basilières, *Black Bird* (Toronto: Knopf, 2003).

24. This shift also affected the fortunes of other figures, such as the secular martyr figure Dollard des Ormeaux. As Rudin points out, the older, clerico-nationalist narrative of moral victory in apparent defeat was no longer attractive as the province sought to redefine itself as "successful, entrepreneurial, and ambitious" (Ronald Rudin, *Founding Fathers: The Celebration of Champlain and Laval in the Streets of Quebec, 1878–1908* [Toronto: University of Toronto Press, 2003], 230).

25. For an analysis of the relationship between religion and culture in Québec, see Raymond Lemieux, "Le Catholicisme Québécois: Une question de culture," *Sociologie et Sociétés* 22, no. 2 (October 1990): 145–163. Although contemporary Quebecois continue to shun baptism, cultural identification with Catholicism remains important in the province. Québec's Catholic past informs, albeit perhaps on an unconscious level, its response to a wide range of contemporary issues, notably the "reasonable accommodation" of religious minorities.

26. Lévesque, of course, was the iconic, chain-smoking founder of the separatist Parti Québécois.
27. Mariette Paquin, recorded interview with the author, August 6, 2009.
28. Soeur Claire Gagnon, recorded interview with the author, August 6, 2009.
29. Morisette interview.
30. Ossossané is the ancient Wendat site in Ontario, not the ancient Iroquois site near Auriesville, New York.
31. Francis Gros-Louis, "The Reburial of the Human Remains of My 350 Year Old Ancestors," 1999, http://www.agondachia.com/cemetary.html.
32. Janith English, telephone interview with the author, October 11, 2011. See also Sherri Clemons, "Gathering of Nations Held," *Gyah'-wishatak-ia: The Turtle Speaks* 3, no. 2 (September 1999): 1, 12.
33. Métis participants included young Riel Lamarche and his brother Louis Lamarche, descendants of famed Métis leader Louis Riel. See Roberta Avery, "Indians Reunite to Bury Their Dead," *Toronto Star,* August 30, 1999. For Iroquois participation, see Carey Moran, "Hurons Return, 350 Years Later," *Midland Free Press,* August 10, 1999.
34. Influenced by contemporary Wendat nationalism, residents of the settlement formerly known as Ancien Lorette, near Québec City, now refer to their village as Wendake, the name of their ancient homeland in western Ontario.
35. Georges Sioui, recorded interview with the author, July 26, 2009.
36. "Huron-Wendat Gathering, 1649–1999 Commemoration," Agondachia Association website (no longer available).
37. English interview.
38. Ibid.; Avery, "Indians Reunite." This familial language was in stark contrast to the distanced terminology, such as "osteological material," which Kenneth Kidd had used in his 1953 article (Kenneth Kidd, "The Excavation and Historical Identification of a Huron Ossuary," *American Antiquity* 18, no. 4 [April 1953]: 359–379).
39. English interview; see also her comments in Roberta Avery, "Huron Wendat Reunite," *Indian Country Today,* September 13–20, 1999. English's perceptions of the timelessness of the event were echoed by Sherri Clemons, a participant from Oklahoma, who wrote: "The sage was so strong that it made you feel like you stepped back into time" (Clemons, "Gathering of Nations Held," 12).
40. Gros-Louis, "Reburial of the Human Remains."
41. Jim Wilkes, "After 50 Years, Peace Comes to the Souls of 500 Huron: ROM Gives Back Bones Archaeologists Dug up in 1947," *Toronto Star,* August 29, 1999. For more information on this ancient Wendat ceremony, see Eric Seeman, *The Huron-Wendat Feast of the Dead: Indian-European Encounters in Early North America* (Baltimore, MD: John Hopkins University Press, 2011). Iroquoian variants of the Feast exist and have been practiced

into the twentieth century (Michelle Hamilton, *Collections and Objections: Aboriginal Material Culture in Southern Ontario* (Montreal: McGill–Queen's University Press, 2010), 86–87. Hamilton also briefly mentions the 1999 Ossossané reburial (190–191).

42. Avery, "Indians Reunite"; Moran, "Hurons Return."

43. Jim Withers, "Hurons Reunite after 350 Years," *Montreal Gazette*, August 30, 1999, A9; Gros-Louis, "Reburial of the Human Remains." Much of the contemporary newspaper coverage of the event concurred with the Wendat sense of having been grievously wronged. The *Midland Free Press* opined: "It must have been painful indeed for the descendants of those original Hurons to live with the fact that their ancestors had been removed from their resting place in such a fashion. Most certainly no culture today would consider doing such a thing. . . . One would hope the days of whole-scale removal of the remains from ancient burial sites have long past" ("Solemn Ceremony Rights a Wrong," *Midland Free Press*, August 31, 1999, editorial).

44. Ibid.

45. Wilkes, "After 50 Years."

46. Ibid. See also Withers, "Hurons Reunite"; Avery, "Huron Wendat Reunite."

47. Withers, "Hurons Reunite."

48. Janet Turner, "Huron Descendants Descended upon Midland," *Ontario Archeological Society Arch Notes* 4, no. 5 (September/October 1999): 15–16. See also Withers, "Hurons Reunite."

49. For example, see newspaper coverage already cited and Erik Seeman, *Huron-Wendat Feast.*

50. English interview.

51. Ibid.

52. Ibid.

53. Kidd, in "Excavation," mentions the discovery of six copper finger rings (367, 370) and speculates that they are those of the married female Wendat Catholics Brébeuf said were buried in 1636 alongside their Catholic husbands and the traditionalist majority interred at Ossossané Rueben Gold Thwaites, ed., *The Jesuit Relations and Allied Documents,* 73 vols. (Cleveland: Burrows, 1896–1901), 15:173–175. Rings were also found near Sainte-Marie at Midland, both during formal excavations and, in one exciting incident, by a visiting school group in 1934 (see "Rings Found with Skeletons Thought for Indian Wedding," *Catholic Register*, August 23, 1932.

54. Most of the participants saw the rings as definitively Catholic articles. Indeed many, like English, called them "convert rings," making them explicit (rather than implicit) Christian symbols (see English interview; see also Janith English to Mima Kapches, 1999 letter preserved at AMMS).

55. Georges Sioui, telephone interview with the author, October 11, 2011; English interview.

56. Ibid.
57. English interview.
58. Janith English to Mima Kapches, 1999 letter preserved at AMMS.
59. This location, near Québec City, was where some of the surviving Wendat refugees first fled in 1650.
60. See Georges Sioui, *For an Amerindian Autohistory: An Essay on the Foundations of a Social Ethic* (Montreal: McGill–Queen's University Press, 1992); and Georges Sioui, *Huron-Wendat: The Heritage of the Circle*, trans. Jane Brierley (Vancouver: University of British Columbia Press, 1999).
61. Sioui, *For an Amerindian Autohistory.* The experiences of many young Mohawks were similar. Writes Douglas M. George-Kanentiio (*Iroquois on Fire: A Voice from the Mohawk Nation* [Westport, CT: Praeger, 2006], 48): "We also were told by our teachers of the depravity of the Iroquois and the cruelty of the Mohawks, in particular. Our heritage, prior to conversion, was one of violence, sensuality, warfare, and the vilest elements of paganism. We were historically tainted because our ancestors had burnt alive a number of Jesuit missionaries, and only by submission to the church were we saved from damnation."
62. Ibid.
63. Ibid., xviv.
64. Sioui interview, 2011.
65. Sioui, *For an Amerindian Autohistory*, 40.
66. Sioui interview, 2011.
67. Sioui interview, 2009. See also *For an Amerindian Autohistory*, 40, 44–46, 49–51. Sioui's characterization of the Iroquois's intention of forcibly creating "one people" with the Wendat, the better to confront the French, is seconded by other historians, notably Jon Parmenter (*The Edge of the Woods: Iroquoia, 1534–1701* [East Lansing: Michigan State University Press, 2010], particularly 70–75). Parmenter notes that Jogues himself viewed the Iroquois strategy in this way (60).
68. Sioui interview, 2009. A similar argument is made by Gerald Alfred, a Mohawk political scientist who, writing of Champlain's initial 1909 offensive against the Mohawk in 1609, notes: "The hostility and misunderstanding engendered by this initial confrontation defined the Mohawk-French relationship at least until 1667. Although only 191 French were killed—38 in captivity—and another 143 were taken captive by the Mohawks and other Iroquois during this sixty-year period . . . far less loss than the Iroquois suffered through war and disease, the resolution of this problem was to become a French preoccupation for many years" (*Heeding the Voices*, 30).
69. Religious divisions between traditionalists and Christians quickly became as problematic in Iroquois circles as they had among the Wendat. For a fascinating account of Iroquois religious divisions in the colonial era, see Daniel Richter, "Iroquois versus Iroquois: Jesuit Missions and Christianity

in Village Politics, 1642–1686," *Ethnohistory* 32, no. 1 (Winter 1985): 1–16. For excellent case studies regarding contemporary religious divisions among the Mohawk, see George-Kanentiio, *Iroquois on Fire,* for Akwesasne–St. Regis, and Gerald F. Reid, *Kahnawà:ke: Factionalism, Traditionalism, and Nationalism in a Mohawk Community* (Lincoln: University of Nebraska Press, 2004) and Alfred, *Heeding the Voices,* for Kahnawake.

70. Reid's career choice to work high above the world, constructing the steel skeletons of skyscrapers, was a popular one for young Mohawk men from the 1950s to the present. For more information, see Edmund Wilson, *Apologies to the Iroquois* (Syracuse, NY: Syracuse University Press, 1959).

71. "Owen Reid" (pseudonym), recorded interview with Theresa Sharrow, September 10, 2010.

72. "Sister Ursula Little" (pseudonym), telephone interview with the author, June 24, 2010.

73. The various causes of the Mohawks' eventual abandonment of the valley named for them in upstate New York is addressed at some length in Alfred, *Heeding the Voices,* 33–51.

74. "Sister Ursula Little" interview.

75. "Owen Reid" interview.

76. "Cecilia Pafford" (pseudonym), interviews with the author, June 10, 2010, and August 9, 2010.

77. "Cecilia Pafford" and "Agnes Pafford" (pseudonyms), interview with the author, June 10, 2010.

78. "Cecilia Pafford" interview, August 9, 2010. Pafford's perspective is echoed by Michael Coren, "You Hate Me? Thanks: Every Insult Can Be Considered a Victory for Catholics," *Ottawa Sun,* November 7, 2009.

79. Assumptions about culpability can be played on, as Margaret Atwood warns in her dystopian novel *The Handmaid's Tale,* where women unsuspectingly kill political prisoners they are told are sadistic rapists.

80. According to Catholic tradition, a martyr is a martyr not because of what she suffers but because of the *cause* for which he suffers. Medieval Catholics, however, constantly confounded these two, as have Catholics ever since. See Brad Gregory, *Salvation at Stake: Christian Martyrdom in Early Modern Europe* (Cambridge, MA: Harvard University Press, 1999), 47–50.

81. This divisive yet transformative logic of martyrdom has been harnessed by some of the twentieth century's most powerful social movements for change, such as Mahatma Gandhi's pacifist revolution in 1940s India and Martin Luther King Jr.'s civil rights movement in the United States several decades later. For an interesting handling of contemporary martyr figures, see Lacey Baldwin Smith, *Fools, Martyrs, Traitors: The Story of Martyrdom in the Western World* (New York: Alfred A. Knopf, 1997), especially the later chapters, which explore John Brown and the Rosebergs; see also Castelli's excellent chapter and epilogue discussing Cassie Bernall, the

popular martyr figure of the Columbine high school massacre (Elizabeth Castelli, *Martyrdom and Meaning: Early Christian Culture Making* [New York: Columbia University Press, 2004], 172–203).

82. See also Richard Lundstrom, "A Hard Look at American Catholic Folklore: Mohawks, Martyrs, and Myths," *Akwesasne Notes* (July 1973): 22–23.

83. For the perspective of the chief Royal Ontario Museum negotiator on the repatriation, see Mima Kapches, "Ossossané Ossuary: The Circle Closes," *Archaeology of Eastern North America* 38 (2010): 1–15.

6. The Naked and the Dead

1. "Sarah Oldfield" (pseudonym), recorded interviews with the author, July 26, 2009, and June 3, 2010.

2. Kahatsiohareke is a traditionalist Mohawk cultural and linguistic center in upstate New York, founded in 1993 on the site of an ancient Bear Clan village. It is seen by traditionalists as the fulfillment of the prophesy that the Mohawk would one day return to their ancestral lands.

3. For the perhaps unintended effects of such martyrdom art, see Donald L. Boisvert, *Sanctity and Male Desire: A Gay Reading of Saints* (Cleveland: The Pilgrim Press, 2004).

4. Lilly Fiorenza, recorded interview with the author, June 11, 2011; telephone interview with the author, June 17, 2011.

5. "Agnes Pafford" (pseudonym), interview with the author, June 11, 2010.

6. "Alice Duchene" (pseudonym), interview with Theresa Sharrow, August 30, 2010.

7. "Sister Ursula Little" (pseudonym), telephone interview with the author, June 24, 2010.

8. The Ravine was acquired in 1895, only a decade after the shrine's founding. But the fact that it was partially "filled . . . to make it flatter for the pilgrims" ("Father Richard Fisher, SJ" [pseudonym], telephone interview with the author, June 2010) has made archaeological work there exponentially more difficult.

9. Anonymous, "Down the Hill and up to Heaven," PG 81, no. 3 (1970).

10. For examples of this "giant reliquary" language, see PG 79, no. 1 (1968). The Auriesville shrine sold bottles of the Ravine's water for many years as a sort of secondary relic.

11. The signs reproduce brief excerpts from Jogues's long narrative of his 1642 captivity among the Mohawk, during which Goupil was killed. See Rueben Gold Thwaites, ed., *The Jesuit Relations and Allied Documents*, 73 vols. (Cleveland: Burrows, 1896–1901), 31:53–63.

12. Text of the signs in the Ravine, reproduced in Anonymous, "Down the Hill." Canadian authors, writing about the Martyrs' Shrine, also attempted to encourage pilgrims' vivid sense of almost hallucinatory en-

gagement with the martyrs by reflection upon their still-lingering presence in the places they had once walked. Wrote J. G. Shaw in his oft-reprinted pamphlet *Saints Lived Here: The Story of the Martyrs' Shrine* (Midland, ON: Martyrs' Shrine, 1930): "the ground my foot presses against was walked by an exhausted man who would not lie down because God had created him to serve Him. This hill I am climbing was climbed by a discouraged man who would not give up because he was in possession of the Faith and there were people around him who did not have it. That little stretch of flat ground down by the river was home for ten years to men who left the highest standard of living to sleep in bark cabins, feed on rotten fish with corn mush, and consort with man-eating savages because Christ said go ye and teach all nations."

13. Molly Milot, recorded interview with the author, September 21, 2010.

14. "Alice Duchene" interview.

15. Mohawk religious identity, of course, has always been variegated. Segments of the Mohawk population became Catholic in the seventeenth century, but the majority retained their traditional ways. Some later accepted various varieties of Protestantism. For more on Iroquois religious identity, see Christopher Vecsey, *The Paths of Kateri's Kin* (Notre Dame, IN: University of Notre Dame Press, 1997); David Blanchard, "To the Other Side of the Sky: Catholicism at Kahnawake, 1667–1700," *Anthropologica* 24, no. 1 (1982): 77–100; Edmund Wilson, *Apologies to the Iroquois* (Syracuse, NY: Syracuse University Press, 1959).

16. "Sister Ursula Little" interview.

17. Tekakwitha was canonized in October 2012. She is often presented as the first native person to be recognized as a saint. This popular perception overlooks Juan Diego, the seer at Guadalupe (though he may be a mythical rather than a historical figure) and Saint Rose of Lima, who was of mixed indigenous and Spanish descent.

18. "Sister Ursula Little" interview.

19. For more on the dynamics of native appropriations of Kateri, see Paula Elizabeth Holmes, "We Are Native Catholics: Inculturation and the Tekakwitha Conference," *Studies in Religion/Sciences Religieuses* 28, no. 2 (1999): 153–174, and Darren Bonaparte, *A Lily among Thorns: The Mohawk Repatriation of Káteri Tekahkwí:tha* (Akwesasne, NY: The Wampum Chronicles, 2009).

20. "Natalie Lamoureux" (pseudonym), telephone interview with the author, July 20, 2010.

21. "Father Richard Fisher, SJ" interview, 2010.

22. Matthew 7:16.

23. I would like to thank Steve Catlin, archivist at the Midland Martyrs' Shrine, for taking me to see this hidden bas-relief at Midland in 2008.

24. Father Bernard Carroll, telephone interview with the author, June 24, 2011.

25. Father Wynne to Mother Nealis, personal correspondence, January 14, 1925, preserved at OLMSA.

26. Father Jim Kelly, telephone interview with the author, June 24, 2011.

27. See, for example, the minutes of the Ontario Conference of Catholic Bishops for June 30, 1988 regarding Chihoatenwa, JAC, B302, #14.

28. Carroll interview.

29. During this period, the shrine revised its written materials, running new editions stripped of "offensive statements and pictures (v.g., barbarians, heretics, pagans, etc) . . . and taking into account recent studies on the most up-to-date historical interpretations of the Huronia experiment." See William Russell, SJ (principal author), *Preliminary Report of the Martyrs' Shrine Sub-Committee, Presented to the Commission on Ministries, Upper Canada Province of the Society of Jesus,* October 6, 1968, JAC, E601, #20. Homilies at Midland during the 1970s also began to reflect this new ethos, reflecting, for example, upon "the Indian people who died for their faith" (*Homily of Sunday, August 29, 1976,* printed in MSM 40, no. 4 [Winter 1976]: 5). They increasingly stressed Catholic "recognition of the contribution made by native Christians to the building of the Church in Canada" (Tim Lilburn, "Remembering the Legacy of Native Christians," MSM 43, no. 2–3 [Summer–Fall 1979]: 9). It was likely around this time that the Shrine began publishing a series of pamphlets entitled "Heroic Native Christian Series," though the lack of dates on these publications make this difficult to verify. See, for example, A. J. Macdougall, *Joseph Chiwatenhwa: An Apostle with Apostles* (preserved at JAC, Box 302, #5).

30. Ibid. The Canadian Alliance in Solidarity with Native Peoples also made an analogy between the anti-Semitism of traditional Catholic theology and subsequent persecution of the Jews.

31. David Stanley, "Sermon for the Feast of the Canadian Martyrs," MSM 36, no. 4 (1972).

32. Message of Pope John-Paul II at the Midland Martyrs' Shrine, preserved at AMMS, Fonds Farrell FPIE.

33. Kelly interview.

34. Russell, *Preliminary Report.*

35. These pivotal encounters between native peoples and the Midland Jesuits left few archival traces, but they have been preserved in the memories of still-living Jesuits, such as Father Jim Kelly.

36. John Robinson, recorded interview with the author, June 11, 2011.

37. Kelly interview.

38. Catherine Verrall, letter to Hon. Rueben Baetz, Minister of Tourism and Recreation, on behalf of the Canadian Alliance in Solidarity with Native Peoples, October 27, 1984, AMMS, File F2C, Ste. Marie Huronia Historical Parks, 1983–1985.

39. Ibid.

40. Ibid.

41. Father Alex Kirsten, recorded interview with the author, August 28, 2010.

42. From its opening in 1968, Sainte-Marie provided a week's history training for all of its staff, providing a spur for the shrine to do the same. See Russell, *Preliminary Report,* 15.

43. Carroll interview.

44. In seeing work with aboriginal people as being central to the identity of Canadian Jesuits, Farrell was a bit like Jean-Pierre Chazelle, though far more sensitive.

45. *Brébeuf's Dream* was the title of a documentary film produced by the shrine about its new programs.

46. The deaconate program had actually been running since 1972, but until the construction at Anderson Lake it had no permanent home.

47. Kelly interview.

48. Institution of such an event had been one of the recommendations of a special subcommittee exploring ways of making the shrine more relevant in the post–Vatican II era. See Russell, *Preliminary Report.*

49. Ibid.

50. Ibid.

51. "Olivia Desjardins" (pseudonym), recorded interview with the author, June 12, 2011. Many of these crutches are now stored alongside the discarded bas-relief in the basement of the priests' residence.

52. Ibid. Of course, the Ojibwe did not have the same immediate link with the martyrs in the same way that the Iroquois or Wendat nations did.

53. Robinson interview.

54. Ibid.

55. Kelly interview.

56. Jean McGregor-Andrews, recorded interview with the author, June 11, 2011.

57. Father Kelly (interview) reiterates that in the early 1980s the event attracted "bus loads from North Bay and Sioux Saint Marie with hundreds of people."

58. Father Carroll (interview) correctly notes that this tiny group is dwarfed by the "tens of thousands" of Anishnabe Catholics living in northern Ontario.

59. McGregor-Andrews interview.

60. Aboriginal residential schools in Canada were run by a number of different religious bodies, not just the Catholic Church, though, under the auspices of several different religious orders, it did run more schools than any other entity. The Anglican Church was a close second. The Oblates of Mary Immaculate, a Catholic religious order, have apologized for their involvement in residential schools, as has the Canadian Federal

Government. The Catholic Church as a whole, however, has made no such apology.

61. Kirsten interview.

62. Carroll interview.

63. For example, now-deceased Jesuit provincial Father Jim Webb praised Chihoatenhwa as "having given his life for his faith" and presented being in "solidarity with the native peoples of today" as the religious and civic duty of every Canadian Catholic.

64. Carroll interview.

65. Steve Catlin (interview with the author, August 27, 2010) sees the recent decision to assign pastoral care of the majority-Ojibwe parishes of Christian Island to the Jesuits as an indication that a promising new era of Jesuit–native engagement is imminent.

66. Ibid.

67. Ibid.

68. Anonymous, *Biography of Father Tom Egan,* OLMSA, Egan files, 1994. Though the two shrine directors shared a common mission, to open their shrines to greater native involvement, their chronology is different. It is Egan who is the earlier of the two figures, serving as shrine director at Auriesville from 1968 to 1981, whereas Farrell's tenure was later, from 1980 to 1996.

69. Ibid.

70. "Father Richard Fisher, SJ" (pseudonym), telephone interview with the author July 1, 2009.

71. Ibid.; "Sister Ursula Little" interview; see also Matt Roche, SJ, *Obituary of Father Thomas F. Egan,* Egan files, OLMSA, 1994.

72. Roche, *Obituary.*

73. *The Pilgrim* is one of the longest running Catholic periodicals in the United States. Founded in 1884, it has been publishing ever since.

74. Egan rushed to the defense of the Mohawk when he felt the mass media "placed all the Mohawks in a bad light." But Egan himself was not without insensitivities, for example, referring to native women as "squaws." See PG 80, no. 1 (1969).

75. Contemporary ultraconservative Catholic pilgrims still see traditional Iroquois culture in much the same way. A National Coalition of Clergy and Laity homily in September 2012 characterized the Iroquois as worshipping "war gods" who demanded "human sacrifices."

76. Egan, "Pastoral Letter," 1972; Egan, unpublished homily, 1976, preserved at OLMSA.

77. Egan, "Homily," 1976, PG 88, no. 2 (1977).

78. Egan, "Pastoral Letter."

79. Ibid. See also PG 84, no. 3 (1973).

80. See, for example, PG 82, no. 1 (1970); 87, no. 3 (1976); 88, no. 3 (1977); and 83, no. 2 (1972).

81. "Sister Ursula Little" interview.

82. "Cecilia Pafford" (pseudonym), interview with the author, August 9, 2010.

83. Egan, "Pastoral Letter"; see also PG 84, no. 2 (1973).

84. "Cecilia Pafford" interview.

85. Ibid. Her charge is seconded by "Natalie Lamoureux" (interview): "more people are becoming traditional, they fill up the longhouse until it is standing room only. But they depend on us [Catholics] to translate the language. . . . They didn't grow up with the language."

86. Pafford's comments that language and liturgy are central to her identity is not unique. Other respondents express a similar sense of indebtedness to Catholicism for the preservation of their ancestral language. See PG 84, no. 3 (1973). Her strong linking of language, identity, and religion bear striking similarities with nineteenth-century Quebecois clerico-nationalism.

87. "Cecilia Pafford" interview.

88. The sacristy is the part of the church (generally hidden from the view of the congregation) in which priests and altar servers don their vestments and make other preparations for mass.

89. This impression of being on display for whites is shared by other native people who visited Auriesville, including Natalie Lamoureux (interview).

90. "Cecilia Pafford" interview.

91. "Sister Ursula Little" interview.

92. "Father Richard Fisher, SJ" interviews, 2009, 2010.

93. Robert Boyle, "Christmas Message" 1982, OLMSA.

94. Ibid.

95. Dorothy Domkowski, interview with the author, June 4, 2010.

96. Ibid.

97. Beth Lynch, interview with the author, June 4, 2010.

98. PG 88, no. 2 (1977).

99. The significance of the dig as the only fully excavated Iroquois village in the United States was signified by its being placed on the National Register of Historic Places by the U.S. Department of the Interior in 1973.

100. "Sister Ursula Little" interview.

101. "Natalie Lamoureux" interview.

102. Ibid.

103. For a study of the repatriation of Iroquois false-face masks, see Ruth B. Phillips, *Museum Pieces: Towards the Indigenization of Canadian Museums* (Montreal: McGill–Queen's University Press, 2011), 111–131.

104. Ibid.

105. "Agnes Pafford" (interview) suggests that many from Akwesasne agreed to go on pilgrimage to Auriesville under the misapprehension that they were going to Fonda, though she stops short of alleging deliberate dissimulation.

106. "Natalie Lamoureux" interview.
107. Lynch interview, 2010.
108. Ibid.
109. "Natalie Lamoureux" interview.
110. "Sarah Oldfield" interviews.
111. "Father Richard Fisher, SJ" interview, 2009.
112. Lynch interview, 2010.
113. Lilly Fiorenza also expresses similar antiecumenical ideas (interview, June 17, 2011).
114. Beth Lynch, recorded interview with the author, June 2009.

7. Pilgrims' Progress

1. This statue is in Battleground Park, in Lake George, New York.
2. All of the quotes attributed to Hellman in these paragraphs are from his inaugural homily for the NCCL's Fifteenth Annual Pilgrimage of Restoration, delivered on September 22, 2010.
3. For a general account of Catholic ultraconservatives' reaction to the Second Vatican Council's liturgical reforms, see Michael W. Cuneo, *The Smoke of Satan: Conservative and Traditionalist Dissent in Contemporary American Catholicism* (New York: Oxford University Press, 1997), 22–30.
4. Molly Milot, recorded interview with the author, September 21, 2010.
5. "Margaret Middleton" (pseudonym), recorded interview with the author, September 22, 2010.
6. For an account of the rise and beliefs of Catholic ultraconservatives, see Cuneo, *Smoke of Satan*.
7. The Jesuit writer Francis X. Talbot was the first to attempt to determine with any exactitude the path followed by Isaac Jogues as he was taken into captivity in 1642, efforts that he publicized in "The Bloodstained Trail of Isaac Jogues" (*America* 47 [September 17, 1932]: 565–567); "Where Father Jogues Was Ambushed" (*America* 47 [September 24, 1932]: 589–591); and "The Torture Trail of St. Isaac Jogues," *Historical Records and Studies of the United States Catholic Historical Society* 23 (1933): 7–86. For a critique of his efforts, see Lucien Campeau, "Un site historique retrouvé," *Revue d'Histoire de l'Amérique Française* 6, no. 1 (June 1952): 31–41.
8. For a description of the effects of Vatican II on Catholic laypeople, see James M. O'Toole, *The Faithful: A History of Catholics in America* (Cambridge, MA: Belknap Press of Harvard University Press, 2008), 199–265.
9. NCCL website, http://www.national-coalition.org/index.html; emphasis in original.
10. Many other Christian groups, including "Quiverfull," also stress the need to cede control of reproduction to God. See Kathryn Joyce, *Quiverfull: Inside the Christian Patriarchy Movement* (Boston: Beacon Press, 2009).

11. For an overview of ultraconservative Catholic views on contraception and abortion, see Cuneo, *Smoke of Satan*, 59–79.

12. Mike Emig, recorded interview with the author, September 22, 2010.

13. The group's gender expectations skewed the quantity and quality of my interviews. Female NCCL pilgrims were generally much busier than their male counterparts. Most were constantly wrapped up in an inaccessible bubble of prayer. Mothers were particularly occupied. For example, in one ten-minute interview with "Sarah Clarke," our discussion was interrupted no less than seven times with child-related issues. Men, both lay and clerical, had much more free time. Priests walked independently of any particular brigade and were thus largely exempt from their constant regime of prayer, song, and reflection. NCCL executives and members of the Safety Patrol (all of them male) had far more opportunities to interview. Rapport with female respondents was also more fragile. Generally, women seemed to enjoy the interview process less than the men and seemed to regard me more as an anomaly or intruder than did their male counterparts.

14. Michael Meier, recorded interview with the author, September 22, 2010.

15. This seemingly playful exchange reflects disturbing views on domestic violence in some ultraconservative circles. One priest of the St. Pius X Society suggested that to me victims of violence should be seen as "lucky" (rather than abused) because their suffering gave them the valuable opportunity to redeem themselves (through passive suffering) and potentially their abusers (by their martyr-like witnessing).

16. Gregory Lloyd, telephone interview with the author, June 24, 2010.

17. Ibid. Cuneo (*Smoke of Satan*, p. 4) also notes the "masculinized" ethos of ultraconservative Catholics.

18. Interestingly, Canon Hellman sees Jogues as a man who, through suffering, learned how to love like a woman. His comments epitomize the ultraconservative idea that women are "naturally" loving and compassionate, whereas men must work to acquire these qualities. Canon Andreas Hellman, recorded interview with the author, September 22, 2010.

19. "Sarah Clarke" (pseudonym), recorded interview with the author, September 22, 2010.

20. Meier interview.

21. Hellman interview.

22. Suzy Buchanan, "Trouble in Paradise: N.H. Town Split by Radical Traditionalists," Southern Poverty Law Center, Intelligence Report, no. 126 (Summer 2007).

23. Hellman homily, September 22, 2010.

24. Ultraconservatives' strong belief in and fear of purgatory and hell adds something special to their perception of the martyrs. Like the Catholics of centuries past, they admire martyrs' attainment of heaven.

25. E-mail from Gregory Lloyd, September 16, 2010. Ironically, it was Lloyd who was not able to attend the event.

26. 1 Corinthians 4:9. Gabriel Lalemant, we will recall, quoted this same verse to Brébeuf after their capture, and Isaac Jogues also used the verse to comfort himself during his repeated captivities.

27. St. Pius X Society pilgrimages have a similarly reparative slant, as does a Polish walking pilgrimage to the Midland Martyrs' Shrine in Ontario. Pius X pilgrims, like the NCCL, march in "brigades" while listening to excerpts of the *Jesuit Relations.*

28. Michael Emig and his son Joseph, recorded interview with the author, September 22, 2010.

29. O'Toole finds similar adamancy in his interviews of contemporary ultra-conservative Catholics. See O'Toole, *The Faithful,* 298–301.

30. Meier interview.

31. Hellman interview.

32. NCCL pilgrims resisted discussing contemporary native peoples, constantly turning discussion back to the seventeenth-century groups who encountered the martyrs. All interviewed suggested that aboriginal attempts to revive the traditional spiritual practices of their ancestors were "artificial." When challenged that their own traditionalism could face similar criticism, pilgrims denied the similarity.

33. "Sarah Clarke" interview.

34. Lloyd interview. Lloyd's comparison of the supposed persecution of NCCL members and that of native peoples seems less forced when one takes into account Catholic conflation of different types of suffering.

35. Hellman interview.

36. Milot interview, 2010.

37. "Peter Miller" (pseudonym), recorded interview with the author, September 22, 2010.

38. "Sarah Clarke" interview.

39. Canon Dolan homily, 2012 NCCL Pilgrimage of Restoration.

40. For a fascinating account of Goan-Canadian Catholic life see Kathryn Carriere's doctoral thesis, *Brown Baby Jesus* (University of Ottawa, 2011).

41. Father Patrick Coldricks, recorded interview with the author, August 28, 2010. This will be the only reference to this lengthy interview.

42. Other Midland officials, such as Steve Catlin (interview with the author, August 27, 2010), also note the great reverence displayed by Hindu pilgrims.

43. The exception to this general rule is the Polish Walking Pilgrimage, an event much like the NCCL's.

44. By contrast, in earlier days, when the Native Prayer Days were large enough to require many chartered buses, these motor coaches frequently became mobile prayer units under the direction of Jean McGregor-Andrews and her husband (McGregor-Andrews, recorded interview with the author, June 11, 2011).

45. For example, when I requested to ride with the Goan group in one of their chartered coaches, I was told that "the bus ride isn't part of the pilgrimage."

46. In some cases, some elements of regional identity are stressed over others. Grassroots organizers of the Goan pilgrimage decided to make the event exclusively Konkani-speaking, effectively snubbing those who speak other languages.

47. The rainbow of ethnicities and nationalities of the priests stationed at Midland reflect both increasing Canadian diversity and the decline of domestic vocations for the priesthood. For a more critical view of Canadian multiculturalism, which argues that only the least threatening aspects of immigrant culture and religion are in fact accepted, see Neil Bisoondath, *Selling Illusions: The Cult of Multiculturalism in Canada* (Toronto: Penguin, 2002). For an account of the lives of Asian Catholic immigrants in Canada, see Terence Fay, *The Faces of Canadian Catholics in Canada: The Asians* (Toronto: Bayard Press, 2009).

48. Father Alex Kirsten, recorded interview with the author, August 28, 2010.

49. Coldricks interview.

50. This anecdote was related to me by Steve Catlin (interview).

51. Kirsten interview. Kristin's comments reflect the rethinking of the theology of martyrdom also prevalent at the time. In his book *Jean de Brébeuf* (Québec: Bellarmin, 1993, 246–258), Jesuit theologian René Latourelle sought to transform it from an act stressing the hatred of the martyrs' assailants to an act displaying the martyr's own self-sacrificial love for them.

52. The "push me, pull you" dynamic of "gatekeeper"-guest negotiations at contemporary Midland mirrors that observed by Franca Iacovetta in the postwar era (Iacovetta, *Gatekeepers: Reshaping Immigrant Lives in Cold War Canada* [Toronto: Between the Lines, 2006], 95–98). As she notes, such a dynamic tacitly assumes that it is the "gatekeepers'" prerogative to select the aspects of new Canadians' cultural heritage that are acceptable to the mainstream.

53. Pilgrimage organizers are sometimes defiant in their essential disinterest in the martyrs. One Goan organizer was adamant that their event was "mostly based on getting the Goans together and having a mass in our local language." Their primary devotion, he stated, was "to Mother Mary and our Catholic religion" rather than the martyrs, "whose history may not be known to many of us."

54. Kirsten interview.

55. It is unclear when Brébeuf's home, "la Boissée," finally fell into ruins. *Les Amis* internal documents suggest that the charming, thatched building was still standing in the 1950s.

56. Gilbert Gauroy, interview with the author, June 15, 2008.

57. Pierre Bunel, interview with the author, June 15, 2008.

58. Suzanne Guenon, interview with the author, June 15, 2008.

59. This sense of the martyrs as "new saints" is accentuated by the fact that their cult in France is very much a postcanonization phenomenon. Images of the martyrs were sometimes used in postwar stained glass made to replace windows shattered in the bombings (as at Dieppe, St. Lô, and Condé-sur-Vire).

60. This statement, of course, applies more to Europeans than to aboriginal traditionalists, many of whom express a strong sense of religious and cultural continuity with ancestors, particularly when performing traditional ceremonies.

61. There is a microcult dedicated to Jogues in Orleans and to Daniel and de la Lande in Dieppe.

62. *Les Amis* seem unaware that there is an American cult of the martyrs and do not fly an American flag at their chapel. Their focus on Brébeuf in the singular, as well as their feeling of kinship with Canada, based largely on linguistic ties, helps to explain their preference for Canadians.

63. "Cantique à Saint-Jean-de-Brébeuf," archives of Les Amies de Jean de Brébeuf.

64. The Friends' interest in the other North American martyrs is pretty much nonexistent.

Epilogue

1. Notes Allan Greer, on the Jesuit recovery of the body of Charles Garnier: "the rescuers have to sift through carnage and debris, passing over dead Indians bodies and also wounded, but still living Indians bodies, until they find what they have been seeking: one lifeless, but immeasurably precious European body" (Allan Greer, "Colonial Saints: Gender, Race and Hagiography in New France." *William and Mary Quarterly* 57, no. 2 (April 2000): 323–348.

2. Their deaths also show their influence, powerful and ambivalent, on Wendat society. It is significant that the anonymous ex-Wendat ex-Catholics who killed them retained significant aspects of Catholic belief and ritual they exhibited in their "unbaptism."

3. It remains unclear whether the slaying of René Goupil represented the will of the majority or a minority faction.

4. Of course, no one can be martyred against his or her will because, in a truly amazing piece of circular logic, if a given individual fails gracefully to accept imminent death, then by definition this person is not a martyr.

5. As Brad Gregory correctly argues, it is not that martyrs are suicidal or wish to die for no reason but rather that they do not wish to live at any cost, particularly if they are put in a position where living would, in their

view, involve the adulteration or denial of their religious beliefs (Gregory, *Salvation at Stake: Christian Martyrdom in Early Modern Europe* [Cambridge, MA: Harvard University Press, 1999], 103–105).

6. Rueben Gold Thwaites, ed., *The Jesuit Relations and Allied Documents,* 73 vols. (Cleveland: Burrows, 1896–1901), 34:31.

7. "Ariel's Song," from Shakespeare's *The Tempest,* act 1, scene 2.

Acknowledgments

Perhaps appropriately for a book that presents the deeply and sometimes painfully personal side of the cult of the North American martyrs, this work grew from two seminal conversations. The first was with Georges Sioui, my colleague at the University of Ottawa, who vividly described for me his "first lesson in Canadian history" at a parochial school on a native reservation in Québec in the 1950s. He and his fellow six-year-olds, he related, were instructed by the nuns who taught them to kneel and pray for forgiveness for their ancestors' role in the slayings of *"les saints martyrs canadiens"* and to thank God for his providence sending these holy men to save their people from sin and barbarism.

The other discussion was with Jesuit historian and archivist Father Jacques Monet, SJ. He revealed to me that the central altarpiece at the Midland Martyrs' Shrine, which purportedly shows simply the eight slain missionaries resplendent on clouds of celestial glory, has an intriguing secret. During a thorough renovation of the sanctuary in the 1980s, he disclosed, the lower portion of the painting, which depicts in graphic detail the martyrs' torture at the hands of their native tormentors, had been ingeniously disguised, allowing it to hide in plain sight. Monet's revelation made me realize that images of martyrdom often serve as something of a barometer of changing theological and cultural values. During periods of their waxing influence, the violence of the martyrs' deaths has often been celebrated as a triumphant storming of heaven's gates. But when questioned by indignant native critics, these images are sometimes amputated, sometimes abandoned. For sending me down the rabbit hole of research and reflection which eventually resulted in this book, my thanks.

What Georges Sioui and Jacques Monet inspired, my family sustained. This book could not have been written without the loving support of my husband, Mark, who was a constant source of encouragement and fresh insight throughout the long, intense process of research and writing. Sophie and Danny, my children, were models of patience while visiting shrines and archives, cathedrals and convents on both sides of the Atlantic. Peter Anderson, Simon Evans, and John Anderson each read multiple drafts of every chapter, providing what were invariably trenchant and helpful critiques and suggestions, while Stephanie Evans, Rosemary Lewis, and Maya, Madeleine, and Anna Anderson served as emotional bulwarks.

Indeed, the writing of this book often felt like something of a group effort, not simply because of my family's invaluable participation, but also because interviews were so important to evoking the more recent permutations of the martyrs' ever-dynamic "afterlife." I acknowledge my heavy debt of gratitude to my many respondents: francophones, anglophones, and Mohawk-speakers, native traditionalists and Catholics, Canadians, Americans, and French citizens alike for their willingness to share with me their valuable insights, fascinating experiences, and passionate perspectives on the martyrs and their legacy. Because some of those interviewed participated on the condition of anonymity, I gratefully acknowledge them here under the pseudonyms I created for them in this book. My grateful thanks to Darren Bonaparte, Suzie Champoux, "Alice Duchene," Chief Janith English, "Father Richard Fisher, SJ," Sœur Claire Gagnon, Bob George, Father Jim Kelly, SJ, "Natalie Lamoureux," Père Roch Lapalme, SJ, "Sister Ursula Little," Père Gilles Morissette, SJ, "Sarah Oldfield," "Agnes Pafford," "Cecilia Pafford," Mariette Paquin, "Owen Reid," and Tharani Tharmalingam.

I would also like to warmly express my thanks to each of the organizations that allowed me to participate as an observer in their respective pilgrimages. Thanks to Gregory Lloyd and Mike Meier of the National Coalition of Clergy and Laity for so generously permitting me to walk with their group's 2010 Pilgrimage of Restoration. My grateful acknowledgments to "Sarah Clarke," Mike Emig, Canon Andreas Hellman, "Margaret Middleton," "Peter Miller," and Molly Milot for their valuable insights on the contemporary cult of the martyrs in the United States and for their kindness and hospitality while we were on the road together. My sincere thanks also to the organizers of the first-ever Goan pilgrimage to the Midland Martyrs' Shrine, particularly Walter R. Dos "Romeo" Remedios and Father Patrick Coldricks, SJ, for his unfailing good humor and his generosity with his time. My deepest regards and gratitude also go out to the organizers of and participants in the 2011 Native Prayer Days, particularly "Olivia Desjardins," Jean McGregor-Andrews, and John Robinson for their insightful comments and gracious welcome. I would also very much like to express my gratitude to Les Amis de Jean de Brébeuf: Pierre Bunel, René and Suzanne Guenon, and Gilbert Gauroy for their invaluable insights and warm welcome to Normandy. Many thanks to all of the other French friends who so kindly assisted me: Père André Metz, SJ, of Rouen, Brigitte Kavanaugh, Sylvie Howard, Mimi Bonnefoi of Josselin, and Sœurs Marie de l'Enfant Jésus and Marie-Colette of Pont l'Évêché for their kind assistance in researching their spiritual ancestor, Catherine de Saint-Augustin. *Mille fois merci!*

This project would have been impossible without the assistance of those at the twin sanctuaries that have long honored the eight martyrs: Our Lady of Martyrs Shrine in Auriesville, New York, and the Martyrs' Shrine in Midland, Ontario. Instrumental in leading and shaping the martyrs' cult in the twentieth century, they are vital sites at which to observe both its current dynamics and tensions. The rich, yet underexploited archives of both shrines were invaluable in helping me chart the fascinating backstory of the sometimes cooperative, sometimes competitive transnational campaign to canonize these eight men as North America's first saints.

Special recognition is due Steve Catlin, archivist of the Midland Martyrs' Shrine. Steve was indefatigable in helping me to access information and imagery and always generous in drawing on his own formidable knowledge of the martyrs, their era, and their veneration in our always lively conversations. I will always be especially grateful to Steve for taking me "backstage" at Midland, allowing me to explore the rich and hidden layers of the shrine's retired imagery and the sloughed-off skin of its previous institutional incarnations. I am also indebted to Father Bernard Carroll, SJ, Father Alex Kirsten, SJ, and John Zurakowski and for their unfailing assistance.

Beth Lynch of the Our Lady of Martyrs Shrine was another important contributor to this project. I appreciate her always provocative and thought-provoking comments. My sincere appreciation also to Father George Belgarde, SJ, Dorothy Domkowski, Joanne Freeman, Lily Fiorenza, and Father Peter Murray, SJ. Without the contributions of all of these individuals, my attempt to sketch the recent history and contemporary dynamics of the martyrs' afterlife would have been stillborn. Thank you all so much for everything you did to make this book possible.

Institutions as well as individuals were critical to the genesis of this work, providing the necessary financial support, research assistance, and intellectual challenges necessary to sustain this project over its multiyear gestation. I gratefully acknowledge the indispensable and generous financial support of the Social Sciences and Humanities Research Council of Canada. I also appreciate the fantastic support of the University of Ottawa for its faculty's research. My particular thanks to Dean of Arts Antoni Lewkowicz and to Huguette Bourgeois, Josée-Anne Cyr, Lucie Hotte, Pierluigi Piovanelli, and Leslie Strutt for their generous support, in myriad ways, of my research. I would also like to thank colleagues outside of my institution for their help. My gratitude to Kathleen Cummings and Robert Orsi for their insightful and invigorating commentary on my manuscript. Thanks to Paul-André Dubois, Jean-Guy Goulet, Louis Painchaud, and Don Smith for their kind interest in this project.

While ethnographic fieldwork was indispensable to this project, so was archival research. I would like to extend my especial thanks to Père Robert Bonfils, SJ, of the Archives Jésuites de la Province de France in Vanves, Nancy Fay and Lorraine Gadoury of the National Archives of Canada, Suzie Hudon of the

Centre de référence de l'Amérique française in Québec City, Mima Kapches of the Royal Ontario Museum, Jessica Ehrenworth of the City of Toronto Archives, Father Jacques Monet, SJ, and Jasmine Miville-Allard of the Archives des Jésuites au Canada in Montreal, and Bill Brodeur, Rosemary Vyvyan, and Jan Gray of Sainte-Marie-among-the-Huron Historic Park. I also thank the helpful staff members of the Bibliothèque Nationale de France, Paris, and the Archives départementales of Calvados and Maine-et-Loire. Four University of Ottawa students, Paul Gareau, Colette St-Onge, Gabriel Jones, and Theresa Sharrow (who conducted some of the interviews for this book in Mohawk), also deserve special recognition for their excellent research assistance. Thank you!

Several scholarly projects also aided immeasurably in the development of this work. Joel Martin and Mark Nicholas pioneered an innovative interdisciplinary colloquium on native peoples and Christianity in which I was a participant. Ann-Marie Plane and Leslie Tuttle also solicited my contribution to their exciting volume on early modern dreams and visions. I am grateful to all four scholars for their invitation to participate in these projects. Chapters 1 and 2 of this work thus contain brief excerpts from Emma Anderson, "Blood, Fire and 'Baptism': Three Perspectives on the Death of Jean de Brébeuf, Seventeenth-Century Jesuit Martyr," from *Native Americans, Christianity, and the Reshaping of the American Religious Landscape*, edited by Joel Martin and Mark A. Nicholas, copyright © 2010 by the University of North Carolina Press (www.uncpress.unc.edu); and from Emma Anderson, " 'My Spirit Found a Unity with This Holy Man': A Nun's Visions and the Negotiation of Pain and Power in Seventeenth-Century New France," from *Dreams, Dreamers, and Visions in the Early Modern Atlantic World*, edited by Leslie Tuttle and Ann Marie Plane, copyright © 2013 by the University of Pennsylvania Press.

I am also grateful to Dean Julie Byrne for her kind invitation to showcase my research as a public lecture at Hofstra University and to Caroline Galland and Bertand Van Ruymbeke for the opportunity to present my work at a bilingual European forum on Colonisation and Confessionalization held in Amsterdam in 2011. I would also like to acknowledge the American Academy of Religion, Canadian Catholic Historical Association, French Colonial Historical Society, and the American Historical Association for the many chances afforded me to present my developing research in their scholarly fora, there to receive the encouragement and stimulation that helped me to further refine my ideas.

Last but not least, I am inexpressibly grateful to my editor at Harvard University Press, Kathleen McDermott, for her belief in this project and for her tenacity, patience, and unfailing insight. I would also like to thank Andrew Kinney and John Donohue for all of their hard work in taking this book from pipe dream to reality.

Index

Cannibalism; Catherine de Saint-
Augustin; Condé-sur-Vire, France;
Iroquois; Jesuits; Lalemant, Gabriel;
Lazare; Martyrdom; Martyrdom art;
Martyrs' cult; Miracles; Ragueneau,
Paul; Relics; Saint-Ignace (place);
Torture; Traditionalists; Wendat
Bunel, Pierre, 350, 351, 356, 444. *See also*
"Boissée, la"; Condé-sur-Vire, France;
Friends of Jean de Brébeuf; Gauroy,
Gilbert; Guenon, René

Cannibalism, 19, 48, 91, 93, 243, 258,
289, 306. *See also* Goya, Francisco José
de; Native postwar rituals; Soul return;
Torture
Canons of Christ the King, 310, 314,
323–324, 325, 326–328, 331, 332.
See also Hellman, Andreas; National
Coalition of Clergy and Laity; Slaves
of the Immaculate Heart of Mary;
Ultraconservative Catholics
Captivity, 5, 10, 11, 14; purpose of
captive-taking, 17, 47, 367; behavioral
expectations for captives' behavior,
17–18, 45, 47, 48, 74; preliminary
torture of all captives, 18–19, 39–42;
captivity of Isaac Jogues, 23–25, 26, 28,
59, 74, 158, 296, 362, 365, 367; captives
at Saint-Ignace, 39–42; native captives
as witnesses to martyrs' deaths, 159,
368–369; mock captivity at tercentenary, 203–205. *See also* Adoption;
Jesuits; Jogues, Isaac; Native postwar
rituals; Soul return; Torture
Carroll, Bernard, 266, 270–271, 274,
282–284, 347, 445. *See also* Martyrs'
cult; Midland Martyrs' Shrine;
Vatican II
Casot, Jean-Joseph, 96, 108. *See also*
Hospitalière nuns; Jesuits; Martyrs'
cult
Catherine de Saint-Augustin, vows of, 54;
departure for Canada, 55, 60; mystical
relationship with Jean de Brébeuf,
55–56, 76–85; relationship with Paul
Ragueneau, 56–57, 64–65, 70–72, 76;
early years in Canada, 60–62; and
Brébeuf's relics, 70–72; death of, 85;
reactions to, 85–86; revelation of
mystical life of, 86; commemoration by
Ragueneau, 86–87; contributions to
martyrs' cult, 86–87, 231; effects of,

86–87; mixed reception of Ragueneau's
biography in France, 87–88, 94. *See also*
Brébeuf, Jean de; Hospitalière nuns;
Jogues, Isaac; Martyrdom; Martyrs'
cult; Miracles; Ragueneau, Paul; Relics
Catholic Minorities, Catholic minority
pilgrims at the Midland Martyrs'
Shrine, 1–2, 173–177, 315–316, 339,
341, 342–343, 373; Quebecois' new
status as a religious minority after the
Union of the Canadas, 7, 100–101,
103–104, 109–111; American Catholic
minority, 7, 103–105; Ultraconservative
Catholics' self-perception as a victim-
ized minority, 7–8, 316, 329–330, 339,
342; Wendat Catholic minority in
seventeenth century, 31–35, 69–70;
contemporary native Catholics perceive
selves as martyred minority, 250–251.
See also Martyrs' cult; Midland
Martyrs' Shrine; Native Catholics;
"Native Prayer Days"; Our Lady of
Martyrs Shrine; Pilgrimage; Ultraconservative Catholics
Catlin, Steve, 278, 283, 445. *See also*
Midland Martyrs' Shrine; Native
Catholics; "Native Prayer Days";
Saint-Ignace (place)
Cayuga. *See* Iroquois
Chabanel, Nöel, 4, 175; longing for
martyrdom, 30; death of, 50, 53, 159;
nomination for beatification, 156;
revulsion for native peoples, 156, 368;
"vow of persistence" of, 156; similarity
of his death to Chihoatenhwa's, 156;
in martyrdom art, 161; celebration of
tercentenary of death of, 191, 204;
analysis of, 363, 364, 366. *See also*
Blood; Douart, Jacques; Honareenhax,
Louis; Jesuits; Martyrdom; Martyrs'
cult
Chaumonot, Pierre Joseph Marie, 135.
See also Jesuits; Parkman, Francis
Chazelle, Pierre, 108, 120–124, 173.
See also Jesuits; Martyrdom; Martyrs'
cult; Ojibwe; Oshawana; Petrokeshig
Chihoatenhwa, Joseph, death of, 33,
67–68, 156; conversion of, 67; as a
martyr, 67; and religious factionalism
at Ossossané, 67; similarity of his death
to Chabanel's, 156, 210; in art at
Midland Martyrs' Shrine, 269–270,
275, 277, 283; contemporary *causa* of,

Lady of Martyrs Shrine; Tekakwitha, Catherine, Saint; Ultraconservative Catholics

Manifest Destiny, 132, 136–138. *See also* Historiography; Parkman, Francis; Protestants; Shea, John Gilmary

Martin, Félix, 106–109, 120, 132, 173. *See also* Bourget, Ignace; Chazelle, Pierre; Collège Sainte-Marie; Historiography; Jesuits; Martyrs' cult

Martyrdom, conceptual "slipperiness" of term, 6, 8–9; as "spectacular," 6, 12, 21–22; and *in odium fidei,* 9–10, 50, 66, 68–69, 103, 363, 365–366; and asceticism, 14–15, 44–45; as means by which Jesuits understood predicament of the 1640s, 17, 20, 31, 53; "living martyrdom," 20, 83; and conversion, 20–21, 23, 27; and reward in afterlife, 21–22; Jesuit longing for, 24–26, 29–31, 44–45, 55, 218; volunteerism and, 29–30, 60, 114–115, 220–221, 223, 224, 264, 366, 367–368; euphemisms for, 29–30; and mysticism, 30–31, 36, 55–56, 76–85; "morphing" of in colonial North America, 45, 46–48, 365–367; in early Christianity, 46–47; "feminization" of, 55–56, 80–81; reevaluation of in eighteenth-century art, 89–94, 96; narrowing of in nineteenth century, 155–156; critiques of martyrdom in the twentieth century, 220–221, 223, 224; and moral superiority, 251–252. See also *In odium fidei;* Jesuits; Martyrdom art; Martyrs; Martyrs' cult; Reparation

Martyrdom art, 1–2, 90; conventions and taboos of, 90–93; in the eighteenth century, 90–94; in the seventeenth century, 92; in the nineteenth century, 99–100, 105, 106; increasing racialization of, 117–120; and Quebecois collective identity, 118–120; continuation of conventions in twentieth-century photography, 206–207; in the Chapel de Jésuites in Quebec City, 218; controversy over at Our Lady of Martyrs Shrine, 255–256, 257–265, 284–286, 287–289, 302–308; nature of, 256–257; editing or hiding of, 265–269, 307–308; controversy over at Midland Martyrs' Shrine, 265–273, 279–280,

284. *See also* David, Étienne; David, Jacques-Louis; Goya, Francisco José de; Légaré, Joseph; Martyrs' cult; Midland Martyrs' Shrine; Nealis, Mary Margaret; Our Lady of Martyrs Shrine; Poulter, Gillian

Martyrs, names of canonized martyrs, 4; how each man died, 4–5, 66–67, 362–363; other possible interpretations of their deaths, 5, 36–37, 48–49, 362; inherent subjectivity of term, 5, 8–10, 52–53, 114–115, 360–361, 370; exclusion of native martyrs, 5, 69–70, 119–120, 156–157, 361–362, 368–370; self-perception of, 6–7, 10; how term is used in this book, 9; Jesuit desire for martyrdom in 1640s, 14–15, 16–17, 20–22, 23, 25, 27–28, 30–31, 44, 55; expectations for martyrs' behavior, 21, 33, 45, 73, 366; Jogues's death "ups ante" for other Jesuits, 29, 44, 60, 367–368; exclusion of Jacques Douart as, 35–36; in early Christianity, 46; compared to North America, 46–48; intervention of martyrs in lives of living, 55–56, 58–59, 70–71, 150; deaths as attracting new missionary recruits, 56–57; Jesuits presented as martyrs by Catherine de Saint-Augustin, 56, 70–72, 76–79, 81–83, 87; by Paul Ragueneau, 56–57, 65–69, 71–72, 87; and French colonial identity, 73–74; *habitants* as martyrs, 114–115, 116–117; *les braves* as martyrs, 116–117, 125–127; elevation of, 146, 150–151, 161–162; exclusion of Anne de Nöue, 155–156, 368. *See also* Ahatsistari, Eustache; Brébeuf, Jean de; Chabanel, Nöel; Chihoatenhwa, Joseph; Daniel, Antoine; Douart, Jacques; Garnier, Charles; Goupil, René; Jogues, Isaac; la lande, Jean de; Lalemant, Gabriel; Native martyrs; Nöue, Anne de; Onaharé, Joseph

Martyrs' cult, establishment of colonial martyrs' cult, 5, 7, 55, 65–70, 76–85; and Catholic minorities, 1–2, 7, 13, 315–316, 333–348; and ultraconservative Catholics, 3–4, 8, 13, 309–314, 316–333, 341–342; threats to the survival of the cult in the eighteenth century, 7, 13, 87–97; nineteenth-century revival of the martyrs' cult in

2014. 03. 06   39.95 (34. 95)